The Spanish Speakers
in the United States

The Spanish Speakers in the United States

A History

Peter J. Duignan
and L. H. Gann

University Press of America, Inc.
Lanham • New York • Oxford

Copyright © 1998
University Press of America,® Inc.
4720 Boston Way
Lanham, Maryland 20706

12 Hid's Copse Rd.
Cumnor Hill, Oxford OX2 9JJ

Library of Congress Cataloging-in-Publication Data

Duignan, Peter J.
The Spanish speakers in the United States : a history / Peter J.
Duignan and L. H. Gann.
p.   cm.
Rev. ed. of : The Hispanics in the United States / L. H. Gann and
Peter J. Duignan. 1986.
Includes bibliographical references and index.
1. Hispanic Americans—History. I. Gann, Lewis H. II. Gann,
Lewis H., 1924- Hispanics in the United States.
E184.S75D85 1998   973'.0468—dc21   98-39212 CIP

ISBN 0-7618-1258-X (pbk: alk. ppr.)

⊖™ The paper used in this publication meets the minimum
requirements of American National Standard for Information
Sciences—Permanence of Paper for Printed Library Materials,
ANSI Z39.48—1984

About the Book and Authors

Hispanic peoples are the fastest growing minority in the United States, yet the literature on Hispanics as a group is very sparse. This is the first large-scale survey to cover the history, politics, and culture of all major Hispanic groups (including Cubans, Mexicans, Puerto Ricans, and Chicanos) in the United States. The authors begin by examining the Spanish legacy of the Southwest, the beginnings of large-scale Mexican immigration into the borderlands after the turn of the century, socioeconomic changes brought about by World War I, and changes in the demographic composition of the nation as a result of later immigration. They next discuss in detail the national debate over immigration, asking, for example, whether immigrants compete for jobs and social services, whether the Immigration and Naturalization Service is capable of handling the flow of immigrants, and whether employer sanctions are just. They also describe the immigrants themselves—their educational levels, occupational backgrounds, and experiences in adapting to life in the United States—stressing the difference between the various groups in these areas. Finally, Drs. Gann and Duignan look at Hispanic culture, including politics, education, sports, and social problems. This pioneering study argues that immigration is a positive experience for both the newcomers and the local communities into which they settle.

L. H. Gann and **Peter J. Duignan** are Senior Fellows at The Hoover Institution. Drs. Gann and Duignan are coauthors of *The United States and Africa: A History* and of *The Middle East and North Africa.*

Contents

Preface

Hispanics form both one of the oldest and one of the most recent groups of immigrants in the United States. Spanish speakers came to parts of the Southwest before the Pilgrims arrived in New England. Yet the bulk of the Hispanic newcomers settled in the United States in this century, a large proportion of them after World War II. A vast and impressive amount of work already has been done on the history and sociology of particular national groups. Ours is the first to deal with the Hispanic peoples in the United States as a whole.[1] The present work attempts to provide a synthesis based on secondary sources, as well as on personal interviews and visits to the border region and to American cities with large Spanish-speaking populations. Our book, however, is not a history of the Spanish-speaking peoples. We concentrate on the problems of the present, although we do attempt to set these in a wider historical context.

The subject is difficult to define because Spanish speakers vary as much among themselves as do most Americans. Most Spanish speakers are not immigrants; there are Spanish-speaking Californians, New Mexicans, or Texans whose ancestors lived in the Southwest long before their respective states became part of the United States. The Hispanics, like the vast majority of other Americans, have come from many different countries including Mexico, Puerto Rico, Cuba, Nicaragua, El Salvador, Honduras, Spain, and Argentina. Some of them are proficient in Spanish, although others have lost the use of their ancestral tongue. Some are indifferent to their cultural inheritance and regard themselves as unhyphenated Americans; others have a strong commitment to their Hispanic legacy. Some are rich and some are poor; some are conservative and some are radical; some are fair-skinned and some are swarthy or black.

Spanish-speaking Americans, moreover, differ in the ways in which they define themselves. Most Mexican Americans, for instance, agree that they are of mixed origin, that they form part of *la raza,* a term that connotes—unlike the Nazi concept of pure race—a sense of a common past and a common destiny. But Americans of Mexican descent are far from agreed on what to call themselves. In New Mexico, the descendants of the early Spanish-speaking colonists often refer to themselves as *nuevo mexicanos* or *hispanos* (old-stock, Spanish-speaking people). In Texas, names often used are *tejanos* or *latinos*. Some descendants of early Spanish-speaking pioneers prefer to call themselves "Spanish Americans," a term that to their critics may suggest social snobbery or an unjustified desire to conceal their Mexican past. The term "Chicano" had a somewhat pejorative sense in the first part of the present century. Some Mexican Americans, especially those of an older generation, still strongly object to the term, but many young Americans of Mexican descent have taken up the term as a badge of pride.

Puerto Ricans face similar problems of self-definition. Some fair-skinned Puerto Ricans (a minority) simply merge into the general white population; some dark-skinned Puerto Ricans, especially those born in this country and no longer able to speak Spanish, believe that their future lies in merging with the blacks. Cubans are equally divided, though for very different reasons: some see themselves as a vanguard destined to free Cuba from Communist tyranny; others look only to remaining in America.

The primary links between these different groups remain their religion and the Spanish language, but Spanish-speaking immigrants (like German-, Yiddish-, and Italian-speaking immigrants) begin to modify their original tongue soon after they arrive. "Elevator" has become *elevador* instead of *ascensor*. Many Puerto Ricans in New York say "guachiman" for watchman, "rufo" for roof, "moppa" for mop, and "estore" for store. The Puerto Rican accent differs strikingly from the Mexican, and both groups in turn smile at Castilian with its lisp.

But even Spanish may get lost. American children of whatever ethnic ancestry are notoriously reluctant to learn their parents' language. The new, much-heralded, ethnic consciousness commonly centers on music, cookery, crafts, and sports. The ethnic revival usually stops where the irregular verbs begin. No one who has ever tried to teach a foreign language to American school-children will imagine that there is an ethnic ground swell anywhere among them, let alone a widespread desire to acquaint themselves in the original with the masterpieces of Neruda or Calderón.

Despite this diversity, and despite numerous conflicts within the various Hispanic groups, there is also a sense, however diffuse and disparate, of a wider Hispanic consciousness. Since World War II, the expansion of Spanish-language radio and television programs has strengthened the Spanish speakers' sense of community. So have migration within the United States and the rising rate of intermarriage between members of different Spanish-speaking nationalities and their offspring. So have bilingual education and university programs in Chicano or Hispanic studies; so have bureaucratic programs instituted to promote Hispanics to better jobs, especially in the public sector and in academia. Above all, immigration from Mexico, Puerto Rico, Cuba, and to a lesser extent, from other parts of the Caribbean and from Central and South America, has changed the country's demographic composition. (According to the 1980 census, 6.4 percent of the population stated that they were of Hispanic origin; 56 percent of this group described themselves as white.)

The current high rate of immigration, both legal and illegal, has already set off a vigorous political debate. No one can be certain about the future, but we submit that Spanish speakers will leave a new imprint on the United States and that their importance in this country will increase.

In referring to specific national groups in this country, we will use terms that originally were customary and were acceptable to those to whom they referred. We therefore will speak of Spanish-speaking Californians in the nineteenth century as *californios* and of militant Mexican-American students during the second part of this century as *chicanos*. In alluding to Spanish speakers in general, we will talk of Hispanic Americans. We will not use the term "Anglo," but will instead call them English-speaking Americans or Anglo-Americans.

Our study raises wider problems regarding not only immigration but the character of the American nation as a whole. From their early beginnings, the American colonies contained numerous settlers who spoke tongues other than English, especially German and Dutch. Mass immigration from continental Europe during the last century produced the notion of the "melting pot," in which different ethnic groups would be fused into a new people.

During the 1950s, and even more during the 1960s, the pendulum swung the other way. Assimilation, once welcomed as a national ideal, began to be despised among the learned, though not for racist reasons. As John Higham, a doyen of American immigrant history points out, Milton Gordon's *Assimilation in American Life* (1964) was the last major contribution to the assimilationist tradition.[2] Thereafter, revisionists took over. Patriotism of the traditional variety dropped out of fashion in academe; the "melting pot" was derided. Immigrant history, all too often, turned into martyrology—a tale of exploitation and denial, bad enough for "ethnic" whites, but hellish for dark-pigmented peoples. Scholars emphasized the ills of American society, past and present, and also the immigrants' many grievances—sometimes to such an extent that readers might be left to wonder why anyone troubled to come to the United States from abroad in the first place or why they stayed after being treated so badly.

There was, at the same time, a new stress on "roots" (used as the title of a successful television series on the history of a black American family). Ethnicity earned praise to such an extent that broader concepts regarding a common American nationality with common national interests were lost. Revisionist scholars had a pervasive distrust for the "establishment," or for white middle America, or for the capitalist system, or for industrial society in general. This distaste easily blended with romantic regrets for vanished rural societies. Alternatively, or in a complementary fashion, critics contrasted the real evils of an extant capitalist society in the United States with the imagined splendors of a socialist society yet to be built. Pluralists now dominate immigrant studies. According to Higham, they fall into two categories: the "soft" pluralists who believe that cultural differences between the various immigrant groups are cultural assets to be cherished and preserved for their own sake, and the "hard" pluralists who are interested in the various ethnic groups primarily as components of an exploited working class.

We ourselves are rooted in an earlier tradition. We are not unaware of the ills that beset American society. We are, however, disinclined to idealize the preindustrial past; nor do we romanticize ethnic roots. We recognize the value of cultural diversity. But we also value the dynamic qualities inherent in American society that enable it to assimilate foreigners, and we think more highly of capitalism's capacity for self-regeneration, its opportunities for social mobility, and its commitment to civic liberty than do its critics. We sympathize with those who—to use Lenin's phrase—have voted with their feet to come to the United States; this sentiment comes easily because one of us is himself an immigrant, and the other is of immigrant stock. We are not unfamiliar with the evils of racial and ethnic prejudice. But prejudiced thinking and hostile stereotypes regarding other nations and cultures are not limited to capitalist societies or to relations between white-skinned and dark-skinned peoples. Medieval Englishmen were capable of denouncing the Welsh and Irish in terms that would have suited a Ku Klux Klan wizard reviling blacks. On the whole, we regard the American immigrant experience in a positive light.

Our book attempts to blend several disciplines. We try to deal with the salient aspects—sociological, cultural, economic, and historical—of particular immigrant groups and their problems. Having worked previously in African studies, including the sociology of empire builders, we are particularly interested in the comparative dimension. We also attempt to make policy recommendations. In doing so, we are conscious of our limitations. When professors recommend policies, they can do so only in their capacity as well-informed citizens. But all the problems we raise are subject to intense public discussion, and we have found it impossible to remain uninvolved. We hope therefore that this study will make a contribution to an ongoing and necessary public debate.

We are indebted to those scholars who have read our manuscript as a whole or in part—Barry Chiswick, Mark Falcoff, Roland A. Alum, Edwin Harwood, Barbara Held, Santiago Rodriguez, Alvin Rabushka, Ellwyn R. Stoddard, Mario J. Paredes, and Ramon Gutierrez. Their willingness to assist us does not necessarily imply agreement with our view; nor are they responsible for any mistakes in our work. We also wish to thank the Hoover Institution, the Earhart Foundation, and the Weingart Foundation for their generous financial support.

L. H. Gann
Peter J. Duignan

Preface to the 1998 Printing

Much has happened since this book was first published in 1986 under the title *The Hispanics in the United States: A History*. The impact of the 1986 law legalizing 1.3 million illegal immigrants was not anticipated. The newly legalized brought in millions more; undocumented workers kept coming. States such as California, where 40 percent of immigrants settled, bore a heavy burden in providing health, education, and local services. In California the continued influx of immigrants led to a backlash and the adoption, in 1994, of Proposition 187 denying schooling and welfare benefits to illegal immigrants. By 1996, in part because of this growing anti-immigrant movement, Congress passed two laws. This epilogue then replaces the original conclusion and attempts to bring up to date the 1986 book and to consider the impact of the 1996 laws as well as to reassess the arguments for and against immigration in the perspective of the new laws and the conditions of the United States in 1998. We attempt to give a balanced account but conclude that, while immigration overall is a good thing, American economic conditions no longer require large numbers of older, unskilled, semiliterate people. In today's world, the United States should admit only 500,000, not a million plus people each year. Those admitted should be skilled, speak English, and not be old or infirm. No one should be admitted who might become a burden on the welfare system. Fewer refugees should be allowed in, reunification of families should be limited to young members of the nuclear family. And better efforts should be made to control our borders, ports and airports to keep out illegal immigrants and find people who overstay their visas. No more amnesties; welfare benefits should be means-tested, and families that cannot support their relatives should not be permitted to sponsor their immigration. Bilingual education is discussed and rejected; the learning of English should be a primary purpose of education. Americanization, not multiculturalism, should be the goal of schools.

Peter Duignan
May 20, 1998

Part I

The Stage Is Set

Chapter 1

The Hispanic Legacy

For more than a century, Latin American thinkers and politicians have pondered the disparity in wealth and power between Spanish-speaking America on the one hand and the United States on the other. The "giant of the North" has, in this same period, invited suspicion, hatred, and admiration. Yet if a statesman familiar with both North and South America had been asked two centuries ago to forecast the future course of these two empires, he certainly would have predicted Latin America's future predominance over North America.

Two hundred years ago, the United States had just gained its independence; the states formed no more than a loose chain of territories wedged between the Atlantic Ocean and the Allegheny Mountains. The population in 1790 was less than four million (3,172,000 whites and 757,000 nonwhites, mostly blacks). Most English-speaking Americans lived in rural areas. When the American Revolution began, there were only five towns with more than eight thousand inhabitants in all of the North American colonies.

The Spanish-American dependencies seemed infinitely more splendid. Their population probably exceeded English-speaking America's by more than four times. Alexander von Humboldt, the famous eighteenth-century German traveler and savant, reckoned that Spanish America at the end of the eighteenth century contained about 3.25 million whites, 5.5 million *mestizos* (of Spanish-Indian lineage), 7.5 million Indians, and .75 million blacks.[1] At the end of the eighteenth century, Spain's American provinces enjoyed greater prosperity than ever before.

Given Spanish America's growing prosperity, the Spanish-speaking peoples at the end of the eighteenth century seemed destined to rule over the greater part of what is now the United States. The border of the Spanish empire extended to the Missisippi River. (By a secret compact concluded in 1762, France transferred its claims to "Louisiana," an enormous region west of the Mississippi, to Spain; the Spaniards remained in formal possession until 1800, when the country was retroceded to France. In 1803, Napoleon finally sold the territory to the United States.) Florida was a Spanish territory. (That area came into American possession between 1819 and 1821.) "New Spain," the present-day Mexico, extended far into what is now the American Southwest.

In addition, the Spaniards held a substantial stake in what might be called the Caribbean plantation frontier. Cuba had been a Spanish possession for centuries. Under a succession of liberal viceroys, Cuba at the end of the eighteenth century had begun to expand its economy. French planters fleeing from the slave revolts in Haiti established coffee estates in the Oriente province. During the 1820s, expatriate capital from the Latin American mainland, from Spain, and from foreign countries sought profits in great sugar plantations. An expanding sugar frontier gradually pushed into the rich and uncultivated lands of the central province, conferring on Cuba a decisive lead over its competitors in the Caribbean and Brazil. Relying on competent management, economies of scale, and substantial reserves of land, the Cuban plantation owners were able to import increasing numbers of African slaves as well as Indians from Mexico, giving to Cuban magnates much in common with plantation owners in the American southeast. The island of Puerto Rico (*Porto Rico*) was run in a similar fashion. From the end of the eighteenth century, immigrants from the Canary Islands, French émigrés from Haiti, and Spaniards from Santo Domingo introduced new ideas and new marketing methods. Coffee and sugar cultivation spread, turning Puerto Rico into a valuable possession of the Spanish crown. In short, the Spanish challenge to English-speaking America at the end of the eighteenth century was indeed formidable.

The inner strength of this empire, however, in no way corresponded to its outward splendor. On the contrary, the empire suffered from bitter internecine disputes. The *peninsulares,* Spaniards from Europe, generally held the highest positions in church and state, though a few were found in the lower strata. Below the *peninsulares* stood the *criollos* (whites born in the colonies), who included landowners, businessmen, and professional people. Below the whites stood the *mestizos,* children of unions (usually, though not necessarily, illegitimate) between whites and Indians. They were a new breed, Latin Americans par excellence, distinguished both from *criollos* and *peninsulares* (the latter often referred to disparagingly as *gachupines*—those who wore shoes with heels rather than sandals). Most *mestizos* were landless and they occupied most of the intermediary positions in society. Most of them depended on wages and made their livings as craftsmen, soldiers, foremen, petty traders, and laborers. They spoke Spanish, went to church, and formed the bridge between Spaniards and Indians. Some Indians became partly integrated into the Spanish establishment, but most of the Indian population remained outside Spanish-speaking society. The great majority of Indians continued to speak their own languages, follow their own customs, and farm the land in the traditional manner. Although they did most of the unskilled labor on the haciendas, they formed an underclass of outsiders.

A balance sheet of Spanish imperial rule over the centuries is hard to draw up, for there were many different forms of colonialism within the Spanish empire, and conditions differed widely even within the borders of the same viceroyalty. But, overall, Spanish rule was harsh. Its legacy helped to create forms of social organization that placed Latin America at a grave disadvantage vis-à-vis the Anglo-Americans. At the beginning of the nineteenth century, the United States was a bourgeois country without a feudal past. Much of Latin American society, on the other hand, was seignorial in kind, shot through with caste privilege, and widely, though not universally, dependent on peonage. Whereas the United States had been shaped in the spirit of the Protestant middle-class, Spanish America was molded by the ancien régime. It was with good reason that Alexander von Humboldt remarked on the striking parallels between the Indians in Mexico, Peru, and New Granada on the one hand and the serfs of backward Mecklenburg and Livonia on the other.[2] For all its vigor and vitality, Spanish America at the beginning of the eighteenth century widely resembled the most backward parts of central and eastern Europe.

This imposing empire proved incapable of maintaining its cohesion, and when the French, under the Emperor Napoleon, invaded the Iberian Peninsula in the first decade of the nineteenth century, the Spanish overseas empire began to collapse. Most of Spanish America gained its independence, but splintered into a number of separate republics. This disintegration of Spanish America into a congeries of independent states did not occur for lack of statesmanship or ability—postindependence Latin America did not want for great thinkers and leaders. But the Spanish possessions in Latin America were diverse in nature and scattered, split apart by great rivers, mountain ranges, deserts, and, above all, by distance. Had Latin America retained its political unity, the course of world history might have been different. However, the forces of history and geography alike proved too strong for those who hoped for a united South American commonwealth. By 1825, after seventeen years of bloodshed, the Spanish-American empire lay in ruins. Cuba, the "ever-loyal isle," and Puerto Rico remained the last outposts of Spanish imperial might in the Americas until the end of the last century. On the mainland, a divided company of independent states faced the difficult task of rebuilding their shattered prosperity.

The northernmost of these secession states was Mexico, a powerful country—on paper. The regions under Mexican control, real or nominal, extended over some two thousand miles—all the way from San Francisco to the borders of Central America, a stretch equal to the distance from

San Francisco to Lake Huron or from London to the Ural Mountains. The new republic, however, labored under difficulties that might have driven the boldest to despair, for war had shattered Mexico's previous prosperity. Few foreigners would come to Mexico where life and property seemed unsafe. The government exercised but scanty control over the outlying provinces, and the constitutions, based on the North American example, did not work. Mexico, in fact, was a byword for political instability. During the three decades that followed independence, Mexico passed through something like 45 changes of government, countless military rebellions, "pronouncements," coups, and several foreign incursions. The country's various forms of government included a monarchy, a federal republic, a centralist republic, and a dictatorship.[3] There was a bewildering array of parties, but politics meant essentially minority politics. The ruling group constituted one-tenth of the population; all others were excluded from power.

The machinery of government was weak, communications scanty, and the military forces defective. The new government accordingly tried to solve the Indian question by simply denying its existence. All Indians were declared citizens, but their social conditions remained unchanged; if anything, they worsened. In some ways, the Indians' predicament resembled that of southern Italian peasants upon Italy's unification: the Indian cultivators, like the peasants in the *mezzogiorno*, were conscripted to fight for causes they did not understand. They were obliged to pay taxes to a central government (run by city folk) of professional men who were often unsympathetic to, or ignorant of, peasant problems and beliefs. Rich landowners and urban businessmen gradually began to encroach on the communal lands. Mexico faced problems of an almost insoluble kind, problems that the United States, a land without peasants, was spared. These problems continued to worsen; by the 1850s, Mexico's existence as a nation seemed at stake by reason of the Indians' bitter resistance to the central government.[4]

Mexico's northern frontier comprised several regions: coastal California and scattered settlements in parts of the distant interior of Arizona, Texas, and New Mexico. All of these regions developed largely in isolation from one another. There were some lateral communications (the most important being the Old Spanish Trail from Santa Fe to Los Angeles, pioneered by Antonio Armijo in 1829). But the main roads led to Mexico City. The frontier provinces remained hampered by distance, isolation, lack of markets, and lack of capital.

The richest of the borderlands was California, where the Spaniards had occupied a narrow band of territory along the coast. These California outposts were too remote and numerically too insignificant to have played any part in the war against Spain. Nor were they initially affected by Mexico's independence. To the citizens of Mexico City, California was like the end of the world. Spanish-speaking Californians, for their part, came to speak of Mexico as *la otra banda* (the other shore). The Mexican government did not hesitate to send political prisoners and petty crooks to California in order to encourage colonization. By treating California as a kind of Siberia and by its neglect of the province, the central government rendered itself so unpopular that the native born ceased to call themselves *españoles* or *mexicanos*, and insisted on being known as *californios*. *Liberalismo* (liberalism) seeped into the far north and, with it, came calls for local autonomy, freedom from clerical control, separation of civil from military power, secularization of the missions, and the sale of the *californios'* lands. The *californios* managed to attain most of these demands peacefully. In 1836, they took over the provincial government, which had been regarded by the great landowners as their private fief; by 1846, 46 *ranchos*—like the missions of old—produced soap, wine, and cloth for their own needs. The *rancheros* grazed sheep, horses, and, above all, enormous herds of hardy scrub cattle which were slaughtered for their hide and tallow. Traders coming by sea from the United States or Great Britain took away larders of tallow and bales of dry skin; in return they brought in dry goods, salt, agricultural implements, and such small luxuries as the frontiersmen could afford.

Spanish-Mexican society impressed many visitors by its charm and what appeared to be its insouciance. It was a society where family links were intensely strong, where a man's or woman's first allegiance lay with his or her kinfolk. Male predominance went unchallenged, much more so than in English-American society. As Richard Henry Dana, a well-known writer of the period, put it: "The jealousy of . . . husbands is extreme, and the revenge [for adultery] deadly and almost certain."[5] It was a society in which men worked hard when they had to but were not preoccupied with saving, investment, and economic progress, as Anglo-Americans understood the terms. It was a society in which enjoyments were colorful and communal—with religious processions, dances, evenings of singing and guitar playing, cock fighting, bull fighting, bearbaiting, horse racing, and sumptuous dinners for the well-to-do; a society that valued courtesy, formality in manners, and an intense sense of personal honor.

For all its charm, it was also an unstable society. No matter which faction exercised power, governments were disinclined to honor those civic liberties dear to the Anglo-American tradition: distinctions between the various branches of government, a free press, and a free parliament. The majority of the people remained without civic rights as Anglo-Americans understood them. There were no real cities and there was almost nothing like a middle class in the modern sense. The Spanish-speaking settlements were strung out in a narrow band along the coast, the vast interior remaining unoccupied and undefended. The *rancheros* were not aristocrats in a European sense, the Spanish crown already having abolished most of their legal privileges before Mexico attained independence. They regarded themselves as members of a rural gentry; but these gentlemen were ill equipped both psychologically and economically to defend their position once the Anglo-Americans took over the country.

In New Mexico and Arizona, in contrast to California, the Spaniards tried to build on Indian foundations. New Mexican society came to rest on extensive seignorial privileges. Among the Pueblo Indians, for instance, the conquerors imposed labor services. At the end of the seventeenth century, there were extensive Indian revolts. But the Spaniards returned and developed a distinctive frontier economy dependent on the hardy *churro* sheep. The sedentary Indian communities in the borderland benefited in some respects from their association with the newcomers. The Pueblo Indians received some protection against the attacks of Comanche and Apache raiders, and they improved the techniques of irrigated farming they had practiced for centuries. The Indians also paid a heavy price when the strangers from the south levied tribute in the form of textiles and hides. Worse still, the newcomers introduced infectious diseases, such as smallpox and measles, against which the Indians had no natural resistance—scourges that had already ravaged Mexico in the sixteenth century, and which proved more destructive in terms of human life than all the Spaniards' firearms.

Neither Spaniards nor Mexicans could make much headway against the Apaches on their own ground. Far from being able to expand into the interior, the colonists remained surrounded on three sides by warlike nomadic communities, and sometimes even had difficulty securing their communications to Mexico against marauding warriors.

Nevertheless, New Mexico's Spanish-speaking population slowly increased, concentrated for the most part in the central part of the Rio Grande valley. About one-quarter of the population was Pueblo Indian; the remainder included many Hispanicized Indians who had converted to Catholicism. The main centers were Albuquerque, Santa Cruz de la Cañada, and Santa Fe (the latter originally founded in 1609 on the site of a prehistoric Indian village). During the eighteenth century, Santa Fe developed a substantial trade in sheep, wool, pelts, and wine, chiefly with Chihuahua but also with the Plains Indians. During the early nineteenth century, Santa Fe became the center of a considerable commerce with the United States. Goods were carried first by pack animals, and from 1822, by wagon trains over the Old Santa Fe Trail from Independence and Kansas City, Missouri. The residents of New

Mexico henceforth were able to trade with the Anglo-American frontiersmen much more easily than with Mexico, just as the *californios* could more readily traffic with Boston merchants by clipper ship than with Mexican suppliers by the overland route.

In most other respects, Spanish-speaking society in New Mexico differed considerably from California's. Fearful of Indian attack, the New Mexico cultivators preferred to live in small townships in which each home—with its thick adobe walls, barred windows, and heavy doors—might serve as a fortress. The rule of the *patrón* over his peons was much tighter than in California, where the availability of ranch land militated against the emergence of a peon class and where ranching did not require nearly as much labor as irrigated or flood-plain farming along the river valleys in New Mexico. During the period between Mexican independence and the outbreak of the Mexican-American War, substantial numbers of Mexican immigrants made their way into New Mexico, especially into the area between Socorro and El Paso on the Upper Rio Grande River. New Mexico also developed a substantial sheep-farming industry as well as its own class of artisans—weavers, smiths, and *santeros* (carvers of wooden saints' statues).

In addition, Mexicans built up a small mining industry. Copper was produced at Santa Rita, in the southwestern part of New Mexico, and mule trains took the ore to Mexico City, where the metal was minted into coins. Mexican prospectors also discovered gold in the Sierra del Oro, between Santa Fe and Albuquerque. Lack of capital and the high cost of transport presented the mining industry with difficult problems and thereby helped to prevent the emergence of a proletarian class. New Mexico remained a semifeudal society dominated by a small oligarchy of *criollo* landowners, soldiers, and parish priests.

By far the most exposed part of Mexico's northern border was Texas, where Spaniards had established a few settlements as a safeguard against an assumed French threat. In 1718, for instance, they built the township of San Antonio, where the eighteenth-century Governor's Palace, the Cathedral of San Fernando, and the Franciscan mission San António de Valero continue to provide visual evidence of the colonizers' religious faith, artistic taste, and that fusion—characteristic of the frontier—between church and state. However, the Spanish system of maintaining influence through mission stations and *presidios* did not work well in a distant borderland whose warlike, indigenous peoples could be neither converted nor conquered.

At the end of the eighteenth century, Mexican *latifundistas* (great landowners) began to make their way, together with their retainers, to the banks of the Rio Grande and beyond. In the grasslands along the Nueces River, cattlemen found unexpected security from raiding Apaches and Comanches. Marauding horsemen did not care to enter the south Texas triangle, where the climate was too warm for the bison herds on which depended the livelihood of the Indians. The cattle ranches were stoutly defended by Mexican *vaqueros*, almost as expert as Apache warriors in fighting on horseback, tracking men or game, and finding their way in the wilderness. The expanding Anglo-American frontier in Louisiana created a growing demand for Texas cattle, as did the development of sugar plantations in the Caribbean. In addition, the Mexican settlers cultivated a variety of staple foods that furnished their main diet.

Altogether, Mexican colonization in Texas had three great achievements to its credit. The pioneers were the first to set up great cattle ranches in what is now the United States. They also created a new lifestyle, that of the *charro* (a tough cowman inured to hardship and skilled in ranch work, a splendid fighter, and a loyal retainer to his lord). And the Mexicans introduced their own Spanish-derived system of land titles, along with other features of Spanish law, thereby putting a permanent imprint on the southernmost part of the region.[6]

The Mexicans did not penetrate far into the interior. San Antonio, Goliad on the San Antonio River toward the Gulf, and Nacogdoches near the Louisiana border were their main settlements. As far as the Mexicans were concerned, the vast interior remained *tierra despoblada* (empty acres). Unlike California and New Mexico, Texas thus lay dangerously exposed to Anglo-American infiltration. Whereas the southernmost Mexican settlements in Texas were separated from the Mexican heartland by a huge expanse of semiarid land, no mountain ranges or desert wastes divided borderlands from the main centers of Anglo-American settlement. Instead, rich alluvial plains stretched from the plateau to the Gulf, and the rivers could be crossed in all seasons and at almost any point without much difficulty. New Orleans was much closer to San Antonio than was Mexico City. Weakened by internal dissension and beset by economic difficulties, Mexico was strategically ill placed to defend its northern borderlands.

In summary, the Spanish-speaking immigrants had made a considerable contribution to the development of the Southwest. They had created the first sheep farms and the first cattle ranches; they had introduced a variety of Mediterranean crops; they had pioneered the earliest mining industry on the frontier; they had developed a distinctive dry-land civilization represented by the adobe house and church, the mule train, the ox wagon, and irrigation works. The singular culture of the *charro* evolved a working idiom whose terms—rancho, lasso, bronco, corral, and rodeo—are now understood by English-speaking people throughout the world.

The Spaniards had implanted in the Southwest their traditional system of colonial values, symbolized by the presidio, the mission station, the church, and the fair—together with a set of economic attitudes that took for granted strict control of the economy by the state, with regulation of land tenure, commerce, town planning, and irrigation. Mexican independence introduced some modifications of this tradition. Indians and *mestizos* received the right of citizenship, at least in a formal sense. Local legislatures had come into being to represent the interests of the elite; but the mass of *mestizos* and Indians, who made up the lower classes, continued to live in the most humble circumstances. The *mestizo* sharecroppers, or *medieros* of New Mexico and Texas barely managed to keep body and soul together. The Indians were poorer still, some of them reduced to virtual enslavement. Frederick Jackson Turner's famous thesis notwithstanding, the frontier and freedom were far from synonymous.

The Mexican-American frontier differed strikingly from that of the English-speaking Americans who were shaped in their earliest stages by the canoe, the ax, and the log cabin; later by the moldboard plow, the chapel, the schoolhouse; and finally by the railway track and barbedwire fence. On the whole, Mexican influence in the northern borderlands remained exceedingly tenuous, confined to a few "islands" of settlement. When Mexico proclaimed its independence, the total number of Spanish-speaking people in what are now the states of California, New Mexico, Arizona, Utah, Nevada, and Texas was only about sixty thousand. As claimed on Mexican maps of the period, settlements were scattered over an enormous area of more than 850,000 square miles—over nine times the size of Great Britain. In the best of times, this huge borderland would have been difficult to settle and difficult to defend. But at a crucial moment in its history, Mexico found itself facing an Anglo-American challenge. It proved ill equipped to hold onto its northern patrimony.

Initially, U.S.-Mexican relations were excellent. Mexicans appreciated the moral support given by North Americans to the cause of independence in Central and South America; Mexico modeled its constitution on that of the United States. The few Americans who visited Mexico—men like Joel R. Pointsett, the first American minister to Mexico—returned with a most favorable impression. Southern plantation owners in particular felt a bond of sympathy with *criollo* landed magnates. Well-to-do American merchants in California were proud to marry into "good" local families. Most Americans, however, knew little of civilized life in Mexico, and few Mexicans had the slightest knowledge of cultured American society in Boston or New York. Few educated Americans had a command of Spanish; few cultured Mexicans spoke English. The two nationalities formed their impressions about one another primarily from the frontiersmen they met in remote border communities. The original stereotypes of Mexicans and Anglo-Americans thus derived from frontier confrontations, and these images in turn colored national stereotypes as a whole.

A great deal of popular history notwithstanding, Spanish- and English-speaking frontiersmen did not always clash; violence was the exception rather than the rule. Narrative historians, journalists, and television script writers have one thing in common: a preference for dramatic and bloody events over the humdrum life of every day. This preference is apt to distort the past as well as the present. The point bears repeating that the great majority of Anglo-Americans and Spanish-speaking Americans who met on the border rarely, if ever, drew a knife or fired a pistol in anger. They came to trap, to farm, and especially to trade, for commerce was essential to life on the frontier. The pioneers never were wholly self-sufficient. A whole range of goods—muskets, rifles, salt, coffee—had to be brought in from outside. California's early cattle economy, as we have seen, depended heavily on Yankee merchants and Yankee ships. New Mexico increasingly turned to the United States as Sante Fe became an important local trade center, as American and New Mexican merchants played a growing role in the development of the province, and as New Mexico's provincial government became reliant on income derived from custom duties. Trade benefited everybody, not only the *ricos* (the upper class) but also artisans, miners, and cowhands willing to buy imported goods. New Mexicans exchanged bullion, horses, and mules for American-manufactured knives, axes, guns, textiles, and the like. American traders and trappers settled in New Mexico, married local women, converted to Catholicism, acquired land, and became pillars of society. American merchants did the same in California.

A number of these early American pioneers—hunters, ship's captains, ranchers, merchants, army officers—developed a liking and respect for Spanish-speaking people, not only *caballeros* with their courtly bearing and elegance but also plain folk with their equally distinguished manners. "A common bullock driver delivering a message," wrote Richard Henry Dana, when he visited California in 1833–34, "seemed to speak like an ambassador at an audience."[7]

Many Mexicans reciprocated these good feelings. "The industrious, honest North American settlers," resolved the *ayuntamiento* (town council) of San Antonio in 1832, "have raised cotton and cane, and erected gins and saw mills. Their industry has made them comfortable and independent while the Mexican settlements, depending on the pay of soldiers among them for money, have lagged far behind."[8] Mexicans, the city fathers complained, are obliged to buy their blankets, hats, and

shoes from the Americans because Mexico lacks the requisite manufacturing plant. Increased American immigration would afford a new
source of supply, would help to protect the interior from Indian invasion,
would build roads, and would develop commerce with New Orleans
and New Mexico. American ideas of good government, moreover, resembled those held by Mexicans more nearly than those held by European
immigrants. These views expressed the opinions of the Mexican elite
and they were echoed in California, where some of the landowners
looked to an increasing number of immigrants for the purpose of
expanding trade, raising the value of real estate, and reducing the sense
of provincial isolation.

Part of the Mexican lower class expressed its admiration for its
English-speaking neighbors by adopting some of the Anglo-Americans'
habits. In fact, the process of Anglicization on the frontier began long
before English language schools, English radio broadcasts, English television programs, and other instruments of "cultural imperialism" had
made an impact on Mexican-American popular culture. The "very
humble people" of Nacogdoches, Texas, wrote with disgust that cultured
Mexican army officers during the course of an official mission in 1828
were "ignorant not only of the customs of our great cities, but even of
the occurrence of our Revolution. . . . Accustomed to the continued
trade with North Americans, they have adopted their customs and
habits, and one may say truly that they are not Mexicans except by
birth, for they even speak Spanish with marked incorrectness."[9]

Favorable impressions, however, came to be outweighed by the poor
opinions that Spanish-speaking and English-speaking Americans held
about one another. On the part of the upper-class Mexicans, there was
a mixture of social disdain for North American frontiersmen and a
sense of apprehension regarding the future.

In Mexico itself, anti-Americanism had literary springs as well. Many
educated Mexicans used the term *anglosajones* (Anglo-Saxons) as a word
of abuse. In the cities, the educated often imbibed their views of Anglo-
Saxons through the European romantic movement, through Spanish and,
above all, French authors. Continental romantics such as Heine disliked
the Anglo-Saxons (especially the British) because they associated the
Anglo-Saxons with the real or alleged ills of the industrial revolution.
Materialism, irreligion, greed, philistinism, and lack of aesthetic integrity
supposedly were Anglo-Saxon qualities—different from the profound
virtues of the folk that were thought to inhabit the souls of Germans,
Poles, Frenchmen, or Mexicans.

Ethnic prejudice flowered with equal exuberance on the northern side
of the Mexican border. Indeed, a deep sense of hatred pervades a good
deal of early Anglo-American writing concerning the Spanish-speaking

people along the American frontier. Militant Protestants censured Mexicans for their adherence to Catholicism and their supposed superstition, disloyalty, lechery, drunkenness, and subservience to priests.

Many Americans also looked down on Mexicans for their darker complexion and mixed racial origins. *Californios*, a mixed people, were supposedly cowardly, ignorant, lazy, and addicted to gambling and alcohol. American pioneers equated the Mexicans' social system with poverty and feudal subordination. "Half naked and scantily fed, they [the New Mexican peons] are content with the miserable pittance doled out to them by the proud lordlings whom they serve," wrote Rufus B. Sage, an American pioneer, just before the outbreak of the Mexican-American War. As Sage described them, the peasants lived in miserable adobe houses, cramped and unsanitary, without the most elementary amenities, and even without proper furniture. "The entire business of the country is in the hands of the rich . . . and as a natural consequence, the rich know no end to their treasure, nor the poor to their poverty." This state of affairs was not likely to improve, for superstition was universal; education was confined to the priests; "gambling, swearing, sabbath breaking" were the rule; life and property were both equally unsafe.[10] Interethnic hostility, in other words, did not spring from color prejudice or nationalist xenophobia alone. Ethnic tensions, on the contrary, reflected a wider conflict between two mutually incompatible societies.

The immediate cause for war between Mexico and the United States derived from disputes over Texas. A remote province poorly controlled from Mexico City, Texas was being overrun by non-Mexican immigrants, both legal and illegal. These newcomers were Germans who brought their own system of mixed agriculture to Texas, and Americans, primarily from the Southeast, who grew cotton and other subtropical crops with the aid of slave labor and who also acquired a stake in cattle farming. By the 1830s, the newcomers heavily outnumbered the scanty Mexican population. Mexico did not object to immigration, provided that the colonists would adopt Mexican citizenship, abide by Mexican laws, become Catholics (at least in a formal sense), and pay taxes (including customs duties designed to make Texas trade with Mexico rather than with the United States). Foreigners, after all, had come to Mexico of their own free will; they should be obedient to the customs of Mexico.

The American settlers, for their part, were determined to maintain those "inalienable rights" to which they had been accustomed in the United States. They objected to what they regarded as corrupt justice, excessive taxes, discriminatory laws against Protestants, an inefficient and remote administration, and Mexico's resolve to outlaw slavery (a decision that especially alienated the Southerners who made up the majority of the American colonists). The Americans in Texas likened their condition to that of their forebears under British suzerainty, and, in their view, both history and equity favored their cause. The borders of the newly independent states in Latin America were of relatively recent vintage. The new states did not as yet enjoy the unchallenged legitimacy they were to acquire in the twentieth century. (Both "Great Columbia" and the "United Provinces of Central America" broke up into smaller states during the 1830s.) Spanish-speaking *californios*, *tejanos*, and *nuevo mexicanos* themselves were far from united in their loyalty to Mexico. Hence, the American colonists in Mexico (including a minority of *tejanos* willing to fight against Mexican rule) felt perfectly justified in their endeavor to break away from Mexico.

Secession became inevitable when President Antonio López de Santa Anna resolved to maintain his tottering government by placing himself at the head of a centralizing dictatorship, dissolving the Mexican Congress, and proclaiming the end of Mexican states rights. By doing so, he aroused not only the American colonists in Texas but also Mexican advocates of states rights from Texas to California. In 1836, Texas proclaimed its independence from Mexico. Mexican forces tried to reconquer the territory but failed.

Texas (the "Lone Star state") gained short-lived international recognition as a sovereign commonwealth. Mexico, though unreconciled to its loss, ultimately might have accepted the Texas fait accompli, but on no account would the Mexicans countenance the annexation of Texas by the United States. To the Mexicans, Texas was the first line of defense against their greedy neighbors whose talk of "manifest destiny" and voracity for land seemed to represent a never-ending threat. The loss of Texas, it was feared, would result in the loss of New Mexico and California. To Mexican patriots, Mexico's very existence seemed at stake, for, if the country did not resist, it might ultimately be partitioned like the former kingdom of Poland.

Circumstances, the Mexicans believed, temporarily favored them. America was engaged at the same time in a dispute with Great Britain over Oregon. Great Britain supposedly had a material stake in the independence of Texas. And the Americans were not to be overly feared; Mexico's armed forces outnumbered them by five to one—at least on paper. The American army was fit only to fight Indians, and undisciplined American volunteers would be no match for Mexican professionals. Mexico's population of seven million amounted only to about one-third of America's; but the Mexicans despised the Americans as money-grubbers and believed (as did the Japanese and the Germans in the twentieth century with equally little justification) that the Americans were too soft and too materialistic to fight. Remembering the Yankees' blundering attempt to invade Canada in the War of 1812, the Mexicans held American military power to be of small account. Their contempt for American power was strengthened by President James Polk's attempts to buy Texas and California for hard cash.

The Mexican view of the United States, moreover, was widely shared in Europe. The *London Times* thus felt convinced that the "invasion and conquest of a vast region by a State which is without an army and without credit is a novelty in the history of nations."[11] Tocqueville, on the other hand, later gave a brilliant explanation for the Americans' military superiority. He argued that an "aristocratic" people would prevail in the earlier stages of a conflict; a "democratic" people, on the other hand, would get the better of its opponents in the latter stages of a war, by which time the "democratic" people would have gained a decisive superiority. Tocqueville, therefore, expected further American expansion at the Mexicans' expense.[12]

The Americans were bitterly divided over the war against Mexico. The principal advocates of war derived from the ranks of Southerners who wanted to safeguard slavery as an institution within the United States by the creation of a new (possibly several new) slave states. Abolitionists and antislavery proponents, on the other hand, looked upon the acquisition of Texas as a slave-owners' conspiracy designed to subvert American freedom. President Polk planned to decide the issue by a program that would satisfy both the slave states and the "free soil" states: he would acquire not only Texas but also Oregon and California, thus extending America's boundaries to the Pacific Ocean.

California played a particularly important part in President Polk's calculations. The territory was as rich a prize as Texas. Its connection with Mexico was tenuous and its Spanish-speaking population was tiny. Moreover, California threatened to become a political Texas as English-speaking immigrants began to arrive in the country by sea via Cape Horn, and later by land via the Oregon Trail. These newcomers were a hard-bitten lot, very different from the handful of Americans who had arrived in California during the 1820s and the 1830s. The new immigrants had no intention of assimilating into Mexican society; they believed in America's "manifest destiny." They deliberately settled in northern California, away from effective Mexican control. Some of them began a rising of their own, the Bear Flag Revolt, which later merged into the broader Mexican-American War.

President Polk's interest in Mexico was all the greater because he feared (mistakenly, it turned out) that the British had designs on California. Its acquisition would give the British an overwhelmingly powerful position in the Pacific, where they already held the Australian colonies, New Zealand, and British Columbia. President Polk would have been willing to get his way by cash rather than by cannon. The Mexicans, however, were determined to resist, and, in 1846, Mexico and the United States went to war.

Aided by difficult terrain, the Mexicans fought with great resolution. It is reading history backward to imagine that the outcome of the war was a foregone conclusion; this is a misconception later promoted by the propaganda of Whigs and abolitionists who stigmatized the conflict as a plot to bring more slave-holding states into the Union. The Mexican infantrymen, tough and inured to hardship, were formidable opponents; and the artillerymen and engineers performed with distinction, enhancing Mexico's military reputation in arms. Incidents such as the last-ditch defense of Mexican positions by youthful officer cadets—*los niños héroes*, the hero children—live on as a legend in Mexican memories. But the Mexicans were divided internally between the centralists—who wished to establish a semimonarchical form of government—and the federalists— who stressed states rights. Competition between rival factions weakened the soldiers' resolve, as they were "recruited" by one army and then another. There was as yet little sense of a common nationality. Regionalism was intense, especially in outlying communities such as Santa Fe, where the only link to the rest of the country was a wagon train that came every year, or perhaps ever second year, to bring in supplies and take out pelts to Chihuahua city. The Americans, by contrast, had a greater sense of national cohesion. Also, the Americans were brilliantly led and displayed the same capacity for rapid improvisation and daring offensive strikes that later served them in the Civil War. Mexican leadership and Mexican supply arrangements, on the other hand, in no way did justice to Mexican valor. In the end, the Americans achieved a shattering success, one no European army at the time could have equaled, and Mexico was compelled to sign peace terms at Guadalupe Hidalgo, near Mexico City on February 2, 1848.

Under the terms of the treaty, Mexico agreed to cede to the United States both California and New Mexico, a vast territory approximately half the size of Mexico at the time, though containing only about 1 percent of its population. In addition, Mexico relinquished all claims to Texas and the Mexican-American boundary was set at the Rio Grande. Most of this territory was only nominally controlled from Mexico; in California, the voice of Mexico City had ceased to be heard. From the territory acquired by force of arms, the Americans in time created the states of California, Nevada, Arizona, Utah, New Mexico, and Wyoming and gained parts of what are now Kansas and Colorado. In exchange for this territorial cession, the United States agreed to pay Mexico the sum of $15,000,000 and to assume the claims of its own citizens against Mexico of $3,250,000. The Americans promised to respect the Mexicans' religion and property in the newly conquered lands. Mexicans desirous of returning to Mexico would be allowed to do so; while those who neither left nor declared their intention to remain Mexican citizens would acquire American citizenship.

At a negligible price in money and in men, the United States acquired huge new territories, extended its power to the Pacific Ocean, and more or less assumed its present shape. (The Americans, in 1853, rounded off their new possessions by the so-called Gadsden Purchase, by which Mexico sold the regions that now comprise southern Arizona and southern New Mexico.) Fortunately for the peace of both countries, the United States refrained from annexing the relatively well-populated Mexican heartland, a solution called for by ultrachauvinists in the United States. Had the Americans given way to the "All-Mexico Movement," the conquerors would have had to subdue a large and disaffected Spanish-speaking population that might have embarked on a prolonged guerrilla war. Conflicts between Americans and Mexicans continued on the border as private citizens continued to lead filibustering expeditions across the border and as cattle rustlers kept southwest Texas in turmoil until the 1880s. But the new boundary was no longer effectively challenged. War confirmed the absolute supremacy of the United States on the American continent.

The Treaty of Guadalupe Hidalgo was only one of several harsh territorial settlements imposed on the vanquished side following nineteenth-century wars in Latin America. (For example, Paraguay lost heavily after a disastrous war against the Triple Alliance of Argentina, Brazil, and Uruguay, 1865–1870.) In the eyes of Spanish Americans, however, the Treaty of Guadalupe Hidalgo was different in that it involved the loss of Latin lands to Anglo-Saxon conquerors. The "giant of the north" was thereafter looked upon with much greater suspicion than before. The Mexicans saw themselves as the aggrieved party, forced to defend their homeland against an overweening opponent. The early admiration for the United States, which had led Mexico to emulate American political institutions, gave way to widespread bitterness. The *corridos* (popular ballads) continued to tell their tales of Mexican bravery and Yankee greed.

Mexican opinion in the newly conquered lands was divided. About two thousand Mexicans proudly refused to accept American sovereignty and migrated to Mexico. Others—with rifles in hand—continued to resist the Americans. But the overwhelming majority, about eighty thousand, decided to accept American rule. Subsequent critics notwithstanding, the Treaty of Guadalupe Hidalgo was not comparable to twentieth-century treaties—either those imposed by Hitler on his enemies, or the settlement in Eastern Europe after World War II that involved the enforced migration of something like fifteen million people from their homelands. The great majority of Mexicans believed that life under the Stars and Stripes would be no worse, and perhaps would be better, than life under the Mexican Tricolor, an impression heightened by the unfortunate experiences of many *californios* who did make the move to Mexico. Mexico, the majority of *californios* and *tejanos* argued, had been unable to defend them. Since the courageous resistance of *californios* had received no effective support, Mexico no longer had a claim on Spanish speakers' loyalty. As acting governor of New Mexico Juan Bautista Vigil y Alarid stated in 1846: "The power of the Mexican Republic is dead. . . . No one in the world can resist the power of him who is stronger. Mexico had been our mother; it was only just that we should weep at her tomb. But it was better to become citizens of the United States than be subjected to a European nation or to share the fate of Poland, that had been partitioned among its neighbors."[13]

Chapter 2

Spreading the Eagle's Wings

The new lands incorporated into the United States differed widely in geography and social composition; the American impact on them also varied. In California, the American occupation authorities at first tried to maintain the old order. They accordingly enforced Mexican law, utilized Mexican administrative procedures, and appointed *californios* to leading positions in the local government. The first constitutional convention, assembled in 1849, contained a number of Spanish-speaking delegates and took some account of their wishes. For instance, the convention decided that all new state regulations and laws should be translated into Spanish. The *californios*, some of whom were of mixed ancestry, also were successful in preventing Indians from being disenfranchised.

But the discovery of gold in California in 1848, followed by the great Gold Rush, shattered the old order, and the Spanish-speaking people became an insignificant minority. (Within the first two years of the discovery of gold, they amounted to 15 percent of the population; by 1870, they numbered only 4 percent.) Under the weight of the new immigration, California society, with its seignorial traditions, antiquated methods of production, and aristocratic insouciance, cracked like a matchbox under a sledgehammer. Modern critics, such as Rodolfo Acuña, blame primarily the Anglo-American racism for the *californios'* demise. Racial prejudice was indeed strong; it found expression in intense anti-Oriental as well as anti-Hispanic feeling, and it existed not only among backwoods miners but also among the well educated. The fires of prejudice were stoked by intellectuals, including literary men and educators proud of their supposedly progressive views. David Starr Jordan, the first president of Stanford University and an uncompromising advocate of world peace, never tired of pointing out to Irishmen, Greeks, Jews, Italians, and Mexicans that they could not measure up to the Anglo-Saxons' exalted standards.

More important still, were economic factors. Early California was a violent and ill-policed land. Faced with Mexican competition, many of the early Anglo-American miners responded with pistol and gun. The newcomers heavily outnumbered the *californios*, who were looked upon as foreigners who recently had been vanquished in war. The atmosphere was further poisoned by repressed sexual jealousy in a society composed largely of young men who may have envied the Spanish speakers their women folk. The Anglo-American immigrants also had a deep-seated fear about the uncertainty of their livelihood in the mine fields. Mining was a high-risk occupation; there were no social services and no family connections to help one out of bankruptcy. The Anglo-Americans' apprehensions grew as new competitors began to arrive from Latin America.

The Spanish speakers included Peruvians, Argentinians, and Chileans (mostly skilled men—including bakers and bricklayers). The most numerous group, however, was the so-called Sonorans, from northern Mexico. They were distinguishable from other Latin Americans by their strange dress—white pantaloons, sandals, and sombreros. They were swarthier, more Indian-looking than the *californios*, and more "primitive." Also they would work for lower wages than the others. The Sonorans incurred odium not merely because they were foreigners, but because they appeared to represent the old seignorial system adapted to the mining industry and were therefore a threat to the very structure of American society. A mixture of restrictive legislation, litigation, vigilante activity, blackmail, beatings, and murder caused the Spanish speakers to flee from the northern mines. The Spanish speakers were further blamed when some of them took to banditry, thereby occasioning greater vigilante action. Anti-Hispanic discrimination had become institutionalized.[1]

Gold field lawlessness made an even more profound impact on existing land rights. Many of the newcomers had an anarchic strain; they respected neither tradition nor property rights, whether claimed by men of Nordic or of Mexican descent. As placer gold became exhausted, many miners turned to such pursuits as farming, squatting on the lands of *californio* magnates. The Treaty of Guadalupe Hidalgo explicitly guaranteed existing property rights; but this was difficult to enforce, given the divergent nature of two contrasting systems of landownership—the traditional Hispanic land grants involving enormous concessions to a handful of families, and the Anglo-American system of individual ownership through quitrent deeds. Faced with mass immigration and dependent on a weak and creaking governmental machine, the U.S. authorities were in no position to make good their promises. In 1849, an estimated two hundred *californio* families were said to hold about fourteen million acres in parcels from one to eleven leagues (one league equals forty-five hundred acres). The magnates depended on extensive forms of cattle-farming which required but a minimum of labor. Thus, unlike feudal lords of an earlier era, the magnates were unable to mobilize substantial levies of armed retainers in defense of their property. Most landowners also lacked the liquid capital that would have enabled them to tide themselves over bad times, to defend their rights in court in the endless legal battles that ensued upon the American conquest, or to modernize the industry.

The assault on the *californios* was two-pronged. Squatters moved onto their lands and sometimes physically harassed the rightful owners. And lawyers and politicians questioned the magnates' titles in the courts. In 1851, Congress, under pressure from California legislators, passed the Land Act of 1851, which required the landowners to prove their titles before a land commission. The commissioners themselves were honest men, but, by placing the onus of proof on the landowners rather than upon those who questioned existing titles, the act nevertheless put the *californios* in a difficult position. Their case rested primarily on usage and custom, whereas the commissioners demanded documentary proof which the magnates could not easily supply. As cases dragged on and appeal followed appeal, the cost of the proceedings proved ruinously expensive. And even if the *californios* won their cases in court, many lost their land through the high cost of lawyers' fees, the shady practices of land sharks, or outright seizure by squatters.[2]

The *californios'* troubles did not end with those occasioned by the law's delay. From the late 1860s, the demand for California beef—the landowners' staple product—began to drop as a result of competition from superior Texas beef. During the early 1860s, the California cattle industry suffered from rains, floods, and subsequent droughts. Some *rancheros* managed to survive these disasters and even to profit from the subsequent expansion of the farming industry resulting from the building of railways and the employment of new farming techniques. Some successful *californios* married into Anglo-American families and became indistinguishable from their neighbors. However, many more proved unable to adjust to the needs of capitalized farming for a mass market. The *californios'* ignorance of English and of American legal procedure, high rates of taxation on unimproved land, heavy burdens of debt coupled with high rates of interest, unbusinesslike management techniques, and a commitment to maintaining traditional lifestyles— all contributed to the *californios'* demise as a social class. This is not to say that large aggregations of land disappeared from California. On the contrary, the state saw every gradation in farm size, from the small family farm to the giant estate. But even the so-called baronies gradually changed their economic function as cattle raised for the hide and tallow trade gave way to sheep, and then to wheat, and later on to fruit, wine, and citrus in the course of an unplanned social revolution.

A small minority of Spanish-speaking Californians benefited from the new order. Albert Camarillo, a distinguished Chicano historian, ascertains that between 1860 and 1880 there was a small increase in the percentage of Spanish-speaking townsmen in southern California who made their living in the professions or in business. Some gained a modest degree of prosperity as physicians, attorneys, hairdressers, harness makers, or clerks. In Los Angeles, by then a growing city, this widely dispersed middle class maintained a living standard far superior to that of the rest of the Spanish-speaking population.

Most of the Spanish speakers, however, suffered from the decline of the traditional ranching industry and from the decline of the traditional rural crafts associated with ranching. In southern California, the percentage of skilled Spanish-speaking workers diminished strikingly, while at the same time there was a noticeable increase in the percentage of semiskilled and unskilled workers, many of whom found jobs in the growing tourist industries, in manufacturing, and in large-scale farming enterprises in the hinterland. As Camarillo has shown in his pioneering study, the Mexican pueblos became encapsulated in sprawling cities in which the Spanish speakers were reduced to the status of a despised minority.[3] The old plazas came to resemble an *Altstadt* in an industrialized German city, where the historic core commonly deteriorated into a picturesque backwater and where housing conditions were at their worst.

This was what happened in Los Angeles. Founded in 1781, Los Angeles began as a settlement with a mixed population of Spaniards, *mestizos*, and a number of black slaves. After the Mexican-American War, the pastoral economy declined; more and more Anglo-American and also European newcomers came to the township. As historian Pedro Castillo points out, the Mexican *barrio* by 1880 had become a well-defined ethnic enclave and a slum.[4] Most of its citizens, like the majority of Spanish speakers in California, had become members of a semiskilled or unskilled working class, working no longer for landed magnates but for Anglo-American owners of farms, factories, and workshops.

What accounts for the *californios'* relative lack of success? An obvious explanation centers on racial and ethnic prejudice, which prevented *mestizo* workers from finding a foothold in the trade unions, which confined Spanish speakers into segregated barrios, and which excluded them from an equitable share in political power. But Spanish speakers were not alone in facing such discrimination. Other immigrants (Italians, Portuguese, and Armenians) also had to cope with numerous social disabilities; Orientals, in fact, were not allowed to own land. But the European immigrants, coming from countries more developed culturally and economically than Mexico, often were better equipped by social training and background than Mexicans to make use of new commercial opportunities. Armenians, for instance, improved their fortunes as craftsmen, truck farmers, and small-town traders. Italians and Portuguese profited form the market economy by starting new California industries, such as fishing, viticulture, truck farming, and the restaurant trade. The Italian immigrants who managed to get as far as the West Coast were, on the whole, better educated and better placed financially than their compatriots who had landed on the East Coast and ended up in crowded urban ghettos. Poor immigrants found work on the farms of Irishmen and Germans who had arrived earlier in the United States. The Italians, with their widely acknowledged habits of industry and economy and their specialized skills in truck farming, benefited from being able to acquire land cheaply. They introduced into the San Francisco Bay Area such cash crops as garlic, broccoli, eggplant, zucchini, bell peppers, artichokes, and grapes. By 1900, Italian farmers monopolized truck farming in the Bay area. This in turn gave employment to Italian businessmen.[5]

The Spanish speakers, by contrast, lacked the Italians' experience in truck farming and business. The *californios'* social structure was more archaic than the Italians', and the former failed to develop an urban bourgeoisie. Although the Spanish speakers had many different skills, their special training as *rancheros* (ranch hands), harness makers, horse-shoers, and leather workers was linked to a traditional ranching economy, and their qualifications became increasingly difficult to sell as the California economy was transformed.

California's nineteenth-century history had a streak of violence, but its tradition of bloodshed was minor compared to that of Texas, a state conceived on the battlefield. To the original struggle for Texan independence, Mexicans had brought an element of vengeance from their own internecine dissensions. Anglo-Americans contributed an equally grim legacy: enmities borne of social and racial prejudice, the injustice associated with slavery, and the ferocity derived from lengthy Indian wars. The most fundamental cause of lawlessness, however, did not come from ethnic or class hostilities between Mexicans on the one hand and Anglo-Americans or Europeans on the other. The root cause of trouble lay in the inability of Mexicans and Americans alike to enforce the most elementary requirement of government—a respect for law. Under the Treaty of Guadalupe Hidalgo, the United States bound itself to prevent incursions of Indians from north of the Rio Grande into Mexico. In 1852, the U.S. Army's effective strength amounted to no more than 10,000—and that tiny force was expected to police a sub-continent.

Not surprisingly, the job of pacifying the borderlands proved totally beyond the army's ability. In 1852, only twenty-three hundred men were stationed in the Department of Texas; of these, less than six hundred did garrison duty at border posts on the Rio Grande. Indians continued

to raid Mexico from the American side. In addition, Comanches and
other warriors set themselves up on the Mexican side of the border
and carried out forays into Texas and New Mexico. The Indians were
joined by American and Mexican desperadoes, who were armed as
effectively as the American soldiers and often were more familiar with
the countryside.

On the Mexican side of the border, law and order were enforced in
an equally ineffective fashion. The central government was not necessarily
anti-American; in fact, it welcomed American support against the
unsuccessful designs of Napoleon III to turn Mexico into a French
vassal state. But the central government exercised little power in the
remote border provinces, where landed magnates controlled the local
government, raised their own forces, and conducted struggles for power.
According to their American critics, there was a definite alliance (originally for the disposal of stolen cattle) between Indians, Mexican officials,
and influential *rancheros*. The distinction between the bandit, the freedom
fighter, and the successful entrepreneur was tenuous. Juan Nepomuceno
Cortina, a well-known raider at the time, has become a hero to modern
Chicano nationalists who claim he was a guerrilla leader who fought
the hated gringo establishment with the support of lower-class Mexicans,
a patriot determined to avenge slights inflicted on Mexicans by "Anglos,"
and a social reformer resolved to rectify the injury done to Mexicans
by American land sharks. But Cortina also was a major contractor who
supplied the expanding Cuban market with cattle rustled from American
ranches.[6]

By the beginning of this century, the invention of the internal
combustion engine was about to provide lawmen with additional means
against mounted raiders—the truck, the armored car, and the scouting
plane—and rural banditry had become a thing of the past. From the
standpoint of improving ethnic relations, however, pacification in Texas
had been delayed too long. A pattern of violence, discrimination, and
contempt made Texas probably the worst state in the Union for the
Mexican American.

New Mexico had a social pattern all its own. Here the Spanish
colonizers encountered the kind of people they preferred, sedentary
Pueblo Indian villagers, rather than nomadic hunters. The conquerors
set up a seignorial system common in the south, where a small class
of *patrones* held sway over indigenous peoples dwelling in villages and
practicing customary forms of tillage. In the Rio Grande region especially,
the population remained overwhelmingly Spanish speaking, and *hispanos*
continued to advance both east and west of the Rio Grande River
valley. The landed magnates retained their accustomed influence based
on peonage and traditional family alliances. Anglo-American immigration

was slow to develop and the *hispanos* commanded a numerical majority in the territory throughout the nineteenth century. Even as late as 1912, a generation after the railways first reached the region, the Spanish speakers still represented 60 percent of the population, and their preponderance continued until the 1940s.

New Mexico's history was not a particularly happy one. As *hispano* sheepmen moved onto the eastern plains, they clashed with English-speaking cattlemen, chiefly Southerners and Texans who were moving westward and came to dominate the southeastern part of the territory. The cattlemen's hatred for the sheep farmers, whose flocks ruined the pastures for horned beasts, merged with ethnic hatreds to produce bitter local clashes, such as the Lincoln County War of the 1870s, in which rival range organizations came to blows and in which Mexicans were caught in the middle. This era of New Mexican lawlessness produced its share of Mexican-American folk heroes, including Elfego Baca (one of the great fighting sheriffs of the frontier).[7]

There were bitter conflicts over land and bitter complaints about the chicanery of lawyers and about the law's delay, apparent injustice, and expense. Nevertheless, a good many *hispanos* managed to participate in the growing market economy and also to safeguard for a time their political position. In doing so, they benefited from the territory's long-continued "colonial" status. Whereas California and Texas reached statehood right (or almost) at the beginning, New Mexico—until 1912— remained a territory subject to Washington's control; hence the power of Anglo-American immigrants counted for a great deal less than it did in Texas. *Hispano* landowners continued to play a major part in the territorial legislature where, at least until 1859, all sessions continued to be held in Spanish. The influence of the magnates depended in part on their ability to work with influential merchants and ranchers of Anglo-American extraction, many of whom were tied to *hispanos* by bonds of friendship or marriage. When New Mexico reached statehood, the *hispanos* made a determined attempt to entrench their political rights. (The New Mexico Constitution specified that no citizen's rights could be abridged because of his race, color, creed, or inability to speak or write either English or Spanish.)

The persistence of the magnates' influence was double-edged in its effects. In parts of New Mexico, the accustomed seignorial relationship, with its traditional subservience and poverty, continued for a long time. A *hispano*-dominated territorial assembly initially refused to abolish peonage or Indian slavery. These practices were outlawed only by an act of Congress in 1867, a measure more honored at first in its breach than in its observance. Until 1891, *hispanos* successfully opposed public education for the territory because they feared that their children would be Americanized in the public schools and because they preferred a system under which youngsters were taught the Spanish language and the Catholic religion.[8]

Despite their political skill, the traditionally minded among the magnates could not prevent the economic transformation of New Mexico, which fortunately developed along lines very different from those in Mexico. Railways, the development of coal and copper mining, and the development of commercial farming had contradictory effects on the *nuevo mexicanos*. Many traditional freightmen, unable to compete with the steam engine, lost their jobs. *Nuevo mexicanos*, displaced from their land, formed vigilante organizations such as *La mano negra* or *Las gorras blancas* which sabotaged the property of homesteaders, ranchers, and railway companies responsible for fencing off land and inhibiting the free movement of Spanish-speaking sheepherders and their flocks.

The Spanish-speaking upper class lost its power and prestige as land increasingly passed into the possession of English-speaking immigrants and as financial power came to rest with eastern capital. But at the same time the territory's economy became much more diversified and New Mexico was spared the overriding power of the *hacienda* that continued to afflict Mexico. *Hispano* villagers found liberty and new economic options by working in the mines, on the railways, in agricultural processing industries, and in other occupations that freed them from the magnates' exactions. Peons escaped the conditions of semiservitude that continued to prevail on the *haciendas* of Mexico as they had in New Mexico. Romantic reconstructions of the seignorial past notwithstanding, wage workers in a capitalist economy improved their material condition, their health, and the health of their children. New kinds of merchandise—sewing machines, iron stoves, iron bedsteads, canned food, mass-produced shoes, shirts, blankets, cakes of soap—began to spread from the mining townships into the villages. Along with these goods came new attitudes that contributed to the gradual erosion of seignorial privileges and traditional patterns of life, patterns that look attractive in storybooks but from which the real peon of the past desperately wished to flee.

By the time New Mexico attained statehood, Spanish Americans and Anglo-Americans had arrived at a new compromise. The *hispanos* were by no means happy with their situation, but they preferred the United States to Mexico. In fact, they came to consider themselves superior to the immigrant Mexican workers from the south who in turn entered those poorly paid and unpleasant jobs that *nuevo mexicanos* began to relinquish. The *nuevo mexicanos*, like the *tejanos* and the *californios*, increasingly differentiated themselves from the newcomers by insisting on their status as *hispanos* or as Spanish Americans rather than as

Mexicans. From the Anglo-American standpoint, the problem of the borderlands—once an external problem—now became internalized. Spanish, or mainly Spanish-speaking enclaves, such as the borderland town of Laredo, survived; but the Southwest as a whole was firmly incorporated into the politics and culture of the United States.[9]

American expansion into the vast southwestern landmass was followed by the opening of what might be called the eastern maritime frontier. When Latin America gained its independence, Spain continued to hold on to a number of Caribbean islands, including Cuba and Puerto Rico. Despite contemporary propaganda, Spanish rule was not wholly unprogressive. Cuba had a railway engine before the United States and an entire railway system before most of Europe. The Cuban economy nevertheless remained extremely vulnerable because the bulk of the island's exports went to the United States. The Cubans had a host of grievances—social, economic, and political. The Cuban enemies of Spain benefited from the proximity of the United States as a privileged sanctuary. During the 1860s and 1870s, Cuban cigarmakers sought escape from the ravages of counterinsurgency war by settling in Key West and Tampa, Florida, as well as in New York, where Cuban manufacturers helped to set up a new industry. The Cuban exiles gave aid and comfort to expatriate freedom-fighters, men like Jose Martí, Cuban poet, patriot, and apostle of Cuban independence, who spent a good deal of time in the United States and garnered substantial support from Cuban expatriates. In addition, exiles arrived in New York from Puerto Rico, including Ramón Emeterio Betances and Santiago Iglesias Plantín (founder of the Socialist Party in Puerto Rico). Expatriate Puerto Ricans in New York published a revolutionary newspaper *El Postillón* and participated in the intense intellectual life of the various exile communities.

With support in both North and South America, the revolutionaries in Cuba once more took up arms, in 1895. A government-in-exile operated in New York, headed by Tomás Estrada Palma. The New York junta assisted the Cuban rebels with men, money, and ammunition, and for a time the insurgents' hope ran high. However, the Spaniards struck back with vigor, and Spanish methods of counterinsurgency in turn produced in the United States bitter hostility toward Spain. The Cuban issue occasioned a bitter struggle within the United States between interventionists (composed, oddly, of humanitarians and imperialists) and those who wanted the country to stay out of the war. Very few Americans sympathized with the Spanish ruling power, and there was no Hispanic lobby to sustain the Spanish cause. Spanish-speaking intellectuals, whether Cubans, Puerto Ricans in New York and other eastern cities, or Mexicans in the Southwest, overwhelmingly considered colonial Spain a foe. European Spaniards in the United States lacked influence and were few in number. During the nineteenth century, most Spanish emigrants settled in Latin American countries where they could speak their native language. During the 1890s, the number of Spanish immigrants to the United States slowly increased and subsequently accelerated (from 8,731 during 1891–1900 to 27,935 during 1901–1910), but the total remained small. Those Spaniards who did come to the United States lacked political influence and did not necessarily sympathize with their home government. They considered themselves as Asturians, Catalans, Gallegos, Basques, or natives of the Canary Islands rather than as Spaniards. The strength of their provincial loyalties reflected the diversity of the Spanish homeland itself.[10]

Another small Spanish-speaking group from Europe consisted of Sephardic Jews, whose ancestors had been expelled at the end of the fifteenth century and who had carried an archaic form of Spanish to various parts of the Mediterranean. Some, who converted to Catholicism and were known as *marranos*, reached high office under the Spanish crown. Their numbers included Luis de Carvajal y de la Cuera, probably the first highly placed pioneer of Jewish provenance to come into the region now covered by the United States. (He advanced to the rank of governor-general of New Leon in what is now Texas; he colonized the region around Tampico; but, subsequently, in 1590, he died in a dungeon during the Inquisition). The Sephardim as a whole did not reach such heights. They remained a distinct subgroup within the Jewish community, mostly small traders and craftsmen, with their own ritual, Spanish folklore, and ballads derived from the Middle Ages. They created for themselves mutual aid societies, synagogues, and even their own newspaper (*La América*, published in New York between 1910 and 1925, the first Judeo-Spanish periodical in the U.S.)[11] But the Sephardim counted for little in terms of influence or numbers and were unable to build an enduring communitywide structure. They had no sense of identification with Spain and they lacked the political and financial influence acquired by their Ashkenazic (German-speaking or eastern European) co-religionists. Moreover, Sephardim in no way seem to have communicated with other Spanish-speaking groups in this country.

In the end, the interventionists within the United States won the battle, and in 1898 the United States entered the war. A small American army landed in Cuba. Admiral George Dewey destroyed most of the Spanish fleet, and, in the closing days of the war, American forces occupied Puerto Rico. Spain's internal position was as perilous as its military situation, and, in October, a peace conference assembled in Paris. Spain ceded Puerto Rico to the Americans. Puerto Rico's commercial value at the time was negligible, but President William McKinley was convinced that Spain's complete banishment from the Americas was a prerequisite for permanent peace and believed that the United States should keep the island for its strategic importance.

The Spaniards would have preferred to hand Cuba over to the United States rather than to grant independence to the island. Annexation would have involved the taking of a $400 million Spanish debt incurred in part by Spanish warfare against the insurgents. Many well-to-do and well-educated Cubans also would have welcomed U.S. annexation in order to assure sound government and the protection of their property. The Americans, however, refused to take the island. Had they done so, they would have acquired a Spanish-speaking Quebec impossible to assimilate.

The results of the war were far-reaching. The United States emerged as a Caribbean power. American troops occupied Cuba from 1899 to 1902; American physicians helped to eradicate yellow fever from the island, thereby contributing to a demographic revolution; and Americans attempted to reform the civil service and the schools. In 1901, Cuba received a republican constitution that subjected the island to a limited form of American supervision.[12]

The new dispensation had unintended consequences. The majority of the traditional Cuban upper class thereafter turned from their accustomed civic duties to business, foreign travel, and social life as government increasingly fell into the hands of professional politicians and military men. Cuba's political structure continued to bear many of the authoritarian features that had characterized Spanish colonial rule. The contrast between Cuba's political tradition and an expanding economy modeled to some extent on the example of the United States created "a serious vacuum of legitimacy" that the postcolonial politicians could not fill.[13]

Puerto Rico, after a brief period of military governance, became (for all intents and purposes) a U.S. colony. The Americans never created a colonial service or a colonial office on the British model; but, in 1900, Congress, under the so-called Foraker Act, provided for the civil administration in Puerto Rico. Spanish colonial rule was by no means as unprogressive as American interventionists had assumed. When the Americans arrived, they found that the Spaniards had built many roads and had begun work on a telegraph and telephone network, that racial prejudice was not as severe as in the United States, and that many cultivators farmed their own land. Nevertheless, the Americans encountered a highly stratified society, one that in some respects resembled the seignorial society soon to be overthrown by the revolution in Mexico.

Agriculture formed the people's main livelihood. The coastal plains and the larger inland valley depended primarily on the cultivation of sugar, a plantation crop. Plantation society comprised two main social classes: the hacienda owners and their workers. Between them stood a small group of artisans—blacksmiths, and carpenters, as well as the overseers—or *mayordomos*. The *hacendados* typically resided in a nearby city and left the management of their estates to a baliff, often a member of the lord's extended family. The workers lived as squatters on plantation land and usually worked as sharecroppers in lieu of paying rent. The landless workers were compelled to carry workbooks, and they could not leave the plantation until they were free of debt.

In the coffee-growing districts of the interior, social stratification was somewhat less rigid. Even in the interior, however, there was a fundamental division between the large landowners and the landless. As the nineteenth century advanced, the introduction of hulling machinery made the cultivation of coffee increasingly profitable. The larger haciendas (many of them owned by newcomers from Spain) increasingly encroached on the smaller farms, the owners of which had little recourse other than to sell their land and find work on other men's holdings. There also was a substantial number of smaller holdings, but the distribution of good land was lopsided—2 percent of the island's 39,000 farms contained about 70 percent of the cultivable land. The mass of the population lived at subsistence level.[14]

Communications were restricted physically as well as socially. By the turn of the century, there was only a single surfaced highway in the country, a military road linking San Juan and Ponce. Governance under the Spaniards was authoritarian, and the fiscal system struck hardest at the poor. Most of the revenue came from customs duties and sales taxes on imported food. Illiteracy was widespread. By the late 1890s, only about 13 percent of the population knew how to read and write. And disease was rampant. Under these conditions, few could afford the price of a steamship ticket to the mainland, and few of the landless knew about the advantages that emigration offered.

In 1910, there were reportedly only 1,513 Puerto Ricans in the United States (a great underestimation); of these, one-third lived in New York, where they found employment in industries processing tobacco and manufacturing ropes. Settling in Spanish Harlem and later also in Brooklyn, this community consisted not only of young, single men employed in unskilled and semiskilled occupations; there also were owners of restaurants, *bodegas* (grocery stores), and *botánicas* (shops selling medicinal and culinary herbs); and there were pharmacists, priests, and other men and women with a professional education. There were Latin dance bands, clubs, and newspapers (for instance *La Prensa*, initiated in 1913, New York's most important Spanish newspaper), and even a sophisticated journal, the *Revista de artes y letras*, which published poetry.[15] By this time, some visible improvements had changed the economic conditions of the island itself. The Americans did away with the traditional system of justice (whereby an accused person could be held incommunicado for indefinite periods of time), introduced a fiscal system based on the taypayer's ability to pay, and created a new kind of sanitary system. Within a quarter of a century after the American annexation, the island's health services had improved immeasurably, and 1,200 miles of public roads had been built, connecting all cities and towns as well as all parts of the interior. The island was served by railway, cable, and shipping services; motor trucks came into general use; and the island became an important distributing center for the Caribbean, with several steamship services carrying both passengers and freight. The Americans for the first time created a free and compulsory system of education. By 1923, 213,321 children attended school, the highest rate of attendance in the Caribbean.

American enterprise also wrought far-reaching changes in the island's agricultural system. By the time of the American occupancy, nearly all the land suitable for sugarcane had been brought under cultivation. Production thereafter failed to expand because the sugar mills were antiquated and methods of production remained backward. American investments, improved methods of cultivation, new irrigation works, the introduction of fertilizers, the availability of American markets, and the development of banking and communications all produced great changes. Foreign trade grew in an extraordinary fashion, from $16,602,000 in 1910 to $185,323,000 in 1925.

Concurrently, there was a striking demographic shift. Benefiting from improved health care and improved living conditions, the population expanded from an estimated 950,000 in 1899 to 1,416,000 in 1928, an average increase of about 16.3 percent over a period of ten years.[16] The island, however, became completely tied to the American economy; by 1920, an estimated 75 percent of the population depended on the sugar industry. Shattering rural isolation and promoting demographic growth by tying the island to the economy of the United States, the Americans and Puerto Ricans set up what was, by the standards of that period, a model colony. At the same time, they unwittingly created the conditions that led to mass emigration from the island to the United States. Overall, the Americans—within half a century—had enormously expanded their dominion and had placed under their flag both a Spanish-speaking land frontier in the Southwest and a maritime frontier in the Caribbean.

Chapter 3

Mass Migration from Mexico Begins

Although a widespread stereotype suggests that nineteenth-century Mexico was a backward, sleepy land, the country in fact achieved striking progress. Mexico astounded foreign observers by its remarkable changes under Don Porfirio Diaz' dictatorship. The *Porfiriato* from 1876 to 1911 achieved for Mexico precisely what successful colonial governments were priding themselves on doing for Africa. Diaz put an end to internecine warfare, encouraged foreign capital, safeguarded private property, and assisted in the creation of roads, railways, harbors, telegraphs, and post offices. Mexico's indigenous upper class began to fuse with the middle class into a national bourgeoisie endowed with considerable resources. British, French, and, above all, American lenders helped to create a booming oil industry. By 1910, mining had become big business, a start had been made in manufacturing, and Mexico's National University had acquired an international reputation—as had Diaz's advisers (the so-called *científicos*, who preached a gospel of hard work and economic progress).

But the *Porfiriato* rested on narrow social foundations, and, in 1911, the regime collapsed with unexpected suddenness. The Mexican revolution was a long drawn-out process, punctuated by coups, countercoups, executions, bloody fighting, and more fighting.[1] The revolutionaries' program for land reform did not get underway until President Lázarao Cárdenas achieved office (1934–1940). Within six years, Cárdenas had liquidated most of the big estates—45 million acres were distributed in the form of *ejidos* (communal lands owned by groups of peasants). Land reform, however, met innumerable problems: lack of capital, irrigation, skills, and marketing facilities. The revolutionaries did succeed in breaking the social and political power of the *hacendados* as well as the secular power of the Catholic Church.

The revolutionaries, however, had aimed for more. They wished to relieve poverty, promote social justice, reduce or eliminate the distinctions of social class, and create a more efficient system of production. Unfortunately, the revolution did not solve the problems of the Mexican countryside. The distribution of land among the poor failed to do away with landlessness, at a time when the population rapidly increased and striking disparities continued in the prosperity of the various regions. Mexicans in the areas adjacent to the United States came to enjoy a standard of living higher than the poverty-stricken regions of the center and south, those areas that also were apt to provide the largest number of emigrants to the United States and to receive the greatest number of Mexican repatriates.

Land reform did not necessarily lead to improved methods of cultivation or increased production. Owners of *minifundia* (tiny plots) were ill equipped to bring about changes in the methods of production. Well-to-do landowners, fearing loss of their farms, all too often invested their savings in urban areas rather than in the countryside, a common experience in countries subjected to the expropriation of estates. In Mexico, agricultural change was apt to lag behind urban change with far-reaching consequences for Mexico's future social stability. The new Mexican bourgeoisie, nationalist and committed to the revolution, remained tied to the state in a manner unknown in North America. In a sense, the Mexican revolution, like the *Porfiriato* before it, continued in the royal tradition of Spain.

The revolution also had the unintended consequence of uprooting vast numbers of people and became itself a great propellant that pushed Mexicans across the border.

"My father died when I was six years old," a newspaper owner from Mexico recorded in the early 1930s. "My mother and my aunt set up a dress-making shop. My sister and I made the cardboard boxes and the hair for the wigs. My mother was making good money until the first revolution came. Orozco's soldiers in 1912 took all our silk goods and hair goods and Singer sewing machines, and burned the stores for which we supplied goods. . . . Then I went to work in my uncle's printing shop. . . . But in 1913, the revolution of Carranza and Villa against Huerta began. . . . The revolutionists came to our city. . . . They remained in the shop until my uncle returned. . . . The officer hit him on the head with a pistol and told the rest of us he would shoot us all if another paper came out. . . . I was only 15 years old, but I joined the Villa-Carranza army against Huerta. [The Villa army having been defeated] I later deserted. . . . I came to the United States on October 4, 1915 with 40 cents [and] finally got a job as a railway worker."[2]

The newcomers to the United States also comprised a number of middle- and upper-class people: intellectuals or political men who had adhered to Diaz or who had backed the wrong side in the postrevolutionary upheaval, and businessmen with good connections beyond the border. Mexican Americans, or light-skinned Mexican Americans with

European features wishing to separate themselves from the lot of the common people, increasingly separated themselves from the newcomers and emphasized a "Spanish" or "Latin American" legacy.

"In Mexico, I was a merchant," recorded an educated labor migrant in Chicago in the early 1930s. "Here I am a working man. . . . I am not ashamed of being a Mexican. But I am not proud of the Mexicans in Chicago. They are mostly Indians of the lower uneducated classes of peons. In Mexico, they lived in *chozas* and were servants. Here they live in tumbledown houses and being unused to having money, spend it. . . . In Mexico, they never mixed with people of learning or a little study. When they come to this country, they still keep apart."[3]

Some Mexican Americans of the upper class further cultivated the delusion that old-time residents of the Southwest were of "pure" Spanish blood and thus racially superior to Mexicans. The tendency of long-settled Mexican families to Hispanicize their heritage went with a growing literary appreciation for the supposed "Spanish" or "Mediterranean" legacy of the Southwest, an appreciation that had no conceivable relevance to the lives of those ordinary working men and women who had begun to make their way to the North during the 1890s and the early 1900s. By this time, railway construction, the expansion of commercial agriculture, and the development of manufacturing and service industries in the Southwest created a new demand for labor. Above all, the United States provided a sanctuary for refugees fleeing from the bloodshed and misery occasioned by clashes between Mexican revolutionaries, with the United States playing its accustomed role of providing a refuge for political losers.

Rich or poor, conservative or revolutionary, the majority of Mexicans in the United States continued to take a keen interest in the politics of their native country, especially in the fortunes of the Liberal Party in Mexico. Mexican revolutionaries relied heavily on American-imported arms. Mexican radicals also derived inspiration from militant American organizations such as the IWW (International Workers of the World). More important still, Mexicans in the United States—just like immigrants from other countries—created an unofficial network, tied by links of kinship, friendship, and common geographical origins. This aided subsequent immigrants by providing information about jobs, lodgings, and even family contacts in a new country. At the same time, the clamor for more unskilled workmen from Mexico grew louder as Oriental immigration was restricted, though by no means eliminated, through the Chinese Exclusion Act of 1882 and the so-called Gentleman's Agreement between the United States and Japan (an agreement no gentleman would have signed). The number of Mexicans in the United States increased rapidly. They came initially from the Mexican state of Guanajato, then from Michocan, Jalisco, and Zacatecas. They later came from Durango, San Luis Potosi, Aguascalientes, Coahuila, Sinaloa, and Tamaulipas.

Well-established Mexicans deplored the departure of their compatriots. Newspapers warned the migrants against the wiles of *enganchadores* (recruiters), and editors thundered against the "Yankee contempt" with which Mexican workmen were apt to be treated beyond the Rio Grande. But even the critics of emigration did not deny that those who left their country had good reason for doing so because of "the high taxes which weigh heavily on the people" and the "bossism" prevalent in Mexico, where the *cacique* (the local patron) was wont to rule his bailiwick with a heavy hand.

There were many causes for the increased emigration from Mexico. According to his critics, Diaz unwittingly promoted emigration by interfering with the villagers' traditional land rights leaving them with no alternative but to go abroad to make a living. Mexico's food production declined and the people's condition worsened. This does not explain why, for the first time, Mexico's population should have begun to register a rapid increase under the *caudillo*'s peace. Most likely, the development of the mining and petroleum industries added to the growth of the Mexican railway system and created a mobile labor force composed of men no longer willing to accept the age-old subordination to a *patrón*.

Learning that more cash was paid for their labor on the American side of the border, Mexican workmen increasingly made their way to the United States, where they usually gathered in Mexican neighborhoods. To the immigrants' natural desire to associate with men and women of their own background was added the Anglo-Americans' widespread ethnic prejudice. Many southwestern communities invoked property restrictions against Mexicans, often enforced through "restrictive covenants" against leasing or selling accommodation, a form of discrimination also extended to Jews, Armenians, and other "undesirables." There also was segregation in schools and other public facilities.

After the turn of the century, the total number of Mexican immigrants remained small. The 1910 census reported 162,000 Mexicans—probably an underestimation—compared to 1,088,112 Canadians and 5,670,611 Germans. The Mexican and Mexican-American communities were far from cohesive. They included men and women who were born or permanently settled in the United States as well as short-term immigrants. They had an intelligentsia of their own, men and women well acquainted with both Mexican and American politics and trained in professions such as the law, medicine, or pharmacy. There was an incipient Mexican middle class but not as strong as that found among immigrants from Northern Europe; there were far fewer Mexican clergymen, teachers, and newspaper editors of the kind that produced a vigorous church, synagogue, and ethnic press among German and Jewish immigrants at the time. The fate of the early Mexican migrant accordingly lacks the literary documentation available for many other immigrant communities, but there is no doubt that, after the Mexican revolution, the character of Mexican immigration changed fundamentally as the initial trickle became mass migration. Mexican workmen began to seek not only higher wages but also security from the violence engendered by revolution.

Data about war losses or statistics about migrants during a revolution are even harder to collect than figures relating to a settled population in peacetime. Experts calculate that one million people may have died in Mexico during the revolutionary period, the victims of battle, famine, and disease. While the United States flourished, Mexico became more impoverished. A generation earlier, the Mexican-American border separated territories that differed little from one another economically. From the turn of the century onward, the frontier marked increasingly striking differences in economic development and social well-being. The American "pull" became ever stronger as the wage gap between Mexico and the United States widened. According to historian Mark Reisler, an agricultural laborer in the state of Jalisco in 1905 who worked from sunrise to sunset earned about 13 cents per day in addition to some maize.[4] A truck laborer in the United States made $1.25 for ten hours' work. If an entire Mexican family migrated to Texas to pick cotton, it could earn as much as $5 a day, nearly 40 times as much as in Jalisco. The Mexicans' lot in their own country during that period further worsened as a result of a rapid rise in the cost of living. Between 1891 and 1908, the price of many staple foods nearly doubled. Not surprisingly, the United States represented for the labor migrant not a land of bondage but a land of opportunity.

Mexican laborers did most of the railway construction and maintenance work in southern California, New Mexico, and Nevada, where they were willing to work for a lower wage than other immigrants. (The Southern Pacific Railroad in 1908 paid Greek section hands $1.60 per day; Japanese, $1.50; and Mexicans, $1.25.) Mexicans also played an important role in agriculture. In Texas, they harvested cotton and vegetables grown on irrigated land and they cleared the mesquite brush and thorny undergrowth. In California, they labored on the great estates, where they gradually displaced Japanese, Italian, and other workmen. By World War I, Mexicans had become the most important single ethnic group in the agriculture of the Imperial Valley of California, having gradually replaced whites and blacks from the American South, Hindus, Chinese,

Japanese, and others. Mexicans also began to be employed in a variety of jobs associated with mining, smelters, sugar factories, and municipal streetcars. This labor helped to build the new Southwest.

World War I gave a further impetus to this migration. Newcomers from Europe rapidly declined in numbers, as would-be fortune seekers from the Old World put on uniforms or were tied in various ways to domestic war production, and as ships increasingly carried troops rather than tourists or emigrants. War greatly expanded the market for American industrial products, including arms. At the same time, war extended worldwide demand for American food, and more acres were put into production. The use of irrigation and fertilizers, the widening application of science to farming, the development of motor transport, improvements in methods of cold storage, fencing, harvesting, and a host of other new agricultural techniques gave a boost to commercial farming, especially in the Southwest. Citrus fruit (ultimately to become California's premium crop), vegetables, cotton, and sugar beet all boomed at a time when the indigenous American farming population began to diminish.

The development of large-scale irrigated farming in the Southwest transformed traditional labor patterns. For instance, planting an acre of lettuce required almost ten times as many man-hours as the cultivation of an acre of wheat. In the United States, which was untroubled by agitation for redistribution of land, large farms came to play an increasingly important part in the production of such labor-intensive crops as vegetables and sugar beets. (By 1929, California contained 2,892 large-scale farms accounting for 60 percent of the nation's large fruit farms and 60 percent of its large truck farms.) Although these enterprises took no more than 2.1 percent of the land in California, they accounted for 28.5 percent of California's total output. As time went on, agribusiness increased in economic importance.

To some critics of a later generation, agricultural specialization had an iniquitous quality. From the days of the ancient Romans, writers have tended to idealize the yeoman's sturdiness, self-reliance, and independence (though smallholders in the valley of the Ganges or the Yellow River have never generated such praise). The smallholders were hard working, but, in fact, they were also often narrow minded, suspicious, and locked into local hostilities. They labored under economic disadvantages and often were too poor to take risks or too much in debt to introduce agricultural innovation or accumulate capital. Moreover, their economies commonly suffered from underemployment and associated economic ills that mar the idealized image of the unspoiled peasant as the repository of traditional virtue.

Commercialized agriculture required greater capital investment per acre than was normally available on a farm. Increased agricultural costs created new difficulties for those small farmers who failed to keep abreast by specializing in competitive products. The nation as a whole gained because food remained relatively less expensive in the United States than in most other industrial countries. But many petty proprietors, including many Mexican-American cultivators, were forced off the land, especially in New Mexico and Arizona. Disaster might strike in various ways: some lost their farms through tax foreclosures; and others discovered that the creation of national forests, with strict control of federal grazing, forced smallholders to reduce their herds. Family farmers of whatever national ancestry gave up agriculture, as did many hired men who went to the cities to look for more highly paid work. In the Southwest, the large-scale farmers and farming corporations increasingly became dependent on what their spokesmen called "fluid labor," mostly migrants from Mexico willing to work at lower wages than Greeks, Sicilians, or Japanese.

Life was grim for this "fluid labor" force. In an effort to secure as many workdays as possible, many Mexicans and their families became used to a way of life in which workers unflaggingly followed the ripening crops. Groups of families moved together by automobile or truck. A Mexican family might live in more than five places during a single year. If jobs were available, women and children would join the men in the fields, regardless of child labor laws or compulsory school attendance in the United States.

Mexican migrants thus increasingly found work outside the traditional areas of Mexican settlement in the Southwest. The demand for Mexican labor grew particularly in the sugar beet industry. During and after World War I, Flemish and German-Russian workmen gradually worked their way up from "stoop labor" in the sugar beet fields to become tenant farmers or independent entrepreneurs. The Flemings' slot at the bottom of the rural hierarchy increasingly came to be filled by Mexicans. A 1927 Bureau of Labor Statistics survey estimated that Mexicans constituted from 75 to 95 percent of the beet workers in Michigan, Ohio, Indiana, Minnesota, Colorado, and the Dakotas. Work in the sugar beet fields was a particularly disagreeable occupation because, as an official report put it, "the monotony, difficulty, and drudgery of the work, frequently performed in inclement weather, combined with long hours of work and low earnings, make sugar beet field work one which most laborers would avoid if they could find other means of employment."[5]

Tomato picking was even more arduous. Mexican families, dependent on seasonal labor on the farms, also made their way to Indiana where they harvested tomatoes before harvesting sugar beet in Ohio and Michigan. Tomato picking required constant stooping and carrying heavy crates in the broiling sun. Pickers were required to work from daybreak until dark on vines that in the early morning were wet with dew or rain. If a worker mistakenly picked the wrong grade of tomato, he was liable to be paid nothing at all. For this backbreaking work, an experienced adult male worker might earn $1.50 a day; women and children received less. The migrants' living conditions were miserable: they were lodged in barns, tents, abandoned slaughterhouses, abandoned hotels, and even in straw stacks.[6] Their food was sometimes nothing but bread and beans. Not surprisingly, the local people would not take work under those conditions, preferring employment in the local canneries which, although hard, exacting, and ill paid, was preferable to stoop labor in the fields.

In addition, Mexican workers began to take unskilled and semiskilled work in industry because farm labor was seasonal in character. Even at the best of times, Mexican rural workers had to eke out their living during the agricultural off-season by taking up pick-and-shovel work on the railways, irrigation projects, dam construction, cement work, road construction, and power-plant development. (According to a Texas survey completed in 1928, about 75 percent of unskilled construction workers in the state were Mexicans.) An increasing number of Mexicans also obtained jobs in mines and factories, where their pay was considerably higher than on either American or Mexican farms. (By 1914, a peon on a hacienda received a daily wage of about 16 cents; an unskilled, illiterate agricultural worker in the United States received between $1 and $3; mine work netted between $4.50 and $5.) Mexicans began to work in steel, auto, and sheet metal plants as well as in oil refineries, textile mills, and many other enterprises.[7]

This occupational shift was linked to geographical shifts operating in two ways: from the countryside to the city, and from the Southwest to other parts of the United States. Los Angeles remained the greatest Mexican-American center. Even by the 1920s, Los Angeles was a city like no other, a strangely amorphous aggregation that kept spreading outward, taking in more and more independent townships in the process. Los Angeles County in the 1920s constituted 4,083 square miles, an area larger than the state of Connecticut, and it was, even in those days, a tangle of suburbs without a single center strong enough to dominate the entire city. Within the huge conurbation, East Los Angeles became the main Mexican enclave (with more than 90,000 people out of Los Angeles's 1930 total population of one million.) This barrio continued to attract newcomers, both from small towns in California and from Mexico. The barrio provided employers with both a seasonal and an all-around labor force for California's expanding economy. The barrio also afforded some sense of security to immigrants. There was the comforting presence of relatives and friends, or, at the least, fellow countrymen. There were clubs, barbershops, and corner stores where

Spanish was understood. There was a Mexican political consciousness to set against nativistic campaigns among Anglo-Americans. In economic terms, the barrio served as a labor pool for employers; it also offered housing affordable to the poor, however defective by middle-class standards.[8]

In addition to making their way to Los Angeles, Mexicans, especially those intent on remaining in the United States for long periods, began to make their way north and east, beyond the confines of their traditional areas of settlement in the Southwest. Spanish-speaking immigrants settled in Denver, St. Louis, Pittsburgh, and Chicago, where Mexican barrios sometimes paralleled the "Little Polands" or "Little Italys" set up by other communities.

The most important Mexican center in the Midwest was Chicago. Immigration on a substantial scale began in 1916 with the recruitment of about two-hundred railroad track workers from the Texas-Mexico border. The 1920 census counted twelve hundred Mexicans in the city, most of whom worked for the railroads, steel plants, and meat-packing houses. By 1930, the Mexican and Mexican-American community had grown to twenty thousand.[9] Ten years later they may have numbered as many as thirty-five thousand. They settled mainly on the south side, in contrast to Puerto Rican immigrants who usually found homes on the north side.

Overall, the occupational structure of Mexicans and Mexican Americans in the United States by 1930 had undergone a profound change. Popular journalists as well as many academicians continued to think of Mexicans as farm laborers; but, for the first time, the census takers classified slightly over half of the Mexican population in the United States as urban, that is, inhabitants of towns with a population of more than 2,500. Nationwide, only 40.5 percent were employed in agriculture. In the Midwest, the proportion of Mexican town dwellers was even higher: 57 percent of employed Mexican men worked for the railroads and other transport industries.[10]

For the great majority of Mexican townsmen, life was a struggle. Mexicans moved into the hardest and dirtiest jobs, often those vacated by earlier immigrant groups. Like the Polish, Italian, and Irish immigrants who had preceded them, Mexicans found accommodation near the plants where they worked; for example, Chicago's Hull House area in the new west side for railway workers, south Chicago for steel workers, and the back of the stockyard for men employed in meatpacking. Mexicans usually fell heir to the dilapidated housing previously inhabited by East European (and, earlier still, by German and Scandinavian) immigrants. Housing conditions usually were deplorable: worn stairways, inadequate plumbing, and leaking roofs, all of which was preferable to village shacks but nevertheless miserable by urban standards. The Mexicans' troubles were compounded initially by their inexperience and lack of skills. (In the two largest steel plants in the Calumet region in 1928, 79 percent of the Mexicans were unskilled, 19.1 percent were semiskilled, and only 1.8 percent were skilled.) Mexicans, like other foreign immigrants, suffered from their inability to speak, read, or write English well. Like other unskilled and semiskilled workers, they drifted from plant to plant and industry to industry as opportunities changed, from work on the railroad tracks to employment in steel plants and stockyards.

Urbanization produced a host of new problems. In many Chicago neighborhoods, especially in the local stockyards, Slavs and European-born Latins looked askance at Mexicans and tried to keep them out as unwelcome competitors. There was nothing like the residential segregation found in small agricultural townships in California; even in the so-called Mexican city blocks, Mexicans never formed a majority. There were barroom fights and clashes between gangs of different ethnic descent. Mexicans complained that a Polish or Lithuanian-born foreman dealt most harshly with hired hands from Mexico. A Polish or Irish policeman, went another complaint, would think nothing of beating a drunken Mexican, whereas the same officer would be only too happy to take home a boisterous inebriate from his own ethnic group.

World War I contributed not only to the incipient urbanization of Mexican Americans but also to their Americanization. A substantial number of Spanish-speaking Americans served in the armed forces, and, in 1921, returning veterans set up an early Mexican-American organization, the Sons of America. The Sons of America proclaimed their faith in the Stars and Stripes and at the same time sought to end prejudice against Mexican Americans. Mexican workers also formed a variety of welfare organizations designed to provide their members with sickness and death benefits at a time when state-supplied social security was unavailable. These bodies included the *Alianza-Hispano Americana* (founded in Arizona in 1894) as well as societies with a more specific interest in Mexican national traditions, such as *La Sociedad Cervantes* and *La Sociedad Mutualista Mexicana*. In addition, Mexican musicians established bands, athletes formed sports organizations, and there were art, theater, and youth groups.

At the same time, Mexican neighborhoods witnessed the slow expansion of a middle class. Its impact is difficult to measure because it remains the least studied of all Spanish-speaking groups, and also the group most difficult to investigate or even to define. No one knows how many successful professional men of Mexican ancestry changed their names or passed themselves off as Spaniards, Cubans, Latin Americans, or otherwise cut themselves off from the Mexican community by marrying into Anglo-American families. Their number was undoubtedly small, but they were probably overlooked because sociological inquiries in the 1930s concentrated almost exclusively on Mexicans of the laboring class. Mexicans managed restaurants, grocery stores, barbershops, bakeries, and, above all, pool halls, which served as centers of social activity for unmarried young men. This emergent Mexican bourgeoisie met with considerable difficulties. Many of their customers were labor migrants who, poorly paid and dependent on seasonal employment, were apt to ask Mexican shopkeepers for credit in case of need. Hence, a great many Mexican-owned businesses shut their doors when times were bad.

The troubles of a Mexican store owner in no way differed from those of a Jew, Greek, or Armenian who had set up business on the wrong side of the railroad track. In certain other ways, however, the Mexican experience differed strikingly from that of most other European immigrants. The majority of Polish, Jewish, Greek, Italian, or Slovak newcomers experienced immigration as a traumatic break in their lives. Crossing the Atlantic, finding work, and coping with a new country turned into a dramatic tale that grandmother and grandfather never tired of retelling. The great majority of European newcomers were proud to take out citizenship papers: the formal oath of allegiance taken before a judge became an important event in their lives, a rite of passage that entailed a claim to equality with all Americans and one that also enhanced status within the immigrant's community. New citizens also obtained material benefits by being integrated as voters into the big-city political machines or by becoming eligible for employment in the post office, police department, armed services, and other government agencies, or by becoming qualified for federal relief when times were bad.

The Mexican experience tended to be different. The majority of Mexican immigrants, like Puerto Ricans or the French Canadians who settled in New England, for long were apt to look upon themselves as temporary sojourners to the United States. They built up an extensive network of kinsmen and friends—centered in Mexico but often extended into different parts of the United States—provided both emotional and material support. A return journey to Mexico did not entail an expensive trip across the ocean; the "old country" was just south of the border, a few days' travel by bus or railroad. Many Mexicans went home to find a wife; many more kept in close touch with friends and neighbors by means of vacations that were inconceivable to a Polish or Slovak workman. As one Mexican labor migrant put it:

The European comes to remedy, not a temporary but a permanent and absolute evil. . . . They come therefore decided to become American citizens, to adopt the English language, to dwell with their pogency under their new roof. . . . The Mexican immigrant is not prepared to make such a transcendental change; he goes and returns easily by the rails which unite the two countries without any geographical break.[11]

The Mexicans' outlook toward their American abode remained ambivalent. Some disliked the new country:

It is not as happy and gay a life as it is in Mexico. They have no fiestas or serenatas and no places for paseos [walks] in the evening. If you walk in the streets [of Chicago] in the evening, you suffer insults from uncouth persons. . . . It is very cold here in the winter. . . . In the summer it is too hot. The life here is very cheerless in contrast to Mexico. The neighbors are other nationalities and they are very hostile instead of friendly.[12]

Others loved the new country, where even a poorly paid job on the railways might represent a striking improvement. As a track laborer's wife put it:

I like it very much here in the United States. I do not ever want to go back to Mexico to live. Here even the poor people can have what only the rich have in Mexico. I lived in a small town in Michoacan. We had to leave on account of poverty. My husband used to plant corn in Mexico; now he works on the track in Hammond.[13]

But whether satisfied or dissatisfied, Mexicans agreed that their American-born children had changed and that assimilation affected second-generation Mexican Americans just as it affected second-generation Americans descended from European immigrants.

How sorrowfully I have seen innumerable little children of Mexicans who could neither read nor write Spanish. They know that their parents are Mexican because they have heard it from the lips of others, but never from their own parents.[14]

Such children became U.S. citizens by right of birth. First-generation Mexicans, on the other hand, occupied a more ambivalent position. Whereas Puerto Ricans enjoyed the advantage of U.S. citizenship as a matter of course, Mexican immigrants remained reluctant to take out naturalization papers. (By 1930, only 5.8 percent of Mexican-born people in the United States had become citizens.) Their naturalization rate was the lowest of all immigrant groups. Mexicans preferred to take their grievances to Mexican consuls who acted as tribunes for their grievances and even promoted welfare societies and trade unions. As a short-term solution, their choice made good sense. The Mexicans' reluctance to take up citizenship, however, entailed considerable social costs; for instance, urban politics did not function as a ladder of social mobility for Mexicans as it had done for Jews and Irishmen. Intervention in American national politics was likewise out of the question. For a long time there was no "Mexican vote" in the United States comparable to the Czech, Polish, or Irish votes that played their respective parts in the history of the Czech, Polish, and Irish independence movements.

Lacking political power, Mexican Americans exerted almost no influence on the long and bitter controversy concerning future limits to be set on foreign immigration. Yet, the resultant changes in U.S. immigration laws indirectly worked in the Mexicans' favor. Up to 1917, the United States generally admitted immigrants without restriction of nationality—the only major exception being the Chinese, and (by informal arrangement) Japanese. The law insisted only that the newcomers should not be criminals, paupers, physically or mentally defective, or contract laborers—restrictions that sometimes failed to be avoided in practice. The Consolidating Immigration Act of 1917 prohibited the immigration of illiterates over sixteen years of age, and the Immigration Acts of 1921 and 1924 imposed a system of national quotas designed to favor immigrants from northern and western Europe.

The immigration laws represented a new mood of isolationism engendered primarily by American disillusionment following World War I. They also reflected widespread racial prejudices and economic apprehensions shared by the Western world at large, including all the various Spanish-American countries. (For example, in the 1930s, Mexico introduced a national-origin quota that allotted no more than one hundred for such "undesirable" categories as Poles and Rumanians.)[15] Despite the restrictions imposed on newcomers, the United States remained a haven for immigrants, far more generous in its admission policy than any other major power.

In demographic terms, the immigration acts nevertheless had unexpected consequences. In particular, they prevented a large-scale influx of newcomers from Spain and Portugal just when emigration from the Iberian Peninsula and the Iberian islands had picked up momentum.[16] The authorities made some exceptions for skilled workers, such as Basque shepherds, but the total number of Iberian immigrants declined sharply. The majority of Spaniards who made their way to the United States were single men who were better educated and more skilled than the average immigrant. (During the first quarter of the century, 80 percent of the Spanish immigrants were male, 36 percent of whom were either highly skilled craftsmen or professionals.) The Spanish settlements originally centered in New York City, the main port of entry, and in the formerly Spanish regions of California and Louisiana.[17] After the turn of the century, Florida, especially Tampa, developed into the major Spanish center.

The Spaniards' education and cultural self-confidence might have given them a leading place within the Spanish-speaking community, but they displayed little desire to maintain a separate ethnic consciousness within the American framework. Many Spaniards looked upon the United States as no more than a temporary abode. (Between 1899 and 1952, 57 percent of all Spaniards in the United States either returned to Spain or moved to Latin America. Between 1930 and 1940, the total number of Spaniards in the country declined from 110,607 to 85,133.) The Spaniards thought of themselves in more provincial terms as Basques, Catalonians, or Asturians. They were apt to form regional associations, and their national impact remained slight.

The principal, though unintended, beneficiary of the Immigration Acts was Mexico. No quotas were imposed on either Canada or Mexico; American immigration officials could much more easily supervise immigrants coming by ship from Europe than those who crossed America's lengthy frontiers by land. Given America's wartime and immediate postwar prosperity, labor migration from Mexico for a while increased in striking fashion. Between 1918 and 1920 alone, almost 250,000 *braceros* (agricultural contract laborers) crossed the border. The total number of immigrants (both legal and illegal) working in the United States at that time was probably well in excess of 500,000, and this at a time when Mexico's population (according to its 1921 census) amounted to no more than 14,334,000.[18]

The immigrants of the 1920s differed in many respects from their predecessors. Those who made their way across the border in the beginning of the century came primarily from Mexico's central and eastern border states. The immigrants after World War I were more mixed in geographic origin; about half of them came from northeastern border states and the remainder from west-central Mexico. These newcomers played a major part in giving Mexican-American culture its current imprint. They fanned out widely in the United States, from Pennsylvania to California, thereby effecting a striking shift in the geographic pattern of settlement.

The Mexicans' attitude with regard to this population movement was as ambivalent as the Americans'. The majority of literate Mexicans bitterly opposed emigration. According to revolutionary nationalists, Mexico suffered from under- rather than overpopulation and emigrants were regarded as traitors both to the fatherland and the revolution. Mexican employers urged the government to prevent the exodus, and officials in the Department of Migration warned prospective emigrants of the perils that awaited them beyond their border: ill treatment, broken promises, and individual atrocities, including lynchings by angry mobs in remote and lawless districts. The statistics divide the victims of those lynchings into "whites" and "blacks." Mexicans were classed as "whites." No one knows for sure how many Mexicans perished through mob violence, but the proportion of Mexican victims must have been considerable. The number of lynchings began to decline after the turn of the century and rapidly diminished during the late 1930s.[19]

The Mexican press publicized such abuses, but the Mexican workers understood perfectly well that the worst of such outrages was the exception rather than the rule. The workers preferred to rely on the migrants' own "grapevine," that unofficial network of information that also played a vital part in promoting immigration from Europe to the United States. Letters from relatives and friends as well as accounts given of working and living conditions by returning workers carried much more authority than newspaper articles, speeches by politicians, or representations made by civil servants. The Mexican villager who had personal contact with emigrants in the United States was quite well informed of what he might expect on the other side of the border. He was realistic in his economic assessments and felt convinced that whatever hardships might await him beyond the border, he would nevertheless better his condition by taking the road to the north. As an American consul in Mexico put it, "I examined hundreds of Mexican applicants for passport visas. . . . Nearly all had friends in the United States. They told me that they placed no reliance whatever on representations made by their own officials, and felt assured of good treatment in the United States."[20]

The villagers' assessments were shared in part by the Mexican intelligentsia. While no government official said so publicly, Mexican administrators were inclined to regard emigration as a political safety valve. Returning migrants, moreover, often came back with new skills, new ideas, and some cash in their pockets. *El Universal,* one of the leading newspapers in Mexico City, thus opined that migrants to the United States learned habits of temperance and punctuality as well as knowledge of English and new agricultural techniques. Manuel Gamio, a Mexican anthropologist reflecting on the labor exodus in 1931, compared the migrants' stay in the United States to "attendance in a gigantic university."[21]

In the end, Mexican official attitudes turned out to be almost irrelevant. Whatever the Mexican officials did—whether they denied passports to migrants, issued warnings, placed administrative restrictions on recruiters, or tried to cooperate with the Americans—the labor exodus continued. As long as jobs were available in the north, there were hands willing to fill them.

Chapter 4

Slump, Recovery, and World War II

The Great Depression forms a landmark in the history of the United States and of the Western world at large. Following an extraordinary boom, the stock market collapsed and the free market system apparently faced breakdown. By mid–1932, the gross national product of the United States had dropped to half its 1929 value, and something like twelve million people (about one-quarter of the labor force) were out of work. Recovery was slow. By 1940, Europe again had plunged into war, even when orders for American arms, ammunition, food, and other war-related supplies came pouring in from abroad, seven million Americans still were looking for jobs. No immigrant community was hit harder by the slump than the Spanish speakers. The Mexican-American community contained only a small proportion of professional men and independent proprietors; the vast majority of Mexicans, Mexican Americans, and Puerto Ricans were employed in seasonal work or in unskilled or semiskilled jobs that were poorly paid and did not allow saving for a rainy day.

Mexican (and Puerto Rican) immigrants labored under additional disadvantages. They usually remained tied to their respective homelands by birth, blood, loyalty, and, often, by periodic residence. Poverty-stricken newcomers kept pouring across the border, thereby slowing down the assimilation of the Mexican-American community as a whole. As a standard work on Hispanic-American demography explains in the formalized language of sociology:

> An important reason for the relatively slow rate of change . . . is the continuous influx of Mexicans-born from south to north of the border. These immigrants bring with them their traditional demographic and cultural traits and thus reinforce the national traits north of the border. . . . Most of these immigrants have little schooling, a factor that operates against their acquiring the North American's demographic characteristics. . . . Hence the old Mexican culture as it is found north of the border will continue to be reinforced.[1]

This is not to say that there was no advancement. In the Imperial Valley in California, for instance, a substantial number of farm workers saved money to buy real property. Paul S. Taylor, a social investigator, was astonished during the 1920s by "the rapid and extensive development of homeownership" in the area.[2] Realtors almost universally found that Mexican installment purchasers were good credit risks. Having acquired a plot, a Mexican would construct a rough shack upon it. As soon as his personal finances would permit, he built a second (or even a third) small house on his plot, either by himself or with the help of a Mexican contractor. These houses, situated mostly in small country towns on the "wrong side" of the railroad tracks, served their owners as a means of obtaining rental income.[3] Only a handful of Mexicans in the Imperial Valley, however, became farm owners. In this respect, the Mexicans differed from Japanese and Italian workers who managed to lease or buy farms, thereby arousing by their competition intense hostility from older, established farmers. Asked why they did not buy farms, Mexicans answered that they lacked the requisite capital, that they did not wish to commit too much of their scanty capital for excessively long periods, or that buying land in California would make their eventual return to Mexico more difficult. Perhaps equally important was the Mexican laborers' cultural legacy against commercial farming by small proprietors.

Some progress also occurred through promotion to white-collar and blue-collar occupations. In the Imperial Valley, most of the important stores catering to Mexican trade were owned by Orientals, Lebanese, or Jews. All of these stores, however, employed Mexican clerks able to speak English as well as Spanish. Because about half of them came from the laboring class, securing a clerk's position represented a step up the social ladder. A clerk might take correspondence courses to become a bookkeeper, and the bookkeeper's son might become a professional man. Other Mexicans served their own communities as grocers, barbers, and garage mechanics; as owners of auto repair shops, pool halls, restaurants, and small movie theaters; or as bakers, butchers, or tailors. The Mexican community also contained a few wealthy merchants who conducted their businesses along the most modern American lines. These men almost inevitably were middle- or upper-middle-class immigrants from Mexico, not local men who had made good.

The Mexicans' rise into the bourgeoisie nevertheless met with many obstacles. Mexicans often had to cope with social ostracism at school. There was widespread residential segregation, commonly chosen by the immigrants themselves for the sake of having family, friends, and countrymen for their neighbors, but also imposed at times by restrictive covenants in selling urban properties. Mexican merchants (and Puerto

Rican ones as well) were expected by their fellow countrymen to extend credit in a manner not expected of American merchants. Given their geographical and social isolation and the extent of racial prejudice against them, the Mexican bourgeoisie developed slowly. The Mexican immigrants therefore could rely on no more than a handful of their own spokesmen during the bitter debate, set off by the economic slump, concerning the Mexican's future presence in the United States. The most influential Mexican-American organization at the time was known as LULAC (League of United Latin American Citizens), which required that its members be U.S. citizens. A middle-class body, LULAC, also dedicated its efforts to promoting the use of the English language and the virtues of American citizenship. By doing so, LULAC hoped to combat racial prejudice, end social segregation in Texas, and achieve complete political and social equality for the Mexicans. LULAC officially argued against the imposition of quotas on Mexican immigration, yet some of its members in fact favored restrictions on the grounds that the continued entry of poverty-stricken, illiterate workers would not only lead to greater competition for jobs but also increase Anglo-American prejudice against respectable, established Mexican Americans.

The long and bitter debate between those who wanted to admit immigrants and the exclusionists did not give a clear-cut victory to either side. The United States never extended the quota system to Mexico—a significant success for employers who favored immigration. The antirestrictionists in Congress enjoyed support from the formidable lobby representing southwestern agriculture. Even more important was the intrusion of the State Department into the controversy. The State Department did not take a particularly favorable view of immigration as such; during the 1930s and World War II, the State Department opposed increased Jewish immigration to the United States. The State Department was, however, resolved to maintain good relations with Mexico and with the Latin American world as a whole. Secretary of State Frank B. Kellogg vigorously resisted the Labor Department's advocacy for restrictions. And the United States did not attempt to place any barriers on the immigration of Puerto Ricans.

In regards to U.S. immigration policy in general, certain points are worth making at a time when many academicians are convinced that the United States was never a true haven for the oppressed.[4] For all its deficiencies, the United States has remained by far the most hospitable land, and American society has been more open and tolerant to foreigners than that of any other world power, including France, a major recipient of immigrants in the 1920s and 1930s. At a time when statesmen in almost every land tried to protect their respective citizens from the effects of the economic slump by means of ill-conceived tariffs, immigration barriers, and vindictive restrictions on resident aliens, the United States continued to admit more newcomers than any other country. Having been accepted as a legal resident in the United States, an alien enjoyed greater personal liberty than anywhere else on the globe; for instance, his economic survival did not depend on his ability to secure a permit of labor (as in France or Great Britain); nor was he subjected to the increasing supervision and petty harassment that foreigners suffered at the hands of French officials in the *mairie* or the *préfecture.*

The restrictionists nevertheless won significant points at the expense of Mexicans. Up to 1930, Mexicans had officially been considered as whites. In 1930, however, the Census Bureau devised a special racial category for "Mexicans" based upon the rather dubious racial perceptions of the census takers.[5] At the same time, American authorities made some attempt to keep out illegal entrants by enforcing existing laws more strictly than in the past. Immigrants to the United States were required to have visas, although visas might be denied to applicants liable to become "public charges" and to other assumed undesirables. Aliens caught without the requisite documents could be charged with a misdemeanor and deported; persons guilty of reentering the country, having previously been deported, could be charged with a felony and imprisoned for up to two years. The State Department rigidly cut down the number of visas issued to Mexicans and, for a time, excluded most "common laborers" from the United States.

No expert can show precisely how well these restrictions work. By comparison with Western Europe (not to speak of Hitler's Germany, Stalin's Russia, or even General Beck's Poland), America's state machinery remained extraordinarily weak. In 1924, Congress set up a border patrol to keep out illegal immigrants. Troubled by poor standards of recruitment and a high turnover rate, the patrol made a bad start; thereafter, the force rapidly improved its standards and, by 1930, had acquired a reputation for integrity and efficiency. But the border patrol faced an impossible task; and by mid–1928 the force comprised no more than 781 men, including 700 inspectors. Numbering no more than one twenty-fifth of London's Metropolitan Police, the border patrol was expected to supervise borders extending over two thousand miles, unmarked and unrecognizable in many places.[6]

In addition to half-hearted attempts to keep out newcomers, the United States in 1931 organized a series of major repatriation programs at the Mexican migrants' expense. The campaign operated in a dual fashion: local government and welfare agencies, including private bodies, carried out their own repatriation programs; in addition, the federal government made a determined effort to deport illegal aliens from the country. The Bureau of Immigration concentrated its efforts in southern California, where Los Angeles, troubled by the expense of unemployment relief, already had taken an active part in sending illegal aliens back to Mexico.

No one knows exactly how many Mexicans were deported during this period. There were striking regional differences in the manner by which U.S. authorities dealt with Mexican workers in the various border states. But, all in all, the number of people repatriated between 1929 and 1935 must have exceeded 415,000 persons, by far the largest number of aliens of any nationality ever forced to leave the United States. The *repatriados* consisted of many different groups: deportees, aliens fearful of an uncertain status, indigents, and men who were willing to return voluntarily in the hope that revolutionary Mexico would offer them a better future.

The American repatriation program received close scrutiny in Mexico. The Mexican government sought to welcome returning citizens and made plans for colonization projects, highway construction schemes, and the distribution of government lands designed to help returning Mexicans. The Cárdenas administration even originated a repatriation movement of its own, designed to harness the skills of returning migrants for the purpose of national reconstruction. All of these plans, however, came to nought. The colonization plans were poor and affected no more than about 5 percent of all the repatriates, and in the end the colonization schemes collapsed. Many *repatriados*, disappointed by the lack of jobs and low living standards in Mexico, became even more disillusioned by the manner in which official rhetoric contrasted with the lack of bureaucratic accomplishment.

The repatriation programs created among Mexicans in the United States a widespread sense of insecurity, thereby weakening the incipient Mexican trade union movement in the Southwest. Here, organizers in the fields faced well-nigh insoluble problems occasioned by the migratory nature of the labor force, strong-arm methods used by farmers and local law enforcement agencies, internal divisions within the labor unions, ethnic hostility against Mexicans, and the workers' poor bargaining position at a time of mass unemployment. The farm workers confronted a solidly organized lobby, the Associated Farmers of California (organized in 1936), which represented the wealthiest growers, who determined agricultural legislation in the state.

The farm laborers, representing something like 53 percent of California's agricultural population, were ill organized, divided along ethnic lines and distrusted by the "dirt farmers" as well as by agribusiness. The field hands made little headway at a time when agricultural unions wielded scant bargaining power. By the early 1930s, specifically Mexican unions included the Confederation of Mexican Labor Unions (Confederación de Obreros Mexicanos, CUOM), formed in 1928 with a constitution modeled on the Regional Confederation of Labor of Mexico. The CUOM disowned any radical intent. Another union was the Imperial Valley Workers' Union (Unión de Trabajadores del Valle Imperial), formed in 1928 as an independent organization of migrant workmen. This union's strike in 1928 was broken, but some growers did grant small wage agreements. In addition, the worst abuses of the contract labor system, including the withholding of wages, disappeared. A third body was the Confederación de Uniones de Campesinos y Obreros Mexicanos, which in 1933 obtained some minor concessions from the Japanese Growers' Association.

In addition, the communists attempted to enter the field. In 1930, they organized the Agricultural Workers' Industrial League, but it failed to make any real gains for its members as the Depression and widespread unemployment put labor unions at a grave disadvantage throughout the country. Communists also controlled the Cannery and Agricultural Workers' Industrial Union (C and AWIU). But, widespread fears among the growers nothwithstanding, the average migrant worker had no interest in social revolution; he simply wanted a better paid and safer job. Far from increasing, communist and socialist strength declined during the 1930s. (Between 1932 and 1940, the socialist and communist vote in the United States went down from nearly one million to under one-hundred-and-fifty thousand.) By 1935, the C and AWIU had become moribund and was officially dissolved when communists adopted the popular front as a way of working within existing unions.[7]

Public sympathy was not totally lacking for the farm workers' cause. Writers such as John Steinbeck moved their audiences to compassion by their graphic portrayals of "Arkie" and "Okie" farm workers. The Mexicans and Mexican Americans, however, lacked spokesmen of their own. To the general public, the Spanish-speaking farm workers remained invisible men. Migrant families in fact had an extraordinary capacity for making themselves inconspicuous. Many traveled by night because the license plates on their cars were out of date and they were anxious to avoid highway patrolmen. For the same reason, they traveled along back roads, pursuing zigzag routes. They stayed overnight in squatters' camps off the highways or camped along the way, out of sight in a clump of trees, under a bridge, or around the bend of a stream. They drifted into town, not as a procession but in single families—car by car, family by family. Grimmer still were the living conditions of many "undocumented" workers who often were housed in makeshift shelters or even underground dugouts—always fearful of being caught and deported, scared also of being preyed upon by local thugs, yet afraid of going to the police. Not surprisingly, many settled communities remained almost unaware of their presence, even at the height of the season.

The migrants remained equally inconspicuous to the majority of American intellectuals and political men. A few pioneers did excellent academic work—including Emory Bogardus, Carey McWilliams (a lawyer committed to the ideals of the New Deal who also was a fine writer), and Paul Schuster Taylor (the author of a monumental study on Mexican labor).[8] A handful of liberal lawyers, newspapermen, and Labor Department officials took a sympathetic interest in the Mexicans' fate, but academia as a whole remained indifferent to the problems of farm laborers, Mexican or otherwise. On the contrary, an army of luminaries—men such as A. Lawrence Lowell (president of Harvard University), Harvey F. Osborne (president of the American Museum of Natural History), and Roswell Johnson (president of the American Eugenics Society) denounced the way in which Mexican steel workers, miners, and farm hands were said to sully American morals and biological purity.

The New Deal administrators, by contrast, did benefit Mexican Americans, at least in a minor way. The Farm Security Administration set up permanent camps for migrants in centers of employment such as the Salt River Valley, Coachella Valley, and the San Joaquin Valley. The federal Emergency Relief Administration provided some employment during the grim winters of 1934 and 1935. Thereafter, the Works Progress Administration (WPA) provided work for skilled and unskilled men alike, as did the Civilian Conservation Corps (CCC). The "New Deal," however, had serious limitations. Many Mexicans failed to obtain relief payments, either because they were aliens or because they lacked the requisite local residence requirements. Most agricultural workers, whether Mexican or Mexican American, were excluded from benefits payable under industrial accident insurance and from a variety of other benefits. Mexicans often were reluctant to apply for welfare because their pride of family and of manhood forbade them from describing themselves as paupers. Even those who were willing to apply and who were entitled to benefits sometimes failed to gain their share because they were unfamiliar with the complex claims procedures. Also, the Mexican-American vote was numerically too insignificant, too dispersed geographically, and too difficult to mobilize to carry any weight within the Democratic Party. Although President Franklin D. Roosevelt's labor legislation did little for the rural migrant worker, and he took little interest in Mexican Americans as such, to those Mexican Americans who had the vote F.D.R. stood out as the unchallenged champion of the poor. Roosevelt did almost nothing for them, but the majority of

Mexican Americans remain strongly attached to the Democratic Party to this day.

To recapitulate, the Depression struck Mexican Americans, especially the farm workers, with great severity. Enforced repatriation rested on the assumption that the Mexicans sent back to Mexico were unassimilable foreigners. In fact, a number of these Mexicans already had American-born children who attended public schools, spoke English as well as Spanish, watched movies, listened to radio programs, played baseball, and indeed shared the experience of the second generation of other immigrant groups. These children were United States citizens by birth; in deporting their parents, the U.S. authorities unwittingly violated the children's rights. Not surprisingly, the deportation drive left an unfortunate legacy of insecurity and distrust, a legacy that long proved difficult to eradicate from the memories of Mexican Americans.

The outbreak of World War II dramatically changed the climate of both American labor relations and politics. Mass enlistment into the U.S. forces and an expanding and incessant demand for food, raw materials, and engines of war both for the United States and its allies created an enormous new demand for hired hands. War against Nazi Germany also played some part in discrediting the racist ideologies that had been so widely entrenched in prewar society. By 1942, there was no more talk of repatriating aliens. On the contrary, the United States government approached Mexico about a contract labor program that would satisfy the needs of southwestern growers. The Mexican authorities held numerous reservations, rooted in past American job discrimination, as well as a concern for their own expanding wartime economy. In the end, however, the Mexicans felt obliged to aid the United States in a common war effort and they believed that a *bracero* (contract worker) program would benefit the Mexican economy through worker's remittances, by providing unemployed men with jobs, and by familiarizing migrants with American agricultural techniques.

In arriving at these conclusions, Mexican policy makers drew heavily on the work of Manuel Gamio, a noted Mexican sociologist and an authority on Mexican labor migration. Gamio believed that the wholesale emigration of Mexicans to the United States injured Mexico by tempting many of the country's most active young men to leave. As an alternative, Gamio proposed contract-labor arrangements whereby Mexican workers would go to the United States for seasonal work under government supervision.

In some measure, the resultant agreement, concluded in 1942, corresponded to Gamio's hopes. The U.S. Farm Security Administration (later the Department of Agriculture and Labor) signed contracts with individual workers who agreed to labor in the United States for specified periods in specific occupations, usually farming. In return, the U.S. government provided transportation to and from the United States, guaranteed Mexican nationals "the prevailing wage" for the work in which they were engaged, and provided adequate housing and medical services. The United States in fact agreed to be the contractor to whom employers would apply for hiring *braceros*. Mexican workers in the United States would not be conscripted into the armed forces, would not be subjected to racially discriminatory acts of any kind, would be guaranteed repatriation, and would neither deprive Americans of their jobs nor lower their wages.

Despite all these safeguards, there were abuses. The U.S. government departments charged with supervising the project were too understaffed to enforce the promised safeguards. Some, though by no means all, growers violated their contracts by misrepresenting conditions of work and failing to provide the promised standards of food, accommodation, and pay. Texas (widely known as the "Mexicans' Mississippi") acquired a particularly poor reputation in this respect. Between 1943 and 1947, Mexico therefore blacklisted those Texas employers who preferred to hire illegal immigrants (primarily from Guanajato, Jalisco, Michoacan, Zacatecas, and San Luis Potosi) as well as local workers, prisoners of war, students, and even young school children to harvest the crops. A great many *braceros* decided to "skip"; that is to say, they ignored their contracts and struck out on their own for better jobs in the North and West.

The *bracero* program aroused bitter criticism on both sides of the border. According to its American critics, the *bracero* program in retrospect primarily benefited agribusiness by enabling growers to effect changes in crop and production patterns while the growers' own costs and tax burdens were increasing. By contrast, local farm workers found that their wages remained stable or actually declined. At the same time, a great number of Mexicans became familiar with work in the United States. During its 22-year history, 4.6 million contracts were issued to Mexican migrants, most of them from six or seven states in north-central Mexico.[9]

In Mexico, hostility to the *bracero* program was, if anything, even fiercer than in the United States. Mexican employers complained that their country was losing much-needed hands and that migration strengthened Mexico's American competitors in the world market. Catholic clergymen in Mexico deplored what they regarded as the breakup of the *braceros'* families and the moral temptations to which the *braceros* were exposed in the United States. Mexican labor unions, though linked to the ruling party, criticized the program because of anti-Mexican discrimination in the United States and because emigration caused the unions to lose potential members. The Mexican opposition parties, from the *sinarquistas* on the right to the communists on the left, used the *bracero* program as a stick to beat both the governing Partido Revolucionario Institucional (PRI) and the hated Yankees. The PRI found itself in the unenviable position of having to explain why, if the realities of Mexican economic development corresponded to its propaganda, the program was necessary.

Even more damning were critiques based on Mexican nationalism and a diffuse anti-Americanism common among both Mexican and Latin American intellectuals. Conservatives resented the "consumerism," relative social equality, and "unheroic" civilian ethos of Americans. Indigenous employers resented the fact that American corporations, contrary to their reputation, usually paid better wages than local firms. But anti-Americanism found little response among Mexico's poor. The average *bracero* was not ignorant of the ways of the world; only about 20 percent came directly from the countryside. The typical *bracero* was barely literate in Spanish but he was a mature man, usually married and with children to support, and well aware that a *bracero* contract might make the difference between penury and survival for his family.

A *bracero* contract accordingly became a valuable document involving widespread graft. Would-be *braceros* had to bribe local officials to get clearance to apply, once clearance had been obtained, the prospective worker had to make his way to an official recruiting station. His journey might involve a great deal of time and expense because most of the recruiting stations were located near Mexico's northern border rather than in the densely populated central plateau which provided most of the *braceros*. By the time a workman reached a recruiting station, he already had paid about 50 *pesos* (silver coins) to the local "municipal president" for permission to leave the particular township. At the contracting center, the potential *bracero* had to pay another 300 *pesos* or so to an official to gain admittance. In addition, workers had to pass health inspection and run a gauntlet of quotas and security checks.

Even before entering the United States, many Mexican workers had invested fifty dollars or more—roughly half their annual income. Humanitarian-minded planners and social scientists rarely considered the social costs of graft, extremely lucrative for officials on the take. Bribery proved impossible to stop, given the low salaries paid to junior officials, the refusal of most Mexicans to file complaints, and the ever-present attractions of the American labor market. Oddly enough, the *bracero* program actually may have contributed to a stabilizing of labor because those who could afford the *mordidas* were oftentimes returning *bracero* who had set aside money to acquire a new contract. Many *braceros* went back year after year to the same company or grower, thereby perpetuating in some measure the traditional relationship between client and *patrón*.

During the five years from 1942 to 1947, about 200,000 *braceros* made their way to the United States. More than half of them worked on California farms, the rest mainly in other parts of the Southwest. In addition to laboring on the land, *braceros* worked on a variety of other jobs, including transportion and maintenance. The effect on American wages is difficult to calculate. Meier and Rivera's standard work points out that cotton wages in Texas (which had no *braceros*) rose 236 percent during the war years, while in California (which used more than half the *bracero* quota), cotton wages increased only 136 percent.[10] In addition, wages were held down indirectly when, in 1943, the War Food Administration set wage ceilings on asparagus, tomatoes, grapes, and cotton—all crops heavily using *bracero* labor. For all practical purposes, the *bracero* program entailed a subsidy paid by the American taxpayer to the grower. The cost of the program to the federal government amounted to more than $113 million, or $450 per *bracero*, which derived from the expense of recruiting and other guarantees. Large-scale American farming enterprises did well under the system.

Mexico's economy also benefited from the program. Between 1942 and 1947, Mexico received about $318 million from the remittances and savings of *braceros*. These remittances increased in value after World War II, when the *bracero* program was intermittently continued. Precise estimates differ, but *bracero* remittances probably contributed between 1 and 2 percent a year to Mexico's annual income. The importance of these remittances hinged on their "multiplier effect" because each *bracero* supported an average of six people. The *braceros'* remittances, unlike any other source of foreign exchange or aid, went directly into the pockets of the poor.[11]

The *bracero* program also unwittingly attracted increasing numbers of illegal or "undocumented" workmen from Mexico to the United States. Returning *braceros* provided detailed and accurate information to friends and relatives concerning wages, conditions, and jobs in the United States. When asked in the early 1950s why they had come to the United States, 82 percent of the illegal immigrants interviewed stated that they had learned of the opportunities available in the United States by word of mouth. They were realistic; none of them expected to buy a Cadillac or find streets paved with gold. The unemployed man's need for a job as well as his discontent with the red tape and graft involved in the *bracero* program combined to persuade Mexicans to cross the border illegally. During World War II, their numbers remained fairly small, except in Texas. Between 1934 and 1943, about 12,000 illegal immigrants a year were apprehended and deported. The numbers rose abruptly to 31,179 in 1944 and doubled in 1945, continuing upward to 1,089,583 in 1954. In fact, illegal immigration during the years of the *bracero* program was probably as high as it was during the 1970s— with far-reaching demographic effects.[12]

World War II was also remarkable from the standpoint of national morale. In all previous wars, including the Civil War, Americans had been bitterly divided. World War II was the only major conflict in American history that did not create a powerful peace party. There was instead a widespread sense of national resolve, one generally shared by Hispanic Americans. After all, the Nazis' racial cult had nothing to offer to peoples of mixed ancestry, and Puerto Ricans and Mexicans were low on the Nazis' list of national preference. The Mexican ruling party detested fascists on ideological grounds. (During the late 1930s, Mexico, like the United States, admitted a substantial number of refugees from General Franco's Spain.) In 1942, Mexico declared war on the Axis powers and some Mexican units fought with the Allies in the Italian campaign. There was indeed a handful of Mexicans and Mexican Americans who sympathized with Nazi Germany. Known as *sinarquistas*, they opposed American and Mexican involvement in the war and, in addition, called for the return of the Southwest to Mexico. But the mass of Mexican Americans were no more inclined to support the *sinarquistas* than the ordinary German-American was to support the Nazi-inspired *Bund*.

A small number of Mexican Americans sought military careers during the interwar period, even though the fighting services were not a common career choice. In this respect, Mexican and Puerto Rican–Americans differed from Irish and German immigrants of an earlier vintage who often had enlisted in peacetime. By the early 1940s, ethnic succession had left its imprint on the armed forces as well as on every other part of American society. Members of the "old" immigration were plentiful on the armed forces honor rolls, and there were numerous commanders with German and German-Swiss names (such as Eisenhower, Spaatz, Nimitz, Kruger, and Eichelberger).[13]

Hispanic Americans began at the bottom of the military hierarchy, and in doing so they shouldered an especially heavy military burden. According to the 1940 census, the "foreign white stock" in the United States (meaning foreign-born Americans or Americans of foreign and mixed parentage) included 1,076,653 Mexicans (probably a serious under-estimation), 109,407 Spaniards, 69,967 Puerto Ricans, and 65,714 Cubans and other West Indians (not necessarily Spanish speakers). According to Meier and Rivera's history of the Chicanos, more than one-third of a million Spanish speakers (mostly Mexican Americans) had served in the armed forces by the end of the war, the highest percentage of any ethnic community.[14]

Spanish-speaking Americans were highly represented in the armed forces for a variety of reasons. Spanish speakers—particularly the Mexican Americans—included an unusually high percentage of young men of military age, relatively few of whom were skilled workmen, technicans, managers, or engineers eligible for draft deferment or exemption. Service in the armed forces afforded an easy means of naturalization for the foreign born. Hispanics, unlike blacks at the time, were not segregated in the fighting forces. Military service, especially in such fighting units as the paratroopers, marines, and tank corps, satisfied both the Spanish-speaking soldier's sense of pride and his desire to counter calumny. *No dejes que la Raza quede mal* ("Come on; don't make the 'Race' look bad!") was a common injunction to stiffen a wavering recruit during a tough training session.

The Spanish-speaking soldiers came from many different backgrounds. More than 65,000 Puerto Ricans served in the armed forces in World War II. The 295th and 296th Infantry Regiments of the Puerto Rican National Guard participated in the Asian and Pacific campaigns. Many of their members also went as replacements to the 65th Infantry Regiment, a regular U.S. unit composed of Puerto Ricans who fought in Europe. During these operations, 318 died in service and 20 were killed in action.[15] In addition, the U.S. armed forces contained Cubans, Central and South Americans, as well as *españoles* (men from Spain), and Sephardic Jews. The largest group by far, however, consisted of Mexican Americans, mostly city-bred soldiers from the Southwest who were apt to identify themselves in terms of *barrios* (neighborhoods) and were from such places as Maravilla, Chiques (Oxnard), Simons, Jimtown, Limonera, Sespe, San Antonio's "West-Side," Calle Ancha in Austin, "Magnolia" in Houston, Bessemer in Pueblo, "Larrimer" in Denver, El Pachuco, Juariles, or La Smelter.[16]

Their peacetime experience varied. They had worked as laborers, small businessmen, craftsmen, students, truck drivers, farmers, or as just plain *vagos* (vagrants). They differed in speech and background; the *calo* (slang) used by the border people from El Paso and Juarez contrasted with the homespun Spanish spoken by men from remote townships in Colorado or Arizona and with the racy English affected by the native-born Los Angeles men. There were distinctions between the American-born and the naturalized citizens originally reared in Mexico, many of them well versed in Mexican history, poetry, or the art of Diego de Rivera.

The largest group, according to Raul Morin (himself a Mexican-American veteran), were those born in the United States who could trace their ancestry to the original settlers and early immigrants of the Southwest. This group comprised, among others, the "Spanish Americans" from New Mexico and Colorado, the *tejanos* from Texas, and the *pochos* from California. They were the most "American" of all the recruits. For companions, they preferred their school chums or townfolk regardless of racial background; they enjoyed Spanish songs, Mexican *mariachis*, and also the latest American jazz. Among them were many *encartados* (people of mixed ancestry): Mexican Italians, Mexican Filipinos, Mexican Blacks, Spanish Mexicans, French Mexicans, Irish Mexicans, German Mexicans, and English Mexicans. There also were Anglo-Americans who had spent most of their lives among Mexicans, spoke excellent Spanish, and insisted that they were as Mexican as anyone else. In addition, Mexicans often met Spanish-speaking Americans of different ancestry they would rarely (if ever) encounter in civilian life.

Military service, of course, could raise difficult morale problems. To the ordinary G.I., distinctions among the Spanish speakers meant little and he was apt to lump them all together as "Mexicans." Racial prejudice continued in the armed services as it had in civilian life, least of all in the fighting units and most of all in the base camps.[17] "Why fight for America," Morin questioned himself, "when you have not been treated as an American? Do you really think that in the event the United States should win the war, Mexicans will be given better treatment?" In the end, Morin answered these questions for himself in the affirmative, served with a distinguished record, and ended the book from which we have quoted on an optimistic note.

The Mexicans had grounds for complaint, however. Their mood darkened as a result of the "Sleepy Lagoon" case in which several Mexican youngsters were convicted of murder (1943) but subsequently freed by the California District Court of Appeals for lack of evidence (1944). Then there were the zoot-suit riots in Los Angeles (1943). The zoot-suiters (*pachucos*) were second-generation Americans of Mexican descent who organized into city gangs (sometimes armed) distinguishable by their peculiar garb. Fighting between American sailors and zoot-suiters often led to unprovoked attacks on anyone who looked like a Mexican.

In terms of subsequent Chicano nationalist thought, the zoot-suit riots have since turned into one of the crimes of the century. Rodolfo Acuña's college text devotes eight and one-half pages to a series of minor riots and only half a page to the military achievements of 300,000 Mexican Americans. Another scholar, Mauricio Mazon, devotes an entire book to the riots and to what he calls the psychology of symbolic annihilation. He does so in referring to a period in history when untold millions were physically annihilated in concentration camps and forced labor camps abroad.[18] In retrospect, the *pachucos* have become political militants, defenders of *La Raza*. As we see it, this interpretation lacks historical perspective. Racial prejudice was common enough in the American—and British—armed forces during World War II, but brawls did not result from racial antagonism alone. There were brawls between U.S. soldiers and civilians, U.S. soldiers and sailors, and American and British servicemen. Brawls, for some, were just a happy pastime. The *pachucos*, far from being culture heroes, met with bitter disapproval from settled Mexican Americans who, like their Anglo-American neighbors, disliked street-corner gangs of any color. The riots nevertheless brought an extraordinary amount of publicity, and left a bitter taste, especially among those Mexican-American servicemen who had to listen to pejorative comments from their fellow soldiers and to questions like "What sort of citizens are these Mexican zoot-suiters who would beat up our own Navy men?"

The fact remains that Hispanic-American soldiers fought with great distinction. Seventeen infantrymen won the Congressional Medal of Honor and many more gained the Distinguished Silver Cross, the Silver and the Bronze Star for bravery under fire. Many American soldiers of Mexican descent took part in the initial fighting in the Philippines. They had enlisted in the 200th and 515th Coastal Artillery Regiment, composed of men from New Mexico, Texas, and Arizona. (These units went to the Philippines partly because many of their members could speak Spanish.) They took part in the famous defense of Bataan; they later shared in the terror of the Bataan death march and other atrocities inflicted upon the captured Americans by the Japanese. Mexican Americans also served in the National Guard units that helped to man such divisions as the 1st Infantry, the 2nd Armored, and the 3rd Infantry, which fought in North Africa. They subsequently saw combat in Italy in the 36th (Texas) Division, a unit unusual in that it contained an all-Spanish-speaking infantry company (recruited mostly from El Paso and its neighborhood). Many more Mexican Americans and Puerto Ricans saw action in northwestern Europe and in the Pacific.[19]

A reader interested in the individual exploits of Mexican-American soldiers must turn to Morin's account. We can do no more than select two case histories of different backgrounds. Private Silvestre S. Herrera, a former farm worker, entered the army in 1944 at age 27, leaving behind him in Phoenix his wife and three children. Advancing with his platoon (part of the 142nd Infantry Regiment, 36th Division) along a wooded road near Martzweiler in France, Herrera first distinguished himself in a frontal assault on an enemy strongpoint, capturing eight Germans. In subsequent fighting, Herrera stepped on a mine and lost both his feet. Despite intense pain and heavy loss of blood, Herrera—incredibly—continued to pin down the enemy with accurate rifle fire while another squad worked its way around the enemy's flank. To welcome home Pfc. Herrera, Arizona Governor Osborn declared August 24, 1945, to be "Herrera Day."

Another of the many Mexican-American war heroes was Jose L. Holguin, a graduate of Belmont High School in Los Angeles where he had made a name for himself as a member of the scholastic honor society and also in athletics. Holguin, no more than twenty years old, joined the Air Force shortly after Pearl Harbor and rapidly became one of the most outstanding navigators in the U.S. bomber force in the Pacific. In 1943, Holguin's plane was shot down by Japanese fighters in a night raid on Rabaul. Wounded, he was thrown out of his plane just as the aircraft went into a spin and a wing broke off. At the last moment his parachute opened and he survived. With his back badly injured, his jaw broken in two places, and a bullet hole in his leg, Holguin managed to crawl to a stream that led to a large river. He floated down the river, battled the swirling waters, and lived on frogs and berries he found in the thick underbrush along the river's edge. Rescued by indigenous villagers, he was later betrayed to the Japanese, who beat him, starved him, put him in solitary confinement, and used him as a guinea pig in malaria tests. Out of sixty-four fellow prisoners, only six survived. After the second atomic bomb had been dropped on Japan, the prisoners were liberated by the Australians. Holguin continued to serve in the Air Force, a highly decorated man and recipient of (among many other honors) the Air Force Commendation Medal awarded to him in 1955, by which time he had become a colonel.

The returning veterans found a country that in some respects differed considerably from the one they left. The war industries had created a variety of new jobs, and Chicanos as well as blacks began to fill positions previously closed to them. Whether as soldiers, sailors, or workers in war industries, more Mexican Americans began to move outside the *barrios*. There also was a change in attitude. As Morin recalls, the veterans asked themselves: "How long had we been missing out on benefits derived as American citizens? Old-timers had told us, and we also had read in books, how the early [Anglo-American] settlers had invaded our towns and shoved us onto 'the other side of the tracks.' But we ourselves had never made much attempt to move out of there. We had accepted without question edicts, taboos, restrictions, traditions, and customs that our ancestors had brought over from the old country."[20]

The war meant that, for the first time in their lives, Mexican-American veterans received preference over all nonveterans in the purchase of automobiles and new homes, leases and rentals, and civil service employment. Before the war, bank loans had been difficult to get; afterward, veterans became eligible for loans. The housing provisions in the G.I. Bill of Rights enabled Chicanos to purchase houses beyond the *barrios*. The educational grants under the same bill allowed them to train for technical employment and the professions. Mexican Americans entered the medical, legal, and academic fields. Others opened grocery stores, service stations, *tortillerías*, insurance and real estate offices, accounting firms, hardware and drug stores, and enterprises specializing in television and radio repair, auto mechanics, upholstery, painting, plumbing, trucking, carpentry, electrical work, barbering, printing, and cabinet making, in addition to the traditionally "ethnic" occupations of managing Mexican restaurants, *cantinas*, and corner grocery stores.

The experience of war also had positive psychological consequences. The demobilized veteran had shared in a common national experience. He was proud of his uniform, the ribbons he had earned, and his citizenship, and frequently had enlarged the circle of his friends to include Americans from different backgrounds. Soldiers from poverty-stricken homes had experienced standards of comfort taken for granted by the rank-and-file American serviceman but regarded as luxurious by Mexican Americans, Puerto Ricans, and even British soldiers who envied the G.I.'s pay, food, and entitlements. Mexican Americans also developed "a greater race and ethnic consciousness," a new confidence that found expression in postwar politics and in the development of such groups as the Community Services Organization, the American G.I. Forum, and the Mexican-American Political Organization, which we will discuss in a subsequent section.

But the extent of these successes should not be exaggerated. Housing discrimination continued in a variety of ways (for instance, through a system privately enforced by realtors who surreptitiously allotted "points" to prospective purchasers based on ethnic affinity as well as on income, social standing, and existing credit rating). Far from declining in size, the *barrios* grew after 1950 as more and more immigrants entered the country. The majority of Hispanic professional men and women continued to work as lawyers, librarians, clergymen, and teachers while non-Hispanic whites embarked upon careers as architects, engineers, and physicists in greater numbers than the Hispanics. But there were advances. Among Mexican-descended Americans, the proportion of unskilled laborers declined while the percentage of white-collar workers increased. Farm hands ceased to form the most significant proportion of the Hispanic labor force.

The extent of Hispanic advancement is difficult to assess. The impact of war differed from region to region: Texas offered the least opportunity to Mexican Americans, Illinois and California provided the most. And the various Hispanic communities were affected in strikingly different ways. The main beneficiaries were the *hispanos* descendants of the original Spanish-speaking population of the West. Mexican Americans, foreign-born and native (born in America of Mexican parentage), enlarged their share in middle-class or lower-middle-class occupations. The Puerto Ricans fared worst, possibly because the statistical picture was skewed by a heavy impact of semiskilled and unskilled laborers from the island to the United States, and possibly also by reason of an exodus of well-qualified Puerto Ricans from the mainland back home. Nevertheless, war and its aftermath improved to some point the Hispanics' overall position within the United States—with far-reaching consequences for the future.

Part II

Newcomers from
Many Lands

Chapter 5

The Puerto Ricans

The United States has a maritime frontier on the Caribbean as well as a Mexican border on land. This maritime frontier was shaped by American expansion beyond its shores, an experience that in some ways resembled that of Europe overseas. To many Americans, the Western European colonial dominions that had survived World War II seemed at best anachronisms and at worst obstacles to both commerce and liberty. In Latin America, especially in the universities, the American attitude itself towards Puerto Rico also came under fire.

According to their censors, the Americans had reduced the island to the status of a dependent country. The establishment of a Puerto Rican Commonwealth in 1952 had changed the form but not the substance of colonial rule. Legally, Puerto Rico was a self-governing community voluntarily associated with the United States, ruled by a governor and a legislative assembly elected freely by its citizens' direct vote for a period of four years. In fact, Puerto Rico remained tightly linked to the United States. Puerto Rico could not conduct its own foreign policy and thereby remained unable to opt out of the Americans' involvement in the Cold War; it formed an American military bastion; it could not control the newcomers who came to its shores, including political carpetbaggers, speculators, and, more recently, Cuban refugees.

Worse, said the opponents of the American connection, the Puerto Rican Commonwealth could protect neither its manufactures nor its farming industry by placing tariffs on Yankee imports. American capitalism thereby inhibited the island's autonomous economic development: the Yankees decimated Puerto Rico's petty bourgeoisie through "price wars" waged by large American companies against small enterprises in Puerto Rico, they discriminated against Puerto Ricans in hiring and promotion, and they ruled the island through a dependent class of Puerto Rican politicos and businessmen whose operations posed no real challenge to the American presence.[1] Riddled by political and economic contradictions, Puerto Rico, the critics argued, proved unable to provide a living for its sons and daughters. Having arrived on the mainland, Puerto Ricans continued to experience a related pattern of exploitation and discrimination—hence the majority of them remained locked in an unbreakable vise of poverty.[2]

Puerto Rico: Price of Development

In our view, these critiques depend on certain unspoken assumptions. The dynamic nature of American capitalism and of American society and the extent of ethnic and social mobility are apt to go unrecognized. There also exists an idealized image of a vanished rural past, an image that haunts both the books written by many nineteenth-century romantics and the works of many modern leftists. The modern fantasies tend to derive from intellectuals whose knowledge of rural life was not picked up on a family farm, but from lectures, seminars, or subsidized "field trips." Such analyses have other failings. For one, the social ills of the United States, or of urban society in general, are assumed to be everlasting, even when they are at the point of change.

We do not share these assumptions. The traditional *jíbaro* (the village cultivator) had many virtues. He worked hard, prayed with devotion, led a Spartan life, was loyal to his kinsmen and his church; he was a man of his word, was self-reliant, and had his own traditions, including a rich legacy of dances, legends, and songs (some of them, like that of the Sephardim, of medieval Spanish origin). He also was illiterate, superstitious, and beset by diseases against which he could not protect himself—the image of the healthy, sturdy, peasant comes from novels, not from medical reports. He dwelt with his family in a tiny, overcrowded shack, he was apt to go hungry, and his life-expectancy was brief.

In Puerto Rico's popular entertainment, the *jíbaro* wearing his *pava* (broad-brimmed hat) remains an earthy, good-natured man, full of natural wisdom and common sense. Poets, journalists, and academicians who have never handled a machete or fed a pig also hearken back to the splendors of Puerto Rico's folk soul and call themselves *jíbaros* at heart. In doing so, they only fool themselves.

Puerto Rican reality was different. In 1901, the death rate stood at 36.7 per thousand. Malaria, tuberculosis, and yellow fever were an ever-present menace to the countryman's well-being. The traditional *jíbaro* was beset by constant sickness. By 1921, the death rate had dropped to 22.3 per thousand, and in 1941 it stopped at 18.6 per thousand, roughly half the 1901 figure. The "colonial" impact in respect to health was an unmixed good. The American campaign against illiteracy achieved similar successes. Between 1899 and 1940, the illiteracy rate reportedly diminished from 79.6 to 31 percent.[3] At the outbreak of World War II, Puerto Rico's condition already compared favorably with that of the other Caribbean islands, including Haiti and Santo Domingo, which had escaped the assumed taint of recent colonial rule.

This is not to say that all went well under the Stars and Stripes. Quite the contrary. Puerto Rico, before World War II, remained a backward island whose farmers faced a serious shortage of land. Gains in the country's hygienic condition caused the population to nearly double between 1898 and 1940, thereby putting more stress on a depressed economy heavily dependent on sugar. Per capita income before World War II was a mere $118 a year. (Farm work, the main source of employment, paid as little as 6 cents an hour; the construction workers—the laboring elite—earned 22 cents an hour.) The people did not starve, but malnutrition was widespread. Unemployment and underemployment remained countrywide afflictions unassuaged as yet by mass emigration; at this time, even a steamship ticket, considerably less expensive than a plane ticket, was beyond the means of ordinary citizens.

The island suffered from rigid inequality in status as well as in income. According to Dr. José Vásquez Calzada, a Puerto Rican scholar, in 1963 20 percent of the people, comprising the wealthiest families, earned about 51 percent of the total national income; another 20 percent, embracing the poorest families, received no more than 5 percent of the total national income. Development was extremely slow, not because American capitalists were crowding into the island's money markets in search of profits, but because the influx of capital remained relatively small and investors were reluctant to risk their funds in a depressed economy in which sugar provided one-fourth of the island's jobs and two-thirds of its dollar exports.

To cope with its problems, Puerto Rico turned to a peculiar blend of Latin American *personalismo* (government based on personal loyalty to a revered chief), and the North American "New Deal." During the 1940s, Puerto Rico became a laboratory in which American and Puerto Rican progressives experimented, using a variety of social planning and "pump-priming" policies with public agencies and regulatory devices—using all those policies that American academicians, aid administrators, and technical experts attempted to export to the Third World as America's special contribution to post–World War II global development.

The political revolution began in 1940, when new elections broke the political influence of the sugar industry and of the families that dominated the plantation economy. The new government was headed by Luís Muñoz Marín, leader of the Popular Democratic Party (*Partido Popular Democrático*), president of the senate in 1941, and governor from 1949 until he voluntarily stepped down in 1964. His popularity, his personality, his ability to use his own party as a patronage machine, and his flair for dealing with American politicians within the Democratic Party—and for manipulating the American power structure as a whole—gave Luís Muñoz Marín unrivaled influence on the island. Muñoz also was tied by personal friendship and political affinity to José Figueres (a political leader and reforming president of Costa Rica) and to Rómulo

Betancourt (president of Venezuela); all three of them were committed
to the Alliance for Progress, a venture for United States–Latin American
cooperation in the spirit of President John F. Kennedy's "New Frontier,"
which began operation in 1961.

When Muñoz embarked on his political career, he saw himself as
the spokesman of the poor. In their service, he meant above all to curb
the power of the great sugar interests by forcing the sugar companies
to pay higher wages and taxes; in addition, he wanted to weaken them
by breaking up the large estates—to the extent of going into competition
with them. As *líder máximo* (supreme head), he relied on the trade
unions, the bureaucrats, and on the masses loyal to the chief against
the old Puerto Rican families whose sugar estates had given them
domination over the island's society.

Muñoz received support from Rexford Guy Tugwell, a New Dealer
appointed by President Roosevelt to the island's governorship in 1941.
A former college professor, Tugwell had served as an original member
of Roosevelt's "Brain Trust." He had made both bitter enemies and
warm friends for himself on the island by drawing up, in the 1930s, a
plan for redistributing Puerto Rico's sugar island estates. (He was also
the author of a book well known at the time, *The Stricken Land: The
Story of Puerto Rico* [1947]).

Having acquired land through expropriation and land drainage, the
Puerto Rican government went into the business of producing sugar on
a number of "proportional profit farms" (so called because the government
returned profits to the workers in the form of increased wages). The
authorities developed rural housing schemes and also attempted to
diversify agriculture by introducing new crops, building slaughterhouses,
setting up new hotels, opening a cement factory, promoting public works,
generating electricity, and distributing power throughout the island in
the tradition of the Tennessee Valley Authority.

Muñoz intended a revolution in land ownership. However, given the
cohesion of the old Puerto Rican families and their ability to circumvent
legislation by legal means, Muñoz's and Tugwell's original policies proved
difficult to enforce. Many of the new government farms operated at a
loss, beset by rising costs, labor troubles, inefficient management, and
the politics of patronage. Government-owned industries also encountered
serious problems. Wages paid in government enterprises were set more
for political than economic reasons; wage rates often were higher than
the industries could afford. Government enterprises in fact turned out
to be peculiarly vulnerable to labor disputes.

Agriculture at first tended to be neglected in the island's development
plans as a whole, a failing that reflected the fashionable emphasis on
industrialization as the magic cure for underdevelopment. After the early

1960s, however, the government gave serious attention to farming; more was done to improve the productivity of coffee and tobacco growers. In addition, the authorities promoted diversification by encouraging poultry keeping and cattle husbandry. Even so, farming continued to lag far behind the rest of the economy.

The most striking advances occurred in manufacturing. From 1947 onward, Muñoz and his advisers increasingly became convinced that the use of public funds did not work well in constructing and operating factories. Public enterprises tied up an excessively high proportion of public funds, and governmental expertise and government finance proved insufficient to promote industrialization on the scale required by Muñoz's adherents. Moreover, government enterprise made little difference in reducing the island's unemployment. In fact, the very existence of government-owned, taxpayer-subsidized plants may have made the promotion of private venture more difficult. Whatever the reason, the government-owned Industrial Development Company lost money on most of its ventures.

Having committed itself to a new course, the government began to sell public enterprises to private businessmen. Also, the authorities initiated a program, Operation Bootstrap, to attract private capital to the island by means of tax concessions. Muñoz's critics notwithstanding, low wages were not held out as a bait to investors. On the contrary, the government gradually raised minimum wages to bring them up to the standards decreed by the federal government on the mainland. In doing so, the Puerto Rican authorities unwittingly may have encouraged the emigration of poorly skilled youngsters, as Puerto Rican employers, forced to pay minimum wages, began to hire fewer but more highly skilled and highly paid workers. Minimum-wage laws also unwittingly favored large, well-capitalized firms (often expatriate American businesses) over small, struggling local firms anxious to save on their wage bills. In addition, Puerto Rican authorities began an advertising campaign on the mainland designed to create an image of the island as a vacation dreamland of eternally blue skies, deep-sea fishing, surfing and sailing, and of perpetually elegant, smiling women and bronzed young men.

In some ways, Puerto Rico's modernization campaign succeeded beyond belief. Between 1952 and 1964, industry became the islanders' main source of livelihood. By 1964, manufacturing accounted for 23 percent of the national income, whereas agriculture, once the main source of wealth, contributed only 10 percent. Industry began to diversify: in addition to labor-intensive consumer industries such as textiles, footwear, and electronic equipment, the island acquired capital-intensive oil refineries and petrochemical industries. Overall economic growth was breathtaking. Between 1940 and 1964, the GNP increased nearly ninefold and the manufacturing output went up eighteen times.[4]

There also was some redistribution of income. While profits from the ownership of property declined somewhat, incomes from wages and salaries went up proportionately. In 1940, property owners received an estimated 40 percent of the national income; by 1964, their share had fallen to 24 percent. Wages rose in a striking fashion: between 1947 and 1957, wages increased by 52 percent for farm laborers, 72 percent for white-collar workers, and 80 percent for skilled manual workers. The country became increasingly urbanized. Between 1950 and 1960 alone, the percentage of the labor force employed in farming dropped from 31.1 to 19.8 percent. Public housing improved and education and health services expanded.

In theory, economic growth on such a scale should have inhibited mass emigration. In practice, the opposite happened in Puerto Rico— as in so many other countries. As domestic development accelerated, so did emigration. Improvements in education, communication, technical training, and income levels combined to create new opportunities for prospective emigrants. At the same time, economic transformation wrought new hardships. Many traditional jobs disappeared: the fine needlework that once occupied many Puerto Rican women at home was reduced by foreign competition that paid even less than Puerto Rico's wages, and the mechanization of the sugar industry reduced the number of jobs on the farms. The island did develop a middle class of its own, but unskilled and semiskilled labor in 1960 still made up nearly 60 percent of the island's work force compared to 18.4 percent in middle-class professions and 23.6 percent in white-collar occupations or highly skilled mechanical jobs.

Puerto Rico, by American standards, was an overcrowded island. During the Muñoz era, the cities changed their skylines as apartment towers and high-rise condominiums sprang up, increasing numbers of villagers made their way into the cities, and *urbanizaciones* (private housing developments) expanded, along with city slums. Traffic jams became increasingly irksome and air pollution more objectionable as the automobile transformed the island. (By 1960, Puerto Rico had a higher ratio of cars to people than any other country in the world except the United States.) The average Puerto Rican, in other words, ceased to be a *jíbaro* living in the relative isolation of a homestead in the backwoods; more and more he became a townsman, familiar with radio and television, city ways, and, in a certain sense, with American lifestyles.

Most of the Puerto Rican people had come to value the American connection and did not wish independence from the United States. In

1967, 60.5 percent voted for commonwealth status; the vote for American statehood was 38.9 percent; only 0.6 percent of the vote cast was for independence. Thirteen years later, in the elections of 1980, the electorate again overwhelmingly rejected independence. This is not to say that the U.S. connection was universally popular. On the contrary, the number of advocates for independence was larger than the polls indicated because many citizens refused to vote. Even the proponents of the existing commonwealth status found some valid points in the arguments put forward by the *independistas*. But the fact remains that advocates of independence remained a minority, many of whom were intellectuals.

The mass of Puerto Ricans did not share the intellectuals' assumptions. The Americans had succeeded in Puerto Rico where the French in Algeria had failed; the Americans had succeeded in turning the metropolitan connection into a popular cause. The ordinary Puerto Rican truck driver or factory operator did not object to the influx of American capital that created new jobs on the island. They did not wish to lose their American passports and thereby forfeit their right to travel to the mainland and visit freely with uncles and cousins in New York or Chicago. Nor did they want a separate republic. As Manuel Maldonado-Denis, a bitter critic of the American link, a Marxist, and an advocate of independence, noted with regret, "Whatever the reason . . . , the independence movement has not taken root in the worker and peasant sector of Puerto Rican society."[5]

The emigrants had economic reasons for seeking better jobs abroad. In terms of average per capita incomes, Puerto Rico might do a great deal better than neighboring Caribbean islands such as Jamaica, or even a major Latin American country like Mexico.[6] But compared to the United States, a country increasingly familiar to Puerto Ricans through television, radio, newspapers, and, above all, through letters from friends and relatives on the mainland and travelers' reports, Puerto Rican incomes remained pitifully low, especially in the villages. A countryman anxious to better himself was prone to look for a job in a Puerto Rican city. The road to San Juan often then led to New York. Urbanization and migration to the mainland, in other words, were apt to be closely linked. By 1970, about 60 percent of Puerto Ricans lived in urban areas; the traditional image of the Puerto Rican as a countryman ceased to correspond to reality. Another incentive to emigration was unemployment. Between 1952–53 and 1960–61, although unemployment actually decreased from 16 percent of the labor force to 10 percent, many Puerto Ricans remained out of work, a much higher percentage than among mainland Americans.

The mainland (and sometimes Venezuela)—rather than socialist Cuba, reformist Mexico, or authoritarian Argentina—thus became a magnet of extraordinary attraction. The Puerto Rican labor force became increasingly mobile, which happened as well on many other islands in the Caribbean Basin. Foreign (especially U.S.) firms had set up subsidiaries where local employees became increasingly familiar with superior working conditions and pay on the American mainland. Industrial jobs became more and more popular in societies in which work on farms and plantations had been little honored and poorly paid. Changes in the techniques and organization of air travel further facilitated the migrant's lot. By the late 1940s, the cost of economy air fares already had dropped sufficiently to enable passengers to fly from San Juan to New York for less than $50. The trickle of migration became a flood. By 1972, close to 1.5 million people were making the trip back and forth to the mainland every year; Puerto Rico turned into one of the mainland's major sources of immigrants. New York became the greatest of all Puerto Rican cities, with a Puerto Rican population considerably greater than Puerto Rico's capital. In 1970, the Puerto Rican or Puerto Rican–descended population of New York was 817,712; San Juan municipality's population totaled 463,242, and by 1983 New York had almost one million Puerto Ricans.

The consequences for Puerto Rico were complex. Emigration from Puerto Rico in the 1950s and 1960s probably helped to maintain social stability on the island. As Henry Wells wrote in a standard work on Puerto Rico, "The possibility of going to the mainland, even when not acted upon, offered the discontented and the resentful an ever available alternative."[7] Most of the migrants were teenagers and young adults, those who most readily take part in street riots or brawls.

Migration also affected the island's demographic structure, though the evidence is ambivalent. Traditionally, Puerto Rico had a high birthrate, a high death rate, and a youthful population with few aged people, conditions typical of most backward countries at the time. Prior to 1960, however, the island's net population had grown slowly, primarily because of Puerto Rico's high rate of emigration since the end of World War II. From 1966 onward, Puerto Rico's birthrate began to decline in a striking fashion, and the Puerto Rican's average life expectancy increased during a period of a high rate of return migration. Net emigration in 1969 amounted to no more than 7,000 persons out of Puerto Rico's total population of 2,712,000—a substantial number, but in no way a disastrous drain on the island as a whole.

Had times remained good, Puerto Rico might have been able to solve its problems. Unfortunately, its fortunes suffered a disastrous blow when, by the early 1980s, the island's economy began to experience the full effect of a worldwide slump.[8] Many major enterprises closed down, including a multimillion dollar refining and petrochemical complex in which Puerto Ricans had set high hopes. Unemployment reached 23 percent; the construction sector was virtually paralyzed, business and personal bankruptcy grew rapidly, and the government faced grave financial difficulties. About 60 percent of families were below the U.S. poverty line. Only massive U.S. assistance ($4 billion a year) kept the island going. Congress in 1982 took Puerto Rico out of the food-stamp program and gave the island a block grant to cover social welfare programs. Unfortunately, Puerto Rico had become terribly dependent on food stamps—about 56 percent of the population used them, amounting to a cost of $875 million in 1981–82.

Puerto Rico by the early 1980s had become one of the worst instances of a colonial welfare economy, with few of its virtues and most of its vices. Puerto Rican industries lost many of their former advantages when federal minimum wages were imposed on the island and transport costs increased because American ships were required to be used. The tax advantages formerly granted to Puerto Rican industries were curtailed to raise more revenue in the face of growing public expenditure and budgetary deficits. The accelerating pace of rate increases was coupled with increasing costs in energy and raw materials. The public debt grew from 49 percent of the gross national product in the early 1970s to 80 percent at the end of the decade. The United States had become ever more important, not merely as a source of capital and a market, but also as a source of support by way of transfer payments, which rose from 7 percent of personal income in 1970 to 20 percent in 1977. The unemployment rate by 1982 had risen to 22.4 percent. Of those employed, almost one-third had come to rely on government jobs. In addition to food stamps, a monthly welfare check was received by six out of every ten islanders by 1983. Just as many of their relatives in New York had become dependent on welfare and some of them had lost the traditional work ethic, so had a good many islanders. The food-stamp money appeared to have had no positive impact on the economy; it may simply have increased dependency. Critics therefore argued that the money would be better spent on public works jobs in order to help train and to give employment to the unemployed.[9]

Puerto Rico's "economic miracle" stood endangered. Much of the $50 billion or so transferred to the island since the 1940s in transfer payments and capital investments had been squandered. The Puerto Rican economy, heavily entwined in public regulation and state direction, had failed to duplicate the extraordinary development achieved in such countries as South Korea and Taiwan. The "New Deal" in its Caribbean incarnation had failed. Puerto Ricans also stood divided regarding their country's political status. The *independistas* might form no more than a small minority, but commonwealth status rested on shaky foundations.

By the early 1980s, no party—whether committed to statehood or to a modified commonwealth governance—was willing to accept the existing arrangement.[10]

Puerto Ricans in New York

Puerto Ricans had made their way to New York as early as the nineteenth century, and at the time of the Spanish-American War the city already contained a flourishing community. Mass migration began only after World War II, but then rapidly accelerated. By 1980 the number of Puerto Ricans in New York had grown to 860,552, or 12.2 percent of New York's total population. At that Puerto Ricans also constituted 61.2 percent of the city's Hispanic peoples (as against 66.2 percent in 1970). New York remained the core area of Puerto Rican settlement, with a high proportion of first-generation residents; their influx balanced the outflow of Puerto Ricans from New York and helped to keep down the Puerto Rican New Yorkers' average income. To a large extent, the economic fortunes of New York continued to dominate the history of Puerto Rican migration.

In the years immediately following World War II, jobs had been plentiful. New York was still a thriving manufacturing city and a great port, as well as the center of service industries such as banking and publishing. There was ample employment for skilled, semiskilled, and even a good many unskilled workers. When times got harder in the late 1940s, Puerto Rican migration slackened; however, the local economy again began to boom when the Korean War broke out in the 1950s, and many more Puerto Ricans found jobs in American factories. In addition, 40,000 Puerto Ricans volunteered for the U.S. Army.

Puerto Ricans arriving on the mainland after World War II were apt to be somewhat better educated than their predecessors. A higher proportion of them had learned English; a much larger proportion came from Puerto Rican cities and towns. Nevertheless, the great majority of the newcomers began on the lowest rungs of the economic ladder. Like Jewish immigrants from Eastern Europe at the end of the nineteenth century, many Puerto Ricans took employment in the garment industry and made a living with a sewing machine, especially Puerto Rican women famed for their fine needlework and manual dexterity. Other Puerto Ricans began to work in factories unknown in the late nineteenth century, such as electronic equipment or a variety of other light industries. Many more worked as messengers, bus boys, dishwashers, car washers, and in other unskilled occupations requiring little or no knowledge of English. Additional newcomers came on temporary contracts, like Mexican *braceros,* to pick cranberries or do the roughest work on New Jersey truck gardens and chicken farms.[11]

Originally, the great majority of Puerto Ricans in New York City—like newcomers from so many other parts of Europe—had congregated in one major area. In the Puerto Ricans' case, this was East Harlem. Thereafter, Puerto Ricans spread into other parts of the city—from Manhattan to the Bronx and Brooklyn—partly because they wished to avoid overcrowding and partly because of New York's vast program of slum clearance and public housing, which had the unintended effect of breaking up Puerto Rican residential concentrations. Some Puerto Ricans succeeded financially, but many more remained in barrios such as Williamsburg in Brooklyn, the South Bronx, East Harlem, and lower east-side Manhattan, where burnt-out buildings, litter, abandoned cars, and garbage remind visitors of a wartorn city sunk into grim poverty.

By 1980, East Harlem and the Lower East Side remained the two major areas of Puerto Rican settlement. Puerto Ricans, however, continued to move toward the Bronx, especially into its northeastern portion, and into the boroughs of Staten Island and Queens. Overall, Puerto Ricans had greatly expanded outward from their original neighborhoods in the 1950s. Although many of them remained in the same low-income areas they had occupied 30 years earlier, others had managed to find homes in middle-income communities whose residents owned their own houses. Between 1970 and 1980, the number of Puerto Rican householders living in owner-occupied units went up by 62 percent. The gain, admittedly, was a modest one; owner-occupied units constituted no more than 9 percent of all housing units with a Puerto Rican householder. Nonetheless, some improvement had taken place in the Puerto Ricans' living conditions.

In theory, the problem of adjustment for the Puerto Ricans should have been easier than for their predecessors. Unlike European immigrants to New York of an earlier vintage, Puerto Ricans were U.S. citizens. They did not experience the traumatic shock of being illegals, like the Mexicans, or being "screened" at Ellis Island, where families might be split up and sick or "unsuitable" people might be sent back to their land of origin. The Puerto Ricans were entitled to vote; they had a legal stake in the land. Moreover, the Puerto Ricans were the first substantial immigrant group to arrive primarily by plane, rather than by boat or on foot. Communications with the homeland were easy; there was constant coming and going; children could be sent back to be looked after by grandparents on the island if necessary; and the disappointed and the impoverished could return to his native village or town with much greater facility than the nineteenth-century immigrant from, for example, Lithuania or Calabria. The Puerto Rican immigrants probably contained a larger proportion of persons able to speak some English than any other immigrant group except those drawn from the British Isles, or what later became the British dominions. The Puerto Ricans were also the first immigrant group who unwittingly moved into what became, to some extent, a welfare economy with a powerful and intrusive bureaucracy, a high level of public expenditure, and a strong commitment to social planning.

Puerto Ricans seemed specially adapted to fit into America's multiracial society. Unlike any other major immigrant group that had previously arrived on the mainland, the Puerto Rican community contained persons of every possible color and complexion: men and women of European (usually, but not always, of Mediterranean) appearance; *trigue/tnos* ("wheat-colored" people with light brown skins); and *gente de color* (dark or black-skinned) Puerto Ricans who were nevertheless regarded as Puerto Rican compatriots by their lighter-skinned countrymen and who were rigidly distinguished from *morenos* or American blacks. This is not to say that Puerto Ricans were indifferent to color. In Puerto Rico, however, the issue was much more complicated than in the United States. The Puerto Rican upper and middle classes were apt to be more light skinned than the rest, but by no means universally so; a large percentage of the most poverty-stricken people in the mountain towns or *municipios* of the interior, such as Jayuya or Orocovis, were largely of European descent. There were no iron-bound distinctions; intermarriage was common, class counted for more than color, and there was less concern over skin pigmentation than in the English-speaking world.

Nevertheless, many Puerto Ricans met great difficulties in adjusting to New York even when they were healthy and willing to work. In this respect, the fate of the Puerto Ricans—who found themselves in an emerging welfare state—was quite different from that, say, of the London poor in a nineteenth-century free enterprise economy. At the end of the last century, Charles Booth carried out a pioneer investigation entitled *Life and Labour of the People in London, 1891–1903*. This book described human misery on a scale that shocked their contemporaries. Yet, as Nathan Glazer and Patrick Moynihan point out in their classic study previously cited, the army of late nineteenth-century London poor contained remarkably few able-bodied men who had a modicum of education and some skills and who were not mentally unbalanced.

Puerto Ricans in New York, on the other hand, were beset by structural unemployment that hit even young men fit to work, as well as the old and the crippled; jobs were scarce even in times of relative prosperity, such as in the early 1960s. For example, in 1960, 5 percent of all New York males were out of work; 6.9 percent of nonwhite males and 9.9 percent of Puerto Rican males were unemployed. Puerto Rican family incomes remained low: in 1960 the Puerto Rican median family income in New York amounted to $3,811, as compared to $4,437 for all nonwhites; the Puerto Rican median family income was no more than 63 percent of the median income for all New York families.

During the 1960s Puerto Ricans somewhat improved their positions. However, in 1973 the New York State Division on Employment once more reported that unemployment for Hispanic New Yorkers was increasing at twice the rate for the rest of the population. The Puerto Ricans were exceptionally vulnerable. When times were good, their relative position got better; when times worsened, the Puerto Ricans suffered to a peculiar degree.

Puerto Rican misery had many roots. Puerto Ricans—like many other immigrants—were on the whole a youthful community. In 1979 the Puerto Rican median age was 19.9 years, as against 21.1 for Mexicans, 25.5 for Central and South Americans, 36.5 for Cubans, and 29.8 for the general population. The Puerto Rican birth rate was high. Puerto Rican mothers bore children at a younger age than those of any other ethnic group, and they bore more of them. The proportion of children under five among Puerto Ricans in 1970 was double that for the general population. Forty percent of Puerto Rican households were headed by women, whereas that figure was just 12 percent among "Anglos." According to the 1980 census, only 42 percent of Puerto Rican children were living in families where husband and wife lived together; 47 percent stayed with a female householder without a spouse. Comparable figures for all the city's children stood at 58 and 31 percent, respectively. Puerto Rican married couple families formed no more than 51 percent of all Puerto Rican families, while this figure was 69 percent for the city as a whole.

No statistician can of course be quite sure how reliable these figures are. In dealing with census takers and welfare workers, some women may have deliberately concealed the presence of an adult man in the house, so as not to endanger their children's welfare status. But even if the figures cited are not wholly dependable, they do document a high degree of family instability. Translated into everyday language, the statistics point to a large number of harried mothers battling—without a father's help, and often unsuccessfully—to keep their children off the street and to guard them against truancy, drug abuse, and sexual promiscuity.

Puerto Rican households remained large. Their size did decline somewhat over previous decades, but the average Puerto Rican household in New York City contained more persons by 1980 than any other (3.08

persons, as against 2.49). Puerto Ricans accordingly experienced a good deal of overcrowding—not perhaps by the standards of Moscow or Havana, but by the standards of fellow New Yorkers. The federal standard for measuring overcrowded housing is the proportion of housing units with 1.01 or more persons per room. According to this criterion, almost 16 percent of all Puerto Rican households were overcrowded, as against 8.2 percent for the city as a whole. Some improvement had taken place as compared with conditions in the past, but Puerto Ricans as a group remained among the most poverty-stricken of New Yorkers.

Throughout its modern history, the Puerto Rican community in New York remained beset by unemployment, and those Puerto Ricans who did hold jobs congregated heavily at the bottom of the skill ladder. Although their share of white-collar jobs increased (particularly in the city's public services), only a few attained top-level positions. Moreover, many were employed in industries that were losing jobs, and relatively few were in the growth industries. Puerto Ricans in New York might have been better paid on the average than in Puerto Rico itself, but their median average income remained little more than half the average for the city.

Although Puerto Ricans did not bear the stigma of "illegals," as did many Mexicans, they still felt unwelcomed and more discriminated against than Cubans and Mexicans. In New York a million or so Puerto Ricans lived in some of the city's most undesirable conditions. The decline in Puerto Rico's prosperity since 1978 increased the flow to the United States; between 1972 and 1978, more had left than entered the United States. Many Puerto Ricans continued to feel that they were worse off than blacks and therefore should be helped more.

Blacks obviously did not agree and insisted on protecting their benefits. The Puerto Rican leadership remained mostly "white," even though most Puerto Ricans were dark skinned and resented being lumped together with blacks. Blacks thus accused Puerto Ricans of racial prejudice and of choosing as their leaders or offering preferment to lighter-skinned Puerto Ricans. For example, former congressman Herman Badillo and the mayor of Miami Maurice Ferre were light skinned, as were actors Jose Ferrer, Jessie de Guzman, and Paul Julia.

Puerto Ricans also suffered from other psychological disabilities. They were widely stereotyped as muggers and ne'er-do-wells. They were often ambivalent about their U.S. connection. Were they Americans or Puerto Ricans? Would they live on the mainland or return to the island? There was also the question of Puerto Rico's uncertain political status. Was it to become a state of the Union, remain a Commonwealth, or become independent? Puerto Ricans on the island were American citizens but they could not vote for a U.S. president or send representatives to

Congress. They were, however, empowered to vote for island representation and benefit from numerous federal welfare programs. An estimated 60 percent of Puerto Ricans on the island in 1983 received some welfare.

Puerto Rican misery in the United States had many sources. Puerto Ricans often suffered from racial discrimination, especially the darkskinned ones. In addition, many other factors worked to their disadvantage. Adult newcomers to New York commonly found themselves handicapped, not only by reason of their unfamiliarity with the city's institutions, customs, and employment practices, but also because they often lacked fluency in English, transferable skills, and formal education. The Puerto Rican community in New York also suffered from a partial exodus of skilled people back to the island. In terms of material success, an unskilled Puerto Rican was apt indeed to benefit by leaving the island and settling in New York. An upwardly mobile Puerto Rican, however, might often do better by returning home. In this respect, his position differed sharply from that of a Cuban who—once having left his native land—usually neither desired nor was permitted to return to Cuba.

A Puerto Rican with mainland experience, on the other hand, often found that he could secure a highly paid position more easily in Puerto Rico than in New York. In 1970 the proportion employed in professional and managerial positions on the island was three times larger for urban Puerto Ricans than with New York Puerto Ricans. As a U.S. Department of Labor report put it, "migration to the mainland entails the risk of downward mobility for the highly skilled, but offers the prospect of upward movement for those with no skill or working experience. Return migration for Puerto Ricans with mainland experience [on the other hand] generally increases the chance of moving up the skill ladder."[12]

During the early 1980s, however, the occupational pattern of Puerto Rican immigrants to the mainland began to change in a striking manner. More and more professional people began to settle on the mainland. According to 1983 estimates, for instance, more than half the engineering graduates on the island were taking jobs in the United States. The popular stereotype of the unskilled or semiskilled Puerto Rican immigrant has therefore ceased to correspond to the facts.

Nevertheless, a great many Puerto Ricans in New York became heavily involved in the city's growing welfare economy—initially much against their will. Puerto Rican families, blessed with many children, had to look after them under conditions where there were few grandparents, grandaunts, or grandcousins nearby to share in the task of supervising small children, as was customary in a Puerto Rican village or town. By 1960 half the Puerto Rican families in New York obtained supplementary allowances from the Department of Welfare; one-quarter of all Puerto Rican children in the city received some form of welfare assistance.

In theory, welfarism should have proved a blessing. Assimilation of Puerto Ricans should have proved simpler than that of Polish, Jewish, Sicilian, or Irish proletarians who had arrived penniless in New York during the nineteenth century and who largely relied on help from their kinsmen and co-religionists. New York City, by the 1960s, had ceased to be governed by supposedly corrupt political machinery run by Irish precinct bosses and ward heelers; its public expenditure had increased astronomically from a total budget of just over $5 million in 1928 to more than $2 billion in 1960—nearly double the amount spent only ten years previously. More than a quarter of the city's expenditures went to debt service and pensions for the bureaucracy alone, in addition to heavy commitments to education and welfare. According to the *Encyclopaedia Britannica*, 1968 edition, entry for "New York," 18 percent of the 1960 budget went to education, 12 percent to welfare, 11 percent to sanitation and hospitals, 17 percent to debt service, and 9 percent to pensions. Only 7 percent went to police protection and 4 percent to fire protection; the remainder was expended for miscellaneous purposes.

The new, often inexperienced bureaucracy was extremely complex and hard to understand, especially for a poorly schooled immigrant. The old-style Tammany Hall boss and his subordinates had taken pride in making themselves personally known to their constituents; this traditional Irish system of political patronage would have been quite intelligible to Puerto Ricans accustomed to the idiosyncracies of local *caciques* (bosses) on their native island. The Irish ward heeler's life experience was much closer to that of, say, a Ukrainian peasant immigrant than the life experience of a welfare worker with a master's degree in social studies was to that of a Puerto Rican villager. The ward heeler, dependent on local votes for his livelihood, had made a point of taking part in the local life of his community to the extent of attending—with some ostentation—an Easter service in a Russian Orthodox church one day and a wedding in a synagogue the next. The welfare bureaucrat was a very different kind of person. He or she relied on a monthly salary complete with pension benefits that owed nothing directly to the good will of his or her charges. The welfare bureaucrat was apt to be a skeptic or, at any rate, a liberal in religion who was unlikely to attend a traditional service; socially, the welfare administrator would mix with professional peers (men and women trained at universities) rather than with the poor—a behavior pattern increasingly common to the majority of local politicians as well.

The bureaucrat and the ward heeler had equally divergent views as regards the aim of government. The old-time Tammany Hall boss believed that it was his duty to provide police and fire protection together with a few petty favors and hand outs. In this objective, the old system was relatively successful. There is universal agreement among old-timers of whatever racial background that there was far less violent crime in New York slums during the 1920s than there was 50 years later, by which time the expense and scope of government had become monumental. By then, New York's leaders aimed for infinitely more than their less expensively educated predecessors. The new, liberal bureaucrats desired to "improve" the poor, to regulate their lives in a manner that would have been incomprehensible to the city boss.

The new system of bureaucratic control with its universal reliance on paperwork was ill-suited to fit the needs of the unlettered immigrants. Puerto Ricans' names, for instance, might work in their disfavor. In Spanish nomenclature, the mother's maiden name plays a major part; maternal as well as paternal surnames might be used. (Luís Muñoz Marín was a case in point: Muñoz was his father's, and Marín his mother's, surname.) This custom alone helped to confuse New York City records, especially in the early days of migration when a child could well be listed under different parents' names with different agencies. But that was not all. The poorer and more rustic newcomers were apt to change their first names at will, much to the bureaucrats' confusion. Not surprisingly, the poorly educated often failed to see the point of filling out forms and answering questions that seemed meaningless to a villager who had never owned anything but a hut built by himself. He found that by not giving the "right" answer, he might seriously hurt his future or ruin his chances, say, of getting into a housing project. The common-law marriages frequently contracted by Puerto Ricans were apt to cause red tape, as did their informal ways of adopting children, or problems might arise from an inability to fill out complex income tax forms and thereby take advantage of money that might be due to them as return payments from the government.

The immigrant faced other difficulties not experienced by his predecessors. For instance, a Jewish tailor arriving in New York in 1890, jobless and penniless, might start his career by laboring in a sweatshop. He worked for a pittance, but at least he had a job. Two generations later, sweatshops had been outlawed (although they were continued in a surreptitious fashion). There was an elaborate set of regulations concerning minimum wages and working conditions that conspired against the least skilled and the least experienced, men willing to work but priced out of the market by dint of regulation. Having accumulated some savings, the old-time tailor's assistant might open a little shop of his own. But under the new dispensation, his job became infinitely more difficult: the shopkeeper had to be experienced in the art of filling out forms, the intricacies of withholding tax, and a host of other skills that put a premium on formal education not usually available to a poverty-stricken immigrant. Taxi drivers, to give another example, had to buy expensive licenses not required of their predecessors—and so it went.

The welfare state had other unanticipated consequences. Immigrant wives often found that they could find jobs in New York more easily than their husbands, and perhaps earn more. Women, reared to be obedient to their father's or husband's guidance, suddenly found themselves in a position of economic power within the family—a situation that might cause anguish to their men and a sense of psychological ambiguity to themselves. In that household environment their children seemed all too prone to escape parental guidance. In school, the youngsters absorbed American culture of one kind, and in the street they learned American ways of another sort. Both varieties conflicted with traditional ethics of filial subordination. Both varieties directly or indirectly contributed to such evils as juvenile delinquency and drug addiction.

The welfare system, of course, did not create the tensions inherent in a changing economic structure. It did, however, have the unintended effect of further weakening accustomed links of familiar authority. The old-style immigrant had relied on housing provided by private enterprise. As sociologist Joseph Fitzpatrick put it: Two things had been central to the newcomers from Europe—the geographical neighborhood and the religious congregation or parish.[13] The "Little Germanies," "Little Italies," or "Little Irelands" of immigrant history need not be idealized; they contained plenty of misery and discontent. But the newcomers were clustered in particular city areas where the traditions, shops, restaurants, and local customs were familiar to them, and where they consequently felt "at home." The local church or synagogue provided a sense of spiritual and cultural support, a sense of continuity with the past. The private sector provided poor-quality housing, but it was housing that most immigrants could afford. They moved onto blocks where they had relatives and where they might know some *landsleit* (compatriots).

Puerto Ricans at first followed a pattern similar to the earlier newcomers in New York. However, the poor steadily and increasingly became dependent on public housing. "Urban renewal" widely eliminated private accommodation for the poor rather than for the rich; middle-class philanthropists built a rigid system of rent control that made unprofitable private investment in low-cost housing and even small repairs on rent-controlled property. At the same time, there was a pernicious breakdown of public order in "tough" districts and a loss of public control unknown in the supposedly bad old days of Tammany Hall. Landlords were often unable to collect rent and they preferred to abandon their properties rather than pay taxes on their now useless investment. Abandoned housing became subject to vandalism and arson, resulting in the "burn out" of entire city blocks in a manner reminiscent of the destruction occasioned by the London blitz in 1940. As Thomas Sowell, the distinguished economist, put it in a half-joking fashion, New York had more trouble in recovering from rent control than Berlin did from the thousand bomb raids of Hitler's war.

Puerto Ricans, then, were increasingly forced to rely on public housing. Ideally, there was to be no discrimination against them; in practice, however, they all too often found themselves at a grave disadvantage. Long waiting lists naturally worked against newcomers who had not lived in New York long enough to comply with the residential requirements; housing managers preferred stable marital unions to common-law marriages; the authorities would rather house small families; and they preferred to deal with literate people who understood how to fill out forms. As the housing market contracted, the migrants unable to find public accommodation increasingly competed for what little private housing remained. As their rents rose, they crowded together in tiny "flats," thereby involuntarily creating the very slum conditions they sought to escape.

The welfare system thus seemed ill-suited to the needs of the newcomers. By the late 1950s, Puerto Ricans received about 20 percent of New York's outlay on welfare, mostly in the form of "home relief" and "aid to dependent children" (as distinct from programs such as "old age assistance" and "aid to the disabled"). Puerto Rican workmen usually had large families with more mouths than could be fed on the earnings of one, or sometimes two, breadwinners. The city made up the difference by supplementary grants under the category of "home relief," thereby subsidizing both immigrants and their employers at the taxpayers' expense and providing an artificial incentive to swell New York's labor force.

Aid for dependent children (AFDC) was normally given to mothers rearing children without the support of a breadwinner. Because many Puerto Rican working-class households were unstable, there were many women who relied on AFDC to support their youngsters. AFDC had the unintended consequence of giving economic power to the woman rather than to the man, a bitter pill to swallow for males attuned to the traditional notions of masculine dominance—whether or not merited. Moreover, AFDC set up a pattern whereby a poorly paid laborer might actually benefit his wife and children financially by leaving home; desertion, so to speak, might turn into a form of chivalry. Alternatively, AFDC might tempt men into fraudulent behavior by concealing themselves for the duration of an official's visit. The Welfare Department tried to abort such practices by staging early morning visitations, a practice likely to disrupt traditional family life even further. AFDC may also have had unintended consequences in the realm of courtship, although these are hard to prove. By compensating unwed mothers for bearing children instead of helping the father, the conscientious, hard-working male who was willing to marry the girl he had impregnated may have at times found himself discounted as a suitor; he may have been no more highly valued than, say, the tough, devil-may-care street fighter, who was glorified by pop music and pop sociology.

Sociologists continue to dispute the nature of the links between welfarism and illegitimacy. But whatever the connection, Puerto Ricans in New York had a devastatingly high illegitimacy rate. There was a striking rise in the number of female-headed households, as previously indicated, and the consequent disruption of traditional families among Puerto Rican New Yorkers went with an extraordinary and disheartening rise in the number of abortions. By 1980 abortions among Puerto Ricans had exceeded live births by 50 percent.

The Puerto Ricans' increase in female-headed households formed a part of a nationwide trend. By 1980 an estimated 20 percent of all children in the United States were living with only one parent. This state of affairs was encouraged by changing divorce laws, by the increase of women in paid employment, and by overt or covert critiques of traditional family values put forward by feminists, many intellectuals, and entertainers. Certainly the bulk of Puerto Ricans were committed to traditional family values when they first came to New York. Most Puerto Ricans likewise had little desire to go on welfare when they arrived on the mainland. All knowledgeable witnesses agreed that the newcomers preferred work to drawing relief. They placed high value on dignity, independence, and self-respect. However, they had to contend with economic factors not faced by European immigrants at the turn of the century.

During the late 1960s and 1970s, unskilled and semiskilled workers found themselves at an additional disadvantage as industries began to move out of New York, and the city became increasingly dependent on a service economy that required professional qualifications not available to a poorly lettered immigrant. The partial exodus of New York's industries—occasioned in part by rising taxes, an ever-increasing network of regulations, and the departure of many well-paid and well-qualified men and women to the suburbs—went with an expanding welfare economy. This, in turn, contributed to the creation of a new culture of dependency, one in which individual success increasingly came to depend on experience in—and aptitude for—what was perhaps the most ingrown and complex municipal bureaucracy in the Western world.

Puerto Ricans also had to contend with racial prejudice. The extent to which they were discriminated against because of their color is difficult to gauge. Puerto Ricans with European features and light skins had an easier time than their dark-skinned compatriots. The dark-complexioned people met with even greater hostility when they tried to move out of the slums. The American racial system did undergo gradual modification. Nevertheless, the system continued to encourage dark-hued Puerto Ricans to place special emphasis on their Spanish linguistic legacy in order to differentiate themselves from black Americans. Many had expected that a new solidarity would unite Puerto Ricans and blacks as companions in misfortune. In fact, however, there was often bitter rivalry between the two: for jobs, between opposing neighborhood gangs, and between welfare recipients. In addition, Puerto Ricans clashed with Irish on the West Side and with Italians in East Harlem. Puerto Ricans, like South Europeans, also had to cope with a harsh climate and an alien social environment: *hace muy frío*—it is very cold; *la gente es fría*—the people are cold. These became standard complaints in the barrio and had been equally familiar to Armenians and Sicilians in the past.

How did the poor adapt to life in a city slum where drug use was common and unemployment was an ever-present threat? The task was difficult. The poorly skilled could find only sporadic and insecure jobs at a time when many manufacturing industries had moved out of New York. Such jobs as were available derived mainly from small, under-capitalized, and marginal business ventures. All too often work was poorly paid and seasonal in character. The strains imposed by under-employment were apt to lead to marital instability and child abuse. Above all, there was the ever-present threat from crime—a greater menace by far to the poor in the barrio than to the rich in suburbia. Puerto Rican New Yorkers were particularly exposed to violence. In 1976 the percentage of males admitted to New York state correctional facilities for murder or homicide stood at 17.3 for Puerto Ricans, 13.3 for blacks, and 10.0 for whites. The corresponding figures for drug offenses were 25.3, 10.4, and 17.5. There was a poverty-stricken underclass that was composed of Puerto Rican and black males between the ages of 15 and 30, who in this respect greatly resembled one another. They were far more likely to be convicted of crimes than whites and were more apt to father illegitimate children whom they failed to support. This subproletariat also contained a great reservoir of tough and able men. It was, for instance, this subproletariat that had traditionally provided many first-class soldiers to their respective countries—from Wellington's Redcoats to today's U.S. Airborne forces. Unfortunately, however, society all too rarely found ways for using such aptitudes in peaceful pursuits.

We have dealt with the problem of crime at greater length in a separate chapter. At this point we wish merely to reiterate that the underclass did not form a single undifferentiated group. It was not strictly separated from the working poor. Even big city gangs were not homogeneous; they contained normal youngsters as well as psychopaths; the dangerous criminals among them formed a minority. For the prevalence of crime in the big cities, American theoreticians blamed racism, unemployment, lack of housing, and marital instability. In doing so, they overlooked the slums of European cities such as Glasgow, Scotland, where similar conditions prevailed but where the homicide rate remained a tiny fraction of New York's and Chicago's. Given the failure of the authorities to enforce law and order in the slums, conditions in many poverty-stricken quarters in great U.S. cities in some measure resembled those of late medieval England.

To cope with this challenge, the Puerto Rican poor in some respects behaved remarkably like English gentle folk during a late medieval age of anarchy. *The Paston Letters*, a collection of English family documents dating from the fifteenth century, depict life in a society steeped in violence, where men and women depended almost wholly on their family connection. The Pastons formed part of a sword-bearing gentry caught in the throes of ongoing strife. They survived by seeking powerful patrons among the highest ranks of the aristocracy and by maintaining the cohesion of their clan. They trained warlike young men in the arts of seizing a neighbor's land and castles, and they encouraged bookish young men to become lawyers and to further the family fortunes by suborning juries and manipulating the courts. The Pastons counted themselves equally fortunate when a younger son with a clerical vocation entered the Catholic church and exalted the family name by gaining influential positions within the clerical hierarchy or by leading a saintly life. The women were expected to marry for profit and to abide by the family's collective decision with regard to matrimonial matters.

The Puerto Rican poor on New York's Lower East Side adopted what were in some ways comparable strategies. The original immigrants were quiet and law-abiding, but, forced into an environment with other ethnic groups (blacks, Italians, and Irishmen had established gangs), the newcomers responded similarly, and sometimes bettered the instruction. For the Puerto Ricans, the large family acted as a weapon for self-defense, an insurance against poverty, and an investment portfolio for the future. As Jagna Wojcicka Sharff, an American anthropologist, put it, the family trained the children into distinct but complementary social roles.

The "street representatives," tough young men handy with fist and knife, would act as the family's protector and avenger. They also engaged in irregular work, sometimes connected with the sale of drugs, gambling, or mugging. Contrary to public belief, such activities did not yield large sums. A street vendor of drugs in 1980 would earn no more than $25–50 a week; a telephone operator for a "numbers" game made $75–90 a week. Stealing, mugging, and fencing (selling stolen goods) counted as the most hazardous and least lucrative occupations. The main profits from the drug traffic and games of fortune went to outside entrepreneurs who organized these operations and received a large percentage of the money. The remainder largely went to the street representative's family. The street representative was also expected to defend the honor of his mother and sisters, and as he grew more mature, he was apt to join a gang. As Sharff comments, "most street representatives began playing hookey seriously in junior high school. They leave school completely at the age of 16 or 17, by which time they often have had unpleasant encounters with the police, the court system, and the jails."[14] Few street representatives lived to a ripe old age. Among 36 households studied by Sharff, six men between the ages of 19 and 30 were killed in drug-related incidents during the two and a half years of research. The certainty that some boys would not survive to maturity caused families to wish for many sons. The Puerto Rican slum family thus prized girls who bore many children; young mothers also helped with housekeeping and contributed cash derived from public assistance to the family household.

In addition, the slum family valued the wage earner—the young woman, or more often the boy—who would take a steady job and contribute to the family's financial well-being. The wage earner might be teased for his gentle and law-abiding manner, but the macho standards applied to the street representative were not applied to the boy who brought home a regular paycheck. The family's greatest hope for the future went to the "scholar-advocate," usually a girl who did well at school, completed her secondary education, and sometimes went to college. Such girls did not help with the household chores. They were likely to get secretarial or administrative positions and could understand the ways of the welfare bureaucracy; they might "marry up" and move out of the slum, thereby likewise adding to the resources of the household. The large family thus acted as a kind of social security system to which each family member contributed according to his or her talents, and on whose cohesion all depended for survival.

To this family group, the Catholic Church contributed less than its priests would have liked. Puerto Ricans—the point bears repeating—were the first major group of immigrants who came to New York at a time when an extensive welfare economy had come into existence. Puerto Ricans therefore had less of an incentive to rely on the church as a welfare organization than did, say, Jewish, Armenian, or Irish newcomers of an earlier generation. Moreover, the church was not their own in the way the synagogues had peculiarly been to the Jews or the Gregorian church to the Armenians. The problem is well elucidated by a survey, carried out in the early 1980s by the Catholic church's pastoral research office in the archdiocese of New York. Investigators found that the church's Hispanic parishioners derived mainly from the ranks of the poor. The church had made considerable progress in training priests and laymen in the Spanish language, an important consideration for a community that, unlike so many other Catholic immigrant groups, had failed to bring its own priests to the new country. The church's efforts clearly made some gains. More than half the respondents said that they felt welcome in the church or that they read the Bible; the great majority professed a belief in a personal God who cared for man's condition.

General support for the church, however, translated poorly into the kind of statistics that church leaders normally use to determine fidelity to the church. Church attendance remained poor; large numbers of parishioners knew little about key beliefs held by the church. Traditional folk beliefs continued to mingle with orthodox doctrines, as they would in any peasant society. Even more disturbing to the clergy was the erosion of traditional beliefs among second-generation Hispanics. In fact, the more that Hispanic youngsters were exposed to secularized American culture and education, the more likely they were to share the notions held by their non-Hispanic neighbors. Assimilation appeared to entail a loss of both ethnic and religious identity.[15]

The church continued to work actively among Puerto Ricans to help them maintain their family life, values, and religious beliefs. Catholic groups such as the North East Pastoral Center for Hispanics offered support and tried to counter images of Puerto Ricans as lazy, retarded, and dangerous. The East Harlem Council for Human Services provided secular support services, as did the National Puerto Rican Forum. The Forum gave skill-training, job placement, and relief and legal counseling. The Forum operated five training centers in New York, and as many as twenty thousand Puerto Ricans per year were trained at these centers. The Forum claimed to place 80 percent of those trained. (See Chapter 11 for other support groups.)

Given the difficulties that beset Puerto Ricans, their social advancement was nevertheless noteworthy. By and large, the mainland-born Puerto Ricans occupied in 1970 a position roughly equal to that of Italian-Americans twenty years earlier. Whatever the stereotype, the bulk of the Puerto Rican population did not belong to the underclass, and they neither shunned work nor broke the law. While Puerto Rican women as a group had more children than the rest, this high fertility remained concentrated among those who never managed to go to high school. The Puerto Ricans' rate of intermarriage suggested that social links with other ethnic groups were becoming more numerous among those who chose to stay on the mainland. The Puerto Rican community remained one of the youngest and, overall, one of the more poorly educated groups in the United States. But when compared with people of the same age and education, Puerto Ricans earned comparable incomes.[16]

How did this advance take place? Many second-generation Puerto Ricans went to college and thereafter made their way in various professions or the public services. Others attained distinction in sports, the entertainment business, or academia. More important, the proportion of semiskilled and unskilled workers declined considerably between 1950 and 1970 among the Puerto Ricans, whereas the percentage of persons in skilled and white collar occupations went up. Puerto Rican workers greatly expanded their initial foothold in trade unions as carpenters, bricklayers, hotel workers, garment workers, painters, electricians, and teamsters. Others began in the family restaurant or ethnic food business, as owners of corner stores serving a Spanish clientele. Some of these pioneering firms later vastly expanded; for instance, Goya Foods Inc. was founded in the 1940s by a Puerto Rican immigrant.[17]

During the 1970s, Puerto Ricans also spread farther into other parts of the United States; there were substantial Puerto Rican communities as far afield as Hartford, Chicago, Newark, Boston, Philadelphia, Cleveland, and Los Angeles. In 1980 only 49 percent of the Puerto Rican population on the mainland was living in New York state, as opposed to 64 percent in 1970. Puerto Ricans formed the second largest Spanish-speaking community in the country, numbering more than two million people, or 13.8 percent of the Hispanics on the U.S. mainland. In fact, Puerto Ricans on the mainland were beginning to approach the numerical strength of their compatriots on the island itself (estimated at 3,300,000 in 1980). The Puerto Ricans who moved out of New York constituted many of the most enterprising people in the community, and relocation often went with upward social mobility. Nevertheless, Puerto Ricans as a whole continued to face considerable difficulties. In the late 1970s the majority of Puerto Rican adults on the mainland were still first-generation immigrants, and they remained the most ill-favored of all Hispanic groups.

Chapter 6

The Cubans

The Cuban revolution formed a milestone in the history of Latin America. The upheaval reshaped Cuban society and also led to a major exodus that influenced considerably the composition of the Hispanic peoples in the United States. Polemical studies concerning the revolution and its antecedents now crowd the shelves of university libraries. The prorevolutionary school, on the whole, has obtained the better of the argument in academia, finding expression not only in *Granma* (organ of the Communist Party of Cuba), but also in the magisterial columns of the most recent *Encyclopedia Britannica*. According to the new orthodoxy, Cuba was an economic and political vassal of the United States, run by former President Fulgencio Batista in the American interest. Cuba's prerevolutionary economy was essentially agrarian, characterized by extensive farming (that is to say, the cultivation of large acreages with a minimal outlay of capital); by a monoculture (making Cuba heavily dependent on the production of a single crop—sugar); and by extreme dependency on the United States, which furnished Cuba with the bulk of its foreign capital and markets. Industrial production was limited to a few branches using domestically produced sugar, nickel, and tobacco. Stagnation and the "structural deformation" of the economy were made worse by graft in high places, by prostitution and gambling, and by pervasive inefficiency. Cuba, at the time of Fidel Castro's takeover, therefore remained in an "essentially underdeveloped condition."[1]

Cuba: Revolution and Its Aftermath

The facts of Cuba's economic and political history, however, differ greatly from this version. From the outbreak of World War II to the end of the 1950s, Cuba in fact experienced striking economic expansion. Between 1941 and 1958, the national income tripled (from $678 million to $2.21 billion). Industrial wages compared favorably with average per capita wages in countries as varied as Belgium, Austria, Mexico, and Egypt.[2] Judging by such indicators as per capita income, literacy, the availability of medical care, the proportion of persons employed in farming and manufacturing, and the extent of urbanization, Cuba ranked considerably higher than Mexico, a country widely praised at the time by Castro himself for the "progressive" nature of its economic institutions.

There was certainly a great deal of discontent in Cuba, reflected by an increase in emigration to the United States after Batista's *coup d'etat* in 1952. But there was no mass migration comparable to what took place under Fidel Castro. In the economic sense, prerevolutionary Cuba enjoyed a number of advantages. Widespread misconceptions notwithstanding, Cuban agriculture, for instance, was being progressively mechanized. By 1958, Cuba had one tractor per 117 cultivated acres, compared to one tractor per 153 in the Soviet Union, one per 162 in East Germany, and one per 373 in Mexico. Farm wages in Cuba substantially exceeded those in European countries like Austria or Portugal, not to mention Mexico. (Comparative figures for a daily wage per eight-hour day in 1958 in these countries, respectively, were $3.00, $1.13, and $0.93.)

Land ownership was less highly concentrated in Cuba than in Mexico, Argentina, or the United States. Cuba, moreover, was not just one gigantic sugarcane field. In 1958, the value of the country's agricultural output was said to amount to $734 million; refined sugar accounted for $452 million of the total. While sugar did dominate the agricultural economy, Cuba also produced substantial crops of rice, beans, bananas, and coffee. Between 1939 and 1958, the amount of land devoted to sugar decreased substantially. Sugar accounted for four-fifths of Cuba's exports and was the main source of foreign currency, but exports and national production are not necessarily identical; the sugar industry, including the industrial processing and distribution of the crop, in 1954 amounted to about one-quarter of the national income. Cuban society accordingly did not match the conventional mode of a monoeconomy. In 1953, only 41.4 percent of the population was engaged in agriculture; of this, just over half was employed in the cultivation of sugar; hence "monoculture" accounted for less than one-quarter of Cuba's total labor force. By the 1950s, Cuba in fact provided a livelihood for a substantial bourgeoisie, including a considerable number of independent farmers.

The U.S. stake in Cuba's agricultural economy was diminishing. U.S. control of the sugar industry declined from about 70 percent in 1928 to about 35 percent in 1958. Moreover, the sugar mills and other U.S.-owned plants were apt to be the most modern and efficient in Cuba— those that paid the highest wages and that normally would make the best agreements with the Cuban trade unions. As Theodore Draper points out in the classic cited below, the U.S. investment in Cuba easily could have been bought back with Cuban investments outside the islands. And Cubans were far from hating Americans; they were not accustomed to using derogatory terms such as *gringo* to denote *norteamericanos.*

Cuba had an expanding economy, and the islanders had one of the highest literacy rates and living standards in Latin America.

Nor was Batista simply an unthinking reactionary without any thought in his head but to kill "Reds," a lackey of the oligarchy. Batista, like many modern Latin American dictators, came from a modest background; the well-to-do in Cuba considered him a rude and vulgar upstart. In 1937, the Cuban dictator formed an alliance with the communists and, in return for their support, permitted them in 1938 to set up an officially recognized trade union federation, the *Confederación de Trabajadores de Cuba*. Batista for the first time allowed the Communist Party to obtain legal status, to elect senators and representatives, indeed to become a major national force. His marriage of convenience with the communists for a time turned Batista into a democratic hero, a spokesman apparently for a Cuban versian of the popular front—this at a time when the popular front had failed in Spain and many surviving re-publicans sought refuge in France, the United States, and Mexico. When Batista, then out of power, staged a military coup in 1952 to regain the presidency, the Cuban communists initially put the blame on "Yankee imperialists" rather than on their former ally. Batista's new regime permitted the Communist Party organization to continue. The break in communist-Batista relations came only after an abortive, but well-publicized, attack made by Fidel Castro on the Moncada Barracks in Santiago de Cuba in 1953.[3]

Batista's domestic policy in many ways resembled that of Muñoz Marín in Puerto Rico. Batista and Muñoz had more in common than Batista's subsequent critics would like to admit. The 1940 constitution provided for the creation of a welfare state in which the central government received extensive powers to regulate the economy, and in which in-dividual citizens became entitled—at least on paper—to extensive social welfare services. Labor received concessions, and governments, after 1940, usually looked with favor at demands for higher wages and price control, even though these might result in decreased efficiency and reduced production. If revolution were produced merely by poverty, economic stagnation, and the reluctance of governments to intervene in the economy on behalf of the underdog, Cuba should have been the last of the Spanish-speaking countries in the New World to undergo a social cataclysm.

Cuba's problems derived not so much from poverty, but, at least in part, from an exceedingly uneven rate of development. Cuba had a growing urban sector but a backward hinterland that lagged far behind the cities, with a middle class too large for the economy to sustain.[4] Social tensions increased. There were striking disparities of income between city and countryside; there were equally noticeable tensions within rural communities. The great mass of the agricultural population had no stake in the existing regime; nor did the mass of Batista's soldiers, recruited from the villages and disgusted by their miserable pay, their lowly social status, and the manner in which their leaders enriched themselves.

Above all, there were serious tensions within the Cuban middle class. The white population of Cuba consisted, in descending order of social esteem, of *criollos* (old Spanish), *gallegos* (new Spanish immigrants, many of them from northwestern Spain), and *polacos* (Eastern European immigrants, many of them Jewish). A substantial number of Cuba's shopkeepers, artisans, and petty entrepreneurs were Jewish, Spanish, or Chinese immigrants who had come to Cuba after the turn of the century and had helped expand the economy, but who were not native to the country. The United States poured investments into the sugar industry, railways, a variety of public utilities, and, above all, into the land. As Theodore Draper states: "The only business in which the Cubans had a monopoly was politics."[5] The Cuban bourgeoisie contained within its ranks a large body of men and women unhappy with the foreigners' apparently excessive stake in the economy and dissatisfied, above all, with their own scanty professional prospects. Their fathers might have been of Spanish or other immigrant stock with money in farming and business, but their sons flocked in large numbers to the liberal professions, the civil service, and politics. The economy, however, could not provide employment for so many professionals and would-be politicians. Not surprisingly, the anti-Batista revolution gained its leadership and its initial strength primarily from dissident middle-class people—from lawyers without briefs, physicians without patients, and professors without students—all imbued with a naive trust in the redeeming qualities of a popular revolution and in their own ability to master the forces they would unleash. These young men and women subsequently received support from other discontented social classes, especially the most poverty-stricken members of the peasantry. But it was middle-class dissidents, as usual, who provided the original leadership and motive power of the revolution.

The frustration of the middle-class dissidents became intolerable when, in 1952, Batista staged his *coup d'état*, thereby alienating numbers of men and women who could not reconcile themselves to what they regarded as a usurpation of power. The working class initially was relatively quiescent—as long as Batista's regime did not touch its economic prerequisites; and the mass of agricultural workers and peasants remained passive. But the middle class had been the political class par excellence; Batista's coup exacerbated its internal divisions, especially those between the middle-aged and the young, the backward *sierra* (highlands) and the more advanced *llano* (plains), and the unemployed and the relatively well-paid union man. Increasingly isolated, lacking significant support from any class of the Cuban people, and unable to rely even on its own army, Batista's regime began to disintegrate.

By 1958, Cubans of all classes had become disgusted with the regime. The revolution, started by small guerrilla bands in the mountains, acquired a truly popular character. The withdrawal of U.S. support for Batista persuaded the last of the survivors that the game was up for Batista. Victory for the revolution turned out to be all the more striking because Castro, like so many communists before and after him, had at first skillfully concealed his Marxist-Leninist convictions and worn the camouflage of a nationalist leader with a commitment to social justice. By disguising his ultimate objectives, both to his own followers and to liberal opinion abroad, Castro obtained support not merely from Marxists all over the world, but also from liberal newspapers, such as the *New York Times,* and the liberal establishment in American universities. By the end of 1958, Batista's cause was lost; he fled Cuba, and a new era began.

Castro achieved power on what might be called, broadly speaking, a "popular front" ticket designed to appeal to both liberals and radicals of many different stripes. Once in power, Castro rapidly moved to the left. In 1959, anti-communism officially became a state crime; in 1961, Castro issued a declaration stating that he was a Marxist-Leninist and that he would remain a Marxist-Leninist to his dying day.

At the same time, Castro successively broke with his former allies. The middle class was excluded from political participation and its economic power was shattered. Dissident intellectuals suffered brutal persecution. There was a mass exodus of specialists, technicians, and academic people. The exiles took abroad much of the technical knowledge and skills that the revolution desperately required. The industrial workers lost the right to strike. Far from distributing the land to tillers, Castro collectivized most of Cuban agriculture, and industries were national-ized—with disastrous effects to the economy. Castro provoked a break with the United States by confiscating American investments, and Cuba increasingly became dependent on Soviet subsidies and Soviet trade. Backed by Soviet military might, the Cuban Communist Party claimed for itself not merely a monopoly of political power, but immunity from all criticism and the right to control every aspect of national life.

In the eyes of its defenders, communism had aligned Cuba with the progressive forces of mankind, laid the foundations for a new society, diversified Cuba's economic production, and freed the island from political and economic dependence on the West. In 1959, argued the Cuban communists, 99 percent of Cuba's trade had been directed to the capitalist countries and only 1 percent to socialist countries. By 1982, 69 percent of Cuba's commerce went to socialist countries and only 31 percent to capitalist countries. The oppressing classes had been destroyed. Firmly allied to the Soviet Union, Cuba supposedly faced a glorious future.

In fact, life in Cuba became far more oppressive than it was before, and people by the thousands began to flee the island. Castro progressively tightened the screws and imposed a system of control over Cuba's citizenry far beyond the restrictions imposed on the people by traditional Latin American oligarchies. There were no more elections of any kind. Professional organizations and trade unions became mere instruments of state control. The authorities enforced far-reaching restrictions on internal travel. The media turned into crude instruments of propaganda, exhorting the people to never-ending sacrifices for the fatherland. The government constructed a thoroughgoing system of block vigilance committees to encourage political denunciation. The secret police (*Seguridad del Estado*) set up a sophisticated system of repression modeled on those in Eastern Europe. Deviations from the official line were punished by a variety of sanctions, ranging from short confinement in jails and prison camps (*granjas*) to long sentences of forced labor and possible execution.

Political control was accepted with an equally strict system of economic repression, one that affected the entire nation. The small farms were eliminated, and, after 1968, all remaining businesses and shops were confiscated, including the private cooperatives or "mutualist" medical systems that had given service primarily to poor and middle-income people.

The Cubans also faced difficult problems concerning their dependence on sugar exports. During the early 1960s, the authorities attempted to reduce the reliance on sugar as the country's economic mainstay. Then they reversed their policy, hoping to improve the output of sugar by relying on central planning and collective incentives combined with campaigns in education and improved facilities for health and education to improve the living conditions of the rural workers. The government's difficulties, however, turned out to be much greater than expected; the economy as a whole remained in dire straits, with chronic absenteeism among the workers and a widespead black market of a kind common to centrally planned economies.

Cuba, like other communist countries, developed a "new class" of privileged party functionaries known as *mayimbes* or *pinchos*, who were exempt from official rationing, obtained privileged access to services of all kinds, and enjoyed professional advancement, good housing and access to luxury goods. Discontent further increased when, from the

1970s onward, Cuban troops became actively involved in so-called wars of liberation in Africa. By the early 1980s, forty thousand Cuban soldiers were deployed in various parts of Africa, primarily in Angola and Ethiopia; about one-sixth of Cuba's armed forces was stationed abroad. Foreign service was unpopular, and some recruits unwilling to fight joined the ranks of those who preferred to live abroad.

Repression in turn created an almost universal sense of frustration. The public was increasingly reluctant to accept the party's double-speak—the unbridgeable gulf between reality as defined by the party and reality as experienced by the man in the street. By the early 1980s, a combination of poor management, improvident expenditure of public funds, unwise investments, bureaucratic interference, foreign adventures, the militarization of national life, widespread absenteeism, poor working morale, inadequate incentives, and a defective system of distribution had combined with political and religious repression to reduce Cubans to near despair.

Whereas by 1981 the average per capita income for Latin America as a whole had risen to about $1,500, Cuba's per capita income stood at no more than $834. Cuban propaganda was wont to contrast the rising living standards of the Cuban people with the supposed misery of American blacks. But, in fact, Cuba's GNP amounted to less than one-tenth of the total income earned by blacks in the United States. Black American expenditures on recreation, vacations, and on automobiles alone nearly equalled Cuba's entire GNP.[6] Revolutionary hopes notwithstanding, Cuba continued, as in prerevolutionary days, to rely largely on the export of sugar for its hard currency. (Sugar, in 1981, amounted to 84 percent of Cuba's exports, compared to a 68 percent share taken by oil for Ecuador and a 58 percent share taken by coffee for Columbia.) The country faced a heavy foreign debt and a serious balance-of-payments problem. To a considerable extent, Cuba survived only by repression and through massive aid from the USSR, estimated at $3 billion a year in 1981. Ironically enough, the Cuban authorities by 1982 had begun to ask for investments from Western capitalists in socialist enterprises on the grounds that the new order in Cuba could offer such advantages as low-cost and "disciplined" labor, a low rate of taxation, and free repatriation of profits.[7]

The demographic impact of the communist revolution was staggering. Within less than two decades (from 1960 to 1969), roughly one million people, or 10 percent of Cuba's population, sought refuge abroad.[8] Cuba suffered from a loss of population equal to a hypothetical exodus from the United States in which every inhabitant of fourteen states (Alaska, Arizona, Arkansas, Colorado, Connecticut, Delaware, Hawaii, Idaho, Maine, Montana, Nebraska, and Nevada) left their country for exile overseas. Overall, the communist takeover in Cuba brought about what was, considering Cuba's population, the greatest population shift in Latin American history—a human disaster of cataclysmic proportions.

Cubans in the United States

The Cuban exiles sought refuge in many different countries, including Spain, Mexico, and Puerto Rico. The overwhelming majority, however, turned to the United States, which Cubans continued to believe was the land of opportunity par excellence and the world's most generous country as far as the admission of refugees is concerned. During the Batista regime, something like 15,000 Cubans left their island, mainly for political reasons. By the standards of subsequent Cuban emigration figures, these numbers were small; and they were balanced to some extent by immigration into Cuba from other countries in the Caribbean and from Europe. The Cubans' ability to enter the United States depended on the vagaries of U.S. immigration policies. Equally important was the Cuban Communist Party's ever-changing line with regard to emigration, as well as the twists and turns of U.S.-Cuban relations.

Initially, the United States adopted a reasonably friendly attitude toward the new regime on the grounds that Castro represented progressive and nationalist forces. In 1959, however, Castro confiscated U.S. investments in banks, industries, and landholdings while embarking upon a bitter propaganda campaign that denounced the United States as the enemy of mankind. After a long series of Cuban provocations, the United States in 1961 broke off relations with Havana, by then firmly aligned with the USSR and the Warsaw Pact. Cuban refugees, recruited from an all-party coalition, financed and aided by the CIA, and trained in Florida and Guatemala, attempted in 1961 to invade Cuba at the Bay of Pigs, but President John F. Kennedy at the last moment denied air support to the invaders and the venture collapsed. U.S.-Cuban relations further deteriorated during the Cuban missile crisis (1962), after which Cuba increasingly identified itself with the USSR.

The Cuban refugees' experience varied enormously. Some left Cuba legally and others escaped, often under the most terrible conditions. The first Cubans to depart were drawn mainly from the ranks of the fallen dictator's former supporters; their departure represented the classic pattern of postrevolutionary migration. The American public was apt to believe that these exiles were primarily government officials, bank presidents, senior military officers, merchants, and landowners—those whose power and privileges were threatened by the revolution. In fact, the early emigrants were far from homogeneous in their social composition; they did, however, include a disproportionately high number of former businessmen, entrepreneurs, and professional men. But they were soon joined by disillusioned members of the revolutionary regime. There also were many defections from the Cuban merchant navy—so many that, by 1962, nearly all the merchant marine captains appointed during the pre-Castro era had left the country.[9] These refugees also included almost all of the Cuban Jews; by 1983, no more than 750 Jews were left in Cuba out of the nearly 15,000 Jews who had lived on the island before the revolution.

The social basis of the refugees broadened during the 1970s. The introduction of rationing, the ongoing socialization of the Cuban economy, and the growth of political repression induced increasing numbers of ordinary men and women to go into exile. By the end of the 1970s, the United States was home to a substantial Cuban population. Immigration from Cuba alone amounted to more than the legal immigration from the whole of Latin America.[10]

The exile population in the 1970s came primarily from the laboring class, representing a higher percentage of blue-collar workers, especially skilled workers, than existed in the Cuban population as a whole. Professionals made up 44.5 percent of the refugees in the United States during the early years of the Castro regime; by 1974, their share of the newly arrived exiles had dropped to 13.9 percent. Conversely, the working-class exiles represented only 19.7 percent of those entering the United States in 1961, but by 1974 their representation had climbed to 45.9 percent of those arriving. As a result, the Cubans living in the United States began increasingly to resemble in their social composition the Cubans on the island.

During the 1970s, most Cuban immigrants to the United States were members of the working class.[11] This group had modest educational and occupational backgrounds similar to immigrants from Europe. They benefited, however, from the work of previous middle- and upper-class Cuban émigrés of the 1960s. About half of the Cuban immigrants worked in Cuban-owned or managed firms and earned somewhat better wages than those who worked outside this enclave. According to Alejandro Portes, this was not true for most other immigrants to the United States who earned lower wages working in an enclave economy.[12]

The émigrés also included a small number of thugs, homosexuals, mental patients, and ne'er-do-wells released from Cuban prisons and encouraged to emigrate to the United States (something like 4,000 out of the 125,000 involved in the 1980 Mariel exodus, to whom we will refer in the chapter dealing with crime). Scholars like Oscar Lewis had believed that the so-called culture of poverty could not exist in a socialist society because such a culture derived from internal contradictions found only within a capitalist order. In fact, Cuba produced its own underworld of alienated men and women whose lives were marked by vice and despair. Used to an underground existence, trained to evade the tentacles of an all-powerful party, such people were apt to become particularly ruthless when they decided to break the law. Though highly publicized by both the U.S. media and Castroite propaganda, these criminals, comprised only a very small proportion of Cuban émigrés.

Overall, the newcomers to the United States tended to be better educated than those of their countrymen who remained behind, although the pattern began to change during the mid-1960s. Urban people were overrepresented compared with the rural poor, especially those from Cuba's most backward regions. The exiles tended to be older than their countrymen, although age levels dropped when the government increasingly put difficulties in the way of legal departure, and when would-be defectors increasingly were compelled to use illegal means to make good their escape.

The exiled population also diverged from Cuba as a whole in racial makeup. According to the Cuban census of 1953, about 72 percent of Cuba's population consisted of whites. In the U.S. Census of 1970, on the other hand, almost 95 percent of Cubans in the United States identified themselves as Caucasian. Black Cubans apparently believed that racial oppression in the United States was more severe than in socialist Cuba, a belief encouraged by Castro's propaganda. Nevertheless, the share of black emigrants gradually increased, amounting to about 10.2 percent in a sample studied by Juan M. Clark, whose work we have extensively consulted. (Comparisons are difficult to make, because Latin and Anglo-American definitions of "black" differ in a striking fashion.)

What made them leave Cuba? U.S. sociologists interested in the subject have tried to distinguish between political and economic motives. According to Francisco R. Wong, the Cuban refugees included a substantial number of traditional immigrants who came to the United States in search of a higher living standard. Raul Moncarz and Antonio Jorge also refer to the widespread "psychological dependence" on the United States that supposedly characterizes many Cubans, as well as deliberate U.S. government attempts to discredit the Castro regime and the willingness of U.S. authorities to assist those who have defected.[13]

The use of such categories, however, obscures the enormous differences that distinguish totalitarian from nontotalitarian countries. Immigrants from, say, Mexico or Puerto Rico may freely leave their respective homes and return at will. In a fully-fledged Marxist-Leninist dictatorship, migration—like every other aspect of life—is strictly controlled by the ruling party. The differences between so-called economic and political motives, therefore, recede. A shopkeeper whose shop has been confiscated, a worker compelled to work overtime without pay, or a peasant sentenced to forced labor for some trivial offense has grievances in which political, economic, and ideological strands become inextricably intertwined. As "Silvio," a former Castro supporter and a ship's mechanic, put it:

> In Cuba we worked without hope. Here, in the U.S. the young people study and have a chance. In Cuba it is work, work, work, and then the salary is not enough. . . . The quotas of food allowed are a great abuse. The *pinchos* members of the "new class," have no problems, but the majority of the population does not have enough to live. They have to buy necessities on the black market at very high prices, which they often cannot afford. Another feeling that drags you down is that little gets accomplished because of bureaucracy. . . . Then at meetings the people are told to do voluntary work. . . . everyone approved because they were afraid to say no. Naturally, all of these things made the people very bitter.[14]

But, above all, there was the terror: the never-ending fear of denunciation, arrest, forced labor camp, or firing squad. No wonder, concluded "Lorenzo," another refugee, "almost all of the youth of Cuba want to leave, and if they could, they would."[15]

By 1980, 803,226 Cubans, nearly 10 percent of Cuba's population, resided in the United States, and Cubans had become the third largest Spanish-speaking community in this country. Most Cubans in the United States were urban dwellers; their "capital" was Miami, the second largest "Cuban" city in the world after Havana. Almost 60 percent of Miami's population was counted as Hispanic in the 1980 census; demographers estimated that, in five years, Latins would become a majority in Dade County (Florida), outnumbering non-Latin whites by 43 percent to 42 percent, and that they would dominate local politics.

The Cuban diaspora was not confined to Miami. The 1970 census already found Cubans living in every state of the Union, except Wyoming and Vermont. The well-educated on the whole were more mobile in a geographical, as well as a social, sense than the poor; on the average, Cubans living outside Miami turned out to have a better formal education and a higher income than those in Miami. But no other city had quite the same attractions as Miami. Many Cubans indeed returned to the city from other centers in the United States; the so-called Mariel exodus from Cuba in 1980 further magnified Miami's importance. Miami is geographically close to Cuba; its climate is similar to Havana's; it served as the Cubans' principal port of entry. Once a substantial community had been established, it was apt to grow, as newcomers found an extensive network of business, cultural, religious, and charitable institutions to receive them and kinsmen, friends, or even former neighbors to give them welcome. The immigrants found restaurants and shops to their liking; those unable to speak good English could get by with their knowledge of Spanish. Cuban-owned banks, industries, and stores provided jobs; Miami, in a sense, became home away from home.

The impact of the Cubans on Miami was profound. By the early 1980s, Coral Gables, Southwest Miami, and most of Hialeah bore a Cuban imprint. By 1979, almost 600,000 Cubans were living in Dade County, where they made up an estimated 85 percent of the Hispanic population, comprising in turn about 40 percent of that county's total inhabitants. Far from placing a burden on the city, the immigrants transformed its economy. Before 1959 Miami had depended largely on tourism and on money spent in the city by elderly pensioners who had moved to Florida from the Northeast. The Cubans, with their skills and enterprise, turned Miami into what some have called a "new capital city of Latin America" (or "Little Havana").

Attracted by the Hispanic atmosphere of the city and the climate, increasing numbers of Latin American tourists filled the city's hotels (five million tourists in 1978). Latin businessmen invested large amounts in real estate, probably $1 billion annually by 1980. Miami became a major banking center; by 1978, only New York had a larger number of banks specializing in international transactions in the United States than Miami. More than 90 multinationals doing business with Latin American opened headquarters in Miami. By the end of 1982, experts estimated that international commerce generated $4 billion in state incomes and had created 167,000 jobs. The annual Trade Fair of the Americas produced $68 million in 1983, and a free-trade zone for business in Latin America was worth $10 million a month.

Cubans also diversified the city's economy in other ways. Cuban workers labored in the garment industry, Cuban farmers planted new crops and introduced new techniques and ways of food processing, especially in the sugar mills. Cubans also contributed to the local accumulation of capital. Between 1970 and 1978, the assets of savings and loan associations in Miami rose from $3 million to $12.5 million; the deposits in commercial banks from $3.2 million to $7 billion.

The Cubans also made a major contribution to Miami's urban renaissance. According to widespread stereotypes, immigrants create slums which then have to be "cleared" through government "renewal programs." Miami's urban recovery, on the other hand, came mainly from private enterprise, especially Cuban. In 1960, Miami's city center was run down and its buildings were deteriorating rapidly. Cubans began by settling in a decaying residential section close to downtown, where rents were low and many stores had shuttered their windows.

The Cubans began to purchase their own houses, to remodel and improve them, and eventually they moved from "Little Havana" into Hialeah, Westchester, and other suburbs, while the newcomers moved into houses their predecessors had left.[16]

In addition to making their homes in Florida, a substantial number of Cubans moved to other cities; above all, to west New York, Jersey City, Newark, Bridgeport (Connecticut), and—to a lesser extent—to Los Angeles and Chicago, as well as to San Juan, Puerto Rico. This outward movement was initally slow because the Cubans were inclined to look upon their stay in the United States as temporary. Dade County, however, was unable to provide jobs for all the newcomers. In addition, the federal government set up the Cuban Refugee Emergency Center in Miami for the purpose of assisting needy Cubans with a variety of social services, and also to aid their move to other cities.

In resettling Cubans outside Florida, the authorities hoped to help the refugees find jobs equivalent or similar to those they had held in Cuba. Cubans, like many other refugees before them, had to overcome a variety of obstacles to their advancement: lack of proficiency in English (a particularly serious matter for a professional man or woman), legal restrictions, and ignorance of their new locality. The refugees also had to contend with ignorance on the part of both private groups and public agencies about the quality of the foreign applicants' educational background and professional experience. Some suffered from psychological disorientation as a result of their experiences in Cuba and the difficulties encountered in becoming accustomed to a different society.

Florida, by reason of its geographical position, became a convenient center for semiclandestine and clandestine activities against the communist regime, sometimes with and sometimes without the knowledge of U.S. authorities. The refugees maintained contacts with a widespread underground movement in Cuba, drawn mainly from the labor movement but also from a variety of other groups, including the peasantry and the liberal professions.[17] In time, however, the Bay of Pigs disaster, the consequent American decision to abandon thousands of men and women to Cuba's secret police, and subsequent negotiations designed to improve relations between Washington and Havana helped to weaken the resolve of many militants.

Unfortunately, the skills required for underground warfare, including such activities as the smuggling of arms, the production of illegal documents, the organization of cells (small working groups), and the laying of ambushes also can be utilized for ordinary banditry carried out by the greedy, the cynical, or the disappointed. As hope for the liberation of Cuba declined, Miami also became a center for gun-running, dope smuggling, and related forms of gangsterism linked to Latin

America. Miami's legal trade to South and Central America came to be paralleled by an illegal commerce. The ordinary Cuban resident in Miami, of course, had no part in illegal activities. In 1971, Miami's police chief, Bernard Garmire, explained that Cubans accounted for only 5 or 6 percent of the crime in the city, even though they composed, by then, about 30 percent of the population. At the same time, Cubans increasingly resolved to remain in the United States permanently. Whereas, in 1970, only 10 percent of Miami's Cubans were citizens, ten years later 177,000 had become naturalized; 86.4 percent of the noncitizens indicated that they intended to take the oath of allegiance to the United States of America. Exile politics increasingly turned into U.S. politics as a greater percentage of Cuban-descended voters than of American voters in general took the trouble of going to the polls.

In terms of social advancement, Cubans in the United States performed in a manner closer to that of the Western European than to the Puerto Rican or Mexican immigrant. By 1978, the median income for all U.S. families stood at $17,640; Cubans, $15,326; Mexicans, $12,835; blacks, $10,879; and Puerto Rican, $8,282. The Cuban median family income rose in a rapid fashion—from $5,244 in 1967 in Miami to $15,300 in 1977. There was a similar shift in the Cubans' occupational structure. By 1970, about one-fifth worked in middle-class occupations, as professional workers, administrators, managers, and proprietors. Just over one-third made their living as skilled workers or in white-collar jobs; about 45 percent held unskilled or semiskilled jobs. Eight years later, the number of persons in middle-class positions had increased to 30 percent. The percentage of white-collar workers, craftsmen, and semi- or unskilled workers had declined somewhat, despite the subsequent arrival of numerous newcomers drawn from the Cuban workingclass.

The Cuban immigrant community in the United States also differed from Mexican and Puerto Rican immigrant groups in that the Cuban community contained a substantial number of men and women drawn from the upper-middle and upper classes of their respective countries—well educated and with a strong commitment to the literary culture of Spain and Spanish America. Cubans from traditionally wealthy or distinguished families often faced peculiarly difficult problems of psychological adjustment. Having lost their wealth and accustomed social standing, they thought of their former homeland with a considerable degree of ambivalence, remembering their former social position as more resplendent in retrospect than it had been in fact. They had to make their way in a country where a family name distinguished in the "old country" suddenly meant little or nothing, a country where age, far from adding to social esteem, counted against them in the struggle for jobs.

In many cases, upper-class Cubans were outdone by countrymen of more modest social background whose youth or special commercial or technical aptitudes gave them an edge in the battle for success. (By 1980, the Cuban community in Miami contained approximately two hundred millionaires; on a less spectacular level of affluence, more than 70 percent owned their own homes.) Cubans did particularly well in banking; by 1978, they controlled 14 of 67 local commercial banks. They formed numerous independent businesses, such as restaurants, stores, furniture manufacturers, garment plants, and cigar factories; between 1967 and 1980, the number of firms owned by Cubans in Miami increased from 919 to 18,000.

Even for the most fortunate Cubans, exile was not easy. Many newcomers suffered homesickness and worried about their country and those they had left behind, friends and relatives they might never see again. Many of the immigrants were middle-aged people for whom psychological adjustment to the new country—with its strange and sometimes repugnant customs—was harder than for young people. (By the late 1970s, the median age of Cubans in the United States stood at about 36—much older than the median age of any other Hispanic group.) The Cuban exiles' peculiar demographic composition derived in part from the manner in which a disproportionately large number of middle-aged, middle-class men and women were forced to leave the land of their birth. For whatever reason, Cubans found themselves obliged to provide for a relatively large number of dependent, elderly relatives.

As sociologist Douglas Gurak indicates, the Cuban community also had to cope with a striking demographic imbalance between men and women. Normally, immigrants to a new country at first contain more men than women. During the 1960s and 1970s, Cuban women, however, outnumbered men; 58 percent of the Cubans who arrived during the 1965–1973 airlift were women. The proportion began to change with the 1980 exodus; this brought the number of new arrivals to an all-time high of more than 125,000, 70.2 percent of whom were men. The reasons for these changes are to be found in Castro's changing emigration policy; the consequences were straightforward—continued pressure toward marriage outside the Cuban community.[18]

The Cubans also faced economic problems. Cuban businessmen met with bitter criticism from leftists who argued, without any justification, that the immigrants' relative success was owed to special favors extended by the U.S. government to victims of communism. Cuban intellectuals at times encountered discrimination in academia, where the newcomers were censured for their real or alleged political views. The average Cuban's income for the time being remained lower than that of the average non-Hispanic white. Settlement of Cubans initially involved more downward than upward mobility. Though the great majority of Cubans worked hard, their average position after ten years' residence in the United States did not equal their position prior to emigration. Their experience was not, of course, surprising. The emigrants had to leave their property behind; their professional credentials often were not recognized; they lacked the social and professional contacts they had enjoyed at home. But this does not mean that the Cubans remained where they were. A study of Cubans in northern New Jersey shows that over half of the immigrants had to accept lesser occupations than those they were accustomed to before leaving their country. However, from their first U.S. occupation to that held in 1978, 38.1 percent experienced moderate to high degrees of social mobility.

Success often went to well-trained professional people, but not necessarily so. An enterprising taxi driver or trucker might enjoy more success by bettering his condition and "Americanizing" his lifestyle, than his one-time social superiors. For some Cubans, of course, success did not come at all; as was true for other refugees, there was much poverty among the newcomers. In 1976, about 17.1 percent of Cuban families subsisted below the official U.S. poverty line, though that poverty line would have been acceptable to a working-class household under Castro's regime. Conditions were particularly bad in metropolitan New York, where more than one-third of the Cubans lived in poverty (34 percent in the Bronx, 35 percent in Manhattan, and 39 percent in Brooklyn).[19] Of all these centers, the northeastern part of New Jersey formed the main center of Cuban settlement, the "second capital" of Cubans in the United States.

What of the Cubans' cultural adaptation? It was influenced to some extent by their ability, on the average, to rise more quickly on the social scale than Mexicans or Puerto Rican–Americans.[20] Successful Cubans behaved like other successful Americans of immigrant stock—they moved out of "ethnic" neighborhoods. Some took pride in a lavish social life; they entered their names in social registers modeled on those of old Havana; they joined social clubs, the primary qualification for which increasingly became the ability to pay a substantial fee rather than the possession of an appropriate background bank balance. Still, many Cubans continued to have problems: the elderly did not know English, their housing costs rose, and they felt lonely. And the young dropped out of school at a rate higher than that of other whites or blacks.

Most Cubans did not come to the United States because they preferred the American way of life or because they meant to make money, but because life in Cuba had become intolerable. Most were determined to preserve what they regarded as the best features of Cuban culture, a difficult undertaking for a group cut off from its homeland. The effort proved easiest by far in Miami, which soon became a bilingual city where a Cuban refugee could dine out in a Cuban restaurant, buy his groceries in a Cuban corner store, obtain information about world events from local Cuban radio and television stations, seek entertainment in a Cuban night club, buy Spanish books in a Cuban bookstore, attend Cuban plays, and listen to Cuban musicals or song recitals. Cuban artists plied their trades, Cuban academicians found jobs at American universities, and Cuban scholars produced their own learned journals (for instance, *Cuban Studies,* published by the Center for Latin American Studies at the University of Pittsburgh). The Cuban community in Miami also set up its own private schools which taught Spanish and stressed Cuban history and culture while emphasizing traditional family obligations and traditional discipline.

To a remarkable extent, Cuban academicians like Alejandro Portes and the anthropologist Oswaldo Ignacio Morales-Patiño became interpreters to the United States, not only of Cuban culture but of Spanish-American culture as a whole. This was not easy; initially, Cubans had a reputation for being more concerned with "racial purity" than were other immigrants from the Caribbean. Cubans were distrusted at times as "whites" or as political reactionaries; a Cuban might be jokingly referred to as a *tuve* ("I owned"—a man or woman who boasted too much of real or imagined former wealth, a weakness common among refugees from any land).

There also were other psychological differences between Cubans on the one hand and Puerto Ricans or Mexicans on the other. Only the Cuban community contained a large percentage of political exiles committed to the overthrow of a communist regime. In this respect, the Cubans resembled far more, say, the Polish or Croatian immigrants, who came to the United States after World War II, than the Mexicans and Puerto Ricans. When many Mexican or Puerto Rican intellectuals turned to antiestablishment politics in the United States, most Cubans looked upon the United States as a refuge against tyranny. Having acquired U.S. citizenship, Cubans were apt to vote for the Republican Party, whereas Mexican Americans and Puerto Ricans generally preferred the Democrats.

The Cubans, more than any other Hispanic group, therefore tended to identify themselves with the social status quo in the United States. They displayed to the full the immigrant conservatism that characterized so many newcomers from Europe in the nineteenth century, men and women who had come to the United States to escape from the landlord, the army recruiter, the pastor, or the bureaucrat; people who generally liked the land of their choice because it so often provided them with greater economic opportunities and more political freedom than they had enjoyed in the old country. As far as the Cubans were concerned, their community in Miami appeared to be a successful example of cultural adaptation.

Admittedly, not all was well. The Cubans, like the Germans, Jews, Chinese, and others before them, aroused a good deal of resentment for their active presence. As one Cuban put it: "We came too fast, too many were successful. Some of us are too arrogant, too loud—and play dominoes till 2 in the morning."[21]

Many Anglo-Americans resented hearing Spanish whenever they went shopping, or having to speak it, for that matter.[22] There were fears about rising crime rates and soaring housing costs. Many blacks became embittered at the extent of the Cubans' success, all the more so because most Cubans were white. Cubans were accused—quite mistakenly—of owing their relative economic success to refugee assistance extended to them by the federal government. In fact, such aid to Cubans amounted to much less per capita than subventions received by Puerto Ricans in New York who, on the average, did less well than the Cubans. There was competition for apartments and for jobs. And there was a bitter reaction against bilingualism, with slogans like "Let them learn English." Such difficulties however, were not new in American immigration history. In all probability, the passage of time will permit solutions, and the mass of Cubans will assimilate.

Chapter 7

Strangers from Many Lands

In addition to Mexicans, Puerto Ricans, and Cubans, the United States has received an ever-growing number of newcomers from other Spanish-speaking lands. The flow from Central and South America was small as long as there were no immigration restrictions on applicants from the Western Hemisphere.[1] Ironically, Latin American immigration increased greatly after 1965, when Congress abolished the traditional quota system and imposed a limit of 120,000 per year on immigrants from the Western Hemisphere.[2]

Spanish-American immigration into the United States formed part of a wider pattern involving migration among various Latin American countries. Historically there had always been a good deal of interchange among neighboring American states, but, overall, no Spanish-speaking country—whether Spain, Mexico, or Argentina—could rival the United States as a haven for emigrants from Central and South America as a whole. In normal years, no country in the world was as willing as the United States to accept legal newcomers.

Generalizations with regard to the U.S. impact on South America are hard to make. According to critics, this impact was wholly evil. The United States supposedly kept Latin America and the Third World in general in a state of economic dependency—hewers of wood and haulers of water for the developed North. Yet Latin American critics of the United States might, with more justice, have censured the United States for the progressive and often disruptive nature of its impact. In terms of America's total investments overseas, the sums placed in Latin America counted for little. (In 1970, the total value of U.S. foreign-invested assets amounted to $78.090 billion; of this amount, $12.201 billion was in Latin America.) Nevertheless, in Latin American terms, these investments were vast. Not surprisingly, Latin American nationalists and socialists alike looked upon the U.S. influence with distrust.

American corporations overseas transmitted new technical and managerial skills as well as capital. American companies usually provided higher wages and better working conditions than did the majority of indigenous employers. For instance, the United Fruit Company, often mentioned in the anticapitalist folklore of Latin American socialism, paid relatively high wages and provided health measures, new crops, scientific research, and new marketing methods. Equally disruptive was the impact of American missionaries, college teachers, Peace Corps volunteers, and entertainers who wittingly or unwittingly often stood for values directly opposed to authoritarian rule or traditional concepts of religion, family cohesion, and personal honor which had sustained Latin American institutions in the past.

There also was the influence of the American military, which provided new weapons, new forms of military technology, military education, and civic responsibility. This influence became institutionalized through the creation of war colleges modeled on the National War College in Washington, D.C. As Willard L. Beaulac, former U.S. Ambassador to Argentina, points out, a high percentage of Latin America's recent revolutions have been associated with the war colleges, where soldiers studied civilian as well as military problems and where civilians were indoctrinated with the army's idea of how public affairs should be run. "War colleges in Latin America, by their very nature, spark revolution."[3] In addition, American academicians, technical experts, and political advisers brought new ideas into the realm of social planning. During the 1960s and 1970s, they were committed to exhorting the ideals of the New Frontier and the Great Society overseas. Many of them preached the advantages of central planning.[4] The United States, in a sense, also had a disruptive influence through what might be called its international demonstration effect: despite the growth of its welfare state and despite the expansion of the regulatory powers assumed by federal agencies, the United States remained a much more open society than any of its southern neighbors.

To many Latin American intellectuals, the United States was a country steeped in soulless materialism. But the masses did not necessarily share this viewpoint. On the contrary, for many ordinary people the United States was to be envied because it afforded its people a relatively high standard of living, because it was free of revolutionary turmoil and civil war, and because it was a land that combined liberty and stability with economic opportunity. Whether liked or disliked, the United States became for Latin America a new cultural magnet, one that rivaled or exceeded Western Europe in importance, a land where an ambitious man might obtain an advanced education, new ideas, a new job, or new professionl opportunities. From the 1950s and the 1960s onward, there was a striking increase in emigration to the United States from a variety of countries in Spanish America. The newcomers were men and women from every class in society. The total figure of legally admitted immigrants from South America (especially Argentina, Colombia, and Ecuador) increased nearly threefold, as did the number of

Spaniards. Newcomers from the Dominican Republic (technically part of North America) multiplied about nine times. During the 1960s, the aggregate of these Spanish-speaking immigrants amounted to 450,600, more than the total number of Mexicans (443,300) and nearly twice the total number of Cubans (256,800). (During this period the total number of German and Italian immigrants was 200,000 and 206,700 respectively.)

The countries and peoples involved in these movements are so diverse that generalizations are difficult. Even small countries like Honduras or El Salvador offer enormous contrasts in social structure. The Central American countries in turn differ greatly among themselves; the contrasts among the South American countries are no less striking. All told, the newcomers added further color to the already complex Hispanic palette in North America.

The Dominican Republic

From the 1960s onward, the Dominican Republic began to make a major contribution to the new immigration. The Dominican Republic, which once formed part of the Spanish empire in the Caribbean, is a mountainous land comprising about two-thirds of the island of Haiti. (The adjacent Republic of Haiti occupies the other third.) The Dominicans, like the Puerto Ricans, are a racially mixed people. The condition of Santo Domingo in many ways resembled Puerto Rico's a generation or two earlier. By the late 1950s, illiteracy still stood at 50 percent; only 10 percent of the labor force was engaged in nonagricultural pursuits—primarily agricultural processing industries, construction, and services. The majority of the people relied on farming for their livelihood, with sugar as the main crop, followed by tobacco, cocoa, tropical fruits, and hides. Most manufactured and capital goods came from abroad, mostly from the United States.

During the 1950s and 1960s the Dominican Republic experienced bitter turmoil, which ended in 1966 when Joaquin Balaguer became president. Thereafter, the economy and health conditions improved and education expanded. By the late 1970s, about 90 percent of the student-age population received some level of education. Also during the 1970s, the GNP expanded considerably, reaching a growth rate of 13.2 percent in 1976, with a per capita income of about $800. The island ceased to be a planter society; the traditional landed oligarchy no longer predominated. The new ruling group consisted mainly of industrialists, businessmen, civil servants, and professional people. By the late 1970s, only a few *latifundia* remained mostly state- or foreign-owned. The country was self-sufficient in major staple foods like rice, and the network of communications had improved beyond recognition.[5] At the same time, the country's urban population expanded greatly, amounting to perhaps one-half of the island's total inhabitants by the early 1980s. The country developed airports, seaports, radio stations, and a telecommunications network. Dominicans were placed in ever-increasing contact with the outside world.

Unfortunately, however, the relative prosperity attained during the early 1970s stood on slender foundations. The country had to cope with both a constant population increase and the multiplication of small, uneconomic landholdings (*minifundia*). Many of the industries and services were controlled by the state through an unwieldy bureaucracy; many public services were government monopolies. The growth of the government sector resulted in considerable measure from the confiscation of the enormous wealth accumulated during former dictator Rafael L. Trujillo's term of office. Nationalization, however, led to inefficiency— state enterprises usually turned out to be the ventures most incompetently run and most subject to nepotism and corruption.

With the global recession of the early 1980s, sugar prices decreased disastrously. The country was burdened with a huge foreign debt ($1.2 billion in 1982), and unemployment grew to nearly 30 percent. Conditions were even worse in the villages, where jobs were harder to find than in the cities. Declining incomes from sugar and exports such as rum, as well as the high cost of imported gasoline and machinery, nullified plans to modernize the sugar industry.[6] Many Dominicans sought jobs overseas; by the early 1980s, about 10 percent of the country's population was estimated to live abroad, mainly in the United States.

The Dominican exodus to the United States was accompanied by corresponding migration from Haiti to Santo Domingo, where Haitians did much of the stoop labor in the sugar fields. Many of these Haitians, hired on contract, declined to return to their own poverty-stricken homeland at the expiration of their engagement, thereby burdening San Domingo with new ethnic and social problems while contributing to anti-Haitian prejudice. While Haitians increasingly performed the most poorly paid agricultural work—a familiar immigrant pattern—Dominicans increasingly sought jobs in the industrial and service industries of their own cities and in the United States. Between 1960 and 1975, the number of their arrivals in the United States increased from 756 to 13,081, not counting temporary visitors and illegal immigrants.[7]

The Dominicans, unlike the Puerto Ricans, were not U.S. citizens. Some Dominicans preferred to be identified as Puerto Ricans for purposes of immigration; others called themselves Cubans for purposes of prestige. In certain respects, the Dominicans' pattern of settlement showed some parallels to the Puerto Ricans'. The Dominicans settled in well-defined enclaves in New York (in the northern half of Manhattan and the Corona–Jackson Heights area of Queens). These areas were, on the whole, distinct from the Puerto Ricans'—not because of ethnic hostility between the two groups, but because of the newcomers' natural tendency to settle where they already had friends and relations. From New York, the Dominicans fanned outward into other manufacturing cities of the Northeast. In addition, some went to Miami, where they reinforced other Spanish-speaking groups drawn from Cuba and other Latin countries. New York, however, remained the Dominicans' main haven, and roughly 90 percent of Dominicans continue to live in that city.

Other parallels exist between Dominicans and Puerto Ricans. The Dominican Republic, like Puerto Rico, had been exposed to U.S. cultural and financial influence. Even before coming to the United States, many Dominican newcomers were familiar with some aspects of American culture. Baseball was the Dominicans' national game. "Lassie," "Los Duques de Hazzard," and "Plaza Sesamo" were familiar features on Dominican television screens. And American power was visible on the island itself. In 1965, U.S. troops landed in the Dominican Republic to end a brief civil war and left-wing penetration. American investors had put funds into the sugar industry and the incipient manufactures of the Dominican Republic. Many Dominicans, like many Puerto Ricans, initially migrated from their village to a major city within their own country, and from there to the United States.

During the 1960s, the *campesino* increasingly moved directly to New York. Again like Puerto Ricans, Dominicans took advantage of inexpensive transport; they readily moved to and from the United States and easily maintained links to their families at home. Dominicans and Puerto Ricans alike were apt to emphasize their Spanish background, partly in order to avoid identification with American blacks. Dominicans, like Puerto Ricans, often assumed that their residence in the United States would be temporary, or that they could earn enough money to buy land in the United States or set up a small business. A substantial number, however, either failed to save sufficient funds to return or decided that they preferred to remain in the United States. After settling in New York communities, the newcomers both cooperated with and clashed with immigrants of an older vintage—Jews, Greeks, Irish—collectively known to the more recent settlers as *los judíos*, the Jews, but in fact meaning whites. Like previous immigrants, the Dominicans formed their own associations. In time, the Dominicans became increasingly habituated to life in the United States, and began to take out naturalization papers, although initially at a slow rate. Thereafter they took an increasingly active part in local politics, especially through the Democratic Party and through organizations such as LUPA (Latins

United for Political Action), in which they aligned with Puerto Ricans and other Hispanics.

Widespread stereotypes to the contrary, the majority of the new Dominican immigrants came from an urban rather than from a rural background. Theirs was not an emigration of a starving people; they were success-oriented migrants, men and women who had already amassed enough money to seek better jobs in the United States. Some of them secured admission to this country through questionable means; but the effort involved in surmounting legal barriers may have favored the immigration of particularly motivated people. Studies conducted during the late 1970s suggest that a high proportion of newcomers by that time were well-educated, highly trained, urban, middle-class people. This finding diverges from previous investigations that characterized Dominican emigrants as drawn from rural backgrounds and a low socioeconomic status. Many Dominicans came from the Cibao region, a relatively high income area. About 30 percent had left in search of better incomes; 18 percent for educational purposes; and 14 percent to join relatives. (These reasons for emigration obviously would overlap.) By the early 1980s, this had become a mass movement: between 300,000 and 500,000 Dominicans had come to live in the United States, representing close to 10 percent of the Dominican Republic's total population.

Initially, the occupational distribution of Dominicans in New York resembled that of the Puerto Ricans. About four-fifths of Dominican New Yorkers worked in semiskilled and low-skilled occupations—in textile mills, as machine operators, in restaurants and hotels, and as janitors, maintenance men, domestic servants, and so forth. They at first were heavily underrepresented in professional and managerial, as well as clerical and skilled positions. Nevertheless, the Dominicans' family incomes soon exceeded the Puerto Ricans ($11,800 for Dominicans in the United States, compared to $7,972 for Puerto Ricans, $14,182 for Cubans, and $16,284 for Americans of non-Hispanic origin in 1977).

The difference in performance between Puerto Ricans and Dominicans clearly was not a result of less discrimination on the part of Anglo-Americans, who frequently could not differentiate the two groups. Dominicans were not U.S. citizens on arrival; they were among the most recent newcomers in New York; they initially contained few people with a postsecondary education; and they needed some time to get adjusted in the new country. The Dominicans, however, may have benefited from the persistence of more traditional values. They were known to priests as good Catholics. Among Dominican New Yorkers, more children were born to traditional husband-headed families than to female-headed families. Among Puerto Ricans, the reverse was true. Whatever the reasons, some Dominicans gradually improved their positions. By opening grocery stores or barber shops or small agencies, or by taking up skilled work in non-unionized professions. Others turned to white-collar work. Well-educated Dominicans increasingly found jobs in local governments or corporations requiring men and women to speak Spanish as well as English.[7]

Central and South Americans

During the 1950s, Central America had supplied but a handful of immigrants to the United States. Thereafter, the tempo rapidly increased, as civil strife in Central America became ever more bitter: between 1961 and 1978, a total of 38,900 El Salvadoreans, 35,700 Panamanians, 35,500 Guatemalans, and 28,000 Hondurans legally entered the United States. Except perhaps for Costa Rica, these countries generally suffered from the most severe social problems connected with civil liberty and land. There also were widespread internal dissensions, with the spread of Marxist-inspired guerrilla wars. During the 1960s, strategists such as Che Guevara had placed their hopes in small bands of dedicated revolutionaries who would establish "foci" of resistance in inaccessible regions; these men would, so to speak, light the fuse that would set off massive revolutionary conflagrations among the peasants. This strategy everywhere led to disaster. It was replaced by the well-tried Leninist policy of setting up united fronts, with Cuba and the Soviet bloc providing funds, propaganda, training facilities, and arms. The "united fronts" vowed national resistance against "Yankee imperialism" and its puppets. But, once having attained power, the Marxist-Leninist cadres shifted direction, from an alliance of all "progressive" forces to the establishment of Marxist-Leninist dictatorships.

Nicaragua was the first Central American country to fall. In 1979 the Sandinistas triumphed. Thereafter, they gradually disposed of dissidents, including those within their own ranks, and began the long march toward a Marxist-Leninist society. They also increasingly provided backing to revolutionary forces in adjacent countries. Revolution in Central America, as in Cuba and Vietnam, led to emigration on an enormous scale. By the early 1980s almost 200,000 Nicaraguans had left their country, including Eden Pastora ("Commander Zero"), formerly the main Sandinista spokesman, who, in 1983, proclaimed a war of resistance against his former friends. The government, for its part, imposed a rigid system of censorship and intensified its own system of revolutionary repression against dissidents.

The authorities in Nicaragua, in conjunction with their Cuban allies, in turn provided weapons, funds, training facilities, bases, and propagandistic support for Marxist guerrilla forces in El Salvador. There was a mass exodus of Salvadoreans seeking to escape terror from both the left and right. Unwelcome alike in the neighboring Central American territories and Mexico, many Salvadoreans made their way to the United States, both legally and illegally. By 1983, officials estimated that the number of El Salvadoreans in the United States amounted to as many as 500,000.

El Salvadoreans were not the only refugees to arrive from Central America. The Sandinistas in Nicaragua became involved in a partisan struggle of their own, directed both by ex-Sandinistas disillusioned with the new regime and by more conservatively minded Nicaraguans, with some covert U.S. support. Civil war in El Salvador and Nicaragua led to widespread bloodshed and a pervasive sense of insecurity.

By the early 1980s, the ravages of revolutionary war extended to Honduras, which is likely to become another important supplier of immigrants to the United States. Honduras became a key region in the struggle for El Salvador as leftist forces began to use Honduras as a base for channeling weapons and supplies from Nicaragua and for staging attacks on the Salvadoran army. Honduras by this time had been seriously affected by the worldwide recession, which reduced the sales of Honduras' agricultural exports. Land reform, implemented from 1975 onward, created problems of its own. On top of all their other troubles, the Hondurans faced a major refugee problem; by 1983, there were 46,000 refugees in the country, including 18,000 Salvadoreans.

Not surprisingly, the spread of guerrilla war led many Central Americans to emigrate. By 1983, roughly one-tenth of all Salvadoreans had left their country. Between 200,000 and 300,000 of them were estimated to have found homes in Los Angeles, which thereby became the world's second-largest Salvadorean city. Many of these newcomers depended on support from local churches, including El Rescate, an organization backed by the Southern California Ecumenical Council to help Central Americans find refuge. Most of these newcomers were illegal immigrants. Saddened in many cases by the loss of relatives, and homesick, jobless, and fearful of being caught, they all too often looked to the future with despair. The plight of the "feet people" threatened to equal the misery of the "boat people." Should Marxist-Leninists succeed in their objective to establish Marxist-Leninist regimes throughout Central America, emigration of Central Americans would accelerate to an extraordinary extent.

By contrast, newcomers from such countries as Chile, Argentina, and Uruguay—Latin America's "Far South"—conformed more closely to the pattern of Western European immigration to the United States during the post-World War II years and involved primarily urban people of middle-class or skilled working-class backgrounds endowed with a formal education in the academic or technological fields.[9] The Argentines and Chileans who came to the United States did not face hunger at home; their motives for emigrating were more complex. Some Argentinians departed because they were fearful of left-wing terrorists or right-wing repression or of their country's economic future, or because they were Jewish and worried about the long-term prospects of their community. Others left for economic reasons—because the Argentine economy was in decline or because they anticipated that the United States would provide more opportunities for their children. Many of them were professional men who contributed to their land of adoption through a great variety of specialized skills in the performing arts, sciences, literature, medicine, and architecture (a discipline of high social prestige in the Hispanic world and one in which Latin Americans have excelled).

Overall, these emigrants from Central and South America have little in common except the Spanish language—often pronounced in strikingly different accents, depending on the immigrant's country of origin. The possession of a common language did not necessarily give the newcomers a sense of belonging to one Hispanic community. On the contrary, the newcomers differed in national, ethnic, and cultural background; and they resented the Americans' frequent unwillingness to differentiate between different stocks. As Lt. Ray Calletano, a police officer in the popular television series "Hill Street Blues" put it trenchantly:

> "Chief Daniels, esteemed colleagues: it is with great pride that I accept and thank you for this award. [But] . . . why huevos rancheros? Why margaritas? Why do you assume that all Hispanic people like that kind of food? . . . You go to all this trouble to give this banquet in my honor, and nobody even bothers to find out that I'm Colombian, not Mexican or Puerto Rican. And furthermore, phrases like 'credit to his people' and 'fine Puerto Rican American' tend to stick in the throat of a man who has been a citizen of this country for 22 years!"[10]

The newcomers included a substantial number of college teachers who tried to get away from the pressures of politicized universities in Latin America or who found better research facilities and improved chances of promotion in the United States. They also contributed heavily to journals such as *La Raza* (a well-written Spanish newspaper published in Chicago).

Regional preferences differed greatly. Central Americans were apt to prefer the western states, Guatemalans favored Los Angeles, and some Hondurans made their homes along the Gulf coast. But others moved to the Northeast, particularly to the New York metropolitan area, and New York soon contained the world's largest urban population of Puerto Ricans, Hondurans and Panamanians. Most of the Dominican immigrants settled initially in New York, before fanning out to other parts of the United States. There were massive settlements of Central and South Americans in Chicago, Miami, Los Angeles, San Jose, and San Francisco. The newcomers often replicated the political divisions of their own countries and formed their own national associations, for leftists on the one hand and conservatives on the other.

To chronicle the experience of each South American immigrant group would take a separate book. We will focus on the Colombians, whose experience differed strikingly from the Dominicans'. The first Colombians to settle in the United States were primarily educated men and women— nurses, pharmacists, and technicians who arrived after World War I and lived in the Jackson Heights area, a pleasant, middle-class section of New York City. A combination of rural unrest and political violence, known as *La Violencia*, impelled many more Colombians to leave their homeland during the 1950s and early 1960s. These newcomers were drawn from a much wider spectrum than the middle-class pioneers of Colombian settlement. Their movement into the United States was accelerated by the mechanization of agriculture and by the advancing pace of industrialization, which forced many farmers and craftsmen out of their traditional jobs. The population of Colombia continued to grow at a rapid pace, and there was widespread unemployment—at a time when the price of airfares to the United States was rapidly decreasing.[11]

By 1970, about 27,000 first- or second-generation Colombians were living in New York City, the vast majority of them whites. They formed essentially a middle-class community that strongly distinguished between the Colombians and other Hispanics, especially Dominicans and Puerto Ricans. The Colombians' sense of distinctiveness derived in part from their claim to speak the purest Spanish in the New World and from a sense of having come from good family backgrounds. (Colombians called their Jackson Heights neighborhood "Chaperino," after a Bogotá middle-class suburb.) Colombians in New York City tended to be somewhat younger on the average than the population as a whole, and their relative youth may help to explain the fact that the Colombians' average income at the time remained somewhat below the median wage. A relatively youthful community will not, after all, contain many men and women who have arrived at the peak of the earning power. They were well equipped, however, for the competitive situation they encountered in New York. They were somewhat better educated than the average New Yorker, and they had a lower birthrate and smaller families on the average than their fellow citizens. Married Colombian women typically held paid jobs outside the home. In an economic sense, the Colombians in New York had become fully adjusted to the country of their choice.

The Colombian community in Chicago, numbering about 3,500 foreign born in 1970, followed a somewhat different pattern. The Chicago community contained a substantial number of *costeños*, denizens of Colombia's coastal region and derived from African, Indian, and Spanish ancestry. The Spanish Colombians in the cities of the interior traditionally enjoyed economic advantages because they were reputedly "white" (in the Latin sense) and lived in cities where opportunities for social betterment were traditionally superior to those available in the countryside. As education improved in the coastal regions, ambitious *costeños* with the appropriate diplomas but the wrong social background and skin color emigrated to the United States. The Colombian community in Chicago contained many dark-complexioned professional men and women—doctors, engineers, accountants, and architects who brought their families to the new country. They usually entered the United States via Miami, then moved on, settling first in apartments on Chicago's far north side until they could purchase homes in the affluent suburbs. The *costeños* were Catholics; they sent their children to parochial schools so they could study English and Spanish and retain respect for traditional values. The *costeños* became fully integrated into the Chicago middle class; they mixed with one another or with Cubans, but only infrequently with Spanish Colombians (a most exclusive group), Mexicans, or Puerto Ricans. In Chicago, as in New York, Colombians were slow to take out naturalization papers, participate in American politics, or form political alliances with other Spanish-speaking communities.

Making It in the United States

What of the overall impact of the United States on the newcomers? According to its many home-grown and foreign critics, the United States by the 1960s had become a new Egypt. If America's critics were to be believed, it is difficult to understand why any sane man or woman sought admission into, much less chose to remain in, a house of bondage in which there was no real choice except between the paradox of Victory of the spirit despite physical hunger or:

To exist in the grasp
of American social neurosis,
sterilization of the soul
And a full stomach.[12]

Although racial and ethnic prejudice thrive in the United States just as in Latin America, the economic condition of the various Spanish-speaking communities in the United States differed too greatly to permit racism to be the primary explanation for these communities' disadvantages.[13] We will refer to the Hispanics' general position in U.S. society again in our conclusion. At this point we will merely say that, by 1970, Central and South Americans had achieved by far the highest levels of education and income among the Spanish speakers; in this respect, they most resembled the Cubans. Central and South Americans had on the whole a better formal education than the rank and file of their fellow Hispanics in the United States. The professional distribution among Central and South American men corresponded generally to that of non-Spanish whites in the United States. Immigrants formed a disproportionately high percentage of those Hispanic-descended people who had "made it" in the United States. The professional distribution among Central and South American women remained somewhat less favorable than that of non-Hispanic white Americans; the differences reflected the higher degree of female emancipation in the United States compared to Latin America at the time.

The relative economic success attained by South American immigrants in the United States had little to do with political agitation or the exercise of political power. The South Americans, like the Cubans, contained a considerable number of persons who had not yet taken out U.S. citizenship and generally were unwilling to participate in wider Hispanic political alliances. Yet it was the Cubans and South Americans who were economically most successful in comparison with other Spanish speakers in the United States. Racial or sexual prejudice played little or no part in restraining the immigrants in the race for advancement. Had the Anglo-American's assumed sexism and ethnic chauvinism been as predominant as the critics of American society assumed in the 1960s and 1970s, South and Central American women should have been at an even greater disadvantage than their menfolk; in fact, these women's median income exceeded that of non-Spanish whites in a number of age groups.

Overall, the median earnings of the various Hispanic communities in the United States came to be arranged in a hierarchical order in which the immigrants' cultural background, the region in which they lived, the age composition of their communities, the number of earners in each family, and their education counted for more than their racial background. In terms of relative performance, the Cuban experience was similar to that of white immigrants from other countries. According to Barry Chiswick, a leading expert on immigration, white immigrants who had been in the United States only a few years earned about 10 percent less than the native-born. After becoming fully adjusted to the country of their adoption, the newcomers did better than the rest; white immigrants who had spent twenty years or more in the United States received salaries on an average 6 percent above the native-born. The Cuban rise to prosperity was somewhat slower, but Cubans too eventually reached parity with native-born whites. Cubans who had stayed in the United States for ten years earned 16 percent less than native-born whites. Cubans who had been in the United States for twenty years or more made 3 percent more money than native-born whites. In some manner, therefore, the United States remained a land of opportunity.[14]

Taken on their own, of course, such statistics have a lifeless quality; they cannot give an account of the enormous disparities that exist between members of the same class or even the same family. Many so-called middle class families lived in a working-class manner; the husband, his wife, and perhaps a grown son or daughter labored long hours in unfamiliar jobs in unfamiliar surroundings, and lived frugally so as to save money or to train for a better career. The statistics also conceal the numerous blue-collar and domestic workers who sought an economic foothold so that they might send money home or get a family member to join them in the United States. The statistics do indicate that, on the whole, the rate of progress among the various Hispanic communities remained strikingly uneven, with South Americans and Cubans at the top, Mexicans in the middle, and Puerto Ricans at the bottom. But such generalizations are of little relevance to the fate of individuals from any of these groups—except insofar as newcomers of middle-class provenance or with middle class aspirations did better than the rest. By the late 1970s, however, all Hispanic communities had secured at least some advances within their respective occupational structures.

What of the newcomers' broader integration into the country of their adoption? Integration involved two separate, but related, processes: partial and selective merging into the Hispanic communities, and assimilation into U.S. society as a whole. Spanish-speaking Puerto Ricans, Argentinians, and Salvadoreans shared the same language and also certain cultural traditions; they enjoyed similar kinds of music; they typically professed the same religion. There also was a good deal of intermarriage. Rates of mixed unions, both with Hispanics of other national provenance and with non-Hispanics, varied widely from region to region and from one national group and one social class to another. Mexican Americans from the Southwest, for example, were less likely to seek spouses from outside their own communities than Hispanics in a big city, such as New York (where some immigrants married U.S. citizens, frequently non-Hispanics, in order to remain in the United States). But even in New York there were striking disparities. Whereas 29.5 percent of Puerto

Ricans wedded non-Puerto Ricans, 56.1 percent of Central Americans did so. South Americans, Central Americans, and Cubans also were far more ready to wed Americans of non-Hispanic ancestry than were Puerto Ricans or Dominicans. But, overall, mixed unions increased in a striking fashion, especially in the second generation.[15]

The creation of a broader Latino or Hispanic consciousness, on the other hand, met with many obstacles. The Hispanic definition was in part imposed by bureaucratic fiat, not by the Hispanics' own initiative. Many Hispanics—for instance, Chicano nationalists—refused to accept the label. So did the Spaniards, who preferred to be known as *españoles*. The Latin Americans themselves came from numerous sovereign states, each with its own history, traditions, separate loyalties, and sometimes long-standing animosities. The ties established by a common language, by radio and television programs, by "Hispanic" music, or by advertising directed to the "Hispanic" market seemed too fragile to serve as a permanent bond. The various Hispanic groups arrived at different times; their major components settled in different parts of the United States. They wielded disparate political influence. Even in a single city—such as San Francisco or Chicago, meeting grounds of many Hispanic groups— Hispanics, including those from the same country, remained divided in a social sense. They might select different social identities, and often did so by the choice of their neighborhood. Not surprisingly, the Hispanics failed to act as a single cohesive unit even in local politics.

Overall, the immigrants from these many lands behaved in a manner strikingly similar to that of earlier ethnic groups. As A. J. Jaffe, Ruth M. Cullen, and Thomas D. Boswell have shown in an important study, the newcomers in the long run learned English, especially the young. To give one example, 1,204,058 persons aged 5 years and older in New York City in 1980 spoke Spanish at home. Of these 72.4 percent were said to speak English well; only 27.6 percent did not have a good command of the language. The Hispanics' socioeconomic status tended to improve in the second and third generations; their fertility declined as their formal education improved. The pace of assimilation differed greatly between one general community and another, but there was a clear trend toward convergence. Hispanics of every national derivation increased their demographic stake in the major U.S. cities. Ultimately, they would merge with the U.S. population at large.[16]

Part III

The Porous Frontier

Chapter 8

The Borderlands

The "frontier" always has had a romantic ring in American history. "Border" or "borderlands," on the other hand, commonly have incurred suspicion. The Mexican-American border regions for long were remote and backward regions where robbers, raiders, and revolutionaries found a ready haven. In the twentieth century, however, the borderlands have seen rapid development, both on the Mexican side and, even more so, on the U.S. side, where economic growth formed part of a process that has entailed a shift of population and industries from the northern "snow belt" into the southern and southwestern "sun belt." The United States–Mexico border today is the most frequently crossed international boundary on earth. Even Laredo, a small town in Texas with no more than 70,000 people, registered more than twelve million lawful crossings annually in the early 1980s. The total number of legal border crossings amounted to something like 180 million. In addition, large numbers of illegal migrants, *mojados*, make their way across the border each year, only about 20 to 30 percent of whom are caught.

The Main Geographical Regions

The borderlands are both vast and varied. The northern parts of Mexico contain more than 40 percent of the land but only one-fifth of the population. About one-half of this land is desert or near desert; almost all the arable lands that can be cultivated without irrigation have been under crops for a long time. The farming industry centers on those regions where irrigation is available for instance, the Mexicali Valley, parts of the lower Rio Grande region, and the Rio Fuerte Basin in Sonora. Manufacturing, commerce, and tourism account for the major part of the region's income, and those occupations naturally link the Mexican borderlands with their northern neighbor.

The Mexican north does not form an integrated whole. The Sierra Occidental divides the north into eastern and western portions. The highways and roads lead mostly from north to south, toward Mexico City. A motorist traveling by car from Ciudad Juárez to Nogales (separated from one another by only 375 miles by air) must cover 1,611 miles if

129

he wishes to remain in Mexican territory. As John Price, a Canadian sociologist, points out in his excellent study of Tijuana, these geographic divisions have far-reaching economic consequences.[1] They render the Mexican north more dependent on its northern neighbors than it would be in a different geographical setting. The lay of the land also divides Mexican immigration to the northern provinces into separate eastern and western streams. The geographical division of the north also has some influence on whether an emigrant to the United States decides to go to California (the recipient, on the average, of about half the Mexican emigration into the United States) or to Texas (which receives just under one-quarter of the annual Mexican immigration to the United States).

Within the Mexican border region, the nine major border municipalities occupy a special position. They have per capita incomes that range up to three times the Mexican national average; about one-fifth to two-thirds of the wages earned by their residents derive from the United States. In addition, the border municipalities collect about 70 percent of the money spent by foreign tourists in Mexico and conduct more trade with the United States than with the Mexican interior. Although the commercial balance with the United States is unfavorable to the northern border region—because the area lacks sufficient exports of its own and because it is geographically remote from Mexico's main industrial zones in central Mexico—the border lands make up for this imbalance by receipts from Mexican workers in the United States, by assembly plants, and by the expenditures of American tourists.

On the American side of the border, there are several major economic configurations, intimately linked with neighboring regions in Mexico. San Diego, on the Pacific coast, began its career as a Spanish presidio; the arrival of the transcontinental railway in 1887 changed this small Mexican village into an English-speaking city; it subsequently developed into a major naval port and a manufacturing center with a strong emphasis on defense industries, high technology, and research. San Diego's expansion occurred when Baja California, the neighboring Mexican province, was as yet little inhabited. The growth of southern California's economy, however, stimulated development south of the border. The growth of such cities as Tijuana, Ensenada, and Tecate in the northern part of Baja California had a reciprocal impact on the San Diego conurbation.

The American impact was not all for the good. According to Niles Hansen, an American economist and an expert on the border regions, urbanization in Tijuana was originally promoted by entertainment industries of a dubious kind that were designed to serve Californians who wanted to spend money in a relatively permissive country in race tracks, gambling casinos, dance halls, and bordellos.[2] In more recent times, Mexican growers have supplied American customers with marijuana and other drugs. The "tourism of vice" had an unfortunate effect on the images held by both Mexicans and Americans about their respective neighbors on the other side of the border. All too many Mexicans saw their visitors as drunkards, gamblers, and whoremongers, while many Americans imagined that the Mexican border towns were no more than centers of vice.

In fact, this image today bears no relation to reality. Tijuana has only a few hundred prostitutes who deal with foreigners; there are few drug peddlers; the Mexican authorities have clamped down on pornography; abortion now is less common in Tijuana than in California. Very few Mexicans in the border cities earn their money by pandering to crime or depravity; for decades, the border cities have received most of their income from manufacturing and legitimate trade.

The population of the border region continues to grow. If existing trends continue, Tijuana by 1995 will have a population larger than San Diego and its suburbs. As the cities expand, so does the traffic across the border. In 1977, the number of U.S. citizens crossing the San Diego-Tijuana Station numbered 14.6 million persons. The number of Mexicans going the other way was still larger—immigrants, both documented and undocumented, as well as tourists. In 1981, Mexican tourists spent a record $1.5 billion in the United States, an increase of nearly 50 percent over the preceding year. The sharp decline in the value of Mexican currency in 1982 interfered gravely with this traffic. Nevertheless, even devaluation and the restrictive measures taken by governments on both sides of the border could not break the bonds that inextricably link the borderlands on both sides of the frontier.

The Imperial Valley forms a border zone of a different kind. The valley is hot and dry with an average rainfall of only about 3.5 inches per year; it actually lies below sea level and, prior to 1900, remained a virtually uninhabited wasteland. The construction of a series of great dams and canals, including the All-American Canal in 1940, turned the valley from arid waste into flourishing farmland that supports truck crops, alfalfa, cotton, and sugar beets, as well as livestock. The valley's farming economy depends on large farms organized by corporate enterprise. Farming in the Imperial Valley owes a great debt to the immigrant Mexican workmen who replaced workers of European or Chinese origin. After World War II, and especially during the 1960s and 1970s, farms increasingly mechanized their operations; as a result, agricultural employment declined and more laborers turned to urban occupations.

The El Paso, Texas, economic region also has distinctive problems. Before the coming of the railway, El Paso was a dusty adobe village. The arrival of four railroads in the 1880s changed El Paso's economic position, not only with regard to its own region on the U.S. side of the border but also in relation to northern Mexico. Dependent on customers and workmen drawn from both sides of the border, El Paso became a major manufacturing center with oil refineries, a copper refinery and smelter, cement plants, clothing manufacturers, and major defense installations.

El Paso occupies a special demographic position among U.S. cities: 62 percent of its people are of Hispanic origin (1980 figures). El Paso and Ciudad Juárez (on the other side of the border) benefit from their symbiotic relationship in many different ways. The residents of Juárez prosper from tourism, expanding commerce, and the ability of commuters to work on the U.S. side of the border, El Paso profits from the influx of Mexican workmen and the purchases of Mexican customers.

The tight links that exist between the two cities also create problems. El Paso's large and growing Hispanic population suffers from high unemployment; here, as elsewhere, the poor all too often speak only Spanish. Their position is not improved by local tax arrangements. El Paso has one of the nation's highest local tax rates, but the citizens probably do not get full value for the money spent on their behalf.

The southern border region of Texas is unusual in that although San Antonio, its major metropolitan core, is a considerable distance from the border, it remains closely linked to the border zone. In 1980, 53.7 percent of its population was of Hispanic origin. Tourism and commerce with Mexico played an important part in the city's economy. (According to a 1973 estimate, San Antonio's retail trade with Mexican citizens accounted for 25 to 30 percent of the city's income in this sector.) Laredo, the oldest continuously settled site in Texas, depends even more than does San Antonio on the proximity of Mexico, including its twin city of Nuevo Laredo. The Laredo region's economy relies on ranching, oil, gas, tourism, and international trade. It also is one of the largest inland ports of entry into the United States. More than five million automobiles cross the border every year; without Mexican customers, most of the city's freight forwarders and brokers and many resale merchants would not survive. In 1979, Laredo's mercantile and service sectors accounted for 50 percent of the city's employment; manufacturing contributed only 7.9 percent. Most of the workmen employed in industry were unskilled; 95 percent of the labor force was Mexican American. In addition, the local economy depended heavily on commuters from Mexico, including numerous farm workers.

The lower Rio Grande Valley, including the counties of Hidalgo and Cameron, again has characteristic features of its own. It contains a sprawling metropolitan area with multiple urban centers, including Brownsville, McAllen, and Harlingen, which together constitute about 40 percent of the county's population. During the 1970s, all these cities experienced rapid growth, as did Matamoros and Reynosa, the principal cities on the Mexican side of the border. The valley as a whole forms an interconnected community of more than one million persons. Its economic mainstay continues to be farming. The valley has become a major producer of citrus fruit, cotton, vegetables, grain, sorghum, and sugar cane. In addition, there are food-processing, apparel-manufacturing, and other industries. Manufacturing, however, faces many difficulties because of the distance from major markets. The construction of new natural gas pipelines from Mexico and the further development of tourism may help to alleviate the situation.

Relations between Mexicans and Americans in the Rio Grande area were at their worst during the nineteenth century, when boundary disputes, quarrels between Anglo-American ranchers and Mexican land grantees, and local banditry were at their height. During the twentieth century, the construction of railways and the division of ranches into irrigated farmland led to rapid economic development within the valley. Older hostilities between Texans of Anglo-American and Mexican origin were succeeded by social disputes as the *barrios* of Brownsville and neighboring cities filled with Mexican nationals, who performed the toughest and least-paid jobs on the farms and factories. The English-speaking population declined and the Spanish speakers increased, so much so that, by the late 1970s, they accounted for 80 percent of the valley's total population. More than half of them lived below the poverty line and 90 percent of all families in this category consisted of Mexican Americans.[3]

In general, the borderlands have a higher demographic growth rate than either Mexico or the United States. The Mexican and United States portions of the border are tied to one another by tourism, trade, labor migration, and manufacturing. They cannot help but profit from cooperation over such technical issues as water, waste disposal, transportation, and pollution. Each side of the border is tied more closely to the other than to its mother country. People wander back and forth across the border—over 180 million legal border crossings are registered each year. Border officials could detain all travelers and search their vehicles; but if inspectors were to stop all cars and buses, this would create enormous traffic jams and cause intolerable delays to both American and Mexican tourists. For better or worse, the Mexican and U.S. sides of the border are, like Siamese twins, tied to one another for life.

Some Current Controversies

The borderlands have had a bad press. During the nineteenth century there were complaints of violence and ethnic hostility. Modern critics are no less harsh. In 1976, for example, the governors of the U.S. border states issued a joint statement concerning the borderlands, speaking of the poverty and conflict that always have stalked these regions. "This is explained," the report stated in convoluted officialese, "by the existence of many innate friction-laden features, chief among which is the greatest disparity in per capita income between any two bordering nations in the world. This disparity has led to an ever-growing imbrogliation of the region's economy."[4] Such "imbrogliation," according to the governors, takes many forms: illegal immigrants "contribute heavily to the increasing levels of domestic unemployment"; "local cities cannot solve their own problems"; and traditional "individualistic approaches" cannot cope with assorted questions such as "protectionism, immigration, smuggling, crime, unemployment, industrialization, transportation, pollution, energy, water, tourism, [and] education." According to the governors, the region's economic health is declining; the border regions occasion "a pernicious drain on the overall economies" of the four border states. The borderlands therefore require special treatment, for "the region's problems are of common economic and social characteristics" that transcend existing jurisdictions. Not surprisingly, bureaucrats argue, the assumed "uniqueness and severity" of these afflictions require for their solution a new official entity, well funded and endowed with broad powers, to be known as the "Regional Planning Action Commission."

This gubernatorial consensus notwithstanding, there is no clear evidence that the borderlands are declining. According to Niles Hansen's excellent study, personal incomes in the borderlands varied greatly: in the San Diego region, they were higher during the 1970s than those in the United States as a whole; in most other borderland regions they were lower. On the other hand, the rate of increase in the various borderland communities was higher in the borderland cities than in the United States as a whole. Between 1969 and 1977, the percentage of change in annual per capita income amounted to 81.6 for San Diego, 80.8 for El Paso, and 131.9 for McAllen, compared to 91.6 for the United States as a whole.

The governors believed that the region's problems have a common economic and social character. In fact, the subregions differ greatly among themselves in their geographic layout, immigration patterns, demographic composition, levels of income, economic structure, and crime rates. Contrary to public stereotype, cities with a high percentage of Spanish-speaking inhabitants are not necessarily more crime-ridden than others. Miami, with its large Cuban population, by 1982 had become the nation's crime capital, much of its violence being linked to the drug trade. On the other hand, El Paso, with its Mexican and Mexican-American majority, had the lowest rate of murders and robberies among the country's major cities.

The borderland debate raises broader questions about immigration from Mexico, its nature and effects, questions we shall discuss at length in the following chapter. Demographers, the point bears stressing right here, have cause to question the widespread assumption that the U.S. borderlands and, in a wider sense, the United States as a whole have become the main vent of Mexico's surplus population. Between 1820 and 1972, only 3.6 percent (1.6 million) of the total known legal immigration of 45.5 million into the United States came from Mexico. (These figures are, of course, subject to dispute; the true figures may well have been somewhat larger.) By the early 1970s, this had changed. Mexico sent more legal migrants to the United States than any other country; even so, these newcomers represented only 13.6 percent of the total U.S. legal immigration. Mexico's population at the time was growing by about a million and a half persons per year; the United States received only about 3.3 percent of Mexico's annual population increase. The use of Spanish in the United States has increased greatly; nevertheless, the bulk of Americans continues to trace their ancestry to northern Europe, especially the British Isles and Germany.

Current concepts concerning the effects of urbanization in Mexico also need revision. The shantytowns along the Mexican border form reservoirs of immigration. Their denizens—peasants uprooted from the countryside—supposedly live in a state of social disorganization and anomie, their one ambition being to better their lot by coming to the United States where they probably will make less than an American citizen because of their pitiful background. Such interpretations fill many tomes of sociological literature; in the past the Chicago School of sociology made similar assumptions about Polish immigrants in the United States during the 1920s; these immigrants supposedly were subject to social anomie and condemned to a life of misery and crime.[5] But such generalizations regarding social disorganization in the *barrios* either of Mexico or the United States today may be as misleading as those made with regard to the Poles in Chicago in the 1920s.

A recent study by Antonio Ugalde examines the *barrio* of San Felipe del Real Adicional, situated on the western edge of Ciudad Júarez, Chihuahua, place of transit for *braceros* and wetbacks going to the United States and a center of attraction for thousands of migrating and transient peasants.[6] Ciudad Juárez is separated from El Paso by the Rio Grande River, both towns are set in a semiarid, treeless desert, and both are shrouded in traffic dust and smog. The citizens of Adicional are mostly migrants; 92 percent of the respondents consulted by Ugalde have come to the city from outside, mostly from the north central plateau of Mexico. They leave their villages because they hope to find higher-paying jobs in town or because droughts have made life too difficult in the countryside. Contrary to what might have been expected, few respondents moved to Adicional with the thought of subsequently crossing the border to find more remunerative employment in the United States. The migrants of Adicional, like nineteenth-century newcomers to the United States, rely heavily on relatives for information about Ciudad Juárez for help in overcoming the initial hardships of the city, and for finding jobs, temporary housing, food, and practical advice. Far from disintegrating in the city, kinship ties remain strong and play an important part in helping the migrant to adjust. The newcomers find life difficult; there is a great deal of unemployment. But the immigrants act as economic men: they make rational decisions and try to better their condition.

Some theoreticians claim that the rapidly expanding cities of developing nations derive special difficulties from an overgrown tertiary sector. The transfer of rural dwellers to this tertiary sector supposedly forms one of the main causes of unemployment. The labor pattern of Adicional and other Latin American cities investigated by Ugalde does not confirm this theory. Most of the newcomers look for jobs in industry, especially in construction. Far from being demoralized, they work hard and are anxious to save, which they do in part by building shanties to house themselves and their families. The shanties gradually improve as the new settlers invest time and money in their property. Whereas subsidized public housing projects constructed at the taxpayers' expense are apt to look good at the beginning and then gradually deteriorate, the self-constructed shantytowns look miserable at the beginning but improve in time as the newcomers improve their little houses and make them more habitable.

Ugalde's findings do not square with commonly held assumptions concerning the slum dwellers of the border. Governor (later President) Miguel de la Madrid voiced a typical opinion when he stated that "The people who come . . . are so temporary that they don't know how to handle themselves as citizens. Where do they live? Old shacks, maybe, with a color television because they can take that with them. The kids go about on the streets; soon they become delinquent, and then they become addicted to drugs. These people lifted up their roots where they came from, but they have not been planted here."[7] If theoreticians concerned with the progressive "miserization" of Third World slums are to be trusted, the citizens of Adicional will in fact be worse off as time goes on.

Ugalde's investigations, however, do not accord with such notions. Despite the ever-present burden of unemployment, the citizens of Adicional gradually better their lot. Even though Adicional is a poverty-stricken neighborhood, its people are better off on the average than

Mexicans at large. Not everybody gains, but many do. Of Ugalde's respondents, 23 percent stated that they were worse off than their fathers had been, but 38 percent claimed that they were better off than their fathers, and 31 percent indicated that their condition was about equal to their fathers.

The people of Adicional are not illiterate. In fact, their literacy rates are higher than Mexico's as a whole. Far from being politically apathetic, they take an active interest in politics and also join local organizations of various kinds. Urbanization does not lead to excessive drunkenness, gambling, or sexual depravity. There is a high percentage of common-law rather than church-sanctioned marriages in Adicional, but there is no evidence that the men and women who have contracted such unions are sexually less responsible than anyone else. Nor are slum dwellers necessarily ill-informed. More than four-fifths of Adicional residents own radios, one-third own television sets, and one-tenth have managed to buy cars. Current theories regarding the assumed evils of urban anomie notwithstanding, the people incline toward neither crime nor political radicalism.

This is not to say that Adicional is a well cared for community. Few children complete grade school, medical conditions are deficient, housing conditions are crowded and unsanitary, and unemployment (and disguised unemployment) are ever-present problems. But the stereotype concerning the crime-prone, immoral, disoriented, radicalized, pessimistic, apathetic, helpless, and despairing men and women who supposedly inhabit the borderlands has little basis in fact. "Through hard work they [the residents of Adicional] have built the neighborhood, often laboring together in communal works. And the slow but steady improvements in Adicional over the past years have contributed to many of the residents' sense of purpose about the future."[8] Slum dwellers who move to the United States are not therefore the worst and most depraved of their nation; on the contrary, they usually have accepted the principles of hard work and self-help that have made the United States thrive.

All labor migrants of course do not come from cities. Many come from villages, and their decision to leave has profound effects on the countryside. According to its critics, the effects of labor migration on indigenous villages are disastrous, and the critics often have a point. A massive exodus of young people may well produce major social disturbances, and a substantial body of modern field studies exists to prove the case. For instance, James Stuart and Michael Kearney, investigating a poverty-stricken community, San Jeronimo in Mexico, stress that labor migration to the United States produces a rural shortage of labor; hence, food production declines; something like 80 percent of the food now consumed in San Jeronimo derives from external sources.

Migration to the United States, in the authors' opinion, does not produce genuine wealth for the village.[9] But there also is a great deal of evidence pointing to different conclusions. The more fortunate labor migrants sometimes manage to save money and, on their return to Mexico, rent land or buy a lot and a house in the small country town of their origin, or purchase cattle, improved pastures, or irrigated land. Money acquired in the United States provides foreign aid of the grass-roots kind that passes directly from the giver to the recipient without clinging to the palms of bureaucratic intermediaries.

As we see it, academicians err when they deny ordinary villagers the capacity to make enlightened economic choices. Setting up a rural store may be both a profitable and a beneficial form of investment, one that provides *compensinos* with much-needed goods and services, and thereby stimulating production. The purchase of a house may provide the new owner with a valuable asset for his old age; the purchaser also may improve the state of Mexico's housing stock by taking care of, and perhaps improving, his newly acquired asset. A truck or a tractor, bought by a local man conversant with local needs, may make a more valuable contribution to the village economy than an expensive and unwanted project, enforced from the outside by bureaucratic planners and apt to arouse hostility rather than political support from its supposed bene-ficiaries.[10]

It is certainly true that labor migration removes young men from the villages. But this does not mean that their departure necessarily lowers agricultural productivity, or that their enforced stay in the villages would cause more crops to be grown. Much depends on local methods of production, a fact well established by economic anthropologists in Africa. Agricultural yield, moreover, depends on a great variety of other factors—the accessibility of markets, the quality of marketing available to farmers, the availability of transport facilities, fertilizers, machinery, and know-how, as well as the quality of the soil and climate. To prevent young men from leaving a village may not enhance productivity; on the contrary, such a prohibition may well promote more rural under-employment and occasion more misery than existed before.

Nor is it true that labor migration, including "circular" migration to and from the village, is necessarily the choice the poor make. A study by Kenneth D. Roberts suggests that any hard and fast destinctions between "traditional" and "modern" agriculture in Mexico may leave much to be desired.[11] Villagers depart from farms in both "traditional" and "modern" regions in the Mexican countryside for the purpose of finding work in Mexican and U.S. cities. A young man's decision to leave his home is taken with the advice of his entire family; the family in fact is engaged in elaborate planning on how to dispose to the best advantage the available manpower. Migrants do not necessarily come from the poorest villages; they may in fact come from the most prosperous rural communities.

Roberts found that in the Bajio region of Mexico, for instance, there is a good deal of prosperity. Farms are well developed; rural incomes are substantial. Yet families send selected members to work in the United States. The Bajio households are able to do so because they have an income sufficiently high to take the risk of paying a migrants' travel expense and maintaining him for a time in the United States, even if he cannot immediately get a job there. In the Mixteca Baja area, on the other hand, the people are poor. Primitive techniques and undesirable soils cause farm incomes to be insufficient for the bare needs of a household and there are few local opportunities for wage labor. Hence, young men often leave the village permanently, rather than becoming "circular" labor migrants. Migrants cannot afford a trip to the United States. Instead, they seek work in Mexican cities, where they can rely on an existing network of established people from Mixteca Baja. Far from preventing labor migration to the United States, economic development in the rural periphery may in fact enourage it.

We also cannot agree with Marxists who regard labor migration as a purely capitalist phenomenon. One million of the citizens of Yugoslavia, a socialist country, were working abroad by the late 1970s, mostly in West Germany. These migrants made up about 5 percent of Yugoslavia's population and nearly one-fifth of its labor force. Psychologically, the West had become Yugoslavia's new frontier; men driven by ambition or despair were moving northward into a life of uncertainty and possible achievement. The migrants sent back about $2 billion a year; their earnings constituted one of Yugoslavia's most important sources of hard currency. Yugoslavia at the same time was suffering from serious unemployment; about 500,000 men were out of work. As Dusko Doder, an American journalist, put it: "The migrant system alone was preventing high unemployment from becoming intolerable. It is inconceivable . . . that Yugoslavia's economy could survive the double burden of reabsorbing one million expatriate workers and losing their remittances over a short span without catastrophic consequences."[12]

The Border Economy

When American and Mexican negotiators signed the Treaty of Guadalupe Hidalgo, the borderlands on both sides of the new frontier remained of marginal importance to the two contracting parties. The Southwest played only a minor part in the U.S. economy. Mexico's northern provinces for the most part remained lightly populated and poverty stricken. During the twentieth century, there was a decisive shift. Within the United States, the center of gravity began to shift from the so-called snow belt to the sun belt, turning California into the most populous state of the Union. In Mexico, the northern border states since 1940 have attained the highest growth rate of any region in the country as a whole.

The extent of recent development is astonishing in both demographic and economic terms. The combination of a falling deathrate, high birthrate, and a high rate of immigration gave northern Mexico one of the highest rates of increase in the world. Most of the people live in cities; indeed, the proportion of town dwellers is higher in the border states than in Mexico in its entirety (85 percent for the border states in 1970, 60 percent for Mexico as a whole). By contrast, the U.S. border regions are relatively backward within the context of the U.S. economy. For instance, they have a high, though declining, dependence on government employment. (In 1976, about one-fifth of the American work force drew paychecks from government; in the borderlands, the figure stood at 33.4 percent.) The borderlands also were overrepresented in terms of the number of persons employed in trade—the figures varying from 28.9 percent of nongovernment employment in California to 33.1 percent in Texas, compared to 26.2 percent for the United States as a whole. Shopkeepers, wholesale merchants, insurance companies, and forwarding agencies catered not only to the inhabitants of the American borderlands but also to hundreds of thousands of Mexicans. Americans cross the border in large numbers in order to obtain medical and dental help, for entertainment, to get their cars repaired, or their hair cut. Americans also buy sugar, rice, vegetables, meat, and baked goods, bottled beverages, furniture, prescription drugs, gasoline and diesel fuel, as well as a great deal of other merchandise. Mexicans come to the United States to purchase clothes, cars, car parts, technical appliances, canned goods, liquor, cigarettes, and many kinds of American food.

Manufacturing employment in the borderlands, by contrast, traditionally was low because of the region's remoteness from the major American markets. The shift of American industries from the heartland in the Northeast and the Great Lakes region to the South and Southwest began to change the situation. Industrialists willing to relocate their plants commonly find that wages (and taxes) are lower in the borderlands, that trade unions are not as powerful as in the Northeast, and that climatic conditions are more pleasant than in the snow belt. Hence, markets in both the borderlands and Mexico have grown.

Some border regions have experienced industrial growth reminiscent of those of mid-Victorian England, even when industrial employment in the rest of the United States was declining at the expense of service industries. Whereas industrial employment in the United States as a whole between 1969 and 1976 dropped by 6.1 percent, manufacturing employment in California rose by 4.5 percent; in New Mexico by 19.4 percent; and in Arizona and Texas by an astounding 49 percent and 51 percent, respectively. This development in turn was intimately linked to the economic fortunes of Mexico. In prosperity as in crisis, the economies of Mexico and the United States remain tightly linked.

The economic problems that face Mexico and the United States alike became magnified along the borderlands, where the ordinary problems of immigration became further complicated by the need to accommodate commuters. A substantial number of Mexican citizens continued to live in Mexico while holding jobs in the United States; some crossed the border daily; others worked several days or even weeks between trips home. No statistician can determine precisely how many commuters arrived in the United States at various times, but scholars estimate that, by the mid–1970s, many hundreds of thousands of persons in Mexico became directly dependent on the earnings brought home by such commuters.

No statute in American law specifically established the commuter system. It was legalized by administrative rulings by the Immigration and Naturalization Service in 1927, which merely institutionalized a practice dating from the nineteenth century.[13] The official justification was simple: the United States had long established peculiarly close relations with both Mexico and Canada; hence, their respective citizens should be exempted from certain general requirements of the immigration laws, even though Congress had not specifically provided for such exemptions.

Border crossers were numerous and important to the border economy. A report by David North claimed that by 1970 the border-crossing work force numbered at least 100,000.[14] The number in 1983 probably exceeded this figure by two or three times. The border crossers were apt to be young, poorly educated in a formal sense, and prone to do unskilled labor, mostly farm work or construction. Originally consisting mainly of young men, the border crossers by the early 1980s contained an increasingly high proportion of women and families with children.

North's report asserted that the border crossers took jobs from U.S. residents, depressed wages, and hurt labor unions. About half of those who crossed the border were green card holders, reforms would have to deal with this group. North recommended reducing the number of green card holders, forcing employers to live up to labor laws, and developing plans to improve the border area economically. (Since his report of 1970 much of this was done.) North also wanted to force employers to hire locals.

Mexican government officials, by contrast, claimed that Mexican citizens living along the border and working in the United States spent approximately 60 percent of their incomes in the United States; the remainder was taken back to Mexico. Most border employees appeared to pay state and federal taxes, as well as sales taxes on goods purchased. These taxes and purchases amounted to tens of millions of dollars for each state along the border and for the federal government. For example, ten thousand commuters came into San Diego daily from Mexico in the 1970s; their estimated earnings were $48 million. An estimated $28 million remained in San Diego and $20 million returned to Mexico. In addition, more than 5,500 seasonal workers made their way to San Diego each year. They earned about $13 million and spent about 80 percent of this locally.[15]

Americans, like Mexicans, remained as ambivalent about the commuter system as about any other aspect of immigration. Employers in the border region argued that they needed alien labor; the Mexican authorities realized that the commuters' earnings formed a valuable source of income. Shopkeepers on the United States side of the border did not want interference with their alien customers, especially in communities like San Diego, Nogales, Eagle Pass, Laredo, Hidalgo, and Brownsville, in which retail trade was highly oriented toward Mexican clients and suffered severely whenever the Mexican currency depreciated in value.

The U.S. State Department saw as its primary duty the protection of diplomatic relations between the United States and Mexico, not the interests of American labor. On the other hand, unions and workmen, including Mexican Americans, complained that commuters kept wages down and were hard to organize, and that their presence in the United States increased unemployment, a particularly serious issue at a time (June 1982) when seasonal unemployment in the United States had reached 9.5 percent, representing about 10.5 million Americans. According to labor, and to labor-oriented spokesmen like Senator Edward Kennedy, the commuters' presence in the United States was all the more deleterious to the interests of organized labor because of the high rate of joblessness in the border areas as well as the widespread practice of using the commuters as strikebreakers. (Their use in this capacity was outlawed by federal legislation in 1967, but such laws proved hard to enforce.) To cap it all, the commuter practice made it even more difficult to control illegal immigration.

The precise effects of the commuter traffic on wages are not easy to establish, especially in the border regions that typically suffer from wage rates lower than those in the United States as a whole, as well as from a higher incidence of reported federal wage-law violations. Employers paid little attention to the difference between "wetbacks," residents, and commuters. Despite widespread misconceptions, commuters on the whole labored in much the same kinds of occupation as permanent residents and received more or less the same remuneration given resident workers in the same enterprise.[16] The commuter problem, in other words, can not be solved in isolation, but will have to wait for a more general settlement of the immigration question as a whole.

Hoping to relieve the problem of unemployment, the Mexican government in 1965 established the so-called *maquiladora* (assembly plant) program. This took advantage of provisions in the U.S. tax code permitting foreign-based subsidiaries to assemble abroad products manufactured in the United States, and then to export this merchandise back to the United States, subject only to a restricted tax. By the mid-1970s, the *maquiladoras* had come to employ about 80,000 Mexican workmen along the border, mainly in electronics and textile factories. In 1977, electrical and electronic goods accounted for 38 percent of *maquiladora* production and 63 percent of their labor force. In addition, *maquiladoras* turned out a vast range of other merchandise (sewing machines, aircraft parts, office equipment, and the like). Between 1966 and 1976, the value of *maquiladora* products entering the United States jumped in value from $7 million to more than $1 billion. By 1983, more than 130,000 Mexicans were employed in 600 factories that brought in approximately $2 billion a year to Mexico. *Maquiladoras* turned into Mexico's second- or third-leading dollar earners.

The *maquiladora* program aroused bitter controversy. According to its proponents, Mexico benefited from foreign capital; more Mexicans found jobs than before (especially in such cities as Ciudad Juárez, Nuevo Laredo, and Matamoros, the chief beneficiaries of the program). The workers employed in assembly plants formed part of a stable labor force—not an army of migrant laborers such as the *braceros*. Thousands of Mexican women employed in the *maquiladoras* found economic independence of a new kind and more workers than ever before acquired a regular income. Stable employment led to the emergence of consumer credit to finance local purchases. Participation in a social security program made workers and their families eligible to receive benefits and services otherwise unavailable to them. Mexico acquired an increasing amount of foreign exchange. Workmen employed in the *maquiladoras* had more cash to spend than before; hence the *maquiladoras* benefited shopkeepers on both sides of the border. From the U.S. standpoint, lower production costs in Mexico translated into lower prices for U.S. consumers and overseas trading partners. Moreover, there were clear advantages to the United States in placing such plants just across the border rather than in distant cities.

Juárez and the area across from San Diego developed into the leading *maquiladora* centers. Juárez provided jobs for 40,000 people in 115 factories. By 1973, more than 135 plants were operating in Tecate, Tijuana, and Ensenada, employing 17,191 Mexicans with a payroll of $47 million. San Diego's Mexican links were even tighter. Between 1965 and 1974, an estimated 147.6 million Mexican visitors crossed the border at San Ysidro alone to buy goods and to work in San Diego. In 1979, Mexicans spent an estimated $120 million in San Diego.

According to U.S. businessmen, American workers did not lose jobs as a result of these *maquiladoras*. On the contrary, they created more employment on both sides of the border and they enabled U.S. goods to remain competitive in world markets. *Maquiladoras* also benefited Mexico in a variety of ways. Far from keeping the country in a state of economic dependency, they gradually performed more and more complex operations, thereby improving skills and also producing spin-off industries and services required by the *maquiladoras*.

Critics pleaded a very different case. According to American trade unionists, the *maquiladoras* competed unfairly with American labor by utilizing lower-paid Mexican hands at the expense of American workers. To Mexican nationalists, the *maquiladora* program was one more way of increasing Mexico's economic dependency on the United States. Because of the fragmented nature of assembly work, the men and women employed in the *maquiladoras* would not develop new skills. The so-called spread effects of the *maquiladoras* were minimal; the assembly plants used U.S. equipment; their output went mainly to the United States; and a high proportion of the workers spent their income across the border without benefiting Mexico.

The *maquiladoras*, said their Mexican critics, had other disadvantages. They did not lessen unemployment in the border zone because any absolute increase in jobs would merely attract more immigrants from the interior. The *maquiladoras* operated under a form of internal colonialism, for the new factories remained under the control of foreign corporations, their ability to set industrial policy undermined Mexican sovereignty, weakened local initiative, and represented yet another departure from the ideals of the Mexican revolution.

We do not share these assumptions. We are impressed by the ways in which foreign investment and foreign skills helped to promote manufacturing enterprises in other countries in the past. During the early nineteenth century, the rise of manufacturing in Belgium, the Rhenish Province of Prussia, and northern France owed a considerable debt to British expatriate enterprise which, at the time, incurred similar criticism. As we see it, both sides have gained: Mexican workmen have a stake in getting new jobs; and American workmen have a vested interest in enriching their neighbors because poor men cannot buy merchandise that Americans produce. Also, there are clear advantages to the United States from a program that places new industrial plants just across the border rather than in a distant land overseas. As an American manager of a *maquiladora* put it: "If we were located in the Far East, there wouldn't be a plant in Tucson fabricating our components, nor would we be buying our materials from General Tire and other companies in the U.S." From the Mexican standpoint, there were evident advantages to an arrangement that provided new jobs. For all their complaints, Mexican nationalists would have been even more displeased had the Americans decided to shut down the *maquiladoras* and prohibited investment across the border.

Given the facts of interdependence, what policy should the United States pursue with regard to the borderlands? Policy will depend on the manner in which the border is perceived. Some regard the border as a barrier that separates the United States from Mexico. The border, in their view, should be controlled to avoid leaks that might adversely affect the territorial integrity of the United States. Such, at least in theory, is the approach of government agencies that deal with immigration, naturalization, and customs, and of lobbies that favor immigration control and zero population growth.

A very different view is held by a scholar like Ellwyn R. Stoddard, who looks upon the border as a binational zone, stamped to some extent with a culture of its own, part Hispanic, part Anglo-American.[17] The Mexican and U.S. frontier lands are tied by trade, migration, and culture; they also face common problems of a prosaic kind—control of rabies, pollution, and mosquitos; crime; housing; the allocation of water; the provision of transport; industrial development; tourism; and so on.

The border is not well served by existing modes of governance. As Stoddard points out, the U.S. borderlands wield but scanty political influence; border policies for the United States are mainly formulated by people who live far from the region, commonly in the Northeast. Conditions are not much better in Mexico, where the administration is highly centralized and where policy makers in Mexico City have only a limited understanding of border culture. Policymakers are often ill acquainted with traditional frontier customs; they are naive in assuming that the reports obtained from local authorities accurately portray existing border conditions or that statutes framed in ignorance of border conditions in fact meet with compliance on the spot.[18]

To cope with these problems, the border in practice has developed a modified law of its own, made up of informal local arrangements and compromises. The most superficial observer who joins a throng of Mexican labor migrants crossing the border on foot through the winding tunneled crosswalk that links San Ysidro on the U.S. side to Tijuana in Mexico can test the validity of Stoddard's observations. If the tourist on foot should attempt to present his passport to the border guards (as he would on arriving by air in Mexico City or New York), he is apt to be waved on.

How can these issues be resolved? According to Stoddard's sensible advice, the United States should change its laws to extend technical services into the southern "buffer zone" in Mexico. (At the time of this writing, such a pragmatic transborder system worked only for aircraft in a 30 mile zone on each side of the border, within which pilots from either country might freely use the airspace.) The extent and cost of such an arrangement would have to be negotiated between the United States and Mexico.

By the early 1980s, a number of agencies were facilitating cooperation along the border. These included the International Boundary and Water Commission and the Pan-American Health Organization, sponsor of the U.S.–Mexico Border Health Association; both of these operated on an official level. There was informal exchange through such bodies as the Customs Brokers Association, chambers of commerce, the Border State University Consortium for Latin America (a consortium of universities that provides information about border problems), as well as the Association of Borderland Scholars. Examples of binational planning include the Railroad Relocation Project in Brownsville, Texas, a program promoting cooperation between Southern California and the Baja Norte, and the joint work conducted by civic and religious groups.[19]

Even more essential is cooperation between local authorities on both sides of the border. This is particularly difficult to organize because Mexican and U.S. cities, counties and *municipios* differ widely in their respective powers. Mexican cities might well need a body such as the Organization of U.S. Border Cities and Counties. Mexican *municipios*, however, lack the autonomy and the financial powers enjoyed by U.S. cities. When local agencies cooperate, they all too often do so by circumventing official channels. As Stoddard puts it, they have to create new border customs. This aspect of borderland expertise creates enormous disparities between the reality of how border jurisdictions work and official reports and statistics that are brought in from federal or state officials. On a daily basis, local border officials carry on foreign policy with their sister cities and counterparts through a network of informal linkages in the public and private sectors.

Far from discouraging this state of affairs, U.S. and Mexican policy alike should—in our view—promote such procedures by giving more power to local authorities, including the right to make effective local arrangements. U.S. and Mexican policymakers would do well, as we see it, to study effective transborder cooperation of the kind that ties the Austrian Bundesländer, German Länder, and Swiss cantons in the triangle linking the three adjoining countries along their shared frontier in Central Europe, to the common benefit of all.

Chapter 9

Immigration, Legal and Illegal

The history of the Western world is a history of migration. During the nineteenth century, Germans, Jews, Englishmen, Irishmen, and others sought homes for themselves overseas—in the United States, Australia, Canada, Argentina, and elsewhere. During the twentieth century, the highly industrialized countries themselves attracted an increasing number of newcomers from the rural periphery from countries as far afield as Turkey, Algeria, Sicily, and elsewhere. During the long era of prosperity, from the end of World War II to the 1970s, the pace of immigration increased, and by 1984 the countries of Western Europe faced the difficult task of integrating an estimated total of fifteen million foreign residents. There also was the problem of how to deal with illegal immigrants (amounting in 1984 to an estimated 400,000 in France alone). This inflow paralleled mass immigration of Mexicans, Puerto Ricans, Central Americans, and many others into the United States.

The International Setting

The guest workers in Western Europe at first received a hearty welcome. They took jobs the local people did not want and they relieved a pressing labor shortage in the receiving countries. The immigrants learned new skills and accumulated capital that helped their own countries modernize. The worldwide recession that began in the 1970s and continued into the 1980s caused a reassessment of these optimistic views. As unemployment increased both in Western Europe and the United States, foreigners increasingly were seen as a threat to indigenous workers. Host countries began to doubt the wisdom of letting temporary workers bring in their families and use the generous welfare services of the state. The costs of providing housing, education, and health and other social services to immigrants appeared ever more onerous. Experts had long maintained that the migrants (mostly young, single men) did not receive as much in services as they paid in taxes. But, as the migrants brought in families, the use of social services increased both in Western Europe and the United States. The migrants themselves acquired new wants and new aspirations.

In general, the newcomers continued to work in certain industries and occupations. Most found jobs in small companies and businesses, performing manual work (88 percent in West Germany, 77 percent in France, 73 percent in the United States). They tended to concentrate in construction and manufacturing work; they also worked as domestic servants and as waiters and cooks in hotels and restaurants, and, to a lesser extent, as farm laborers, especially in the United States.[1]

Initially, most of these newcomers looked upon themselves as temporary sojourners. Illegal Mexican workers caught by the Immigration and Naturalization Service (INS) stated that they returned home about every six months.[2] But, in spite of this initial expectation, more and more tended to stay. The composition of the illegal immigrant population in the United States gradually began to resemble more and more the makeup of the legal immigrants. Originally, most of the undocumented aliens in the United States were young and single men. A case study of nonapprehended aliens conducted in Los Angeles among clients of the One Stop Immigration Center found that nearly one-third were women, many of them with family ties in the United States. The clients of One Stop Immigration Center were, on the average, between 25 and 30 years old; many had stable work histories in the United States; more than 70 percent were married. They no longer fitted the conventional image of the young unwedded male who took the trip *al norte* as a temporary expedient.[3]

The recipient countries developed diverse and contradictory methods to cope with the resulting problems. There were attempts to assimilate immigrants by compulsory language classes (adopted by local authorities in Sweden, for instance, where immigrants by 1984 made up an estimated 9 percent of the population) or by on-the-job training as part of a comprehensive labor market policy. Some Western European experts proposed to admit only single men for short-term contracts; others suggested that immigrants be paid to leave (a policy adopted in West Germany, where, by 1984, about three hundred thousand had accepted favorable repatriation terms). A more radical method was to keep out foreigners altogether. The recession of the 1980s led to a crackdown on immigration in countries as diverse as France, West Germany, and Mexico. In France, François Mitterand, before coming to power, called for a liberalized immigration policy. After attaining the presidency, he in fact tightened the immigration laws, strengthened the border police, embarked on a policy of "repulsion," ended an amnesty program adopted in 1981, and set fines for employers convicted of hiring illegal aliens.

Mexico adopted an even more rigid policy. In 1983, the Mexican government limited the number of refugees it would accept from Latin American and Caribbean countries on the grounds that illegal immigrants from Central America were taking jobs from the native born. The Mexican government increased patrols along its southern border, tightened visa regulations, and began to strictly monitor refugee activities. The Mexicans in fact adopted the very policies for which they criticized the United States, even though the number of refugees involved in Mexico (150,000) was a small fraction of the number of illegal immigrants that came to the United States. The U.S. record in receiving and caring for refugees was much better than Mexico's—a point studiously ignored by Mexican censors of this country.

The United States, for its part, confronts a special problem not shared by any other country. The border between the United States and Mexico divides a wealthy from a poor country; the wage gap between the two countries is the largest that exists between any two states in the world sharing a common border. Mexico's very proximity to the United States facilitates immigration, legal and illegal, from Mexico. So does the enormous economic wage disparity (by a ratio of nearly 8 to 1) that continues to exist between the United States and its southern neighbor.

One difference between the United States and other host countries receiving immigrants lies in the treatment the immigrants get and in their numbers. The United States attracts more legal immigrants than all other countries of the world combined. Cubans, Nicaraguans, Vietnamese, Cambodians, Poles, and East Germans all seek asylum from the political and economic oppression associated with Marxism-Leninism. Mexicans, El Salvadoreans, Columbians, and Argentinians, as well as many others, look for economic and social advancement *al norte*. The United States is infinitely more humane than most countries and more willing to receive newcomers than almost any other country in the world; the United States is also more permissive in the administration of its immigration laws and in the facilities granted by courts to litigants. Whatever the deficiencies of the United States immigration laws, it is obvious that no man in his right mind would prefer to be an illegal Guatemalan immigrant in Mexico, or even an illegal Jamaican immigrant in Canada, to being an illegal immigrant in the United States.[4]

Numbers

No one knows how many people cross the border every year from Mexico to the United States, nor how many stay. In regard to legal immigration, the figures show a considerable increase from the 1950s. Between 1951 and 1960, 299,811 Mexicans legally entered the United States. Between 1961 and 1970, the number had risen to 459,937. Legal immigration from Mexico continues at a high rate. More newcomers

legally entered the United States from Mexico during the 1970s than
in any prior decade, despite new restrictions by which the United States
in 1977 kept down the quota of any one Western Hemisphere country
to a total of 20,000 persons. (This limit did not apply to the admission
of immediate relatives of U.S. citizens; the number of such close family
members continued to snowball as newly enfranchised citizens in turn
asked for admission of their own, often numerous, kinfolk.[5])

Far more numerous are the illegal, "undocumented aliens" who every
year enter the United States either by crossing the border surreptitiously
or by presenting fraudulent documents. These newcomers are of many
different nationalities—including Vietnamese, Cubans, Koreans, Pak-
istanis, and Jamaicans—although Mexicans and other Spanish-speaking
people from Latin America account for most of them. The United States,
during the 1970s and 1980s, has become the most important haven for
illegal immigrants and refugees.

Economic reasons are the main attraction, especially in Mexico, for
the largest number of illegal immigrants to the United States. During
the Nixon administration, government spokesmen variously estimated
the number of Mexicans illegally present in the United States to be
between six and twelve million. Under the Carter administration, the
Census Bureau estimated this figure to be between four and six million.
According to a statement made in September 1984 by the Immigration
and Naturalization Service, about three million illegal immigrants entered
the United States each year, most of whom returned to their respective
home countries. In 1983, the service arrested more than one million
aliens attempting to enter the United States illegally. Mexican government
studies put the number of "undocumented" Mexicans at between less
than half a million to even more than one million present in the United
States at any one time, depending upon the season. David M. Heer,
an American scholar, believes that official estimates in the past have
grossly overestimated the number of illegal aliens in this country. He
argues that conjectural figures accepted in the past have not taken into
account the fact that the net flow of newcomers is always less than the
gross flow. According to his findings, the annual net flow of undocumented
aliens between 1970 and 1975 ranged only from 82,300 to 232,400
persons. Estimates with such a wide range of variation clearly have
little practical value; in some cases, they depend more on the writer's
political proclivities than on well-documented research.[6]

In striving for more accurate figures, however, the researcher faces
formidable obstacles. Illegal immigrants do not advertise their presence
in the United States, nor do the guides who take the migrants across
the border, the friends and relatives who shelter them, or the employers
who provide them with jobs. The figures collected by the INS concerning

the number of illegal Mexican aliens apprehended in the United States have a somewhat higher claim to credibility. They show a stupendous increase from 1965, the year in which the *bracero* program expired, bringing to an end the legal but temporary labor migration of previous years. Between 1965 and 1979, the number of apprehensions by the INS rose from 55,300 to 976,667.[7] By 1985, Mexico's economic situation had further deteriorated. Burdened by a huge foreign debt and a high rate of inflation, stricken by terrible earthquakes, and loaded by a huge bureaucracy, the Mexican economy was tottering, and emigration to the United States seemed likely to accelerate.

By this time, illegal immigration had reached what might be called a critical mass. The INS was overwhelmed by numbers. Elaborate networks had developed to help the newcomers. Relatives, friends, and well-wishers provided accurate information with regard to ways and means of getting into the United States, finding jobs, and obtaining schooling, medical care, welfare, and unemployment benefits. At the same time, there was an occupational and demographic shift. During the 1950s, most "wetbacks" were young single men, with scanty schooling, who usually looked for jobs in agriculture.[8] By the 1980s, the newcomers from Mexico had become better educated (80 percent were literate in Spanish and had 8 years of education). In addition, many more older men and women and children had come to the United States. Long-term residency in the United States increasingly was the norm.[9] Illegal aliens at the same time began to move into more highly skilled and better paid jobs. Some of them also benefited from the increasing sophistication of a new underground industry that specialized in the manufacture of forged documents of all kinds—social security cards, birth certificates, testimonials, and the like. Such offenses were not generally regarded as high priority cases by U.S. attorneys, who preferred to deal with far more serious crimes.

Although the immigration laws contain both civil and criminal provisions, their enforcement continues to be hampered by the ambivalent attitude of the United States population as a whole. In theory, Americans say they want their immigration laws observed. (A 1982 Roper poll states that 80 percent of those questioned wanted immigration reduced in its entirety; 91 percent supported a crackdown on illegal immigrants.) But, at the same time, the average American looks upon most illegal aliens as hard-working job seekers. As Edwin Harwood has reported, denunciations of illegal aliens usually are made only when the alien personally troubles or offends some individual who "gets even" with "Juan Martínez" or "Pablo Gonzales" by reporting him to the INS. Personal grudges rather than the desire to enforce the immigration law apparently account for most tips received by the INS.[10]

In addition, the illegal immigrant's cause enjoys support from most of the press, from civil rights lawyers, and from church groups, some of which provide shelter and other help. The churchs' activities in some ways parallel those of the "underground railway" that hid runaway slaves before the Civil War. To many liberals (and many Latin Americans), the United States immigration laws lack legitimacy, a criterion normally not applied by such critics to the immigration laws of foreign, including Latin American, countries.

Inspired by a strong commitment to civil rights, the federal courts during the 1960s and 1970s increasingly sided with groups previously neglected, or supposedly neglected, by American society: minorities, the poor, or those criminals regarded by psychiatrists as sick in mind. The courts, however, simply reflect the ambivalence felt by the average American, who might well remember an aged grandparent of his own who speaks broken English. Personal interviews indicate that even those Americans who want strict enforcement of the immigration laws as a general practice are apt to hedge when it comes to someone they know; most Americans in fact assume that an illegal alien who has lived and worked in this country for a considerable time and who has acquired property and public standing should be allowed to remain in the United States, even though such preferential treatment in effect discriminates against those foreigners who obey the law and wait patiently in the queue for a visa.

What sort of person is the average illegal immigrant? There are illegal immigrants of many types and nationalities. A high proportion comes from Latin America. According to David M. Heer's estimates, 39 percent of all resident aliens born in Latin America were undocumented, and 49 percent of all resident aliens were born in Mexico.[11] Many of these newcomers are unmarried young men who are somewhat better educated than the ordinary Mexican; about two-thirds of them come from villages, mostly in central Mexico; about one-third come from urban areas; only 11 percent originate in the Mexican border regions. Such are the conclusions of an authoritative study carried out in 1978–79 by the National Center of Labor Information and Statistics, an agency of the Mexican government. According to its findings, eight out of ten undocumented Mexican workers are men; half of them are 30 years of age or younger; 55 percent are married; they have an average of five years of schooling. They primarily seek work in California (47 percent), Texas (27 percent), Illinois (7 percent), and Colorado and New Mexico (6 percent), with the rest going to other parts of the United States. Before coming to this country, 60 percent had worked in agriculture, about 8 percent in white-collar jobs; but, in all cases, they earned much less than in the United States. Having settled here, they find jobs in farming (36.1

percent), blue-collar occupations (36 percent), and services (23.5 percent); only 4.5 percent work in offices.[12] The nationwide figures, however, conceal the extent of diversity. By 1982, for instance, small business had become the primary employer of undocumented alien workers from Mexico in northern California. Mexicans no longer worked only as gardeners, kitchen helpers, or nursery employees; they also had found jobs in the electronics industry, the restaurant business, and construction enterprises, all of which had become heavily dependent on Hispanic labor.

What sort of lives do the illegals live? Again, conditions vary enormously. Some (those who stay) have become fully integrated into the local community; they own their own houses and hold responsible positions. No one knows that they lack the proper documentation, and the local police have better things to do than to investigate their immigrant status. Many more undocumented wokers live as a part of an alienated subculture. These people feel stigmatized as job stealers, thieves, and vagrants while assigned the hardest and most unpleasant jobs; they dread being apprehended by undercover agents of the INS or by the police.[13] The most recent arrivals suffer from a special sense of insecurity; those who have stayed in this country for a lengthy period and have close relatives and friends to help them in their underground existence have less apprehension regarding the future. Illegal immigrants are far more likely to believe that their employers cheat them than legal residents. The undocumented workers do indeed constitute an alienated group.

Despite widespread public misconceptions, the bulk of the undocumented workers do not engage in crime. On the contrary, they wish to avoid trouble with the police or to be conspicuous in any form. Some newcomers even fear to go out to eat, to visit a bar, or even to see a movie. They generally avoid getting drunk in public; they try not to get into fights or drug dealing. Most of them dream of returning to Mexico one day to set up a small business of their own, but few of them in fact go back. On the contrary, they keep coming, often at great risk. For all its manifold disadvantages, the United States still seems a land of opportunity where the *mojados* can escape from poverty.

Illegal immigration is likely to continue to increase as public knowledge spreads through the network of friends and kinsmen regarding the changing nature of jobs in the United States, the INS's administrative weaknesses, the nature of U.S. legal loopholes, and the extent of social and welfare services an illegal alien may claim. The INS's hands are further tied by a lack of sufficient judges, courts and jails; hence most aliens are permitted a "voluntary return." The FBI, moreover, lacks facilities to fingerprint all the aliens who have crossed the border. The increase in the flow of illegal immigrants has contributed to changing the attitudes of the courts. In the past, when fewer illegal aliens entered the country, the INS was able to prosecute more illegal aliens for criminal offenses than at present. During the 1970s and early 1980s, however, the courts increasingly have handed down rulings adverse to the INS's enforcement activities. The "due process" requirements for successful convictions have become more onerous from the INS's standpoint.[14] Unless the offender pleads guilty, a public defender must be hired, the accused must be apprised of his rights; and court actions are drawn out endlessly.

For many illegal aliens, voluntary return and even deportation have become no more than an unpleasant nuisance as the use of falsified documents continues to spread and as the immigrants and their advisers become more skilled in using the law. For instance, a reputed alien can simply claim U.S. citizenship, thereby throwing the burden of disproving his claim on the INS, which has more pressing claims on its duties.[15]

Statistics concerning the total number of illegal aliens are thus difficult to collect in the United States. But even if scholars had at their disposal more accurate documentation regarding the extent of illegal immigration, its demographic consequences would be difficult to assess. Many Mexican immigrants, both legal and illegal, do not in fact desire to remain permanently in the United States. A field study of undocumented Mexican workers on a Texas ranch concluded that the average *indocumentado* has no intention of remaining in the United States; he has come to find a job that is better paid than in Mexico. By obtaining employment in the United States, he can save money to support his family in Mexico. But he does not wish to cut his ties with Mexico, and he does not wish to surrender his Mexican citizenship; he would rather live in Mexico than in the United States. (In this respect, Mexican labor migrants today do not differ very much from those southern and eastern European peasants and workmen who came to the United States just before World War I, more than 55 percent of whom returned home.)[16]

What of the long-term demographic effects of this immigration? Mexican immigrants, indeed the Hispanic population as a whole in the United States, have a higher rate of fertility than Anglo-Americans. Spanish speakers will account for an increasingly large proportion of the U.S. population. Between 1970 and 1980 alone, the nation's Mexican-descended population nearly doubled; at the same time, they became more geographically dispersed than they had been previously. According to Census Bureau reports published in 1982, the Spanish-speaking population in the United States in 1980 was 14.6 million, with striking growth rates in California, Texas, and Florida, and large-scale Hispanic concentrations in the cities of El Paso, San Antonio, Los Angeles, San Diego, San Jose, New York City, Miami, Denver, and Houston.

As a result of immigration, both legal and illegal, and of natural population increases on the part of Hispanics, the United States has experienced a remarkable demographic change. The Hispanic growth rate in California amounted to about four times the general rate. Most notable was the increasing growth rate of Hispanics in or near the Los Angeles Basin—Los Angeles, Orange County, Riverside, San Bernadino, and Ventura.) Texas also witnessed an Hispanic growth rate higher than the rest of the population, even though the state also attracted many immigrants of non-Hispanic origin. The most spectacular increase in a major urban area occurred in Harris County (Houston). Hispanics came to form a majority of the population in 25 counties, and close to the majority in an additional 15 counties. New York City likewise saw an increased Hispanic influx; although that city lost something like one million people during the 1970s, Hispanics increased by more than 300,000 and, by 1980, accounted for about one-fifth of the city's population. New Jersey received increasing numbers of Puerto Ricans and Cubans from New York. In the Midwest, Hispanics were concentrated in Chicago, where they formed about 15 percent of the population. And Hispanics occupied an equally important position in Florida, especially the southern part.

It was only in New Mexico, Arizona, and Colorado—all traditional areas of Hispanic settlement—that the Hispanic growth rate failed to equal that of other communities. In New Mexico, the Hispanics' rate of increase was surpassed by an Anglo-American influx from outside. Most of the English-speaking newcomers settled in Albuquerque; the Hispanics in the southern part, on the other hand, began to gain on the English-speaking population, perhaps because of the immigration of Hispanics from nearby El Paso and Mexico. In Colorado, the bulk of the Hispanic people was concentrated in the Denver region and, to a lesser extent, in Colorado Springs, Greeley, and Pueblo. Because of the significant number of Anglo-Americans who settled in the state, the Hispanic growth rate did not keep pace with their neighbors'. The same is true in Arizona, where Anglo-American immigration caused their growth rates to outstrip the Mexican-Americans'. Overall, however, there was a striking demographic shift in the Hispanic Americans' favor.

This population growth has led to widespread fears that the United States is being "overrun," that the country faces "Latinization," or that it will ultimately turn into a Third World country. Existing growth figures, however, need to be kept in perspective. During the 1970s, the total number of all legal immigrants as a percentage of the decennial population growth amounted to 21.9 percent—a considerable figure indeed—nearly one-third higher than the figure attained during the 1960s

(16.5 percent). Yet, this percentage was much less than that attained during the first decade of the 1900s (39.6 percent).[17]

Nor are there any statistical indications that in the future Spanish speakers will take over the country. Projections made by demographers regarding the Spanish-speaking population vary; they depend on changing assumptions made with regard to future fertility and migration trends. Hispanics certainly will form a major part of some states, including California. A 1982 report by the State Department of Parks and Recreation concluded that Hispanics would, by the year 2000, total 25.6 percent of California's population compared to 40.4 percent for non-Hispanic whites, 33.9 percent for blacks, and 32.7 for Asians.[18] In regard to the Hispanic population by the year 2000, even the highest alternatives chosen for the purpose of estimating the future population growth of Hispanics between 1980 and 2000 assume a growth of only from 6.4 percent to 9.9 percent of the total U.S. population—hardly an increase of inordinate proportions.[19]

Pro-immigration Arguments

No nation is as ambivalent about immigration as the United States. The French in the past have given refuge to millions of foreigners, but any newcomer who wants to earn a living in France without being able to speak unaccentuated and grammatically correct French finds himself an object of paternal correction at best and a victim of derision and discrimination at worst. Swiss and Germans are glad to recruit guest workers on contract as long as times are good, but even those educated in Central Europe are apt to complain of being overrun by foreigners in terms that would be characterized as racist in the United States. Citizenship in the mind of the American public represents voluntary allegiance to the United States, an allegiance that any naturalized foreigner can fully share. Henry Kissinger can describe himself as an American in a way that Benjamin Disraeli (a Jew) and George Frederick Handel (a native-born German naturalized in Britain) could not describe themselves as Englishmen. Immigrants and their descendants constitute only a minor proportion of the citizens of Western European countries; with the single exception of the American Indians, every inhabitant of the United States is an immigrant or is of immigrant extraction.

Accordingly, there is a substantial body of opinion in the United States that welcomes extensive, sometimes unlimited, immigration. Like many political alliances, the pro-immigration forces are strangely assorted. Some Chicano nationalists, for instance, argue that the United States has no right to limit Mexican immigration into the Southwest because those territories were stolen from Mexico by the Anglos in the first place. In their view, Mexican immigration will strengthen the Chicano community within the United States and thereby aid the cause of radicalism. At the very least, the argument continues, the U.S. immigration problem is an international one that cannot be solved by unilateral U.S. action. The Mexican government has even demanded to be consulted over U.S. plans to restrict immigration from Mexico.

Some conservatives also value both legal and illegal immigration, but on very different grounds. In arguments expressed privately rather than publicly, they praise the Mexican immigrants' willingness to work hard and their refusal to join unions. Some opponents of feminism hope that improperly educated or uneducated Mexican women will bear many children and that these women will respect and obey their husbands. According to conservatives committed to the view that a high birthrate is desirable, the demographic future of the United States would be in danger without the constant influx of new immigrants, whose presence in the United States prevents the American population from aging too quickly and from ultimately declining in numbers.[20]

Other pro-immigrant arguments stem from findings of sociologists who argue that immigrants tend to be more motivated and therefore more apt to succeed than their stay-at-home countrymen or than native-born Americans. Thomas Sowell has found that blacks who migrate to the United States from the West Indies have higher average earnings than native-born black Americans. European immigrants do equally well. Barry Chiswick, an American economist, has ascertained that despite language and cultural barriers, European immigrants on the average surpass the earnings of the white native-born Americans within fifteen years after arriving in the United States.[21]

Immigration in economic terms represents a transfer of skills received without cost to the receiving country at the expense of the immigrant's country of origin which developed the immigrant's mind and muscle. A high proportion of legal immigrants admitted during the 1970s occupy well-paid professional and managerial positions; some critics of the United States even blame Washington for encouraging a "brain drain" that deprives foreign countries, especially those of the Third World, of desperately needed skills. Illegal immigrants have much less formal training in science, technology, and management than legal immigrants; but, even the so-called unskilled (the fruit pickers and laundry workers) need physical and moral aptitudes that must be developed at someone's expense.

The strongest support for pro-immigration policies comes from free enterprise economists. Although immigrants encounter widespread resentment on the grounds that they take work away from Americans, these fears are baseless, at least in the long run. Far from taking jobs, the newcomers in fact create new work both for themselves and others; the immigrants require housing, shoes to wear, cars or bikes to get to work, bread to eat, and books to read. Furthermore, in many cases the immigrants do jobs that Americans will not or cannot do. How many Americans want to pick fruit in California or cut spinach in Michigan? How many Americans want to do apartment-project landscaping or housekeeping chores or restaurant work in any city in the United States? Without immigrant labor, many growers say, American housewives could not so readily afford the grapes, oranges, lettuce they now buy in the supermarkets. And prices in service industries and the restaurant business are kept lower because of low-paid labor.

The advocates of immigration admit that some unskilled Americans suffer from the competition of foreigners, although the correlation is unclear. (U.S. cities with a high proportion of Hispanic immigrants do not suffer from higher rates of unemployment than cities with a scanty Latin population.) But native-born U.S. workers should not complain too much; they enjoy a competitive advantage over newcomers because they already know the language, the culture, and the job. Nor are American workers simply helpless victims of circumstances. Faced with competition, they have new incentives to find better jobs or acquire further training. To the extent that the wages of unskilled men and women fall, the benefits of additional training become greater. Consequently, immigration leads to a greater self-investment in education.

The spokesmen for the free flow of immigrants discount opposition from the zero growth population lobby, which now forms an important segment of the anti-immigration alliance. According to this lobby's critics, there is no link between population density on the one hand and poverty on the other. Both Singapore and Hong Kong are densely populated city-states; nevertheless, their respective populations are both better fed and more prosperous than those of Mali, Niger, or Chad, in which small populations have vast acres at their disposal. The causes of hunger do not derive simply from overpopulation, which itself is a question-begging term. Hunger all too often is man made. Deprivation is rife in Uganda, not because Uganda's land resources are inadequate but because its relative prosperity was shattered by internal dissensions, tyranny, foreign invasion, and the consequent breakdown of authority.

The advocates of immigration further argue that, far from placing an undue burden on the U.S. welfare system, the immigrants contribute as much or more than they take out. Only aliens legally admitted to residence in the United States are entitled to participate in public assistance programs; illegal aliens are not eligible for such aid (though in fact many receive it). Further, the advocates argue that undocumented workers are unable to collect significant amounts of welfare. As Julian

Simon points out, immigrants do not normally bring parents or grand-parents along to be supported by social security; hence, the immigrants' contributions benefit native-born senior citizens without adding greatly to the current number of beneficiaries.[22] The welfare system, moreover, is in trouble. As the U.S. population ages, there will not be enough young workers to keep the system going by the end of the century (unless the United States makes profound changes). Far from discouraging the influx of young workers, we should welcome these men and women and incorporate them into the welfare system.[23]

Because the debate on this issue is bitter and involved, some detailed studies deserve to be cited. A Department of Labor investigation reported in 1976 that the particular group of workers under consideration had in fact contributed more to the public coffers than they had taken out (77 percent of the study group reported that they had social security taxes withheld, and 73 percent stated that they had federal income taxes deducted from their earnings; only 27 percent had used hospitals or clinics; 4 percent had collected unemployment insurance; and 5 percent had received welfare payments). A study by the San Diego County Human Resources Agency estimated that the county's annual cost in social services amounted to no more than $2 million, compared to the aliens' yearly tax payments of more than $48 million.[24]

Julian Simon, an American economist, states "From the time of entry until twelve years later, immigrants use substantially less public services than do native families. Then immigrant usage becomes roughly equal to the natives'. After about 2–6 years, immigrant families come to pay as much in taxes as do native families, and after that they pay substantially more . . . Immigrants contribute more to the public coffers than they take away from them."[25] Wayne Cornelius, one of the country's leading experts on immigration, similarly argues that illegal immigrants do not readily seek medical care, primarily for fear of being detected and deported.[26]

Even if restrictionists were to succeed in making the United States impose effective barriers on illegal immigration, the pro-immigrationist argument continues, the social cost would be too heavy. Immigration control is all too apt to reflect merely the controllers' social, racial, or "eugenicist" prejudice.[27] By excluding aliens, moreover, the United States would harm its neighbor. Mexico, in its present economic crisis, would suffer yet another devastating blow if it were deprived of the remittances sent home by illegal as well as legal immigrants to the United States, or if Mexico were to lose the social safety valve furnished by the emigration of young and able-bodied men to the United States.[28] More than 150 years ago, Heinrich Heine, one of the most insightful of German poets, saw the connection between the ability of Germans to emigrate abroad and their consequent failure to stage an effective revolution at home. It is not in the interest of the United States to contribute to a social revolution in Mexico.

The effective control of migration, moreover, would endanger domestic liberty for native-born Americans. Illegals might indeed be stopped at the border if the United States were willing to use East German methods of border control—complete with mine fields, police dogs, barbed-wire fences, and a Berlin Wall surrounding U.S. border cities. But, how many Americans would welcome the methods employed by the GDR's National People's Army and its People's Police? How many Americans would want to carry national identity cards or be under an obligation to report any change of residence to an *Einwohnermeldeamt* (a West German citizens' registration bureau)?

Economic common sense and political equity alike, the argument ends, require a liberal immigration policy. The United States would do better to leave immigration to the unfettered system of supply and demand instead of relying on the designs, however well meant, of planners, politicians, and bureaucrats.

The Case for Restriction

The coalition of those who wish to restrict immigration is as disparate in its composition as the informal alliance of those who favor the newcomers. Critics of an open immigration policy include barroom patriots who dislike foreigners and also many—though not all—trade unionists who regard immigrants as possible competitors. (The International Ladies' Garment Workers Union favors illegals on the grounds that they have helped to revitalize the garment industry. The United Automobile Workers has repeatedly changed its stand on the question.) Other opponents of immigration comprise zero population growth advocates and environmentalists, Mexican employers who dislike having their trained workers moving *al norte*, and traditional American conservatives who assume that the newly enfranchized citizens of Hispanic ancestry will vote for the Democratic Party or, worse still, "Latinize" the United States. The list extends even to Latin nationalists who believe that U.S. capitalism will debase the newcomers. Some Latin intellectuals share the snobbish contempt expressed by Jaime Carrero, a Puerto Rican professor reared in the United States, for the "Jet/Neoriqueño," a young man of dual background, probably a worker who has made money on the mainland, whom the learned writer castigates as an idiot.[29]

But there are more reasonable critics of immigration. They distinguish, for one thing, between legal and illegal immigration. Legal immigration may be acceptable, within bounds. Illegal immigration must be rejected.

As a U.S. Senate report puts it, "Evasion represents such a widespread violation of the immigration law that the viability of the law is called into question."[30] The average illegal immigrant is not a criminal. On the contrary, he or she is a hard-working, sober person who wants to earn an honest living and doesn't have the slightest interest in overthrowing the established order. By its very nature, however, the presence of several million illegal aliens extends the scope of the growing "second economy" in the United States, an economy in which members must operate to some extent outside the legal framework. Worse still, failure to control the U.S. borders encourages serious crime, against the illegal immigrant and may have encouraged the massive smuggling of narcotics from Latin America to the United States. The typical labor migrant, the point bears repeating, has not the slightest connection with the American, Venezuelan, Colombian, Cuban, Corsican, and other gangsters who control the drug traffic. But all residents of the United States suffer in some measure from the sense of illegality promoted by the U.S. failure to enforce its laws.[31]

The INS's inability to effectively deter illegal immigration constitutes a form of discrimination against legal immigrants who comply with the law. Control over the number of newcomers who wish to come to the United States is a matter of national sovereignty. Mexicans or any other foreigners who deny to the United States the right to regulate the entry of aliens on the grounds that this is an international matter proclaim a double standard—one that the governments of Latin American (or European) countries themselves would never adopt.

Nor can Mexicans rightfully claim special privileges of access for their nationals to the southwestern states, though Chicano and some Mexican nationalists do so on the grounds that these lands once belonged to Mexico. The present boundaries of the United States are recognized by international law. Again, we have the double standard. No German, after all, would dare claim the right to migrate to Gdansk (formerly Danzig) or to Kalingrad (formerly Königsberg), on the grounds that these had for centuries been German cities.

The problem of illegal immigration, however, must also be seen in a wider context. The present century has seen an enormous growth of the world's population. Demographers dispute whether the expected population of our planet will crest at 8, 10, or 12 billion, but none doubts that humanity is expanding at an unparalleled rate. Of more significance, the rise in the world's population is spatially uneven. The peoples in many parts of the Caribbean Basin, Central and South America, Asia, and Africa are experiencing growth of a particularly striking kind. (Latin America and the Caribbean, between them, now have more than 350 million people to feed.) Mexico's 67 million people have an astonishing birthrate of nearly 3.5 percent; if present growth rates continue, Mexico will double its population within 22 years.)[32] Transport facilities have vastly improved over the last 30 years; the transistor radio, cheap newsprint, and television programs increasingly familiarize the peoples of the Third World with the opportunities offered by the United States. So does the informal information network created by immigrants already resident in the United States. By the early 1980s, Mexican immigrants were being joined by newcomers from Haiti, Colombia, and Nigeria; even Bangladeshis were beginning to enter the United States illegally, having exhausted their asylum claims in West Germany.[33] The spread of Marxism-Leninism in Central America has created a more immediate problem much closer to the United States. If these neighboring states experience continued civil war and revolution, then the present inflows, still modest at present, could become a torrent.

According to scholars David North and Allen LeBel, present immigration policies will lead to a two-class society in which much of the most unpleasant labor in the country will be done by illegal foreigners.[34] Unlike the Polish and Irish navvies, who did so much of the pick-and-shovel work of this country during the nineteenth century, undocumented aliens will not be eligible for citizenship; they will form a permanent underclass—serfs in what is supposed to be a free and egalitarian society. Lacking legal status, they will be much more easily subject to exploitation than native-born or legally admitted aliens. The new underclass will depress wages for the native-born unskilled, especially the blacks; the mere presence of illegal aliens will discourage technical innovation and the multiplication of labor-saving devices in industry.[35]

Given the absence of reliable statistics, no one can be quite sure how far the underclass argument applies. Not all illegal aliens are poor or exploited; a substantial number now work in relatively well-paid jobs. Nevertheless, investigations by Mexican as well as by U.S. scholars give general support to those who fear not only the emergence of a new group of underprivileged people but also further competition against native-born citizens who lack skills and ambition.

The most important restrictionist arguments, however, hinge on the issue of the welfare state. During the "new immigration" at the end of the last century and the beginning of this one newcomers generally were left to their own devices. The poverty stricken among them received assistance from members of their own ethnic groups—through the benevolence of friends, fraternal lodges, lay organizations, churches, temples, or charitable societies. Powerful political organizations, such as Tammany Hall in New York, disbursed funds in support of their clients, but there was no welfare state in the present sense of the term.

Even Franklin Roosevelt's New Deal operated within narrow limits by present-day standards.

During the 1960s and 1970s, poverty programs in the United States expanded in an extraordinary fashion. Between 1959 and 1975, the total transfer payments to the poor in the form of housing subsidies, food subventions, and medical aid alone rose from $997.6 million to $14,072.5 million.[36] In the same period, the courts widened the range of those legally entitled to receive welfare. The Supreme Court, for instance, removed residency as a requirement for welfare eligibility. In 1982, in an even more important decision, the Supreme Court invalidated a Texas state law that withheld public funds from the education of illegal aliens. This decision was likely to force state and local authorities into additional expenditures and to set off further lawsuits obligating state and local authorities to furnish additional social services to illegal aliens.[37] At the same time, the courts weakened the exclusionary criterion of becoming "a public charge," a criterion previously used to keep out undesirable immigrants.

The problem was further complicated by tax and welfare frauds. Cheating, of course, was not invented by foreigners. Political scientists of all hues agree that an expanding welfare system and a growing tax burden increase the temptations to citizens of whatever ethnic ancestry to maximize the benefits received, regardless of their contribution, and to minimize the payments entailed under the system. Immigrants, both legal and illegal, are no exception to this rule. According to statements made by individual Internal Revenue Service (IRS) agents, many single Mexican men, for example, claim numerous deductions for family members. However, the IRS lacks the capability to investigate the claims made by transient aliens, especially when these would entail inquiries in Mexico. Many aliens unlawfully present in this country use bogus names and social security numbers. Many more—no one knows how many—make use of public hospitals or draw Aid For Dependent Children payments for children not born in the United States, an illegal procedure. When investigations are conducted through special screening projects to uncover welfare use by illegals, claims made by unauthorized aliens turn up in sufficient numbers to warrant concern.

The extent of such claims is difficult to evaluate in statistical terms. Illegitimate welfare claims are widespread, though no one knows their exact numbers. Scholars have drawn attention to the laxity that characterizes many welfare administration agencies and to the manner in which many welfare administrators actually discourage their clients from taking so-called dead-end jobs that would keep them off the welfare rolls. Moreover, there are good reasons for questioning research findings, arrived at in the mid–1970s, that purport to show how illegal immigrants put more into the welfare system than they took out. The samples used in the mid–1970s were apt to be statistically skewed.[38] They derived primarily from surveys of illegal aliens apprehended by the INS. By far the greatest number consisted of healthy young men in employment, men whose families usually remained in Mexico. A statistician would naturally expect from such a group a low incidence of welfare utilization and a high degree of tax withholding (which is involuntary on the worker's part). Many of them, moreover, arrived in the United States at the time of their apprehension, hence they had not yet gained either the opportunity or the requisite knowledge to become involved in welfare programs. No departmental records produced by government agencies were used in these studies; the data on tax payments and the utilization of welfare services in fact came from the illegal immigrants themselves and from informants who had a vested interest in understating the extent of the services they had used.

Studies made since 1979, by scholars including Maurice Van Arsdol, arrived at very different results in regard to the illegal aliens' proclivity to make use of social services.[39] These investigations dealt with un-apprehended aliens who, though unlawfully resident in the United States, had become more thoroughly integrated into the general population and were more representative of today's illegal residents as a whole than their predecessors. Not surprisingly, men and women habituated to life in the United States had begun to make use of its welfare facilities. Van Arsdol's study used data concerning a relatively stable group of illegal immigrants from Mexico, men and women whose mean length of stay in the United States amounted to four years; 12.4 percent of them indicated that they had received some form of welfare. In a more recent study, David Heer surveyed women of Mexican descent who had given birth to children in Los Angeles County hospitals. Heer found that at least 13.3 percent of all live births in Los Angeles County in 1980 and 1981 were to illegal immigrants of Mexican descent. About one-fifth of the women illegally resident in this country indicated that their families used AFDC, food stamps, and Medi-Cal (California's medicaid program).

The figures cited above do not support any stereotypes of the illegal immigrant as merely an idler who comes to the United States to live on the taxpayer's generosity. However, these surveys do show that there is a higher social cost to illegal immigration than that assumed by early investigators. Illegal immigrants of non-Mexican descent were, if anything, more likely to make use of welfare payments than were Mexicans. For instance, a survey of nonapprehended Dominican and Haitian illegals in New York City conducted by Charles Keely and his colleagues indicates that 13 percent of the Haitians and 29 percent of the Dominicans received unemployment insurance—a higher percentage than prevailed for illegal Mexicans.[40]

What of the total cost involved in illegal immigration? Again no one knows the answer. Illegal aliens are now eligible on the national level for benefits such as social security, medicare, income tax credits, workers' compensation, and temporary disability insurance. In some states, there also exist general assistance and temporary disability insurance. The children of illegal immigrants obtain free education; hospital care commonly is provided, and even welfare payments have been made.

Illegal aliens used to shy away from making claims. But recent studies, such as those carried out by David North, have shown that undocumented workers have increasingly become welfare-wise, and have begun to seek transfer payments to an ever-growing extent. The Los Angeles County Department of Public Social Welfare between 1979 and 1980 rejected 19,088 individuals claims because the applicants lacked legal alien status (saving the country an estimated $50 million dollars a year); two years later, the department identified 35,153 ineligible alien claimants. Such claims increased at a rate of more than 30 percent a year in Los Angeles County, despite the fact that they were not being paid. A study published in 1984 by the Washington, D.C.-based Urban Institute found that, overall, Mexican immigrants paid considerably less in state taxes than the state paid in services for them, the difference amounting to an average of $1,739 per household. This difference derived in part from the highly progressive nature of California's tax system, which exacted proportionately much higher tax rates from the rich than from the poor, and from the high proportion of Mexican children per household in comparison with the overall population. The National Council of *La Raza*, in response, noted that the study excluded data regarding the fiscal impact of Mexican immigrants on the federal level. The inclusion of federal data, argued *La Raza*, would lead to a different evaluation, for undocumented immigrants use federally funded programs less than state and locally funded services.[41]

Despite such objections, however, no expert doubted that there were costs to illegal immigration, not only in southern California but also in other parts of the United States. For instance, the state of Illinois in 1982 conducted a one-day sampling of all initial unemployment insurance claims filed by persons presenting an alien identification document. Officials found that 46 percent of the cards presented were counterfeit. The investigators projected that, if the day in question were a typical one (a reasonable assumption to make), illegal aliens using this technique were receiving unemployment insurance benefits at the rate of $66.2 million a year.[42]

Los Angeles County is unusual in having evolved an effective and relatively inexpensive technique for identifying illegal aliens among the hundreds of thousands of applicants for welfare, a technique worthy of study by other jurisdictions. All applicants must document their legal presence in the United States; the native born must present birth certificates; naturalized citizens must present their papers; aliens are obligated to complete the so-called alien status verification form. Los Angeles County thereby avoids the substantial welfare costs borne by other jurisdictions with less effective systems of identifying illegal aliens.

Los Angeles was not alone in scaling down assistance to undocumented aliens. In recent years, when the overwhelming majority of Americans had become resolved to end illegal immigration altogether, cutbacks were made in a variety of ways, in Washington and the state capitals, and through the legislative and executive branches of government, although without a consistent plan. The largest of these cuts affected refugee cash assistance, which diminished sharply after 1981. Michigan, New Jersey, and Ohio denied general assistance benefits to illegal aliens. Nevertheless, illegal immigration continued to create many indirect costs. In Los Angeles, officials estimate the city's illegal residents at about 1.1 million people, one-seventh of the total population of the city. In 1980–81, Los Angeles spent $214 million on health care, welfare, justice, law enforcement, and other services (excluding education). Some of these costs indirectly derived from the large number of illegal aliens in the county; others were occasioned by direct costs of services (such as emergency ward and maternity ward medical services) that the county could not reasonably deny to illegal aliens. Studies undertaken in other parts of the United States also indicate that there are high costs to illegal immigration. A survey completed in Illinois in 1982, for instance, suggests that more than $450 million had been paid annually in unemployment benefits to illegal immigrants in that state.

Illegal immigrants also are accused of displacing Americans from jobs. These changes come not only from Anglo-Americans, but also from Hispanics and black Americans. According to information made available to us by Edwin Harwood from his forthcoming book *In Liberty's Shadow*, surveys conducted in 1983 by Lance Tarrance Associates and Peter Hart Research Associates, 58 percent of Hispanic and 82 percent of black American respondents thought that illegal aliens were taking employment from Americans. Fifty-seven percent of Hispanic Americans looked to tough restrictions against illegal aliens, and 60 percent to legislation prohibiting employers from hiring undocumented aliens. In this respect there is a striking divergence between the bulk of the Hispanic population and those who considered themselves to be their ethnic leaders. This difference is not surprising, for it is the unskilled (including the unskilled Mexicans already in this country) who bear the adverse costs of immigration, not the skilled. The cost of immigration to the American-born poor go beyond the competition for jobs and welfare benefits. Continued immigration, especially illegal immigration, is apt to contribute to gang violence as poor, native-born youths feel threatened by newcomers. Immigration might accelerate the trend toward predominantly Hispanic schools, thereby limiting the exposure of students in such schools to spoken English. As more Hispanic children go to school, their parents will call for more bilingual teachers—this at a time when instructors with such qualifications remain in short supply and will continue to remain so, especially in the sciences.

Problems then exist. How severe are they and how widespread? This is hard to answer, for all questions concerned with illegal immigration are related to those connected with the "second economy," that huge, unrecorded, untaxed sector of the United States that works underground and has steadily grown with the regulatory state. The best of scholarly opinion disagrees on the subject of illegal immigration: Julian Simon, for instance, argues that there is no real clash of interest and that undocumented workers even constitute the "ultimate resource," one that significantly adds to the U.S. economy.[43] A good many recent investigations, however, arrive at contrary conclusions. About 30 percent of the U.S. labor force currently performs jobs that require low skills in industry, service occupations, and agriculture. These are the positions most sought for by illegals. Their presence may well explain in part why certain industries continue to pay low wages and resist mechanization. Don Huddle, of Rice University, presents evidence from his field work in Houston, Texas, to prove his case that illegal workers do take jobs from U.S. citizens. Employers, according to Huddle, prefer to hire illegals because they are more docile, do not join unions, do not draw on workmen's compensation, and will work for longer hours without overtime, and because less than half have any taxes withheld or paid by employers.

It is the poorest and most vulnerable Americans (youths, blacks, and women) who suffer most from the illegals' competition. The presence of undocumented workers thus forms an invisible subsidy to the employers of illegal workmen and to those consumers who make use of the illegals' services. It is the unskilled American, himself often black or Hispanic, who pays the main cost.

The Immigration and Naturalization Service

Over the years, government departments, like military regiments and corporations, are apt to develop their own individualities. The INS (known to many Mexican Americans as *La Migra*) has proved no exception. The INS is the government agency Mexican and other immigrants first make contact with in the United States; its importance for shaping ethnic relations is hard to overestimate. For the greater part of this nation's history, the INS did not exist. In 1891, Congress provided for the appointment of a Superintendent of Immigration, who reported to the Secretary of the Treasury and did little more than count arrivals and make reports. In 1903, the Bureau of Immigration and Naturalization came under the Department of Labor and Commerce.[44] In 1913, this agency divided into separate departments; Immigration and Naturalization likewise split into two separate bureaus, both placed under the Department of Labor. The role of the department grew after World War I, when unemployment, racist considerations, American nationalism, and subsequent fears of alien-inspired subversion contributed to the Quota Act of 1921 (revised in 1924 as the National Origins Act).

In 1924, the United States set up the border patrol under the Bureau of Immigration. The patrol at first contained no more than 450 men, drawn from the same civil service register used for the appointment of railway mail clerks. Their pay was poor and promotion was slow; their work was arduous and their numbers were totally insufficient to supervise the borders. The New Dealers made some administrative changes: in 1933, Immigration and Naturalization were combined into the INS; in 1940, control over this agency passed from the Department of Labor to the Department of Justice, where it has remained.

The INS, however, continued to be exposed to contradictory currents; policy shifted to and from between those who wanted massive immigration to supply the farms with migrant workers and those who wanted to keep the immigrants out. The border agents exercised far-reaching powers of search, seizure, and arrest, authority that made them unpopular. The service as a whole remained understaffed and underfinanced as it faced the undesirable task of enforcing incompatible policies.

During the first half of the 1950s, Congress made some attempt at comprehensive immigration legislation, the first such effort since the Quota Act and National Origins Act of the 1920s. The Immigration and Nationality Act of 1952 (known as the McCarran-Walter Act) left the Western Hemisphere nations without numerical restriction, race and sex, however, were excluded as criteria for citizenship through naturalization. Amendments to the McCarran-Walter Act, passed in 1965 and 1976, created a complicated system of preferences for immigration that stressed family reunification and refugee status. Illegal immigration, nevertheless, increased by leaps and bounds, and so did the work of the INS.

At the same time, the demands made by laws and citizenry alike on the immigration service grew in an extraordinary fashion. But there was no corresponding rise in the resources of to the service. In 1974, half a century after the creation of the border patrol, its authorized strength amounted to no more than 2,122. The Americans, in other words, devoted no more men to controlling their enormous borders than were employed as police officers in a city the size of Milwaukee or St. Louis, a state of affairs inconceivable in either Western or Eastern Europe.

The service continued as a whipping boy for every faction in the American immigration debate (conducted, at the time of writing, over the so-called Simpson-Mazzoli bill). In the past, moreover, the INS suffered from inadequate leadership, when leaders were selected for purely political reasons. The Department of Justice shows little interest in the INS. No substantial lobby calls for the allocation of additional funds for the INS or defends INS officers accused by civic groups, ecclesiastical organizations, or local elected bodies of "abrasive" or "insensitive" conduct in enforcing the law of the land. Not surprisingly, morale within the INS has suffered.

The INS also understandably has failed to resolve the problems that exist from its contradictory functions as a service organization and as a law enforcement agency. The INS bears responsibility for administering laws relating both to the exclusion and to the naturalization of aliens. The service inquires into the right of admission into the United States; adjudicates requests on the part of aliens for benefits under the law; guards against illegal entry into the country; investigates, apprehends, and removes aliens guilty of law violations; and examines alien applicants who wish to become citizens. The INS, moreover, is expected to provide information, counsel, and school textbooks to prospective citizens; to protect national security through the supervision of the U.S. borders; and to stem the inflow of illegal drugs in cooperation with local, state, and such federal agencies as the Drug Enforcement Administration.

To this day, the resources available to the INS in no way correspond to its enormous tasks, the very range and magnitude of which cause confusion. Experts, such as those responsible for the report entitled *The Tarnished Golden Door* (issued by the U.S. Commission on Civil Rights in 1980), have called for far-reaching reforms, including the abolition of the border patrol and the separation, as far as possible, of the department's enforcement and service functions. Reform, however, cannot occur in a vacuum. As Edwin Harwood, the American sociologist already cited in this study, points out, civil servants cannot improve their organization until society tells them exactly what functions the organization should serve. As they stand at present, U.S. immigration laws cannot be enforced.[45]

By the early 1980s, the INS was undermanned, underfunded, and neglected by the Department of Justice, as well as by the Office of Management and the Budget. In 1982, Congress did authorize a substantial increase, to $428 million. But no one knows if these additional resources will suffice to cope with a problem that has increased enormously from the early 1960s, when apprehensions amounted to less than 100,000 a year.

INS inspectors are supposed to be tough in enforcing the law. But practice belies that image. The INS seeks criminal prosecutions for only a very small percentage of aliens and U.S. citizens involved in the violation of immigration laws. The INS in fact takes a lenient line, even though it might invoke criminal prosecutions in almost every instance where such cases are involved. The American public is itself extremely ambivalent. When an illegal alien commits a serious crime, public opinion is aroused, and the INS is called upon to enforce the law as strictly as possible. But when illegals are wanted as workers, the INS, in carrying out its duties, may incur censure for allegedly acting like a "green Gestapo" or as "storm troopers." The public is likewise in two minds about assisting in law enforcement. The INS may receive tipoffs from aliens or citizens with a personal grudge against an illegal immigrant. A citizen, however, will rarely denounce an illegal alien without some personal cause. An illegal alien, once having succeeded in getting a home or a stable job in the United States, obtains strong public support; many Americans then come forward to defend the alien's right to remain. This ambivalence is shared by INS inspectors, who would rather prosecute criminals than illegal aliens who work hard and live peaceably.

To a great extent, immigration law enforcement by the early 1980s had become law without enforcement. Convictions were ever harder to obtain, given the growing complexity of the law and the pro-immigrant bias displayed by many judges. For instance, people caught smuggling aliens routinely entered plea bargains that reduced the felony of "transporting" to the misdemeanor of "aiding and abetting" entry without inspection. The ordinary alien who made a false claim for U.S. citizenship was unlikely to be prosecuted. Unless vicious crimes were involved, INS officers had difficulty getting their cases taken up by public prosecutors. When sentences were meted out, they were apt to be quite lenient. The scarcity of detention space and of judges to hear cases meant that the situation could not easily be remedied.

If the laws were tightened, the border patrol at present would remain too small to enforce them. By 1983, the border patrol numbered 2,300 agents, with only 300 to 400 agents along the southern border at any one time. The vast increase in the inflow of aliens, the extension by the courts of Fourth and Fifth Amendment rights to aliens, and the grant of the Miranda warning to aliens have contributed to the weakening of the border patrol. Even if border deterrence were to improve dramatically, the immigration courts and the INS detention centers could not cope with the large numbers of apprehended illegals.

The INS suffered from a loss of authority in other ways. Law suits initiated by civil rights groups and immigration activists, and hostile publicity received by the INS in the media made the INS anxious about its image. Contrary to the impression given by many newspapers and television commentators, the day-to-day enforcement practices followed by INS agents were lenient compared to the sanctions that were available to the INS under the law.

Many aliens learned that the best way to get into the United States was to violate the law and that the best way to stay in the country was to use the law's generous provisions to delay deportation with frivolous appeals. This problem threatened the very integrity of the law itself, thereby removing the incentive for law-abiding aliens to wait abroad until they could immigrate legally. Unless something was done, a frustrated public might call for an end to legal, as well as illegal, immigration.

What Is to Be Done?

The so-called Simpson-Mazzoli bill (Immigration Reform and Control Act, 1982) was defeated by Congress. The bill would impose penalties on employers who hired undocumented workers; it would allow 6 million illegal aliens estimated to be living in the United States to petition for legalized status and amnesty; the bill also would strengthen existing smuggling and deportation laws and allow a limited number of so-called guest workers into the country. The bill, however, came under heavy fire from Hispanic and black groups fearful that employer sanction would lead to discrimination against minorities, a concern shared by civil rights activists of all colors. Conservatives called legalization of undocumented workers an unjust reward for those who had broken the law. Growers and the U.S. Chamber of Commerce called for weaker sanctions and more guest workers. The AFL/CIO opposed the hiring of foreigners as temporary workers. The unions also feared that provisions for the importation of workers under the so-called H-2 program would expand, thereby taking jobs from unemployed U.S. citizens and legal immigrants.[46]

There were, however, more deep-seated objections, both to the Simpson-Mazzoli bill and to similar measures. These included a bill, passed by the Senate in September 1985, containing four major provisions: illegal aliens resident in the United States since January 1980 would be eligible for the legalization of their status; employers convicted of knowingly hiring illegal aliens would face designated penalties; additional resources would go to border control services; and an existing program, known as "H-2," would allow workers temporarily into the country for labor on farms. Objections to such measures hinged, above all, on the actual machinery of law enforcement. As Edwin Harwood points out, increased funding for the border patrol, as was envisioned under the Simpson-Mazzoli bill, might indeed lead to the apprehension of more aliens than previously had been caught. But, in fact, they merely would be returned under the penalty of the "voluntary return" option and be free to reenter again in the near future. In other words, the price of being caught remains small, much smaller than in any European country. Even if the laws were to be tightened, the criminal provisions at present could not be realistically enforced because the federal judges and prosecutors are already overburdened with more serious cases, and the U.S. lacks the detention and prison space for "real criminals" who sometimes receive reduced sentences, or even probation, because of the pressure on the prisons. Immigration officers, moreover, continue to work under a number of handicaps, including federal decisions in the constitutional area that weaken their ability to prosecute alien smugglers and other offenders. Inspectors might indeed screen more carefully for fraudulent visa entrants; yet such activities would surely inconvenience legitimate travelers.

There are other ambiguities. For instance, the Immigration and Nationality Act of 1952, as subsequently amended, rendered illegal the harboring, concealment, and transportation of illegal aliens. But, in a blatantly political move designed to please large-scale agricultural employers, the legislature added the "Texas proviso." Under its terms, "employment (including the usual and normal practices incident to employment) shall not be deemed to constitute harboring." Businessmen, in other words, could not be punished for giving jobs to illegal aliens. However, by abrogating the Texas proviso and placing heavy fines on corporations found guilty of having given jobs to illegal aliens, the tide of illegal immigration might be reversed; employers, to all intents and purposes, would then act as unpaid government agents to keep the foreigners at bay.

In practice, however, such proposals will not work. Employers, as Harwood shows in the paper cited previously, are ill qualified to determine immigration status between illegal aliens and lawful aliens authorized to work, when illegal aliens make false claims and use fraudulent documents. Employers are not trained to distinguish the difference between forged and genuine documents presented by job applicants. Even if businessmen were willing to try, they would run the risk of lawsuits if they denied jobs to applicants who presented the identification required for verification. Employers, moreover, would risk charges of racial discrimination by civil rights groups and Hispanic activists because personnel officers would be more apt to deny jobs to Hispanics suspected of being illegal than to reject European applicants. Furthermore, forcing firms to act as unpaid immigration inspectors would raise their costs at a time when American firms face severe challenge from foreign competition.

The amnesty provisions included in the Simpson-Mazzoli bill raise similar difficulties. As Harwood shows, fraud already has become so common that the administration of future amnesty provisions would be difficult to enforce. Amnesty petitioners are likely to be numerous; according to a congressional estimate in 1984, about 1.75 million aliens might apply for amnesty if 1982 were selected as a cutoff date. Many of these applicants would be tempted to produce forged papers to substantiate their claims. Given the large caseload facing federal prosecutors and courts, the scanty manpower resources at the INS's disposal, the ambivalence of the American public with regard to illegal residents, and the way in which immigration lawyers and federal judges have chipped away at those provisions of the existing law intended to check fraud, a general amnesty is not likely to restore the effective enforcement of the immigration laws and would lead to another flood of illegals willing to gamble on future amnesties.

Are any other solutions in sight? A thoughtful study, *The Dilemma of American Immigration*, rejects a number of possible alternatives.[47] The authors discount, as we do, any system of employer sanctions on the grounds that it would tempt employers to avoid trouble by discriminating against job applicants who "look Hispanic" or "look Asian." They oppose the creation of a national identity card. Such a project could lead to the institution of internal passports; it also would create an administrative nightmare, for identity cards would have to be provided not only for several million immigrants but for more than 230 million U.S. citizens. Amnesty would encourage further illegal immigration and throw a greater load than before on the income transfer and social service system, a burden that would bear most heavily on low-skilled native workers. These workers would face both increased competition in the labor market and increased competition for scarce social services. The authors equally oppose occupation-specific labor certification. The decision to admit or not to admit immigrants following certain professions would be influenced by domestic lobbies. Such interest groups—physicians, nurses, pharmacists, or whatever—would exercise substantial pressure on their own behalf, without countervailing pressure from the widely dispersed consumers.

Additional foreign aid to Mexico also will be equally incapable of providing a solution. Whatever its merits, the border industrialization program discussed earlier in this book is bound to attract migrants from the remote areas of Mexico to the frontier cities. From there, workers may be tempted to cross into the United States in search of higher wages; the *maquiladoras* therefore may actually encourage immigration to the United States. With equal justification, Cafferty and his co-authors of *The Dilemma of American Immigration* argue against measures to make naturalization in the United States more difficult to obtain for foreigners than it is at present. An important difference between the United States on the one hand and most European and Third World countries on the other is found in the manner in which the United States encourages the naturalization of foreign immigrants. This country should not abandon that tradition. The option open to an alien of becoming a citizen is a central part of the American creed; this possibility prevents the emergence of hostility between immigrants and the native born.

What of illegal immigration? F. Ray Marshall, an American economist and a former Secretary in the Department of Labor in the Carter administration, has a suggestion that ought to be seriously considered. He argues that the United States must be able to enforce its laws, but that the INS (with a nationwide force of only 700 investigators and 2,000 border patrol agents) is in no position to do so on its own. (The 1985 budget, proposed early in 1984, did provide for one thousand additional law enforcement positions, raising the agency's budget by $41.1 million to a total of $574.5 million; but even this increase was small in relation to the enormous task the INS is expected to carry out.) According to Marshall, effective enforcement of the laws against illegal aliens might best be entrusted to the Department of Labor. Instead of recommending a system of national identity cards, Marshall proposes a system of work authorization numbers, recorded in a national databank. The social security number carried by each lawful resident in the United States could be adapted to this purpose. The system would not require workers to carry or to present to employers any identification card. Nor would employers be required to determine the right of any applicant to work in the United States. Job applicants instead would inform employers of their work authorization number. The employer would call the work authorization agency's toll-free exchange and receive immediate verification of the immigrant job applicant's work authorization. The system would work rather like a credit card and would be equally effective. A similar program using visa numbers or cards issued in Mexico by American officials also merits consideration.

Legislators would still face many difficulties. The United States would require laws barring the employment of aliens not authorized to work. Administrators would have to design a system of inspection that would enable them to check the numbers allotted under the system. The Social Security Administration would have to release personnel data on both citizens and legal residents to prevent illegals from using borrowed social security cards or phoney numbers. The INS still would face the difficult task of making status determination. Above all, the United States would have to reform the court system, an extensive task with implications that go far beyond the immigration questions.

In addition, the United States must make effective provision for temporary migrant workers. Widespread beliefs to the contrary, not all newcomers wish to remain here. In many cases it is the unsuccessful immigrant who stays in the United States because he is unable to make enough money to pay for the return trip or because he has become entangled in the social system. Commonly, the successful migrant goes home to invest his earnings in land or a small business. The United States cannot do without migrant workers because in this country, as in other countries, there are a substantial number of jobs that the native born or the assimilated immigrant cannot do—because it is seasonal work or because of the social stigma that has become attached to such occupations.

How should the immigrants be selected? Congress should set periodic quotas for permanent immigrants. These quotas must be adjustable for varying economic and political circumstances; they should be nonracial in spirit and application. The size of the annual quota should depend on congressional decision. We agree with Cafferty and his associates who set the basis of .2 percent of the population for determining the number of resident alien visas to be issued annually. This number seems justifiable by the historical proportion of immigrants to the total population that continues to be easily absorbed; at the same time, it allows for a generous number of admissions (about 500,000 a year).

The quota will have to take account of two major desiderata—the legitimate needs for family reunification and the desirability of admitting skilled rather than unskilled newcomers. There should be no limits on the admission of close relatives of adult U.S. citizens (parents, spouses, and dependent children.) Citizen sponsors, however, should be required to guarantee financial support and medical insurance for their relatives during the first five years in the United States. We do not recommend similar exemptions for the relatives of resident aliens. In setting quotas,

Congress should do away with annual country ceilings. A point system would make provision for awarding advantages to characteristics that enhance a newcomer's productivity in the United States—including schooling, vocational training, on-the-job training, knowledge of English, and the possession of funds. A smaller number of points would go to applicants who have close relatives in this country.

The points system seems to us of particular merit. We agree with the authors of the *The Dilemma of American Immigration* who argue that by emphasizing kinship relations and by practicing limiting law enforcement we have allowed a high proportion of low-skilled immigrants into this country. Their presence, while benefiting certain employers, depresses the wages of the most underprivileged Americans and also widens inequalities of income. The United States, instead, should encourage the immigration of highly trained and highly skilled persons who will add more to the country's productivity than those who have few or no technical qualifications.

Cafferty and his associates also make useful recommendations for an immigration tax, recommendations with which we agree. This would be levied on all foreign immigrants, including temporary sojourners. The tax should not be overly burdensome (we suggest 5 percent on all earned income) and would be paid in addition to the federal income tax. Revenue might be used to defray the expense of processing immigrants and to provide assistance for social projects in areas disproportionately affected by immigrants. At the same time, the United States should give encouragement to foreign visitors who come to these shores as students, businessmen, or tourists. Red tape, as Cafferty and his coauthors show, might be cut down by a computerized system for checking visa numbers as visitors leave the country; such a system would help the INS to keep track of visa overstayers and reduce illegal entry.

The provision of social services for immigrants has become a major source of controversy and also of hostility toward immigrants. We recommend, as does the *Dilemma* study, that all classes of immigrants and visitors be admitted only with proof of medical insurance. We do not advocate a federal health insurance program; we suggest insurance through private companies. Immigrants would not be entitled for regular income transfer programs (such as food stamps, ADC, medicaid, supplemental security income) during their first five years in the United States unless the immigrant suffers an unanticipated disability. Workers meeting state requirements, however, would be entitled to benefits. As *The Dilemma of American Immigration* states, employers presumably will have paid the necessary premiums. Temporary workers and other immigrants will have social security taxes withheld; it is only fair that they should be as eligible for social security benefits as U.S. citizens.

These suggestions appear to us eminently practicable. We reject, however, as do Cafferty and his associates, a new *bracero* program. Temporary immigrants should be allowed to change their work as they please. Prospective employers should provide medical insurance, social security tax payments, and guaranteed return transportation, in addition to a wage at least equal to that of the federal minimum wage, and not less than the prevailing rate for the job.

These suggestions, whatever their merit, will turn out to be unworkable unless the administrative powers of the INS are strengthened and unless the courts refrain from weakening the machinery of control. Overall, the United States needs a strong, purposeful policy, and one that can in fact be enforced.

Part IV

Life in the United States

Chapter 10

The Rise of New Hispanic Cultures

The first Spanish-speaking intellectuals in North America were missionary priests. They wrote, preached, and taught in Spanish to spread the word of God; nothing was further from their minds than to create an independent Spanish North American culture. As the missions' power waned, learning became gradually, though not wholly, secularized. During the years following the Mexican-American War, Spanish-language newspapers increased in numbers and circulation from California all the way to Texas. These provincial papers printed not only news and editorial comments, they also provided a literary vehicle for the works of Spanish-speaking poets, essayists, and social commentators. These journals found an ever-growing audience among the many educated men and women included in the massive migration of Mexicans to the United States that followed the Mexican revolution. Such people were familiar with Mexican literature and politics; they read and discussed the works of literary men like Ricardo Flores Magón, Silvestre Terrazas, and Ignacio E. Lozano (editor of *La Prensa*, a Spanish-language newspaper in San Antonio, a city that housed many well-to-do refugees from Mexico). They and their readers looked to Mexico and to a high culture of Spanish derivation; they regarded themselves as members of *la clase mejor*, the "better class"; and, although they criticized the Mexican revolution, they looked upon themselves above all else as Mexicans.

By the 1930s, however, the intellectual and social climate had changed greatly. The Mexican-American community had come to include a substantial middle class: owners of restaurants, grocery stores, and barber shops; contractors; and also some professional people—doctors, dentists, lawyers, pharmacists, and teachers. Many of these people were bilingual; some spoke only English. They no longer limited their reading to local Spanish newspapers or to books imported from Latin America or Spain. Some of them had appointments at universities and colleges or at English-language newspapers and publishing houses. Whereas the traditional rich tended to back the conservatively minded *Alianza Hispano Americana*, the new middle class was more likely to join such organizations as the League of United Latin American Citizens (LULAC) to support the struggle for civil rights.

Among the intellectuals, there was a good deal of support for the moderate left. These included the writer George I. Sánchez, a professor at the University of Texas, who, in 1940, published a classic study, *The Forgotten People*. This described Mexican Americans in New Mexico as victims of imperialism, swept aside by the relentless march of territorial aggrandizement. Another influential writer was Ernesto Galarza who later wrote a harsh critique of the *bracero* system, *Merchants of Labor* (1964), and also wrote articles, produced films, organized farm workers, and supported mass campaigns to improve the laborer's lot.[1]

These men called for justice and a better world—but not for separate political and social status for the Chicano people. They looked to full integration within the United States, at a time when the Mexican-American community had become linguistically diverse. The Spanish spoken in the Southwest was widely varied. There was the street slang of Los Angeles, remnants of archaic Castillian in New Mexican Spanish, and there were expressions known to Chicanos alone, not to Mexicans. Conversational Spanish was in constant flux. A literature founded on a *patois* risked the danger of quickly becoming dated, as the language of the streets changed along with altering social conditions and transitory idiomatic fashions. Afrikaans employed by Dutch-descended settlers in South Africa assumed a permanent form through the authority of standard dictionaries, grammars, and a magnificent translation of the Bible. Chicanos lacked this linguistic infrastructure. Should intellectuals write in English or in Spanish? And if in Spanish, what form of Spanish should Chicano intellectuals adopt?

The Spanish spoken in the Southwest was identified in the public mind with the poor. Mexican Americans suffered not merely from the racial but also from the cultural prejudice of Anglo-Americans. Many Mexican-American school children had sorry tales to tell of being insulted by a classmate or an unpleasant teacher, or of being discouraged or forbidden from speaking Spanish at school. Anti-Spanish prejudice extended even to some major institutions of learning. At Stanford University during the 1950s, Spanish could not be offered to fulfill the foreign language requirement for graduate studies in history on the grounds that the language of Cervantes and Calderón was not a suitable vehicle for scholarship. American educators were prone to believe that Mexican Americans, unlike other Spanish speakers throughout the world, spoke a debased form of Spanish. American scholars and educators were not alone in their censure; they received unintended support from men of letters of the Spanish-speaking world (including Mexico), who criticized the supposed corruption of Spanish by the penetration of

English in the Southwest. Even in New Mexico, where the Spanish language was strongly entrenched, well-to-do Mexican Americans were apt to abandon their native tongue in the hope of raising their social position.

Social and political pressure, however, did not lead to the extirpation of the language. In New Mexico, for instance, the House of Representatives used both English and Spanish until 1953, when Spanish was deemed unnecessary because all Spanish-speaking members had become fully bilingual. Nor did Spanish turn into a bastardized language. Contrary to popular belief, the average Spanish-speaking person in the Southwest does not actually mix Spanish and English, but normally relies on one language alone while using selected words or phrases from the other for emphasis, comic effect, or nuance. Spanish and English alike remained accessible instruments for Mexican-American writers to use.[2]

The Chicano Revival

From the 1960s onward, Chicano activists set out on a new course. The world seemed in turmoil, the Western colonial empires in Africa were in disintegration, and Franco-African and black West Indian intellectuals discovered the real or supposed merits of *négritude*. The United States experienced student militancy, the Black power struggle, and campus revolts on the part of leftist professors and students. Conventional business values fell into disrepute; on television screens throughout the United States, businessmen were being (and continue to be) vilified for their assumed selfishness, philistinism, or even criminality.[3]

Given the changed climate of opinion and the mood of millenarian euphoria on many U.S. campuses, Chicano intellectuals, like their Anglo-American confreres, called for far-reaching political and social change. Generalizations about the Chicano revival are difficult to make because the movement was divided into many local groups, with many differences of opinion in regards to the tactics and the strategy to be pursued. But all looked to a cultural renaissance in the development of a militant literature that would take pride in Hispanic heritage and in the formerly despised term "Chicano."

Literary militance found expression in *El Grito: Journal of Mexican-American Thought*, the first Chicano journal, founded in 1968, and also within the ranks of the National Caucus of Chicano Social Scientists, founded in 1973 at New Mexico Highlands University. Equally important were periodic academic gatherings, such as a statewide conference held at the Santa Barbara campus of the University of California in 1969 and the Chicano Youth Liberation Conference at Denver, Colorado, in the same year. Radical Chicano thought thereafter found expression in

Aztlán: Chicano Journal of the Social Sciences and the Arts, first published in 1970 at the University of California at Los Angeles. The achievements of established artists and thinkers of Hispanic descent—including exiles from Spain, Pablo Casals, the cellist, and George Santayana, the philosopher; immigrants from South America such as the Venezuelan-born Eliseo Vivas, a conservative political scientist; and Puerto Ricans such as the actor José Ferrer, and Jesús Maria Sanromá, the classical concert performer—seemed to bear no significance to the pioneers of *Chicanismo*. The Chicano intellectuals looked for inspiration from the people, or what they perceived to be the people.

Chicano militants often were divided about their Iberian heritage. Cultured Chicanos admired great Spanish poets like Federico García Lorca, whose use of ordinary words to create elaborate images was replicated in Chicano verse. But, to many Chicano intellectuals, Spain, with its imperial legacy, was an oppressor nation whose *conquistadores* had ravaged Latin America, raped brown women, and imposed the stigma of both illegitimacy and social inferiority on their *mestizo* offspring. Chicano intellectuals accordingly were much more ambivalent about the masterpieces of the Cid or Cervantes than, say, Afrikaner intellectuals were about the great works of Dutch literature or, Irish Americans, who proudly read Yeats and Joyce.

Chicanismo, for its part, attempted to reach the masses. According to its proponents, the Chicano people had been reduced by Anglo conquest to political and cultural dependency and a status of presumed invisibility. Chicanos must create a new history and a new literature that would serve social as well as esthetic and academic functions. Their work should elucidate the Chicanos' unique culture, illuminate Chicano identity, and inform Chicano politics. Pioneers like George I. Sánchez had put their faith in the Western liberal tradition; Chicano intellectuals, while recognizing the worth of such ambitions, must go beyond them, and call for more far-reaching social change.[4]

Chicano concerns found expression, to some extent, in Cesar Chavez's National Farm Workers Association. Chicano writers sought to influence the people through various *teatros*, especially the Teatro Campesino founded by Luís Miguel Valdez, a poet and college teacher, and an alumnus of the San Francisco Mime Theater. The staff of the *Teatro Campesino* consisted solely of agricultural workers. The movement used *corridos* (popular ballads) based on traditional folk songs for political purposes. *Teatro Campesino* plays also served political objectives in the propagandistic style popularized during the early 1920s in the Soviet Union and in leftist cabarets that flourished in Berlin after World War I. There were no subtleties; there was no attempt at characterization;

their purpose, Valdez claims, was to inspire the audience to social action. A typical play showed a wicked grower (bearing a signboard identifying his profession) thrown to the ground by a virtuous worker, who released his opponent only after the capitalist bloodsucker had signed a contract.[5] One of *El Teatro Campesino's* best plays, *Los Vendidos* (*The Sellouts*) was made into a film by the El Centro Campesino Cultural.

At its most radical, Chicano thought found expression "The Spiritual Plan of Aztlán," formulated during a Chicano youth conference in Denver, Colorado, in 1969. According to this document, the Chicanos came from the northern land of Aztlán, the home of their forefathers. The Chicanos were the "people of the sun"; the call of their blood was their destiny. Chicanos formed "a bronze people with a bronze culture"; they formed "a union of free pueblos"; they were Aztlán. The people of Aztlán recognized no "capricious frontiers on the Bronze Continent." Aztlán belonged to those who worked the land by the sweat of their brow, "not to foreign Europeans" or to "gringo" invaders.[6]

Chicano history to them was a tale of martyrdom that Puerto Ricans and Cubans did not share. Furthermore, the Chicano nation had been enriched by a deep spiritual experience. According to Armando B. Rendón, a Chicano writer, Chicanos might justly claim "a union with the cosmos. . . a cosmic sense of spirit . . . an *alma Chicana* [a Chicano soul]." In Rendón's view, the concept of *La Raza Unida* was a reassertion of a "cosmic Chicano existence." Anglo-American society, by contrast, was but "a bastard issued from the promiscuous concubinage of several hundreds of ethnic and racial peoples who have cast their cultural identities into the American melting pot." North American culture was "destructive of personal dignity . . . callous, vindictive, arrogant, militaristic, self-deceiving, and greedy." Anglo-America was "spoiled and immature"; it was "a cultural cesspool."[7]

The Chicano mystique found its most striking early formulation in a work entitled *I am Joaquín*, by Rodolfo ("Corky") Gonzáles, of Denver, Colorado, son of a migrant worker, a onetime professional boxer, farm worker, civil rights activist, lumberjack, educator, playwright, and publisher. His narrative poem was called "undoubtedly one of the most significant pieces of creative literature that has as yet been written by a Chicano."[8] In his verse, Gonzáles expresses disdain for the Chicano who has attained economic success and thereby has sold out his brother. Gonzáles despises technical civilization; he calls for an end to the self-stultifying struggle for riches. He looks to his Indian heritage and to cultural withdrawal from Anglo-America; he takes pride in Chicano *machismo*, Chicano womanhood, and Chicano faith. He will have nothing to do with that monstrous technical and industrial giant called progress;

he will have no share in Anglo success; he refuses to be absorbed by those who reject him and his parentage.[9]

I am Joaquín represented only one of the many strands in early Chicano thought, although it was the most visible. Inspired by an intense romanticism, this form of *Chicanismo* faced irresolvable contradictions. Even though it stressed cultural separatism, its proponents came from the best-educated Anglicized stratum of the Mexican-American people. Many of them had gone to college; their upbringing and culture were very different from the manual workers whom the poets extolled, but who rarely read the poets' verse. A real man, in the Mexican-American workingman's or workingwoman's estimation, was supposed to be *feo, fuerte y formal*: ugly (that is to say, roughhewn and rugged), strong (forceful, competent, capable of taking responsibility), formal (in the sense of being well-mannered, Spartan, and civic-minded). These ideals essentially were those of the traditional upperclass; they would have been as acceptable to the colonel of a Prussian grenadier regiment as to the headmaster of a British public school. Such ideals bore little resemblance to the values of most progressive American academicians in the 1960s and 1970s, men and women commonly wedded to a romantic school of self-revelation, self-development, and the search for self-identity—infused all too often with self-indulgence and self-pity.

The Chicano writers looked for originality, for a literature that would be all of their own. But all too often, the new Chicano mystique merely reflected notions common among European romantics, who also had frequently wallowed in the supposedly mystic qualities of the blood, the soil, and the folk while decrying the decadent materialism of the West. Following the romantic tradition, some *Chicanista* intellectuals also subscribed to the postrevolutionary cult of the Indians, a cult that had been widely indulged in by intellectuals and politicians in Mexico. This self-identification, however, was as artificial as the self-identification of romantically inclined professors and *Oberstudienräte* with farmers and fishermen in nineteenth-century Germany. As Robert E. Quirk, an American historian, puts it: "A Mexican of the politically effective class, proud to proclaim himself as Indian, would be highly indignant to be called that by a foreigner. Rather it is the ideal Indian, the mythic Indian, the Indian on a monument, who recalls the past glories of an Aztec empire. This empire ceased to exist in 1521 and therefore contributed almost nothing to Mexico's post-conquest civilization. What the Indians are today has little to do with Aztec kings."[10]

Early Chicano intellectuals, moreover, failed to take adequate account of their own people's cultural diversity. Mexican Americans, like black Americans, are a mixed people. Mexican-American culture constitutes a cultural blend of Indian, Spanish, and other European elements.

Narciso Martinez, a genuine folk artist of the 1930s, a great accordion player, worked as an agricultural laborer and played at fairs and *cantinas* during weekends.[11] He learned a great deal from the German- and Czech-descended Texans he met around Corpus Christi. Many of his marvellous waltzes, polkas, and *Schottische* may well remind a listener of music heard in a beer cellar in southern Germany. Conversely, Western country music, with its never-ending tales of personal misfortunes and its didactic tone, owes an equally great debt to the *corrido*, the Mexican folksong sung to the accompaniment of a solo guitar. A popular artist like Johnny Cash is in a sense the heir of Mexico as well as of the English-speaking frontier. As Manuel A. Machado, a Mexican-American scholar, says: "The cultural *mestizaje* [racial mixture] that occurred in Mexico also blended with the Anglo to produce a value system within the Mexican-American community that is itself hybridized. Therefore the rejection of Anglo values by the Chicanos is really rejection of one element of the Chicano culture.[12]

Chicano theoreticians called for cultural secession from what they regarded as the Anglo establishment. They sometimes exalted even violence under the slogan of *venceremos*. But, with a striking lack of consistency, many worked through the very institutions they professed to despise. They accepted university posts, a strange choice for those revolutionaries who denounced others for permitting themselves to be co-opted by the powers that be. Chicano militants also looked to the "Anglo" law courts and the "Anglo" bureaucracy to defend their rights. Chicano writers reached the public through respectable publishing houses such as Prentice-Hall or Macmillan. *Teatro Campesino* productions were telecast on public television and subsidized by such organizations as the Carnegie Foundation. Whatever the revolutionaries might proclaim in theory, they devoted much of their efforts in practice to what Germany leftwingers at the time called "the long march through the institutions." The Chicano movement thus overwhelmingly benefited professors, teachers, ethnic politicians, and other professional men and women more than the masses. (A poll taken by the *Los Angeles Times* in 1983 showed that only about half of the Latins in California were aware that a Chicano Movement had taken place—a rate of recognition only slightly higher than that of non-Hispanic Americans.)[13]

By about 1973, the original Chicano movement, with its narcissistic and romantic elements, had lost its impetus, as had the radical student movement that had supplied much of its power. The movement had made a positive impact in encouraging an increased commitment to education in general and to Chicano consciousness in particular. But the movement failed to furnish effective intellectual leadership. Thereafter, as Chicano scholar Robert Vasquez points out, the movement further divided.[14] "Internal colonialism" ceased to be the predominant focus; class issues attained increasing importance. Chicano intellectuals sought a broader audience, and Chicano writers examined a much wider range of subjects than did their predecessors. Chicano theoreticians looked to many modes of expression, all the way from surrealism and even punk rock *à al chicana* to many varieties of Marxism, both orthodox and dissident.

Perhaps the most influential of these Marxist *Chicanistas* was Juan Gómez-Quiñónes, a poet and historian, who re-examined the Chicano past as a series of cumulative events and created a system of periodization in order to elucidate the Chicanos' evolution. He accepted the realities of class division among Mexican Americans; he pointed to their divergent interests, and he tried to link their conflicting attitudes about assimilation into the dominant Anglo culture to class status. To Gómez-Quiñónes, the intellectual's proper role was to clarify cultural values and to introduce new ideas for the purpose of bringing about progressive change.[15]

In formulating his views, Gómez-Quiñónes, like other scholars, ran up against formidable difficulties. What about those actual proletarians— truck-drivers, steel workers, lumbermen, auto workers—who liked living in the U.S., felt proud of their American citizenship, and saw no need to overthrow the system, or even to familiarize themselves with the views of a progressive intellectual vanguard? A common reply was: they had been seduced by bourgeois propaganda and the power of advertising. But if one class could in fact impose a false consciousness on another class, against the latter's true self-interest, what became of the Marxist theory of revolution? There were other problems. Were the civic liberties granted by "bourgeois democracy" truly as formalistic as many Marxists asserted? If so, why could dissident Marxists express their views only in bourgeois countries, and not in socialist states, where the party line ruled supreme and where intellectual experimentation outside the party's framework remained under an interdict? Why did the revolution in Cuba suppress the Afro-Cuban subculture on the grounds that race and color have no meaning within the framework of economic determinism? Had not Marxism itself turned into an ideological weapon for the defense of a new class of party functionaries and ideologues? Gómez-Quiñónes and his friends gave no effective answer to such questions.

Failures and Achievements

The Chicano struggle took a variety of forms. The campaign for cultural advancement gained particularly strong support from Chicano student organizations. In Los Angeles in 1968, college students formed an organization called United Mexican American Students, with representatives from various local associations. A similar body sprang up in the San Francisco area, the Mexican American Student Confederation. A third group was the Movimiento Estudiantil Chicano de Aztlán, which turned into an umbrella organization for a large assortment of college and university groups.

Resorting to a variety of tactics—from political persuasion to demonstrations, sit-ins, teach-ins, walkouts, and "trashings"—Chicano activists protested against poor schools and called for the dismissal of allegedly prejudiced teachers and administrators, and for new curricula that would acknowledge Chicano contributions to American society. In addition, militants campaigned to set up Chicano study programs at colleges and universities, especially in the Southwest. A Mexican-American Graduate Studies Department was set up at San Jose State University in 1969; a Chicano Indian University, D.Q.U. (Deganiwidah-Quetzalcoatl University), opened its doors near Davis, California, in 1970. Many alternative schools emerged in cities across the country.

In addition, new research organizations came into being that made a major contribution to scholarship. These included, among others, the Chicano Studies Research Center (CSRC) at the University of California at Los Angeles. CSRC in 1980 received a grant from the Fund for the Improvement of Post-Secondary Education to develop instructional materials in Chicano studies, and subsequently investigated such topics as Mexican-American relations, Chicano women's history, and Chicano politics. Other Chicano research centers came into being at universities in Stanford, California; Austin, Texas; within the University of California system—including Berkeley, and San Diego; and at Dominguez Hills (part of the California State system). These cooperated with major Mexican institutions like the Universidad Nacional Autónoma de México.

There also was striking expansion in the field of Mexican-U.S. relations and in what became known as frontier studies. A full account would require an academic Baedeker. We can here mention only a few major centers. The Center for U.S.-Mexican Studies at the University of California at San Diego developed into the nation's largest program of advanced research and teaching devoted to U.S.-Mexican relations. Conceived on the lines of the interdisciplinary Center for Advanced Study in the Behavioral Sciences at Stanford, the San Diego Center brought together students in many related fields. Whereas institutions such as the Centro de Estudios Frontizeros del Norte de Mexico and the Center for Inter-American and Border Studies at the University of Texas at El Paso concentrated on the borderlands, the San Diego Center sought to investigate U.S.-Mexican relations in their wider setting and also to involve in its work nonacademic professionals—public servants, trade unionists, educators, and businessmen.

Particularly noteworthy were efforts to coordinate such studies. In 1982, the Chicano Studies Center at UCLA, the "flagship" of Chicano studies in the United States, formed a consortium with Chicano studies centers located at Stanford, Austin, and the Puerto Rican Studies Center of New York (CUNY) to conduct work on such subjects of common interest as demography, migration, and related problems. Of particular significance was the work done on the Mexican-American borderlands, a subject that produced an extensive literature of international import.[16]

There also were more specialized ventures. These included, among others, the Southwest Voter Registration Education Project (SVREP) in San Antonio, Texas, which collaborated with the Center for Mexican-American Studies at the University of Texas at Austin in a series of important studies on Mexican-American demography and voting patterns. A third organization was the Freedom International Foundation at Houston, Texas, which, like SVREP, was a nonprofit educational and research organization that promoted scholarly conferences and research. In addition, private enterprise discovered the importance of the growing "Hispanic" market. Organizations like CHIPS (Continuing Hispanic Profile Study) were designed to elucidate subjects of special interest to businessmen a ("brand awareness," "ad awareness," eating habits, shopping habits, and so forth).

The Chicano movement generated a great deal of sincere commitment, and it gave an impetus to popular interest in Hispanic culture. The movement did not, however, succeed in its original objective of radicalizing the Chicano masses. The average Hispanic voter simply did not believe that U.S. society constituted one of the most repressive, intolerant, and racist the world had ever seen; that brown-skinned and black-skinned peoples within the United States were in a state of incipient revolt; that there was an identity of interests between the masses of the Third World and the black and brown minorities within the United States against the exploitative forces of Western capitalism; that all Mexican Americans instinctively sympathized with the heroes of the 1910 revolution; or that only a few minority of *tío tacos* ("Uncle Toms") strove for success in American society. Nor did the bulk of Mexican Americans identify themselves with the Indian American. And they had never done so in the past. (Indeed, Mexican movies shown on Spanish television to Hispanic audiences almost invariably used actors and actresses with strikingly European features.)

Above all, the militants never grasped the strength of the social conservatism that inspired the mass of ordinary people in the barrios. Genuine working-class parents, having gone to great lengths to send their sons and daughters to college, had no wish to see their children become revolutionaries; they preferred their offspring to learn architecture, medicine, or computer science.

Chicano activists and their allies point to alienation and distress among the masses, both immigrant and native born. But, as public opinion polls indicate, most Americans, Hispanic or otherwise, do not share the sense of alienation and unhappiness found among literary intellectuals.[17] Hispanics questioned in 1985 actually expressed a higher degree of confidence than Americans as a whole in such major institutions as churches, banks, newspapers, public schools, Congress, big business, organized labor, and television. Their response provides no comfort to those who regard the Hispanics as alienated people ready for revolt. Minority status per se need not create misery. Minority status is distressing because it is so often coupled with low income and social status. But, many people of Mexican heritage in fact may be subject to less stress than whites or blacks, especially with regard to low educational attainment or family separation and divorce. Mexicans may not depend as much for their self-esteem on scholastic diplomas as do their white or black fellow citizens; and a system of extended kinship makes Mexicans perhaps less reliant on the immediate family for social support. And immigration is apt to be a more positive experience for many migrants than some academics assume.[18]

The precepts of *Chicanismo* also met with intellectual dissent within the Mexican-American community. The critics include Manuel A. Machado, whose book *Listen Chicano: An Informal History of the Mexican American* lambasts not only politicized Chicano studies programs, but also run-of-the-mill schools of education throughout the United States.[19] *Hunger of Memory: The Education of Richard Rodriguez* is an autobiographic essay by a Mexican-American writer and lecturer who worked his way up from working-class origins through an excellent education in Catholic schools and private and public universities, and who rejected *Chicanismo*.[20] In fact, only a small percentage of Mexican Americans chose to identify themselves as Chicanos.[21]

Many, though not all, of the early Chicano intellectuals played down the extraordinary diversity within the Chicano community. But, in fact, the Mexican-American electorate differs widely in age distribution, income, education, and linguistic preference. The Chicano philosophers played down the progress of Anglicization at a time when the percentage of Mexican Americans who spoke only Spanish was declining.[22] For example, *Chicanismo* at first discounted the growing importance of the Mexican-American or Hispanic market, when the Spanish speakers' purchasing power was attaining significance within the national economy. And *Chicanismo* snubbed the Mexican-American middle class at the very time their entrepreneurship, especially in small business ventures, was becoming a dynamic factor.

In their search for a *Chicanismo* mystique, Chicano romantics, though not necessarily the Marxists among them, created a mirror image of the "Anglo" barroom patriot's image of the Mexican American. In academic terminology, the Mexican-American value system is supposedly oriented toward the present, nonintellectual, not success-oriented, fatalistic, traditional, and family centered. These values are said to contrast with "Anglo" values that are future-oriented, intellectual, aimed towards success and self-determination, acquisitive, progressive, and individualistic. Such generalizations, of course, do not deal with real people—bartenders, auto workers, shopkeepers, and bank managers. Together with jokes about drunken Irishmen, grasping Jews, and "dumb Poles," they deserve to be relegated to the realm of ethnic fairyland.

Academic *Chicanismo*, moreover, suffered from more practical impediments. Older university departments were apt to look askance at the academic respectability of the new Chicano departments, in which the professors were overwhelmingly liberal or radical. Conservatives of whatever kind—traditional patriots, members of the "moral majority," Evangelical Christians, "reactionary" Cuban exiles, advocates of a free market economy, or opponents of "approved" causes like the Equal Rights Amendment—had at best only a slender chance of attaining teaching positions in the new departments. Ideological isolation often became a serious matter in such departments during the early 1980s, when the United States slithered into a depresson, when students increasingly called for "saleable" and "practical" skills, when enrollments in the new departments declined, and when both financial and academic support began to wane.

By the early 1980s, *Chicanismo* had failed to reconcile the varying Chicano groups. *Chicanistas* remained divided among themselves even on such key issues as the relationship between the Chicano and the Mexican peoples. *Chicanismo* had failed to produce a single major work of literature or scholarship acceptable as a model for Chicano intellectuals as a whole. And, all too often, *Chicanismo*'s very symbols had become commercialized, a fate shared by the protest movements of the 1960s. Frequently, the academic *Chicanismo* novelists' labored plots and the complexity of the poets' language, imagery, and symbolism made their works difficult to understand and dependent on an audience of college teachers and students. Even within academia, there often was a failure to sustain adequate academic interest in Chicano subjects. A major inventory of Mexican-related research in the United States and abroad, published in 1982, provides details of 338 research projects currently being pursued on a wide variety of topics; of these, only 38 concerned

Chicano studies.) For non-Hispanics, involvement remained limited to a handful of philanthropic academicians who accepted *Chicanismo's* romantic self-image at the "Anglo's" expense.[23]

Nevertheless, the Chicano revival has substantial achievements to its credit. A full discussion would require a book, and we will simply mention some salient features. By the early 1980s, the Chicano movement had contributed to advances in scholarship by academicians such as Alberto Camarillo, Leo Estrada, Juan Gómez Quiñones, Armando Guitierrez, Isidro Ortiz, Antonio Rios-Bustamente, Armando Valdez, William Velasquez, and many others. And the movement produced a series of journals specifically devoted to Chicano subjects.

There also was a distinctive body of Chicano writing, poetry, folklore, novels and plays. Given their diversity, it is impossible to write of a typical Chicano work of art. Common to them all are discontent with the real or assumed plight of Mexican Americans and a desire for change. The poetry tends to be protest poetry or poetry of self-affirmation.[24] Well-known authors include Rafael Jesús González, Francisco Jiménez, Ricardo Sánchez, "Corky" González, and Alberto Heredia. Writing under the pseudonym of Alurista, Heredia attempted to create bilingual verse (neither fully Spanish nor fully English) in which he deplored the manner in which Chicanos had forgotten the magic of their ancestral Indian culture. José Montoya drew on his experiences as a migrant worker; Rafael Jesús Gonzáles wrote in a Whitmanesque vein about the Chicano plight. In addition, Chicano writers made a contribution to the art of the novel. Prominent authors include Ricardo Vásquez, Raimundo Barrios, José António Villareal, Salvador Rodriguez del Pino, Miguel Méndez-M, Tomas Rivera, and, above all, Rodolfo A. Anaya, author (among other works) of *Bless Me Ultima*, a story of life in New Mexico in the 1940s written in a plain, direct, and unpretentious style that differs strikingly from the flowery effusions of the "Spiritual Plan of Aztlán."[25]

Much use was made of folk heroes, such as Murieta, Villa, and Zapata, in Chicano literature. More important from the standpoint of mass consumption, the Mexican superhero found his way into comic strips. Marbarito C. Gárcia created a new character, *Relámpago* (Lightning), who uses supernatural powers to break up drug rings, smash motorcycle gangs, and foil bank robberies. Bearing in one hand the flag of the United States and in the other the Mexican banner, *Relámpago* provides an alternative to the glamorized bandit of old.

Some of the most successful forms of Chicano culture were found in graphic arts, music, painting and moviemaking. In New Mexico and California, Catholic missionaries during the Spanish period employed local artisans to paint and carve representations of Jesus, the Virgin, and the saints. The *santero* (village artist) became a respected member of the local community; during the twentieth century, mass-produced pictures and plaster statues helped to put him out of business. The tradition of religious art, however, continued. Modern Chicano artists like Estebán Villa and Manuel Hernández Trujillo derived inspiration from the work of both traditional *santeros* and modern painters, including the Mexican masters of the murals. Some of the Spanish-speaking artists stress their ethnic background, but others do not. Those that do have been influenced by pre-Columbian and Mexican traditions.

In addition to filmmaking, a subject discussed subsequently, the most significant influence on Chicano artists comes from the Mexican muralists Diego Rivera, Juan Orozco, and David Alfaro Sigueiros, all of who combined Spanish and Indian heritage in their work. Ethnic consciousness led some Chicano artists to form groups such as the Mexican American Liberation Art Front and Con/Sofo, which attempt to aid Mexican-American artists and to project in art forms the Chicano experience. The sculptor Medellín, for example, projects a strong Mexican, indeed a pre-Columbian style, while Luís Jiminez is very modern. Other prominent Chicano painters include António Gárcia (muralist), Porfírio Salinas (landscapist), Edward Chávez, and Melesio Casas.[26]

Puerto Rican and Cuban Contributions

Interest in Hispanic culture was not limited, of course, to Mexican Americans. The Puerto Ricans' situation in some ways differed from, and in certain respects resembled, the Chicanos. Puerto Rico had a substantial university system of its own, comprising both public and private schools and offering an advanced education to more than 120,000 students in 1981. The major institutions were the University of Puerto Rico, founded in 1903, with 50,000 students distributed over three campuses; the Inter-American University of Puerto Rico, established in 1912, with 11,000 students; and the Catholic University of Puerto Rico, created in 1948, also with 11,000 students. In addition, there were various smaller universities and regional colleges. By 1981, more students received a postsecondary school education in Puerto Rico than in Denmark, a more populous and considerably wealthier country than Puerto Rico.[27] Puerto Rico built up an extensive literature and a scholarly tradition of its own with bonds to France, Spain, and the various Latin American countries (but, unfortunately, too-little known in the United States). The Instituto de Cultura Puertoriqueño, the Academía de Artes y Ciencias de Puerto Rico, and the Editorial Universitaria, Universidad de Puerto Rico published Puerto Rican belleslettres. Puerto Ricans living on the United States mainland had no difficulty purchasing such works or in obtaining advanced academic instruction provided (in Spanish) in the island commonwealth.

Puerto Rican intellectuals on the mainland who were committed to *hispanidad* thus possessed a more accessible outlet than did Chicanos, for many of whom Mexico was a foreign country whose language they did not know well. Unlike Chicano militants in the Southwest, Puerto Rican radicals in New York or Chicago did not think of reconstituting an idealized national home on the American mainland; the Puerto Rican militant was far more likely to call for independence from the assumed American colonial yoke. Nevertheless, in many ways Puerto Rican academics on the mainland came to share the varied political and cultural convictions that animated their Chicano compatriots. Like the Chicanos, the Puerto Ricans were divided among those who sought cultural assimilation in the United States, those who wanted to preserve their Hispanic heritage within the existing social and political framework of the United States, and radicals who linked the cause of Puerto Rican culture with the cause of revolution.

The moderates supported groups such as *Aspira* (set up in 1961 to enable more Puerto Ricans to get an education). The Puerto Rican Legal Defense and Education Fund, a middle-class organization, fought against discrimination in the manner of the Jewish Anti-Defamation League. Puerto Rican leaders also called for bilingual education, special courses in Spanish and Puerto Rican history, and "community control" of education—a subject we treat in a separate chapter. New academic institutions came into being. Antonia Pantoja, founder of *Aspira*, set up the Universidad Boricua in New York and Washington, D.C., to provide advanced training for Puerto Rican students while involving them in research regarding Puerto Rico. At this time, Puerto Rican scholars like Frank Bonilla and Lloyd R. Canino attained academic prominence. Puerto Rican studies centers appeared at a variety of community colleges and universities. With the coming of Dominicans and Ecuadoreans, these centers became Hispanic or Caribbean centers rather than Puerto Rican. Puerto Rican student organizations became active, and often militantly leftist in their political orientation. In addition, Puerto Rican intellectuals attempted to create new forms of socially committed literature through such organs as the *Revista Chicano-Riqueña* and through such works as Juan Soto's *Spiks* (1973) and Piri Thomas's *Down These Mean Streets* (1967), cast in a mood of somber social realism. The work of Oscar Lewis, a Jewish American associated in a broader sense with this movement, reflected a similar mood. His *La Vida: A Puerto Rican Family in the Culture of Poverty* (1965) attempted to combine anthropological investigation with a general critique of capitalism in a work of literary achievement, though his concepts regarding the "culture of poverty" met with widespread dissent from Puerto Rican intellectuals.

Other artists with a social message included Pedro Juan Soto, who created a wealth of short stories, novels, and experimental dramas that depicted the misery of slum life in New York; poets Pedro Juan Pietra and Jesus "Papoleto" Melendez; as well as more traditional writers like Juan Aviles. Their work found an audience in institutions such as *El Museo del Barrio*, a center for poetry reading and workshops as well as for exhibitions by Puerto Rican artists in New York.[28]

Overall, in our view, these works of social realism are open to criticisms similar to those applicable to much of Chicano literature. The social realists, while claiming to speak for the poor,. in fact wrote about, but not for, the poor. For all the progressive writers' disdain for the bourgeosie, their books were read mainly by college audiences. The social realists were apt, moreover, to disregard entire dimensions of social reality. They assumed that the mass of Americans, or at least the mass of Hispanics, was downtrodden and alienated and that the men and women who enjoyed life and successfully managed their affairs were somehow unworthy of artistic consideration, or even ordinary respect.

The Cubans' experience differed strikingly from both the Chicanos' and Puerto Ricans'. Before the revolution, a substantial number of Cuban intellectuals sympathized with Castro. After Castro had forced Cuba's intellectual life into a Marxist-Leninist straitjacket, officially sponsored literature and scholarship became as unimaginative and uninspiring as in the Eastern bloc. Many of Cuba's most outstanding writers went to jail or into exile, including Armando Valladares, who was released from prison in 1983 after 22 years of misery. Valladares' poems were smuggled out of Cuba and published in Paris and Miami during the 1970s (one volume was entitled *From My Wheelchair*, based on a hunger strike that had temporarily paralyzed the poet's legs. Valladares' works, comparable in manner to Alexander Solzhenitsyn's, belong to the history of Cuban rather than of American literature. As Castro's repression intensified, more and more names of distinguished Cuban émigrés crowded the pages of the directory of Cubans abroad.

For Cuba, the mass emigration of intellectuals became a cultural disaster comparable to the emigration of German and Jewish intellectuals from Germany during the 1930s. By the early 1980s, even Fidel Castro had come to realize the extent of Cuba's cultural loss; instead of denouncing all émigrés as fascists and renegades whose departure had benefited Cuba, Castro came to ascribe Cuba's economic crisis in part to the loss of so many educated men and women since the revolution.

Cuba's loss proved North America's gain. The Turkish Sultan, upon receiving a multitude of distinguished Jews expelled by Spain at the end of the fifteenth century, supposedly expressed wonder at the Spanish monarch who impoverished his own kingdom by sending so many talented people into exile to enrich the Turkish monarch. Americans had good reason to sympathize with the Ottoman ruler's point of view. The history of Cuban culture in exile remains to be written. We can do no more than list in a footnote a few names that indicate the variety of talent that came to the United States.[29]

Contrary to Castro's propaganda, these exiled intellectuals were not, for the most part, right-wing conservatives. They were people of every conceivable shade of opinion, including many who had originally supported the Cuban revolution before breaking with Castro. However, they had certain features in common. They were apt to suffer from a dual sense of isolation: a sense of distance from their English-speaking neighbors, with whom they could not communicate in Spanish, and a sense of remoteness from the majority of the Latin American literary intelligentsia. Among Latin American scholars and literary men, the socialist revolution in Cuba had aroused almost universal approval. However, this approval was not unmixed with criticism. In 1971, for example, Castro jailed Cuban poet Heberto Padilla, who was forced to make a humiliating "confession" to regain his freedom. The Padilla affair led to numerous protests. Some intellectuals, such as Mario Vargas Llosa (the Peruvian novelist), broke with Havana. But, overall, the intellectuals preferred the Cuban regime to right-wing dictatorships; they generally regarded socialism as morally superior to capitalism, at least in the abstract; and they continued to regard the United States as a bastion of reaction. The Cuban exiles in this country, unable to share these assumptions, could make little impact on this solid orthodoxy. They did make a distinct contribution to the critique of Marxism-Leninism as it operated in their own country. But, perhaps lacking the requisite literary and personal connections, they did not make a wider impact on the English-speaking world, unlike those intellectuals associated, say, with the journal *Commentary* in the United States or *Encounter* in Great Britain.

In day-to-day politics, the majority of Cuban refugees long considered themselves exiles destined to return to their homeland after its liberation. Whereas Puerto Rican and Chicano militants would bitterly criticize or condemn American culture, most of the Cubans who found refuge were grateful to the United States for their freedom and for the prosperity they achieved for themselves and their families. And, whereas Chicanos and Puerto Ricans could travel to Mexico or Puerto Rico without hindrance, the Cubans were cut off by political barriers. They looked upon Cuba as early nineteenth-century Poles or as late nineteenth-century Irish-Americans regarded their respective home countries—as enslaved lands to be freed from a tyrannical regime.

Émigré Cuban intellectuals of course have made, and are making, an important contribution to American cultural life—as artists, university instructors, journalists, architects, and the like. Cuban as well as non-Cuban scholars have contributed to such publications as *Cuban Studies/ Estudios Cubanos* (published by the Center for Latin American Studies at the University of Pittsburgh and concerned with developments in revolutionary Cuba rather than in the United States). In the manner of previous immigrant groups, Cubans also have developed an active "ethnic" press. But there has been no attempt to build a new Cuban-American culture, comparable to Chicano culture with its uneasy blend of romantic longings, ethnic liberation, search for self-esteem, and call for social reconstruction.

The Hispanic Media, Sports, and Entertainment

The confluence of immigrants from many Spanish-speaking countries created a new market for Spanish reading material that all Spanish speakers could understand. By the early 1980s, the United States had become the fourth largest Spanish-speaking nation in the world; one of the largest groups of Spanish speakers was to be found in Los Angeles. Immigration into the United States opened a great and expanding market for newspapers, books, and radio and television shows—for cultural artifacts of every description—with far-reaching consequences for the future of the United States.

Although the annals of the Spanish-language press in the United States remain to be written, the history of the foreign-language press in the United States has followed a fairly consistent pattern. At the beginning when even educated immigrants often lacked an adequate command of English, standards often were high, as distinguished literary men contributed to the foreign-language press to gain an audience. Subsequently, the newcomers become Anglicized, and standards in the foreign language press dropped—fates of publications like the German-Jewish *Aufbau* in New York or the Yiddish-language press in the same city.

Only the future will show whether or not the Spanish-language press in this country suffers a similar fate. Given the size of the Spanish-speaking population, prospects for its own press are good. Most Spanish-language newspapers do not deal exclusively with Spanish-speaking peoples per se, but with national, local, and international news. In recent years, local newspapers have been developed to treat ethnic affairs or interest groups; for example, César Chávez's farm workers union publishes its own newspaper, *El Malcriado.* Others include *El Gallo*, of the Crusade for Justice in Denver, and *The Latin Times*, of Chicago. About 30 Chicano newspapers are published currently.[30] There is even a Chicano Press Pen Association. National magazines like *Regeneración* and *La Raza* have a long history; general magazines, including *Nuestro, Somos*, and *Agenda*, are mostly in English. Commercial publishers have not been anxious to publish Chicano authors in Spanish because the market was believed to be small. There are, however, some Chicano distributing centers and publishing firms (El Dorado Distributors, Cultural Distribution Center, Quinto Sol, and La Causa Publications); equally important, though sometimes neglected by scholars, are journals devoted to the growing Hispanic market, including *Hispanic Business* and *Hispanic Business Magazine.* The major publishing centers for Hispanic studies tend to be located at university presses (for example, UCLA, UCSD, the University of Texas, and Notre Dame University).

Altogether, the Spanish press in the United States has greatly expanded: by 1983, more than one hundred newspapers were being distributed. It is as diverse in its composition as the Hispanic population. But, for the most part, it bears little resemblance to what the architects of *Chicanismo* hoped to achieve. Far more typical than *Chicanismo's* academic writers were television personalities and journalists, including Grace Soto and Virginia Maese, cofounders of the new English-language magazine for Hispanic women *Latina* (established in 1982). Soto and Maese provide articles not about *Chicanismo*, but about celebrities, health, fashion, films, cookery, and general news—a typical woman's magazine in any culture. For better or worse, Hispanic audiences in the United States have turned out to be not all that different from their compatriots.

Ethnic cultures in the United States traditionally have made a major impact in such areas as music, food, the performing arts, and athletics. These areas share certain features. In the first three, an entrepreneur's foreign descent is no disadvantage; on the contrary, his national heritage adds a touch of the exotic that customers value. All four activities transcend linguistic boundaries, require no subventions from private foundations or from the taxpayers' pocket, and serve as avenues for social advancement.

Music and sports, moreover, enjoy the advantage of being exempt from the suspicion of elitism that haunts so many progressive American educators. Music and sports—unlike algebra or chemistry—appeal to a wide circle of spectators who feel competent to judge the performances they watch; they prize excellence, and their concept of excellence becomes part of popular culture.

The Mexican music performers often started as farm laborers or fruitpickers who learned an instrument and played by ear without being able to read musical scores. Gradually, the more skillful or fortunate became more professional, went on regular tours, and were accepted by record companies specializing in ethnic music. The most successful musicians also gained a reputation in other styles, including rock music. Outstanding performers included Flaco Jimenez, a noted accordion player, whose *corridos* covered an immense variety of subjects: the tale of a dreadful hurricane ("Victimas del Hurracan Beluah"), praise of a young Mexican-American soldier fighting for his country in Vietnam ("El Pade de un Soldado"), and the tragic-comic ballad concerning a *mojado*, lacking a green card (an immigration permit), who loses both his car and his girlfriend to dastardly Anglos ("Un Mojado Sin Licencia").[31]

Other aspects of the Hispanic musical heritage promoted by Mexican-Americans include *flamenco*, music and dance originally from Spain but enriched by artists from many Latin American countries. Mexican-Americans gained equal renown as singers in a variety of art forms: classical; Spanish, Mexican, and New Mexican folk songs; and American country-western, where artists such as Freddy Fender and Johnny Rodríguez acquired reputations for themselves. All of these arts transcend the narrow bounds of campus-centered *Chicanismo* or purely "ethnic" music. Their influence on American culture therefore has been profound and is certain to grow. Other Spanish-surnamed musicians include Xavier Cugat, "Tavares," Charo, Carlos Montoya, Pepe Romero, and Vicki Carr.

The Cuban impact has been equally important. Cubans have achieved fame as classical performers (one example, Alberto Bolet y Tremoleda, an outstanding violinist and cello player). Cuban impresarios in Miami have staged traditional operettas as well as song recitals and classical works. A substantial number of entertainers have performed popular Cuban music on records produced and manufactured in Miami or New York. Younger musicians have learned to mix Latin rhythms with contemporary soul and rock in styles known throughout the world. Puerto Ricans also have acquired fame both as classical musicians (Jesús Mária Sonroma and Graciela Moreno) and in popular music (Tito Puente, Noro Morales, and José Feliciano).

Of like significance is the immigrants' impact on American cuisine. Tortillas, tacos, carnitas, carne asada, and chile verde are familiar to restaurant-goers all over the United States. Ethnic outsiders also have made their way into beauty competitions. Intellectuals might despise the "Miss America" contest, just as they disdain so many other forms of entertainment pleasing to their fellow citizens. But for millions of Americans, beauty contests provide a magnificent spectacle. And viewers of non-Anglo-Saxon background have experienced personal satisfaction as "acceptable" models have expanded.

Another road to success has led through sports. The achievements of "ethnic" athletes always has been a source of pride to their respective communities, as well as a means of dispelling hostile images with regard to any particular immigrant group. The history of sports in the United States has seen an ethnic succession from one lowly paid unskilled immigrant group to the next, especially in baseball and boxing. Baseball, unlike tennis, requires no expensive courts; amateur teams prove their prowess in vacant city lots. Boxing is a useful skill in a tough neighborhood, especially for those who want to avenge ethnic slurs. Excellence in athletics, moreover, has the quality of total verifiability. Even the most fair-minded jury is apt to disagree bitterly on which candidate merits the Nobel Prize, but on the running track or football field, or in the boxing ring, there is no room for argument.

In recent years, Hispanics have dominated the world middle and lightweight classes.[32] Hispanics also play a major role in professional baseball. There have been fewer Hispanic basketball and tennis stars, but mention should be made of Rosemary Casals (Spanish), Orlando (Pancho) Gonzáles (Mexican-American) and Raul Ramirez (Mexican), as well as Guillermo Vilas of Argentina. Chi Chi Rodriguez (Puerto Rican) and Lee Trevino (Mexican American) are top-ranked golfers, and many Hispanics are jockeys.

In addition to gaining acclaim on the playing fields or in the boxing rings, Hispanics gained fame on the Hollywood movie screen in what might be called the "ethnic" as well as the national market. Every moviegoer in the United States knows the names and faces of artists Jose Ferrer, Rita Moreno, and Anthony Quinn, even though few of their fans know that these artists are respectively of Puerto Rican or Mexican origin. Desi Arnez (Cuban) for years had the best comic series on TV "I Love Lucy"; he also had a successful career as a band leader and a movie actor. Freddie Prinze, Tony Orlando, Geraldo Riviera, and Erik Estrada (all Puerto Ricans) have had successful TV careers. And there are many Hispanic dance groups performing in the United States, and actors and dancers abound.

Films, television, and radio programs in the Spanish language occupy a very different position. Filmmaking remains one of the few art forms in the modern world that is enjoyed equally by intellectuals and the mass of the people. By the early 1980s, over two hundred films had been made in the United States by and about Mexican Americans, Puerto Rican Americans, and Americans from other Spanish-speaking nations. These films transcended the narrow bounds of campus-centered *Chicanismo*, attracting viewers from the general public as well as the

Spanish-speaking population. To promote their distribution, Adan Medrano, himself a filmmaker, and Don Cardenas set up the Bilingual Communications Center in Denver, Colorado. The new organization sponsored its own "Cinefiesta" as part of the Denver International Film Festival. By the early 1980s, Latin films had attained such quality that Cardenas and Medrano were fully justified in speaking of an "artistic renaissance."[33]

Many of these films had a didactic quality: they were designed to educate the general public in the role played by Spanish-speaking peoples in the United States. Such movies included *Seguín*, the biography of Juan Seguín, an unsung hero of the Texas war for independence from Spain; another was *Chuco*, which re-examined the zoot-suit riots of the 1940s and castigated racial stereotypes portrayed in the media. The new Latin films, however, also dealt with problems affecting humanity as a whole. The movie *Atrapados*, for example, explored the fate of two strangers trapped beneath the rubble of a shattered high rise apartment building; its air of hope and courage would appeal to any viewer with an experience of civil catastrophe or war. In 1983, *The Ballad of Gregorio Cortez* became a national success on the American screen. The movie was based on Américo Paredes's *With His Pistol in His Hand*, published in 1958, which told the story of a Mexican sheriff killed in 1901 during a tragic gunfight, an incident that had found its way into many *corridos*. Equally noteworthy were *El Norte* (a movie that won wide acclaim in 1984) and the film version of *Zoot Suit*.

Spanish-language movies served a restricted audience. Spanish television, on the other hand, became a major business enterprise, given the size of the Hispanic market (estimated at $40 billion in 1980). U.S. television producers long had ignored this specialized market while, conversely, English-language programs were beamed to Latin American countries in such numbers as to arouse harsh criticism of "cultural imperialism." Mexican reaction was so bitter that, in 1974, the Mexican government banned numerous American television series, including "Ironside," "The FBI," and "The Fugitive" on the grounds that these programs promoted "non-Mexican values" and excessive violence.

But then the tables turned. In 1960, long before *Chicanismo* had become a force on American campuses, a group of Mexican television magnates—including Miguel Alemán Valdes (a former President of Mexico and a major investor in the Mexican tourist industry), Rómulo O'Farril (owner of numerous Mexican newspapers), and Emilio Azcarraga (an electronic media tycoon)—began to investigate opportunities offered by the Hispanic market in the United States. Their efforts resulted in the creation of SIN (Spanish International Network), linked financially to Televisa, the Mexican television empire. By 1980, SIN included 82 affiliates: nine linked by satellite, six regular stations, six low-power stations, and the rest on a cable system. Mexican television, controlled by Mexicans in Mexico, had become a cultural power in the United States, a fact far from welcome to its *Chicanista* critics. (Puerto Ricans on the eastern seaboard, by contrast, heavily depended on telecasts from the island.)

KMEX-TV, in Los Angeles, became a major enterprise with live shows from Mexico, spectacular musical and cultural programs (with a strong emphasis on Mexico), news, athletic events, and the like. WNJU, an alternative language network, beamed Spanish news and entertainment to the large Hispanic community in the New York area. Subsequently, CBS made arrangements for bilingual television series, and the FCC decided to permit a major increase in the number of VHF channels serving specialized audiences.

According to the Broadcasting Cable Yearbook, 23 Spanish-language television stations operated within the continental United States in 1980, nearly as many as in the whole of Spain (28).[34] SIN in 1983 was estimated to reach more than three million Spanish speakers. The various telecasts differed greatly in content, style, and political orientation. SIN presented world events from a liberal-leftist standpoint, but not all Spanish telecasts followed this pattern. Nor did Spanish-speaking viewers confine their attention to Spanish programs only. Television itself helped to create a bilingual market. Overall, the Spanish-language media justified neither the worst fears of their critics nor the brightest hopes of their supporters. Most of the Spanish television stations—like their English-language counterparts—provided a steady fare of news, sports (including soccer), commentaries, musical programs, and full-length features imported from Mexico and other Spanish-speaking countries. Some of these films were of high quality. Many others, with such titles as *Extraños Caminos del Amor* ("Strange Ways of Love"), *La Vil Seducción* ("Vile Seduction"), and *Quiero Gritar Tu Nombre* ("I Wish to Cry Out Your Name"), were given to extended close-ups, noble sentiments, and facile plots.

The extent of television's political impact is uncertain, but one thing is clear: Spanish-speaking audiences are as diverse, but also as enthusiastic in their support of the new medium, as is any other ethnic group in the country. Like every other ethnic or special interest group, they fought against such demeaning or supposedly demeaning stereotypes as the "Frito Bandito" advertisements.

In addition, the growth of the Hispanic market led to a striking expansion of Spanish radio stations. By the late 1970s, there were more than five hundred Spanish-language radio stations in the United States.

According to their critics, these stations had numerous deficiencies, including lower frequency power than stations broadcasting little or no Spanish. The radio stations lived by advertising, by their real or supposed "ability to sell its audience as a consumer market."[35] They provided few opportunities for local Chicano artists and depended heavily on records made in South America. Worst of all, from the intellectuals' standpoint, their audiences were largely in lower-income neighborhoods.

Between them, however, television and radio broadcasting became a major cultural force and often—unexpectedly—an instrument of cultural adaptation to American society. The Spanish-language programs primarily served large Spanish-speaking audiences in New York, San Francisco, San Antonio, Los Angeles, and Miami. According to the 1980 census, 11.1 million Americans spoke Spanish at home, although three-quarters of them also used English. But, in many cities, there were much larger concentrations of Spanish-speakers; fully 40 percent of San Antonio's population and 36 percent of Miami's used Spanish at home, with the older Hispanic people being far more likely to speak Spanish well than those between the ages of 5 and 17.

In general terms, sociologists could point to two conflicting, yet complementary, trends. On the one hand, the spread of education and the impact of the media caused Spanish speakers to turn to English, as European immigrants had done in the past. According to the 1980 census, 5 percent of American adults lived in homes where Spanish was the main language; but, of these adults, more than two-thirds spoke English well. On the other hand, there was a new demand for Spanish—not the *patois* of the streets, but grammatical Spanish pronounced in the fashion acceptable in Latin America. Mexican Americans complained at times that too many posts went to foreigners from Mexico or Cuba rather than to Chicanos. Station managers, for their part, argued that many American-born Mexicans failed to speak perfect Spanish and therefore could not easily hold their own in the rapid give-and-take of a talk show. Television experts found that, far from being incompatible, a sound knowledge of good English and good Spanish went hand in hand.

Overall, Spanish broadcasting and television did not eliminate English services; they complemented them. The majority of TV owners watching Spanish programs in San Antonio and East Los Angeles watched English more than Spanish programs. Only 21 percent devoted more time to Spanish than to English telecasts. According to one sample, audiences paid attention to radio and television in making up their minds on how to vote; but 60 percent of the same sample stated that such media were not important in influencing their electoral decisions. However,

Spanish-language television and radio, like Spanish films and Latin music, did succeed in transcending the national limitations of particular Hispanic audiences.[36] Mexican Americans, Puerto Rican Americans, Cuban Americans, and Spanish-speaking "Anglos" all contributed to new arts and came to serve a wider community.

Chapter 11

Hispanic Politics

From the day the United States declared its independence, American politics was to some extent ethnic politics. Ethnicity played a part even in the struggle against George III. A number of minorities had sided with the Crown: American Indians generally gave support to the British; so did many settlers from Scotland (especially the ill-assimilated Highlanders). A popular toast during the War of Independence went to "the free exportation of Scotchmen and Tories."[1] The power of diverse ethnic lobbies differed widely. Nineteenth-century Irish immigrants—able for the most part to speak English, and familiar with the art of agitating and organizing against their British overlords—were concentrated in a few major cities and came to play a major part in urban and ultimately in national politics. Voters of Scandinavian and German ancestry wielded much less power because of their relative geographical dispersion in midwestern farming areas.

From Notables to Organization Men

Spanish-speaking Americans always played some part in the local politics of the Southwest. But nationwide they were one of the last ethnic minorities to make their power felt. Many factors conspired to reduce their influence in public affairs. At first they were weak numerically, for the bulk of Mexicans and Puerto Ricans only entered the mainland United States only after the turn of this century. Mostly poor and ill educated in a formal sense, they were largely confined to the geographical periphery—New Mexico, southern California and southern Texas—and to New York. They were exposed to all kinds of disability, political and racial; they lacked unity.

Political influence initially centered on the great landowners, and their relatives and friends. In California, as we have seen, the Mexican magnates lost their land and power. In parts of Texas and New Mexico, the *patrón* managed to hold on to his traditional position; *Hispano* notables continued to exercise leverage in local government through their ability to deliver the votes of their clients through the *hacienda* system, and through the ability of the *patrón* class to stake out claims in corporate enterprise. In New Mexico, for instance, Miguel António Otero became a prominent businessman, with interests in land and railway companies; he also served for three terms as a member of the U.S. House of Representatives. His son Miguel Otero, Jr., attained the territorial governorship of New Mexico under President William McKinley. By organizing Mexican-American voters and obtaining control over some federal appointments, he created his own political machine and ran an efficient administration.

The Mexican middle and lower-middle class, by contrast, at first played a miniscule role in politics. They had a stake in retail trade and in serving local markets; but for the most part they lacked the capital or technical expertise to build major business enterprises. If anything, their part in local affairs diminished, as often the Mexican *pueblo* became engulfed by a larger English-speaking city and as the *pueblo* was reduced to a *barrio*. As successful Mexican Americans left the *barrio*, and indeed often changed their names, the masses often found themselves deprived of what might otherwise have become their natural leaders.

A Spanish-speaking intelligentsia thus at first hardly existed, and the villagers found themselves bereft of educated spokesmen. As mass emigration from Mexico began after the turn of the century, a considerable proportion of the Mexican laborers in the Southwest consisted of newcomers and labor migrants—men and women without a vote and harder to weld into unions or political parties than any other segment of the laboring poor. Many of these newcomers looked for help to Mexican consuls accredited to the United States, rather than to local politicians or to local courts with their apparently incomprehensible procedures.

Military service during two World Wars and the gradual growth of a Mexican American middle class gave a new impetus to political organizations. In 1921 returning veterans formed the Order of the Sons of America in San Antonio. The League of United Latin Americans (LULAC), formed in 1923, in Corpus Christi, aimed at civil and social equality, full integration of Spanish-speaking Americans, improved education, active participation in U.S. politics, and an end to discimination in schools and jobs. LULAC developed into an effective lobby which later issued its own journal (*Latino*), prepared guides for voters, issued a newsletter (*Aviso*), and conducted studies of legislation affecting Hispanics. With branches in 41 states, LULAC is the nation's oldest and largest Hispanic organization. But, given the size of the Hispanic population, LULAC's membership remains limited. In 1983 LULAC had 110,000 members, compared to 317,00 members listed in 1975 in the Polish National Alliance, one of several bodies serving the Polish community in the United States, a community little more than one-third of the size of Hispanics in this country). Other political bodies include the American G.I. Forum, the Mexican American Political Organization, the Political Association of Mexican American Organizations, and the Community Service Organization.[2]

The 1960s witnessed the rise of many additional groups, organized as lobbies, staffed by men and women trained as lawyers, educators, or administrative experts, skilled in dealing with government agencies, and determined to improve welfare, education and other services for Chicanos. They depended on gifts from private foundations and, even more, on federal, state, and local government funds. Much of their success hinged on their ability to extract funds from official sources, and in this respect they differed strikingly from earlier ethnic organizations, which lacked access to government funds and depended much more heavily on private benefactions from their members.

One of the most important of these newer bodies was the Mexican American Legal Defense and Educational Fund (MALDEF), set up in 1968, and centered in San Francisco, with offices in other cities, including Denver, Los Angeles, and Washington, D.C. MALDEF sought to give educational assistance and to protect the legal rights of Mexican Americans through legal action. In addition to cases relating to voting rights, public accommodation, and job discrimination, MALDEF took on issues relating to social welfare, municipal rights, consumer protection, and the like.[3] The same year, 1968, also saw the creation of the National Mexican-American Anti-Defamation Committee, which hoped to profit from the lessons of Jewish Americans.

Another important body was the National Council of La Raza (NCLR) of Washington, D.C., a private, nonprofit organization, founded in 1968 as the Southwest Council of La Raza to organize Chicano groups (100 groups were affiliated in Arizona, California, Colorado, New Mexico, and Texas). It became known as a resource and information clearinghouse, a coordinating and funding source for local Chicano organizations. NCLR trained entrepreneurs, researched Chicano voting patterns and participation, and worked on bilingual and bicultural education projects. In 1970 the council moved to Washington, D.C., to act as a pressure group.[4] There also were more distinctly pedagogic bodies; for example the Mexican-American Educators, organized in the 1960s to encourage the advancement of Chicano teachers and administrators and higher education for Chicano students. The group also served as a clearinghouse on Mexican-American education. The National Association for Chicano Studies, formed in 1972, worked mostly in the western U.S. to build Chicano political, cultural, and educational awareness.

The Puerto Ricans at first were slow to organize. Many of them were labor migrants who initially turned for help to the Office of the

Commonwealth of Puerto Rico, set up in 1949 by Luis Munoz Marín. As the community grew, the importance of the agency diminished, and a number of private organizations began to take over many of its functions. These included ASPIRA, an educational association; the Puerto Rican Teachers Association; the United Bronx Parents; and others. But for a long time voters failed to go to the polls. Such neglect was a response in part to the major parties' indifference to the Puerto Ricans' voting potential. In New York, there was usually a last-minute drive to corral the "Spanish" vote through the Mayor's Committee on Puerto Rican Affairs, but the special needs of the Puerto Rican working class usually was last on the politicans' agenda.

With increasing immigration after World War II, the Puerto Rican vote became somewhat more influential. At the same time, Puerto Ricans began to organize in a more effective fashion. In 1958, they formed the Congress of Organizations and Puerto Rican Hometowns, an association of 57 civic, cultural, and political organizations in New York City, designed to serve as a link between its member groups and city and state officials and also to promote civil rights, voter registration and the abolition of literacy tests for Puerto Rican voters in New York State. Five years later, in 1963, Puerto Ricans set up the National Association for Puerto Rican Civil Rights, modeled in some measure on the NAACP and affiliated with the Leadership Conference on Civil Rights. In addition, Puerto Ricans created the National Puerto Rican-Hispanic Voter Participation Project. This was fashioned on the older Mexican-American organization and designed to improve Puerto Rican voter turnout in cities like New York, where Puerto Ricans, though numbering between 13 and 15 percent of the population, provided only 6 percent of the voters in the 1978 and 1980 elections for the New York State Assembly. The Association of Puerto Rican Executive Directors (ASPIRA) was founded in 1961 in New York City by Puerto Rican professionals who believe that education was the way to develop youth. ASPIRA devoted itself to encouraging Hispanics to complete high school, to pursue further studies, and to work for their communities. This was accomplished through high school clubs, youth services, scholarship programs, and by advocacy and research. ASPIRA of America, founded in 1980, coordinated the efforts of six groups (in Puerto Rico, Pennsylvania, Illinois, Florida, New Jersey, and New York) and provided a linkage system between groups and city, state, and federal agencies.[5] Another important group was the National Puerto Rican Forum, Inc., of New York City, founder of ASPIRA, and the largest and oldest nonprofit Puerto-Rican community-based organization in the United States. Founded in 1957, the forum steadily pursued its objectives of social and economic improvement of Puerto Ricans and other

Hispanics by job training and placement, market and survey research, economic development, and advocacy.[6]

The Puerto Rican Legal Defense and Education Fund was incorporated in 1972 to help the Puerto Rican community achieve equal rights and opportunities by providing legal representation and promoting legal education through its professional development program of recruiting and training Puerto Rican lawyers. Other groups in New York City concerned themselves with youths (Mobilization for Youth), drugs (Promesa), community-based organizations (Progress), the elderly (Puerto Rican Association for Community Affairs), and the family (Puerto Rican Family Institute). There also were Casita Maria, Inc., the East Harlem Council for Human Services, and others.[7] All of these groups, Mexican and Puerto Rican alike, looked to the integration of their people into American society through established court procedures, welfare agencies, and existing party politics.

In terms of party politics, the support of Mexican Americans overwhelmingly went to the Democratic Party. They backed Franklin D. Roosevelt and the New Deal. Roosevelt himself did little for Hispanic Americans, but the New Deal agencies benefited Hispanic Americans to some degree and created a lasting sense of gratitude. The Truman administration in 1948 completed the integration of the armed forces. John F. Kennedy was even better liked by the Hispanic voters: during the 1960 election, something like 98 percent of the Mexican-American vote went to Kennedy over Richard Nixon. Kennedy had personal charisma; he was a Catholic; he had a beautiful wife who spoke Spanish; above all, he had the support of his entire family, his family was popular, and the voters appreciated family links. Mexican-American support for the Democrats declined somewhat when George McGovern ran for the presidency; he won no more than 85 percent of the Mexican-American vote. But in 1976 Jimmy Carter brought the percentage up to 92, deliberately appealing to the Hispanics through advertising in Spanish, and profiting also from the general *desconfianza*, the spreading distrust of the federal government heightened by the Watergate scandal.

The Puerto Rican vote also went to the Democrats in overwhelming numbers—though not necessarily for the same reasons. Puerto Ricans, like blacks, on the whole had more trust in the federal government than did Mexican-Americans, partly because of the Puerto Ricans' share in public employment in New York. Puerto Ricans were impressed also by the New Dealers' connection with Munoz Marín, the apparent success of New Deal politics on the island itself, and the part played by the Democratic Party in building welfare agencies, both on the federal level and in New York. The Puerto Rican poor hoped for justice from the federal courts and the government bureaucracy.

Mexican Americans were more ambivalent in their attitude. The lawyers working for MALDEF also looked to the federal courts, but on the whole Mexican Americans were more likely than Puerto Ricans to distrust *los federales*—those federal officials whom Mexicans met in the guise of immigration inspectors or police officials. Mexican Americans contained among their ranks a large number of men and women lacking American citizenship and not entitled to welfare services. Into the 1980s, Mexican Americans continued to be underrepresented both in the federal and the state civil service in comparison not only to Anglos but also to black Americans. Despite their excellent fighting record in wartime, Hispanics did not enlist to anything like the same extent in the peacetime armed forces, despite the military's pioneer role in integrating minorities.[8]

In terms of electoral power, the so-called Spanish vote at first counted for little outside certain regions such as New Mexico. Hispanic politics for long remained confined to the middle class, which was small in number and disparate in composition. For the masses, there was a sense of discouragement. Henry Barbosa Gonzalez records that when he first entered local politics, in 1950, there was no person with a Spanish surname on the primary ballot in what to all intents and purposes was a one-party state.[9] Gonzalez descended from Spanish settlers in northern Mexico on his father's side and from Scotch-Irish Presbyterian stock on his mother's, yet his acquaintances assured him that he was *un loco*, a madman, for even trying to gain public office. Gonzalez had started in the humble job of a probation officer in Bexar County; subsequently, he became family relocation director for the San Antonio Housing Authority; in 1950, he managed to be elected a San Antonio city councilman and later gained a seat in the U.S. Congress, the first Texan of Mexican origin to achieve that office.

Gonzalez' success was hard won, for the entire system of representation seemed to work against men and women of his background. The complex arrangement of electoral districts had not been designed to keep Hispanics from being elected; but it operated in their disfavor, taking no account of the growth and distribution of Mexican Americans. In California, for instance, East Los Angeles became the major Mexican-American center, with an estimated Hispanic population of more than 600,000 in 1971. East Los Angeles, however, remained divided into nine state assembly districts, seven state senate districts and six U.S. congressional districts—all of them with non-Hispanic majorities. In city elections, Mexican Americans faced similar difficulties. Most cities in the Southwest had adopted a system of at-large elections, introduced originally for the purpose of avoiding the real or supposed corruption of machine politics. In practice, the system worked against political representation of Mexican Americans who tended to be concentrated in particular wards, and who therefore would have benefited from a system allowing each ward or district to vote for its own candidate. Not surprisingly, Mexicans failed to make their potential power felt at the polls. In 1970, no more than eleven Mexican Americans held office in California (compared to 392 non-Mexicans); and there were only 98 Mexican-American city councilmen (compared to 1,594 non-Mexicans).[10]

Mexicans living in the United States, moreover, were slow in securing naturalization, much slower than immigrants from Europe. The median age of Hispanic voters remained low (about half of them were under the age of twenty). And a high proportion of Mexican and Puerto Rican voters belonged to the working class, which generally has a lower voter turnout than the middle class.

There also were striking disparities that made common action difficult. Mexican Americans and Puerto Ricans, for example, seemed to share no common interest. The various Mexican communities themselves were divided by regional differences. For example, Texas has both a poorer racial climate and greater concentrations of Hispanics in its cities than does New Mexico, a more conservative state where *hispanos* always have held a substantial stake in politics and have sharply differentiated themselves from the Mexican immigrants, nicknamed *surmatos.*

Not that the picture was wholly bleak. Hispanic Americans developed their own class of political notables, men who won their spurs in city and state politics and subsequently advanced to higher office. Among Puerto Ricans, one of the most outstanding of these was Herman Badillo. He made his mark as a lawyer, and, within the Democratic Party in New York, as Bronx Borough president and as city commissioner; in 1970, he became the first mainland Puerto Rican to be elected to the House of Representatives. (By 1977, the New York community had placed into office one congressman, two state senators, four state assemblymen, and two city councilmen.)

As we have indicated before, Puerto Ricans in New York remained a youthful community, much of it poverty stricken. Their political elites were subject to many constraints. James Jenning, a political scientist, identified three distinct groups among them: "poverty-crats," or welfare program administrators; bureaucrats; and elected politicians. The "poverty-crats" depended on federal or city money, an unstable power base, as funding for programs fluctuated. The bureaucrats were limited by the requirements and ethos of their position. The electoral politicians enjoyed greater freedom, though this of course was circumscribed by the need to please their Puerto Rican (and sometimes also non-Puerto Rican) constituents and by the need to form electoral alliances. The political leaders differed from traditional European ethnic politicians in being better educated, more apt to support reform groups, and not as strongly tied to party loyalty. Most of them had completed college and made their living in professional, technical, managerial, or administrative positions.[11]

Mexican Americans also have made additional progress. The 1974 elections led to the elevation of two Mexican Americans to governorships. Jerry Apodaca, governor of New Mexico, had served in the New Mexico State Senate, where he was chairman of the Democratic caucus. Raul Hector Castro, governor of Arizona, was a naturalized citizen born in Mexico; he made a name for himself first as a superior court judge, later as U.S. Ambassador to El Salvador and then Bolivia. But nationwide, Hispanic Americans remained of minor account in public affairs.

The Republicans might have tried to garner Mexican-American support in states like California, where the Mexican-American vote can, in theory, swing elections. Republicans could have appealed to Mexican-American and Puerto Rican voters on social issues—such as crime, homosexuality, and abortion—on which the so-called Latin vote usually took a conservative position. Republicans could have made a pitch for the small businessman; and they could have attempted to address an essential fact: that the Mexican American is worth something as an individual human being, that personal qualities are worth more than any organization. But, as a Mexican-American scholar said: "Republican campaigners do not make the pitch that individual endeavor, supported by extant legislation, will accomplish more than any welfare program. . . ."[12]

The Republicans also might have attempted to gain Mexican-American support over such issues as racial discrimination, improved education, or the abuse often received by poverty-stricken Mexicans in regions like southern Texas. Republicans might have paid attention to Chicano "laundry lists" outlining abuses in schools and of the police.[13] But the Republicans generally failed to make use of their opportunities among Hispanics. There were some exceptions. In 1968, Manuel Lujan, son of a former mayor of Santa Fe, secured election to Congress, the first Republican to represent New Mexico in the House for 46 years. Lujan was not, however, an ethnic politician. He appealed to businessmen and to those who approved of his commitment to encourage industrial expansion into rural areas. Overall, the Republicans neglected the Hispanics, with one major exception, the Cubans.

The Cubans generally distrusted the Democrats, whom they considered "soft" on communism and whom they censured for Kennedy's perceived betrayal of the Cuban invasion at the Bay of Pigs. The Cuban impact on U.S. politics was at first limited. The Cubans initially considered themselves as merely temporary residents in this country. They were, moreover, divided into a variety of organizations, unable to present a united front.[14] The vast majority was united in its hatred of the Castro dictatorship; but, even in this matter, Cubans differed widely in their prescriptions for future action—from joining small groups devoted to armed insurgency (and sometimes involved in crime), to constitutional agitation, or even to engaging in negotiations (*el Diálogo*) with the Cuban authorities for the purpose of allowing émigrés to visit relatives at home. (This policy may have contributed to the massive exodus of Cubans from the port of Mariel in 1980.) Overall, however, the Cubans looked upon the left as their opponents, and their sympathies overwhelmingly went to the Republican Party.

Politics: The Changing U.S. Scene

The 1960s and the 1970s saw a profound change in the country's political climate. The United States became committed to social transformation through the New Frontier and the Great Society. There were far-reaching changes in the administrative power structure—much more than the effects produced by demonstrations, processions, and ritual fasts staged by student militants. The judicial branch vastly increased its power, both on the federal and the state level. Courts assumed what to all intents and purposes were both legislative and executive functions.[15]

Judges increasingly became convinced that the courts must play an active role in reforming the nation, on the grounds that the constitution was a "living law," to be used creatively and in a flexible form for an "evolving society." The courts therefore inclined to extend rights to promote general social equity. The process of liberalizing the judiciary accelerated in 1978, when the Omnibus Judgeship Act established seven new federal judgeships and 35 additional circuit judgeships (all lifetime appointments). A high proportion of these went to candidates active in Democratic Party politics; President Carter was able to appoint nearly half of the members of the federal bench. A mere 3 percent of these nominees defined themselves as "conservative" in one poll—even though self-professed conservatives were more than ten times as numerous in similar polls taken in the country at large.

There was an equally striking transformation of the federal executive. No matter who occupied the Oval Office or which party controlled the executive, agencies concerned with civil rights issues increased both their personnel and functions. The Carter administration merely accelerated existing trends through the Labor Department, the Equal Employment Opportunity Commission, the Justice Department, Health, Education and Welfare, and other agencies. Their senior civil servants were overwhelmingly committed—like the liberal judges—to what they regarded as the humanization of society through social action. These beneficient ends were to be attained by means of eliminating racial injustice, the planned redistribution of wealth, the enhanced regulatory power of the state, and a striking increase in public expenditure designed to benefit the poor.

The politics of welfare assumed a new shape. It came to rest on complex and shifting alliances between public agencies, their spokesmen and supporters in Congress and state houses, an activist judiciary, and a great variety of social or ethnic lobbies and protest groups. To its proponents, the evolving welfare state stood as a monument to a new morality. According to its critics, the new order benefited the diploma-bearing professionals more than the poor; the evolving tax system was deeply regressive; "public goods" spending channeled more tax money to wealthy than to needy Americans; and even environmental and minimum-wage standards, designed to help the deprived, rebounded to the benefit of the prosperous and the well educated. Whatever the rights and wrongs of this controversy, the growing welfare state increased the range of "public goods" available for distribution among the electorate. By doing so, the new order added to the strife among competing lobbies, ethnic or otherwise, to secure a fair share of these goods to their respective members.

Ethnic lobbies further increased their strength through the Voting Rights Act of 1965 and subsequent court decisions bearing on the subject. Originally conceived to protect the voting rights of blacks in the South, the law was expanded in 1975 to cover language minorities in the Southwest, including Hispanics unable to speak English. The new legislation forbade discriminatory election devices, such as literacy tests and the poll tax; it attempted to safeguard minorities against gerry-mandering schemes apt to dilute the strength of minority voters; it required bilingual ballots in areas where one particular minority exceeded 5 percent of the vote. The Justice Department was empowered to review changes in voting procedures—from moving a single polling site to redrawing political boundaries. In the Southwest these provisions applied to the whole of Texas, portions of Arizona and New Mexico, and four counties in California (King, Merced, Yuba, and Monterey). As a result of this and related measures, both the black and the Hispanic vote considerably increased in power—to the consternation of conservatives unable or unwilling to do their electoral homework on the minorities.

The new politics, with its increasing emphasis on minority rights, developed at a time when Mexican, Puerto Rican, and Cuban Americans began to make some limited but real gains in the economy. Hispanics, for one thing, increasingly found their way into skilled trade. According to a Census Bureau survey completed in 1972, Hispanic males over the age of fourteen, while still heavily underrepresented in managerial and professional jobs, provided about the same percentage of craftsmen as many other ethnic groups (19.6 for Hispanics; 21 for Germans; 19.2 for English, Scottish, and Welsh; corresponding percentages for managerial and administrative positions were 6.5; 13.9; 15.8). At the same time there was a striking and as yet ill-documented expansion of Hispanic businesses. A few of them made the headlines or found their way into reference books—for example, specialized entrepreneurs, such as Oscar de la Renta, a Dominican fashion designer who opened what became a famous salon; and Cuban-born Roberto C. Goiceta, chairman of the Coca Cola Company. But the typical Puerto Rican, Mexican, or Cuban businessman ran a store or a restaurant, a garage or repair shop, or a barber's salon. Studies completed by the U.S. Bureau of the Census in 1972 and 1978 confirmed that enterprises owned by Hispanics remained heavily concentrated in retail trade and related services. In 1977, 62 percent of these firms belonged to Mexican Americans, 16 percent to Cuban-Americans, and the rest to Puerto Ricans and Hispanics of other ancestry.

The total worth of "Hispanic" business is hard to estimate. Calculations, for one thing, raise the complex question of who is or is not Hispanic. Should Dr. Luis W. Alvarez, a Nobel laureate in physics and a director of the Hewlett-Packard Company, be classified as such? He is of Spanish-American descent on his father's side and Anglo-American on his mother's side. The late Freddie Prinze, a popular entertainer, was of mixed Puerto Rican and Hungarian descent. It is a difficult problem to solve, even for Hispanic activists who complain, for instance, that Spanish-speaking immigrants from foreign countries are much better represented in higher educational institutions in the United States than are Puerto Ricans or Chicanos. Under the rubric of "Hispanic," "Latin," or "Spanish" origin—goes the complaint—these aliens benefit excessively from affirmative action programs.[16] Calculations concerning the net worth of American business also involve the "second economy," which operates outside the scrutiny of the IRS. (Its value, in 1981, was estimated by Peter M. Guttman, an economist, at $420 billion in unreported incomes.[17] The bulk of this staggering sum was probably withheld by big business, but small shopkeepers and craftsmen also bore some responsibility for the huge tax deficit.)

Provisional estimates differ greatly. The highest, put forward in 1983 by KMEX-TV, claimed that Hispanics had a national spending power of $50 billion annually. Others were more cautious. Jesus Chavarria, a business expert, put the total worth of Hispanic business receipts in 1977 at some $10.4 billion. In comparison with the gross receipts of all American firms combined (estimated at $3.9 trillion in 1976), the gross value of Hispanic commercial ventures did not amount to much.

Nevertheless, their overall earnings were far from insignificant, approaching, as they did, Cuba's entire GNP ($12.5 billion in 1978). Even more striking was the growth rate of Hispanic business. Between 1972 and 1977 the receipts of small business ventures operated by Hispanics went up by 74.8 percent. The rate of business formation among Hispanic enterprises exceeded the rate for all small businesses in the United States, 52.6 percent to 30 percent.[18]

The growth of Hispanic small business was all the more impressive because it occurred when small entrepreneurs were facing increasing difficulties as a result of the growth of federal regulations. By the 1970s, even a petty shopkeeper needed to be half a lawyer-accountant; he also required more initial capital than had been necessary in the past. Despite these impediments, Hispanic businessmen gradually began to build up a stake in the economy.

The Politics of Militance

Radicals, however, committed to a materialist interpretation of history, were little inclined to take account of these far-reaching social changes. Many of them believed that the hour of revolution had come and that the minorities (blacks and Hispanics), as well as the disinherited of all colors, would take the leading part under the leadership of a progressive vanguard, primarily composed of revolutionary intellectuals.

Marxist claimants for the leadership of the impending, and supposedly inevitable, revolution were many. The Communist Party of the USA (CPUSA), the oldest Marxist party of the existing Marxist-Leninist groups, and also one of the most loyally pro-Soviet in the world, set up a number of united fronts, the most important being the National Alliance against Racist and Political Repression and the Trade Unionists for Action and Democracy. The former served as the party's main vehicle for influencing Hispanic and black opinion; the latter attempted to play a similar role within the labor movement. The party also maintained a special Puerto Rican Commission and a National Chicano Commission to facilitate work among Hispanics. But, right from its beginnings, the CPUSA established a poor record in Hispanic eyes by failing to appoint Hispanics to positions of leadership. Eastern-oriented and loyal to Moscow's line, the party never gained a Hispanic mass following.

There also were other socialist groups—Maoists, Trotskyites—but all of them were subject to splits on sectarian and personal issues and lacked the capacity for mass action. To make matters worse from the Marxist-Leninist standpoint, the revolutionary parties were equally divided in their respective home countries.[19]

There also were a number of underground organizations dedicated to what they called the "armed struggle." These were groups representing every conceivable brand of Marxism-Leninism. They included the Black Panthers and *Venceremos* (the latter dependent on militant Hispanic students), groups that promised to its members personal self-fulfillment as part of a supposedly irresistible force in history. More important were the *Fuerzas Armadas de Liberación Nacional* (FALN), a Puerto Rican organization formed in 1975 through a fusion of minor groups. FALN took credit for various bombing incidents on the mainland. In 1976, for example, FALN assaulted a number of targets in Chicago and Manhattan, including business establishments and police stations. Attempts to continue the struggle persisted; in 1983, the Mexican police arrested a Puerto Rican, William Morales, who ran a training school for Puerto Rican and Central American terrorists from a house in Mexico.

All of these underground organizations shared similar weaknesses. They were apt to be armies of officers; their memberships fluctuated; the cadres split on issues both political and personal. Neither the intellectuals nor the *Lumpenproletariat* of the big cities proved amenable to revolutionary party discipline. Violence, though widely publicized, made neither a military nor an economic impact on this country. The United States indeed remained a violence-prone country, but deaths occasioned by political terrorists accounted for no more than an infinitesimal fraction of Americans who lost their lives through street crime, gangsterism, or private vengeance.[20]

In theory, armed action should have been more effective. The United States contained many different ethnic groups; there was much poverty; the borders were ill controlled; the slums were poorly policed. Fraudulent documents were easily available to malcontents, and so was support from outside the United States, specially from Cuba. Militant socialists in the Kaiser's Germany had once called for *Volksbewaffnung*—for arming the masses. A century later the United States had, in fact, achieved this aim. This country had more privately owned firearms than the rest of the world combined. An American could freely buy a serviceable Mauser, Lee-Enfield, or M.1 rifle for the price of taking his wife or girlfriend for dinner in a good restaurant. But most Americans were in no mood to follow the militants. The revolutionaries revered Mao Tse-Tung, Ho Chi Minh, Castro, and Che Guevara. The public at large admired General MacArthur, Presidents Eisenhower, Reagan, and Carter, the Rev. Billy Graham, Pope John Paul II, and Sir Winston Churchill, and Queen Elizabeth II, Rosalyn Carter, Mother Teresa, and Margaret Thatcher.[21] There was no way revolutionaries could reconcile such differences.

The revolutionaries also failed to take adequate account of what might be called immigrant conservatism. Immigrants to the United States might complain of all manner of social injustice. But immigrants, unlike refugees, throughout American history had come to the United States of their own free choice; they looked on the "old country" with considerable ambivalence. Migration, to the United States as to other countries, often had been an act of personal revolt. The immigrants wanted to get ahead, to escape from the restraints that had beset them in their parent societies. Many newcomers to the United States, moreover, had bitter memories of socialist or would-be socialist regimes, whether of the Marxist-Leninist variety, practiced in Cuba, Poland, East Germany, and Vietnam, or of the moderate reformist kind represented in Mexico by the governing Partido Revolucionario Institucional, with its institutionalized systems of bribery and privilege.

From the revolutionaries' standpoint, things were no better on the island of Puerto Rico. However much the Puerto Rican militants might disagree among themselves, they all stood for independence. But, by the 1960s and 1970s, economic and personal ties between the island and the mainland had become too close to make independence a popular issue. Too many Puerto Ricans were living in the United States; too many Puerto Ricans migrated periodically from the mainland to the island. Most of the islanders were divided, not only over independence but also over the question of whether to seek statehood within the United States or to retain the existing commonwealth status. They worried more about economic problems, such as unemployment, than about Puerto Rican sovereignty. (In the gubernatorial elections of 1976, the *independistas* polled only 6.43 percent of the popular vote.) Overall, the militants of every hue throughout Puerto Rico and the U.S. mainland remained poorly organized and devoid of mass support; they spilled more ink than blood.

During the 1960s and 1970s, radicals also made attempts to politicize youth gangs and to organize new gangs that would not be subject to the control of cadres, but organized on the principle of "democratic centralism"; these groups would operate in that twilight zone between illegality and legality. Profiting from the experience of black power advocates, Chicano and Puerto Rican radicals set up organizations that would defuse gang warfare while combining neighborhood help with political propaganda and self-defense. The Young Lords Organization (YLO) in Chicago, for example, sought to convince its Puerto Rican supporters that the real enemy was not the rival "Latin Kings" or the "Paragons" or the "Black Eagles" but the Anglo-Saxon power structure. The Young Lords organized sit-ins, tenant strikes, communal self-help, and what euphemistically became known as "confiscation."[22] They inspired the formation of similar groups in other cities, notably New York. Members styled themselves *compañeros revolucionarios* and prided themselves on their revolutionary purity. Some gangs, at the same time, managed to obtain grants from city governments or federal welfare agencies, which thereby sought to "co-opt" the radicals. All these organizations, however, suffered from internal schisms, excessive reliance on students and dropouts, and an unstable membership. Criticisms by Omar Lopez and Tony Baez, senior office holders within the YLO, regarding the Chicago group applied, to a greater or lesser extent, to them all:

> The Chicago group is made up largely of high school dropouts and some who didn't finish grammer school. The New York chapter evolved out of a political organization . . . most of whose members had either graduated from or dropped out of colleges in or around New York. The Chicago people felt that the New Yorkers were preoccupied with ideological refinements whereas they had neither the time nor the educational background to concentrate on ideological work . . . Lack of ideological clarity in Chicago was part and parcel of . . . lack of organizational discipline . . . inadequate internal political education; frequent changes in leadership. . . .[23]

The organizations founded on the philosophy of *Chicanismo* operated on a different set of principles. Their adherents did not call for armed insurrections; they did not favor a "back-to-Mexico" movement; their organizations were not monolithic; and their methods were essentially legal. They relied heavily on charismatic personalities and on their ability to use the media for political purposes. One of their foremost leaders was Cesar Estrada Chávez, the son of a migrant worker trained in politics through the Community Service Organization (CSO).[24] In 1962, he resigned from the CSO to organize migrant farm workers in California. His National Farm Workers Association, after bitter struggles against the rival Teamsters Union, gained massive successes in farm workers' strikes against the growers. Supported by college students, civil rights activists, and militant clerics, Chávez performed miracles of organization. He linked his union to the powerful AFL-CIO; he also employed buyers' boycotts as a political and economic weapon. In the end, he succeeded in obtaining for his members the principle of the "closed shop." To his admirers, Chávez was a great leader. To his detractors, he was yet another labor czar, who also appealed to the urban chic and who burdened workers with compulsory unionism, linked to heavy dues and union discipline. The ultimate results of the Chavez brand of unionism were not all of the kind expected by his supporters;

the growers increasingly mechanized their operations, and Chávez himself had to cope with intraunion challenges from dissident members and from a striking decline in membership. At the same time, there was a drop in official funding for California's Agricultural Labor Relations Board (established in 1975 under Democratic Governor Jerry Brown), as George Deukmejian, the next, Republican governor, accused the board's Democratic nominees of slanting their decisions in the union's favor. The union's very success to some extent militated against its own power. By the early 1980s, the grape pickers had ceased to be disinherited people. Their wage rates and benefits had greatly improved over the pittances they received in the early 1960s, while the growers themselves increasingly looked for a labor force more stable and better remunerated than before.

Reies López Tijerina, another charismatic personality, chose a different path. His *Alianza Federal de los Publos Libres* sought to gain international visibility by militant methods, by staging a raid on a courthouse, and similar actions of a symbolic rather than an insurrectionary kind. Tijerina challenged the manner in which, in his view, the United States had failed to abide by the provisions of the Treaty of Guadalupe Hidalgo. Tijerina attempted to get Mexico to bring diplomatic pressure on the United States to assure the Hispanos in New Mexico of having their land restored and their culture vindicated. Tijerina also sought cooperation with the black civil rights activists in a major national demonstration, the Poor People's March. *Hispano* members of the *Alianza*, however, objected to the predominant position assumed by the (black) Southern Christian Leadership Conference. Such disagreements reflected the broader tensions between Hispanics and blacks in large cities, such as Los Angeles and Phoenix, where powerless people of every race clashed with ethnic rivals in gang fights and competed for the same jobs.[25]

Some of these urban groupings attempted to transcend the limitations of a street gang. They included the Brown Berets, a militant Chicano organization which, among other things, tried to fight against the drug culture. The Berets took a paramilitary stance, seeking support from the youth of the *barrios*, and law enforcement agencies took the group's tough postures seriously—with disastrous effects for the Berets. The Berets were not in fact very radical. They stood for a "ten point" program that emphasized practical issues like housing, food, and jobs. The Brown Berets failed to appeal to the imagination of liberals, and therefore proved unable to manipulate the media, as Chávez had done. They also lacked the discipline that Chávez imposed on his union members and consequently suffered from constant factionalism.

The most outstanding of the new organizations was the *Partido de La Raza Unida*, founded in 1970 and led by José Angel Gutíerrez, Chairman of the *Congreso de Aztlán* which administered the party's national effort. *La Raza* meant to operate as a third party, drawing its support from the growing Chicano population. Where Chicanos held a majority, they should seek power through gaining elective offices; where they wielded the balance of power as a third party, they should exert their authority for the good of the Chicano people; where the Chicanos formed a minority, they still should be able to influence government. Given the burgeoning power of the Chicano mystique, argued *La Raza* leaders, the Chicanos could exert a leverage even beyond their numbers in predominantly Chicano regions, such as southern Texas, northern Mexico; various parts of Arizona; and in Colorado and California. In years to come, they might even run Chicano city-states.

In theory, this strategy should have worked. Black politicians, after all, managed to become a power by mobilizing black voters to support mayoral candidates in large cities like Chicago, Los Angeles, and Atlanta. In practice, *La Raza* gained only limited success. In the 1972 election in Texas, *La Raza* made the first and most successful bid on the part of a third party to run statewide candidates. Thirty-four percent of the respondents in a sample taken by a political scientist identified themselves with *La Raza Unida*.[26] But *La Raza* failed to maintain its impetus when other contenders also began to put Hispanic names on the ballot. In local politics, *La Raza* gained seats on various school boards and local councils. In Crystal City, Texas, for instance, Chicanos, led by Gutierez, in 1977 obtained control over the municipal government, including the school board, the police, and other administrative agencies. But *La Raza* displayed particular weaknesses. Derided as "radical," *La Raza* encountered interference from state authorities. The governor, for example, issued repeated denunciations of *La Raza Unida* and succeeded in getting the federal government to delay program monies initially earmarked for Crystal City. *La Raza Unida* leaders failed to retain electoral support as the voters came to look upon them as merely another set of politicians out to line their own pockets, while the bulk of the people continued to live in poverty.[27]

Political cultural nationalism began to weaken after 1975. The militant 1960s became a memory; the Spanish-speakers' lot improved; many *barrios* began to fragment, as its better-off citizens moved to the suburbs. *Chicanismo* no longer seemed relevant to immediate needs—skills and jobs. Gonzáles' Crusade for Justice in Colorado and his support for *La Raza* weakened; there was a striking decline in enrollments in his alternate school.

The Chicano movement also was beset by structural problems. It was highly fragmented and beset by *personalismo*. The 1970 *Directory of Spanish-Speaking Community Organizations* listed 800 organizations, most of which were Chicano. These organizations subscribed to a great variety of goals and their leadership was splintered. There were too many generals and too few privates—too few professional organizers. There were divisions between middle-class bodies and those drawn from the *barrios*. The Chicano militants were beset by a lack of cash, and they failed to develop methods of fundraising. Many organizations existed precariously on membership dues and on funds from dances, dinners, and raffles. Others looked to contributions from professional people and businessmen who, more often than not, were more interested in maintaining their newly gained status.

Some service agencies managed to get help from foundations (including the Ford Foundation) and governmental agencies. Funding of this kind, however, created its own problems: dependence on fluctuating outside sources; reluctance to offend actual or potential donors; and struggles among rival organizations over funds. Many of the new groups, moreover, directed themselves only to one or two salient issues of crucial importance to a local community. Once the issue was resolved, or appeared to be resolved, membership was apt to decline.[28] Given the heterogeneity of its organizations, the Chicano movement failed to develop a common ideology. Many radicals who used revolutionary rhetoric in fact proposed not an armed insurrection but militant integration into Anglo-American society. They called for better housing, increased opportunities in education and employment, and equality and justice within the system.[29]

Predominant were the politics of brick, mortar, and cement. All too often, it was the Mexican side of the streets that lacked maintenance. "Mexicans voted for guys like Roosevelt, Truman, and Carter and the damn streets still didn't get paved. The Mexicans elected two or three city councilmen and they're paving everything in sight."[30] From Houston to San Jose, politicians found that drainage, schools, and paved streets were more emotional issues than bilingual education, immigration, or *Chicanismo*. Some militants understood the importance of these more concrete issues. But many more did not, and the electorate as a whole saw no reason to believe that radicals were better able to cope with such questions than were run-of-the-mill politicians. Radicalism, moreover, had little ideological appeal; only insignificant numbers of the Mexican-American electorate identified themselves as radicals. Insofar as they went to the polls, the bulk of voters instead preferred to take their cue from parties of a more conventional kind.

The Politics of Integration

By the 1970s, the radical dreams that had inspired so many Chicano and Puerto Rican activists had evaporated. Ethnicity continued to play an important part in American politics, but American society was too vast, too heterogenous, subject to too many conflicting pressures, and too individualistic in character to facilitate the permanent mobilization of any one ethnic group for party purposes. The majority of Cubans might vote Republican; the majority of Puerto Ricans and Mexican-Americans would continue in their allegiance to the Democratic Party; both did so, not simply for reasons of ethnic solidarity, but for concerns of a more general nature. Politicians trading on their ability to "deliver" any one particular vote at election time were apt to deceive both themselves and their allies. Hispanics, like their fellow Americans, thought in terms of ethnicity, but not only in terms of ethnicity. They differed in national origins, class affiliation, and life styles. They were overwhelmingly out of sympathy with radicalism.[31]

Their political sympathies were equally diverse. The Cuban community generally continued to side with the Republicans, and Cubans continued to feel strongly about the communist regime in Cuba. (In 1981 Cuban Americans set up their own political action committee, the National Coalition for a Free Cuba, headed by Carlos Benitez.) Cuban academics in the humanities complained of political discrimination against them on the part of liberal-leftist faculty. In domestic politics, the picture was less clear. Whereas the business community generally sympathized with "Reaganomics," other Cuban Americans veered more toward the center. Hispanic support for the Democrats remained more reliable than that of European ethnic minorities, but much less so than that of blacks.[32]

By the 1970s and the early 1980s, Hispanic voting power had begun to make an impact. The demographic surge of these decades had produced its effect. By 1982, 40 congressional districts had a Hispanic population of over 20 percent (one in New Jersey, one in Arizona, three in New York, two in Illinois, four in Florida, seventeen in California, three in New Mexico, nine in Texas). In seven districts, Hispanics held an absolute majority (one in New York, one in Florida, five in Texas).

Hispanics had increased their economic power and increasingly made their voice heard, especially on the local level. In Florida for instance, Cuban Americans attained the mayorality in Tampa, Hileah, and Sweetwater. A Cuban-descended Puerto Rican, Maurice Ferre, became Mayor of Miami. (Ferre, a Democrat, by profession an engineer, and a man of great wealth, thereafter met with challenges from conservatively minded Cuban Republicans; but, at the time of this writing, he still enjoyed substantial backing from some Cuban intellectuals and from the bulk of Miami's black and white population.) Cubans did less well in New York, where they clashed with the Democratic Party, the office holders of which looked askance at the newcomers. Puerto Ricans and Dominicans, by contrast, became increasingly influential in the politics of New York City. (Dr. Rafael España was appointed Special Adviser on Hispanic Affairs by Mayor Koch in 1980, the first Hispanic adviser in the mayor's office.) The Hispanic vote proved particularly important in the Southwest, a region that had gained in national importance through the shift of population and of industries from the "snow belt" to the "sun belt." The Hispanic vote also profited from action on the part of the Justice Department and various state legislatures for the purpose of redrawing electoral districts to benefit minority candidates. Mexican Americans therefore secured representation in growing numbers on school boards, town councils, and other official bodies. Hispanic influence in politics by no means corresponded to the Hispanics' growing demographic strength—even in the Southwest, which contained the greatest concentration of Hispanic voters in the United States. Still, in 1983, there were more than three thousand Hispanic officials in the United States.

In addition, Hispanics began to make an impact on national politics. By the beginning of the 1970s, there were five Hispanic congressmen and one senator. President Reagan subsequently made a number of Hispanic appointments. One was John Hernandez, appointed acting administrator of the Environmental Protection Agency. Another was Dr. Jesse Soriano, Director of the Office of Bilingual Education and Minority Language Affairs. Eleven Hispanics were elected to the 98th Congress. All of them benefited from the increased turnout of Hispanic voters. (In Texas, for example, the number of Hispanic registered voters increased from 488,000 to 830,643 between 1975 and 1981.) And all of them gained from the redrawing of electoral districts. Nearly all secured election in districts where the Hispanic vote exceeded one-half of the electorate. They did not much differ from their non-Hispanic colleagues; they were well educated; they had been active in state or municipal politics; they made their living as lawyers, in business, or in the professions. A substantial number of Hispanics in public life had served for a time in the armed forces, another integrative experience.

In 1977, the Congressional Hispanic Caucus was formed for Congressmen of Hispanic heritage or for those representing Hispanic population centers. By 1983, the Caucus had 140 members. The caucus worked to meet the needs of Hispanic-Americans; it published a monthly newsletter *Avance*. (In October 1983 the Hispanic Caucus was instrumental in blocking passage of the Simpson-Mazzoli bill.) The National Association of Latino Elected and Appointed Officials (NALEO) was founded in 1979. Sponsors included a variety of commercial undertakings, such as the United California Bank, civic organizations, and trade unions. Headed by Edward J. Avila, former field representative for Congressman Edward R. Roybal, NALEO operated as a nonpartisan group that sought to face Hispanic issues transcending party lines. NALEO, which refused to accept government funding, concerned itself with such problems as voter registration, research (through the NALEO Public Policy Institute), the development of Hispanic business, census questions, legislation of special concern to Hispanics, and the like.

In addition, Hispanic leaders in 1983 formed a new organization, Hispanic Force '84, for the purpose of unifying Hispanic voters to give them greater political impact and integrate them into mainstream politics. Formed under the leadership of New Mexico Governor Tony Anaya, Hispanic Force in theory meant to transcend partisan politics; but, in practice, it became identified with the Democratic Party.

The Hispanic electorate remained somewhat ambivalent in its ethnic loyalty. A Spanish surname did not by itself guarantee Hispanic support. In California's primary election of 1982, for example, former state Health and Welfare Secretary Mario Obledo, running against Los Angeles Mayor Bradley, a black, drew only 4.7% of the vote, a figure far below the proportion of Hispanics estimated to have voted. The candidates, in fact, downplayed their ethnic background when speaking outside their local communities. "I'm Hispanic secondary to the fact that I'm a candidate and I'm an American," argued congressional candidate Martinez. His fellow Mexican American Torres, took an identical stance. "I ran a non-Hispanic primary campaign. My having a Spanish surname is incidental. . . ." The nonracial approach proved successful in Denver, Colorado, where voters in 1983 elected Frederico Peña, a young Mexican-American lawyer, to the office of mayor. Peña's electoral victory shattered yet another preconception: that cities will not vote for an ethnic minority candidate until the aspirant's own ethnic group forms a majority or near majority. Denver's Hispanics at the time of the election numbered no more than 18 percent of the city's population; yet Peña managed to win with a demand for new leadership and civic innovation.[33]

More important than ethnic prejudice in politics was the continued failure of many Hispanic Americans to make full use of their voting power. While Hispanic voting strength increased, and would continue to do so in the future, a gap remained between the turnout rates of Mexican Americans and others. In the 1982 elections in Texas, 38 percent of registered Mexican-American voters went to the polls, compared to 54.4 percent of non-Mexican Americans.[34] In California, Mexican Americans were even slower to cast their vote; in the 1982 gubernatorial elections, the Republican candidate's victory owed much to the Hispanics' reluctance to go to the polls. As a professional analyst commented,

"Had Hispanics turned out on a level conforming to pre-election estimates, the incremental vote for Bradley would have been enough for him to win."[35] In Chicago, on the other hand, the Hispanic vote helped Thomas Washington become mayor. Nevertheless, Hispanics vote at about half of the rate of the non-Spanish-speaking population.

What accounts for the Hispanics' relative reluctance to cast their votes? According to a widespread mythology, they are politically "apathetic," or their "political culture" militates against their participation in the democratic process. Statistical evidence does not bear out the stereotype. It indicates that Mexican Americans are perfectly capable of understanding the ways of democracy and that they take pride in exercising their civic functions. (Eighty-four percent of a sample taken in Texas in 1973, and 86 percent of a sample taken in Wisconsin in 1966 stated that the Hispanics generally gained a sense of satisfaction from going to the polls.)[36] Mexican Americans, moreover, created many organizations of their own in the past; Mexico itself has a rich legacy of political action. There is clearly something wrong with explanations based on the Mexican Americans' supposed sense of "futility, docility and resignation."[37]

The differences between Mexican Americans and Puerto Rican Americans on the one hand and their non-Hispanic fellow citizens on the other are rather of a structural kind. Low educational attainment produces low voter registration and voting. The Hispanics' traditional political organizations serve communities containing many labor migrants. Their memberships tend to fluctuate; their financial resources are limited. Their organizations serve many different purposes: they offer mutual-aid benefits to help their members in emergencies; they make extensive provision for the involvement of members' families in organizational activities; they often are designed to deal with particular issues and crises; they place great emphasis on the personality of individual leaders; and they stress ethnic pride.[38] These characteristics are not peculiarly "Latin"; they are just as likely to be encountered among first-generation European immigrants in the United States.

Above all, voting behavior is shaped by demographic and sociological factors. The Puerto Rican and the Mexican-American community alike contain a high percentage of children (unable to vote) as well as a large proportion of young men and women, who are less likely to go to the polls in any community than are their elders. The Mexican-American and Puerto Rican community, by the 1970s and 1980s, still contained a much higher percentage of working-class people than most other ethnic communities in the United States. Working-class voters, on the whole, are less likely to go to the polls than middle-class people; hence, Hispanic voter participation was apt to remain relatively low. (The Hispanic population also has a larger number of noncitizens: 13.1 percent, in comparison to 1.2 percent for other immigrant groups.)

The Mexican Americans, moreover, have within their ranks a large number of persons who have chosen to retain their Mexican citizenship. Their national preference does not necessarily exclude political participation; there are many Mexican Americans who listened earnestly to advice on political matters given by their fathers or grandfathers who had not taken out naturalization papers. Failure to accept naturalization, however, considerably affects voting statistics. Organizations like the Southwest Voter Registration Project tried to rectify this situation. Such efforts were impeded not only by what was widely misnamed voter apathy, but by organizational disarray within the Department of Immigration and Naturalization. During the early 1970s, an alien's application for naturalization was processed fairly speedily; ten years later, the ever-growing workload, the shortage of well-qualified personnel, and administrative inefficiency had enormously slowed down the process. Applicants for naturalization found that their files had been mislaid; letters had been lost; two years might elapse between the time an application for naturalization was received and the moment the applicant could take the oath of allegiance.

The Puerto Ricans had no citizenship problems. Some even doubted that they should be included among the Hispanics. They were disunited about federal block grants to their island. They were not sure if block grants would help Puerto Rico's general development more than the ongoing food-stamp program, on which more than half of the island's population had become dependent. On the island itself, more than 85 percent of the eligible voters went to the polling booths. In New York, on the other hand, only 15 percent cast their ballots. The difference in voting behaviors had little to do with civic consciousness; many Puerto Ricans felt that, because they were residing only temporarily on the mainland there was no point in filling out a ballot. However, the longer the Puerto Ricans remained on the mainland, the more they were apt to vote and to understand the way the system worked. For a long time, the Puerto Ricans lacked an equivalent for the Mexican Americans' Southwest Voter Registration Education Project. Then, in 1979, the National Puerto Rican Coalition (NPRC) was formed to increase voter participation. Leaders of various Puerto Rican organizations made up the NPRC and acted as a pressure group in Washington, D.C.

By the early 1980s, sociologists and organizers active for both the major parties were as yet surprisingly ill acquainted with the composition of the various Hispanic electorates in the United States. But, at least for the Southwest, the Southwest Voter Registration Education Project had drawn a clear profile of the average Mexican-American voter. Older citizens of foreign stock, unable to speak English, poorly endowed with cash or a formal education, were least likely to vote. The educated English speaker was most likely to go to the polls. Overall, the regular voter was likely to be not a youthful radical but a solid citizen aged 45 years or more.[39]

As a voter, he or she is likely to obtain relevant political information from TV rather than from the radio or the newspaper. The voter pays a great deal of attention to the opinion of his or her spouse, and, to a lesser extent, to the Democratic Party, Mexican-American officials, relatives, and community leaders—in that order of priority. Older Mexican Americans are likely to identify themselves with the Democratic Party; younger Mexican-Americans are more apt to describe themselves as independent or undecided. Mexican-Americans are more likely to style themselves as liberal or a moderate than conservative; but a high proportion—44 percent, according to Robert Brischetto's research—will not bear any one of these labels. (Brischetto's sample shows the following breakdown: 14 percent conservative; 27 percent moderate; 18 percent liberal; 2 percent radical; 42 percent not willing to accept any such identification.) The average voter is in fact ambivalent: "liberal" on economic issues; extremely conservative on social issues, such as crime, the family, religion, schooling, and, above all, abortion. Only 14 percent of Mexican-Americans in Brischetto's sample favored the legalization of abortion.[40]

Surprisingly, Ronald Reagan in the 1980 presidential election gained at least 25 percent of the Hispanic vote. His supporters included the bulk of the Cubans, who received a number of new appointments—for example, Professor José Sorzano was named to the U.S. delegation to the U.N. The shift in the Hispanic vote as a whole was not as significant as that experienced by the major white ethnic groups—Polish, Italian, and Irish. Nevertheless, the 1980 election stood as a signal of an electoral integration not anticipated by Chicano activists. Working-class people of all ethnic backgrounds continued to lean toward the Democrats, but working-class homeowners were increasingly likely to support the Republicans.

During the 1984 elections, the Republicans further improved their position among Hispanic voters. At the time of this writing, estimates differ widely about the number of Hispanic votes cast nationwide for President Reagan. According to NRC's figures, it was 32 percent, according to the CBS-*New York Times*, 33 percent, according to ARC-*Washington Post*, 44 percent. The Spanish International Network (SIN), in a preliminary breakdown on election night, put the Hispanic Reagan vote at an even higher figure—47 percent in Florida (with its heavily Cuban population), 51 percent in California, 42 percent in New York,

33 percent in New Mexico, 32 percent in Texas and Illinois, and 45 percent nationwide. By the end of 1984, 51 percent of Hispanic respondents in a Gallup poll stated that they would vote for Reagan were the election to be held again.[41] Reagan clearly benefited to an extraordinary extent as the first Republican candidate to take serious account of Hispanic voters as a national force.

How will this diverse electorate affect the country's future? Can Hispanics acquire a wider consciousness with regard to their common interests? Experts in the early 1980s were divided; Chicano scholars, especially, continued to stress the separate nature of Mexican-American concerns. There were, however, distinct indications that social class was beginning to outweigh in importance the old national affiliations. The intermingling of Spanish speakers in San Francisco, Los Angeles, New York, and Chicago, the impact of the new Spanish media, the policies pursued by the Catholic Church, the courts, and the federal bureaucracy— all probably contribute to the strength of growing Hispanic identity. But, in a sense, the Hispanic voter, who no longer sees himself as primarily a Dominican or a Puerto Rican, is himself the product of Americanization.

In terms of party politics, the impact of the Hispanic vote by the early 1980s had increased considerably. In terms of issues, immigration was perhaps the most important. In 1983, the Simpson-Mazzoli bill went down to defeat through the efforts of a broad and disparate coalition, of which Hispanics formed an important part.

Within the Democratic Party and within Congress, Hispanic power is likely to grow.[42] Hispanics will continue to insist on ethnic pride. They will reject anything that even faintly smacks of ethnic discrimination. They call for a liberal stance on immigration; they continue to defend bilingual ballots. The Hispanic caucus in Congress also is certain to act as a pressure group for good U.S. relations with Latin America. Cuban and Nicaraguan refugees apart, the majority of Hispanics tend to oppose U.S. intervention in Central America. In foreign affairs, however, the congressional Hispanic caucus is not likely to gain the same influence as the Jewish lobby attained in the matter of U.S.-Israel relations. Latin America is too vast and too divided, and the Hispanic community in the United States is too divergent, for such a consensus.

In regard to social policies, Hispanic voters are ambivalent. They continue to favor the welfare state, a natural choice given the high Hispanic poverty rate in cities like New York. But Hispanic voters by no means back all welfare policies in an unconditional fashion. (Nearly two-thirds of the Hispanic electorate backed the conservative position in the controversy over California's Proposition 13, designed to reduce the property tax on householders.) Hispanics generally oppose illegal immigration and support penalties for employers of undocumented aliens. Contrary to what radicals had assumed in the 1960s, there is Hispanic support neither for socialism nor for ethnic separatism. Hispanic voters for the most part prize bilingual education. But, even in Texas, where Mexican Americans form a strong bloc and where Spanish radio reaches more Hispanic listeners than does English radio, English newscasts and newspapers are more important as trusted sources of information about political events than are Spanish programs.[43]

Concerning sociocultural issues of a more general kind, most Hispanic voters retain their convictions. They have, on the whole, little sympathy for gays and lesbians. There are, moreover, profound cleavages between the interests of an auto worker—Hispanic, black, or Anglo-descended— on the one hand, and, say, an ecology-minded college professor or a militant feminist on the other. Overall, the Hispanics stick to traditional values. On certain controversial issues, Hispanics veer even further to the conservative position than the bulk of their countrymen. For instance, by 1983 a higher proportion of Hispanics favored a U.S. withdrawal from the U.N. and the creation of a compulsory national identity card than did the rest of the population.[44] Most Hispanics are also reluctant to side with the big spenders in the realm of economic policy. The majority of Hispanics dislike high taxation and dread inflation, though not to quite the same extent as whites and blacks.[45] Overall, Hispanic voters, far from requiring leadership on the part of a self-styled progressive vanguard, have realistic expectations of what the two major parties are likely to do for their respective voters. (According to a 1985 Gallup poll, Hispanic respondents nationwide believed that Republicans served better than Democrats the interests of business and of white-collar and skilled workers. The Democrats, by contrast, were regarded as more likely to do well for small businessmen, farmers, labor union members, and unskilled workers).[46]

Overall, the Hispanic electorate is as varied and ambivalent over many key isues as the United States is as a whole. For better or worse, Hispanics in American politics have begun to act in a manner not dissimilar to their fellow Americans'.

Chapter 12

Bilingual Education

Whenever a teachers' convention meets and tries to find out how it can cure the ills of society, there is simply one answer; the school has but one way to cure the ills of society and that is by making men intelligent. To make men intelligent, the school has again but one way, and that is, first and last, to teach them to read, write and count. And if the school fails to do that, and tries beyond that to do something for which a school is not adapted, it not only fails in its own function, but it fails in all other attempted functions. Because no school as such can organise industry, or settle the matter of wage and income, can found homes or furnish parents, can establish justice or make a civilised world.[1]

—W. E. B. DuBois

No one better understood the true purpose of primary and secondary school education than the author of these introductory lines, W. E. B. DuBois, perhaps the greatest of black radical scholars in the United States. Yet, throughout the history of American education, DuBois's sound assumptions have met with unceasing challenge. Throughout their history, Americans have attempted to use education for pragmatic aims of the most contradictory kinds: for the purpose of saving souls, turning out good citizens, for turning the foreign born into good American citizens, or—more recently—for giving students a better understanding of human sexuality. Foreigners typically have criticized American education. A century before Dr. Benjamin Spock tried to humanize American education, Sir Charles Dilke, a British traveler to the United States, commented with amazement on those American children who "never dream of work outside school hours, or of solid reading that is not compulsory," and who were forever "ill-mannered" and "far too full of self-assurance."[2]

The Struggle for Bilingual Education

In addition to becoming a religious battleground, schools frequently became involved in ethnic issues as successive immigrant communities attempted to use the classroom to maintain their respective linguistic and cultural heritages. Germans, for instance, though supposedly a well-assimilable group, sometimes went to extraordinary lengths during the nineteenth century to use every conceivable institution—public schools, parochial organizations, churches, gymnastic associations (*Turnvereine*), and even glee clubs (*Liedertafeln*)—for the purpose of strengthening *Deutschtum* on American soil, an issue of bitter controversy.[3]

During the 1960s and 1970s a nationwide debate developed over bilingual education. In the eyes of orthodox educators, bilingual instruction—in the child's native tongue and in English—should be transitional. The child's home language should be used for teaching purposes, so that students will acquire cognitive skills and avoid academic retardation. English should be taught as a second language only until the student becomes proficient in English, at which time native-language instruction should end. In theory, attention would continue to be paid to the child's heritage and culture. But the basic purpose, at least of federal legislation, was to get students to transfer into all-English classrooms as fast as possible, without falling behind in other subjects.

But the English-speaking public generally insisted that English should remain the sole language of instruction in schools. The use of native languages was resented by the descendants of earlier immigrants, whose forebears had struggled to learn English. Anglo-Americans feared it would usher in multi-lingualism and artificial attempts to preserve ethnic cultures.[4] Bilingual education, according to its critics, might turn into an instrument to increase ethnic employment in schools and to achieve the political, economic, and social goals of Hispanics. Bilingual education became for many Hispanics a civil rights issue and also a means of obtaining heightened respect for their culture, an instrument for fighting discrimination against non-English-speaking groups, and a device for obtaining jobs and increasing the Hispanics' political leverage.[5]

Spanish-speaking Americans were in fact slow to emulate their European predecessors' demands for bilingual education. Organizations such as the League of United Latin American Citizens, the Mexican-American Political Association, and the American GI Forum, while not unmindful of their Hispanic heritage, stressed political, social, and economic equality for Mexican Americans and attempted fully to integrate Mexican Americans into American life. LULAC thus placed special stress on ending *de facto* segregation in school and job discrimination.

From the 1960s onward, the emphasis shifted from socioeconomic to broader and often contradictory objectives set by educational reformers. Some of them, making use of newly popular theories of "alienation," defended bilingual education for children reared at home in a language other than English by stating that its use in the classroom would prevent "inward maladjustment." The emotional fabric of the Mexican-American child was said to be often overextended. In this view, the child was "disturbed, confused, and disoriented as the result of being pulled between two worlds," neither of which was capable of providing that "sense of security necessary for learning experiences" and of belonging. Coming from the love and warmth of his home into an unsympathetic school, the child supposedly underwent traumatic experiences that might lead him into anxiety, retreat from society, or into crime.[6]

The demand for bilingual education came from many sources. Cuban immigrants, many of them highly educated, called for quality schooling for their children, an education that would preserve the Cubans' Spanish culture. Bilingual education also was said to be essential for the purpose of gaining a new sense of self-pride for the Hispanic poor, this in a country where Spanish enjoyed low esteem, and where too many authors of school books, teachers, politicians, professors, advertisers, and even producers of television programs supposedly conspired to demean Spanish speakers by casting them into stereotyped characters. The most radical attacks on the existing system—launched when student unrest was at its zenith throughout the country—came from members of *La Raza Unida*, which then advocated biculturalism as a political weapon in the struggle to set up a "third politics" for the purpose of gaining power in predominantly Chicano regions.

Bilingual education also came to be considered essential because of the relatively poor performance of so many Puerto Rican and Chicano students and because of their high dropout rate from schools and colleges. Spanish-speaking educators stated that there were at least five reasons why Hispanics drop out. Many Spanish speakers fell behind early in their education because they did not know much English; by the time they reached high school, they were discouraged. Many complained of bad teacher attitudes toward Hispanic students because of the students' color, accent, and poor English skills. Students did not hear enough English spoken at home or in the barrios and received little help in reading and writing English in the home. Failing to see the relevance or economic benefits of further education, they left school to find a job as soon as they could. Moreover, a high percentage of illegitimacy, concubinage, and abandoned mothers and children among Hispanic slum dwellers created a poor environment for learning and staying at school.[7]

As we have stressed in other chapters, Hispanics, while better placed than blacks, also suffered more severely from unemployment than members of the so-called majority. Overall, Hispanic college graduates did best, followed by high school graduates; high school dropouts were at the bottom.[8] Clearly, argued the advocates of bilingual education, more suitable courses of instruction would help to improve the Hispanics' economic as well as educational position. Faith in education commonly went with a characteristically American creed in the combined power of cash, gadgets, and the correct pedagogical method taught at almost every school of education in the United States. As Manuel H. Guerra said, "There is nothing about the bilingual problems of the Chicano child which money, electronic laboratory equipment, and appropriately trained, understanding teachers cannot solve."[9]

The call for educational reform fit the mood of the 1960s and early 1970s, when the ideals of the New Frontier and Great Society seemed as yet untarnished, when educational expenditure in the United States had ballooned, and when there seemed to be no limit to what pedagogues, well supplied with funds, could accomplish for the betterment of mankind. Between 1952 and 1972, public expenditures for education in schools and colleges increased more than 700 percent, from $8.4 billion to $67.5 billion. The number of educational employees tripled, from 1,884,000 to 5,646,000.[10] If money alone could buy excellence, the United States should have entered a golden age of public instruction instead of seeing declining standards in many schools.

Commitment to upgraded education for the poor was accompanied by determined attempts to desegregate schools. In 1964, Congress passed the Civil Rights Act and a year later, the Elementary and Secondary Schools Education Act (ESEA). The federal government, through the Department of Health, Education, and Welfare, became actively involved in desegregating public schools throughout the United States. At the same time, both politicians and educators turned to "compensatory education" to uplift the children of the poor and to "Americanize" immigrants. The Bilingual Education Act of 1968 was designed as yet another means of facilitating the learning of English by youngsters with a different mother tongue.

The parallel campaigns to integrate schools and to upgrade standards of Spanish-speaking and other students did not, however, easily run in harness. Both Hispanics and blacks had experienced widespread segregation. According to a report issued by the Civil Rights Commission in 1970, one-third of all Mexican-American students were attending schools defined as "ethnically imbalanced." In some districts, for example, in Houston, Texas, administrators used the argument that Mexicans were legally white in order to accomplish token desegregation through mixing Mexican-American and black students. At the same time, Mexican Americans complained that the use of ESEA compensatory funds for improving the lot of "disadvantaged" Mexican Americans created negative self-concepts among Mexican-American children. The concept of "cultural deprivation," used widely in the educational reforms of the late 1960s, ran counter to the Mexican Americans' pride in their language and culture. Although the civil rights movement made conscious efforts to eliminate hostile stereotypes from textbooks and courses, there was little attempt to present minority cultures in a positive fashion.

Puerto Ricans were equally outspoken in their criticism. In New York City, ASPIRA, a Puerto Rican cultural organization, assisted by the Puerto Rican Legal Defense and Education Fund (PRLDEF), took the Board of Education to court several times. The first suit began in 1972; in 1974, Puerto Ricans gained the "ASPIRA Consent Degree." In 1975, the plaintiffs again took legal action for failure to implement the consent decree—specifically, for failing to develop a method for identifying children in need of bilingual education. The court ordered the Board of Education to carry out the 1976 decree; in 1978, the contestants arrived at an agreement whereby the Board of Education would report both to ASPIRA and PRLDEF—without, however, solving all the points at issue.

At the same time, educators of many different national origins built an extensive network of Chicano studies, Puerto Rican studies, Cuban studies, Latin American studies, ethnic studies, and bicultural or multicultural education programs at many northeastern, midwestern, and California colleges and universities. Directed by such scholars as John Vasquez, Gilbert Sanchez, Emilita Stone, Edna Acosta-Belen, and Isabel Sirgado, these programs made an important and long-overdue contribution to American education.[11] A new journal, *The Bilingual Review/La Revista Bilingue* (1974), began to discuss language problems. All of these efforts combined to form a powerful lobby to push for bilingual education and to mobilize more federal funds for this and related purposes.

Their complaints became more outspoken as the Hispanics' political power increased and as the federal government unwittingly favored their cause through a new statistical definition. Until 1970, the definition "Hispanic" was limited to those born in Spanish-speaking countries or to U.S. citizens with Spanish surnames. The 1970 census broadened the term to include both racial origin and Spanish-language speakers, irrespective of their birthplace. This resulted in a dramatic increase in those officially defined as "Hispanic," from 3.1 million in 1960 to 9.1 million in 1970, and to 12 million in 1978. Even the latter figure seems too conservative because it does not take illegal immigrants into account.

At the same time, the Hispanic cause acquired increased status within the federal bureaucracy. In 1967, the Inter-Agency Committee on Mexican-American Affairs was set up as a coordinating body for cabinet-level programs; in 1970, a permanent cabinet committee was formed to serve as a forum for Spanish speakers. Growing numbers of Hispanic Americans obtained appointments to the staff of the Civil Rights Commission, the Equal Employment Opportunity Commission, the

Department of Health, Education, and Welfare, and the U.S. Office of Education. By their philosophies and the composition of their personnel, these bodies overwhelmingly were committed to the liberal cause. Self-styled progressives among the federal bureaucrats, judges, college professors, journalists, and congressional members and staffers formed an informal but powerful lobby committed to institutional change.

The *Lau v. Nichols* case stands out as another landmark on the road to bilingual education. In a major case brought against the school district of San Francisco, alleging discrimination against Chinese school children, the Supreme Court in 1974 decided that the provision of equal facilities, textbooks, teachers, and curricula for youngsters unable to speak English did not mean equality of opportunities—and all school districts were thereafter required to take "affirmative steps" to rectify the deficiency. In the following year, the Office of Civil Rights issued a memorandum (cumbrously entitled "Task Force Findings Specifying Remedies for Eliminating Past Educational Practices Ruled Unlawful Under Lau versus Nichols") outlining procedures to be followed by school districts providing bilingual and bicultural education. The 1976 California Bilingual-Bicultural Education Act followed a similar philosophy. This act represented a major policy shift: bilingual education would no longer aim simply at a transition into the American mainstream but would strive for the maintenance of separate ethnic cultures. Only those teachers with appropriate social and bilingual credentials were now deemed qualified to provide bilingual education.

The call for bilingual education became louder as the number of foreign-born children unable to speak English rapidly increased in the public schools. (By the early 1980s, for example, the San Francisco Unified School District contained 27,786 children with only a limited command of English; 48 percent of all students came from non-English-speaking homes.) At the same time, Spanish-speaking intellectuals—widely supported by the universities—called for affirmative action programs in employment and also for bilingual programs in schools. The federal government responded sympathetically to this demand, and, by 1978, the Bilingual Education Act was funding 518 bilingual, bicultural projects in 68 languages ranging from Spanish (about 80 percent of the total) to Chinese and Vietnamese. Separately, HEW's Office of Civil Rights instructed 334 school districts to begin bilingual and bicultural classes or face a potential termination of all federal school aid. Altogether, more than $500 million had been spent on these various ventures. Yet, not one cent of federal aid went to the large number of "Saturday Morning Schools," in which foreign-born parents, dissatisfied with the language instruction as well as the disciplinary standards in public schools, privately organized and financed classes in a broad variety of tongues (German, Russian, and Chinese) taught by volunteers along traditional lines and with traditional values.

The Case For and Against Bilingual Education

Bilingual education raised many troubling controversies—for example, in the field of Hispanic-black relations. Blacks and Hispanics for a time had collaborated in common campaigns against racial discrimination. The massive disbursement of public funds, however, naturally led to struggles over the allocations among different ethnic communities. Some Mexican-American activists argued that they had gained less than blacks from the poverty programs of the 1960s, or that Hispanics were less fairly represented than blacks in the state and federal bureaucracies. Equally controversial was the issue of desegregation. Assuming that Hispanic children should be taught in the parental home language, they would have to be separated from other students; this would lead to the separation they were decrying—at a time when public schools were in fact becoming more segregated with the increase of Hispanic children nationwide. (According to a study prepared by Gary Orfield for the U.S. House of Representatives, more than 60 percent of Hispanic students in the western United States were attending *de facto* segregated schools by the early 1980s.)[12] In addition, there were practical considerations. What was the value of bilingual education for the job market during a nationwide depression, when the larger issues involved not merely getting jobs for Hispanics but also protecting them against layoffs from jobs they already held?

Revisionist scholars broadened the campaign for bilingualism and biculturalism into a broad critique of American society.[13] The melting pot, in their view, had failed—or had never worked in the first place. "Americanization" had injured not only the Spanish-speaking peoples, but also the many ethnic minorities whose history in the United States allegedly was one of continued cultural and economic degradation. Far from having served the newcomers, American schools always had been prone to reinforce existing ethnic, racial, and social class hierarchies. Those immigrants who had succeeded in entering the middle classes during the early twentieth century had done so not because of, but in spite of, their schooling.[14]

Bilingual education might have gained wider acceptance if its advocates had been content to describe bilingual education as no more than a transitional bridge to assimilation. Many academicians, however, went further. They linked bilingual education with bicultural education, and bicultural education with cultural separatism or "affirmative ethnicity," and "affirmative ethnicity" with a far-reaching critique of traditional

American values. By doing so, they alienated the great mass of conservative and middle-of-the-road voters who continued to comprise the overwhelming majority of the American electorate. The biculturalists, like their liberal and left-wing political allies, misjudged the temper of the nation as a whole. They assumed, as did President Carter in a well-publicized speech delivered in 1979, that the United States was in a state of spiritual malaise, that a sense of disenchantment had struck at the very heart, soul, and spirit of the American people, and that public opinion was ready for a fundamental change. A widespread "ethnic revival"—one transcending the Hispanic community—supposedly reflected a wider disenchantment with the white, Protestant, Anglo-Saxon establishment by the white ethnics and their descendants.

These assumptions in fact were quite mistaken. The bulk of Americans liked their country and its institutions.[15] The so-called ethnic revival did not, for the most part, represent a serious challenge to American patriotism. A delight in *Oktoberfests* and zithers, tartans and pibroch, and Swahili names and bongo drums did not necessarily signify nationalist yearnings for Blacks, Lithuanians, Esthonians and Latvians. Much of the ethnic revival represented a further step toward Americanization. Foreign-descended Americans with names like Wieruszowski, Gregoriades, and Katzenellenbogen demanded parity of esteem with their fellow citizens. The ethnic revival had little to do with serious efforts to study a foreign literature or language. For all practical purposes, the ethnic revival was apt to end where the irregular verbs began.

Bilingual education encountered criticism not only on patriotic but also on more narrowly technical grounds. For instance, the General Accounting Office in 1976 issued a report, *Bilingual Education: An Unmet Need*, which charged that the U.S. Office of Education had failed to specify how effective bilingual education should be provided, how to train teachers, and how to produce suitable teaching materials. The USOE itself commissioned a critical report in 1978 that concluded that "most of the children did not need to learn English, [and] that those [who] did were in fact acquiring it; and that to the degree that children were already alienated from school, they remained so."[16]

This report led to the amended Bilingual Education Act of 1978, which limited the number of English-speaking children in the program to no more than 40 percent, involved parents more, required bilingual proficiency in both languages, and expanded programs to include not only speaking but reading and writing as well. At the time of this writing, 26 states required bilingual education. The current goal is to improve the programs, concentrate on teaching English, and teach the native language only in transitional, not maintenance, programs, thereby gaining more local support and better trained teachers.

The National Association for Bilingual Education by 1983 was pushing for transitional bilingual programs, not for language maintenance. It accepted the primacy of English but wished to treat the native tongue as a second language. The American Federation of Teachers opposed maintaining the native language because, it claimed, this would keep the child from becoming proficient in English and from becoming assimilated.

When Ronald Reagan secured the presidency in 1980, his adminis- tration did not embark on as radical a shift in policy as its right-wing supporters had hoped. There was, in many fields, a good deal of continuity between the Carter and Reagan administrations. The Reagan administration, for instance, did not attempt to put an end to bilingual education, but Washington's previous sense of commitment declined. The political tide moved in the opposite direction, as officials, like Virginia Attorney General J. Marshall Coleman criticized proposed federal rules on bilingual education as unwarranted intrusions on states rights. Bilingual education came under heavy fire because of its costs, the expected growth of new financial burdens, the paucity of basic research in the field, the lack of qualified teachers, and the programs' real or supposed lack of success.

In 1982, as part of the Reagan's "New Federalism," the Department of Education announced that school districts in the future would not be held accountable for federal bilingual agreements that required native language instruction for children speaking little or no English. The states, according to the new theory, knew best how to spend federal education dollars. The new administration also attempted to change existing tests for civil rights compliance, particularly in the field of equal educational opportunity. Henceforth, the bilingual program ini- tiated by any state would no longer be judged by its results, but by its intentions. A number of states began to modify existing laws. In 1982, for example, Illinois—for long the bellwether state in the field of bilingual education—was considering far-reaching changes, such as: eliminating the requirements to teach bilingual history and culture as part of the bilingual program; having local school boards decide the means and extent of parent and community involvement in bilingual programs; and giving school districts the power to set their own standards.[17] The Twentieth Century Fund, in a report published in 1983, came to similar conclusions. Instead of bilingual education, the report favored "language immersion." The report called for an end to teaching in any language except English and said that U.S. government support should be limited to training in English.

The Reagan administration, in drawing away from bilingual education, took account of this profound shift of opinion in Congress, among educators, and in the public at large. Hostility to bilingual education had many sources: resentment at falling standards of education and discipline in many of the nation's schools; disenchantment with changing fads and fashions in education; growing resistance to an ever-increasing tax burden; growing unemployment, which resulted in enhanced competition for jobs; and concern about continuing foreign immigration. (By the early 1980s, two-thirds of the American public wanted the numbers of newcomers to the United States to diminish rather than to increase.)[18]

Opposition to bilingual education was accompanied by growing hostility toward multilingual ballots. The legislature, in 1975, amending the Voting Right Act of 1967, required multilingual ballots and election information to be printed for non-English readers. Advocates of the change argued—giving little or no evidence for their contention—that minority-language groups were discriminated against by having to use English-language ballots. In fact, the overwhelming majority of voters in the country can read English; under existing legislation, foreigners must be proficient in English to acquire U.S. citizenship. The experiment turned out to be costly and divisive. In 1982, Senator S. I. Hayakawa introduced legislation to make English the only official language, thereby in effect abolishing multilingual balloting. As of this writing, the future of the controversy remains in doubt.

U.S. courts also have had to take notice of bilingualism. California and New York lead in the numbers of court interpreters who serve Spanish speakers. (In California, since 1978, interpreters also are required in Arabic, Cantonese, Korean, Japanese, Portuguese, Tagalog, and Vietnamese.) The California Court Interpreters Association, founded in 1971, has more than five hundred members and is the largest organization of its kind in the United States. One-fourth of all federally certified interpreters work in California.

In 1982, the Bilingual Education Act was due for renewal. Hearings were held in 1982 and 1983. The Reagan administration wished to change part of the Act in order to fund a greater variety of educational programs, to be determined by the local authorities, but designed to concentrate on training in English. Senator Walter D. Huddleston wanted to go even further; his bill (S 2002) would ensure "that an extensive course of English instruction is an integral part of the bilingual education program and that participation in the bilingual education program will in most cases be limited to one year and for other purposes."[19] The administration opposed the one-year limitation on bilingual education programs but supported other aspects of the bill. Secretary of Education T. H. Bell remarked that government support for bilingual education grew from $7.5 million in 1969 to $134 million in 1982 and provided help for between 1.2 million and 3.5 million children.

Numerous pressure groups, however, continued to lobby for bilingual education, including the American Coalition for Bilingual Education, the National Advisory Board for Bilingual Education, and the National Clearinghouse for Bilingual Education. Administrators of several state bilingual education programs opposed the one-year limitation on the program and attacked the "total immersion in English" approach.

But there were doubts about bilingual education, not only among Anglo-Americans but also among some Hispanics. A good many Mexican Americans came to believe that the new programs might in fact retard rather than advance the progress of those who seek to make it in American society. Richard E. Ferraro, president of the Los Angeles School Board, was one of their number. "When you're talking about language," he argued, "English is essential for success in this country." John Alvarez, a young Californian of Hispanic descent, put it more graphically: "Many of our people prefer to speak English. They get pissed off when you speak to them in Spanish."[20]

Conditions of course differ widely from one Hispanic group to another, from one part of the country to another, and even from one city to another. By stressing linguistic skills, bicultural programs may have diverted Hispanic students from making their way in such fields as engineering and computer science, seriously neglected by Chicanos and Puerto Ricans, nearly half of whom graduate in fields that are less financially remunerative.[21] Many Mexican Americans understand little or no Spanish; but, according to Gallup pollsters, by 1982 English was widely spoken in many Hispanic homes, and nearly half of Hispanic children spoke English with their friends.[22]

Bilingual education, with its inherent critique of the melting-pot theory, had become part of the educational system at the very time that the melting pot had begun to work. Television, radio, advertising, the automobile, rock music, sports, and fashions in clothes all transcend ethnic divisions. Intermarriage for most races, including Mexican Americans, was on the increase, especially for second-generation immigrants (Puerto Rican New Yorkers forming the main exception). By the early 1980s, about one-fourth of all Mexican-American marriages in California were mixed.[23] Even the Hispanic media employed English, with Spanish as a second language. Fifty-four percent of Spanish speakers prefered to read and speak in English. The editors of the magazine *Caminos* claimed that 85 percent of their readers read articles in English first.[24]

Bilingual educators were accused of disregarding such developments; they often admitted to bilingual programs children who were proficient in English. A U.S. Office of Education-sponsored investigation of 38 bilingual projects for Hispanic Americans judged that about 70 percent of the pupils involved used English rather than Spanish for the purpose of taking tests.

Bilingual education also met with massive criticism from those who did not object to bilingualism as such, but who argued that bilingual programs often interfered with a proper teaching of English. These critics (including experts working on a 1983 Twentieth Century Fund study) considered bilingual education an ineffective teaching tool. It was a mistake to assume, they argued, that there was no alternative between the "sink-or-swim method," on the one hand, and bilingual education conducted in a foreign tongue, on the other. There was an answer: teach English to the foreign born in English; and provide this instruction in special courses adjusted to the students' special needs. Students would then immediately be forced to use the new tongue. They would be less likely to be inhibited in responding to a question in English if they knew that the teacher might not know the pupil's home language, or might not know it well. Despite the massive expenditures on bilingual education, there was no evidence that it had been more effective than the old-fashioned way of teaching English through English, a method used in Los Angeles and many other major cities during and even before World War I. This method, one might add, also has proved its utility in Israel, where *ulpanim* (special language schools) effectively teach Hebrew to Israel's polyglot immigrants in Hebrew.

As it was, the critics went on, bilingual education had turned into a massive political pork barrel. During the mid-1960s, to give a specific instance, Los Angeles managed with only two language consultants, paid on the same modest scale as ordinary teachers. By the mid-1970s, Los Angeles had engaged a director of bilingual education, two assistant directors, and eleven advisers, all of who received much higher salaries than the best-paid classroom teachers. Bilingual education therefore was apt to accentuate the besetting weakness of American public education: the disproportion in pay, power, and prestige between the classroom teachers and the administrators. Bilingual education, moreover, had created a new political lobby of bilingual supervisors; aides; counsellors; instructors; publishers of textbooks; producers of films, tapes, and other aides; and professors in education providing courses in bilingual education.[25]

The concept of bicultural education raised further difficult questions. How, in fact, should any ethnic culture be identified? What was German culture? Goethe's or Dr. Goebbels's, Marx's or Bismarck's? Should the schools try to transmit Hispanic, Mexican, Mexican-American, or Chicano culture, a question far from theoretical for members of a community who have defined themselves in many different ways. A survey conducted by Carlos Arce at the University of Michigan's School of Social Research found that 46 percent of the Mexican-descended respondents chose to be called Mexicans, 21 percent Mexican Americans, and only 16 percent Chicanos; the remainder picked a variety of other labels or none at all. Corresponding figures elicited by the Southwest Voter Registration Education Project for San Antonio and Los Angeles for Mexican-American voters were 20 percent, 50 percent, and 7 percent.)[26]

Biculturalism seemed to entail additional disadvantages. Well-qualified bilingual teachers were hard to recruit, particularly in the "hard sciences," and especially when U.S. schools were suffering a grave shortage of science instructors. This deficiency was all the more serious during a period when the United States was lagging behind Japan and other industrialized countries in the teaching of languages, mathematics, and scientific courses in high school.

Much to its disadvantage, bilingual and bicultural education came to be linked, for many of its academic defenders, with the assumption that the classroom should provide therapy as well as instruction. But, as Mary Ellen Goodman and Alma Beman, have pointed out in their investigation of a Houston slum, Mexican-American working-class children are well-adjusted.[27] They appreciate their grandparents, they respect their fathers as the family's money-earner and supreme court of discipline, and they love their mothers. Mexican children have a realistic appreciation of their chances in future life. They aspire to better jobs than their parents held, but they are not seduced by the glamor and riches they see on television. The mood of Mexican-American working-class people in Houston is expansive and optimistic. They find that "Anglo" prejudice has lessened and that industrialization has improved the workers' lot.

We too see no merit in theories that turn "Anglo" color and racial prejudice into a single-causal explanation of social ills. Racial prejudice assuredly exists in the United States, as it exists everywhere else in the world. Racial prejudice, however, is crisscrossed by class prejudice and, above all, by prejudice linked to the facts of ethnic succession. The most unpopular ethnicities in America are those who have arrived last in this country—not necessarily the most dark-complexioned.[28] Racial prejudice alone does not explain why the children of some immigrant groups—Chinese, Vietnamese, Jews, and Cubans—on the average do better in classrooms than those of others, including blacks, Puerto Ricans, and Mexicans. The explanation for their performance differential derives from a variety of social factors which are difficult to disentangle. One of them is family size: parents who have only a few children can spend more time and money on their individual upbringing. Equally important is the content of education, both at home and at school. In Wilhelminian Germany, for example, Protestants were more likely to explore the sciences than Catholics and therefore enjoyed a natural advantage in an economy apt to pay better salaries to engineers and scientists than to teachers of Latin. A similar distinction has now arisen in the United States between Asian students on the one hand and Chicano and Puerto Rican students on the other. There are proportionately more Asian graduates in computer sciences, engineering, and other scientific pursuits than Chicano or Puerto Rican graduates; hence, the Asians enjoy a natural advantage in the struggle for well-paid jobs. Puerto Ricans and Chicanos would profit financially by being guided into the hard sciences.

Above all, learning begins at home, and parental value preferences are more important than those of the pedagogues. People of Mexican heritage do not on the whole appear to be as distressed by low educational achievement as are blacks and whites.[29] Moreover, children from a middle-class family, or from a family aspiring to middle-class norms, enjoy educational advantages: mother and father will help with the homework, buy books, and lavishly praise good grades; they will censure a boy when he comes home, blood-stained but proud, from a fight on the school grounds. Such children will have a better chance than youngsters from a home where the television set or the stereo blare at full blast, where books are scarce, and where a man is thought a man for occasionally coming home drunk and enjoys a macho reputation for his prowess in a barroom brawl. Teachers can help to reinforce the values of the home, but they cannot be expected to do the parents' work. Nevertheless, schools can play a major role in creating an environment that supports high expectations and has a clear focus and a strong instructional leadership that can help the poor as well as the rich student.

Overall, one of the tragedies of bilingual and bicultural education has been that its growth coincided with the spread of educational norms that many parents dislike—permissiveness, submission to peer pressure, hostility to "elitism," and enforced busing. The disenchantment with education was accompanied by a major demographic shift: by the 1980s, only one-third of the students in big-city schools were "white." The middle class had attempted to fashion the schools in its own image. After 1920, the high schools attempted to include all American youths within their scope; the educators achieved this objective during the 1950s. In doing so, they primarily sought to prepare children for white-collar jobs or for employment in skilled trades; but, as the school system expanded, its achievements all too often seemed to contract.

The growth of the educational establishment and the educational bureaucracy—and their seeming loss of purpose—has accordingly coincided with public disillusionment with the schools, this is evidenced by the growing number of school bonds, once popularly supported, that now are often rejected by the voters. (Between 1957 and 1967, the electorate approved 73 percent of school bonds; between 1968 and 1976, the number had dropped to 48 percent.) There was bitter and sustained criticism of U.S. educational performance. According to the National Commission on Excellence in Education, only about one-fifth of all seventeen-year olds in the United States were able to write a persuasive essay; no more than one-third could solve a mathematical problem requiring several steps. The U.S. Chamber of Commerce in 1983 found that 35 percent of the corporations in one survey had to provide remedial training in basic skills for new employees.[30] If schools are to serve the special interests of the poor, they must get away from courses in "life adjustment," driver education, and "family living." They must restrain widespread antipathy to "elitism" in academic subjects. They must instead offer incentives to learning and promote academic excellence.

Multilingual and Multicultural Education:
A Positive Approach

How is excellence best obtained? The schools' achievements ultimately must depend on well-qualified teachers who are well paid and who are not burdened by paperwork extraneous to the classroom. And they must enjoy the public's respect. Education also needs a sense of purpose. As we see it, the supreme object of education should be to turn out citizens who can take a worthy part not only in earning a living but also in governing and defending the republic.

The foreign born and their children must be encouraged to learn the national language, an indispensable means to success. Given the enormous diversity of the U.S. population, there is no single formula for attaining linguistic competency. The children, say, of a foreign-born professor who teaches in an all-English-speaking college town require no bilingual education program. Their parents will know English and probably will help with the children's homework. The youngsters will pick up spoken English on the playground, as well as in the classroom. The theory of linguistic immersion works at its best with such people.

The position, however, is quite different in a multilingual city like San Francisco, Los Angeles, or Miami, where a large proportion of the students are "limited-English-proficient." Such students are looked down upon by their Anglophone schoolmates for "talking funny," are apt to associate only with their own kind, are unable to make use of the instruction offered to them in a regular public school, and thereby waste both their own time and the taxpayers' dollars. According to the National Institute of Education, the limited-English-proficient students aged five to fourteen number about 2.5 million; within twenty years, their number might rise to 3.4 million. Altogether they speak more than 80 languages (about two-thirds of them use Spanish); they come from every conceivable socioeconomic background; and their cultural and education backgrounds vary enormously. They profess almost every religion known on earth. They present a most difficult linguistic problem to educators. The Santa Clara School District in California, to give one example, in 1983 provided education in an astonishing variety of tongues, ranging from Spanish to Vietnamese, Cantonese, Mandarin, Korean, Tagalog, Japanese, Portuguese, Cambodian/Khmer, and Lao. A 1980 report from the Los Angeles schools stated that non-English-speaking pupils, or students with a poor knowledge of English, between them numbered 110,000 and spoke 87 different languages. Los Angeles at the time spent almost $46 million to furnish these youngsters with bilingual education.

San Francisco, traditionally one of the nation's most polyglot cities, is another case in point. At the end of 1982, the city contained 27,786 students with a home language other than English. They spoke 27 languages. San Francisco's record in the past was a troubled one. Students unable to converse in English had been sent to a special Continuation High School, where they had mixed with truants and delinquents and learned to use drugs and get into trouble. It was the deficiencies of the San Francisco school system that, in 1974, caused the *Lau v. Nicholas* case to go to the Supreme Court.

San Francisco thereafter developed a system remarkable for its intelligence and effectiveness, one that could serve as a model for other cities with a polyglot immigrant population, whether in the United States or Europe. Students incompetent in English were tested for their academic competency and their ability to speak English and then placed in appropriate schools; they also received help with immunization and other services. The Bilingual Education Department developed a variety of programs to meet different needs, including programs for students unable to read or write in any language, the handicapped, and also gifted students.

In addition to setting up special programs in the public schools, San Francisco established special education centers for members of particular ethnic communities in which children were taught in their own language until they were sufficiently proficient in English to transfer to public schools. The syllabus was practical and "success-oriented," with classes in reading, writing, hygiene, nutrition, social studies, and English on the primary level, to which were added mathematics, history, geography, art, and music in the intermediate daily program.

San Francisco took another step of major consequence in 1979, when the city opened Newcomer High School to provide a transitional education program for foreign-born youngsters (grades 9 through 12; ages 14–17 years) unable to speak sound English. The new high school provided thorough instruction in English as a Second Language (ESL); bilingual classes in such fields as social studies and mathematics; and also such electives as art, cooking, typing, and office management. After spending a year at Newcomer High School, students transferred to a district public high school or an appropriate vocational school or college. Youngsters sent to district high schools received continued ESL instruction and bilingual "support" classes in other subjects until they were able to profit fully from all English-speaking classes.

On the surface, the staff at Newcomer faced an almost impossible task. Their students included youngsters from all over the world: Asia, Latin America, the Near East, and Europe. Many students had gone through experiences that might cause anyone's hair to turn grey. The following are entries in the Newcomer High School Yearbook (1981–82):

> Noraworg Phuovieng is 16 years old and he comes from Laos. He arrived in this country only 3 months ago. Noraworg's father was a soldier with the Laotian army but as the Communist regime became more and more oppressive, he and his family decided to defect to a free country. Noraworg still remembers where they managed to take a boat to Thailand. . . .

> Ever Gomez is 14 years old. . . . He was born in El Salvador, now being torn by a bloody civil war. Ever and his mother fled their native country because his father disappeared after he had been to a political rally . . .[31]

For these youngsters, Newcomer High School turned out to be a haven where they benefited from small school size (about 500 students), from the efforts of a highly qualified and gifted staff, and from the experience of meeting other youngsters from all over the world. We were impressed by what we saw: an elderly Chinese-born instructor teaching history in the manner of a traditional storyteller; a chef simultaneously imparting a knowledge of cookery and practical English; and a teacher who had fled from Southeast Asia explaining, in a social science class, the significance of the words "refugee" and "immigrant" by a mixture of simple English and enjoyable ham-acting. There were no serious disciplinary problems. Attendance figures were outstanding, ranging from 93.8 percent in 1979–80 to 97.3 percent in 1982–83. Test scores also were good. Newcomer turned out to be exactly what a well-run school should be.

Many American cities must accommodate themselves to immigrants and refugees, most of them poor. They strain city budgets for housing, education, and health care. In 1983, Los Angeles authorities estimated that 27.1 percent of the city was foreign born. Sixty-two percent of its children in kindergarten and more than 40 percent of the children in the first five grades were Hispanic. In the coming years a majority of the students in Los Angeles schools will be Hispanic. Hundreds of millions of dollars are being spent in bilingual education in the United States with the federal and state governments providing most of the money.

Los Angeles also worked under great pressure to provide bilingual education to some 110,000 students (1983) who spoke 87 languages. There was no separate school for non-English speakers; bilingual classes were taught in local schools. Ninety percent of the students in bilingual programs were Hispanic. The goal has become transitional instruction— not language maintenance or bicultural education, as it was in the late 1970s. (Lack of money and bilingual teachers made language maintenance impractical.) As in San Francisco, Los Angeles administrators pointed to better attendance figures and test scores for bilingual students.

In New York City there were, at the time of this writing, 70,000 in bilingual education programs out of 900,000 students. Most language training was in Spanish, but 52,611 students were taught some subjects in their native language and 17,000 or so received instruction in all subjects in English. To support this program New York City obtained $16 million from the federal government. On the other hand, there was little bilingual education in the Denver school system; teaching was done primarily in English, even though one-third of Denver's 62,000 students had Spanish surnames. Only about 4,000 students receive bilingual training (and that in English); only a few schools provided tutoring in Spanish.

Texas has experienced a massive increase in immigration since the late 1970s: by 1983, about 260,000 children there were in bilingual programs, which cost $50 to $75 million a year. Poor border communities were overwhelmed as children illegally crossed the border to be educated. Tests showed that the majority of these children did not develop even minimal skills in English. The federal government had to assist local schools suffering from large immigration. Federal courts insisted that children of illegals should be educated and that the federal goverment should pay the bill. Local communities along borders were mostly poor; forced to dilute their education resources to include illegals, the children of citizens found themselves disadvantaged through poor education.

Miami, on the other hand, had one of the most advanced bilingual programs in the country. More than 95,000 out of 220,000 students in 1983 were in bilingual education programs. English speakers learned some Spanish, and Spanish speakers received intensive English instruction, plus training in basic academic courses in their native language. Dade County is heavily populated by Spanish speakers (40 percent),

Miami has 56 percent. In the school system, 39 percent of the students were Hispanic. There was much public discussion about bilingual training in the schools, especially its slow pace. But the debate was less heated than in the past, and there was less opposition to bilingual education.

In 1983, there were more than 660 teachers in the program, with a budget of $17 million. The average school day for those not proficient in English was: two hours of instruction in English, 30 minutes of Spanish (or other languages), 90 minutes of instruction in Spanish in academic subjects (math, social studies, etc.), and the remainder of the day spent on studying subjects in English. Once the students had become proficient in English, they would do one hour a day in Spanish at the high school level, and 30 minutes at the primary school level.

What of the future? Generalizations are hard to make because standards of bilingual education, like those of education throughout the United States, differ enormously: there are some deplorable, some mediocre, and some superb schools. No single formula can be applied to every community, but there should be a common sense of direction. Some critics of multilingual education fear that, by encouraging it, the American taxpayer may unwittingly turn the United States into another Lebanon, Cyprus, Belgium, or Canada—countries torn by ethnic-linguistic strife.

We do not share these apprehensions. American society, as we see it, is too mobile and assimilative in character to be frozen into permanent ethnic molds. There are indeed great ethnic aggregations, but these are in constant flux as families continue to move out of "ethnic" neighborhoods and new ethnic groups move in. (For instance, Vietnamese and Chinese replace once-solid Spanish-speaking neighborhoods in Los Angeles or San Jose.) No immigrant group in American history has ever succeeded in forming its own "Quebec."

The Franco-American example is indeed instructive in this respect. Franco-Americans from Canada possessed in the Province of Quebec a territorial base adjacent to the United States, a base not available to any immigrants from Europe. Between 1870 and 1929, about one million French-speaking immigrants made their way from Quebec to New England. French clergymen, journalists, educators, and politicians dreamed of permanently entrenching French civilization in New England. They created their own schools, newspapers, trade unions, and religious congregations—to little avail. The men and women from Quebec became "Franco-Americans," and thereafter Americans. It was not until the 1970s that Franco-Americans cautiously tried to reidentify themselves ethnically. Franco-Americans thereafter succeeded in creating bilingual education programs; for instance, the University of Maine at Orona set up a Franco-American studies program.[32] But for all the New England bumper stickers showing a frog and the legend *le français—je le parle par coeur* ("French—I speak it by heart"), New England will never join Quebec. In the same way, Spanish would die out in time if the border were closed. Hispanics will remain an ethnic group but not a language group, according to Calvin Veltman, a sociolinguist at the University of Quebec who has studied Chicanos.[33]

In regard to the best manner of teaching English, our own approach is eclectic. There are several ways in which a language can be taught—the United States does not have to tie itself down to any one of them. The variety and flexibility of U.S. education has in fact always been its strength. There is a case for the "sink-or-swim" method (one from which refugee children from Central Europe profited in the 1930s). There is a case for special English instruction in English. There is also a case for well-run bilingual classes. The choice among the different methods should be left to the local education authorities who are most familiar with local desires and needs.

We consider that the maintenance of foreign immigrant cultures should be a matter of private, not of public, endeavor. We do wish to stress, however, the value of maintaining the intellectual capital represented by the foreign-born students' existing language skills. We also wish to enter a plea for upgrading the teaching of foreign tongues and of the geography of foreign countries. All too often in the United States, the best—or the only—geography teaching is done by travel bureaus with their posters.

Cultural considerations aside, the United States has become far more dependent than in the past on foreign trade. There is increasing need for merchants, bankers, diplomats, and soldiers able to communicate in foreign tongues, yet this country has been remiss in educating a sufficient number of men and women with the requisite linguistic skills. Yielding to demands for "relevance" and the students' pressure for easy grades, American schools, colleges, and universities have long ignored language requirements. (Between 1966 and 1979, the percentage of U.S. colleges and universities insisting on a foreign language as a qualification for admission dropped from 34 percent to 8 percent—at a time when America's foreign commerce continued to increase as a proportion of the national GNP, from 6 percent in the 1940s to 17 percent in 1982.) U.S. schools and colleges contain too many youngsters who cannot speak, read, or write any language correctly—regardless of their national origin or native language. This deficiency is deplorable, as is the mind-set that assumes competence in one language to be incompatible with the command of another. On the contrary, a student fluent in Spanish can more easily acquire good English than a student who is incompetent in either tongue.

The United States, the point bears repeating, must seek to turn the tide of a linguistic ignorance. Compared with such countries as Switzerland or Holland, the United States is poorly equipped in the teaching of foreign languages, often with deplorable, and sometimes even tragic-comic, results. (To give one example: sales of the Chevrolet Nova automobile were said to have dropped in Latin America because "Nova" [*no va*] signifies "no go" in Spanish.) Far from spending less on maintaining linguistic proficiency, Americans should spend more. Spanish in particular has an important part in this country's educational future, given America's stake in the Latin American world. Spanish in fact might well be encouraged as the first foreign-language elective in schools and universities in such states as Texas, New York, California, and Florida. But Spanish, like all other languages, can best be taught if students are given a grasp of grammar and orthography, those traditional skills frequently derided by experimental education theoreticians.

Similar considerations apply to the teaching of history. U.S. schools on the whole have grossly neglected history, especially world history. American culture is in many ways antihistorical; too many research institutions are concerned with public policy; too many government departments and educators act as if history began last week. Students at every level, whether English or Spanish speaking, quickly get the message. Few students of any linguistic background can intelligently explain why Mexicans celebrate the "Cinco de Mayo" as a national holiday or why, for that matter, Ulstermen once a year should act as if the Battle of the Boyne (1690) had been fought yesterday. Chicano nationalists justly may be criticized for some grotesque distortions; they are fully justified, however, when they call for a better understanding of history—not only of the numbers of minorities that have enriched the United States, but of the countries from which they came.

Overall, American schools should seek to preserve our multifarious heritage and extend it; and they should endeavor to blend traditional with innovative skills in education. In regard to methods for attaining this goal, conservative and liberal educations alike can do no better than to learn from W. E. B. DuBois, whose introductory observations at the beginning of this chapter may also serve as its conclusion.

Chapter 13

Affirmative Action and Nationhood

From the beginnings of their nation, Americans were less class-conscious than Europeans. But what Americans lacked in class prejudice, they made up in racial prejudice. The civil rights struggle in the United States—from the emancipation of the slaves in the mid-nineteenth century to the struggle against residential, scholastic, and job discrimination during the mid-twentieth century—was dominated by the color issue. Other ethnic clashes insensibly came to be subsumed under this overriding concern.

The final campaigns against institutionalized ethnic inequality were fought after World War II, a conflict that identified racism with Nazism. In 1954, the U.S. Supreme Court unanimously outlawed racial segregation in public schools in the historic *Brown v. Board of Education of Topeka* case, a decision welcomed as much by Mexican Americans in the Southwest as by black Americans in the South. Of equal consequence was the Civil Rights Act of 1964, designed to outlaw racial discrimination altogether.

The civil rights campaigners had two principles in common: they believed in equality before the law and a "career open to talent." No U.S. citizen should be permitted to suffer any disabilities because of his or her racial or ethnic descent, national origin, or religion. But, thereafter, the civil rights alliance began to splinter. Traditional liberals were content to remove all formal barriers to civic or economic advancement; following that, competition in the free market should determine success. Such, for instance, was the position of many Jewish Americans who earlier encountered "quotas" that limited their admission, say, to prestigious medical schools. Such was the position of most legislators who had put the Civil Rights Act on the statute book. Senator Hubert Humphrey, for instance, while guiding the bill through the Senate, assured his colleagues that the bill did not require an employer to achieve any kind of racial balance in his work force by giving preferential treatment to any individual or group. Under the provisions of the Civil Rights Act, employers were held liable only for their own "intentional" discrimination, not for societal patterns in the work force. According to Humphrey, vague claims of "institutional racism" were not to be countenanced.[1]

Origins and Rationale

After the 1960s, the focus of the civic rights struggle began to change. The shift of policy found expression in a series of decisions in federal and state courts. Equally important was the changing role of federal agencies: their powers increased and so did their personnel and their organizational complexity. According to the new philosophy, equal opportunity was not enough; policymakers should endeavor to correct the statistical imbalance that continued to exist in employment, living conditions, and income among the various ethnic communities. An entire network of agencies applied their collective skills to right these wrongs through executive actions. They included the National Labor Relations Board (set up in 1935), the U.S. Commission on Civil Rights (1957), the Equal Employment Opportunity Commission (1965)—all independent agencies—and the Office of Federal Contract Compliance, (established in 1965 within the U.S. Department of Labor). Others were the Department of Health and Human Services (known as Health, Education and Welfare until 1980, when the Department of Education became an independent agency), and the Minority Business Development Agency (part of the Department of Commerce).

Guided in the main by liberal civil servants, these agencies gradually expanded their scope, with support from the courts and from sympathetically inclined legislators, academicians, and public interest groups, all of which desired equitable representation for all ethnic communities throughout every sector of the economy. Black Americans were the reformers' original concern; other "disadvantaged" peoples, recognizable by skin color or sex, also came to be subsumed under the category of disadvantaged, requiring help through affirmative action in staffing, promotion, and contracts.

Hispanic Americans had but a minor share in initiating the new order. Mexican- and Puerto Rican-American civic organizations originally followed an assimilationist policy. During the 1930s, activists had demanded that Mexican Americans should be classed as "whites"; nothing was further from their minds than a quota system. Hispanic-American civic right associations only gradually became converts to the new concept, which was pushed with special vigor by black Americans, whose political power greatly increased during and after the 1960s and greatly exceeded the Hispanics', especially in city government.[2]

But the most effective force for affirmative action was not the civic rights leaders, black or Hispanic, but the welfare bureaucracies—no matter which party held power. Affirmative action rested on presidential executive orders and on "guidelines." In 1968, the Office of Federal Contract Compliance (OFCC) issued guidelines alluding to "goals" and "timetables" and "representation." In 1970, under the Nixon presidency, OFCC further strengthened these guidelines in the direction of "result-oriented procedures." New guidelines issued in 1971 stated that "goals and timetables" entailed materially increased utilization of minorities and women; "underutilization" was defined as underrepresentation in any particular job classification in relation to what might reasonably be expected by their availability. The burden of the proof—and remedy—was placed on the employer.

The Reagan administration, though avowedly hostile to affirmative action, did not in fact greatly diverge from its predecessors. Civil rights activists censured the administration for weakening the enforcement of antidiscrimination and affirmative action rules applied to contractors doing business with the federal government. But the main executive orders remained in force. The president himself took care to appoint women, blacks, and Hispanics to noncareer positions. (By the end of 1981, his appointments included 877 women, 130 blacks, and 80 Hispanics out of 2,865 posts.) Agencies concerned with civil rights issues continued to promote affirmative action programs, much to the distress of Reagan's conservative supporters.[3]

Affirmative action cannot easily be reduced to a single denominator; its programs operate in many different, and sometimes divergent, fashions. Disputes existed regarding the criteria to be used. Should affirmative action attempt to provide representation to each minority on the basis of its absolute population ratios within the local community, the state, or the nation? The most constructive planners argued that the object of affirmative action was not to provide an artificial representation—one that belied existing cultural, historical and economic realities—but to "eliminate artificial barriers created by past or present discrimination or by ignorance of possibilities."[4] Selection criteria not relating to job performance should be removed. Candidates should be chosen according to their availability in the labor force. A shipping company, in other words, could not be censured for failing to engage a Mexican-American captain when no applicants were available. A university, on the other hand, might be faulted when none of its professors in the Spanish department were of Hispanic origin, if every qualified Puerto Rican, Mexican American, or Cuban candidate had been rejected.

But a guiding principle remained. "Disadvantaged" groups were entitled to "specific goals" for the apportionment of jobs and government contracts, even though hard-and-fast "quotas" were disallowed. In 1983, to give an example, government officials and Hispanic rights leaders announced agreement on a plan that, by 1990, would be expected to give Hispanics 14.7 percent of entry jobs in the U.S. Postal Service division in the San Francisco Bay Area. The consent decree, approved by the local U.S. District Court, settled a seven-year old racial discrimination lawsuit filed by Incorporated Mexican-American Government Employees. The postal service promised to freeze its hiring lists for certain designated positions until several thousand Hispanics who had failed the civil service tests since 1972 would be able to take them again; special recruiters would be hired to seek out Hispanic applicants. Applicants, however, would not be given special treatment in the sense of being placed ahead of others with higher scores. Another agreement obliged the University of California at Berkeley to hire 26 more women and five more minority professors by 1986, and an extra 49 women and 45 minority professors after 1989.[5]

The affirmative action issue posed fundamental questions. According to its advocates, affirmative action was to be a temporary device, to be enforced only until all distinctions between the races arising from past discrimination had been eliminated. But, in fact, the architects of affirmative action set no time limits to their programs; nor did the law precisely define the conditions that would justify the ultimate abolition of the programs. Temporary programs therefore were apt to become permanent programs. Although affirmative action was limited originally to blacks, a small minority, affirmative action rapidly extended to embrace Hispanics, Native Americans, and women—until, absurdly, the "minorities" to be favored embraced the majority, about 70 percent of the American people.

Affirmative action therefore helped to create new political cleavages among its actual or presumed beneficiaries spawning a backlash among those who had not been favored. The programs also put a new premium on political action to control the affirmative action machinery operated by such agencies as the Department of Labor. The affirmative action program also posed questions that went far beyond the apportionment of jobs: What should be the role of the free market? What kind of nation should the United States be in the future? Did the rights enshrined in the Constitution and the Bill of Rights apply only to individuals? Or were there special group rights to be accorded to minorities historically "deprived" through discriminatory action on the part of the majority? The question was debated in the Supreme Court in disputes such as the *Bakke* and the *Weber* cases.[6] By 1984, the issue as yet remained unresolved.

On the face of it, the advocates of affirmative action seemed to have a strong case. No matter how much progress blacks and Hispanics had made, their median family incomes remain at the bottom of the ladder; white and yellow people, on the average, rank above the brown, black, and red. Affirmative action, according to its sponsors, is essential for shattering this economic hierarchy of color. Like aid to the Third World, affirmative action has been defended on many contradictory grounds: as a means of preserving social stability, as a reparation for real or alleged injustice in the past, as an instrument for the redistribution of wealth, and as a beneficient form of social planning. Sociologist Christopher Jencks has put the argument in a persuasive way. Ethnic minorities have experienced discriminatory treatment for generations, he says. Such discriminatory treatment must be outlawed. But it is not enough to pass "color-blind" laws. Given the pervasive nature of American racism, neither blacks nor Hispanics can begin the race for economic advancement from the same starting point. Unemployment remains rife among blacks and Hispanics, especially among the young. This is not surprising, for blacks and Hispanics have failed to obtain the same kind of work experience available to their white compatriots. Unless the government takes positive action, riots once more will devastate the big city slums.

Past injustice, Jencks goes on, is not easily repaired. Good jobs usually demand information skills and personal contacts that can be acquired only when a man or a woman holds a position as good, or almost as good, as the new post for which the applicant applies. Since blacks, and to a lesser extent Hispanics, have not had access to such opportunities in the past, and since they have experienced great difficulty in attending good schools, "color-blind" hiring rules will tend forever to exclude the less favored from good jobs. Furthermore, most good positions carry an implicit guarantee of tenure as long as the employee performs at an acceptable level. Because most good jobs have been filled under Jim Crow rules, and because the turnover in such jobs tends to be low, a system guaranteeing minority members fair access to the positions that fall vacant in the future will not provide a fair share to minorities for at least a generation.

Admittedly, Jencks continues, reverse discrimination creates inequities. Affirmative action has in fact tended to benefit well-educated minority persons and those with steady work habits, rather than the desperately poor. Young blacks who lack educational qualifications or steady employment histories have benefited little from existing programs; they may have suffered from the manner in which such programs operate. An employer knows that if he fires a minority worker, the dismissed employee can appeal to the Equal Employment Opportunity Commission (EEOC). To fight such an appeal is expensive. Therefore, if a personnel manager considers "high-risk" applicants, many of whom may have to be fired, he may well pick a "high-risk" white rather than a "high-risk" black. In addition, EEOC investigations take special note of promotion rates. This practice may make an employer reluctant to hire blacks considered unlikely to earn promotion. Indulging in such practices is, of course, illegal, but this does not make it unusual. Reverse discrimination may occasion resentment among whites and heighten white prejudices, as black and brown people are promoted with qualifications inferior to those of their "Caucasian" competitors. Nevertheless, such troubles are a modest price to pay for policies that, on balance, already have increased, and will continue to increase, the minorities' earning power.

Affirmative action, Jencks's argument continues, does entail government intervention; and "big government" is now in disrepute. But its record in racial matters has been much better than the critics allege. American public opinion, considers judges and civil servants less self-interested than corporate enterprise. Americans, in fact, have devised a governmental system precisely for the purpose of getting officials to police big business, and judges in turn to police officials. This system has served America well. The time has come for the minorities to make use of the self-same machinery that other interest groups—farmers, industrialists, builders, and shippers—have employed successfully in the past. All these groups have managed to manipulate government intervention for their own good. There is no reason why blacks and Hispanics should be expected to sacrifice themselves on the altar of unlimited free competition when no one else shows a similar inclination.[7]

By contrast, free enterprise economists, such as Thomas Sowell and Walter Block, believe that affirmative action may in fact have had counterproductive consequences because of its arbitrary nature and because of bureaucratic interference in the operation of the free market. Sowell shows that Hispanics and blacks were making substantial gains before the advent of affirmative action. He emphasizes that the dynamism inherent in the free enterprise system has, in fact, benefited all the various ethnic groups that have successively arrived at our shores, even though their initial progress often seemed slow. Italian Americans in New York, for example, suffered from all the ills that later afflicted Puerto Ricans: overcrowding, unsanitary facilities, and poor health. Italians, in fact, did much better in Buenos Aires than in New York.[8] But Italians in the United States have gone up in the social scale, despite all the disabilities from which they suffered, and despite a high rate of initial return migration (52 percent for the period from 1861 to 1914).

Adversaries of affirmative action programs also point to the cost of enforcing them. These costs are borne by the general taxpayer, who is responsible for meeting the salaries of the bureaucrats charged with enforcing the programs, and by the general consumer, who has to pay higher prices to compensate firms for the added expense of employing more administrative staff to comply with the law.

The Politics of Racial Classification

The political questions involved are intractable; they raise, for example, complex problems of ethnic categorization. Assuming that entire ethnic groups have rights over and above those of individuals, how exactly are these groups to be defined? The definition of "blacks" seemed straightforward; essentially it followed the tradition of North American racism, once bitterly expressed in the jingle: "If you are white—you're all right; if you are brown—stick aroun'; if you are black—hold back." Any man or woman with a known African forebear was black. Only in America would Alexander Pushkin, the greatest of Russian poets, a man with an African great-grandfather, be described as a "black" poet, a definition incomprehensible even to the most bigoted of Russian chauvinists.

In trying to define other disadvantaged groups, such as Mexican or Puerto Rican Americans, North Americans followed the same pattern— one that had no meaning in Latin America, where racial and class definitions were confounded to a much greater extent than in the United States. There were Puerto Ricans of purely Spanish or Corsican descent; there were Puerto Ricans mainly of African descent; but no Puerto Rican was likely to describe a dark-skinned Puerto Rican millionaire as black. The same held true in Mexico or Guatemala, where a very light-skinned peasant, living in an Indian village according to traditional ways, would not be regarded as a white, but as Indian, irrespective of pigmentation.

In attempting to define "disadvantaged" groups, American civil servants labored mightily to fit Mexicans, Puerto Ricans, Cubans, Dominicans, and Argentinians—a heterogeneous collection of the most varied ethnic backgrounds—into the American racial mold by constructing a new category known as "Hispanic." Puerto Ricans or Mexican Americans had not originally defined themselves as Hispanics; their leaders had not agitated for the establishment of such a category; Congress had not legislated the new ethnic definition; it came only by administrative fiat. The new category, in turn, became a working tool for demographers and statisticians. Its creation and use in public policy reflected a wider concern on the part of egalitarian reformers in the courts, the media, and the civil service with the real or supposed unfairness of competition in American society. As a public opinion expert put it in a semipopular book: "Blacks, women, Spanish-speaking minorities, gays, undocumented workers, Indians, the physically handicapped, older people, ex-mental patients, ex-addicts, [and] ex-convicts" all had suffered discrimination.[9] Hence, "moral exhortation, consciousness raising and, increasingly, the force of law" were brought to bear on all those who opposed the reformers' grand design. The new crusade made a special appeal to the educated, to professionals, and above all, academicians.[10]

Under this new dispensation, Chileans, Puerto Ricans, Cubans, Dominicans, and Mexicans all became "Hispanics," and all were part of a vast and heterogenous collection of the disinherited—as distinct from "whites." The term "Hispanic" first appeared in U.S. census forms in 1980. But how were Hispanics to be distinguished? Who precisely was a white? Civil servants supplied the answer. For instance, Standard Form 181 of the U.S. Office of Personnel Management, entitled "Race and National Origin Identification," gave a detailed definition. A white was a person "having origins in any of the original peoples of Europe, North Africa or the Middle East, except persons of Mexican, Puerto Rican, Cuban, Central or South American, or other Spanish cultures or origins . . . " Who was Hispanic? "A person of Mexican, Puerto Rican, Cuban, Central or South American, or other Spanish cultures or origins. Does not include persons of Portuguese culture or origin." Who was black? "A person having origin in any of the black racial groups of Africa, except Hispanics."

These definitions had a spurious air of exactitude. In fact, they raised more questions than they solved. North Africans were classed as "white." But who is a North African—a Mauritanian, an Egyptian, a Moroccan? Some Moroccans have their origin in the "black racial groups of Africa," and some have light skin or a European appearance. Are they both white? An Algerian is clearly "white" under the current classification, however swarthy his complexion. A blonde Castilian and a red-haired and blue-eyed Uruguayan, on the other hand, do not count as "white"; they rank as "Hispanics," together with Puerto Ricans of the darkest as well as the lightest hue.

The racial classifier's troubles did not stop at this point. What happened when an employee refused to classify himself racially? Or, worse, what was an agency to do when an employee deliberately furnished a "wrong" classification? The tortured language of the "Conversion Procedures for Agencies, Attachment 1 to FPM Ltr. 298–10" (from the Office of Personnel Management, dated August 17, 1980), revealed the extent of bureaucratic perplexity. If an official refused to provide the data required by the agency, "then the agency is authorized to and will identify the employee's race or national origin as that which the agency visually perceives to be the correct classification for the employee." In other words, the agency would decide John Lopez's "Hispanic" status and Muhammed Abd al-Aziz's "white" status by looking them straight in the eyes!

If the employee provided what is evidently "wrong" information, the bureaucrat faced even greater difficulties. In such a deplorable case,

"The agency will counsel the employee as to the purpose for which the data are being collected, the need for accuracy, the agency's recognition of the sensitivity of the data, and the existence of procedures to prevent its unauthorized disclosure." If the employee, however, proved obdurate and stuck to his chosen classification, the agency was bound to accept it. Self-identification thus remained a bastion of personal integrity. But suppose a majority member were to classify himself as a member of a minority, say a Hispanic or a Native American, for the purpose of getting a minority appointment or a minority contract.[11] The law, by the early 1980s, provided no answer for this situation. If "cheating" were to become widespread, it would surely endanger the purpose of all affirmative action programs. But if fraudulent claims to minority status were to be prevented, the United States would have to create a national classification scheme and this country might follow the U.S.S.R. and South Africa on the road to the documentary definition of everyone's racial ancestry. Such classification schemes, moreover, might become increasingly complex, as new ethnic pressure groups came into being, and as the federal bureaucracy acquired more manpower to tackle new tasks.[12]

The Case Against Affirmative Action

The Civil Rights Act of 1964, as we have pointed out, aimed at securing equality of prospective opportunity; the legislators thought in terms of individual, not of group, rights. Subsequent court decisions and administrative regulations shifted the emphasis in a direction not intended either by the framers of the Constitution or by legislators: toward parity of retrospective results, the "correction of imbalances," and the creation of group rights. The constitutional division of functions (among judiciary, legislature, and executive) has given way to the confusion of functions. The new policy represents the social preferences of a new coalition made up of activist judges, reform-minded civil servants, progressive academicians, and minority leaders. Their policy reflects neither the will of the country's elected representative nor that of the nation at large.

The new policy reflects a legitimate public policy commitment to fight racial discrimination in the job market. Well-run affirmative action programs in business or the academy do not interfere with the maintenance of technical standards. But affirmative action also has raised serious problems of a fundamental kind. All too many advocates of affirmative action believe that the differences in economic status achieved by differing ethnic communities derive only from discrimination practiced in the present or past by majority members against members of ethnic minorities. If a given minority is "underrepresented" or "overrepresented" in comparative wealth or status, the resultant inequality must have been occasioned in the first place by discrimination. The extent of discrimination therefore can be measured through numerical representation.

These fundamental assumptions are mistaken. As economists Thomas Sowell and Barry Chiswick point out, the social processes involved in creating comparative inequalities are much more complex. They are greatly influenced, for example, by the median age of various groups. For the United States as a whole, the median age is 28 years. For Mexican and Puerto Rican Americans, it is 18 years; and for blacks, 22 years. For Italian and German Americans, on the other hand, it is 36; for Irish, 37; for Jews, 46. Clearly a group with a high median age is bound to contain more members who have acquired an advanced education and who have managed to succeed in their respective careers than are groups with a lower median age. At the extreme ends of the spectrum stand Jewish Americans and Puerto Rican Americans: just over half of the Jewish Americans are 45 years old, while only 12 percent of Puerto Ricans are that age. Such age differences play havoc with all gross statistical comparisons, for age has a major impact in regard to income, occupation, unemployment, and crime.

Differences in age in part reflect differences in the number of children per family. Puerto Ricans and Mexicans have much larger families than Orientals, Jews, or Irish. About half the Mexican Americans and Puerto Ricans in the United States are infants, children, or teenagers. They are either too young to earn money or can contribute but little to the family income. Until children have grown up, they may in fact represent an economic burden. Money spent on their care cannot be devoted to expanding a family business, getting a better professional qualification, or sending older children to college. As Sowell puts it, to compare any group's representation in adult jobs with their representation in a population that includes many young children is to compare apples and oranges.

Similar difficulties apply when the age of marriage is taken into consideration. For example, half of all Mexican-American women marry in their teens, whereas only 10 percent of Japanese-American women marry that young. As Sowell points out, little imagination is needed to show how the age of a woman when she marries must affect her opportunities for college attendance or a lucrative career—quite apart from such factors as racial or gender discrimination.

In addition, geographical distribution plays a major role. Income differences between California and Arkansas, or between Alaska and Mississippi, are greater than income differences between blacks and whites. As Sowell shows, no ethnic group in the United States has an income that is only half the national average; but members of a given ethnic group in one location often earn less than half of the income of members of the same ethnic group residing elsewhere. Mexican Americans in the Laredo or Brownsville metropolitan districts in Texas earn less than half the income of Mexican Americans in the Detroit metropolitan area. Virtually no two American ethnic groups have the same geographical distribution pattern. Blacks live in the low-income South in greater proportion than do most other Americans. This distribution pattern itself has far-reaching social consequences. While Mexican Americans and Puerto Rican Americans earn more than blacks nationally, blacks outside the South earn more than either of these Hispanic groups.

More important still are wider cultural differences, which are discussed at length in Sowell's *Ethnic America: A History*. Many social differences among ethnic groups reflect historical differences that existed before they ever set foot on American soil—for instance, the disproportionate share of Jews in the clothing industry, Germans in beer brewing, and Mexicans in farming. Much depends on the length of residence of any given group in the United States and the consequent degree of acculturation. Also important are such social values as the commitment to formal education traditionally evinced by, for example, the Jews and Chinese. As we have previously mentioned, sociological studies suggest that working-class people of Mexican heritage, by reason of their cultural background, may feel less distress or status deprivation because of low educational attainments than many of their "Anglo" compatriots.

Discrimination certainly was been rife in the United States. Few languages have as offensive a vocabulary of interethnic abuse as American English: niggers, spades, chinks, gooks, kikes, micks, greasers, spics, dagos, and so on. Past discriminaton, however, does not explain why Jews, Japanese, or Chinese all have higher average family incomes than Anglo-Saxons. Neither does it explain why, for example, West Indian blacks do better on the average than black Americans.

The fate of any ethnic minority, in other words, depends on factors much more complex than those that can be subsumed under the concept of discrimination. Family cohesion is one important factor. "Latchkey children," who must fend for themselves while their parents are at work, are more likely to get into trouble than children from a family where the mother stays at home and where there are grandparents, aunts, and cousins nearby. Family cohesion, in turn, may be undermined by factors that have nothing to do with racial discrimination and that cannot be rectified by affirmative action. Family cohesion may be affected by migration; by the abuse of drugs or alcohol; even by ill-advised urban renewal schemes or ill-conceived welfare projects. When traditional

ethnic neighborhoods are disrupted by "slum clearance" and the construction of huge apartment blocs, juvenile crime commonly goes up,
as a mother living on the eighth floor is less able to watch what her
children are doing in the streets than she was in the old neighborhood.
Aid-to-dependent-children projects, to give another example, may encourage the disruption of families by driving away the male bread earner
and by unwittingly providing an unwed mother with no incentive to
practice birth control.

Does this mean that ethnic origin should never be considered in
hiring men and women for particular jobs? In our opinion, such a
conclusion is unwarranted. Ethnic origins indeed should be considered
where the *functional purposes* of the job are involved. A police force
composed only of Irish Americans will be less efficient in serving a
Hispanic neighborhood than a police force containing officers of Hispanic
as well as of Northern European descent. Functional underrepresentation
is not an imaginary problem. In 1982, for instance, Hispanic police
officers remained seriously underrepresented in many of California's
major towns, especially in Los Angeles.[13]

But affirmative action with numerical quotas as a universal principle
of equity—divorced from its functional aspects—does not appeal to us.
The poor need help, but not necessarily the kind that liberal reformers
prize most. One of the most important services the nation can render
to the poor is to protect their lives and property. There are parts of
Los Angeles, for instance, where street gangs maintain a turf carved
out three generations earlier, where sons follow fathers into the same
gang, and where babies are tatooed with a gang's name before they are
baptized. Reports compiled by the Los Angeles County Sheriff's office
have in fact identified 405 gangs with a known membership of about
30,000. These people are not all criminals; many of them fight only
when provoked, and only about 5 percent of gang members are "shooters"
(those who attempt to kill). Los Angeles, nevertheless, has one of the
worst problems of gang violence in the nation. Extortion, drug smuggling,
robbery, and murder are rife. A youngster of any race in this environment
grows up under a tremendous social disadvantage. This disadvantage
does not derive from racial discrimination alone, but from the inability
or unwillingness of society to enforce its laws.

This deficiency in turn has many causes, among them: the leniency
of courts; the weaknesses of the police; the abuses of the prison system;
the law's delay; and fashionable values that exalt rebels and outlaws or
that consider the consumption of drugs to be socially acceptable, if not
chic. Instead of pushing affirmative action, judges, civil servants, and
academicians (the argument continues) would be better employed to
plead for the protection of the poor people's lives and their property.

Public money might, in fact, be better spent if the United States were to take a leaf out of the history of Imperial Germany and more deliberately encourage technical education. Above all, boosting family stability can do more for minorities, especially the Puerto Ricans and blacks, than any affirmative action program.

Affirmative action deserves attack on other grounds as well. Though commonly described as a leftist cause, affirmative action ignores the most fundamental assumptions of the classical left by underplaying the reality of social class. This is not surprising. Affirmative action derived from the civil rights movement, and the civil rights movement's early leaders came from the South, where all blacks had suffered from oppression, irrespective of their social station. The leaders of the civil rights movement, in fact, were drawn mainly from the ranks of well-educated blacks—ministers, teachers, and lawyers—rather than from the ranks of the poor. The *Chicanismo* movement, as we have pointed out, also derived from the well educated, not the poor. Similarly, the affirmative action campaign primarily benefits middle-class people (for instance, businessmen profiting from minority contracts, and professors applying for jobs).

As Richard Rodriguez has written: "Those least disadvantaged were helped first, advanced because many others of their race were more disadvantaged."[14] In regard to the mass of the working class, economist Walter Williams, a black conservative, argues that affirmative action has not produced positive results. Its primary achievements thus far have been to split the traditional coalition between Jews and blacks, and to give the false impression that the hard-won achievements by blacks came through gifts, not merit.[15] Or, as a highly regarded black candidate accepted for a faculty position in a major university said, "I hope I am not being considered because I am black . . . I have no need or desire to be a token."[16] Furthermore, minimum-wage laws may actually have hurt poor people (including Hispanics and blacks) by reducing their employment opportunities. Commitment to ethnic quotas also produced inconsistencies when blacks came to be "overrepresented" in certain public sectors (such as the army and the welfare bureaucracy).

Above all, the future of affirmative action entails fundamental decisions regarding the American nation. Ours is a nation of immigrants or of their descendants. Despite many injustices and abuses, the nation has done well by its immigrants—as suggested by their general ability to come, to stay, and—in the case of Europeans and Asians—to surpass in income the native born after 10 to 15 years of residence. The United States has achieved unparalleled progress in improving the living standards for its people and in correcting racial bigotry in social life as well as politics.[17] Despite the aspersions cast upon it by its numerous critics, the United States is, in our view, the world's most successful multiracial society—much more successful than India, the U.S.S.R., Yugoslavia, Cyprus, or any other that one of America's censors might care to choose.

The American achievement has been of a kind that seemed impossible to many earlier observers. Even as brilliant a scholar as Lord Acton, the great nineteenth-century liberal Catholic, considered the task of integrating every racial group into one nation to be impossible. "If the Americans were to admit the Indians, the Chinese, the Negroes to the rights to which they are justly jealous of admitting European emigrants, the country would be thrown into disorder, and if not, would be degraded to the level of barbarous races."[18] The American achievement was brought about through the integrative power of a free market economy and under a constitution that enshrines the rights of individuals, not of groups. The alternative of creating group rights for Hispanics, blacks, women, gays, or other minorities seems to us forbidding.

Ethnic identity, as Nathan Glazer, a doyen of American immigration history, points out, is a matter of choice in the United States. Even within the same family, one brother or sister may fervently side with the family's original ethnic group, another half-heartedly, a third not at all.[19] Any attempts on the part of the government to define rigidly a person's ethnic membership will run into trouble in a country where ethnic boundaries are often ill defined and where individual freedom is prized above all. Bureaucratic or judicial intervention, designed to create clear ethnic boundary lines in perpetuity, is unlikely to succeed. In the short run, such interference will produce only divisive effects. The old pattern of ethnic accommodation in the northern cities, for all its deficiencies, allowed for the resolution of ethnic conflicts through all manner of bargaining. The new bureaucratic and judicial constructs may lead to greater inflexibility. If group rights were to be permanently enshrined, the United States might one day resemble, at best, the long defunct Austro-Hungarian monarchy—and, at worst, a Lebanon of continental proportions.

Chapter 14

Hispanics and the Church

The Catholic Church remains one of the Hispanics' major cultural institutions. Far more Hispanics go to church than to universities; far more Hispanics read the Bible than books on *Chicanismo*. Nearly four-fifths of the Hispanics in the United States are Catholics. Hispanics are certain to make a major impact on the Church in the United States, for they are, on the average, more youthful and bear more children than their fellow Catholics descended from other stocks. Hispanics also are bound to influence the Church's future ethnic composition, and they will add to its national diversity. (The City of San Francisco alone has 18 distinct Hispanic groups, including an estimated 60,000 Nicaraguans and 50,000 Salvadoreans.) Their religious commitment varies widely—from indifference to enthusiasm.

Pastors and Their Flocks

Hispanic Americans, like their fellow citizens of all other ethnic groups, form part of a society that respects religion. A 1983 Gallup study found that churches, followed by the military, rank highest in national esteem, with organized labor and television at the bottom. A high percentage of Americans are willing to support their religious preferences with hard cash: 29 percent of the Gallup respondents contribute 5 percent or more of their income to their churches.[1] Widespread misconceptions to the contrary, American teenagers are neither subject to religious scepticism nor disillusioned with technological progress.

On the other hand, leaders in American society have less confidence in the Church than does the public at large; the public schools, colleges, courts, entertainment industries, and bureaucracies in this country overwhelmingly prefer secular values and individualistic norms. Many Hispanics, by contrast, arrive in the United States with very different cultural assumptions, especially with respect to the extended family. It is of course easy to overestimate the differences between Latins and Anglo-Americans in this respect. A careful study of Anglo-American families would show that practices differ widely—as they do among

Hispanic families—and that among many English-speaking Americans, family obligations range far beyond the immediate nuclear family. Similarly, there is evidence that romantics have exaggerated the extent of family cohesion among Hispanic Americans. But this probably represents only a difference of emphasis. For many Hispanic people, kinfolk include not only relatives by blood and marriage, but also relatives by ascription, such as godparents, and "relatives" chosen from a sense or respect for friendship or old age.

In the United States, the Church did a great deal for the various immigrant communities from Europe. In Mexico, on the other hand, the Church did not play a similar role. The Church was associated with Spanish overlordship, and the Mexican middle class (unlike the middle classes in Poland) developed a strong anticlerical tradition, reinforced by French examples. When the United States acquired the Southwest, the Catholic Church in the region was in disarray; many of its mission properties were taken over and sold to local land owners. The new American bishops labored under many difficulties. They had to administer enormous parishes with a small number of clergymen, many of them padres on horseback. They lacked revenue and supporting staff. There were few clergymen of Mexican ancestry. The bulk of the Catholic priests in the Southwest came from Ireland, France, Spain, and Germany. Anticlerical sentiment among the early Mexican immigrants, such as it was, lost none of its strength when the newcomers saw the Church run by men of different national origins (Irishmen of an earlier generation had complained of French and German priests in their parishes).

By comparison with the colorful, vivid, communal Catholicism of the Mexican village, with its processions and fiestas, American Catholicism often seemed colorless and impersonal. In any case, the clerical pioneers (including, among others, Obate Fathers from France, Spanish Franciscans, and Immaculate Heart, Vincentian Fathers, and others) faced administrative problems of staggering difficulty. The migrant nature that characterized so much of the Mexican labor force continued to affect religious, as well as secular, life. Churchmen could not easily set up stable parishes, just as trade union leaders experienced difficulty creating stable unions, and school principals had trouble keeping youngsters at school.

When mass migration began at the turn of this century, the Church's difficulties became even more forbidding. The immigrants were unaccustomed to parochial schools, religious instruction, and regular attendance of Mass; many of them had been influenced by the anticlericalism that infused the Mexican revolution. To American Catholics, with their austere Irish, part-Jansenist, traditions, the new immigrants seemed potential converts rather than practicing Catholics. For their part, most Mexican immigrants stood aloof; it was the Church that had to reach out to the immigrants.

Initially, the Church could do little more than keep the faith alive. Subsequently, Catholic benefactors in the Midwest and East began to pour in money to develop what they regarded as mission work among Mexicans and to defend the newcomers against the real or assumed temptations of Protestantism on the one hand and the secularism of the public school system on the other. The drive to set up a parochial school system in the Southwest proceeded slowly. Encountering few Mexican children in parochial schools, the Church attempted to build a Mexican-American priesthood, tied to its parishioners by links of family and tradition. The Church remained firmly committed to Americanization, which was to occur through instruction in citizenship, classes in English, and youth activities of the kind prompted by the Catholic Youth Organization.[2]

In Cuba and Puerto Rico, the Catholic Church at first faced similar problems. The breakdown of the Spanish empire in the Caribbean led to an exodus of the Spanish priests who had staffed many of the parishes. American Protestants did their best to convert the masses, although with minimal success. American clergymen and brothers and sisters generously responded to the call for what they regarded as a kind of mission work in Puerto Rico. The leadership of the Puerto Rican church, therefore, typically passed into non-Hispanic hands.

The position was no better on the mainland, where only a small number of Hispanics had joined the Church, even though 30 percent of Catholics in the United States were Hispanics. By 1983, fifteen bishops in this country were Hispanic; among 1500 Hispanic priests, only 183 native-born, Spanish-surname priests were to be found in the United States. In the Northeast by the late 1970s, for example, only 50 Hispanic priests had been born in the United States, about 90 had come from Latin America, and 160 from Spain.[3] Most of the priests were of non-Hispanic origin. Indigenous Mexican-American or Puerto Rican-American priests were few in numbers. These two national groups lacked a large reservoir of educated youth; moreover, the Church may have failed to extend its policy of finding vocations—commonly practiced among Irish-American, Polish-American, or German-American children in parochial schools—for the children of Mexican and or Puerto Rican immigrants.

There are many reasons why there are so few Spanish-surnamed priests. The church may have been guilty in the past of subtle prejudice in believing that Hispanics were not good material for the religious life. The Spanish speakers do not appear to have been actively recruited in schools anywhere in the United States. The early Catholic Church was a missionary church dedicated to assimilation and acculturation. It did not recruit local youths but, instead, brought in Irish, French, and German priests. Many Puerto Ricans came to New York as single men. Then, too, broken homes were not uncommon in Spanish-speaking families, and churchmen did not look for vocations in homes where family unity was weak or where illegitimacy was the practice. There also might have been a stigma attached to being a Spanish speaker in the Southwest. Some churchmen, like other Americans, tended to believe that Hispanics were lazy and lacked dynamism.[4] The most fundamental reason that there are so few Hispanics in the Church may be that few attend Catholic schools—only 8 percent. Traditionally, vocations were nurtured in Catholic schools. The cost of a Catholic education may have been too high for Spanish-speaking immigrants.

By the early 1980s, 400 English-speaking American priests in the Archdiocese of New York had learned Spanish, though not all of them had attained equal proficiency. The ethnic composition of the brothers and sisters was similar (300 sisters from Spain; 200 from various Latin American and Latin Caribbean countries; and only 30 from the U.S.). The predominance of what was partly an alien clergy, of course, paralleled the situation of Sicilian, Polish, or Slovak immigrants of an earlier generation; nevertheless, it was hard to bear for many Hispanic parishioners.

The problem of cultural identity became particularly telling in areas where many Spanish-speaking groups commingled. In Puerto Rico, the Dominican Republic, El Salvador, Cuba, Hispanic people looked upon themselves as members of the particular national group from which they derived. While all Hispanic communities shared a common language and certain cultural traditions, they did not regard themselves as "Hispanics." Yet, in a city like New York, governmental agencies (and, to some extent, the Church) considered them as Hispanics first, despite the enormous differences that existed both between Cubans and Puerto Ricans and within each of these communities.

These differences affect religious practices as well as secular values. Among the poor in Puerto Rico and Cuba, the Indian and African legacies have contributed to the creation of syncretic creeds—spiritism among Puerto Ricans and *santería* among the Cuban poor. Among many of the uneducated, these cults wielded great power. Even the most casual observer can judge the extent of their power by walking into one of the many *botánicas* (shops that sell herbs and cultic implements) in Puerto Rican neighborhoods. Many adherents of these cults still regard themselves as Catholics, even though churchmen traditionally look askance at these syncretic practices.

Although Hispanics are overwhelmingly Catholic, they are largely nonpracticing (about 30 percent go to church in New York City, one study showed). Hispanic Catholics, especially the poor among them, do not stress duty to church and parish as much as, say, Irish Catholics do. They are more apt to emphasize personal belief and folk religion (full, in rural areas, of older forms of magic). The bulk of Spanish speakers, at least in New York, do not know much about many major church beliefs—60 percent could not name a single one of the seven sacraments, nor had they heard of the Second Vatican Council.[5] Erosion of beliefs and practices increases with the second-generation Hispanics.

There also are differences of emphasis between orthodox Catholics of Puerto Rican or Mexican descent and those from Northern Europe. All Catholics believe in the intercession of the saints and the Virgin Birth. But the saints—especially the Blessed Virgin—enjoy particular reverence among Puerto Rican or Mexican congregations; images of the saints and of Mary are everywhere; Mary is an ever-present mother who concerns herself with the personal lives of the faithful. *Personalismo* also plays a strong part in the relations between the priest and his flock. As a Catholic source puts it, "Priest X" is a good priest if he fits in well into the community, if he is personally friendly and warmly involves himself with the lives of his parishioners.[6] For most Hispanics, *padre* is not merely an honored form of address; the *padre* is indeed expected to be a father—more so perhaps than in an Anglo-American community, whose members are more likely to accord the title to a priest simply because of his office.

The *padre's* work in a poverty-stricken community is particularly difficult. He has to deal with problems that stem from a high crime rate. (In 1976, the percentage of males admitted to New York State correctional facilities for murder or homicide stood at 17.3 for Puerto Ricans, 13.3 for blacks, and 10.0 for whites. The corresponding figures for drug offense were 25.3, 10.4, 17.5.)[7] The priest must care for families where out-of-wedlock births are common. (Between 1956 and 1976, the figure rose from 11 percent of the total to 46 percent—second only to the rate among blacks.) Whatever the explanation—economic and social pressure, or the impact of government-funded programs—the stigma of illegitimacy is enormous. Woman-centered households have become numerous in the Puerto Rican community, where almost half of the married couples wind up as single-parent families. Here, the pastor's duties are heavy. Many inner-city priests are overworked and complain of "burn-out," which is exacerbated by the fact that priests in the "Spanish apostolate" often suffer from isolation within the church; they feel left on their own and often complain of insufficient understanding on the part of those in authority. They must deal with an enormous range of social problems; they find that in poverty-stricken communities much of the priest's time is given to menial matters, such as paying bills and maintaining buildings, rather than to taking care of souls.

In addition, the Catholic Church must deal with competition from other religious groups, including evangelical churches and from new churches. All of these have made active efforts to seek converts, and many have achieved success. What attracts the proselytes? The attractions are many: intensive Bible study, festive singing among people who like religious music and active congregational participation in church services; the use of Spanish in prayers, hymns and sermons; and family-centered activities. As Catholic dignitaries are wont to observe, the evangelicals speak Spanish and explain the Bible. It was not without justification that the Mexican Bible Institute in Texas announced that, for Texas, the 1980s would become the "decade for Hispanic Baptists." Other Protestant denominations—Jehovah's Witnesses, the fundamentalist Church of God, and the Mormons—reported similar success stories. Many Hispanics have become Protestants, while at the same time a minority has stopped going to Church altogether. (According to Gallup polls taken in 1985, 18 percent of the respondents described themselves as Protestants and 70 percent as Catholics; the remainder indicated no affiliation.)[8]

The Protestant "storefront" church has become a powerful religious and cultural factor in the slums. There are Catholic estimates that just under 10 percent of the northeastern Hispanic population has ceased to identify itself as Catholics and has joined other religious congregations.[9] The churches, particularly the Evangelical ones, have facilitated Hispanic leadership and have encouraged Hispanic religiosity by insisting on a commitment to practice. They share with spiritism and *Santería* the ability to make Hispanics "feel themselves." Many Hispanics also were attracted to a sect because of their social conservatism on such issues as abortion, crime, homosexuality, and traditional family values. Affiliation to Protestant churches, of course, may not do much to change voting behavior. (The majority of evangelical Christians in the United States voted for Carter, not Reagan.) But, in terms of religious choice, the Protestant challenge remains serious.

Insofar as they attend church, however, the great majority of Hispanics in the United States (an estimated 80 percent) remain Catholics. They are linked to a worldwide organization that commands the allegiance of most professing Christians in Latin America; they adhere to a body that has shaped the various cultures of all Latin nations, and one that has increasingly become conscious of its growing membership in, and far-flung obligations, to the Third World. The Catholic Church, like its Protestant competitors, is therefore exposed to a dual pull: the social conservatism that characterizes the greater part of the congregation and the commitment to social change, held most strongly by self-styled progressive clergymen.

What has the Church done to cope with these problems? The U.S. Catholic Conference/Secretariat for Hispanic Affairs, based in Washington, D.C., has established pastoral centers in New York City, Miami, San Antonio, South Bend, Los Angeles, and Yakima, Washington. Acting as an arm of the Catholic Church, the Secretariat since 1945 (when it was called the Bishops' Committee for the Spanish Speaking) has been a national advocate for Catholic Hispanics. It is supported by the National Catholic Conference of Bishops. Its newsletter, *Encuentro,* is published six times a year. During the 1940s and 1950s, the Bishops' Committee was concerned mainly with the social and economic problems of Mexican Americans in the Southwest and migrant farmworkers in the Midwest. In 1968, the committee was included in the U.S. Catholic Conference (USCC) as the Division of the Spanish Speaking, with Pablo Sedillo as its first national director. The USCC regional offices for Hispanics were made autonomous in 1974: and the national office was raised to the rank of a Secretariat, working with the National Council of Catholic Bishops and the USCC.[10] An important agency working with legal and illegal immigrants is the Catholic Migration and Refugee Service, with more than 15 offices throughout the United States.

Much has been done by the Catholic Church in the Northeast, the main area of Puerto Rican and Dominican settlement, a region where there long has been a strong tradition of social work and where churchmen could draw on the help of numerous scholars. The various religious orders embarked on a major effort. Catholic parochial schools came to play an increasing part in the education of Hispanic children. Between 1977 and 1981, the percentage of Hispanic students in Catholic elementary schools in the Archdiocese of New York, for example, went up from 21 percent to to 24 percent; in secondary schools, the increase was from 14 percent to 16.3 percent. Contrary to widespread assumptions, the private schools have begun to appeal to some poor people as well as to the middle class and the rich.

First and foremost, however, the Church's work hinges on the parishes. The Church has tried to appoint more priests qualified by their knowledge of Spanish and Hispanic cultures to work in parishes that contain numerous Puerto Rican, Dominican, or Mexican-American churchgoers. The Church has attempted to deal with social problems through the traditional corporal works of mercy demanded by the Gospel. And the Church has taken active steps to involve parishioners in parochial projects; including dances, parties, and membership in traditional societies.

In June 1972 the "Primer Encuentro Nacional Hispano" was held in Washington, D.C. This Encuentro was sponsored by the Catholic Bishops of the United States to develop a pastoral plan for the Hispanic-American community, which represented one quarter of the Catholic Church in the United States. In 1973, an Encuentro in the Northeast called for the establishment of the Northeast Regional Pastoral Center. This center developed many programs: advocacy of rights for illegal immigrants and nonunion workers, the "defense of life," and bilingual education. The promotion of vocations for the religious life was a major concern, considering how few Spanish speakers become priests, brothers, or nuns. A program of research, publication, and the production of resource material also was part of the center's work.

The Church also has encouraged such movements as the Hispanic marriage encounter (*Encuentro Matrimonial*), the Spanish language charismatic revival, and the so-called basic community (*comunidad de base*). Diocesan policy towards Hispanics is set by the bishop of the diocese, who appoints Episcopal vicars for Hispanics, directorates, and Hispanic councils. The Church has promoted social work, including Church-sponsored housing, social centers, drug rehabilitation programs, and half-way houses for ex-offenders. All these efforts, of course, have their counterparts in various Protestant churches. The Catholic Church also has created a small "course in Christianity" (*cursillo de cristianidad*). Imported from Spain in the late 1950's, the *cursillo* has grown from small beginnings to affect the entire nation's Hispanic community. Its impact has varied considerably. In places like Los Angeles, the *cursillo* primarily appeals to the elite; elsewhere, it has attained much wider appeal, both among Hispanic and Anglo-American Catholics. Many say without hesitation that the *cursillo* now forms the backbone of the Hispanic apostolate.

In addition, the Church has appealed to Hispanics through the Bishops' Campaign for Human Development. The bishops likewise have broadened the scope of evangelical work through the American Board of Catholic Missions, which finances programs of evangelization through the country, with particular emphasis on Hispanics. The Church has put time and money into Catholic charities; it also has set up new institutions, such as the Northeast Pastoral Center for Hispanics. This provides religious services to individuals—including spiritual guidance and counselling; interdiocesan services; conferences on issues that particularly affect Hispanics (including immigration); the family; religious education, and the like. The Church also has set up major research projects, including a massive enquiry into the condition of Hispanics in New York.[11]

The New York Archdiocesan report on *Hispanics in New York* is a remarkable document, which, it is hoped, will be replicated in other archdioceses, such as Los Angeles. The information in the report comes from a survey of 1,200 Hispanics across the ten counties of the archdiocese, together with a demographic analysis; from "state of the art" papers on specific family problems; and from a series of case studies on Hispanic Catholic living styles, changes in the Hispanics' religious affiliations, and so forth, mostly in poverty-stricken communities.

Such surveys must always be used with caution. Students of public opinion know that those answering questionnaires are tempted to tell the enquirer what he wants to know. Questions of faith and morals, moreover, cannot easily be quantified; nor can they comfortably be fitted into the straitjacket of a standardized questionnaire. Only God truly knows the quality and intensity of a man's beliefs; these cannot be fed into a computer. But, granting all these objections, the report provides a fascinating picture of the Hispanic community in the New York region—a picture that in some ways differs strikingly from the one drawn by literary men committed to a radical critique of U.S. society.

One of the most outstanding of these among Puerto Ricans is Pedro Juan Soto. Born in 1928, Soto, a professor, lived in New York and in Puerto Rico and served in the Korean War. His work reflects the social protest of a group of Puerto Rican intellectuals who are embittered by what they regard as the social and psychological degradation of an entire people. His bitterness found expression in such tales as *Garbatos* ("Scribbles"), a story of alienation in which an unemployed worker, an amateur artist, must contend not only with the physical misery of life in a slum basement in New York, but also with the incomprehension of his own wife; she misinterprets her husband's work as pornographic scribbles and despises him for letting the government take care of the family through welfare checks, instead of looking for proper work. Much of Soto's work—like Piri Thomas's and Oscar Lewis's mirrors a society given to gloom, alienation, and despair.

Up to a point, such impressions of life in New York are truthful enough—but there is another side to it. As the center's survey shows, most Hispanics are Catholics (83.5 percent). Most of them believe in a caring God (77.1 percent), in Heaven (88.3 percent), and in a Jesus who died on the cross and rose from the dead (88.5 percent). Nearly two-thirds share the Church's tenets regarding the existence of Hell. Hispanic believers are somewhat less sure about other teachings of the Church—such as intercession of the saints (only 46 percent believe in this tenet). The majority of Hispanics say their daily prayers (59 percent of Catholics, 72.2 percent of Protestants). Hispanics hold that church attendance is important (81 percent), but not all act according to their convictions in this matter: only 32.8 percent attend mass frequently, and 35.9 percent go to confession once a week or more. Religious practices (burning candles at home; sprinkling holy water; blessing the house) are prized. Even more so is Bible study (56.6 percent claim to do so). The Bible, in other words, is far more important to popular culture than literary work of a secular kind.

The survey is equally interesting in regard to sexual values. The majority of Hispanics oppose birth control (55.2) percent and believe that abortion is morally wrong (64 percent). An even larger proportion (67 percent) find premarital intercourse morally objectionable. Hispanics—like all others—do not always practice what they preach. The Hispanic population in New York has a high rate of illegitimacy. But Hispanics' declared values in general correspond with the Church's more than with those of the secular intelligentsia.

For most Hispanic New Yorkers, Spanish is the language of prayer (74.8 percent use Spanish only; 15.4 percent use both English and Spanish; 9.7 percent use English only). Overall, far more Hispanics are satisfied with the Church than are dissatisfied. Almost one-third state that they would like their sons to become priests (32.7 percent); 49.8 percent feel welcome in the church; 37.7 percent said that priests and ministers displayed a warm and friendly attitude—opposed to 15.4 percent who criticized clerics for being cold and lacking concern for the people. Insofar as there is dissatisfaction, it is more common among Puerto Ricans than Dominicans: "maximum positive experiences" were mentioned by 80.8 percent of Puerto Ricans and 83.9 percent of Dominicans; "maximum negative experiences," on the other hand, were alluded to by 35.0 percent of Puerto Ricans and 22.0 percent of Dominicans. Despite the many economic and social disabilities they encounter, and despite numerous ethnic particularities, the standard sociological indicators nevertheless lead to the conclusion that the experience of Hispanics will resemble that of previous immigrant groups.

The Church and Its New Politics

Clerical policymakers, however, do not seem conversant with such findings. They are particularly concerned with the problem of ethnicity, which the church has faced in dealing with every major group of immigrants who have settled in the United States. The Church always has insisted on its "catholic" (universal) nature. The Church therefore has resisted fragmentation into ethnic churches. Leading divines, however, have become convinced that the so-called melting pot theory of Americanization must be abandoned. According to a statement issued by the United States Bishops' Committee for Social Development and World Peace, in 1981, attempts to create an all-embracing amalgam should be rejected on the grounds that this would be unrealistic politically and objectionable in a moral sense. As the bishops see it, the Church must recognize the strength of diverse national heritages. Newcomers must not suffer the burdens of conformity that were imposed on previous generations of Italians, Poles, Irish, blacks. Believers of alien stocks no longer should be required to separate themselves in a thousand ways from their native communities in order to obtain America's economic and social benefits.[12]

Church leaders therefore have aligned themselves on the side of the "new ethnicity." Whether they were right to do so remains to be seen. No doubt the concern for ethnic cultures has some merit. But, at the same time, Americanization is an ongoing process—indeed, also an inevitable and a legitimate process. Many immigrants, and most of their second- and third-generation descendants, want to be Americans. Immigrants, including the bishops' own forebears, have come and continue to come to the United States of their own free will; they do so both to improve their own economic condition and to profit from the political and social freedoms in the new country.[13]

Similar criticisms apply to the accusations against "Anglo" culture made by such distinguished Hispanic Catholic scholars as Virgilio Elizondo and Steven Arroyo. Their cultural analyses are based on concepts of nineteenth-century German romantics, who contrasted the spirituality and "inwardness" supposedly inherent in the German folk soul with the materialism of the West. Elizondo and Arroyo juxtapose the imagined merits of Latin America against the assumed deficiencies of North American society. North America, in their view, honors trade and the ways of Horatio Alger; in Latin America, by contrast, production from the land is the ideal occupation, and success depends upon harmony with people and nature. In North America, competition is the source of growth; in Latin America, harmony depends upon generous contributions to the common good. North America emphasizes the separation of church and state; Latin America insists on a "holistic concept" of society and on obligations to others. North America supposedly suppresses emotions; Latin America stresses dignity and a sensitivity to life that celebrates both joy and sorrow.[14]

The Church's shift to the left has accompanied to some extent the increasing political importance and numerical power of congregations within the Third World. During the early 1960s, Catholics from Europe and North America still held a majority within the Church. Ten years later, Catholicism had ceased to be predominantly European and North American; Catholicism, moreover, was becoming increasingly an urban religion, a creed of megalopolis. This swing was joined to a crisis within the Church. The postwar years, from 1945 to about 1960, constituted almost a golden age for the Church. An impressive number of able and dedicated men, many of them veterans, had joined the secular priesthood and the religious orders. During the 1960s, the resultant mood of confidence gave way to a widespread malaise, which paralleled a similar sense of disillusionment within academia. The *aggiornamento* (updating) of the Church that followed the Second Vatican Council (1962–1965), convoked by Pope John XXIII, attempted to deal with this ongoing crisis. But, in the conservatives' opinion at least, the new reforms themselves may have contributed to some of the Church's difficulties. In the West (though not in Eastern Europe), the Church experienced falling attendances, declining authority, internal divisions, and a severe diminution in the numbers of the priesthood.

The Church within the United States fully participated in this crisis. During the 1950s and early 1960s, an unprecedentedly large number of the young decided to give their life to the Church. As they began to move toward retirement in the 1980s, the Church has experienced growing difficulties in recruiting their successors. The number of priests, brothers, and nuns has declined; the average age of parish priests began to rise; some parishes found themselves without priests altogether; and parochial schools had to close. The Church tried to cope with these problems by ordaining more deacons (laymen, allowed to marry, but empowered to carry out certain clerical functions, such as conducting prayers and officiating at marriages, baptisms, and burials). By changing its personnel policy, the Church, however, began to face numerous new pressures; it also received complaints from priests who feared that they would become mere clerical functionaries.

At the same time, the American episcopate began to move to the left. Increasingly, the bishops take "liberal" positions, except on abortion and on support to parochial schools. They favor federal power over the powers of states and local communities; they emphasize political action more than evangelical activities as a means of ensuring social action. In 1983, two Catholic archbishops decided to give their backing to the so-called sanctuary movement, a united front made up of various Christian denominations for the purpose of offering sanctuary to Salvadoran and Guatemalan refugees illegally in the United States. By doing so, the archbishops deliberately chose to flout U.S. law that forbade the harboring of illegal aliens, a serious matter for a church whose adherents overwhelmingly back the cause of law and order.

Among the intellectuals within the Church, social criticism of the United States became even more strident; their condemnation of U.S. society drew heavily on the concepts developed by Chicano and Puerto Rican militants. To them, the United States is not the land of the free and the home of the brave; it is a bastion of oppression.

Our country is perishing through the excess of individualism, consumerism, materialism and narcissism. We are the richest and most powerful country of the world, but we are perishing. We enslave others here and around the world so as to nourish the insatiable appetites of our own enslavements. . . .[15]

What is to be done about these evils? The Church, according to ecclesiastical activists, must add a secular plan to its spiritual apostolate. The Church must involve itself in politics for the sake of assuring social justice, both in the United States and in Latin America. As far as Hispanic parishioners in the United States are concerned, the Church must show increased sensitivity toward Hispanic culture and turn both to social activism and to a dialogue with the Church's Marxist opponents.

We remain unconvinced by these arguments. We do not share the distaste for "American materialism," a disdain widespread among intellectuals in this country and abroad. The Church cannot be a political party with a common position on every secular issue. The pastors stand divided over many issues of public policy: conservatives are strong among the parish clergy; leftists and militant liberals are mostly found among young seminarian and certain missionary orders, such as Maryknoll. The Church has proved incapable of arriving at common positions on such concrete proposals as the Simpson-Mazzoli bill on immigration.

In regard to broader questions of American values, we stand far removed from social critics like Elizondo and Arroyo. We see no merit in their hostility to individualism and consumerism as such. Individual freedom and rising living standards are not wrong in and of themselves. They are legitimately sought by immigrant as well as native-born Americans. Nor do we see any point in idealizing Latin Americans at the expense of North Americans. Latin Americans chase the *peso* just as Yankees chase the buck. Nor is there much to be said for reviling, even if only by implication, the Protestants' sense of spirituality.

We also do not share the broader cultural assumptions that have shaped the beliefs of militant churchmen. To them, the profit motive is suspect; they believe that capitalist society is driven only by greed; to them, incomes gained from salaries earned as professors, clergymen, or bureaucrats are somehow more honorable than money made in banking or business. To us, these beliefs are based on economic misconceptions. Further we believe that self-styled progressives like the Rev. William Sloane Coffin tread on dangerous ground when they call for disobedience to American immigration laws. Those who disregard laws on grounds of conscience cannot then complain when their opponents do the same over causes of intense concern to *them*—for instance, on the "right to life" issue. We also are convinced that cooperation between the Church and Marxist-Leninists always has been apt to benefit the latter, to the Church's discredit. Nor would such an alliance prevent defections to Protestantism. The growing power of evangelical Christianity does not spring from commitment to left-wing causes but, at least, in part from the evangelicals' abstention from politics.[16] Instead of seeking a dialogue with Marxist-Leninists, the Church would do better to converse with evangelical Christians and members of the new churches (the so-called cults), who, at least share a commitment to transcendental values rather than to dialectical materialism.

A great many progessive clergymen assume as a matter of course that the mass of Hispanic parishioners want more clerical involvement in politics and a greater emphasis on Spanish language and Hispanic culture. In fact, the Hispanics are divided on these issues. Many Hispanics do not want the Church to meddle in public affairs. Thirty-four percent of all Hispanic respondents in the New York archdiocesan report previously cited opposed any church involvement in the political arena; 17 percent were not sure. Widespread misconceptions to the contrary, the most youthful respondents—those under the age of 25—were those who most strongly objected to clerical participation in the political arena. Eighty percent had no knowledge of clerical involvement in the politics of Latin America—despite the fact that the Church had done its best to secure mass support through backing left-leaning causes.

Nor is there much evidence that lack of clerical commitment to *hispanidad* or failure to provide sufficient services in Spanish are major popular issues. In this respect, as in so many others, the preoccupations of the people at large often are quite different from those of the intellectuals who presume to speak for them. Only 5.4 percent of those respondents in the New York enquiry who had complained of having had "bad experiences" with the Church referred to the Church's alleged "lack of sensitivity to Hispanic cultures"; no more than 3.7 percent stated that they needed services that were not provided in Spanish.[17] In retrospect, the Church—for all its failings—may have done better for its parishioners than church leadership has imagined.

In other words, the Church among Hispanics faces the same essential tasks as it does among adherents of any other ethnic group. The Church stands in the world and must deal with the here and now; but, advocates of the social gospel notwithstanding, the Church must ultimately transcend this world—or lose its mission.

Chapter 15

Perils of Addiction

We make guilty of our disasters the sun, the moon, and the stars: as if
we were villeins by necessity; fools by heavenly compulsion; knaves, thieves,
and treachers by spherical predominance.
—King Lear, Act I, Scene II.

In 1942, Sir William Beveridge, one of the greatest of British civil servants, issued what later became a celebrated report on British social security. Borrowing from Dickens' *Tale of Two Cities,* Beveridge identified the five "giants" that menaced British society: "want," "sickness," "squalor," "ignorance," and "idleness," with drink, drugs, and crime among their offspring. Drinking, drug abuse, and crime vary from country to country and from class to class, but they form an ever-present menace to Hispanics in America, as they do to their fellow citizens.

Drink

The art of fermenting fruit and making wine is an ancient invention. And as soon as men discovered the pleasures of drink, they also became aware of its potential for evil. The United States experienced both throughout its history. Despite their reputation for straitlaced puritanism, colonial New Englanders drank heavily; alcoholism was a prevalent affliction on every frontier; drink helped men (and, often enough, women) over the miseries of life in an isolated military post, a lonely farm, a distant mining township. Alcohol was, and remains, an occupational disease for men who must professionally socialize with other men. Alcoholism also afflicted many newcomers from Europe. Irish workmen were known for their ability to hit the bottle; Slavs were called "clearly the most alcohol-oriented element in the new immigration."[1] Slavs drank far more than Jews, who used wine mainly for sacramental purposes; Slavs also drank far more than Italians, who prized wine primarily for culinary reasons.

Alcoholism is also a major problem for Hispanics. Generalizations are difficult, for conditions vary by national origin, occupational group, and locality. National statistics do show that alcohol abuse is a serious problem for Hispanics. Offenses connected with drinking account for a high percentage of offenses committed by Hispanics nationwide.[2] Other estimates are even more discouraging. A 1975 study in California's Santa Cruz County found that 51 percent of Mexican Americans reported that more than half, often all, of their friends were heavy drinkers; only 25 percent of the "Anglos" gave similar answers.

Because drinking rates are not steady among different national groups, comparative computations are not easy to make. But, according to investigations made by Dr. Hugh Edmandson in Southern California, Latinos moved into the position of the most frequent victims of alcoholism in the mid-1950s, and have stayed there ever since. They have, of course, much competition. Rates for all three major ethnic groups have gone up dramatically since 1965. But, overall, Hispanic Americans—Puerto Ricans as well as Mexicans—have a more serious drinking problem than the rest of the population; the menace of alcohol looms large, not merely through diseases directly related to alcohol (such as cirrhosis of the liver), but also indirectly through deaths occasioned by driving under the influence of liquor, suicide, or killings committed in fits of drunken anger.[3] Drinking and crime also go hand in hand: a majority of crimes are committed under the influence of liquor or drugs.

The majority of Latins, it should be emphasized, do not abuse alcohol. Nor is alcoholism the only, or even the main, threat to Latin health, either in the immigrants' country of origin or in the United States. Patterns of disease follow the wider patterns of culture. In a country like Mexico, communicable diseases, such as influenza and various forms of dysentery, are the principal causes of death. These rank quite low in the United States—even in the poverty-stricken lower Rio Grande Valley; by contrast, Americans are more likely to be afflicted by sicknesses linked in some measure to the stresses and life styles of an industrial society: heart diseases, malignant neoplasms, and cerebrovascular diseases.[4] Alcoholism, however, is one of those afflictions that cross many cultural barriers: Indian tribal warriors, Irish ditch diggers, Mexican factory workers, and Jewish intellectuals may all—for a variety of reasons—choose to drink excessively.

Why do they do so? Why, specifically, do Latins choose to drink? Some experts stress physiological and genetic factors; others argue that nutrition may be involved. Genetic factors may well predispose certain individuals to become alcoholics. But drinking also involves a personal choice and the social attitudes connected with making such a choice. Hence, certain religious groups such as the Mormons, Orthodox Jews, and the Amish manage to avoid the perils of alcoholic addiction. The link between cultural and physiological factors is as yet, however, little understood. Certain populations, including American Indians and their descendants, are said to be more disposed toward alcoholism because of the Indians' particular metabolization process. The evidence for this hypothesis, however, is far from conclusive. Social factors may well have played a much larger role than genetic factors in creating the Indians' vulnerability toward firewater.[5]

Social, rather than genetic, explanations make good sense for the heavy liquor consumption on the part of Slavic immigrants, once stereotyped as inveterate drinkers, condemned by their nature to alcohol abuse. Those who censured the Slavic newcomers for their alcoholic conviviality were prone to miss an important social explanation. The Slav (and the Irish) immigrant performed hard, heavy, ill-paid, debilitating jobs in coal mines, steel mills, and on docks and railroad gangs. Only whiskey could warm him and make him think well of himself and his world again.

Likewise whatever the role of genetic factors, societal considerations seem much more important than hereditary factors in accounting for the Latin's drinking habits. Drinking habits vary enormously from one community to another, and the differences do not follow racial lines. Puerto Ricans and Dominicans, for example, share a similar racial makeup: both derive from a blend of Europeans and Africans. Yet, placed in the same physical environment, in the depressed area of a small New England manufacturing town arbitrarily designated by the researchers as "Newton," Dominicans behave quite differently from Puerto Ricans and also from Guatemalans. Their varying drinking patterns illustrate not merely differing national styles within a small community but also three different social patterns: those of upwardly mobile people, those of welfare dependents, and those of labor migrants.[6]

Dominicans in Newton drink in a moderate fashion; they avoid getting drunk, for such behavior is regarded as unmanly, *indecente*. They only imbibe the best of Scotch whiskies and look askance at cheap drink. Overall, Dominicans in Newton drink much less than they did back home. Their drinking behavior reflects their aspirations for social advancement and their success in climbing the ladder. The first step is taken in the Dominican Republic when a family decides to emigrate in search of something better. Most Dominican migrants first move to New York City's Upper West Side, the South Bronx, or some part of Brooklyn. Both husband and wife are apt to work and save; the most successful couples then find a better residence, in Queens or in a smaller industrial town like Newton. They invest their cash in a house, sometimes even two or three houses, in a neighborhood abandoned by *americanos*. Increased economic opportunities militate against drinking; so does the women's new ability to earn wages. Dominican women acquire increased authority and independence; hence, they curb the alcoholic proclivities that displease them in their menfolk. In Newton, a man can no longer play fast and free with his money; if he does so, his wife may leave him. Of two opposing male ideals, the *parrandero* (the man given to wine, women, and song) and the *padre de familia* (the fatherly provider of the family), the latter is in the ascendant. And he—the *hombre serio*, the conscientious man concerned with the future, the caring husband and attentive father—does not get soused.

Guatemalans in Newton, by contrast, are heavy drinkers. About one-third of the adult Guatemalan men drink to excess; neither friends nor families counsel against such abuse. Guatemalans drink fast, whereas Dominicans sip slowly; Guatemalans imbibe heavily during a long weekend, Dominicans (at the worst) drink heavily only on Saturday nights.

Why such a difference? Both Dominicans and Guatemalans came as immigrants. But Dominicans arrived with their families, and, on the whole, they prosper. Guatemalans travel to Newton as single men, resolved to save money in order to return to Guatemala and start a business back home. Loneliness in a foreign country is hard to bear— an experience as common among Guatemalan laborers in Newton as it is to sailors in foreign ports all over the world. Among Guatemalan labor migrants, hard drinking is apt to be glamorized as manly, as it is so often in the armed services; but at least there is little drug abuse.

The Puerto Ricans' case in Newton is the worst. Some Puerto Ricans of course never touch a drop, but many do. Furthermore, heavy drinkers also follow the dangerous practice of mixing liquor and drugs—cocaine and, to a lesser extent, marijuana. The Puerto Rican custom of making *una bomba* (getting utterly narcotized) has no parallel among other Hispanics in Newton.

What accounts for the discrepancy? About one-tenth of the Puerto Rican male adult population in Newton consists of young men on welfare who drink frequently, have little aspiration for the future, and have no socially legitimate family role. Among Dominicans, the move to the United States is regarded as a major enterprise that attracts the venturesome. Among Puerto Ricans, the departure from the island to the mainland on the whole requires less planning. Puerto Ricans are U.S. citizens; they do not have to make legal arrangements for immigration papers; they are, moreover, entitled to welfare. Receiving welfare is likely to diminish self-esteem among men who feel themselves deprived of their traditional role as economic providers. They lose something of the traditional deference paid to them; their *dignidad* may be impaired; angry and disappointed, they may take to drink. Drink in turn is apt to worsen other family problems; police reports show a much higher incidence of family violence among Puerto Ricans in Newton than among other Hispanics.

A definitive study of alcohol problems among the Hispanics as a whole remains to be written. But, obviously, the patterns investigated in Newton exist for the country as a whole—patterns associated with a youthful population, upward social mobility, labor migrancy, and welfare dependence. There is certainly a widespread *cantina* culture among many young poor people. For them, the bar often serves as a club that substitutes for other voluntary organizations in which poverty-stricken Mexicans do not much participate.[7] Drink temporarily may give a feeling of manliness and security to the uprooted. There is particularly heavy drinking among young men, including students from high school; among these, there is no consistent relationship between socioeconomic status on the one hand and alcohol use on the other. Boys just drink more than girls; sons of the drinking fathers are far more likely to hit the bottle than are the sons of fathers who abstain from liquor.[8]

What can be done about alcoholism? Many heavy drinkers, like many drug users, cure themselves. According to Dr. George E. Vaillant, a leading specialist who studied an inner-city group of alcoholics, more than half rid themselves of their drinking habits, generally without treatment.[9] Alcoholism may or may not be a disease; but it is self-inflicted and is an affliction to which some groups (such as Irishmen or Mexicans) are culturally much more prone than others (for instance, Italians and Jews). Changes in diet, or psychotherapy, may help. But the most successful forms of treatment seem to require addicts to confront their difficulties, to take responsibility for their own condition, and to gain help from a wider support group. Family support is important; the study on the drinking habits of Mexican-American high school students cited above concludes that youngsters are less likely to drink when their parents set a good example, when they know what their children are doing, and when they together go to church.

There are many therapy groups. They include Alcoholics Anonymous (AA), a nationwide organization with chapters in Puerto Rico. Alcoholics Anonymous has Spanish-language as well as English-language chapters. This organization does excellent work; but, as David L. Strong states in his ethnographic report on alcohol usage, AA's "successful efforts in New York and in Puerto Rico are said to involve people who are more middleclass in orientation. The pattern of poverty and governmental assistance [among Puerto Ricans] in Newton may debilitate the necessary orientation for self-help."[10] But even AA does not have all the answers; Dr. Vaillant, mentioned above, found that 95 percent of the patients who were compelled to attend AA meetings relapsed into drinking after treatment.

In addition, community organizations attempt to deal with alcoholism, drug abuse, and counselling for juvenile offenders. By the late 1970s, these included among many others, Ayudate (East Los Angeles), El Proyecto del Barrio (San Fernando Valley), and the Mexican-American Opportunity Foundation (Los Angeles). All of them profited from the efforts of a bilingual staff. Unfortunately, such projects are apt to be limited by an insufficient staff and by an excessive workload; moreover, they must win funding on a yearly basis or face serious curtailments in service. According to Monica Herrera Smith, program coordinator of the Los Angeles County Probation Department, "The number and quality of rehabilitation programs is deteriorating, while concentrations of minorities in prisons and jail increase."[11] Counselling also suffers from other weaknesses as well. Academically trained psychologists by no means agree on the correct cure for alcohol or drug addiction. Their ability to effect permanent cures seems limited, especially when the youngsters whom they have detoxified return to the street corner and the company of their former friends.

Equally important in the reform efforts are the churches, both old and new. Catholics, Lutherans, Episcopalians, and Calvinists all have an honorable tradition of social work. They have been joined by a variety of other groups, including the so-called cults. The Church of Scientology may serve as an example of a new church with a particular appeal to the young. It has developed its own form of psychotherapy, known as "dianetics," which is conducted in Spanish, as well as other languages. According to its own statistics, drug and alcohol abuse among Scientology's adherents is negligible.[12]

Another unorthodox organization is Synanon, which specializes in fighting drug abuse. Equally active are evangelical churches such as the Evangelical Pentecostal Church. The Pentecostals' theology differs radically from the Scientologists'. But both of these churches emphasize individual responsibility, and both seem to effect lasting cures. Both, moreover, create new subsocieties of their own. The Pentecostal churches are not an extension of community life; instead the church is a refuge from community norms. Crises such as ill health, or a prolonged inability to cope with emotional problems, precipitate the decision to join such a congregation. Men who suffered the dual stress of poverty and government assistance turn to a life of hard work. At church meetings among Puerto Ricans in Newton, men and women join in supplications that enjoin people to "leave welfare checks and join God."

Drugs

Drug abuse, like alcohol addiction, is a self-inflicted ill; the history of the use of drugs is probably as old as that of alcohol. Ancient Greek travelers referred with amazement to the tribal Scythians' custom of gathering round the camp fire and throwing herbs into the flames for the purpose of getting "drunk" on the smoke. American Indians employed a variety of drugs; it was from America that tobacco spread to Europe. Westerners learned the use of opium, widely prescribed for medical purposes during the nineteenth century in preparations such as laudanum. During the twentieth century, medical doctors and psychiatrists further dispensed dangerous drugs, including heroin and LSD.

Drug usage began among the highest and the lowest, in the slums and among deviant upper-class people; it was only after World War II that drugs acquired mass popularity. As Joan W. Moore points out in her standard work on the slum culture of East Los Angeles, heroin was almost unknown during the early 1940s; by the mid-1950s, heroin-using cliques had spread to all Chicano gangs.[13] At the same time, the proportion of white addicts in federal narcotics hospitals went down, and the proportion of Hispanic addicts went up.

No one knows how many drug users and addicts there are in the United States. Estimates from the mid-1970s are in the millions, even the tens of millions. These figures are purely conjectural; drug usage fluctuates, and users do not necessarily become addicts, even in the case of heroin. In statistical terms, the health hazards of the drug culture are less than those of alcoholism and cigarette smoking. More people die of the direct and indirect effects of alcohol dependence and cigarette-induced lung cancer than of drug addiction. Nevertheless, the perils of the drug culture are bad enough, given both their effects on the minds of people and on their health and their social habits—for example, criminal activity to pay for their drug habits.

By the 1960s, the consumer's choice of drugs was staggering. There were amphetamines and other pills and capsules working on the central nervous system. There was marijuana, relatively harmless compared with the rest, but still potentially dangerous when taken habitually. There were LSD and other psychedelic drugs, originally associated with the culture of rebellious youth and with the urge for mind expansion and protest. Cocaine (derived from the leaves of the coca shrub originally indigenous to Bolivia and Peru) developed into a major menace; so did heroin. Their use came in particular to be linked to crime, especially in the big cities. As a police officer, trained originally as an MBA at Stanford, stated:

It's a buyer's market [in Washington, D.C.] . . . and . . . in drug work
you are dealing with incredibly complex networks. You go from LeRoy
Putnam, whom I locked up yesterday. He's just a stick-up artist. Then
you get the juggler [carrier] and the holder still on the street level. Next,
the members of the Board of Trade and the city law firms who are bankers
for this type of business . . . there are 15 to 20 different heroin organizations
in D.C. They put out brands of heroin with their own name . . . "Murder
One," "Fast Flight," "Brown Tape."[14]

The drug trade in fact came to mirror legitimate commerce with its
complex marketing, advertising, and financial operations. At the same
time, drug usage, unlike the consumption of wine or liquor, acquired
the charm of the forbidden; it gained a cachet of its own, linked to
fashionable forms of social protest and sometimes to rock music. Drug
usage, in a wider sense, also conforms to the norms of a media culture
in which, day after day, night after night, advertisers enjoin television
viewers to swallow pills in order to relieve the tensions of life. Drug
consumption also spread in other ways; the Vietnam War contributed
to drug abuse; so did poor living conditions, boredom, and inadequate
housing.

Of all the drugs, heroin constitutes perhaps the greatest curse of all.
Added to a multitude of other drugs, heroin has occasioned high death
rates from overdoses; it has contributed greatly to crime and corruption
within police forces, and to a growing prison population; it has enlarged
the army of addicts whose all-encompassing need to buy narcotics may
turn them to theft, robbery, or prostitution. Drug users have developed
their own argot and their own life-styles, linked in turn to a great
underground economy with tentacles in every American city. The drug
traffic has become a major component of American crime.

Drug dealing and drug addiction are connected to widespread unemployment in youngsters, especially minority youth in the cities. Cause
and effect are not easy to disentangle. Some may take to drugs in despair
because they cannot find a job. More important, drug dealing and drug
addiction themselves can cause unemployment. Their beneficiaries and
victims alike will not develop those qualities of punctuality, reliability,
and integrity that are essential for getting and for keeping a job.

Drug addiction is one of the great barriers to social mobility; it also
is an enemy of human dignity, a fact well known both to establishment
reformers and to militant groups like the Brown Berets, who, for a time,
worked to deter narcotics in the barrios. The drug culture, however, is
sustained not just by well-publicized youth gangs and "vice lords," but
by a much broader segment of American society. This includes high
school students, junior executives, and rock singers—who themselves

use drugs, call on their friends to "turn on," and thereby provide the market on which the trafficker's livelihood depends.

Nearly all the heroin and most of the marijuana consumed in the United States come from abroad. International traffic thus involves mercantile cities as far afield as New York, Miami (with its great network of legitimate trade to Latin America), and Los Angeles. Estimates concerning the drug trade differ widely; but all experts agree that Colombia and Mexico provide a large proportion of the heroin, cocaine and marijuana imported to the United States. Mexico also serves as a shipment route for many dangerous substances imported from Latin America. Drug dealing has become a significant part of the borderland's economy. As a veteran border patrolman reported, "It's actually giving Star County [Texas] a building boom." Or, as the foreman of a grand jury probing into the drug traffic expressed it, "A guy [who] for years was picking melons at $10 a day, . . . is suddenly paying a month's electric bill in cash and driving a Cadillac."[15]

Mexico plays an important part in narcotics production, but its extent is unknown. The government has tried to conduct an eradication campaign (*la campaña*) against the cultivation of opium poppies, marijuana, and psychotropics. Mexico's efforts have met with bitter criticism from the United States because of Mexico's real or alleged failure to commit sufficient resources, the lack of adequate control, and the manner in which governmental efforts are impeded by corruption. All of these charges have some substance; all of them, however, equally can be advanced against efforts made to combat the drug traffic within the United States. Mexico's problems are particularly difficult, for the cultivation of poppies and marijuana is much more profitable to a poverty-stricken *campesino* than is the growing of legitimate crops. It is no accident that such key producers of opium and marijuana as the states of Sonora, Guerrero, and Sinaloa are also centers of grinding poverty and rural unrest that lie outside the mainstream of Mexican life. The cultivation of illicit drugs or their exportation to the United States provide a good living to the desperate. To communist countries, such as Cuba and Bulgaria, the sale of drugs provides hard currency as well as a means of weakening the United States. To crime syndicates all over this country, narcotics is an important merchandise, probably far outweighing the importance of liquor during Prohibition.

The Reagan administration in 1982 stepped up the battle against drugs. In 1982 and 1983, the amount of cocaine and marijuana seized at the regional interdiction center set up in South Florida went up by 54 and 23 percent respectively. But smugglers always find new ways to evade controls, and smuggling has become a major border industry. Ultimately, the traffic in narcotics cannot be wiped out by better law enforcement, but only by a fundamental change in American values concerning self-indulgence and self-fulfilment.

How far do drugs impinge on Hispanic peoples in the United States? Research on the subject is slender; existing statistics are inadequate. Among Hispanic Americans, as among all others, there are great variations between one region and another, one social stratum and another, and one national group and another. But the poorest people surely suffer the most, both through crime and addiction. Drug offenses are particularly common among poverty-stricken Puerto Rican townsmen, whose ancestors were ignorant of opiates. In 1976, 25.3 percent of all Puerto Rican men sent to New York State prisons were jailed for drug offenses; the corresponding figure for whites was 17.5 percent, and for blacks 10.4 percent.[16] Addiction forms another major problem. Again, statistics are hard to obtain, but there is a world of difference between the unfortunate *atómico* in a Puerto Rican slum who will shoot or swallow anything to get high and the successful public relations expert who occasionally smokes pot in response to peer pressure. Some users get high for pleasure; many more do so to escape the miseries of life or to escape the psychological afflictions that hit Hispanic peoples perhaps even harder than their neighbors.

Mental afflictions among Hispanic peoples as yet remain to be fully documented. This is a difficult task; experts themselves disagree on how such afflictions are to be diagnosed. Both Puerto Ricans and Mexican Americans utilize mental health facilities to a lesser extent than Caucasions. Facilities are less available to the poor than to the rich. Spanish-speaking psychiatrists are few in number. The value of therapy, moreover, remains a subject open to dispute, especially in therapy groups, the structure of which may be determined by the cultural values of particular ethnic groups. Hispanic patients, for example, are much less likely than Anglo-Americans to discuss their most intimate affairs in public; Hispanics may be less proficient in English; hence, the proceedings in therapy groups tend to be dominated by Anglo-Americans. The number of mental afflictions, however, seems to be high among certain Hispanic groups—for instance, among Puerto Rican New Yorkers—especially among adolescents who supposedly suffer from psychological afflictions at a higher rate than adolescents of other ethnic backgrounds.[17] The position may be no better among Chicanos. According to a study in Alameda County, an urban community in Northern California, "The prevalence of psychological distress among Chicanos is at least as high as in the overall population, notwithstanding previous reports to the contrary."[18]

Drugs and drug-related crime remain a major concern to Mexican Americans. Fifty-three percent of Mexican-American voters in Los

Angeles and San Antonio consider that the government should provide more money for drug programs; 58 percent believe that more funds should go to crime prevention, compared to 34 percent who hold that more should be disbursed on welfare, and 26 percent who want the government to spend more on the big cities.[19] Mexican Americans have good reason for their concern. Drugs are a menace, not only in major cities like Los Angeles, but also in many smaller communities. A 1974 study in Oxnard, Ventura County, California paints a most depressing picture. Nearly 20 percent of the population in Ventura County was Mexican American; but as much as 69 percent of all drug-related arrests in Ventura County involved Mexican Americans. Of all offenders arrested for burglary in the county, 75 percent had previous drug arrests; for Mexican Americans, the figure was 88.6 percent. Twenty-eight percent of the residents in La Colonia, the Mexican-American section, were addicted to heroin, barbiturates, and to a lesser extent, to amphetamines. No wonder Oxnard was locally known as "Hype City."[20]

What occasioned this abuse? The answers given ultimately hinge on contrasting views about the nature of mankind. Are men and women but the helpless playthings of society? Or are they fully responsible for their own actions? We ourselves incline toward the second answer. We are impressed by the manner in which "denial" or "transference" themselves serve as symptoms of addiction: the addict is tempted to deny that he or she is in thrall to a dangerous drug; alternatively, the sufferer blames a spouse, an employer, or a social system for his or her predicament. Men and women, however, are subject to greater or lesser temptations; the nature of these temptations is influenced by society, though the mechanisms involved may be extremely complex. For many sociologists, poverty serves as an explanation—not without excellent justification. (In Oxnard, 71.3 percent of all families in La Colonia in 1972 subsisted on an annual income of less than $5,000.) But physical deprivation alone does not account for drug addiction. Londoners just after World War II lived in a city where many houses had been destroyed by German bombs and rockets; they received little or no coal in winter; they drew a weekly ration that would hardly satisfy the daily needs of a healthy American teenager.[21] Yet there was no drug addiction and little serious crime in the British capital at that time.

Family problems may be more significant. The evidence is uncertain and contradictory. Mexican-American mental health patients from a *barrio* are said to have more trouble with their children than do Anglo-Americans, who report more difficulties with their wives than with their young. School and work disturbances likewise are said to be more common among Chicano men than among non-Chicanos.[22]

Unemployment also plays a part in drug afflictions. Admittedly, there was far more joblessness in the United States and Great Britain in the early 1930s; yet drug usage was small and mainly confined to the rich. But, in a modern society geared toward success and affluence, unemployment may create a particular sense of hopelessness for those who cannot find work. All too many of these people are Mexican Americans. (In Ventura County in 1971, 28.8 percent of Mexican Americans had no employment, compared to 7.7 percent of the rest of the population.) A further point: drugs in California during the 1960s and 1970s became relatively easy to purchase—as they had not been in the early 1930s.

Above all, the lure of a pop culture that romanticizes drug abuse often legitimizes drug usage as a symbol of emancipation on the part of the young against their elders. As stated in the disembodied language of medico-sociological investigators studying drug abuse among young Cubans in Miami, the drug-using group "showed higher levels of behavioral acculturation among the children and wider behavioral acculturation gaps between parents and children than among non-users.[23]

By the early 1980s there was some indication that public authorities were less permissive than before in matters affecting such social issues as drug consumption and divorce.[24] Nevertheless, drugs still were being consumed on a massive scale. No amount of police intervention is capable of greatly diminishing drug consumption; only a massive change in wider cultural attitudes ultimately will do away with this major affliction.

Chapter 16

Crime and Punishment

Violence is as American as apple pie, radicals used to say during the turbulent 1960s. In a sense, they were right. Violence, though not as rife as Western movies suggest, flourished on frontiers that moved inland in advance of judges, jailers, and policemen. In this respect the frontier situation in the United States historically differed from those in northwest Canada and white Rhodesia, where elite forces—the Royal Northwest Mounted Police (later Royal Canadian Mounted Police) and the British South Africa Police, respectively—had already established law and order before there was a mass influx of newcomers.[1]

The situation has been no better in many U.S. cities. These commonly experienced an ethnic succession in crime, as in sports, and indeed every other department of life. Poverty-stricken and unskilled men were apt to indulge in "unskilled" crimes, such as robbery and mugging, offenses that required no more than muscles and the possession of cheap tools (a club, a knife, or an inexpensive gun). As immigrants moved up the social scale and acquired more skills, the lawbreakers among them rose into more highly specialized and profitable spheres of illegality, such as fencing or fraud, or they acquired managerial positions supervising a dependent labor force of toughs, prostitutes, gamblers, and the like.

Crime and U.S. Society

Every ethnic group in the United States—including Jews, Italians, Irish, and blacks—has experienced ethnic succession in crime. Almost every immigrant community has been accused, upon first arriving in this United States, of being particularly prone to breaking the law. Organized crime, although of much earlier origin, received an extraordinary impetus from Prohibition (1920–1933), an ill-conceived experiment in social engineering designed in part to force Americanization on immigrants, especially working-class immigrants. The result was an unnecessary tragedy. As Paul Johnson, a British historian, writes: "America's entrepreneurial market system was in itself an effective homogenizer binding together and adjudicating between ethnic racial

293

groups."[2] Far from Americanizing immigrants, Prohibition reinforced minority characteristics by encouraging specific patterns of crime. Prohibition created new forms of criminal organization, new ways of corrupting public authority, and also enormous new funds that were reinvested in other sectors of the underground economy—gambling, prostitution, and the drug trade. Prohibition turned out to be the start of big-time crime in America. The impact of crime varied from region to region, from city to city. Overall, crime grew during the 1970s, leveled off during the 1980s, nevertheless continuing at a high rate, with a stupendous total of 10.8 million arrests in the United States in 1981 for criminal infractions other than traffic violations.

Generalizations about Hispanic participation in crime are as hard to make as those regarding the role of Hispanics in other spheres of American life. The criminal pattern of a middle-class community, such as that of the Argentinians in New York, differs strikingly from that of the Puerto Ricans, with their large working-class and underclass component. There is no statistical correlation between the number of Hispanics in any given city and the amount of violent crime. Miami has a high crime rate; El Paso and San Antonio have low rates of crime; and all three of them have many Hispanic inhabitants. Crime and society are inextricably interwoven; every social activity—whether banking, building, betting, or boxing—has its seamy underside. Over all, however, Hispanics are as yet little involved in white-collar crimes such as fraud (2.9 percent of all arrests in 1981), prostitution and commercialized vice (5.3 percent), and embezzlement (5.6 percent). Forgery and counterfeiting, useful adjuncts for the purpose of breaking the immigration laws, rank higher, but crimes of violence and crimes against property top the list.

Crime is omnipresent in America. But it is big-city crime, especially muggings and murders, that makes most of the headlines.[3] Its social cost are enormous, particularly for the poor, its principal victims. The high rate of store robberies in the ghettos and *barrios*, for example, has forced many small businesses to close, thereby depriving the neighborhood of much-needed facilities and shattering an important ladder of advancement for would-be grocers, cobblers, and owners of bottle stores. "Mom and Pop" stores have gone out of business. Robberies against bus and cab drivers cause enormous inconvenience by requiring passengers to tender exact change for their fare; the person rejected, often brown or black, must then walk, adding to his already well-founded sense of insecurity, a pervasive social disease of the slum.[4]

Hispanic involvement in violent crime is considerable, although its extent is hard to measure. Arrest records are not particularly good indicators. Police jurisdictions differ in the ways they make up their statistics and in their rate of arrests. Many crimes go unreported; on the other hand, some figures may be exaggerated. Statistics concerning the number of Hispanics convicted for specific crimes throughout the nation leave much to be desired. But, in 1979, about 11.6 percent of the 314,083 persons serving sentences on felony charges in federal and state prisons were thought to be Hispanics. An earlier survey, in 1977, found that Hispanics, mostly Mexicans, accounted for 20.5 percent of California's prison population, and 5.9 percent in the Eastern states, most of these convicts being Puerto Rican. Overall, Hispanic offenders increasingly were involved in drugs and violence. In 1976, the percentage of Puerto Ricans incarcerated in New York for homicide exceeded the percentages for both whites and blacks.[5]

What causes serious crime, and what can be done about it? Why should crime rates have climbed so much during the 1960s and 1970s? These are difficult questions to answer because they involve fundamental judgments about human nature, judgments about which American society is deeply divided. Puerto Rican and Chicano activists stress racial discrimination; according to their interpretation, the discriminatory treatment of minorities causes poverty-striken youngsters to become alienated from society and to then take the path of crime.

Racial discrimination, however, is not universally the immigrant's universal experience. Among long-term Mexican residents, awareness of racial discrimination increases significantly with longer residence in the United States. Nevertheless, even after having lived six years in this country, only 40 percent of Mexican immigrants interviewed had seen evidence of discrimination. In fact, most studies indicate that Mexican immigrants as a whole view American society as positive, beneficent, and egalitarian.[6] Discrimination does not account for the striking behavioral differences observed within the same family; nor does it explain the differential conduct among various dark-skinned groups, such as the Dominicans, Puerto Ricans, and Guatemalans in "Newton" (discussed in the section on alcoholism).

Crime is the product of an unjust social order in general, argue the liberals, fundamentally agreeing with Hispanic activists. Provide jobs, good wages, adequate public services, and good education for the poor, and outlaw discrimination and guns—and crime will be taken care of. It is an attractive thesis, but it does not account for the rise in crime during the 1960s, a period of prosperity and a time when social services were rapidly expanding. Detailed case studies, within or outside the continental United States, moreover, do not bear out purely economic interpretations of crime.[7]

Law-and-order conservatives give a different answer concerning the causes of crime. As traditionalists see it, a clique of permissive politicians, psychiatrists, teachers, parsons, and literary intellectuals—abetted by liberal judges and bureaucrats—has conspired to coddle criminals at the expense of law-abiding Americans. Do away with the courts' "exclusionary rule," abolish the insanity defense, reduce or wipe out parole, and lengthen prison sentences—and gangland will get the message. A tough and coercive approach might work, and speedy and effective justice, for instance, might break up gangs.[8] A cohesive system of justice, designed to isolate malefactors, certainly will protect potential victims: a mugger jailed is a mugger out of business for the term of his imprisonment.

But conservatives are apt to overlook the broader social dynamics of crime. Like an army, crime depends not merely on professional cadres but on huge reserves of potential recruits and on supply and support services that parallel society at large. Tactical successes do not add up to a winning strategy. Nor is there any indication that tough judges and jailers by themselves can stop widespread law violations. If they could, the Soviet Union and South Africa, neither of them wont to coddle law breakers, would be free of crime, and the back alleys of Moscow and Johannesburg would not be—as they are—extremely unsafe at night.

Advocates of a free market economy have somewhat different views of these matters. For rising crime rates, they tend to blame the welfare state. By disrupting family cohesion and diminishing or eliminating paternal authority within the family, such welfare devices as Aid to Dependent Children have eroded the work ethic and promoted social deviance. Minimum-wage laws, by reducing employment opportunities for unskilled youngsters, have had similar effects. Street people, untrained or unwilling to take a low-status job and unaccustomed to punctuality and to habits of saving or foresight, do not do well on the labor market. For this reason, delinquency predicts socioeconomic status better than socioeconomic status predicts delinquency. New York City, for instance, experienced rapidly rising crime rates at the same time the city was enormously expanding its welfare services.[9]

The free marketeers do have a point. But many other factors enter into the equation. For instance, not all welfare states have high crime rates. Sweden, with its all-embracing system that cares for the citizen from the cradle to the grave, has a much lower crime rate than the United States. Nor do all welfare recipients turn to crime, as we have pointed out in our chapter on the Puerto Rican poor in New York; the majority of slum dwellers are law-abiding people, especially the churchgoers. Individual choice plays its part, but so do general economic conditions. There is a striking connection between crime and unemployment, as Paul Garcia, a senior investigator in the New York Department of Correctional Services, points out.[10]

Another argument emphasizes demographic factors. According to this thesis, the rise and fall in crime rates has little connection with the decisions made by, or the opinions put forward by, social planners, theologicians, judges or jailers. Violent crime is explicable, above all, in terms of populations shifts. Mugging, rape, murder, and robbery are occupations for the fit and the young, especially for men between the ages of 15 and 25. One of the major reasons for the striking increase in U.S. crime during the 1960s and 1970s was the post-World War II baby boom. The reduction in violent crime during the 1980s owes more to the declining proportion of youthful males within the population than to better policing; the credit belongs more to birth control clinics than to the law-and-order forces. If such assessments are correct, Puerto Ricans and Mexican Americans will continue to have higher crime rates in the United States until Hispanic families have fewer children.

The demographic argument like the others, merits consideration. But it no more accounts for the whole story, than the explanations that stress poverty, class divisions, disparities in income, or the relative absence of social services. Victorian England had what is by present standards a youthful population and a high birth rate. Victorian class divisions ran deep; London slums shocked even hard-bitten visitors. Yet Victorian England between 1850 and 1890 experienced a striking decline in crime.[11]

As we see it, crime has no single cause; it derives from a conjunction of many circumstances—religious, social, economic, and demographic. Among these factors, we put more stress on family cohesion and religious commitment than do the majority of sociologists. Whether church-going Catholics, Pentecostals, old Amish, Mormons, Scientologists, Orthodox Jews, or followers of Hare Krishna are right or wrong in their respective beliefs, they all have lower crime rates than their fellow citizens. But religious beliefs do not operate in a vacuum. They are held by men and women organized in particular social frameworks. These differ from country to country, and American society is, in some respects, unique.

The United States has a larger and more varied population and more space than any country in Western Europe; the United States is the world's largest and the most populated political entity in which citizens and noncitizens alike can move freely. No other country in the world contains, moreover, as many privately owned guns. The U.S. borders also are more open to immigration—both legal and illegal—than those of any other country on the globe. This country's population is enormously varied, and its composition forever seems to be changing. It is this last factor that renders inappropriate comparisons between the United States and older, more homogeneous countries, such as Great Britain and West Germany. The American immigrant pattern has been infinitely more varied. To give just one example: between 1970 and 1983, more than 2 million foreign immigrants came to Los Angeles County alone, the "new Ellis Island" of the U.S.[12]

Given the ethnic diversity of the United States, given its social, economic, racial, and ethnic cleavages, given its size and its relative lack of social restraints, given the easy mobility of motor cars, forged documents, and guns, sociologists should wonder at the stability of U.S. society rather than at its crime figures. For all their enormous problems, Americans have had good reason to appropriate for their own country the city of Paris' motto, *fluctuat nec mergitur* ("It shakes, but does not sink.").

Law Enforcement

When constabulary's duty to be done
A policeman's lot is not a happy one.
                                                        —W. S. Gilbert

Law enforcement agents in modern America have every reason to echo this plaint of Gilbert and Sullivan. All of them, whether they work for the Immigration and Naturalization Service (INS), the FBI, local police agencies, or the prison service, have image problems. Opinion makers in the universities, churches, and the media rarely possess first-hand knowledge of law enforcement work. They have not experienced the law enforcement officer's widespread sense of social isolation or the sudden tension that grips a police officer or an INS inspector called out on a difficult case. As a Hispanic INS administrator put it, "When one officer faces a hostile group of 50 people throwing rocks, it is only natural for him to feel up-tight, to sense fear, to resort to force that he might not have used in different circumstances."[13] He will feel all the more subject to stress because his decisions may have to be made in a split second, unlike those of a parole board or a university committee.

Schooled in a culture that exalts social criticism, and in most cases personally unaccustomed to crime, intellectuals generally side emotionally with the breakers rather than with the defenders of the law. The general public is almost equally ambivalent, and its ambivalence to the police extends to the *barrios*. According to progressive intellectuals, the poor hate the "pigs." There is indeed much dislike of the police in urban slums. As a case study in a Southern Californian *barrio* indicates, about 35 percent of all respondents blamed police harrassment, prejudice, and "overpatrolling" for conflicts between the police and the *barrio*, a tightly knit community where everyone is related to someone else. About 32 percent of the respondents wanted to reduce the power of the police. But those who feared crime also supported the police. Hence: "The view that Chicanos are uniformly anti-police and supportive of crime should be modified. . . . A significant segment of the barrio . . . are fearful of crime and want to increase police power."[14]

INS officers also find themselves caught between conflicting demands. As we have pointed out in the chapter on immigration, the public wants to exclude illegal immigrants but is unprepared to provide adequate funds for the purpose or to give up their illegal workers. The INS by the 1980s remained understaffed and underfunded, subject to innumerable economies of the kind that led to the grounding of helicopters for want of fuel or failure to replace worn-out patrol vehicles. On the immense task of patrolling its far-flung borders, the United States in 1981 spent little more than the total annual expenditure of just one major U.S. university.[15]

Inspectors have other troubles. They realize that many of the illegal aliens they arrest have the traditional American virtues of thrift and hard work, that illegal aliens are seldom criminals. There is no public prestige attached to arresting undocumented workers in the course of raids on factories; on the contrary, the public is more apt to sympathize with the harried aliens. Inspectors, in fact, would rather work on cases involving drug smuggling, illegal documentation, and the like. Such cases are more interesting and more prestigious than carrying out routine checks of illegal workers. These checks can only be done in a sporadic fashion—to show the flag, so to speak. Washington, D.C., for instance, has only eight inspectors, who had so many duties to perform that they could not effectively investigate illegal aliens. Moreover, Immigration Department employees are counted as second-class citizens within the bureaucratic hierarchy, ranging far behind other investigative agencies, such as the FBI and the Secret Service. The Immigration Department does not get the funding, the public prestige, or even the prison space allotted to other investigative agencies.

To cap it all, inspectors find themselves at the receiving end of intense public criticism. Their censors include progressive clergymen who use their churches as "sanctuaries" to break the law in providing shelter for illegal immigrants; academics; Hispanic activists; employers of immigrant labor, and civil rights agencies. Foremost among these is the U.S. Commission on Civil Rights (founded in 1958), for long staffed overwhelmingly by committed liberals and dedicated to investigative research reminiscent in many ways of the work done by the Fabian

Society in Great Britain, with the difference that, in the United States, the taxpayer foots the bill.[16]

The INS at least forms a unified service; it comes under the Department of Justice and is therefore at least indirectly represented and defended in the cabinet. The various American police forces are unique in the world in that they are split into countless forces, mostly controlled by local authorities. In Britain, which most closely resembles the United States in this respect, there were 167 police forces by the late 1970s; in the United States, by contrast, the estimated number ran to 40,000. These included federal law enforcement bodies (the FBI, the Bureau of Internal Revenue, the Secret Service Division, the Narcotics Bureau, and many others); police forces established by each of the 50 states of the Union; sheriffs and deputy sheriffs in more than 3,000 counties; and police forces subject to cities, boroughs, townships, and villages. They differed enormously in size (with 23,000 officers in New York, 13,000 in Chicago, just under 800 in San Jose, California, and only a handful in small communities.) They equally varied in training, pay, efficiency, and morale. In this respect, as in so many others, the very best and the very worst existed side by side in the United States.

Police recruitment, like recruitment into sports, crime, and the labor force at large, has tended to follow the laws of ethnic succession; the most recent immigrant groups always have been unrepresented or at least underrepresented in the police. As immigrants advance from unskilled to skilled and clerical work, and as they acquire citizenship, they also begin to look for jobs as patrolmen. The New York police, to give one example, was for a long time dominated by the Irish; subsequently, Italians and Jews began to put on the blue uniform, followed later by other ethnic groups. Under this system, tensions between police and public often were accompanied by ethnic tensions and by complaints—both justified and unjustified—of police prejudice and brutality. By and large, Anglo-Americans were most inclined to support the police; Chicanos, according to a detailed case study in a Southern California community, "seemed to fear crime less than blacks, [yet] they apparently feared the police more."[17]

Chicano apprehensions in many cases were well justified. An investigation in East Los Angeles in 1968, for instance, provided clear evidence of differential treatment. The crime ratio for major offenses in East Los Angeles, with a large Hispanic population, and the neighboring (mainly "Anglo") West Valley community stood at 4.9 and 4.8, respectively. But police officers were assigned to these two neighborhoods at the rate of 13.5 and 3.5 per square mile, respectively. In 1968, more than 50 percent of all arrests in Los Angeles were made for drinking offenses. Yet, only 2 percent of all patients in the East Los Angeles Mental Health Clinic

Regional Service had drinking problems. The position was worsened by differential jury representation. A 1969 study indicated that of an eligible Spanish-surname population, only four Spanish-surname people had served on the Los Angeles County Grand Jury during the preceding decade.[18]

Brutal treatment was by no means limited to people without money or influence. In one instance, in 1970, a member of the Los Angeles County Sheriff's Department shot and killed Ruben Salazar, a *Los Angeles Times* journalist, at the Silver Dollar Cafe. Two others also lost their lives, Angel Gilberto Diaz and Lynn Ward. Hundreds of people were beaten by the police at the occasion, the National Chicano Moratorium March, in East Los Angeles. The Sheriff's Department, in defense, stated that 40 of its own officers were injured and 25 radio cars were damaged by rocks and bottles. Whatever the rights and wrongs of what Chicano activists called an Anglo police riot, there was no excuse for what, according to the coroner's inquest, was the unprovoked killing of Salazar; he was struck in the head by a tear-gas projectile fired at close range under circumstances in which no well-trained, disciplined officer would have used a firearm.[19]

Salazar's death occasioned a nationwide controversy. But there were untold other cases that went unreported, cases in which the victims were ill-educated labor migrants without money or influence. In one instance (described to the U.S. Civil Rights Commission), a Chicano involved in a traffic accident in Austin, Texas, was beaten by police investigating the incident. Once handcuffed, he was hit again and taken to a station where he was beaten. He was charged with two counts of aggravated assault and once more was taken to his cell. During the next 10 days he was struck several more times. At least eight officers were involved. The beatings were so severe that he died. The case was not unique. During an 18-month period (1976–1977), 18 Hispanics in Texas died while in police custody.[20]

Reform entailed some major administrative changes. Foremost among these was the recruitment of Hispanic police officers. In Houston, Texas, for instance, the city council announced in the late 1970s that in the future about 20 percent of its recruitment funds would be allocated to attract minority people to join the force. Reforms designed to encourage more Hispanics and blacks to serve in police forces and other public employment throughout the country ran into bitter opposition from opponents of racial quotas and goals. Clearly, public confidence in the police, an indispensable element for the efficient exercise of police power, will best be developed if Hispanic citizens can deal with police officers who are able to speak Spanish, are familiar with the problems of the *barrio,* and are able to gain the backing of the people they are paid to protect. Success in this matter is not unattainable. As the report previously cited pointed out, virtually all Hispanics interviewed expressed a positive attitude toward the progress that has been made up to this point, a success for which Chicano activists can take much credit.[21]

Police reform has many other implications that have affected not only Hispanics but the citizenry at large. Unfortunately, these issues are easier to discuss than to solve. An efficient police department requires adequate procedures to handle citizen complaints and an effective machinery for the internal investigation of abuses. Many police departments have set up Internal Affairs Divisions (IAD) with their own investigators. By the very nature of their task, however, these officers are likely to experience tremendous pressure from their colleagues; hence, candidates may be reluctant to be assigned to investigative positions. IAD work, all too often, lacks prestige and does not count for much in the struggle for promotion.

The best IAD, moreover, cannot accomplish much if the police department as a whole does not enjoy public trust. Many a poor man, of whatever nationality, lacks the time or the self-confidence to report police misconduct, feeling that it is "my word against theirs." When the complainant himself is an offender, his suspicion is likely to be well justified because a jury may be more likely to accept evidence from a police officer—an experienced witness and an established citizen—against a criminal. Especially in cases involving the use of force, jurors may be reluctant to second-guess the judgment of a police officer. No procedural reform, however well designed, can resolve such difficulties by itself; the proper working of a police department ultimately depends on the quality of its officers and on the willingness of a community to support and pay for a well-trained, well-disciplined, and well-remunerated force.

However competent and honest the police may be, there are certain troubles from which no force can escape. The police are expected to suppress crime, but they cannot control the conditions that produce violations of the law. The very people who most wholeheartedly support police efforts to stamp out crime by and large have not experienced personally the inconvenience and tensions that police tactics invariably produce. By contrast, those citizens who need police protection and who most frequently call the police for aid are most apt to be angered by what they either perceive to be police indifference (when the police do too little) or callousness (when the police apparently do too much.)

Violent crime is most common in a slum neighborhood. Policemen are well aware that they are more likely to be attacked in slum alleys than in the streets of a prosperous suburb. Police officers will more likely "overreact" when coping with the poor, rather than with the well-to-do, who, when tempted into crime, will cheat rather than mug their victims. In slums, where street crime is frequent, the police necessarily become intrusive, no matter how well intentioned the officers. Sirens wail, police cars speed down the streets, race through intersections, ignore red lights, dash across sidewalks and into the side lanes. Policemen suddenly jump out of their cars with guns drawn and riot sticks ready. Men drinking quietly, or not so quietly, in a bar suddenly confront officers who rush through the door full of apparent menace. How can a patrolman know that a disgruntled customer had decided to call in a false robbery report? A police department can neither ignore the call nor make it in a gentlemanly fashion. Hence, there is more distrust of the police, and, in turn, perhaps more "overreaction" on the officers' part.

There is no perfect answer. Here, as in so many other areas, Americans must get rid of the notion that, somehow, all social problems have a perfect solution. There is no single answer to crime; and no police force, however well run and well disposed to the public, can prevent all crime. Crime depends on a multiplicity of factors that the police cannot control: the destruction of a traditional neighborhood through urban renewal or freeway construction, the rising demand for drugs, a sudden change in the local economy of a city through the closing down of a major factory leading to massive loss of jobs—the list could go on forever. The best police force under such circumstances can provide no more than the equivalent of first aid. Permanent cures for major social ills are beyond their powers.

Gangs

"Latins are excitable," runs a common Anglo-American stereotype. "They have a quick smile and a quick knife. They are anarchic by temperament; they are macho; they love to fight—even over small matters involving a point of honor. No wonder our cities are prone to gang violence, for hordes of Hispanics keep coming." Ethnic misconceptions of a more sophisticated kind find expression in a musical like *West Side Story*, which portrays the social realities of New York's West Side with even less accuracy than a Johann Strauss operetta represents Imperial Vienna under the Hapsburg monarchy. Chicano activists come up with a different explanation for gang violence. In their view, ethnic minorities lack power and influence; they are alienated from the white power structure; they look upon police officers as representatives of white racism and repression; Chicanos despise the police for their brutality, corruption, and double standards. Most ethnic minority violence in American history has been merely of a retaliatory kind. When Chicanos take to the streets, as they did in East Los Angeles in 1970, they mainly indulge in "commodity riots" directed against property owned by outside white proprietors.[22]

In our opinion, both of these interpretations leave much to be desired. The overwhelming majority of Hispanics do not riot; nor do they belong to gangs or engage in violence. Puerto Ricans and Mexicans are not crime-prone by nature. During the 1950s, for instance, there was not a particularly high rate of delinquency among Puerto Rican juveniles in New York; much of Puerto Rican violence involved crimes of passion against fellow members of the community. It was only as "Americanization" proceeded, that delinquency rates increased.[23]

The scanty evidence available seems to indicate that crime patterns parallel patterns of legitimate enterprise among Hispanics as among all other ethnic groups. Cubans and South Americans, on the average, have been more successful this far in legitimate enterprise than Puerto Ricans and, to a lesser extent, Mexican Americans. Hence, the former also are more likely to have advanced further into the upper levels of criminal enterprise, the world of extortion rackets, large-scale drug smuggling, and so forth. A trained and experienced ex-guerrilla or underground organizer who has gone wrong, or an import-export merchant willing to break the law, clearly has a better chance of breaking into big-time crime than a street-corner thug.

Existing statistics suggest that Hispanic crime has increased over the last twenty years. Miami, for instance, has an underworld of Cuban as well as non-Cuban criminals. In 1983, the United States attempted to persuade Fidel Castro to take back some of the 4,000 criminals, known as "Marielitos," from the Cuban port of Mariel, whence they left in 1980—a very small proportion of the 125,000 Cubans, most of them perfectly law-abiding citizens, who had departed during that exodus. The Puerto Ricans likewise had their share of lawbreakers. Between 1974 and 1979, the number of Hispanic inmates sent to New York prisons went up by twice the percentage figure for all inmates. New York, by 1979, had jailed 4,070 Puerto Ricans; this figure does not include the large number of Central and South Americans and other Hispanics who might not have Hispanic surnames and who were lost in computer printouts as "white" or "black."

Hispanic crime statistics are vitiated further by severe discrepancies in sentencing. According to a Rand Corporation Study in 1983 by criminologist Joan Petersilia, the prevailing system treats the different races in much the same fashion during the arrest, prosecution, and conviction process; differential treatment becomes apparent during sentencing.[24] Hispanic and black felons in California, Texas, and Michigan are likely to receive longer sentences and serve more time than "whites" convicted of similar offenses. The difference is a result not so much of conscious prejudice but of the information received by judges and parole officers used to determine sentences and release eligibility.

What kind of people are these incarcerated Hispanics? They vary enormously, as do the convicts belonging to any other ethnic group. They include educated and illiterate, well-to-do and poor. But, overwhelmingly, they belong to a few major categories. Criminologist Peter L. Sissons has constructed profiles for typical Hispanic offenders in New York. The characteristic non-Puerto Rican lawbreaker is probably a Colombian or a Dominican who may or may not have completed high school and who has received a five-year prison sentence for a federal narcotics violation. The typical Puerto Rican is a 32-year-old male who has not graduated from high school. He is most likely to be a drug offender, although he may have committed other federal offenses, for which he received a five-year sentence on probation or, more likely, a jail term. By contrast, the typical white or black criminal has graduated from high school and may even have gone to college; he is serving a four-year sentence on probation; he is much less likely than a Hispanic to be a drug violator, and he is probably guilty of bank robbery, mail theft, or larceny.

But what precisely is a "typical" offender? This category can be further broken down. Among Puerto Rican prison inmates will be found, at the bottom rung of the ladder, the *jíbaro*, born abroad in a village, who is arrested for crimes of passion, intemperance, or for committing a public nuisance. Alternatively, he might have been unlucky enough to run into a prejudiced policeman who "socked it to him" on a charge that might have been erased from the books had the offender been middle class, well spoken, and suitably apologetic for his offense. Equally pitiful are mentally disturbed or retarded Hispanics, arrested for violent crime, fratricide, child molestation, public exposure, and the like.[25] Distressingly, such men are apt to be recycled over and over again through the criminal justice system without getting proper care. When confined to a maximum security prison, serving long-term sentences, they often become a serious threat to other inmates and staff, and they may be subjected to repeated disciplinary measures when their mental condition is neither diagnosed nor treated. Since few systems have Spanish-speaking psychiatrists or psychologists, and since sick inmates are apt to be looked upon as "fakers," their future outlook is grim. Then there are the young, first- or second-generation Hispanic youths, arrested often for acts of violence, for drug violations, or property offenses (including car thefts, common in a car-oriented society). These youngsters form a standing reserve force for the "non-commissioned" and "commissioned" officers of crime, a subject to which we return in the section dealing with youth gangs.

John Citizen and Juan Ciudadino alike know little or nothing about organized crime. If they live in a big city, especially in a poverty-stricken area, they will be aware of youth gangs. Gang activities make the headlines; readers of local newspapers learn all about the gangs' argot, practices, or real and supposed offenses. Passersby see graffiti sprayed on walls for the sake of staking out territory, expressing defiance, or boosting the author's pride. Gangs come and go; their membership fluctuates. Many of them are perfectly harmless. Some are no more than social clubs whose members may take pride in their cars. The "Excelsior" in San Francisco gained attention by painting a large mural. The "Lords" approached the city for a meeting place. The "Mira Loma" indulged in the more destructive, but not seriously criminal, amusement of climbing down manholes and cutting up telephone lines to shut off electricity and telephone services to local residents. Some gangs, as we have seen in the chapter on politics, try to make their mark on radical politics, though with scanty success. Worse are the gangs that engage in occasional assaults on their elders. Others are insensibly propelled into violence when a "cool gato"—unbeknown to his parents—gets into a fight that ends in an unintended killing. Gangs of this kind are apt to clash with their rivals; but they are not organized for robbery, extortion, or even disciplined street fighting.[26]

Other gangs in a big metropolis like Los Angeles or New York may be much more dangerous. The Lower East Side of New York, for instance, was once a stronghold of European immigrants. When the Puerto Ricans first entered the neighborhood, they were picked on by gangs already established. In time, the Puerto Ricans set up their own gangs, such as the "Dragons." Like other gangs of their kind, the "Dragons" at first served for self-defense; they provided an instrument of ethnic solidarity; and they gave a new sense of group loyalty to youngsters who had become bored with school or wished to escape to the streets from crowded apartments. By the 1950s, the "Dragons" were engaging in neighborhood "wars" with the "Enchanters" and "Sportsmen" (mainly blacks with a white subgang). The combined areas covered no more than a square mile, divided into rival turfs.[27]

Crime, bad enough during the 1950s, continued to worsen in the big cities. There was, for instance, a great deal of serious crime in Los Angeles.[28] A throbbing metropolis with an expanding economy, Los Angeles was much less hostile to Mexicans and offered much better economic opportunities than did most other southwestern towns. The rate of Mexican-American intermarriage with Anglo-Americans considerably exceeded that in most other southwestern communities. Already in the early 1960s, some 25 percent of the Chicanos in Los Angeles married outside their own ethnic group.[29] Enhanced economic opportunities, and increased geographical mobility, however, also contributed to a breakdown of family cohesion and traditional mores; this breakdown in turn played a part in growing crime, partially connected to street gangs. Gangs tied to particular neighborhoods had a tradition dating back at least to the turn of the century. But, decades ago, crime was not as serious and as widespread as it is today. There were fights, but they involved melees with chops, blows, and kicks; firearms remained in the background.

During the last ten years, violence has worsened as guns have become easily available and as most gangs have begun to use and to trade in drugs. At the same time, accustomed bonds of family cohesion have weakened, for a variety of reasons. For instance, public welfare benefits increasingly took the place of private support furnished by families to indigent relatives or aging parents. If a widowed or deserted wife refuses to live with her relatives, she now has the option of relying on public welfare. An expanding underground economy, untaxed and unrecorded, provides increasing incomes for those who manage to make money by illegal or semilegal methods. Streetwise youngsters have more money to spend than before. Guns are more affordable and so are cars (once an unaffordable luxury in the slums). Hence the old-fashioned rumble all too often turns into a motorized foray into enemy territory for the purpose of shooting targeted victims. While gambling or prostitution might provide extra cash, above all there is the "second economy" in drugs to both provide and consume the new income. The increased traffic in, and consumption of, dangerous narcotics such as PCP ("angel dust") in turn enhances the perils of *la vida loca* (the crazy life). Gang members high on "angel dust" are more violent and often become uncontrollable.

The gang cultures are hard to stamp out because they may be linked to neighborhood pride. Gangs offer protection, sex, and opportunities to prove a man's machismo. According to Joan Moore's observations in East Los Angeles, the gang network received reinforcement as other family members joined gangs and as gang members married into the families of fellow members, sponsored children in baptism (*compadrazgo*), and turned into a permanent social institution in many Chicano communities. "Hanging out" with a gang and taking part in fights became for many youngsters a status symbol and a way of life. "Fair fights" (one against one, without weapons) ceased to be the norm; many slum-born youths came to accept a future stay in prison as part of their normal existence. Such a life-style appeared more challenging to many than the dull grind of a high school or junior college. Life in a gang, as we have pointed out earlier, was apt to leave its members unfit for a dull job in a supermarket or bank, where personnel managers look to punctuality, hard work, and obedience in their recruits, qualities that do not flourish on a street corner. By the early 1980s, Southern California apparently had become the nation's largest gang center, with an estimated 800 gangs; Los Angeles alone had more than 100 gangs.

The social composition of these gangs varies considerably but usually shares certain characteristics. Their membership fluctuates; most associates do not descend into serious crime, but find their way into lawful occupations. Of 30 or 40 members in a gang, perhaps no more than three or four may have a reputation for being *vatos locos*, crazy guys, apt to lead their friends into dangerous mischief. It is this small percentage of "core members" who are apt to provide the permanent cadres in the army of crime. A classic study, written in the 1950s, but still valuable, describes these core gang members as "disassociated, hostile, status-involved" youths. For them, most people are "enemies to be manipulated, used, or assaulted, depending on a given situation." There is no honor among such thieves; on the contrary, their associates are "partners in crime, but not friends in the sense of a shared relationship. . . . " Their behavior is dominated by "ego gratifying or rep [reputation]-making acts."[30] All too often, such men end with a knife or bullet in the back. If they survive the perils of the street, they may grow into streetwise older offenders, expert at getting around the law, able to speak acceptable English, employed in drug rings or in a variety of rackets such as loan sharking, fencing, and burglary. But a small percentage makes it into big-time crime, where success is as hard to gain as it is in big-time sports or entertainment. The higher reaches of criminal enterprise are as variegated and competitive as those in legitimate business and are engaged in every conceivable activity—the drug trade, loan sharking, gambling, the smuggling of aliens (a million-a-month business), or in ordinary contraband involving arms, diamonds, high technology, and such like.

Gangs also extend their tentacles into the federal and state prison systems. Law and order, ironically enough, forms one of the greatest problems that beset prisons. All too often convicts are subjected to extortion, rape, assault, and murder. The need for self-protection, the call for ethnic solidarity among poorly educated people unable sometimes to speak much English, the intense psychological pressures occasioned by overcrowding, and the ethnic tensions among white, brown, and black people often reproduce the social conditions of city slums in the jails.[31] A correctional facility is itself a small city; the same tensions that operate in the metropolis operate in the cell block, especially when the prison population keeps rising. Each jail has its own underground economy to produce the funds needed to buy small luxuries, support outside families, or bribe corruptible staff members.

Not surprisingly, then, gangs have formed in prison. These include in California, for example, the "Mexican Mafia" (drawn from southern California) and "Nuestra Familia" (recruited from smaller communities in northern and central California). Both are composed primarily of "state-raised" men, without families of their own, prison-wise, with long previous experience in juvenile hall and orphanages, similar to such ethnic crime organizations as the "Aryan Brotherhood" and the "Black Guerrilla Family." These groups use extreme violence in pursuit of power and economic control. They contrast with *barrio*-oriented cliques that draw on each other for mutual support in a hostile environment where a loner is lost.

How great is the impact of these gangs, and what can be done about them? None of the experts is certain. The very statistics concerning gang violence are confusing and sometimes contradictory; they do, however, indicate a high rate of violence. (To give one example: there were 351 gang-related killings in Los Angeles County in 1980 alone.)

Nevertheless, the gang problem should be kept in perspective. The overwhelming majority of youngsters, including Latin youngsters, in California, Texas, New York, Illinois, are not gang members. According to official estimates, the total number of youth gang members in California in 1983 numbered no more than 82,000. Most of these were not hardened offenders. Troublesome and destructive as gangs may be, they do not dominate Mexican-American society. Even the most casual visitor to East Los Angeles cannot help but be struck by the sense of hard work, the orderliness, and the care that is put into houses and yards by their owners. The threat offered by gangs to American society is negligible compared to the peril posed to the German Weimar Republic by the private political armies of the 1920s and the early 1930s, the Nazi *Sturmabteilungen* or the communist *Rotfrontkämpferbund,* composed of uniformed, well-disciplined, and well-financed youths, too numerous and well led to be controlled by the police.

What is the best way to deal with gangs? Experts have given a great many answers. The conciliatory approach, advocated by many social workers and clergymen at work in the slums, seeks to redirect gangs to peaceful pursuits. In Los Angeles, for example, the Community Youth Gangs Services Project, a $1.3-million Los Angeles County program, attempted to head off explosive encounters before they happened. The project centered on "streetwise" workers who rode through the streets, three to a car. They became familiar with gang members and their families; they gave counsel; they mediated disputes. About 60 percent of the project's 36 workers screened by 1983 were themselves *veteranos* of the gangs with which they were involved. The Catholic United Neighborhood Organization, a community group made up mainly of Catholic parishes, sought to follow a similar course. So did Victory Outreach, a program associated with evangelical Christians, which made an active effort to rehabilitate drug addicts and gang fighters. Similar programs operated in many other cities, including New York, where social workers attempted to redirect gangs from destructive into constructive activities.

Such projects, however, had many pitfalls. All too easily, the would-be manipulators ended up being manipulated. Clergymen or social workers, however well intentioned, found themselves in danger of being regarded as gullible "do-gooders," to be used for favors and handouts. Illegal and antisocial gang activities involved in struggles over "territory," gang "wars," and "peace meetings" might receive legitimacy through the reformers' very presence. Unless the people who work with gangs have a realistic knowledge of gang structure, they themselves might be duped by the fantastic stories circulated by gang leaders, thereby reinforcing the prevailing gang mythology.

Such redirectional programs are in contrast to other efforts made by various police departments. In Los Angeles, for instance, trained officers have made concerted efforts to obtain jobs for gang members and to help them over such hurdles as criminal records and revoked driver's licenses. These endeavors seem more helpful than handouts and "crisis intervention" programs. As Brent Josephson, a Los Angeles police officer engaged in this work, said: "When these kids [hitherto] have pushed on a wall, it has always given way. . . . We [on the other hand] will be solid. We explain right from the start: We're firm. We're not going to quit being police officers."[32]

The tough approach finds support from sociologists like Lewis Yablonski, who insists that violent gangs should never be treated as "legitimate" social structures. The object of official action should not be to institutionalize or legitimize the gang, but to eliminate it. This should be done by detaching fringe members from the hard core and by incarcerating incorrigibles. The record of prisons in rehabilitating convicts up to now has been poor. Prisons do, however, serve a useful function in segregating dangerous men from the rest of society. By targeting dangerous recidivists—drawn primarily from the ranks of youngsters with a record of violence and drug usage, habituated to crime from an early age—and by imposing lengthy sentences on them, society can go some way toward affording better protection to persons and property than now exist.

The choices open to prison administrators are even more limited than those available to policemen. American society makes demands upon prison officers that reflect mutually irreconcilable concepts of what jails ought to accomplish. Prisons are supposed to be places of confinement preventing their inmates from preying on the public; institutions designed to make offenders expatiate their respective crimes; deterrents whose existence serves as warning to potential offenders; and "reformatories" where convicts are improved through education and "therapy." These purposes are contradictory. Not surprisingly, jails and jailers come under unceasing attack for failing to carry them out, especially at a time when the number of inmates confined in jail has risen sharply and when prison expenses have continued to increase.

Prisons, by their very nature, are unpleasant places. No amount of counseling, pastoral care, or therapeutic intervention can make them otherwise. To a convict, the notion that he has been jailed for his or her own good is sheer hypocrisy; no prison reformer will go far if he fudges on the predominantly coercive aspects of jail. Crime, however, also must be seen in its wider social context. Crime is not solely caused by, but is certainly linked to, a weakening in the structure of the family and in social authority. As we see it, social and welfare policies should therefore deliberately aim at sustaining the traditional husband-and-wife family rather than the single-head household.

Religious considerations apart, the disappearance of the single-head household would strengthen the bonds of society; such a change in social habits would do more to fight crime among the young than would the best police and the best jails. The reasons for this are not hard to explain. Single women in charge of a household have more trouble in imposing values and in maintaining family discipline than wedded couples; they also have, on the average, much lower incomes than married people, and financial troubles multiply their personal difficulties. (In 1981, the average income of a woman-headed household with children stood at $11,639; $28,734 was earned by married couples.) Hispanics can only benefit from reversing the trend toward the woman-headed household. Between 1970 and 1980, the number of Hispanic families maintained by women without a husband grew from 15 percent to 20 percent of all Hispanic families; in big cities, the figure was more than 40 percent. A disproportionate number of criminals come from broken homes or women-headed households.

In regard to the coercive aspects of crime control, prison sentences should be used sparingly for nonviolent offenders. "Victimless" crimes, including violations of existing laws concerning gambling and prostitution, should be decriminalized. The police thereby would be freer to deal with more serious threats against persons and property. The primary purpose of prisons—the point bears repeating—should be to segregate the violent. In dealing with convicts, prison officers must insist on (and receive public support in) the exercise of their legal authority. Hardened criminals, romantic misconceptions notwithstanding, are typically authoritarian personalities who respond only to authoritarian treatment; they commonly delight in exercising violent authority, a fact utilized alike by commandants of Nazi and communist concentration camps who used criminals to tyrannize over political offenders.

Courts should "target" recidivists for lengthy imprisonment for the purpose of protecting society. Such career criminals are likely to be those who are young, who use heroin sometimes, and who use alcohol heavily, who have a long criminal career (and thus who started crime at an early age), who have served a long prison term, and whose present offenses involve violence. Gangs like "Nuestra Familia" never should be granted even an implied measure of legitimacy; their members must be dispersed and isolated, both to protect the public and to protect fellow criminals. They should not be confused with neighborhood cliques, based on particular barrios, among whom self-help movements should be encouraged rather than suppressed.

The supreme danger to prisoners does not stem from abusive guards, those stock characters of progressive fiction. The prisoner's main peril springs from violent fellow inmates who terrorize the weak, the timid, and the unpopular (for example, men guilty of sexual offenses against children, or those who have taken a "soft fall"—who have received an unduly light sentence—or who are reputed informers). Prisons must aim first of all at securing the lives and limbs of prisoners and staff. This aim cannot be accomplished until sufficient prison space is built to secure to each convict at least the privacy of his own cell. Above all, prison officers, those overworked, underpaid, and underappreciated men and women, deserve better pay and working conditions.

Many ex-prisoners should be helped in the search for jobs at the end of their sentences. Equally important is the role of education. As Joan Moore points out, the only chance for a *pinto* (a Mexican American who has served time) to get some effective schooling may be while he is in jail. The problems of prison education are not much different from those outside jail. Education must be tough and challenging, leading to recognized and usable qualifications. Education also must be provided in a language that is understood; bilingual programs are essential for inmates who cannot speak English.

Improved education inside the prisons must go with better education inside the inner cities. Such amelioration, however, requires, in our view, a reconsideration of those many humanitarian reforms made with the best of intentions especially in the 1960s and 1970s, reforms made by educators more mindful of conditions in the suburbs than in the slums. Such reforms may have set up serious, though unanticipated, barriers to social mobility. If schools have too little latitude to punish or expel the defiant and the brawlers, their presence in the classroom will interfere with the studies of the ambitious and will provide their fellow students with undesirable models. Grade inflation has had similar consequences. If diplomas and good grades become available to all, the hard workers as well as the idle, the brilliant son or daughter of an immigrant can no longer use an "A"-studded diploma with the same facility as his predecessors as a passport to professional and social advancement.

Unfortunately, many of the programs we have suggested cost money. The problem of crime alone is enormous, given the large number of inmates that enter and leave jails during a given year. In New York alone, about 260,000 persons were arrested every year during the 1970s; of these, 65,000 or so were arraigned in the criminal courts, 28.5 percent of these being Hispanic. Construction costs for prisons are huge. Qualified staffs (including bilingual staffs) are hard to recruit for prison work. Existing prerelease facilities for Hispanic prisoners in 1980 were described as sporadic, poorly coordinated, or nonexistent. Little or no attempt was made to address the complications of language or culture. No public agency operated specifically to find jobs for young minority inmates— a serious omission, given the correlation between recidivism and joblessness. Vocational and educational programs moreover, were poorly coordinated with unions and private firms.

These reforms would cost a great deal of money. Such funds, however, would be well spent; in the end, taxpayers can only expect improved law enforcement if they are willing to pay the price.

Chapter 17

Epilogue

From its very beginning, America has vigorously debated the merits of immigration. (While the colonists wanted more immigrants, King George III called for fewer. One of the crimes imputed to George III by the Declaration of Independence was "Obstructing the Laws for the Naturalization of Foreigners" and "Refusing to encourage their Migration hither.") Since the beginning of the nineteenth century, hostility to immigration has been common in the United States, but it has increased of late. Immigration has steadily increased since 1986, as have welfare costs for these new immigrants. Many critics worry that this increase will change the United States ethnically, culturally, and politically because many of the immigrants are Asian or Hispanic and thus supposedly threaten the nation's European traditions. In 1994, for instance, California voters passed Proposition 187, which proposed denying welfare benefits to illegal immigrants. Also in 1994, the federal Commission on Immigration Reform called for fewer immigrants and for an immigrant registration system that would allow employers to check potential employees' status and avoid hiring illegal aliens. By 1996, four laws were working their way through Congress. One passed the Senate, another passed the House, and a reconciliation bill cleared Congress in late 1996.

All too many immigrants, the argument continues, come to the United States just to get welfare; the newcomers allegedly contribute disproportionately to the crime rate; they also are accused of taking jobs from unskilled whites, women, and blacks. In 1997, the annual number of immigrants was at an all-time high in absolute numbers, but not in relative numbers. The immigrants, moreover, are concentrated in five states (California, Texas, New York, Illinois, Florida) and are therefore highly visible. The presence of so many newcomers entails high costs for local government services such as schooling, medical care, and welfare. Many of the new immigrants (mainly Hispanics) have little education and lack specialized skills or knowledge of English. Overall, the more recent Latino immigrants are less well educated than the native-born. Indeed, the proportion

314

of skilled immigrants may have declined since the 1986 reforms because so many illegals (1.3 million) received amnesty from prosecution and were allowed to remain in the United States. On average, they had fewer than nine years of schooling and, once legalized, they brought in more than a million family members. The economic crisis in Mexico since 1994 has also pushed hundreds of thousands more into the United States. Illegal immigration, especially, has upset Americans, and some politicians, like Pat Buchanan, have called for closing the border and stopping all immigration.

The immigration debate has thus become a personal issue for millions of Americans and perhaps one of economic survival for some high-tech firms. The immigration controversy covers many contentious issues. The United States, for instance, provides generous welfare benefits. How and how much should immigrants, including refugees and elderly people, be permitted to benefit from them? What are the political and social costs of immigration? Do immigrants take jobs from Americans or cause crime? What of the burden thrown on state and local governments? What is the extent and what are the costs of illegal immigration? Are there too many immigrants? How many should there be? Does the United States, in fact, need only skilled newcomers? Now that the cold war has ended, does the United States still need a large refugee program? How can the United States control immigration?[1] These are hard questions to answer.

Historical Background

Public opinion polls taken since the end of World War II indicate a striking decline of ethnic and religious prejudice in the United States. But now a new specter haunts some Americans, fear of foreigners—the "new immigrants." Earlier immigrants came primarily from Europe. In 1965, however, U.S. policy changed decisively and with consequences not fully understood at the time. When the old preference for Europeans was abandoned, the gates were opened to others; henceforth, the great majority of newcomers would be Asians and, above all, Hispanic people from Mexico and other Spanish-speaking countries. Equally important in effecting this shift was the postwar recovery of Europe. Highly industrialized countries such as Germany, Britain, France, and later Italy and Spain, ceased to send abroad large numbers of emigrants but themselves attracted newcomers from Europe's rural or semi-rural periphery, from as far afield as Turkey and Algeria.

316

Epilogue

In the United States, the pace of immigration likewise grew in a striking fashion. (Between 1940 and 1990 alone, more than 18 million foreigners entered the United States legally, and millions more entered illegally.) Each decade saw more newcomers than had arrived in the previous ten years. By 1993, the annual intake amounted to more than 900,000.[2] (In addition to these newcomers who were born abroad, the United States also has a substantial number from Puerto Rico who are not counted as immigrants because the islanders are U.S. citizens who can come and go freely.)

Since 1965, the great majority of newcomers have been Hispanics or Asians. (In 1993, 904,292 foreigners legally entered the United States. Of those, 301,380 derived from the Americas and 358,049 from Asia.) As a result, the ethnic composition of the foreign-born population shifted radically. (See Table 1).

Table 1. Percentage of Foreign-Born by Region of Birth, 1990

	1900	1990
Europe	84.9	22.0
Latin America	1.3	42.5
Asia	1.2	25.2
All other	12.6	10.3

Note: The regional categories shown above encompass many ethnicities. In 1990, for example, more than eighty ethnic divisions constituted "Europe." Source: Susan J. Lapham, *We the American-: Foreign Born (Washington*, D.C.: U.S. Department of Commerce, Economics and Statistics Administration, Bureau of the Census, September 1993).

In a certain sense, the United States has become truly a world nation. Asians include newcomers from China, India, Korea, Japan, Pakistan, Vietnam, Cambodia, Laos, and other nations—an extraordinary mix. Roughly 9 million people who live in the United States are of Asian descent; those of Chinese ancestry constitute 23 percent of the total; Filipino, 20 percent; Asian Indian, 12 percent; and Japanese, Korean, and Vietnamese, each about 10 percent. Asians are America's fastest-growing ethnic group, but only in Hawaii do they constitute a majority. The highest concentration on the mainland—over 35 percent—is in San Francisco. Mexicans form the largest Latin American group, but Latins too have become more diverse than ever—with Cubans, Guatemalans, Dominicans, Chileans, Salvadorans, and a host of others.[3] The newcomers are equally mixed in terms of culture and education.

Americans used to think of immigrants as poor people who would naturally start at the bottom of the ladder. To some extent, this pattern continues because many newcomers lack education and specialized skills and must eke out a living in the clothing, meat, and poultry industries and as domestics, janitors, servers, and farm workers engaged in "stoop labor." But many other immigrants now speak excellent English and have college and postgraduate degrees. According to the 1990 census, the percentage of foreign-born Americans with college and postgraduate degrees was as high as that of native-born Americans. Certain ethnic groups, in particular East Indians, had much higher educational and income levels than the average U.S. citizen. Not surprisingly, East Indians and other Asians do extremely well in U.S. business and academia.

The immigrants also include a substantial body of political refugees (about 10 percent of the immigrant population). Contrary to public expectation, the end of the cold war did not reduce the number of people wishing to come to the United States. The global reservoir of people seeking new homes appears to be getting ever larger. Recurrent crises in Mexico, Africa, the Balkans, and Asia have added to the number of displaced people in the world. Many more wish to leave their present homes in the successor states of the Soviet Union and the former Warsaw Pact countries.

In addition to legal immigrants, a great number of undocumented aliens have come to the United States, evading the scrutiny of immigration inspectors, census takers, and tax collectors. The United States is unique among highly industrialized nations in that it shares a 2,000-mile border with an underdeveloped country, Mexico. With a population of 91 million, Mexico has a substantial surplus of people who look for jobs in the United States because they cannot find enough work at home. The great majority of undocumented aliens come, therefore, from Mexico and from Central America (which in turn also sends illegal immigrants into and through Mexico). Mexico's economic position may further deteriorate, as Mexico still has to cope with an extensive peasantry whose small-holdings become ever less competitive, now that the North American Free Trade Agreement (NAFTA) ensures free trade throughout North America. (Illegal immigrants from Mexico since 1994 include well-educated people—clerks, teachers, doctors, and others—who either can earn more in the States or can no longer find jobs at home.) Undocumented aliens also come from East Asia and Southeast Asia (particularly from China); a much smaller number come from Europe, especially Ireland.

Estimates of the total number of undocumented aliens differ widely and are apt to reflect the ideological orientation of those who make the assessments. In 1976 the Immigration and Naturalization Service guessed that between 4 and 12 million undocumenteds lived in the United States. Later, the estimate was reduced to between 6 and 8 million. A more realistic estimate is that some 4 to 5 million aliens reside in the United States without proper papers.[4] For many reasons, even remotely accurate figures are impossible to provide. No one knows, for instance, the size of the U.S. underground economy. No one can be sure of the illegal residents' collective income. No one can count their numbers, particularly because a great number keep shifting their domicile—from Mexico and Central America to the United States, then home again, as jobs get scarce in the United States, as a migrant gets homesick, or as he or she has saved enough money. In the past, if migrants could not find work or were laid off, they went "home." But the availability of welfare and unemployment benefits now keeps workers here. Recently (1997) it has become more difficult to get in *or* out of the United States because of the strengthened border patrols and fencing; hence more illegals stay in "el Norte" rather than risk being caught leaving or entering. Furthermore, when the 1996 reforms pushed legal immigrants to become citizens to avoid losing welfare benefits, 1.2 million were naturalized. In fiscal year 1997, 1.6 million applied for citizenship; the same number are expected to do so in 1998. These new citizens will have to stay, whereas many would formerly have returned to their homelands.

Diversity, then, is the keynote of the U.S. immigrant population. This diversity is concealed in part by stereotypes and misconceptions about the newcomers. Both are fostered by the crude classification scheme employed by the U.S. Census Bureau and other agencies, which use six separate categories for pigeonholing U.S. citizens and newcomers to the United States—Native Americans, Asian or Pacific Islanders, blacks not of Hispanic origin, Hispanics, whites not of Hispanic origin, and "others." These definitions follow no recognizable system; they were created by bureaucratic fiat. ("Asian" refers to geographic origins; "white" and "black" to skin color; "Hispanic" to cultural tradition.) Nor do these categories take account of broader cultural definitions. An Indian Hindu is classified as "Asian"; so is a Malaysian, an Indonesian, a Pakistani Muslim, a Chinese Buddhist, or a Japanese adherent of Shinto. Culturally, these people differ more than, say, a Catholic from Mexico and a Catholic from Sicily, even though the Mexican is classified as "Hispanic" and the Sicilian as "white."

The "Hispanic" category (created in 1973) is as arbitrary as any. (In the 1980 census, 52 percent of Hispanics also described themselves as

"white.") "Hispanic" comprises people of diverse national backgrounds—
Cubans, Puerto Ricans, Argentineans, Salvadorans, Dominicans, Mexicans,
Spaniards, and others. There are striking variations even within the same
family, say, between a person who grew up in the United States and habitually
speaks English and a relative, a newcomer, who speaks little or no English.
As Carlos Hamann, a free-lance reporter based in El Paso, puts it: "Don't
mix up your categories. The average Mexican American resident here
considers himself a Hispanic from Texas. Call them Latinos, and you will
be slapped; call them Chicanos, and you might get a broken nose."5
  In all probability, the United States will not, in the decades to come,
stick to the present arbitrary system of racial classification. To give a
hypothetical example: Juan Gomez, a blonde Castilian from the Argentine,
would be classified as a Hispanic and hence eligible for affirmative action
privileges. By contrast, João Gomes, a dark-haired Brazilian of mixed
Portuguese, African, and American-Indian descent would *not* be classified
as a Hispanic if he described himself as "white" in the census form and
would *not* therefore be eligible for affirmative action benefits. To use a
real example, the king of Spanish-language entertainment in the United
States is Don Francisco (whose variety show, *Sábado Gigante*, is the longest-
running in TV history). Don Francisco's real name is Mario Kreutzberger.
As a Hispanic, Don Francisco could claim affirmative action privileges,
were he inclined to do so—but his forebears from whom he inherits his
German name, could not have done so were they alive today. Political
lobbyists no more agree on what should be a proper classification system
than do demographers. (For instance, the National Council of La Raza
believes that Hispanics should be considered a race. Other Hispanic activists
reject such a simplistic classification. Some Americans of multiple origin
now call for a "multiracial" category, a request rejected by bodies such as
the National Association for the Advancement of Colored People [NAACP],
which fear a reduction in their clientele.)
  By 2010, Latinos will be the largest minority group in the United States,
surpassing blacks for the first time. Miami is a Latin American city because
of its large Cuban and Caribbean population and because it is a financial
and tourist center for much of Latin America. Los Angeles is second only
to Mexico City in its Mexican population. New York has a large Puerto
Rican and Dominican group; and one in five Chicagoans are Spanish
speakers. But what to call them is in dispute. Until the 1990s there was little
concept of one group of Latin American descent. People preferred to be
referred to according to their national origins: Mexican, Puerto Rican,
Cuban, and so forth. Most still prefer national origin as a primary

identification instead of Latino, Hispanic, or Chicano. The U.S. Department of Health, Education and Welfare adopted the term Hispanic in 1973, and the Census Bureau and other government agencies and larger businesses followed HEW, giving the term national provenance. On the East Coast, Puerto Ricans and Cubans use the term Hispanic; it is generally identified with yuppies and the Establishment. Latinos from New Mexico may use the term "Hispano," but outside the Southwest many prefer the term Spanish to Hispano.

In the West and Midwest the preferred term is Latino, and the term Hispanic is rejected as a government "colonial" term that includes everyone from Latin America and Spain. Latino is more politically charged than Hispanic and Latinos act more confrontationally than Hispanics. Academics and social activists are the biggest promoters of the expression Latinos. Even more militant is the term Chicano, popular in the West, Midwest, and Southwest where most Mexican Americans live. The term originated in California in the 1960s among young, radical, brown-skinned Mexican Americans. Chicanismo stood for a militant civil-rights movement and against the older, more complacent generation of Mexicans and Mexican Americans. "Chicano" came first, then "Latino" became popular because it included more Spanish speakers than just the young and the radical.

In the West and Southwest, universities mostly have Chicano Studies departments; in the Midwest, Latino Studies prevail, and Hispanic Studies programs exist mostly in the East and South. "Chicano" applies mostly to Mexican Americans; "Latino" and "Hispanic" are more inclusive and less confrontational than "Chicano." Most Chicanos reject association with their Hispanidad tradition and associate with the Mexican or Indian people. Some Puerto Ricans and "Newyoricans" have a tension similar to that of Chicanos; they reject the European heritage and identify with an imagined indigenous name or group—Boricuos. In any case, Chicano, Latino, and Hispanic are not racial designations but are cultural and political labels. One should be careful not to use the wrong label.[6]

Another option would be to have a sixth category in the census form—multiracial. There has been a rapid surge in interracial marriages—over 550 percent between 1960 and 1990. (Seventy percent of blacks are of mixed racial heritage; 65 percent of Japanese Americans marry people of other races.) The result would be to end identity politics by racial or ethnic identification; it would end group rights and stress Americanization and the rights of the individual over the group. The category "multiracial" would stop the formation of groups seeking racial preferences and social space.[7] It would also end bilingual education for such groups as Latinos and Cape Verdeans.

Americans are ambiguous with regard to the immigration issue—more perhaps than any other people. According to opinion polls taken in the 1990s, a great majority want to cut down on immigration. But most Americans (except, of course, Native Americans), unlike the great bulk of Germans, British, French, and Italians, know that they themselves derive from immigrant stock. Polls therefore come to strikingly contradictory results: 64 percent of respondents want immigration to be decreased; 78 percent agree that many immigrants work hard and often take jobs that Americans do not want; 55 percent say that the diversity brought by immigrants to the United States threatens American culture; 60 percent insist that immigrants improve the United States with their different talents and backgrounds.[8]

Americans differ from Europeans in a more fundamental respect. In Britain, for example, a naturalized foreigner may achieve high honors as a "British subject." But he or she will never be regarded as "English" (or, for that matter, as Scottish or Welsh)—not because British people are more xenophobic than others but because they define ethnicity by descent. So do Germans. A Volga German who speaks broken German is legally entitled to German nationality. But the German-born and German-speaking son of a Turk who has resided in Germany for many years remains a Turk. By contrast, once a foreigner takes the oath of allegiance in the United States he or she is accepted as an American, even if the new citizen speaks English with an accent, as did former secretary of state Henry Kissinger and former national security adviser Zbigniew Brzezinski. No country in the world is as generous toward its new citizens as the United States.

Americans' ambiguity about immigration is reflected in constant vacillations over legislation affecting immigrants. Periods marked by a massive influx of foreigners have traditionally been followed by an anti-immigration backlash. The arguments pro and con cut across traditional party lines and traditional distinctions between liberals and conservatives. This has always been the case. During the nineteenth century, the Know-Nothings, a third party, bitterly opposed immigrants, especially Catholics, who supposedly plotted with the Pope to subvert Protestant liberties, spread drink, and entrap innocent maidens for servitude in nunneries. Yet the Know-Nothings also strove for social reform and Negro emancipation. For good economic reasons, libertarians, humanists, ethnic minority groups, and employers of wage laborers are united in favoring immigration. They are opposed by an equally heterogeneous alliance made up of old-style barroom patriots, environmentalists, cultural conservatives, trade unionists, and Zero Population Growth activists who want to keep out or restrict the influx of newcomers. The Carrying Capacity Network makes the case against immigration on ecological grounds. By contrast, Molly Ivins, a columnist with liberal credentials as unsullied as the Network's, will have nothing to do with such arguments: "It's not Irish secretaries or French restaurateurs who are about to cut down the last great stands of redwood on private property in California."[9] Senator Dianne Feinstein, a liberals' liberal, wants to reduce immigration, including legal immigration. By contrast, Senator Phil Gramm, a conservatives' conservative, criticizes Feinstein for abandoning the nation's liberal heritage in welcoming strangers.

But anti-immigration sentiments may now predominate, deriving from profound cultural apprehension. The new immigrants, critics say, will transform traditional U.S. culture; sometime in the twenty-first century they may reduce whites to minority status. Look at Miami! In 1960 non-Hispanic whites formed some 80 percent of the population; by 1996 they had become a minority. Cubans and other Latins had revived and expanded Miami's economy—but that gives no comfort to, say, the elderly Anglo American pensioner who objects to Spanish on the school grounds, Spanish in the hospital wards, Spanish on the bus, Spanish on the freeways, Spanish in the stores and banks. Middle-class flight and corruption to boot! Let the last American haul down the flag!

Immigrants also incur blame for rising crime. (Immigrants, on the average, are more youthful and have more children than the settled population. And crime is predominantly a young man's occupation.) Immigrants, it is said, benefit unfairly from affirmative action programs and are a charge on the welfare system. (Elderly immigrants in fact make up one of the fastest-growing groups of people receiving welfare, even though most were admitted to the United States on the promise by their children that they would not become "public charges.") The argument that the presence of so many new immigrants upsets the customary ethnic balance is heard most often in Texas, Florida, New York, and particularly California, where the majority of newcomers have settled. Immigrants, the argument continues, contribute to U.S. population growth at a time when natural resources are supposedly diminishing and getting more expensive (in fact they are increasing and getting cheaper). Undesirable immigrants include asylum-seekers who abuse the U.S. laws designed to benefit legitimate refugees from political persecution. (Applicants for asylum in 1996 included a homosexual fleeing "oppression" and a woman from Togo who claimed she fled her native village to escape the tribal rite of female genital mutilation.)[10]

Hostility is greatest against illegal immigrants. Indeed, many members of a racial minority have joined the anti-immigration lobbies. The Californian taxpayer must spend huge sums to educate immigrant children, to pay for welfare and medical services, and to house illegals in prison. On May 17, 1997, the National Research Council released a 500-page report that estimated that California taxpayers pay about $1,178 each year in state and local taxes to cover services used by immigrants that immigrants' state and local taxes do not cover. In time, the flood will become unmanageable, write Yeh Ling-Ling and Gil Wong, both board members of the Diversity Coalition for an Immigration Moratorium.[11] Many Hispanics feel the same way. (In a 1996 poll, 53 percent of Hispanics in Texas favored reducing immigration, and 35 percent were opposed; in New York the figures were 48 percent to 40 percent; in Florida, 47 percent to 39 percent; in California, 47 percent to 37 percent.)[12] Critics of immigration fear the United States will lose its traditional character and culture. According to the pessimists, the United States has already lost control of its own borders. Optimists deny all such complaints; they say immigrants add value to the United States, create jobs and wealth, and keep the population growing and youthful.

Immigration and the Law

When the United States attained independence, no restrictions were placed on the arrival of newcomers. Newcomers came and left as they pleased. The state made no provision to either hinder or help. For assistance they called on kinfolk, friends, neighbors, their respective churches, and welfare societies (commonly made up of persons born in the same region of the Old Country (*Landsmannschaften* in German and Yiddish). Immigrants were generally welcomed to offset what Alexander Hamilton called "the scarcity of hands" and the "dearness of labor."

It was only at the end of the nineteenth and the beginning of the twentieth century that the United States enacted restrictive measures. Chinese were excluded altogether, in addition to newcomers considered criminal, diseased, insane, or politically subversive. Massive immigration continued, all the more so since transatlantic communications had undergone enormous improvements. (Steam vessels replaced sailing ships, and emigrants no longer risked their lives in crossing the ocean to reach the New World.) But whereas the earlier immigrants had largely come from northwestern Europe, the new immigrants primarily derived from eastern and southern Europe. The new immigrants settled mainly in the big cities and found employment in mining, building, and manufacturing—by 1909 immigrants formed the majority of workers in the biggest U.S. mining and manufacturing enterprises.

After the end of World War I the United States retreated into isolationism. There was a new dread of crime and of political subversion supposedly instigated or supported by foreigners; there were new fears aroused by racist and eugenicist theoreticians who maintained that Slavs and Latins (as well as brown-, yellow-, and black-skinned people) were genetically inferior to British, German, and Scandinavian immigrants. After World War I, the United States therefore set up national quotas, a system retained by the 1952 Immigration and Nationality Act (INA) passed by Congress over the veto of President Truman. Known also as the McCarran-Walter Act, it once more allotted to each foreign country an annual quota for immigrants based on the proportion of people from that country already present in the United States in 1920. The INA thereby continued the national origins system that decisively favored Europe. But in deference to the agricultural interests of the Southwest, no restrictions were placed on migrants from the Western hemisphere, especially Mexico. The INA also established a preference system to assist family reunification, giving first preference to immediate kin, a system that remains in force to this day.

More fundamental still was the change made in 1965 during the heady days of President Lyndon Johnson's Great Society. Since the 1920s, the United States had favored northern Europeans—British, German, Scandinavian, and Dutch people, most of them Protestants. This policy kept out many Catholics (except those who could enter under the Irish and German quotas). There were equally severe restrictions on countries such as Poland, Lithuania, and Russia from which most Jewish immigrants came. The coalition calling for immigration reform thus consisted of the traditional New Deal supporters—liberals, Catholics, and Jews.

In a message to a predominantly liberal Congress, Johnson thus vowed to abolish the national origins quota system, which he considered "incompatible with our best American traditions" and which also conflicted with the assumed solidarity of the nations in the Western hemisphere. Instead, the new legislation would give preferential admissions "based upon the advantage to our nation of the skills of the immigrant, and the existence of a close family relationship between immigrants and people who are already citizens or permanent residents."[13] Subsequent amendments established a ceiling of 20,000 immigrants per country and a ceiling of 290,000 persons to be admitted every year. (The 1980 Refugee Act took refugees out of the preference system, giving new powers to the president to establish the annual limits of the refugees to be accepted.)

It was a major policy reversal whose importance was not fully understood when it was made. The traditional preference given to Europe disappeared—this at a time when the member states of the European Community (EC) were themselves experiencing a new prosperity. Henceforth, Spaniards, Greeks, Portuguese, and Sicilians looked for jobs in Germany, France, and Britain rather than in the United States. In due course, the Mediterranean states of the EC would in turn attract newcomers—mainly from North Africa and the Near East.

Although the 1965 immigration law was debated, its consequences were unforeseen; Senator Edward Kennedy (D-Mass.) was totally wrong in saying what the bill would not do:

> First, our cities will not be flooded with a million immigrants annually. Under the proposed bill, the present level of immigration remains substantially the same.... Secondly, the ethnic mix of this country will not be upset.... Contrary to the charges in some quarters, [the bill] will not inundate America with immigrants from any one country or area, or the most populated and deprived nations of Africa and Asia.... In the final analysis, the ethnic pattern of immigration under the proposed measure is not expected to change as sharply as the critics seem to think.

In fact, contrary to what Kennedy said, immigration levels rose to over 1 million a year, not counting those who were undocumented; immigrants overwhelmingly came from three areas, Asia, the Caribbean, and Latin America (85 percent), and the ethnic pattern changed dramatically away from white Europeans to Asians and Hispanics.

They came to a country that had developed extensive welfare provisions administered by the federal, state, and local authorities. Newcomers became more welfare-wise, as civic organizations and also private legal firms increasingly apprised immigrants of their rights under U.S. law. Illegal immigrants also kept coming in growing numbers. So did political refugees—to an extent that few U.S. legislators had foreseen. By 1986 the United States housed, in addition to more than 1 million Cubans, an estimated 600,000 refugees, mainly from strife-torn Guatemala, Nicaragua, El Salvador, and Vietnam. A church-supported "sanctuary movement" persuaded some twenty cities to declare themselves "sanctuary cities."

The radical 1960s also saw other changes. Since the early part of the twentieth century, immigrants seeking citizenship had been required to demonstrate an adequate understanding of English and of American history and government. The 1965 Voting Rights Act, as amended in 1975 and thereafter, for the first time made a striking inroad in the official position of the English language. New legislation required multilingual ballots in jurisdictions with certain demographic characteristics pertaining to linguistic minorities."[14]

The program of affirmative action, initially popular in the 1960s, later grew less popular, and not only among white males. In 1995, in a *Washington Post* survey, 75 percent of respondents—81 percent of whites and 47 percent of blacks—opposed preferences on the basis of past discrimination. Also, as Michael Tomasky, a committed liberal, put it, "a policy of affirmative action for diversity's sake cannot for long coexist with a policy of open immigration."[15] For why should, say, a wealthy brown-skinned contractor from Mexico City or a prosperous black college professor from Kingston, Jamaica, become a beneficiary of affirmative action when no such assistance is available to an unemployed and disabled white steelworker from Pittsburgh or an unemployed white professor? The multicultural ideals proclaimed by progressive churchmen and academicians were met with equal hostility. Traditional notions of America as a "melting pot" seemed passé to the elites—but not to the mass of voters who expressed their hostility to bilingualism and multiculturalism in various state initiatives calling for English to be recognized as the "official language."

Serious objections also arose to provisions in the law that allowed certain kinds of undocumented immigrants to become legal permanent residents, and eventually citizens. A new program permitted adjustment of the status of undocumented immigrants who could demonstrate continuous residence in the United States as of January 1, 1982. Another clause allowed certain undocumented farm workers to become legal residents through the so-called Seasonal Agricultural Worker (SAW) and Replenishment Agricultural Worker (RAW) programs.

The Seasonal Agricultural Workers' provision of the 1986 Immigration Reform and Control Act (IRCA) granted legal status to more than 1.1 million workers nationwide; it was a failure.[16] It did not stop undocumented immigrants; it merely replaced them with those once legalized under IRCA who had left the fields for higher-paying jobs in town. Some 35 to 70 percent of agricultural workers, it is estimated, carry fake papers that allow them to evade the border patrol and to fool employers.

SAW did not slow the rate of illegal immigration. Instead it spread undocumented workers to other parts of the country. Once in, the farm workers departed the fields for better jobs and were then replaced by other illegals. As a result of SAW, many illegals no longer work only in California or other border states. (Michoacan tomato workers left the California fields for jobs in the meat-packing industry in the Midwest and doubled their wages, to $9.50 an hour.) Since 1986 the SAWs have set up an efficient networking system that sends friends and family in Mexico to jobs first in California, then Nebraska, Wyoming, Minnesota, and even to Maine, where Mexicans, who had been rare, now pick strawberries, blueberries, potatoes, and broccoli. The pattern is now well established: undocumented workers have replaced the more than 1 million who were legalized under IRCA, not only in California but throughout the United States.

Amnesty programs, however, reduced the authority of the United States and respect for its laws. Once granted, an amnesty was bound to raise expectations of further amnesties to come. Having attained citizenship, naturalized aliens were able to bring more relatives into the country, including elderly folk who might become a charge on the U.S. taxpayer. The family-preference policy also had a built-in bias in favor of newcomers from Asia, Latin America, and the Caribbean. The most recent immigrants enjoy the advantages of family preference, advantages not available to those European immigrants who came at an earlier time. In earlier times, immigrants were, in the main, unmarried young men. But as time went on, the family structure of illegal immigrants changed to resemble more and more that of the settled population. When immigrant men brought their families into the country, increased pressure was put on educational, health, and welfare facilities to provide additional services. This was true especially in California, above all in Los Angeles, the U.S.'s new Ellis Island, a huge, multi-ethnic conurbation and now the country's largest port of entry.

Additional legislation that further transformed immigration into the United States included the Refugee Act of 1980 and the Immigration Act of 1990. The Refugee Act of 1980 modernized refugee policy and allowed aliens to declare themselves refugees. The purpose of IRCA was to decrease the numbers of illegal immigrants by limiting their flow and legalizing those who were already living in the United States. The border patrol was strengthened, and employers were penalized for knowingly hiring illegals. As noted previously, IRCA also set up a program to admit agricultural workers when native farm workers were not available. IRCA legalized 1.2 million people previously regarded as illegals. The new legal aliens in 1990 and 1991 then requested visas to bring in their relatives, another 2 million or so. But according to U.S. scholar Frank D. Bean, employer sanctions and a strengthened border patrol did not diminish the flow of illegal immigrants. The Immigration Act of 1990 further revised the 1965 immigration law. The 1990 act aimed to reunite U.S. citizens with their immediate relatives, restrict visas for the unskilled, increase the number of visas to 140,000 for priority workers and professionals if they had job offers, and provide 11,000 visas for investors with $1 million or more in order to create jobs for at least ten U.S. residents. The 1990 act also gave more visas to underrepresented countries, especially Ireland.

Nevertheless, public dissatisfaction with immigration and immigration reform efforts continued to grow. These fears found expression in California's Proposition 187, which passed in 1994 by a vote of 59 percent to 41 percent. The proposition denied California's estimated 1.6 million undocumented aliens access to schools, hospitals, and other welfare services. Although the proposition was struck down in federal court, the size of the yes vote reflected the growing anti-immigration sentiment. Other states have since passed similar propositions.

The case against immigration was also pleaded by groups such as Federation for American Immigration Reform (FAIR), whose opposition to immigration could in no wise be stigmatized as racist. (John Tanton, FAIR's founder and chairman, had previously been a senior officeholder in bodies such as Zero Population Growth, Planned Parenthood, and the Sierra Club.) FAIR's conviction that the country faced an emergency came to be shared more widely than before, especially in California, New York, and Florida. In 1993 alone, more than 900,000 newcomers were legally admitted to the United States, as well as an unspecified number of undocumented aliens.

Nevertheless, especially in the late 1980s, when jobs were created at a rapid rate in California and nationwide, and when influential studies such as *Workforce 2000* warned of impending labor shortages, congressional opinion for a time continued to favor immigration. Congress thus overwhelmingly approved a new bill, signed by President George Bush in 1990. The act raised the then current limit on immigration from 490,000 to 645,000 in each fiscal year until 1994, and to 675,000 annually thereafter. These quotas, moreover, did not include refugees who could show "a well-founded fear of persecution" in their homelands, an easy claim to make in a world where so many governments rule their subjects with a rod of iron. More skilled people would be admitted. Ideological restrictions imposed by previous legislation disappeared. In response to increasingly powerful gay and lesbian lobbies, the act removed a ban on homosexual immigrants, and the secretary of health and human services received authority to remove AIDS and other diseases from the medical list for which a person might be denied entry.

In the end, however, Congress bent to increasing public fears concerning immigration. In 1996, after long and contentious debate, President Bill

Clinton signed a new law, the Illegal Immigration Reform and Immigrant Responsibility Act. Although the new law disappointed those who wanted considerable cuts in legal immigration, it nevertheless instituted great changes. The new immigration act took a hard line against illegal immigrants. To strengthen border enforcement, additional officers (a thousand a year for five years) were to be appointed to the INS, and funds were allocated for a new border fence. The act introduced a pilot telephone verification program that would enable employers to verify the status of newly hired workers and social service agencies to determine the legal status of applicants for benefits. In addition, the law expanded restrictions on the access of *legal* immigrants to welfare benefits. The legislation also prevented immigrants from requesting taxpayer-funded assistance after arriving in the United States; henceforth, U.S. sponsors of immigrants would have to prove a higher income than before so that they would not default on their obligation to the newcomers they sponsored.

The 1996 immigration bill also authorized 600 new investigators to arrest criminal aliens, employers who hired illegals, and visitors who overstayed their visas. It increased penalties for alien smuggling and document fraud; made it easier to expel foreigners who entered illegally, even those who applied for political asylum; and provided full reimbursement by the federal government to hospitals for emergency medical services for illegals.[17]

Equally important was the Personal Responsibility and Work Opportunity Reconciliation Act (1996). The new law vastly restricted the eligibility of most legal and illegal immigrants for federal welfare assistance. The bill grouped foreigners into three major categories for determining their access to welfare aid. The first comprised legal immigrants who had worked in the United States for at least ten years, were veterans, or had been admitted as refugees. The second group, which consisted of "qualified aliens" (most legal immigrants), were not eligible for specific means-tested benefit programs for a five-year period after their entry to the United States. "Nonqualified aliens" as well as illegal aliens and some categories of nonimmigrants with INS permission to remain in the United States were not eligible to receive most federal public benefits or many state and local benefits.[18]

At the time of writing in 1998, experts had failed to agree on the effects of this legislation. Liberals feared that family reunification would be possible only for middle-income immigrants and that poor people would suffer, especially children and the elderly. Conservatives and liberal environmentalists complained that the new legislation would simply encourage aliens of whatever nationality to seek naturalization, thereby enabling them to go on receiving benefits such as Supplemental Security Income (SSI). Conservatives, in particular, censured the legislators for not restricting legal immigration. This was a fundamental mistake, according to experts such as Mark Krikorian, director of the Center for Immigration Studies in Washington, D.C.. Legal and illegal immigration were inextricably linked; one reinforced the other if the same immigrant family included both documented and undocumented aliens and the latter relied on support from the former. And the major issues in the immigration debate—how many and who—were not addressed.

Whatever the pros and cons of the arguments, the country's political atmosphere had changed. There was less confidence in politics and politicians than in the olden days, less faith in experts, less certainty that U.S. resources could sustain an ever-growing population, less belief that the United States could cope with a multicultural future. The rightward shift also led to action by individual states. In 1996, Governor Pete Wilson of California signed an executive order cutting off numerous state services to illegal immigrants and to legals who were not citizens, including welfare, food stamps, prenatal care, and higher education. By doing so, Wilson put into force numerous provisions of Proposition 187, which was approved by California voters in 1994 but thereafter blocked from enactment by the courts. In this, as in many other respects, the United States became more like the member states of the European Union, where hostility to foreigners had grown.[19] In the United States, pro-immigration advocates henceforth stood on the defensive.

The Pro-Immigration Case

The United States is a nation made up of immigrants and their offspring. From its beginnings, the United States has stood indebted to the newcomers and the skills they brought with them. Immigration advocates thus display traditional U.S. optimism. As they see it, Americans can only benefit from immigration. Notable scholars such as Milton Friedman and Julian L. Simon argue that natural resources and the environment are not at risk from immigration. They point to past predictions of ecological disasters and show that these were either exaggerated or mistaken altogether. Take, for example, a report known as *Global 2000*, prepared in 1980 by a group of leading scholars at the request of President Jimmy Carter. The report predicted global crises of famine and disease; the plagues of Egypt would be as nothing compared with the wrath to come. But in fact, the world is getting richer, not poorer.[20] Ecological disaster does not necessarily stand round the corner.

There is no necessary correlation between poverty and a high population density. (Singapore and Hong Kong, two densely crowded urban communities, are far more prosperous than, say, Angola or Mozambique, both of them huge countries with plenty of acres to spare.) The world is not running out of food; urban sprawl does not wipe out prime agricultural land; the world's resources are not "finite." There is indeed "a funding incentive for scholars and institutions to produce bad news about population, resources and the environment." But the world is, in fact, much better off than the doomsayers prophesy.[21]

The U.S. population and income have increased, yet natural resources have not declined; the environment has improved rather than deteriorated, despite massive immigration. In fact, immigration keeps the population growing and the economy developing, which accelerates the positive trends in the availability of natural resources and cleaner air and water.[22]

The Zero Population Growth movement dreads immigrants lest the newcomers have too many children, consume too many resources, and pollute the land. But modern industry, while causing new ecological problems, also creates the means required for dealing with them. (The British, for example, have done away with the pollution-caused London pea soup fogs familiar to Sherlock Holmes; they have also cleaned up the once-polluted Thames, all at a time when new settlers were arriving in the United Kingdom from the Commonwealth.) In any case, argue the optimists, demographers have a bad record in forecasting anything—be it the future size of specific populations or the long-term availability of natural resources.

The fact is that the free market, if allowed to operate, will take care of all these concerns. Immigrants tend to be more motivated and therefore more apt to succeed than their stay-at-home counterparts, or even native-born Americans. Thomas Sowell, a U.S. economist, has found that blacks who migrate to the United States from the West Indies have higher average earnings than native-born black Americans. European immigrants do equally well. Barry Chiswick, another economist, has ascertained that, despite language and cultural barriers, European immigrants on the average earn more than white native-born Americans within fifteen years after arriving in the United States.[23] Asian and Latino immigrants also do well. For example, Chinese and Koreans have helped to revive the economy of Los Angeles and Latinos the economies of Miami and Phoenix.

Immigration in economic terms represents a transfer of skills, without cost, to the receiving country at the expense of the country that developed the immigrant's mind and muscle. Newcomers create work both for themselves and for others since immigrants need housing, shoes to wear, cars to get to work, bread to eat, books to read. Furthermore, in many cases immigrants do jobs that Americans will not or cannot do. How many Americans want to do housekeeping chores or restaurant work? Without immigrant labor, Americans could not so readily afford the grapes, oranges, and lettuce they buy in the supermarkets, although the savings here to farm wages held down by immigrants are minuscule. And prices in service industries and restaurants are kept lower than they otherwise would be because of low-paid labor, most of which is done by new immigrants.

Immigrants may, in some cases, increase the rate of unemployment among American natives with low skills, especially minority and female workers. But if cheap immigrant labor were not available, some jobs would likely move offshore; others would be accomplished through technological or other changes: to self-service gasoline pumps and mechanical grape harvesters, for example. The effect of immigration on wages, Simon concludes, is negative for some special groups but positive for most, and the overall effects are small.

Some unskilled Americans (mostly blacks and women but also Mexican Americans) do suffer from the competition of foreigners because they work for less. Nevertheless, according to the research of Stephen Moore, a Cato Institute expert on immigration, U.S. cities with a high proportion of immigrants do not suffer from higher rates of unemployment, crime, poverty, or high taxation than cities with low rates of immigration. Cities with a high rate of immigration in fact gain wealth faster and increase their respective per capita incomes more quickly than cities with few immigrants. Ironically, cities with the most immigrants—New York, Houston, Los Angeles—are the least anti-immigrant. Some native-born workers do suffer from foreign-born competition. But native-born workers in the United States should not complain too much; they enjoy a competitive advantage over newcomers because they already know the language, the culture, and the job. Nor are American workers simply helpless victims of circumstance. Faced with competition, they have new incentives to find better employment or acquire further training. To the extent that the wages of unskilled men and women fall, the benefits of additional training grow. Consequently, immigration may lead to greater self-investment in education.

Ron Unz, an economist and Silicon Valley entrepreneur, concedes that job competition from foreigners can hurt unskilled native-borns and lead to unemployment, but that that is true for all economic policies in American society. But overall Unz (and free-market economists) argue that foreign workers help reduce the price of consumer goods, thereby raising productivity, which in turn increases the number of jobs—effects that benefit Americans and the economy, and even those who are hurt temporarily.

As for those who would restrict foreigners' access to U.S. graduate schools, Simon argues against that; these foreigners benefit us and their native countries and are one of our best exports. In addition, the melting pot concept helps American high-tech industries by bringing talented people here who were educated elsewhere at someone else's expense. We should therefore make it easier, not more difficult, for talented people to come here.

Whereas skilled workers add significantly to the gross domestic product (GDP), unskilled ones add less than 1 percent, according to George Borjas of the Kennedy School of Government at Harvard. Borjas notes that, with regard to immigration, the two primary questions we have yet to answer are "how many and who?" Efforts in the Senate in 1996 to reduce the number of skilled immigrants were defeated, and no efforts were made to limit the total number of legal immigrants other than skilled ones. That debate did not come up again after the presidential election because the Republicans feared being labeled anti-immigrant.

Immigrants, of course, do not merely perform menial jobs. They also play an important part in new industries where the United States is the world leader—computers, biotechnology, pharmaceuticals, information, and entertainment. T. J. Rodgers, president and CEO of Cypress Semiconductor, a major high-tech firm in San Jose, California, notes that the major Fortune 500 companies have reduced the size of their staffs in order to cut costs. By contrast smaller, innovative, and more flexible firms have expanded and hired more staff. Indeed, firms such as Cypress cannot find enough qualified people. Cypress is not alone in its predicament. The eleven semiconductor companies that comprise the Sematech chip consortium have 17,000 jobs that they are unable to fill. Cypress itself is so short of skilled engineers that the company has started to move design centers abroad.

Critics such as Norman Matloff of the University of California at Davis accuse the high-tech industries of hiring foreigners to keep down the wages of native-born experts. But this is not so. Recruiting an employee from overseas may itself be a time-consuming and costly undertaking when it involves relocating to the United States both the foreign expert and his or her family. Keeping out skilled newcomers may have the perverse effect of forcing U.S. high-tech firms to export jobs. As old industries decayed, new forms of enterprise such as American Express, MCI, and Sun Microsystems have created new work. Rodgers also observes that "our $600,000,000 Silicon Valley company [Cypress] is run by ten officers. Four of them are immigrants."[24] Far from taking work from Americans, they have made the industry stronger. In addition, because the U.S. population is aging, the nation needs a constant influx of young, skilled workers. Without them, there would not be enough young people to pay for the social benefits destined for an ever-growing army of elderly or to help Americans remain competitive in high-tech industries.

From economic issues, we pass to questions of social concern. Do immigrants contribute to rising crime rates? It is well documented that some new Vietnamese, Russian, Israeli, Mexican, Dominican, Chinese, Korean immigrants operate crime rings that target fellow immigrants of their own ethnic groups. The ethnic composition of inner-city gangs has changed (as has that of the law-abiding segments of the population in the inner cities). But according to Joe Cobb of the Heritage Foundation, the number of noncitizens in prison is about the same proportion as the number in the general population. Of the states with the largest proportion of alien prisoners in 1992 (California, New York, Florida, and Illinois) only New York had a greater share of aliens in jail than in the general population. There is no reason to think that crime would necessarily diminish if immigration were stopped. Big-time crime has become globalized; some of the most formidable rackets in the United States are run from places such as Hong Kong and Lima.

The bulk of immigrants are law-abiding, over 80 percent are employed, and they have strong family values. Some 40 percent of immigrant households consist of four or more people, compared with 25 percent of native American ones. Immigrants are more likely than natives to be married (60 percent and 55 percent, respectively), and less likely to be divorced or separated (8 percent and 11 percent). (Figures for Mexican immigrants are even higher— 73 percent of families consist of married couples.) Typical immigrants are less likely to have finished high school, but those who do are twice as likely to have earned doctorates. Immigrants are a little more likely to do paid work than natives, but less likely to work for the government.[25] Contrary to widespread stereotypes, the bulk of the "new immigrants" learn English with as much dedication as the "old immigrants" did. (English self-study courses, massively advertised by private enterprise on Hispanic TV stations, do a flourishing business.) Immigrants are, in fact, remarkably well attuned to the American tradition of self-help and enterprise. They relish consumer goods; they have an even greater interest than American natives in high-quality products and brand names. They like to keep up with modern lifestyles and fashions. The majority do not feel alienated from their work. Immigrants like to make their own decisions without reference to what their neighbors prefer.

Some restrictionists believe that immigrants should be specially selected so that the United States will attract only winners. Peter Brimelow, in contrast, argues that the United States does not need any immigrants at all. But who can predict with certainty any newcomer's economic future? Take the case of Cecil Rhodes, one of the greatest empire builders of the nineteenth century, who founded Rhodesia (now Zimbabwe). Rhodesia later set up Immigrant Selection Boards to recruit "suitable" people. But none of these boards would have admitted Rhodes when he first came to southern Africa as a sickly young man without special skills or academic qualifications, and no capital. Neither would Rhodes have won one of his own Rhodes Scholarships (which required from applicants proven aptitude in "manly sports" as well as academic work). And no immigrant selection board could have predicted that Andrew Carnegie, a youthful Scottish immigrant employed in a U.S. cotton factory, would become a rich man. Yet Carnegie turned into one of the greatest industrial magnates in the United States, a man who provided employment for a huge army of workers. Forecasting of this kind, say the skeptics, is a trade for fools. Furthermore, no one knows how many low-skilled immigrants the United States may need in agriculture, meat-packing, the pig and poultry industries, and so on, to do jobs Americans do not want to do for low wages.

What of the costs inflicted on the United States by immigrants? According to popular opinion, they are horrendous. It is true enough that welfare expenditure, narrowly defined, is greater for immigrants (21 percent; 14 percent for natives). Aid to Families with Dependent Children (AFDC) and Supplemental Security Income pay out more to immigrants than to natives (on average, $404 per immigrant, $260 per native-born recipient). Refugees in particular receive more welfare than natives (see Table 2).

Table 2. Native and Foreign-Born Population, Fifteen Years and Older, Receiving Welfare Payments, 1979 and 1989 (percent)

	1979	1989
Natives	4.3	4.2
Foreign-born	4.8	4.7
Entered 1980–90		4.5
Entered 1970–79		4.7
Refugees 1980–90		15.6

Source: *Population and Development Review*, March 1996, p. 106.

Immigrants also receive more food stamps and Medicaid benefits because they are poorer. By contrast, the costs of schooling and unemployment compensation are about the same for the native-born and immigrants. But immigrants, on average, are younger than the native-born. Immigrants usually arrive healthy and thus receive fewer Social Security and Medicare benefits—by far the most expensive government programs. Complaints about welfare expenditures on immigrants, narrowly defined, are but a "red herring," says Simon.[26] Overall, he concludes, immigrants contribute more to the public coffers than they receive. In fact, the immigrants' relative contribution may have increased over time, rather than diminished.

In any case, welfare expenditures are only a small fraction of total government outlays on immigrants and natives. Schooling costs and payments to the elderly represent the bulk of government expenditures, Simon argues, and natives use more of these programs, especially Social Security and Medicare. Education is a long-term expense but a necessary one if the United States is to remain competitive in the global economy.

Nicholas Imparato, a management professor, and Joseph Costello, a Silicon Valley entrepreneur, argue that traditional notions concerning immigration may have to be revised altogether in considering a new character on the high-tech scene, the "electronic immigrant." Imagine an East Indian programmer, a resident of Bombay. He jointly works as a programmer with a team in California; his work centers on California; his wages are paid by a California company. He communicates electronically with his California colleagues on personal and professional matters; indeed he knows his Californian associates better than his Indian neighbors. He is not an immigrant in the physical or legal sense. But in many ways he resembles an immigrant to the United States in both his economic function and his mind-set. He lives in a world where visas, quotas, and their like have ceased to count.

Pro-immigration groups include the National Immigration Forum, the National Council of La Raza, the American Immigration Lawyers Association, and the National Association of Latino Elected and Appointed Officials. They conclude that the U.S. immigration policy should not hinge solely on a cost-benefit analysis. Politics should also have a moral dimension. Claiming to be the world's bastion of liberty, the United States has a general obligation to admit political refugees from tyrannies wherever these exist. In particular, the United States has close relations with Mexico and should place few obstacles on legal immigration from that country. These obstacles are particularly strong in light of NAFTA. The creation of the North American Free Trade Area is of great benefit to the United States, but the initial costs to Mexico may be high. Mexican peasants cannot compete against some agricultural imports from the United States and Canada but are able to produce fruits and vegetables at a lower price and thus increase their trade with the United States. Mexican village traders may be unable to hold their own against great trading corporations such as Walmart. Hence more and more rural people may have to look for jobs in towns—in the United States as well as in Mexico. Emigration to the United States therefore is a social safety valve; some argue that the United States cannot afford to shut it too tightly, lest the Mexican boiler explode.[27]

The Case against Immigration

Whereas the advocates of immigration are optimists, their opponents incline toward pessimism. Massive population growth, in their opinion, will confront the United States with a wide range of insoluble problems. In 1930, the population of the United States was just under 123 million people; by 1990 the population had risen to nearly 249 million. Census Bureau projections for the future vary; but they keep rising. (In 1989, statisticians calculated that by the year 2050 the United States would have 300 million people; in 1992, the estimate increased to 383 million, and in 1993 to 392 million because of increased immigration and amnestied illegals who, in turn, brought in relatives.) Whatever the value of such projections, the United States will continue to face enormous pressures. The United States shares a 2,000-mile border with underdeveloped Mexico and a maritime frontier with the Caribbean, whose people have a much lower living standard than exists in the United States. A growing number of Haitians, Jamaicans, Dominicans, Cubans, Mexicans, Central Americans, and others will therefore wish to come to the United States for jobs they cannot find at home. Immigration is, in part, a response to trade restrictions; freer trade would reduce the desire to immigrate. If the United States were to open up trade in sugar and clothing, the Caribbean economies would benefit and many would stay at home. Pressures to immigrate will increase as travel further cheapens and as would-be immigrants increasingly can count on help from friends and kin already established in the United States. And the presence of an unlimited supply of cheap, unskilled labor keeps wages low, takes jobs from native-born people, and curtails the modernization of industry and the mechanization of agriculture.

The most important source of newcomers is Mexico. No other Western country borders on a state as economically backward as Mexico. To job seekers from Mexico (and also from Central American countries) the United

States offers enormous attractions. These include political stability, constitutional government, and relative freedom from corruption. The United States affords a greater number and variety of jobs and new opportunities for economic advancement. In addition to these "pull" factors, there are also "push" factors. Mexico faces a long-term demographic crisis. The Mexican population of more than 91 million continues to grow at a substantial rate; it is also much more youthful than the U.S. population. At the same time, well-educated people are being replaced in offices by new forms of high technology. Unemployment and underemployment both remain high. The difference in the growth rate per capita between the United States and Mexico is striking. Conditions similar to those in Mexico exist in much of Latin America. (Mexico has to cope with illegal immigrants of its own, whom it treats much more harshly than the United States treats illegal immigrants from Mexico.) "Obviously, enormous pressures are building throughout the less developed world for emigration, legal or illegal."[28]

Striking also are the number of immigrants from Asia. (Between 1971 and 1990, the Hispanic population of the United States increased by 141 percent, the Asian population by 385 percent.) The Asian population of the United States now comprises many nationalities: Filipinos, Japanese, East Indians, Koreans, and Vietnamese, the largest group being the Chinese (22.6 percent of the Asian population in 1990). A gigantic additional reservoir of emigrants would open up if the U.S. drive for a democratic world order were even partially successful. Imagine a world in which the dictatorships that now run the People's Republic of China, Vietnam, and North Korea were to liberalize and permit free emigration. Untold more millions would wish to come to the United States. Africa is a strife-torn continent from which many might wish to escape. Additional claimants for refuge in the United States might include Russians, Ukrainians, Slovaks, Croats, Serbs, and Bosnian Muslims whose respective homelands are, or could again be, stricken by economic slumps and political turmoil or war.

Zero-population growth advocate Paul Ehrlich does not want to close the "golden door" of immigration but desires to limit population growth by encouraging Americans to have, on average, one child per couple. Immigration, according to Ehrlich, should be limited to less than the sum of deaths plus out-migrants. But for most restrictionists, the solution is simpler: limit immigration. Polls show that the majority of the public believe there are too many immigrants, especially the citizens of California, Florida, Texas, and New York, most of whom think the gates should be closed for at least a few years.[29]

For ecological reasons alone, say the anti-immigrationists, the United States will not be able to cope unless it can radically restrict immigration. No matter whether the newcomers arrive with or without proper papers, their mere presence in the United States erodes the quality of life by increasing the pressure on U.S. natural wealth—water, soil, timber, energy. The immigrants likewise make new demands on public services—housing, schools, hospitals, and welfare agencies. Such pressure will grow all the more since the United States consumes natural resources at a much greater rate than any other country. Do Americans want to live in a country with half a billion people, with even greater traffic snarls, more urban congestion, and more nationwide pollution?

Restrictionists further blame massive immigration for destroying agricultural lands, degrading natural settings, and polluting the environment. Continual immigration will exceed the carrying capacity of the environment, while access to rural and wilderness areas declines. Do American taxpayers want to pay for huge additional outlays on schools, hospitals, freeways, and bridges? Surely not, say politicians such as Richard Lamm, a former governor of Colorado and a presidential nominee of the Reform Party in the U.S. presidential campaign of 1996. Time to call a halt, the restrictionists shout!

Only the elites want large-scale immigration—the masses do not. Such is the argument advanced by anti-immigrationist Peter Brimelow in his book *Alien Nation*.[30] Economic elites need immigrants for cheap labor—housecleaners, nursemaids, busboys, grape-pickers, laborers, gardeners. Roy Beck also argues, in *The Case against Immigration,* that immigration is against the interests of working people, especially those with low or outmoded skills. But immigrants also hurt the middle class by lowering wages. An increase in the labor supply tends to lower wages, but a shortage of workers raises wages, states a 1988 GAO report. The presence of cheap labor from Mexico has kept wages low in California agriculture, for example. Immigrants are responsible for most of the population growth in the United States. If immigration continues at current levels, by 2050 there will be some 400–500 million people. To slow population growth almost all immigration should be stopped, Beck asserts.

Borjas agrees with Beck that immigration does lower wages in some sectors of the economy, such as agriculture, service industries, and construction. Both argue that low-priced migrant labor has been largely responsible for the growing economic inequality in the United States. Economist Robert Dunn of George Washington University states that a large supply of labor from Mexico willing to work for less has hurt the incomes of less-skilled Americans even as economic growth has increased. Borjas thus rejects the economic argument for immigration, which, according to him, can only be defended on political grounds.

Restrictionists such as Beck and Brimelow also contend that the United States does not need foreign investors or entrepreneurs. They say the United States has enough American workers, professionals, and graduate students in the sciences and in high-tech industries and that large numbers of immigrants are not necessary to keep the Social Security system solvent, as some argue. In the United States, the rich are getting richer, and the poor are getting poorer and growing in number because of massive legal and illegal immigration.

According to Brimelow, imported labor of any skill level is not necessary for economic development or technological innovation. He points to Japan, which achieved economic prosperity without immigration. (Japan has only 1.4 million or so resident foreigners; the United States has 25 million). Brimelow forcefully argues the political case for a much regulated and reduced immigration. In *Alien Nation*, Brimelow makes numerous recommendations, some of which came to pass in 1996: double the size of the Border Patrol and increase the size of the INS. But most of his recommendations have not yet been accepted, and many—a national identity card, a new "Operation Wetback" to expel illegal aliens—are not likely to be accepted soon. Brimelow also suggests limiting family reunification to members of a nuclear family, cutting legal immigration from its 1997 limit of 1 million or so to 400,000–500,000 annually, reducing the number of refugees, and lengthening the time of legal residence for naturalization to ten years. In 1997 the U.S. Congress failed to address any of these major problems or whether a literacy and skill level would be imposed. But Congress did revise the welfare reform bill to restore some rights to legal immigrants, especially the elderly and disabled on SSI.

Ethnic leaders, organized in bodies such as the National Council of La Raza, favor immigration because it will strengthen their respective ethnic constituencies. Liberal elites—pastors, entertainers, journalists, academics— derive pleasure from the cultural diversity allegedly created by exotic foreigners. The liberal elites equally enjoy a sense of moral superiority derived from their claimed status as spokespersons for the underprivileged, and as moral role models for the nation at large. But these cultural preferences are not shared by most ordinary Americans.

Immigration has had numerous unintended consequences. The old-style immigrant was usually a European. Most new-style immigrants come from

Asia, Latin America, and the Caribbean, from countries whose political and social traditions greatly differ from those of the United States. Moreover, the new immigrants (much like previous immigrants) have higher birth rates than the natives. Hence immigrants have a disproportionately powerful impact on the demographic composition of the United States. The post-1970 population growth, according to demographer Leon F. Bouvier, is nearly all due to immigration. (Immigrants now account for 37.1 percent of all new population growth; at the peak years of immigration between 1900 and 1910, the figure was 27 percent). The old immigrants, however diverse, all derived from the Judeo-Christian tradition. The new immigrants include Muslims, Confucians, Buddhists, adherents of Shinto, votaries of Voodoo. Given such cultural multiplicity, bilingualism and cultural maintenance programs—anti-immigrationists argue—the United States may split linguistically and spiritually in the future. Does this matter? Did not the United States, in the olden days, successfully absorb Irish, Germans, Poles, and many other nationalities? True enough, argue the anti-immigrationists. But the position has now changed. In the late nineteenth and early twentieth centuries, the United States had a confident core culture. The United States insisted that newcomers should assimilate and learn English—and so they did; there was no bilingual education. By contrast, the new immigrants come at a time when the cultural self-reliance of the United States has eroded. Mexican and Asian activists have learned from the civil rights struggles conducted by black Americans and thus demand bilingual education and seek group rights, "brown pride," and restoration of "brown dignity," while rejecting assimilation and Western culture. The new immigrants, or rather their self-appointed spokesmen, now desire official recognition as groups and proportional representation—requirements incompatible with the operation of a free market. Group rights are demanded in the makeup of electoral districts, in employment, in the award of official contracts, in education, in every sphere of public life. Opposition to such programs is seen as yet one more proof of white America's inherent racism.[31]

Multiculturists want to preserve immigrant cultures and languages, not absorb or assimilate the American culture. (The melting pot metaphor is rejected by multiculturists.) The United States, the anti-immigration argument continues, therefore must restrict immigration and at the same time promote cultural assimilation. Otherwise multiculturalism will lead to political fragmentation and fragmentation to disaster. Imagine the United States as a Bosnia of continental proportions—without a sense of common nationhood, a common culture, a common political heritage, with dozens of contending ethnic groups and a population of half a billion. These problems will become

even harder to face, say anti-immigrationists, because immigration has
exacerbated income inequality in the United States, worsened the economic
prospects of poorly educated black Americans and recent immigrants,
disrupted local communities, and—through sheer force of numbers—further
injured the environment. The United States, argue critics such as Brimelow,
will in the long run cease to be a mainly white nation; its ethnic character
will be transformed—this without proper policy discussion and against the
declared will of America's overwhelming majority. Nativists are accused
of hysteria when they talk about a threatened Mexican *reconquista* of
California. Nativists incur equal censure when they charge foreign-born
activists with holding in contempt the *anglo-sajones* and their values. But
nativist fears merely reflect the ethnic propaganda commonly distributed by
ethnic militants.

More specifically, experts such as Beck, Brimelow, and Matloff do not
merely want to protect the U.S. underclass from foreign competition. They
also criticize U.S. employers for importing highly skilled people. Business
lobbyists now call for at least 140,000 skilled newcomers a year from other
countries. But the United States already has thousands of unemployed
engineers, scientists, computer programmers, and other highly skilled people,
insist Beck and Matloff. Surely, there must be enough Americans to step
into those highly skilled positions that industry wants to fill. (Silicon Valley
executives say not true; that they need skilled foreigners or will have to
ship jobs offshore.) From the industrialists' viewpoint, Beck and Matloff
argue, it is certainly cheaper to pick foreigners; but why should the United
States aim for "a high-tech workforce...that will accept Third World wages
and working conditions?"[32]

For the anti-immigrationists, there are also good political reasons for
cutting down immigration. Latino immigrants today cluster in large
neighborhoods to a greater extent than foreigners who arrived a century
ago. Such clustering slows down assimilation and the learning of English,
according to Hoover Institution economist Edward P. Lazear, as does the
provision of welfare.[33] (Poor people who receive welfare benefits have
less incentive to learn English and adjust to the demands of the new society.)
Latino immigrants in particular now also make political demands of a kind
not made by Sicilian or Greek immigrants a century earlier. As political
scientist Peter Skerry puts it, Mexican Americans "are being seduced by
the new American political systems into adopting the not entirely appropriate,
divisive, and counterproductive stance of a racial minority group."[34]
Mexican Americans, Central Americans, and other Latins are now classified
as part of a new "Hispanic" minority. The leaders who claim to speak on

their behalf demand privileges similar to those claimed for the black minority by bodies such as the NAACP and by white liberals.

The 1996 presidential election showed new Hispanic voting power strengthened by the hurried, massive granting of citizenship to Latinos and Asians (critics claim thousands of criminals were naturalized without proper FBI background checks). The "new citizens" (approximately 1.2 million) were registered to vote by Democratic Party activists and went to the polls in record numbers. They assisted President Clinton to an overwhelming victory in California and tipped tight races in favor of some Democratic candidates for Congress and the legislature, according to exit polls and analysts.[35] Bloc voting, especially by Mexicans, appeared to push Democrats to victory in California and cost the Republicans the governorship in Florida for the first time in recent history. The Latino vote for the Democrats was a backlash for the GOP's perceived anti-immigrant agenda and has huge implications for the future. The Latino share of the vote is increasing rapidly in several key states, helped in part by the 1986 amnesty of 1.2 million illegals and their bringing in another 2 million or so relatives. Between 1992 and 1996 the Hispanic population grew from 7 to 10 percent in California, from 10 to 16 percent in Texas.

These voting changes have all contributed to a new sense of anxiety in the United States that is not confined to angry white males. Take, for instance, East Palo Alto, a Bay Area township near Stanford University. East Palo Alto was once as solidly black as Harlem. In the 1980s East Palo Alto began attracting an ever larger Latino population: between 1980 and 1990 alone, the black population dropped from 60 percent to 41.5 percent, and the Hispanic population increased from 14 percent to 36 percent. Blacks leave East Palo Alto for a variety of reasons. Some feel that they must unfairly compete with Hispanics for affordable housing because, typically, the black purchaser stands on his own, whereas several extended Latino families may pool their resources to rent or purchase a residence. Whatever the cause, regrettably, says Gertrude Wilks, a former mayor of East Palo Alto and the very opposite of a racist, East Palo Alto now feels much more Hispanic. "You almost feel that if you *don't* understand Spanish, you better learn it."[36] And the same lament can be heard in and around Miami, Los Angeles, and San Francisco.

Troubling to many Americans are the political shifts occasioned by mass immigration. Generalizations, of course, are dangerous. Cubans (who occupy a powerful position, especially in New Jersey and Florida) tend to vote Republican, as do Koreans and Chinese. Mexicans, Puerto Ricans (also Arab Americans and others), by contrast, more often support

Democrats. Vice President Al Gore, therefore, organized a group, the Citizenship USA program, to speed up the naturalization of legal immigrants in time for the presidential election in 1996. The White House even pressured the INS to lower standards for the language and history tests for naturalization before the November election. (The Welfare Act of 1996 also had the unintended effect of encouraging many more legal immigrants to apply for naturalization so as not to lose benefits they were already receiving.)

Republicans charged massive voter fraud in the 1996 presidential election, claiming Democrats rushed people through the naturalization process in order to get them to vote Democratic. Fraud was discovered in training programs to teach English and American history and in the implementation of criminal background checks of applicants for citizenship. California governor Pete Wilson charged that 180,000 of the 1.2 million people naturalized through the Citizenship USA program were not checked for criminal records. The controversy continued through 1997, when Republican congressman Robert Dornan of California sued to reclaim the seat he claimed he had lost because fraudulently naturalized Latinos and Asians voted for his Latino opponent. (Congress ruled against him.) Since the INS cannot compel people who have become U.S. citizens to resubmit their fingerprints for FBI background checks, we may never know how many people with criminal records became American citizens, contends Rep. Lamar S. Smith (R-Tex.).

In a 1998 INS study, the agency admits it granted citizenship to more than 38,000 immigrants even though there was evidence that the applicants did not meet the basic requirements for naturalization. The INS office made one processing error in more than 90 percent of the naturalization cases reviewed, and in 87.7 percent of the cases reviewed there was insufficient documentation to grant citizenship. This does not, however, indicate that all the applicants were unqualified; only 3.7 percent of the new applicants (38,850) were ineligible because they did not meet at least one requirement— five years of legal residency, good moral character, or passing tests in history and English. Most of the applicants who failed did so because they did not meet the five-year residency requirement. About 12,000 new citizens were ineligible because they had criminal records. Congressman Lamar Smith, who is chairman of the House Judiciary Committee, repeated the charge that the White House used the Citizenship USA program to the political advantage of the Democrats in the 1996 elections.[37]

Should any of this matter to ordinary Americans who want to preserve their country's existing institutions? Not as far as the mass of new voters are concerned. Few of them are radicals; most of them like their adopted country. These generalizations, however, do not apply to Latino and Chicano activists. Ordinary Americans are offended when Chicano militants deny the U.S. right to control its borders, or when activists call for the restoration of the mythical nation of Aztlán (which they say covered what is now the U.S. Southwest). Most Americans equally dislike the sight of Mexican demonstrators waving the Mexican flag on U.S. soil. Others complained when the INS in 1996 allegedly devalued standards for citizenship "to the point where naturalization is no longer a meaningful experience."[38]

What of the economic burdens of immigrants? The question remains contentious because investigators lack basic data. Estimates concerning the size of the immigrant population vary by as much as 50 percent. There are equal disparities in estimates of the immigrants' incomes, the tax rates applied to them, the range of services included in the estimates, and the range of public revenues. No prophet, moreover, can forecast the future long-term impact that any group of immigrants may make on the economic and political fortunes of the United States (The emigration of so many brilliant Jewish scientists from Central Europe during the 1930s enormously reduced future ability to make an atomic bomb and greatly enhanced that of the United States. But of course no one knew this at the time.)

Nevertheless, immigration entails costs—especially in states with large numbers of immigrants. In the early 1990s, 20.7 percent of immigrant households received either cash benefits, Medicaid, vouchers (mainly food stamps), or housing subsidies; 14.1 percent of native households received similar benefits (10.5 percent of white, non-Hispanic, native households). Second, immigrant households made up of refugees and older relatives receive more welfare for longer periods of time. Immigrant households, especially refugees and older relatives, therefore, spend a relatively large fraction of their lives receiving some means-tested benefit.[39]

These figures are subject to debate. But in general there seems to be widespread agreement that illegal aliens and those without a high school diploma now contribute less to public revenue than those who first came to the United States as undocumented aliens but were later amnestied under the Immigration and Reform Act of 1986. The beneficiaries of amnesty in turn pay less into the public coffers than the native-born. Costs are high for the young. To give an example, a family of four that makes $12,000 a year will pay little or no federal and state income tax; it will contribute only modest sales taxes, property taxes, and, possibly, Social Security payments. But the cost to the state to educate the family's two children will be more than $10,000 a year. The earnings and employment prospects of low-skilled workers (native and foreign-born) have dropped continuously in recent years.

Most immigrants with minimal job skills make little or no progress after their arrival. The cost of providing services to immigrants has added significantly to the fiscal burden of states with a large immigrant population like California.[40] Yet overall immigration is considered a net economic plus for the United States because of the high contributions of those with high school and college degrees. Whereas the poorly educated cost about $13,000 over a lifetime, the educated add $198,000 in net value in taxes paid and welfare benefits deferred.

Most experts agree that immigrants use welfare at a higher rate than the native-born. (According to the March 1994 Current Population Survey (CPS), 6.6 percent of the foreign-born use Aid to Families with Dependent Children (AFDC), Supplemental Security Insurance (SSI), or general assistance; 4.9 percent of native-born citizens use those programs.) Welfare is most concentrated among two special groups—the elderly and refugees. Taken together, refugees and the elderly make up 21 percent of immigrants but account for 40 percent of all immigrant welfare users. (In 1995, some 785,400 aliens received SSI). The number of foreign-born elderly immigrants (those older than sixty-five) is moreover projected to rise from 2.7 million in 1990 to more than 4.5 million in 2010. The main beneficiaries of SSI are Asians, but immigrants from Mexico, Cuba, and the former Soviet Union also use SSI.)

To most Americans this seems absurd. As U.S. Senator Rick Santorum (R-Pa.) argued in an ongoing debate over a new immigration bill, the United States should not become the world's retirement home. The sponsors of elderly immigrants had all signed documents promising that the newcomers would not become public charges. These promises should be honored. Refugees (numbering about one-tenth of the immigrant population), as noted earlier, make extensive use of welfare services. Political refugees tend to be older and less equipped to make a living in the United States than immigrants who come purely for economic reasons, and many older refugees do not learn English.[41] Not all self-described refugees, moreover, have in fact suffered persecution. (Allegedly, members of the Russian Mafia managed to make their way to this country masquerading as victims.)

What of the general burdens imposed by immigrants on the native-born? To begin with, we must point out that some 80 percent of immigrants receive no welfare benefits. Even illegal immigrants have their champions. A high proportion of illegal immigrants find employment in agriculture, clothing industries, poultry and meat plants, and service industries. Their presence keeps down the price of food but also keeps wages low for janitors, restaurant workers, farm laborers, and other unskilled workers. Proponents of agricultural guest-worker programs claim they cannot find enough legal workers and that raising wages would not bring out more workers but would increase food prices greatly. A 1996 report of the Center for Immigration Studies (CIS) in Washington, D.C.—"How Much Is That Tomato in the Window? Retail Produce Prices without Illegal Farm-Workers"—refutes that claim. The report found that a transition to an all-legal work force, by doubling wages and without guest workers, would only increase supermarket prices for fresh produce by about 6 percent and then for only a one- or two-year transition period. After that, prices would be only 3 percent higher.

A federal commission on agricultural workers found in 1992 that there was an oversupply of agricultural workers, widespread unemployment and underemployment, and deteriorating wages and working conditions for seasonal workers. Yet Congress in 1997, pushed by agro-business interests, considered a new guest-worker program of 1 million farm workers. The proposal was a response to congressional efforts to reduce illegal immigration, which provides approximately 17 percent of seasonal labor in the United States. Growers claim they will not have enough workers to pick their crops if illegals or guest workers are shut out. As noted above, CIS scholars deny this claim and insist that higher wages will bring out legal laborers and that growers could adjust to labor shortfalls by mechanization and more efficient use of labor. The California tomato industry provides a classic example of mechanization leading to greater productivity with a greatly diminished work force (from 4,000 to 175 pickers) and higher profits, according to U.C. Davis economist Philip Martin. California has led in the development of wine-grape harvesting. In 1997 about 65 percent of California's grapes were harvested by machine. In one day, one machine does the work of forty hand-pickers. The machine can pick a ton of grapes for fifteen to twenty-five dollars, whereas it costs thirty-five to fifty dollars a ton to harvest grapes by hand. Even undocumented farm workers in the United States experience upward mobility. According to Martin, the average seasonal worker's career as a farm laborer is shorter than ten years. Hence farm workers find it easier to better their lot by shifting, in due course, to a nonfarming job, than to fight for changes in the farm labor market.

There are thus costs to mass immigration, especially illegal immigration. The availability of cheap labor discourages employers from raising wages, rationalizing labor practices, and turning to mechanization. Low wages force some workers, such as those in agriculture, poultry farming, and restaurant work, to seek welfare benefits such as food stamps and emergency room medical treatment. The only offense committed by most illegal immigrants is residing in the country without proper papers. All the same, anti-immigrationists argue, their very presence breeds defiance of U.S. laws. Illegal aliens, moreover, include a minority of criminals guilty of drug smuggling and other offenses. Whether aliens come here legally or illegally, the charge sheet continues, they form new ghettos and change the character of entire cities. The presence of illegal aliens not only keeps wages low but also discriminates against those who are waiting abroad for a visa and those immigrants who have come here legally.

Conventional wisdom claims that immigrants take jobs that natives do not want. This statement, however, does not always square with reality, argues Norman Matloff.[42] In those parts of the United States where there are few immigrants, natives do the least-desirable jobs—but at a decent wage. The United States should not therefore import foreign workers at lower wages at a time when job opportunities for unskilled and semi-skilled workers are diminishing and the income gap between rich and poor Americans is widening. The constant influx of poorly paid workers may also discourage employers from capitalizing their operations and may thereby impede technological progress.

Low wages paid to immigrants, moreover, do not tell the whole story. Another factor is network hiring, whereby news of job openings is spread by tight social networks among immigrants of a particular ethnic group. These alleviate the employer's need to advertise and work in the employer's favor. Once an extended network is established, it stays in place. The chief sufferers are the native poor who may lack the immigrants' extended ties of kinship, provincial origin, and ethnicity.

The adverse impact of immigration on the American poor is not limited to wage employment, say the anti-immigrationists. Legal and illegal aliens alike require space for their children at school. Schools, especially schools in poorer districts, have to adjust to the presence of numerous foreign-born children who have trouble with English and who require bilingual teachers in the most diverse languages. Immigrants receiving low wages compete with the native-born for welfare, public housing, and health care. Immigrants, it is also said, bring in diseases such as tuberculosis and AIDS. Illegal aliens receive welfare benefits via their U.S.-born children who are U.S. citizens and thus eligible for all services. As noted previously, welfare use among elderly immigrants rose 400 percent in the ten years from 1986 to 1996. Indeed, a new class of permanent welfare users has come into being— elderly immigrants. (Despite their model-minority image, about 55 percent of elderly Chinese immigrants were on welfare, mostly SSI, in 1996, whereas 9 percent of natives were.)[43]

Immigrant advocates claim that immigrants create new jobs. But it is not that simple. Although they participate in the work force at the same rate as natives, immigrants have a lower per capita income and therefore consume less. Immigrants, moreover, create enclave economies by shopping at immigrant-owned stores. Their purchases thus benefit other immigrants more than they benefit the native-born. Some immigrants do build new businesses. But as an Urban Institute study found, these also have a lower tax compliance level than native-owned businesses.

What of foreign engineers, computer scientists, and other experts? Matloff points to Softpac of Austin, Texas, which claimed that the software industry needed approximately 40,000 new workers in 1994. This figure is smaller than the 51,000 new computer science graduates produced every year by U.S. universities. Although Softpac cautions against taking its estimates too precisely, these figures certainly call into question the 30,000 work visas granted to foreign computer programmers every year. Softpac also found that between 1990 and 1993 U.S. colleges and universities awarded two bachelor's degrees in engineering for every engineering job opening created through net replacement. The vast majority of technological advances in the U.S. computer field have been made by natives (as documented by the number of awards for industrial innovation given respectively to natives and immigrants). Moreover, what counts in the programming field is general programming talent, not those highly specific skills for which foreigners are often hired. The United States, Matloff concludes, has plenty of suitably qualified men and women already. It is just that foreigners, on the average, are more tractable and come more cheaply.[44] Given these objections, anti-immigration sentiment has become widespread—and not just among Anglo-Saxon whites. For instance, the Latino National Political Survey of 1992 found that 84 percent of Mexican Americans agree with the statement "there are too many immigrants." It is time, say the anti-immigrationists, to heed the people's will.[45] "Wanted: Leaders to Say 'Enough,'" wrote demographer B. Meredith Burke.

Restrictionists stress that immigrant clusters in California, Florida, Texas, and New York greatly worsen existing social problems and put an unfair burden on the states most affected. (Asians now make up 30 percent of the population of San Francisco County; in 1998, Latinos amount to 40 percent or so of the population in the Los Angeles megalopolis.) In general, foreign-born migrants are strongly drawn to large immigrant populations from the same country. Only highly educated migrants move within the United States more in response to the availability of jobs than to the presence of other immigrants who share their heritage.[46] It is time for a change, conclude the restrictionists.

The final word in the debate may be the 1997 National Science Foundation report, which stated that immigration benefits the U.S. economy overall and has little negative effect on the income and job opportunities of most U.S. citizens. Only in a few states with a high concentration of low-skilled, low-paid immigrants with families do state and local taxpayers pay more on average to support education, health, and welfare services that immigrants use.

Mistaken Solutions

Immigration has become a subject of bitter debate all over the Western world, not just in the United States but also in Canada, Australia, and Western Europe. But in the United States the immigration problem is complicated by policies determined by the courts and administrative agencies to create a level playing field between job applicants of different races. Affirmative action was originally practiced to speed up black advancement but was extended to other minorities, including Hispanics and Asians; in time, affirmative action was increasingly defended as an instrument for ensuring "diversity."

Affirmative action, however, had unexpected results. Hostility grew among whites toward Mexican and other immigrants on the grounds that they not only competed with the native-born for housing and social benefits, but obtained unfair advantages in the allocation of jobs and contracts and in college admissions. Affirmative action raised other questions. How valid were the categories used in dividing the U.S. population? Why not a special category for Arab Americans, or for African Europeans? Should skin color constitute a legitimate criterion for ensuring diversity on a college campus? (Admissions officers would surely be in trouble if they were to pursue diversity by giving special advantages to "underrepresented" groups such as Pentecostals, Hasidic Jews, or Scientologists.)

Affirmative action also has had the unintended effect of promoting corruption when, for example, some white firms have used black or Hispanic frontmen to gain contracts. On an individual basis, how could cheating have been prevented when racial or ethnic identity became a valued asset in the market place? The temptation existed for a job applicant or a student seeking admission to a college to invent or find a Native American grandmother or a Hispanic grandmother—easy enough to do as long as racial identity depended on self-identification. To avoid such cheating, the United States could, in the future, require racial identity papers of the kind once used in Nazi Germany or apartheid South Africa.[47] This prospect does not appeal to the bulk of U.S. voters, even though they harbor no sense of historical guilt.

In the field of public education the Americanizing of immigrant children fell into disrepute. The method of teaching English by the "immersion" method was widely replaced by bilingual education (now required by nine states in all school districts with a designated number of limited-English-proficient [LEP] students). In Massachusetts, the enrollment of twenty LEP students in one language group in a district triggers native-language instruction, even if there are only two students in each grade in a separate classroom taught by a certified bilingual teacher. As a result, 40,000 students in fifty-one Massachusetts school districts received bilingual education in 1993–94. Spanish-speaking students, who represent more than half of the LEP population in Massachusetts, are taught to read and write Spanish and also are instructed in Spanish in other academic subjects. Such examples have intensified the debate on bilingual education.

A recent study by the National Research Council, however, found that the arguments in favor of bilingual education were based on a number of myths. There was no evidence of long-term advantages in teaching LEP children in their native language. Further, teaching these children to read in English first, not in their native language, did them no harm. On the other hand, emphasizing cultural and ethnic differences in the classroom was counterproductive. It caused stereotyping, did not improve the self-esteem of minority children, and reinforced the differences of those children from the others. In addition, there was no research support for the idea that teachers who were themselves members of minority groups were more effective than others who worked with children from those same groups. The study concluded that the U.S. Department of Education's management of bilingual education research had been a total failure, that it had wasted hundreds of millions of dollars, had used the research agenda for political purposes to justify a program that had not proven its worth, and had not made its research available to the educators who could use it to improve their school programs.

We would therefore agree with Charles L. Glenn, a bilingual specialist, who insists that there is no reason to spend more years searching for a "model" teaching program while another generation of language-minority students is damaged by inferior schooling. And there is certainly no reason to put any future research in the hands of the Office of Bilingual Education and Minority Languages Affairs (OBEMLA).[48]

We would leave considerable latitude to local authorities to determine their own needs in public education. But we reject "cultural maintenance" as a legitimate object of public education. U.S. citizens and residents alike have an indefeasible right to speak whatever language and practice whatever customs they please in their own homes. But the aim of public education should be to Americanize the immigrants—not to preserve their status as cultural aliens. Bilingualism not only divides Americans but also limits Latinos' job and education opportunities if their English skills remain poor.

The high school graduation rate has risen for whites and blacks since the 1970s, but not for Latinos, whose dropout rate remains very high—30 percent—only slightly less than it was in 1973. The high dropout rate for Latinos is not fully explained by their immigrant status or their limited English proficiency. Recent studies show that a high dropout rate persists among Latino students even if they were born in the United States and speak fluent English—in1997, 21.4 percent of them did not finish high school and 17.9 percent born in the United States did not finish. Both these figures are higher than the dropout rates of 8.6 percent for whites and 12.1 percent for blacks (see Appendix II).

California, because of its large Latino population, has a higher dropout rate than the rest of the country (21 percent to 12 percent). In L.A. County, where most Latinos live, the rate is 28 percent. In California 10 percent of Asians, 12 percent of whites, 28 percent of Latinos, and 33 percent of black students do not complete school. As a result of this high dropout rate many Latinos do not have the level of education necessary for good jobs in the U.S. economy.

But the reasons why Latinos drop out at such a high rate are in dispute. Latino organizations claim it is because of a lack of bilingual education and courses in English as a Second Language. How then can we explain the low level of Asian dropouts, for few schools teach Asian languages though most California's schools are bilingual in Spanish and English? Hispanic students, it is charged, feel isolated and neglected and go to school in high-poverty areas. A fact seldom noted, however, is that Latinos have low expectations about the benefits of education. And Latino culture appears not to place as high a value on schooling as Asian and white cultures do, for example.

Socioeconomic status, not race, can explain the difference in dropout rates between whites and blacks, some experts insist. When one controls for income, the difference in dropout rates disappears between whites and blacks; but the Latino rate is much higher at all income levels. Although black and white dropout rates have dropped significantly since 1972, Latino rates are still much higher than those of blacks and whites (since 1972, the

Latino dropout rate has dropped from 34 to 30 percent). In 1997, the dropout rate for blacks was within 3.5 percent of that for whites.[49]

Latinos: A Profile

Latinos appear to have become the poorest ethnic minority in the United States. The 1995 Census Bureau statistics show that median household income rose for all America's ethnic and racial groups, but declined for the 27 million Latinos by 5.1 percent. For the first time in our history the poverty rate was higher among Hispanics than among blacks. In 1997, Spanish speakers represented 24 percent of America's working poor—up 8 percent since 1985. By 1993, 30 percent of Latinos were considered poor; that is, they earned less than $15,569 for a family of four, and 24 percent of Latinos were in the poorest class, earning income of $7,500 or less. (These figures, however, do not measure AFDC, food stamp transfers, or indeed income in the underground economy.) Still, the drop in income for Hispanics since 1989 has been significant, 14 percent, or from $26,000 to $22,900. Over the same period, 1989 to 1993, black income rose slightly.

The influx of illegal immigrants since 1986 has probably worsened Latino income. But even American-born Latinos have experienced "an almost across-the-board impoverishment.[50] Arturo Vargas, head of the National Association of Latino Elected Officials in Los Angeles, admits that the Latino middle class is growing but claims that most Spanish speakers are trapped in jobs like gardener, nanny, and restaurant worker that will never pay well and from which they are unlikely to advance.[51] Others deny this and say most people move out of these low-paying jobs and are replaced by new immigrants who in turn move on to higher-paying jobs. This has been the experience in agriculture in California, for example, and in restaurant work in Washington D.C., for people from Central America.

The declining income among Latinos is not well understood by researchers, but the economist Thomas Sowell has explained that low income for many groups is caused by lack of education and by the relative youth and large size of Latino families in which the mother seldom works outside the home.

The National Center for Health Statistics recently released a study, *Births of Hispanic Origin, 1989-1993* (February 12, 1998) announcing that young Spanish-speaking women are having children at a higher rate than any other ethnic group. While overall teen birthrates had been declining in the United States, high birthrates among Latina teens, especially those of

Mexican origin, had caused the increase. Latinas gave birth at double the rate of the nation's teens and triple the rate of white teens, announced the report. (Birth to Latina youth rose 32 percent, while teenage birthrates fell among blacks and whites.)

For the first time, the 1995 survey shows Latina teen childbearing rates exceeded those of blacks, even though Hispanics overall have a much higher marriage rate, fewer one-parent families, and are mostly Catholic. At the same time, Latinos for the first time have a higher poverty rate and more out-of-wedlock births than African-Americans, and have the highest drop-out rate from schools and the lowest rate of college graduation.

All of these problems have faced African Americans but now, with a growing middle class and high employment rate, blacks have improved in all these areas and now graduate at a higher rate from high school and college than Latinos. As with blacks, Latino teenagers who have babies are more likely to grow up in poverty with poorly educated parents, low skills, poor English proficiency, and less chance of economic advancement as a result. More Hispanic teenage mothers are married than are black ones, nevertheless 67 percent of Hispanic teenagers and 95 percent of black teenage mothers are unmarried.

Within the Latino community, teens of Mexican origin bore more children out of wedlock than did other Latinos because their population share was higher. But the rate of children born out of wedlock shows Puerto Rican teenagers at 60 percent, Central and South American children at 44 percent, and Mexican-origin teenagers at 38 percent. Paradoxically, although Latinos use contraceptives more frequently, teenage birth rates are up. But the difference in contraception use is small (59 percent for Latinos, 66 percent for whites, 62 percent for blacks).[52] Another disturbing finding of the National Center's study was that Latinos born in the United States were more likely "to give birth as teenagers, to have babies outside of marriage, and to have babies with low birth-weights" than newer immigrants.[53]

As a result of high immigration rates and poverty conditions for many Hispanics, their birthrates are at a record height—18 percent of total births in the United States—yet the Hispanics are only 10.3 percent of the country's population. The highest fertility rate (70 percent) is found among Mexican American women, especially recent immigrants. A high immigration rate and a high birth rate means Latinos are on the way to becoming America's poorest and largest ethnic minority and a major cultural economic, and political bloc in the next few decades. Meanwhile black and white birthrates are declining, so Hispanics in the United States will become a larger proportion of the American population even if immigration is contained.

Furthermore, Latinos (like black Americans) are very diverse: there are middle-class Cubans in Miami and poor Puerto Ricans in New York, and poorest of all are the newest immigrants from Mexico and Central America. Scholars also point to structural changes in the American economy such as the loss of jobs for unskilled and blue-collar workers. There are plenty of jobs in the high-tech economy, but these require higher education levels than most Latinos attain. In 1990 census figures showed that even among American-born Latinos only 78 percent finished high school, whereas 91 percent of whites and 84 percent of blacks did so. In addition, some employers may discriminate against Latinos who speak English poorly and have few marketable skills, seeing them as "disposable" workers. Certainly the presence of millions of new immigrants keeps wages down; the newest Latino immigrants are usually young, poor, and unskilled so take jobs in low-paying industries such as agriculture, poultry processing, and as janitors. This hurts earlier Latino immigrants who must move on to other unskilled jobs if they can find them.

For many scholars such as Frank D. Bean, a demographer, the main reason for the plight of Latinos is education, or the lack of it. Even Mexican Americans whose families have lived in the United States for at least three generations have less schooling than their parents. Latinos have steadily fallen behind non-Latinos in college attendance rates. (In 1994 only 9 percent of Hispanics over twenty-four years of age had college degrees, while 24 percent of non-Hispanics have degrees. (Relatively speaking, but disturbingly, Latinos were doing better in 1975, when 5 percent of Latinos and only 11.6 percent of non-Latinos had college degrees.)

In the Los Angeles Unified School District in 1998, 70 percent of the students are Latinos, and education levels are low because of underfinancing, overcrowding, busing, and bilingualism. Lack of skill in English is a critical barrier to Latino success. Most Hispanic immigrants who come to the United States have low education and skill levels and speak little or no English, and even the children of immigrants born here do not always acquire proficiency in English and drop out at an earlier rate than others. Wayne Cornelius, director of the Center for U.S.-Mexican Studies at U.C. San Diego put it starkly: "Limited English proficiency is the single most important obstacle to upward mobility among Mexican immigrants." Hard work is not enough; only a command of English will give Latinos a chance to rise up the economic ladder. As it is, Latino immigrants to the United States know less English than earlier European or Asian immigrants did. And because Asian students have as yet not pushed for bilingual education they tend to excel in school, have a low high school dropout rate, and a high college graduation rate.

It is estimated that in 1997 there were 7 million Mexican-born U.S. residents—almost 30 percent of U.S. immigrants, a large increase from 7 percent in 1970. Moreover, another 1.5 to 3 million Mexicans migrate seasonally to the United States for twelve months or less. These Mexican immigrants are spreading to suburban areas and more are moving to regions that once had few, if any, Hispanics. The Mexican government now has ninety-five offices in the United States. The *New York Times* on February 4, 1997, reported that Mexican migrant workers worked in the poultry industry in Arkansas, in construction in Atlanta, and with cattle in Idaho; they slaughtered pigs in Iowa, cleaned fish in Maryland, washed dishes in Michigan, harvested tobacco in North Carolina, and baled hay in South Dakota. Even Tennessee has seen an influx of Hispanics to work in the tobacco industry, and Arkansas attracts workers to its chicken-processing plants. Thousands of immigrants work in the 230 meat-packing plants of Iowa, Kansas, and Nebraska, and 23,000 have worked in agriculture in Iowa since 1986.[54] The poultry, pig, and meat-processing industries have been increasingly using illegal workers. Even when the INS deports illegal workers, most eventually return. Employers need more stable workers but either do not pay enough to attract native labor—most pay less than $8.50 an hour—or there is a shortage of local labor. The poultry industry in Arkansas, pig farms in North Carolina, and the beef industry in Iowa and Missouri have all become major employers of illegal immigrants.

The INS has improved its performance in deporting criminals (up from 1,000 a year in 1986 to 50,000 a year in 1997), in enforcing sanctions against employers who hire illegal aliens, and, as a result of new "expedited removal" procedures, in controlling the border (with "Operation Gatekeeper," for example). In fiscal year 1997 through March, the INS levied fines of $3.8 million; in all of 1996 it fined violators only $13.2 million. But this work may not significantly decrease illegal immigration.

Stepping up border patrols has had the ironic effect of pushing people into the hands of ruthless smuggling rings (so-called coyotes) and increasing the number of smuggled immigrants. Witness to this new trend were sixty Mexican deaf-mutes in New York who were forced by those who had brought them into the county illegally to sell trinkets on the streets and live as virtual slaves. Nearly 1,200 illegal immigrants died crossing the border into the United States from 1993 through 1996. (San Diego County had the greatest number of fatalities, 194, along the 2,000-mile U.S.-Mexican border.) In order to avoid being apprehended at border cities, illegals have been crossing in remote areas, and scores have died from drowning and exposure. The second major cause of death has been collisions with cars.[55]

Immigrant Cities

In areas where immigrants have been crowding in, Americans, white and black, have been leaving, citing school crowding, crime, and language barriers. One study of the relationship between the influx of immigrants and the outflow of long-time residents claims that between 1990 and 1996 3.3 million new immigrants moved into ten metropolitan areas and 3.6 million residents left for other states.[56] New York City has absorbed immigrants at a record rate. Thirty-three percent of New Yorkers are foreign-born, and another 20 percent are the children of the new immigrants—by the year 2000, 40 percent of the population will be foreign-born. The newcomers (100,000 a year) have kept the city's population steady and made the economy stronger than it has been for some time. Immigrants, Manhattan Institute scholar Peter D. Salin claims, have helped the city solve some of its problems—suburban flight, erosion of the tax-base, dependency on social services. The new immigrants in New York, Los Angeles, and elsewhere have prevented a "catastrophic" population drain and are less likely to use social services; most have jobs and own their own businesses. About 30 percent of immigrant women are said to arrive with professional and technical training, a level twice that of the 1980s. Immigrant women make up 33 percent of the female population but have 43 percent of the city's babies because they are younger than native New Yorkers. The newcomers are willing to do the low-paying service jobs that keep businesses and the city running. They seldom complain about long work hours and accept poor living conditions and social services. The new immigrants are less crime-prone than the native New Yorkers, even though they are younger. Most also live in two-parent families and behave themselves because they fear being locked up and deported. But the rush of immigrants crowds schools and churches; housing is in short supply and families must double up. Because schools are overcrowded in parts of the city and students receive inadequate attention, test scores are low in New York.[57] Immigration of Europeans into New York city has doubled since the 1960s, but in the mid-1990s the Dominican Republic and Haiti were still the largest source of immigrants. Between 1990 and 1994, 563,000 legal immigrants moved to New York, changing neighborhoods, overcrowding schools, and costing the government large sums to educate them, provide health care and police protection, and house criminals. Russians were 22 percent of the immigrants in the 1990s, up from 9 percent in the 1980s, but the Caribbean and Asia have continuously accounted for more than half of the newcomers. Mayor Rudolph Giuliani insists that the immigrants had been "the key to our success." A 1997 city report also claims that the immigrants have kept up the city's population and stopped urban flight with its resultant lost tax revenue and growth of depressed areas. Without 850,000 immigrants in the 1980s, New York City's population could have dropped 9 percent; instead, it rose 3.5 percent.

The amnesty of illegal immigrants in 1986 and the reunification of families under that act brought greater diversity to New York and other large cities—Mexicans and Senegalese populations increased, as well as Asian. Of New York's 2.5 million immigrants, about 400,000 are illegal. Immigrants from Russia and its former states are now the second-largest immigrant group; the Caribbean remains the top supplier of immigrants— 20 percent of immigrants come from the Dominican Republic. Historically, the flow from the Caribbean has been large, but since the 1980s, 50 percent of Caribbean immigrants have come from the Dominican Republic. As with other Latino groups, Dominican immigrants to New York City are younger on average than natives; and they will create a large second generation. (Mexicans and other Latinos are doing the same thing in California, especially in southern California).

Caribbean immigration, especially of Dominicans and Haitians, has increased since NAFTA became law because the apparel industry fled to Mexico to escape tariffs, creating unemployment. A late 1997 report shows that Dominicans, New York City's fastest-growing immigrant group, have fallen behind other immigrants in the 1990s. It was not always so; until the 1990s Dominicans led all Hispanic groups in income, education, and family stability. But unemployment and poverty have risen among Dominicans; per capita income has declined precipitously, and the number of female-headed households has increased.

What happened? The population grew rapidly, from 125,350 in 1980 to 495,000 in 1995, and most newcomers were poor and uneducated. At this writing in 1998, almost half the Dominicans in the city live below the poverty line. Unfortunately, the Dominicans who arrived in the 1990s faced a job market that needed only skilled and educated workers. The job market for the unskilled has disappeared. Lack of education is a primary cause of the plight of today's Dominican immigrants. In the past many were educated and skilled; the adults now speak little or no English, and 55 percent of the young do not graduate from high school. About 30 percent rely on welfare, and about 49 percent of households are headed by women. As a result, between 1989 and 1997 household income for Dominicans fell 23 percent to $6,099, while the poverty rate rose to 46 percent from 37 percent.

Hispanics now represent 27 percent of New Yorkers; and they have become a powerful force in city politics. They tend to be middle-of-the-road voters who are concerned, above all, with law and order, education, and immigration. The Hispanic Federation, a coalition of sixty groups, is an umbrella organization that focuses political pressure on the most urgent issues. Mexican immigrants in New York City now number more than 200,000. They have carved out niches in the city and in upstate New York and New Jersey, but these are typically low-paying jobs in food service and the clothing industry. An earlier surge of immigration into New York during the 1980s took most of the better, low-skilled jobs and left the newcomers, who were mostly uneducated, unskilled, and not fluent in English, on the lowest rungs of the ladder in labor, living conditions, and earning power. Yet few wish to leave and return to Mexico; most earn more than they did in Mexico and, although their wages are low they are able to send money home. They have no real alternative. NAFTA has not created many new jobs in Mexico, and a recession in 1994 caused thousands more to migrate "al Norte." Many joined friends and families in New York and Chicago rather than California, which has the reputation of being unfriendly to immigrants. A further attraction of New York was the economic revival of the 1990s. More than 100,000 Mexicans moved to the city, and whole neighborhoods of Mexicans sprang up in Queens and other boroughs outside Manhattan.[58]

While New York is becoming more diverse, Phoenix, Arizona, 125 miles north of the Mexican border, is being transformed into a Latino town. The growing economy has brought thousands of newcomers to Phoenix, making it one of the fastest-growing Latino cities in the United States. In one of the most significant demographic shifts in U.S. history, the Latino population is expanding at triple the rate of the non-Latino population. Hispanic culture and business are thriving. Spanish television is growing faster than in any other part of the country, and Phoenix is the number-two market for new Latino businessmen. Latinos spend $5 billion a year in Phoenix and own 79 percent of the businesses in Arizona.

Although Phoenix has more than 375,000 natives of Mexico, it has few of the problems facing the major cities with large Latino populations. Some Latinos in Phoenix are poor, but more are middle class, many of these being entrepreneurs who have settled in Sun Valley. Arizona has drawn Latinos because they regard the state as more tolerant, even welcoming, than California, where illegal immigration and misuse of welfare have created a backlash. Latinos in Arizona, however, have yet to develop political power to match their economic power. None sit on the Phoenix City council, and only one of eight congressional delegates is Latino. Time (and organization) may well bring them political influence to match their economic strength in Arizona.[59]

In 1996 the *Houston Chronicle* published the results of a poll on Texan attitudes toward immigration.[60] Surprisingly, Texas, which has the most Hispanic immigrants after California, supported immigration and policies that favored immigrants. Texans displayed little of the kind of nativistic hostility to immigrants expressed in California through Proposition 187. In California the anti-immigrant vote was about 60 percent but was not just an Anglo American backlash. Latino immigrants, who had been in California for a few years, also voted against continued illegal immigration. Texans, however, especially those who were poor, were concerned that immigrants took jobs from locals, cost taxpayers more in public service, weakened the education system, and raised the crime rate.

While Texans were ambivalent, overall they favored immigration; about half felt the immigration level (1.7 million) was about right. An increasing number feared that immigrants were costly to local government and hurt poor Americans but that their presence was good for the economy.

The people who had the most contact with immigrants viewed them more favorably. Asians were viewed more favorably than Mexicans. About one in four Texans believed that Latinos caused higher taxes, increased crime, and dragged down educational standards. Yet a Rice University pollster, Robert Stein, does not see an anti-immigration backlash such as the one that hit California in 1994.[61] Stein argues that Texas has closer ties with Mexico than does California. It shares a longer border, a longer history, and a greater back-and-forth movement of people and goods. Net migration has not been as politicized in Texas as in California because the Texan economy is more closely tied to Mexico—Texas does $24 billion worth of trade with Mexico; California does $7.3 billion. Texas's larger stake in Mexico and more symbiotic relationship along the border cause Texans to be less interested in curbing immigration. For example, most of the people crossing the border between Brownsville and El Paso go home each night; the illegals mostly pass through Texas.

One sign of this closer relationship is that Latinos in Texas in 1995 were registered to vote at a higher rate (almost 50 percent) than in California (10 percent). While four out of five Texans polled do not believe that immigrants take jobs from the poor, they do believe that the migrants take jobs that Americans do not want. (Studies show that in California, Texas, and elsewhere in the United States, some unskilled whites and blacks do lose out to migrants and are an economic threat to them. One in three blacks believe that migrants take jobs from them.) The misgivings about immigration in Texas, however, have less to do with economic fears than with perceptions that the immigrants do not adopt the English language and

American values. While there is some support for bilingual education, there is more support for making English the official language—two-thirds of those polled would conduct government business in English only. Overall Texans favor immigration, the reuniting of families, and helping the poor. Texans would not strip noncitizens of welfare services as Congress did in 1996. A waiting period of three years seems acceptable to Texans—they do not, however, want people to cross the border just to collect Medicaid, or to have their babies born on American soil just so they can claim citizenship.

The stakes in Texas for winning the Latino vote are high. The Latinos, by 2030, will make up about half the population of Texas. The great majority of Mexican Americans vote Democratic. The Republicans, therefore, must start to pick up a big share of the Latino vote in 1998 and thereafter, or lose Texas. El Paso, Texas's fifth-largest city, will be the big test for Republicans in 1998—only 30 percent of El Paso is Anglo American, and the city usually votes for the Democratic Party. Republican governor George W. Bush is the key to the Republican Party's future in Texas. If he can win reelection, he might carry Republicans to victory in other parts of the state.[62] He had a 92 percent approval rating in El Paso and many Latino Democrats like him and will vote for him. (He is popular, speaks a little Spanish, and makes many appearances with his wife, who speaks Spanish fluently.) Whether this will help the G.O.P. vote among Latinos is uncertain.

Republicans face an uphill fight in Texas because of their support of the 1996 laws on welfare and immigration and because they are perceived to oppose bilingual education and support "English-only" in the schools. On other important issues, however, Republicans appeal to Latinos: they are family-oriented, socially conservative, anti-abortion, and church-going. But most Hispanics in Texas vote for the Democratic Party—two-thirds, and only 14 percent say they are Republicans.[63] As the Hispanic population grows, so will its political power; by 2030 about 49 percent of the population in Texas will be Hispanic. The Republicans thus have their work cut out for them to attract the Spanish speakers away from the Democratic Party.

Even in immigrant-hostile California, attitudes are changing. Asian and Hispanic immigrants are creating a new California, writes Patrick Reddy, a California pollster. In 1996, Anglo Americans were half of the state's population; Hispanics were 32 percent, Asians 11 percent, and blacks 7 percent. If the trend continues, by the year 2000 California, Hawaii, and New Mexico will all be non-Anglo American states. The new ethnics have profoundly influenced the work force: 80 percent of Hispanics are working and, by 2025, two-thirds of California workers will be Hispanic. By 2020, Hispanics are projected to be a majority in California and will change the state's social profile. California will have a lower divorce rate than the United States as a whole; it will have a lower suicide rate but a higher birth rate. Asians and Hispanics have more durable families, a strong work ethic, and thus a healthy life style. But Hispanics in the United States, because they are urbanized and have more children than Asians and Anglo Americans, also have a higher crime rate. And Hispanics in the United States, who on average have fewer than ten years of schooling and a high dropout rate, have lowered California's ranking in educating its citizens. But because Asians are typically better educated than Anglo Americans and have shown strong business skills, and Hispanics have demonstrated a strong work ethic, California will be a better, more prosperous place, says Reddy.[64] Others argue the opposite.

A study, *The Ethnic Quilt: Population Diversity in Southern California* (Russell Sage Foundation, 1997) claims that most minority incomes, particularly those of blacks and Latinos, have dropped since 1960; only Japanese American men have improved their position, from 86 percent of median pay in 1959 to 3 percent more than the median for whites in 1989. The widening economic gap between whites and other minorities, says the study, is caused by the continuing immigration of low-skilled, low-paid laborers, lower education levels among minorities, and discrimination against minorities. The study also claims that the socioeconomic gap between so-called minorities and whites will be more severe in coming years because of undercounting in the 1990 census. (Nevertheless other experts claim a general narrowing of income disparity in the United States.)

Some activists and scholars argue that the presence of a steady supply of illegals in agriculture, and the growth of manufacturing and service jobs in southern California, have kept overall pay down for minorities; the illegals drive others out of the fields and factories because they will work for less. But others insist that new immigration flows do not account for the gap; they claim discrimination keeps minorities from improving their lot. Yet a UCLA study shows steady, rapid, and significant improvement in the conditions of Mexicans and Latinos in general. So if discrimination does not explain the gap; the continuing influx of illegals will. This influx pits Latino against Latino: in agriculture, the later arrivals push out the workers who arrived earlier, claims agricultural economist Philip Martin.

The authors of *The Ethnic Quilt* ignore this fact and err also in claiming disproportionate representation of ethnic groups in certain occupations. They state that while half of working men are white, close to 90 percent of all male lawyers are white and only 3 percent are Mexican American. This, of course, does not prove discrimination. It merely shows that a low proportion of Latinos go to law school, few go to college, and 60 percent do not finish high school. Few ethnic minority lawyers come from families in the lower-income group. Class and education levels, not race, determine the number of professionals in any group. Since the majority of Latinos are born to new immigrants, are young and unskilled, and have young families, it is not surprising that only 3 percent are lawyers or that their wages are low.

While *Ethnic Quilt* contains many useful data and sensible observations, such as information that more Latinos than Asians marry outside their ethnic group, it is wrong in its major conclusion that racism causes minorities to remain poor and that the gap between whites and minorities is growing. Economist Thomas Sowell has repeatedly proved just the opposite.

Rand Corporation researchers Kevin F. McCarthy and Georges Vernez, have concluded that California cannot keep absorbing low-skilled workers and that immigrants should be screened for education and knowledge of English. The authors argue that a skill-based California economy cannot continue to take in large numbers of poorly educated, mostly Mexican immigrants, who put a growing strain on public services and drive U.S.-born workers out of the state. They call for reducing immigration into the United States to about 300,000 annually from its 1998 level of 900,000 or so. Immigration curbs should be increased during times of high unemployment, and English proficiency should be required at all times.

In California, which receives about 25 to 30 percent of U.S. immigrants, the employment market is moving away from low-skilled jobs toward service and technology industries that require a highly educated work force. Yet half of California's immigrants are Mexicans and Central Americans who are mostly uneducated and cannot easily compete in a tight, low-wage labor market.

The United States did benefit from immigration in the past, but times have changed, the researchers claim. The shift toward higher-skill industries has created a widening wage gap between U.S.-born and Latino immigrants and has increased financial pressure on local schools and health care services. Since most (65 percent) of the yearly 900,000 immigrants into the United States gained admission through the family reunification program, the Rand Corporation report calls for reducing family-based immigration, especially from Mexico, Central America, and Haiti.

Critics of the Rand report, however, claim that it ignores immigrants' productive role in the agriculture, manufacturing, service, and apparel sectors. It was probably the presence of low-wage jobs and low-skilled workers that saved L.A.'s manufacturing industries. But Rand experts estimate that 1 to 1.5 percent of California's native-born population has left the labor market since 1970 because of competition from immigrants. Economist Philip Martin asserts in *Migration News* (1997) that the most recent immigrants drive earlier arrivals out of agriculture, and that wages remain low because of this support of illegals willing to work for low wages. As noted earlier, a National Science Foundation report found that although immigrants provided a net benefit to the U.S. economy, the taxpayers of states such as California paid more for education and public services because of these large, young, immigrant households.

Nevertheless, the Rand study conclusions are supported by the findings of two conferences published as *Poverty and Prosperity: Immigration and the Changing Face of Rural California*.[65] Among their conclusions are that immigration, principally from rural Mexico, is fueling unprecedented growth in population, poverty, and public service demands in rural California; upward mobility of immigrant farm workers in rural California is the exception rather than the rule; and public resources available to integrate newcomers are declining even though the number of immigrants is increasing. In effect, *Poverty and Prosperity* supports Governor Wilson's complaint that the federal government does not provide California with enough money to support its immigrants.

Ethnic Los Angeles also claims that Latino immigrants from Mexico and Central America are stuck at the bottom of the economic ladder at low wages and in highly competitive industries, and that the number of unskilled immigrants should be sharply reduced.[66] Asian and Middle Eastern immigrants, however, have moved quickly into elite positions in such fields as dentistry, medicine, and technology. The book concludes that immigrants have caused increased unemployment among African Americans, an often disputed assertion (see, for example, the NSF report), and that Latino newcomers have monopolized entry-level jobs in factories, hotel and restaurant industries, and clothing, manufacturing, and janitorial jobs, an undisputed fact. The study, therefore, paints a gloomy picture for the new Latino immigrants. Gregory Rodriguez of the Pepperdine Institute for Public Policy disagrees with the authors of *Ethnic Los Angeles*. He argues that Latinos are moving steadily into the middle class and are contributing importantly to the region's prosperity. The UCLA study fails to see, Rodriguez claims, the networking and pooling of resources or the growing levels of Latino home ownership. He also argues against the UCLA researchers' thesis that the number of unskilled should be reduced. For Rodriguez an open border offers opportunity and hope for very poor Latinos who, given a chance, could make it in the United States, contribute to the economy, and be assimilated into the American culture.[67]

But California pays a big price for its illegals. The Federal Appeals Court in Washington, D.C., in 1997 once again rejected Governor Pete Wilson's effort to get more federal money for jailed, undocumented criminal aliens (more than 20,000 are held in California prisons). Congress had passed a law in 1994 to allow states to request reimbursement for jailed illegals or to take custody of the undocumented felons—subject to funds made available by Congress in 1994. California received about $64 million, or half of the funds available. In 1995, California received $252 million, about half of the nation's total, but less than the $400 million the state spends. Hence Wilson filed suit in 1996 demanding that the federal government take custody of illegal felons in California or reimburse California for the total prison costs. The courts have twice decided against Governor Wilson on the grounds that Congress's allocation did not cover the higher costs. Earlier Wilson suits demanding reimbursement for costs associated with education and prison were also rejected by the federal courts.

Republicans and Latinos

In the 1996 elections the Republican party was perceived by many to be a party of white males with an anti-immigrant, mean-spirited, and right-wing image. The Republicans lost two governorships and eleven seats in Congress to Latino voters, pollsters claim. They lost many Hispanic votes, especially among the 1.2 million new citizens registered to vote in 1996. (New Latino voter registration was only 11 percent for the Republican Party in the 1990s, and turnout of self-identified Latino Republicans declined 36 percent in 1996.)

How to win back Latino voters remains a major question for the Republicans. One plan calls for ending bilingual education in California by pushing the "English for Children" initiative sponsored by Silicon Valley entrepreneur Ron Unz and educator Gloria Motta Tuchman, which qualified for the June 1998 ballot. But efforts to end bilingual education could be risky for Republicans. Even though some polls show that over 80 percent of Latino parents want their children educated in English rather than Spanish, other polls show that 86 percent of state and Latino voters supported bilingual instruction, and over 58 percent opposed eliminating bilingual education. The Republicans must be careful to get the right message across—that is, that English language competency aids Latinos and gives them access to well-paying jobs in the state's economy. The "English for Children" initiative must not be seen to be anti–Latino immigrant and should emphasize Spanish language instruction while opposing bilingualism. The Republicans, however, cannot control the political debate even though they want to woo Latinos to the GOP. At least the party is paying attention to the increasing political power of the Latino voters; if it does not, it risks becoming politically irrelevant in California and elsewhere.

Since the Republican-controlled Congress passed harsh immigration controls in 1996, its leaders have retreated somewhat from the laws they passed, fearing a Latino backlash. First, Republicans restored welfare benefits to legal immigrants, then they reduced the threat of deportation for refugees and "paved the way for large numbers of illegal immigrants to gain permanent residency."[68] Newt Gingrich, the House Speaker, had maneuvered the amnesty for Central Americans just before Congress adjourned. The reason: the poor Latino turnout in 1996 led Republicans to try to win back the Latino vote.

The Republican Party contains both pro-immigrationists and restrictionists. Facing congressional elections in 1998, and a presidential election in 2000, the Republicans are desperately trying to woo Latino voters, thus the two-month grace period to allow illegal immigrants to obtain "green cards" and visas if they pay $1,000, rather than be returned to their native lands.

The Republicans are sending mixed signals to Latinos because of this split in the party. Businessmen want their employees to get "green cards"; restrictionists want refugees and illegals to go home and apply for visas. Because the Latinos are the fastest-growing ethnic group in the United States and millions were legalized in 1986 and granted citizenship in 1996 and 1997, they have gained political influence in California, Texas, Arizona, and New York. In California, 30–35 percent of the population is Latino and can dominate voting. Up to 1996, Republicans had done well with Cubans and other Latinos because of their pro-business and conservative social attitudes and values. But California's Proposition 187 in 1994 and congressional anti-immigration and welfare laws in 1996 deeply eroded Latino support for Republicans. Even more important was the Democratic effort to register new Latino citizens in time for the presidential and congressional elections in 1996. If Republicans are afraid of being called racists, they should stress that law enforcement is the issue not race. The Republican Party in California has hesitated to back the anti-bilingual initiative (English for the Children) because it might be seen to be anti-Latino. In fact, a large majority of Latino parents oppose bilingual education and want their children to learn English so they can compete in the labor market. But some Republican leaders lack the moral courage to make bilingual education an issue for the party to attack.

The Immigration Debate Continues

Although President Clinton signed the law to strengthen efforts to prevent illegal immigration in September 1996, the debate over immigration has continued.[69] Despite numerous debates in Congress in 1996, most members failed to understand the difference between immigration policy and immigrant policy.[70] The distinctions are clear: immigration policy is concerned with who can come and how many. These days 70 percent of the admitted immigrants are relatives of those already in the United States. Family reunification, then, is the major cause of the continued high immigration figures for the United States. (In contrast, Canada gives priority to immigrants with high levels of skill.) It is unlikely that Congress will do anything about reducing legal immigration in 1998, yet much needs to be done. Although legal immigration is expected to increase by 180,000 to almost a million in 1997, there will be stiff opposition to reducing legal immigration from ethnic and immigrants' rights lobbies and from businesses. The Immigration and Naturalization Service reckons that about 1 million people entered the United States in 1996, an increase of 250,000 from 1995.

Congress has become concerned about the long-term impact of immigration on the country's population growth, the social costs of the system, and the loss of control over further immigrants to the United States through family reunification. Under current law, "chain migration" allows waves of immigrants to bring in their relatives, many of whom are elderly, unskilled, and speak no English and who then become a charge on the welfare system. Cuts in immigration would reduce family reunification or the intake of political refugees and could prevent businesses from recruiting as many skilled foreigners. No consensus has been reached yet on the size of cuts in immigration numbers or where to cut—on numbers admitted, family reunification, employment-related immigration, or refugees.

On February 7, 1997, the INS reported an illegal immigrant population of 5 million, which increases by about 300,000 people a year. Since about 1 million legals and asylum-seekers enter the country each year, minus the 200,000 or so a year who emigrate, the net gain is about 1.1 million immigrants. Another 650,000 people a year come in for three to ten years under various "nonimmigrant" visa categories. Perhaps half of these nonimmigrants stay on. As a result of all these immigrant streams, the Census Bureau estimates that about one-third of the current U.S. population growth derives from immigration. If U.S.-born children of recent immigrants are included, more than half the population growth is the result of immigration. Because levels of immigration roughly doubled between the mid-1970s and mid-1990s, the Census Bureau has had to significantly revise its population growth projections for the twenty-first century. It now projects a U.S. population in 2050 of 400 million (rather than 300 million). Some argue it will be even higher—over half a billion. Most of this population growth (93 percent) will be generated by immigrants who arrived after 1991.

Of the 5 million illegal aliens who were in the United States in 1996, about 2 million (40 percent) live in California, 700,000 (14 percent) in Texas, 540,000 (11 percent) in New York, 350,000 (7 percent) in Florida, 290,000 (6 percent) in Illinois, and 135,000 (3 percent) in New Jersey. According to these figures, about 6 percent of Californians and 4 percent of Texans are illegals. An estimated 54 percent of the 5 million illegals in the United States are Mexican, 7 percent are Salvadoran, and 3 percent are Guatemalan. Most undocumented aliens enter without inspection (60 percent), and 40 percent enter legally at airports and other entry points but overstay their temporary visas. In 1996, most aliens in New York entered legally and overstayed; in California most illegals entered without inspection. Overstayers in New York tended to have more education and higher incomes. Mexican-born persons in the United States number about 7 million; of these, 4 million are legal immigrants, 2 million are illegals, and 1 million are Mexican-born persons who have been naturalized.[71]

Instead of pushing for a lower number of immigrants (from 1.1 million a year to say 500,000 or so), Senator Edward M. Kennedy (D-Mass.) favors only a slight reduction in legal immigration but a sharp crackdown on employers who hire illegals, in order to protect American workers. With the unemployment rate so low in the late 1990s, American workers do not need much protection. Other Democrats would roll back the 1996 welfare restrictions on legal immigrants. Republicans, in contrast, may try again to allow states to deny free public education to illegal children and to end citizenship for children born in the United States to illegal immigrant parents.

No matter where they live, immigrants continue to see the United States as a land of opportunity, but they are also concerned about crime and moral values in their new homeland (*Gallup Poll Monthly*, July 1995). Only Latinos feel they are safer in the United States than in their homeland, but 44 percent of Latinos report significant discrimination (only 23 percent of Europeans report such discrimination). Asians and Caribbeans likewise face greater bias than Europeans. Multiculturalism and cultural maintenance of their original cultures are largely rejected by most immigrants, and 59 percent favor assimilation. Three-quarters of immigrants favor the "melting pot" view of the United States and desire to blend into a unified American culture. Why do immigrants keep coming? About one-quarter come seeking a better job or business opportunity; another one-quarter come to be reunited with family; about 20 percent come for schooling, and 15 percent immigrate for political and religious freedom. Immigrants in general are upbeat about the United States; they would preserve the open door but are as protective of the U.S. borders as the general public is.

What Is to Be done?

Who then makes the better case for America's needs going into the twenty-first century—the advocates of immigration or the anti-immigrationists? An answer is hard to give because there are all too many unknowns. How many aliens reside illegally in the United States? What is their average income? How much do they pay in taxes? How do they use taxpayer-funded services? How many, in particular, live on welfare? What exactly is the role of immigrant entrepreneurship? No expert can be sure.

Nevertheless, agreement can be reached, perhaps, on a number of specific issues. Under international as well as domestic law, the United States, as a sovereign power, has the right to control its own frontiers. Most Americans feel somewhat ambivalent—their own forebears may, after all, have come from abroad. But respondents in public opinion polls (61 percent in 1994) wish to restrict immigration,[72] and believe that the present influx (estimated to exceed 900,000 legal immigrants in 1996) is too high. This view is shared by most Hispanics, who support limits on immigration and welfare—much to the disapproval of Hispanic opinion leaders.[73]

Since the early 1980s, the U.S. labor market has been transformed—the demand for skilled labor has increased while the demand for unskilled labor has diminished. High-tech and the export trade have transformed the American work place—with stark implications for U.S. immigration policies. The United States will find jobs for skilled people; however, the United States does not require many unskilled workers and in the future will need even fewer as agriculture mechanizes and manufacturing plants modernize. Although jobs are scarce and wages have declined for the least-skilled workers and for those who speak little English, the INS still lets in mostly unskilled or semi-skilled people and the elderly. Reuniting families is not a sufficient reason to burden the U.S. economy and welfare system with children and the elderly, the unskilled, semi-literate, and non-English speakers.

Americans are particularly opposed to illegal immigration, though not to undocumented aliens as individuals. (The ordinary citizen will not report an illegal alien to the police or the INS, unless the citizen has a personal quarrel with that particular newcomer.)[74] Illegal immigration is opposed not only by whites but also by minority groups and even by legal immigrants. (California's Proposition 187, directed against publicly funded social benefits for illegal immigrants, enjoyed support among 54 percent of all immigrants, 56 percent of black Americans, 57 percent of Asians, and 59 percent of the general population.)[75] The general public's dislike for illegal immigration is fully justified, for the undocumented alien's very presence in the country is a violation of law. Every sovereign country in the world claims the right to control its own borders—including Mexico, which treats its own illegal immigrants with harshness while lecturing the United States on the subject. Mexico called the U.S. laws that took effect in 1997 anti-immigrant, discriminatory, xenophobic, and damaging to U.S.-Mexican relations. Mexican lawmakers fear the United States will deport hundreds of thousands of Mexican illegal aliens. Central American leaders also raised this fear during Clinton's tour of Central America in May 1997. Nor do we have any patience with those Chicano nationalists who claim for Mexican immigrants a special privilege on the grounds that the southwestern states of the United States once belonged to Mexico. The Southwest was conquered by the United States, developed by the United States, and will stay a part of the nation.

The Illegal Immigration Reform and Immigrant Responsibility Act of 1996 (IIRIRA) which went into effect on April 1, 1997, incorporates a new "expedited removal" process at ports of entry, new grounds of inadmissibility, and a new removal system to replace the old deportation and exclusion systems. IIRIRA toughens penalties on illegal immigrants and threatens immediate deportation if illegals do not turn themselves in. Under the new law, illegals who overstay for more than 180 days will be denied an entry visa for three years; those who overstay for 365 days will be barred for ten years. Under IIRIRA, it is more difficult for aliens to avoid removal from the United States. The INS has received court approval to give an alien two choices: to leave voluntarily at his own expense and not be barred from returning to the United States, or to be removed at government expense and be barred from the United States for ten years. The 1996 law also makes it difficult for class actions to be filed against the INS; in the past, class actions have led to court decisions in favor of Central Americans and Haitians. In June 1997, however, a Florida judge stopped the deportation of 40,000 Central Americans in spite of IIRIRA.

In July 1997, Attorney General Janet Reno halted some deportations of Central American illegals who were threatened with deportation under the 1996 immigration law. The 1996 law had capped suspension of deportation at 4,000 a year. Congress in late 1997 raised the cap to 10,000 a year, but that still left at risk 300,000 or 400,000 Central Americans who had come to the United States during the 1970s and the 1980s, had lived here for years, were employed, and had no criminal record.

The sponsorship requirements of IIRIRA have also been challenged by advocacy groups claiming that Mexicans and Salvadorans have insufficient income to sponsor their relatives for admission. Under IIRIRA, all immigrant family members wishing to enter the United States must have U.S. sponsors who are legally bound to support the immigrant(s), and the sponsor must prove that he has an income of at least 125 percent of the U.S. poverty level—that is, sufficient income to support himself, his dependents, and the sponsored immigrants. These provisions were intended to slow down family reunification of older, impoverished people who might become dependent on U.S. welfare programs. As of January 1995, more than 3.7 million foreigners who applied to immigrate were waiting to enter the United States. Almost all those waiting were in the family reunification category—1.6 million adult brothers and sisters, 1.1 million spouses and children, and 500,000 unmarried adult children. Over one-fourth of the backlog were Mexicans who would have to wait at least four or five years.

The INS budget for reducing illegal immigration was more than doubled to $3.5 billion in FY1997 from $1.5 billion in FY1993. At the end of 1997 permanent immigration staff will have grown to 26,000, but will only have ten more agents in each state. In FY 1996, the INS increased its apprehensions and sanctions of illegal aliens to 1.6 million, up from 1.3 million in 1995. Most returned voluntarily; 72,500 fought their return to Mexico. The Border Patrol caught 380,000 illegal aliens in the first four months of FY 1997, down from 435,000 in the first four months of FY 1995. (The total number of apprehensions in 1996 was 1,507,020.)

Porous sections of the U.S. border were reinforced in 1997. Operation Gatekeeper was extended eastward into California's Imperial Valley from south of San Diego. The aim is to cripple major smuggling rings out of Tijuana which have now moved to the area of El Centro. A similar effort, "Operation Rio Grande," was undertaken in August around Brownsville, Texas. This drive against smuggling rings will be opened westward along the New Mexico and Texas borders to link up with "Hold the Line" in El Paso, "Safeguard" in Arizona, and "Gatekeeper" in California. Efforts to stem the flow of illegals have been hampered by lack of personnel to cover the more rugged areas. Although arrests increased 41 percent in 1997 in the San Diego area and doubled in the El Centro sector, illegals still get through elsewhere along the border.

As noted above, last year's immigration act restricted many deportees' access to appeals and barred suits by people placed into new "expedited removal" proceedings at airports and borders. Also prohibited were class-action complaints against INS policies. In San Francisco, a three-judge panel ruled in May 1997 that Congress acted legally in 1996 in restricting court reviews for some 400,000 late amnesty applications for the 1986 amnesty law. In ten years 2.7 million illegals received legal status under IRCA at a cost of $78.7 billion, or $29,148 per illegal.[76] Yet Congress is considering another amnesty for Central American illegals if they pay $1,000 while awaiting a visa in the United States!

The INS has been lax in finding and deporting illegal aliens who commit crimes and who defraud the United States by obtaining documents from corrupt officials. Until 1998, the INS seldom deported criminals after they were released from prison, and one INS office issued 4,100 work permits to ineligible aliens.[77] The INS defends its poor record by claiming lack of detention space, work overload, the deportation system, and underfunding. At this writing in 1998, there are almost 500,000 illegal aliens tied up in deportation hearings. In August 1997 the U.S. Commission on Immigration (formed in 1990) recommended abolishing the deeply troubled INS and parceling out its duties to other government departments and agencies. The Justice Department would retain responsibility for control of the border and removal of illegal immigrants; the State Department would handle immigration services and benefits such as citizenship requests; and the Labor Department would enforce rules covering the hiring of foreign workers. Congress was briefed on the report, "Structuring, Organizing and Managing an Effective Immigration System," and seemed to support the proposal to separate INS duties along functional lines, perhaps because of exasperation with the INS's inability to cope with massive requests for citizenship, with weeding out criminal aliens, and with cracking down on the flow of illegals.

The commission believes breaking up the INS into its four main components—border and interior enforcement, benefits and visas, work place labor standards, and an appeals process for enforcement actions— will work better than the present system. For example, the enforcement function would include removing legal immigrants and smashing smuggler rings, and would be handled by a new bureau or division of the Justice Department.[78]

But there are other problems stemming from the INS's inability to control America's borders. George Vernez, in a 1996 report of the Rand Corporation, "National Security Migration: How Strong the Link?" argues that there are two immigration-related threats to national security. One is potential loss of confidence in the federal government's ability to protect its citizens from illegal immigrants, drug traffickers, and terrorists. The second threat is the possibility of a massive, uncontrolled flow of migrants across the Mexican border. (An estimated 1 million people are caught crossing the Mexican border illegally each year, but about 300,000 get through.) If Mexico's relatively peaceful political transition were to be interrupted, and its economy were to collapse, the flight from Mexico to the United States might become uncontrollable. Moreover, the ongoing concentration of migrants in the western United States might lead to a divergence of interests between the eastern and western parts of the country. In the East, English would continue to dominate, because the East would still see its future tied to Europe's. In the West, by contrast, English and Spanish would compete for dominance, while the region as a whole would see its future linked to the Pacific Rim. This divergence would grow over time as an ever-increasing share of the population would have its roots in Mexico, Central and South America, the Philippines, Japan, Korea, and China. Already the great majority of the 6.5 million immigrants into California are from Latin and Asian countries. The children of these immigrants account for almost two-thirds of the growth in the population of California.

We are in general agreement with the Personal Responsibility and Work Opportunity Reconciliation Act (1996), which imposes serious restrictions on welfare assistance for certain legal immigrants as well as illegal aliens. Aid should not be available to newcomers unless they have lived in the United States and paid taxes in the United States for a reasonable period. But, in our opinion, some allowance should be made for children, including the children of illegal immigrants. They should be admitted to public schools, lest they become part of a juvenile illiterate and unskilled underclass. We need more skilled workers for the future, not more uneducated alienated ones. The same exception should be made for emergency treatment in hospitals. We do not expect a physician or a nurse about to give emergency treatment to a sick person to ask for that patient's green card or passport. Public health of the entire population should be protected; legals and illegals cannot be separated for health services.

The August 22, 1996, welfare law cut off many federal benefits from noncitizens. The Congressional Budget Office noted that 500,000 legal immigrants would lose SSI benefits in the summer of 1997 under the 1996 welfare law. (Indigent elderly and the disabled get up to $484 a month, $726 a month for a couple.) During 1997 numerous suggested changes worked their way through Congress. The Clinton administration and congressional leaders agreed to restore disability and health benefits to several hundred thousand legal immigrants as part of a deal on the five-year balanced budget plan. (The House passed one such resolution on May 20, 1997 (333 to 99). The amount of money to be spent was $14 million.) Republicans are less supportive than Democrats, but some benefits were restored, such as SSI and Medicaid benefits for elderly and disabled legal immigrants.

The Democrats want to restore SSI and Medicaid not only to all disabled legal immigrants but also to those who became disabled after August 1996. The Republicans, on the other hand, would restore benefits only to those who received them up to August 22, not to those who became disabled after that date. The Republican bill would also deny legal immigrants SSI benefits if the individual who sponsored them earned more than 150 percent of the federal poverty level (about $20,000 a year). A congressional bill would make new immigrants sign legal documents swearing that they will not become public charges while they are noncitizens, and make immigrants subject to deportation if in their first three years they receive welfare for more than twelve months.

Still, in spite of all the complaining, the Welfare Reform Act of 1966 appears to be working. Thousands of people forced from the welfare rolls have found ways to earn through work what they got on welfare. About half have higher incomes than they did on welfare, and the other half have slightly lower incomes, but few have become destitute. The assumption that people cannot get by without welfare has proven wrong in many places. While wages were low on average, (about $170 a week), some still got food stamps to help them get by.[79]

In 1996, low-wage employers such as the Marriott hotel chain, as well as state governors and mayors of cities such as New York, began to promote naturalization in order to shift the cost of providing welfare benefits to the federal government. (Mark Krikorian of *CIS News* made this charge on September 26, 1996.) Restaurant and hotel owners (and New York Mayor Giuliani) were offering citizenship lessons to enable low-paid staff to become citizens so they could collect welfare benefits such as food stamps. In other words, companies such as Marriott, rather than pay a living wage, want the taxpayer to subsidize low wages by giving people food stamps.

Immigrant use of welfare varies widely, according to a UCLA Medical School report issued in 1997. For example, while only 6 percent of poor Mexican immigrants receive Supplemental Security Income, 46 percent of poor Asians and 44 percent of poor Cubans do. In the United States as a whole, about 13 percent of poor people receive SSI checks. A high proportion of Vietnamese and Cubans receive SSI, probably because they came to the United States as older refugees and are entitled to a range of aid programs.

Mexicans, on the other hand, are generally younger and not eligible for SSI or are in the country illegally and therefore unable to get welfare. But Latino immigrants have been poor—22 percent live in poverty, in contrast to 12.9 percent of U.S. natives—and unskilled. Since Latinos are poor, their use of public aid, including public education and other services, is considerable. Because Mexicans account for 28 percent of the U.S.'s foreign-born, are poor, less well educated, and mostly unskilled, they live in poverty at double the rate of U.S. residents. Within fifteen years after arriving, most move out of poverty into a growing Latino middle class who run small businesses, restaurants, and light industries.[80]

A troubling question remains—how should illegal aliens be traced? We welcome the Clinton administration's recent attempts to strengthen the INS and increase its personnel; we agree with the plans to break up the INS. But we reject employer sanctions. As Steven H. Legomsky, a distinguished U.S. legal scholar points out, employer sanctions have indeed created new jobs for Americans; unfortunately, these are in a burgeoning industry that manufactures those fraudulent documents that are now presented en masse by undocumented job seekers to employers. It should not be an employer's responsibility to act as an unpaid immigration inspector. Employer sanctions seem to us just another form of unfunded mandate. Nor do we trust projects designed to set up a central, nationwide registry to create a national identification card. Such systems smack of a police state and would not be acceptable to the majority of U.S. citizens. Such systems, moreover, take no account of the unreliable nature of computer storage. Computerized systems face the ever-present dangers of human error, electronic breakdown, and even sabotage through the introduction of "viruses." American citizens seeking jobs should not be exposed to the vagaries of any such systems. Nor should Hispanic-Americans have to "prove" they are legal! Dealing with illegal aliens is the task of the INS. This agency deserves to be well financed and well staffed. It also merits support by the courts—that is, it should be able to hold quick hearings to determine legality and then implement rapid deportation for those who are guilty of violating immigration laws. Coordination, moreover, must improve between different government agencies. Welfare officers, police officers, and immigration officers should be encouraged and empowered to exchange information efficiently on who is, or is not, a legal resident in the United States

Should children born to illegal aliens in the United States be entitled to U.S. citizenship? At present they are so entitled under the U.S. Constitution, but conservative critics call for an amendment to take away this right. We agree that those who violate U.S. law should not nevertheless gain citizenship benefits for their children. But the Constitution should only be amended for reasons of extreme urgency. This is not such a reason.

What of the economic benefits of immigration? In the olden days, immigration remained unregulated by the state; immigrants came when jobs were plentiful and ceased to come or left when times were hard. The federal government provided no benefits to newcomers who relied for assistance on their kinfolk, neighbors, churches, self-help societies, or local authorities controlled by organizations such as Tammany Hall. Now, in contrast, the United States has a most elaborate welfare structure operating on a federal, a state, and a local level. Immigrants naturally make use of such assistance. As poor immigrants qualify for citizenship, they are likely to go on supporting the welfare state. Their support of a system that benefited them is understandable, but it does not serve the interests of taxpayers at large.

What of the poor and unqualified who wish to come to the United States? The admirable sentiments of Emma Lazarus are expressed in a sonnet engraved on a memorial tablet on the Statue of Liberty: "Give me your tired, your poor, / Your huddled masses yearning to breathe free." Unfortunately the sonnet is a poor guide to present policy. We ourselves would rather bid the world's huddled masses to stay at home and send us the educated and skilled. The great majority of the world's population is desperately poor and uneducated by U.S. standards. If the United States were to follow a truly nondiscriminatory admissions policy, it would have to admit every newcomer who chose to come to these shores. The U.S.'s own poor and unskilled would be the first to object. Public opinion overwhelmingly demands a more restrictive policy that also applies to the admission of immigrants' family members. Family members are now so broadly defined that it is the immigrants themselves who decide who should, or should not, be accepted. The system needs to be altered in such a way that only members of a citizen's immediate nuclear family are eligible for admission, and that once admitted the new entrants must not be allowed to become charges on the U.S. taxpayer for at least ten years.

We once again emphasize, therefore, that the United States should cease to be a welfare agency for poor and aged foreigners. Social benefits such as Medicare, Medicaid, and SSI should be restricted to means-tested U.S. citizens; long-time, tax-paying legal immigrants were excluded in 1996. Legal immigrants who rushed to become citizens in 1996 should have had to wait ten years before qualifying for welfare benefits. (A record number of legal immigrants—1.8 million—sought citizenship in 1997 to avoid losing benefits.)

Illegal immigration was a fluctuating phenomenon that reacted quickly to economic shifts.[81] Illegal immigration in California rose from 100,000 to 200,000 a year in the 1980s and, in response to poor economic conditions, declined to about 125,000 a year in the early 1990s. The 1986–99 amnesty program sent illegal immigrants northward in hope of further amnesties or to be reunited with recently legalized family members. But welfare benefits were tied to citizenship in 1996, and the border was more closely watched so illegals could not get in or out as easily as in the past. The ebb and flow of immigration in response to economic conditions is no longer as fully operative.

In 1996 more than a million immigrants became citizens to avoid losing state and federal benefits. (They would have lost Aid to Families with Dependent Children, SSI, and food stamp benefits.) According to Michael Fix of the Urban Institute, recent U.S. policy induced people to become citizens in order to keep or get benefits, not to accept American values and institutions. The welfare bill has inadvertently helped produce profound changes in the meaning of citizenship. In addition, the INS had been carrying out an active campaign for naturalization and had organized mass swearing-in ceremonies, regardless of whether the prospective citizens spoke or read English or knew much about American history and government. By forcing people to choose citizenship or lose their benefits, the government has inadvertently forced many legal immigrants to stay in the United States without adequate preparation to perform as citizens or to uphold American values.

In more general terms, courts and legislatures alike should be discouraged from further diminishing the difference in status between resident aliens and citizens. The public should likewise insist that U.S. law be upheld—no further amnesties for illegal aliens, which naturally raise the expectation that illegal conduct will once more be rewarded in the future. Stop the reuniting of families with elderly relatives; let in only the immediate family members and the skilled and educated; lower the immigration quota from 1 million to half a million or fewer for a period of years.

The United States, in our opinion, should further restrict the right of asylum. Most professed asylum-seekers are, in fact, economic refugees. Moreover, spokespersons for asylum rights keep trying to extend the criteria according to which asylum-seekers ought to be admitted. Many foreign governments discriminate against homosexuals, persecute feminists, and imprison abortionists. Ought the United States then to admit all foreign homosexuals, feminists, and abortionists? How about victims of ritual genital mutilation of women in sub-Saharan Africa and Egypt? Should they enjoy asylum rights as well? As Mark Krikorian, an immigration expert, puts it, for many U.S. advocates of asylum rights, "the battle over asylum seems to have far less to do with giving shelter to persecuted individuals than with some larger quest to remake the American legal norms and establish victim status for a number of officially recognized groups."[82]

What of immigration's economic benefits and economic burdens? As we have said before, a definitive answer is hard to give, since opponents and proponents of immigration alike must make do with inadequate statistics. Overall, immigrants make a positive and significant contribution to the United States. Common sense, however, suggests that the United States should not admit so many unskilled workers at a time when the U.S.'s own unskilled poor are increasingly hard to employ. Unskilled Americans are the most vulnerable people within the U.S. army of labor; for political, though not for economic reasons, they merit protection in the struggle for scarce jobs. The admission of more poor people to the United States, moreover, would widen the growing numerical disproportion between the poor and the rich— another reason for keeping out poor aliens except those who arrive as guest-workers on limited contracts. Even in agriculture, does the United States really need 500,000 or so *braçeros* each year? If wages were doubled, native labor would go to the fields, according to Philip Martin, an agricultural economist. Doubling wages would have little effect on the prices of food in the markets because labor costs are less than 6 percent of total costs.

U.S. policy, therefore, should favor immigrants with special educational skills, money, or proven entrepreneurial talent. Highly qualified immigrants do compete with highly qualified natives. But natives enjoy natural advantages; they know the country; they know the language; they know conditions. Recruitment costs for foreigners are higher than for natives, perhaps even entailing moving the foreigner's family to this country. Particularly valuable are those highly qualified foreign postgraduates already in this country. (Half the Ph.D.'s in computer science awarded in the United States go to foreign students, most of whom stay in the United States, to this country's advantage.) The present ceiling on skilled immigrants is 65,000 a year. This should be raised and the process made easier, quicker, and less expensive.

Refugees

In 1996, the global flow of asylum-seekers, political refugees, and displaced people declined to 34 million people—a seven-year low—as a result of Western nations discouraging people from seeking safe haven in the United States, Germany, France, and Britain. The World Refugee Survey lists these and eleven other countries as places where guarantees of political asylum have deteriorated. Repatriations have also caused the number of refugees to decline; for example, nearly 2 million people in Africa were sent back to Rwanda, Burundi, and other African countries from which they had fled. Although the United States gives the most money to refugee relief agencies ($389 million in 1996), it is ninth on a per capita basis. The U.S. asylum law that took effect in April 1997 has made it harder to apply for asylum by summarily deporting people who arrive at airports and ports with false documents. Since 1994, German authorities have denied asylum to thousands of so-called refugees and have even sent many Bosnians back to an unstable and dangerous Bosnia.[83]

On June 6, 1997, the bipartisan Commission on Immigration Reform released a report recommending that the White House coordinate refugee affairs through a new office in the National Security Council. (The nine-member Commission on Immigration Reform was established in 1990 and in 1995 issued a controversial report that called for major cuts in legal immigration.) The commission sought to end abuses of the asylum system whereby thousands of people are admitted on false claims of persecution in their homelands. Addressing the reality that most asylum-seekers were economic rather than political refugees, the report called for rapid hearing and speedy deportation of rejected asylum-seekers. Chairwoman Shirley M. Hufstedler insisted that the United States needed "a comprehensive and coherent refugee policy" but did not mention the number of refugees to be admitted. (A 1995 report set a target of 50,000 refugee admissions a year—about half of recent levels.) The report set a floor, not a ceiling, for future admissions and proposed a new system of priorities—at the top those who needed urgent rescue, at the bottom those who were "safe" but needed resettlement. Unaccountably, the commission did not address the growing numbers of people who claim refugee status on grounds of homosexuality, female genital mutilation, forced birth control, or spousal abuse. Restrictionists were disappointed that the commission did not take up this disturbing definition of persecution. After all, as Mark Krikorian, director of the Center for Immigration Studies noted, the world is full of refugees, and the United States has to carefully decide who should be let in.[84] The 1996 law calls for the quick deportation of illegals and refugees from Central America and Mexico. As a result, arrests and deportation of illegals were stepped up during 1997, and judges in various states have delayed the deportation of thousands. The issue is a major concern to Central American nations and Mexico, which fear the return of hundreds of thousands of people who fled the wars in El Salvador and Nicaragua or the economic decline of Mexico and who, if deported, would no longer be able to send billions of dollars back home from wages earned in the United States.

Once again Congress is backing down from tough immigration laws passed in 1996. The Republicans agreed to grant amnesty to 50,000 Nicaraguans and 250,000 Guatemalans and Salvadorans who came here illegally but were allowed to stay on as refugees. HIV victims have similarly claimed and been granted asylum. To many observers, asylum on the grounds of persecution for sexuality or gender is an abuse of the law and could open the immigration floodgates to gays and lesbians from around the world who are HIV-positive. In January 1996, in opposition to a 1996 law barring admission to aliens with HIV or AIDS, the Clinton administration decided to allow HIV infection as a basis for asylum in response to the recommendation of an HIV-AIDS advisory council.

For some time, the immigration problem has been complicated by the refugee problem. Few wish for any more waves of refugees now that the cold war is over and flight from Indo-China has slowed. Many in the United States want not only fewer immigrants but also fewer refugees. Why not settle people persecuted because of their race, religion, nationality, or class near the country from which they flee, in regions that are likely to have similar cultural values and where the language spoken may be similar to theirs? Caring for political refugees in their regions is less expensive and may be more humane than uprooting them and admitting them to the United States.

Refugees make up only about one-tenth of the total immigrant population; the other nine-tenths come to the United States for economic opportunities, for political reasons, and to join family members. In 1994 the U.S. ceiling for refugees was 121,000, but only 112,500 were accepted, mostly from Russia and Eastern Europe but also from East Asia, Latin America, the Middle East, and Africa. In 1995 the ceiling was set at 112,000, and in our opinion this figure is still too high. UN authorities estimate that 50 million people are exposed to political persecution, that perhaps 23 million refugees have left their countries, and that another 25 million are displaced within their own countries in U.N. "safe havens." The United States can admit but a small fraction, yet in September 1997 President Clinton published in the *Federal Register* a proposal to resettle 85,000 refugees in FY1998.

Kathleen Newland of the Carnegie Endowment for International Peace cites three reasons why the U.S. public is turning against refugees. Refugees were welcomed during the cold war because they were voting with their feet and discrediting communism. Now, however, political refugees are no longer popular in Afghanistan, Malaysia, Thailand, Indonesia, Germany, Switzerland, and Canada. (Germany, once one of the world's most generous countries, has amended its constitution to limit the right to seek asylum.)

The "right to leave" is no longer a principle acclaimed worldwide. After all, if people have a right to leave, they have a right to go somewhere, and the choice is usually the wealthy West. Second, the United States is understandably reluctant to take on regimes whose oppressive practices cause refugees to leave. Humanitarian interventionism has been costly and ineffectual. U.S. intervention may have helped somewhat in Haiti, but not in Somalia and probably not in Bosnia. Legitimate political refugees should still be admitted to the United States, but in smaller numbers now that the cold war is over. Studies show that, in time, most refugees become economically self-sufficient but that the old and disabled do not. Nevertheless, refugees in general stay on welfare longer and use it more than the native-born. (Some groups, such as the Hmong people from the Laotian highlands, have had more difficulty adapting to life in the United States than others from societies and cultures that are more similar.)

Standards are now being tightened on asylum-seekers, although one federal judge has stopped the INS officials at airports from deporting them without a trial. Refugee advocates claim that stricter rules on the provision of asylum would mean the persecuted will not be able to seek asylum in the United States. Interdiction at the airports, harbors, or borders seems the best solution. (Most refugees and many legals and illegals probably come in through airports and harbors, as do tourists, students, and businessmen.) The United States is far away for most people and costly and difficult to assimilate into for the elderly and the unskilled from underdeveloped countries, who make up the great number of refugees in the world. Rather than come to the United States and be supported at great cost, refugees should be helped to resettle near their mother country. The Swiss Academy for Development (SAD) has devised a plan that would integrate refugees into the host country where they have settled, if there is little or no chance of their returning to their homeland. Four pilot projects along the Iran/Iraq border (where 2.5 million are housed in border camps) were given financial help to build housing and to create training programs that will help the refugees establish local businesses. So far this approach has been successful and appears superior to the approach of the United Nations High Commission for Refugees (UNHCR), which treats refugees as temporary problems. Better to treat displacement as permanent, and to provide funds for skills training and citizenship in the adopted country. According to journalist Lyn Shepard, the primary SAD guideline "is to resettle refugees permanently in their 'land of first reception'—countries usually similar in culture to their abandoned homelands."[85]

Resettlement programs such as SAD's are humane and relatively inexpensive. A refugee can be resettled, retrained, and made self-reliant for a tenth of the costs of establishing his or her asylum in the United States or a European country."[86] It was therefore irresponsible of the Central Intelligence Agency to offer asylum to thousands of Kurds who worked for the agency in northern Iraq; the Kurds should have been resettled in the region and not brought to the United States

Discussions concerning immigration raise the wider question—what kind of a United States do Americans want for the future? Statisticians in the Census Bureau forecast that, by 2050, whites will barely form a majority and Hispanics will be the largest minority in the country, exceeding black Americans. We ourselves do not think much of such forecasts. For instance, such predictions take little or no account of lower birth rates for immigrants or of intermarriage with other ethnic groups. The intermarriage rate is high for both Latin and Asian people in the United States; moreover, the rate goes up from one generation to the next. The United States will certainly be more ethnically and racially mixed in the future than it is at present. None can be sure, however, how this amalgam will be constituted, especially since future immigration patterns may change. If the number of immigrants is reduced, bilingualism and ethnic preferences stopped, and Americanization encouraged, there will be no danger to U.S. unity.

U.S. Visa Lottery

Once a year, in a global lottery called the Diversity Immigrant Visa Lottery, the U.S. State Department randomly selects applicants for immigration from a computer file. The lottery is for those who have no connection to the United States—no relatives, no job offers—and the object is to add diversity to the immigrant population dominated by Asians and Latinos since 1965. If you win you get a green card, no matter what your skills or age. Only Asians and Latin Americans are largely excluded from the game; mostly Europeans and Africans win.

Congress started the lottery system in 1986 at the urging of an Irish-American lobby. Ireland was guaranteed a fixed number of "winners," and applicants from nineteen other countries became eligible as well. There have been 100,000 winners, with Irish and Poles predominating. But the Irish stopped coming, so in 1993 the 55,000 slots were opened to the world. The Africans got 21,000 visas, Europeans 23,000, Asians 7,200, and Latin Americans 2,500, but China, the Philippines, Columbia, and Mexico got none. Once the green card holders settle in they can bring in their relatives.

The hope is that this system will skew the immigrant pool away from Asia and Latin America.

There is much opposition to the visa lottery from blacks, Asians, anti-immigrationists, and multiculturists. The Clinton administration was planning to abolish the program in favor of family reunification, but legal immigration numbers stayed up so the lottery survived. In the future, cuts to legal immigration will focus first on this lottery program. This program, many critics feel, is a no-brainer; chance alone determines who comes—not skill, not knowledge, and not much cash is required. And no job needs to be awaiting the winner; he has a green card, however, to look for work. The visa lottery, therefore, should be abolished and the category for skilled immigrants raised by 55,000 to 200,000.

Bilingual Education: Yes or No?

Bilingual education has failed to achieve its original objective of teaching children English; the education bureaucracy early on stressed teaching Hispanic-surnamed children Spanish language and their native cultures. Linda Chavez, president of the Center for Equal Opportunity, accuses bilingual education advocates of succumbing to political correctness; the result, she says, is that bilingual education has failed, has undermined the future of the Latino children it was meant to help, and has heightened Latino nationalism and created a sense of victimization among young Latino students.[87] The guiding principle of bilingualism is "cultural maintenance," and some enthusiasts want Spanish to be a second national language. Yet the evidence is clear that Latinos, Hispanics, or Chicanos taught in bilingual programs test behind peers taught in English-only classrooms and earn less money in employment.

The problem began in 1974 when the Supreme Court, in *Lau v. Nichols*, ignored 200 years of English-only instruction in America's schools and said that students who did not speak English must receive special treatment from local schools. This ruling allowed an enormous expansion of bilingual education. Advocates of bilingual education in the U.S. Office for Civil Rights had begun a small program in 1968 to teach English to Mexican American children, but by 1996 it had expanded from a $7.5 million program to one that spent $8 billion a year. The initial objective to teach English to Spanish speakers for one or two years was perverted into a program to Hispanicize Hispanics or Latinos, not to perfect their English or to Americanize them. The federal program requires that 75 percent of tax dollars be spent on bilingual education—that is, long-term native-language programs, not English as a second language. Asians, Africans, and Europeans are in mainstream classes all the time and receive extra training in English as a Second Language (ESL) programs for a few hours a day. Hispanic students, however, are taught in Spanish 70 to 80 percent of the time. Some critics of bilingualism claim that the vast majority of Spanish speakers want their children to be taught in English, not Spanish, and do not want the U.S. government to teach them Hispanic cultures and language. But the bilingual bureaucracy at local and federal levels wants to Hispanicize in part to capture federal funds for schools. Meanwhile, African, Asian, and European students achieve higher academic scores, in part because they are not wasting time in language and culture classes and failing to master the language of the marketplace and higher education—English. Since there are seldom enough bilingual teachers, Asians and Arabs and Europeans go right into classes with English-speaking students. They score higher and graduate more often than the bilingually taught.[88] If the bilingual education system is not reformed, the United States will become deeply divided linguistically. A Latino underclass will not be able to meet the needs of a high-tech work place because their English is poor, and they will grow to resent an educational system that deprived them of a command of English. Since Latino immigration is likely to continue in the future and since Latino birth rates are high, the Latino population will grow. The economic costs of not adequately educating Hispanics will be great, and their economic well-being will be lower than if they were to stay in school longer and focus on English, not on bilingualism, according to Edward Lazear.[89] Lazear argues that much of the anti-immigrant rhetoric in America is generated by government policies that reduce the incentives to become assimilated and emphasize the differences among ethnic groups in the population. Examples are affirmative action, bilingual education, and unbalanced immigration policies that bring in large numbers of Asians and Hispanics, who move into large and stable ghettos.

Rosalie Pedolino Porter, a bilingual education teacher for more than twenty years, is convinced that all limited-English-proficiency students can learn English well enough for regular classroom work in one to three years, if given some help. The old total-immersion system still works best; the longer students stay in segregated bilingual programs, the less successful they are in school. Even after twenty-eight years of bilingual programs, the dropout rate for Latinos is the highest in the country, and few learn English well. In Los Angeles the Latino students dropped out at double the state average (44 percent over four years of high school). Special English-language instruction from day one gets better results than Spanish-language instruction for most of the day.

Hispanic activists now call for limited recognition to be accorded to Spanish—*inglés y más* (English and more) runs the slogan. (Official documents of various kinds are now printed in Spanish and other languages as well as English. At the 1996 Democratic presidential convention, speeches were given in Spanish as well as English.) If this course continues, the demand for recognition of Spanish will inevitably change into a demand for recognition of Spanish as an official language. Such a transformation would give great benefits to Spanish speakers in public employment but leave native English speakers (and speakers of other languages) at a disadvantage. Bilingualism, or multilingualism, imposes economic transaction costs. The political costs are even higher. We do not wish, therefore, the United States to become a bilingual country such as Canada or Belgium, both of which suffer from divisiveness occasioned by the language issue.

Some children are forced into Spanish-bilingual classes because they have Spanish surnames, even though they understand and speak English well and do not speak or read Spanish. As a result they are held back and do not improve in English. Time and again, because they have Hispanic surnames, they are put in classes with immigrant children who speak little or no English. Parents have complained bitterly for some time that all day long their children are exposed to Spanish and only for a few minutes to English. Efforts to get their children transferred are resisted — "We know best" the teacher or principal says. In some reported cases it has taken as long as a year to remove a child from bilingual education even if the child speaks no Spanish when he/she enters the class. Teachers would say, "Isn't it a shame your child doesn't know his native language." Even the Mexican consul-general in Los Angeles justifies supplying native-born Spanish teachers to the county system in order to protect Latino children's Spanish heritage. Why is bilingual education able to continue this way against the wishes of many parents and the almost total failure of bilingual education in most U.S. schools? Bilingual education began about 1967 as an effort to help immigrants, mostly Spanish speakers, learn English. Unfortunately, according to many, "it has become a multi-billion dollar hog trough that feeds arrogant education bureaucrats and militant Hispanic separatists."[90]

In the 1990s, parents in a Los Angeles elementary school had to go on strike to get their children taught in English. One hundred and fifty Hispanic families in Brooklyn's Bushwick district had to sue New York State to get their children out of bilingual classes. An affidavit to the court said a child was put into the bilingual program because he had a Spanish surname even though he spoke no Spanish. By the seventh grade, such children could not read in either English or Spanish. Denver schools are set to limit students to three years in bilingual programs instead of six years because so many of their students have been performing below grade level. In Las Lunas, New Mexico, students protested the lack of English tutoring. In Dearborn, Michigan, the school board was forced to reject $5 million in federal funds for bilingual programs when parents complained. Across the country the story is the same: parents reject bilingualism and want their children to learn English. A *Los Angeles Times* poll in October 1997, showed California voters favored limiting bilingual education 4 to 1; 84 percent of Hispanics opposed it. The most impressive opposition to date is the ballot initiative in California—"English for the Children"—to be voted on in June 1998.

Of course, bilingual teachers and administrators are in favor of keeping their programs: "We know better, we're the teachers," said cochairman Joseph Ramos of the New Jersey Bilingual Council.[91] Misunderstandings abound over bilingual education: it is not about speaking two languages; it is not about learning two languages at the same time; it is not a program conducted mostly in English. Bilingual education is not structured English immersion or English as a Second Language programs in which children are expected to move into English quickly after a year or two of bilingual classes. Transitional bilingual education (TBE) was supposed to have students take most courses in their native languages while they learned English so that they would not fall behind in other courses—this was the rationale in the highly successful Newcomer School in San Francisco and other places. But TBE fell victim to theorists of language education—"facilitation theorists"—who claim that children cannot learn a second language until they are fully literate in their first. This process supposedly takes six or seven years, during which the students are supposed to be taught their native language. Slowly English is worked into the curriculum until the "threshold" is crossed, and then the student can go into English. In other words, children are to learn English by being taught in Spanish. As the principal of a Los Angeles school said, "*loco, completamente loco.*"[92]

When the 1968 Bilingual Education Amendment was passed, Hispanic activists, especially militant Chicanos, seized the chance to get Spanish-language instruction. The U.S. Department of Health, Education and Welfare distributed guidelines to the school districts for setting up bilingual programs. The Supreme Court then ruled in *Lau vs. Nichols* (1974) that non-English-speaking children had a right to special language programs. HEW then expanded the concept to mean bilingual programs for all children from homes where English was not a primary language. So children who spoke perfect English had to attend bilingual classes if their *parents* preferred to speak Spanish or Chinese at home. As early as 1980, there were 500 school districts in the nation with bilingual programs.

The role of the U.S. Department of Education's Office for Civil Rights (OCR) as a micro-manager of bilingual education is disturbing. OCR believes that Spanish surnamed children, even those who speak only English, must have Spanish-language instruction before they begin learning English. The theory is that children from other linguistic backgrounds need to become fluent in their parents' native languages before they attempt to learn English. It is called "facilitation theory" in education jargon. The theory has never really been proved and over the years has been increasingly discredited, yet OCR pushes hard for the system.

School systems are pressured into adopting the facilitation system or face loss of funds and court cases. Even the smallest school districts can be visited and remedial action plans imposed on them. In a case in Denver OCR refused to accept teacher evaluations or parents' wishes to move children out of bilingual classes—really all-Spanish classes. Only standardized test scores would do, OCR opined.

The test, a standardized one for native English speakers, measured English proficiency! A low score meant the student could not leave the bilingual class! Since so little English was taught—one hour a day at most— few students could exit the class and so continued in bilingual classes subsidized and controlled by OCR.[93] OCR is facing a congressional committee inquiry, and it is to be hoped that some reforms can be made.

Yet no one could show that bilingual education was working. That is why "facilitation theory" was introduced; it claimed to show that children needed six years or so to be taught in their native language before they could learn English. Children, it was said, would be cognitively deprived if they were not taught in their native tongue. In practice, this meant Spanish speakers, because no school system could provide bilingual programs for the scores of languages spoken in many states—New York schoolchildren speak 121 different languages. Nor are teachers and students available. In 1993 California had a shortfall of thousands of bilingual teachers.

Crioulo, a dialect of Portuguese spoken only in the Cape Verde Islands, is taught in bilingual programs in Massachusetts and elsewhere in New England. But before the schools could start the program, a Crioulo alphabet had to be invented and written material produced. In the Cape Verde Islands, only Portuguese is taught, but in Massachusetts Crioulo report cards and bulletins in Crioulo are sent home to parents who cannot read them!

And then there was "Spanglish," an attempt in the 1970s to force a combination of Spanish and English on schoolchildren. Such absurdities abound in bilingual education. So desperate are bilingual educators to target students that in one documented case in San Francisco 750 black children were put into Spanish or Chinese classes even though not one spoke either language at home.

TBE has been a failure, has kept many students too long in the program, and has retarded the students' ability to learn either Spanish or English. Immersion programs do much better—80 percent who enter in kindergarten are mainstreamed after three years, whereas only 22 percent of students in TBE programs are moved into mainstream classrooms after the second grade. Most students stay in a TBE program for six years and are not competent in either language when they leave. After six years of TBE one student wrote: "I my parens per mi in dis shool en I so I feol essayrin too old in the shool my border o reri can gier das mony putni gire and I sisairin aliro sceer." This is incomprehensible in either Spanish or English. The parents said the school district claimed the boy was doing fine and was nearly ready to leave bilingual classes.[94] Typically, students in TBE classes get less than an hour's instruction a day in English.

Even though poll after poll in Los Angeles, Houston, San Antonio, Miami, and New York show that parents want their children taught in English not Spanish, Hispanic activists keep insisting on bilingualism, as do academic supporters of bilingualism. The debate has overtones of ethnic politics; it is about Latino power and culture, ethnic pride, so-called victimhood, and preferential treatment through affirmative action. Money and grants are involved; to trigger the receipt of government and state funds a minimum number of students is required. There is a huge bureaucracy of administrators, bilingual teachers, psychologists, and textbook publishers at the funding trough! Money flows from state, local, and federal levels.[95] The issue has been seized by the Democrats to bash the Republicans and paint them as anti-Latinos. (See a special report by House Democratic leader Richard Gephardt.)

Mexican American activists reject assimilation, insist on bilingualism and multiculturalism, and even lay claim to the American Southwest as a part of Mexico. Wave after wave of illegals push inexorably into the United States and find refuge in Spanish ghettos. Many Mexican American politicians and activists claim to speak for these new immigrants. Their message is not pushing assimilation but rather the protection of Spanish language and culture and the theme that the Southwest belongs to the descendants of Mexicans who lost the war of 1848.

Rodolfo Acuña's *Occupied America* is one book that claims the Southwest for Mexicans.[96] Chicano activists (advocates of Chicanismo) push not only for civil rights for illegal Mexicans but also for the return (*reconquista*) of the lost provinces to form Aztlán. Chicanismo demands

Spanish language and culture education, not English or American cultural schooling. The *Movimiento Estudiante Chicano de Aztlán* (MECHA) formed a political party in 1970, *La Raza Unida*, which won control of Crystal City, Texas, and tried to make it into a Chicano city. The party split and has had little political impact since but could easily revive in California or Texas. MECHA survives in dozens of Chicano studies programs in the western United States. Chicano leaders have been courted by the Democratic Party and appear to have a bright future there. Add the newly made Spanish-speaking citizens of 1996 to Chicano activists and Latino politicians and the situation becomes explosive. By the year 2000, 40 percent of the population of California will be Latino, some polls claim.

Mexican American leaders are split; on the one hand they see themselves as an aggrieved racial group and demand group rights and preferential treatment, but on the other they boast of being treated like other downtrodden ethnic groups. The Mexican American leadership is certainly ambivalent: Chicano nationalists claim to be the inheritors of Mexican civilization, but others want to assimilate, have their children learn English, and become Americans as other immigrants did. Unfortunately a few Mexican American politicians such as Art Torres, a former California state senator, play the race card often. MECHA has accused the Republican Party of being made up of racist/fascist European settlers.[97] The virulent, antiwhite high school textbook *Five Hundred Years of Chicano History in Pictures*, boasts of Chicano "resistance to being colonized and absorbed by racist empire builders." Throughout Chicano studies programs in colleges and universities, one sees "a process of racialization and reawakening ethnic consciousness." These feelings are "reinforced and given a political twist by organizations like MECHA, by Chicano Studies departments, by the intrusions of Mexican politicians, and above all by an unceasing flow of new immigrants."[98] Both parties court the Latinos; the Anglo Americans even sang "Viva Mexico!" at a meeting of the National Council of La Raza. No one criticized the executive director of the National Association of Latino Elected and Appointed Officials for saying about the growing Latino population, "We will overwhelm."

At present, therefore, the only basis for bilingual education in California is a mixture of state and administrative decisions and politicians' fear of a backlash from Latino voters if the program is ended. In fact, most Latino voters oppose bilingual education so the Republican Party's failure to back "English for the Children" is a political mistake. Opposition to the Unz initiative comes from the National Association for Bilingual Education, the California Teachers' Association, the National Association of Latino Elected

Officials (NALEO), and the Mexican American Legal Defense and Education Trust, all of whom claim that one year of English immersion for LEP will not be enough.

We believe that the United States should require applicants for naturalization to demonstrate a higher degree of proficiency in English than it does at present. A citizen should be able to read all electoral literature in English. For similar reasons, we oppose those educators in publicly funded high schools who believe that their task is to maintain the immigrants' cultural heritage. Such endeavors should be left to parents, churches, "Saturday schools," the extended family. The role of the public school's teacher is to instruct students in English about American culture. English plays a crucial role in cultural assimilation, a proposition evident also to minority people. (In Brooklyn, for example, the Bushwick Parents Organization went to court in 1996 to oppose the imposed Spanish-English education of Hispanics in the local public schools, arguing that this instruction would leave their children badly disadvantaged when they graduated.) As Ruth Wisse, herself a distinguished educator, puts it, before we encourage ethnic language revivals in the European manner, "we should recall what millions of immigrants instinctively grasped: that English is the most fundamental pathway to America's equal opportunities."[99] (The European experience is likewise clear. "In general, mother-tongue education is unrealistic and unsuccessful. The children of immigrant parents rapidly acquire the language of their country of residence, and are often less comfortable and successful in their parents' mother-tongue.")[100]

A Center for Immigration Studies *Backgrounder* (April 1996) asks the question, "Are immigration preferences for English-speakers racist?" It answers in the negative because one-third of humanity has some knowledge of the English language, and most of these people are nonwhite. Although the immigration bill in the House and Senate had an English requirement for certain employee-based categories of immigrants, it was removed lest it discriminate against nonwhites.

Knowledge of English is an acquired, not an inherent skill—anyone, white, black, or brown, can learn English. Immigrants line up to learn English because they believe that doing so will improve their prospects—and it does, significantly. English is the most widely used language in history. English is the language of science, technology, diplomacy, international trade, and commerce. Half of Europe's business deals are carried out in English, and more than 66 percent of the world's scientists read English. The world's electronically stored information is 80 percent in English. The world's 40 million Internet users communicate primarily in English. Experts conclude that one-third of mankind speaks or understands some English. Selecting immigrants on the basis of some command of the language therefore cannot be discriminatory.

Most Latino parents (81 percent) prefer their children to learn English as soon as possible. They believe, correctly, that English literacy is the key to success in the United States. In California, however, bilingualism is a big business—1.3 million students attend classes at a cost of more than $300 million a year. Bilingual teachers are paid more and schools with bilingual programs get large grants from federal and state programs. Most studies by independent researchers charge that bilingual education is unnecessary and fails in most cases. Most students never really learn to read or write English well, and Spanish speakers leave school at the highest rate of any ethnic group. Bilingual education also defeats efforts to assimilate children into U.S. society and goes against the wishes of most parents. Most of those who favor abolishing bilingual education say that, instead, non- and limited-English-speaking children should spend one year in sheltered English immersion, then go into regular classrooms. Most people seem to agree, except bilingual teachers, administrators, and multiculturists, who would create little Quebecs in states like California, New York, Texas, and Florida. The evidence is overwhelming: bilingualism does not work in most schools, is expensive, and ill serves Spanish speakers to advance and compete in American society.

There are some good bilingual schools—Newcomer School in San Francisco, Main Elementary School in Calexico—but overall, bilingual schools are in chaos. The good schools send a majority to college, whereas most bilingual schools fail to graduate 30 percent of their students.

Bilingual advocates claim that English-only instruction harms Hispanic students by making the acquisition of English difficult and frustrating. They argue that a student must first become literate in his or her native language before learning English. That is nonsense, of course, as tens of millions of children of immigrants who learned English before bilingual education existed can attest. It is also claimed that English-only immersion delays students' learning in academic subjects like math and history and that it prevents parents with limited English from helping their children with their schoolwork. Certainly, parents who speak little or no English cannot help their children in that subject, but since the average Mexican parent has little education in Spanish, he may not be able to help his child in academic subjects in Spanish either.

Defenders of bilingual education misrepresent their case that students in English-only classes have a higher dropout rate, whereas in fact those students graduate from high school and go on to college at a much higher rate than bilingually educated children. In other words, bilingualism may cause Spanish-speaking students to drop out of high school.

The Calexico program is one exception—80 percent of the children speak limited English; but their dropout rate is half the state average. The reasons for this success may be highly motivated and trained teachers, small classes, involvement by parents, and sufficient resources to deal with students' emotional problems and social development.

Few local school systems, however, have the resources of Calexico. Most lack enough trained bilingual teachers for most languages other than Spanish; they lack classrooms to run the programs. The failure rate for students in most bilingual programs is scandalously high—95 percent. Opponents of California's Proposition 227 still claim that teachers and administrators know best and that parents and voters should not be allowed to decide what is best for students. Not many teachers, school branches, unions, or administrative bodies support Prop. 227. They will hunker down behind the recent California School Board decision to let local school branches, which they control, decide what to teach our children.

Yet another anomaly is Spanish immersion for non-Spanish speakers. Escondido Elementary School has had a Spanish-immersion program for three years. Native English speakers are taught mostly in Spanish and are only gradually reintroduced to English until the fifth grade, when instruction becomes half English, half Spanish. The goal is for students to leave elementary school literate in both languages. This special program was developed by parents, teachers, and Stanford University professors who wanted children to learn a second language so that they would be prepared for a multicultural world. There is keen competition for the thirty spots in the kindergarten class.

Two-thirds of the eighty-seven students in Escondido's program are native English speakers, one-third are native Spanish speakers. No English is spoken in the classroom in the first year; the curriculum is the same as in other local schools except that classes are taught in Spanish. For the first two years, instruction in English occupies about 10 percent of the time; Spanish takes up 90 percent. (This is also the format for English-immersion programs.)

The program works on the established premise that children learn languages more easily when they are young: they are not self-conscious about speaking, and they do not worry about using language correctly. Reading and writing are a key portion of class instruction, but only in Spanish.

While the school's program is working very well, it is expensive, labor-intensive, and well staffed, with full cooperation from parents. But this kind of program can work in few places; most have neither the money nor the staff to replicate it. And one can only ask why native English-speaking parents would want to put their children through this kind of Spanish-immersion program. When asked, one parent said that California will soon have a majority of Spanish speakers and she wanted her child to be ready for it. But if the child moves out of California, will she be as ready in English as she would have been if she had not been immersed in Spanish language and culture? Some educated Spanish speakers enroll their children in the program so that they will become familiar with Spanish culture. But they do not seem to be aware that as a result their children will lag behind English speakers for many of their years in school.

The benefits of total immersion are clear, so in an English-speaking culture, English is best. Spanish can be learned in the same way that English is learned in the Spanish-immersion classes. And the Escondido teachers know this because two-thirds of their students are English speakers, not Spanish speakers. Total immersion in English is best, with Spanish being taught as a second language after the first year—just as the opponents of bilingual education want: children learn languages easily in the early years of school. Why not teach in English only in an English-speaking country, and if parents want it, teach Spanish as a second language? Similarly, let Spanish-speaking parents teach Spanish culture at home.[101]

The hypocrisy of many bilingual programs is no better illustrated than by the Adelante Magnet School in Redwood City, California. While bilingual enthusiasts and teachers order total Spanish immersion to teach Spanish speakers English, they insist on total Spanish immersion for English-speaking students to teach them Spanish! And that's what they do at Adelante, where only Spanish is spoken in the classroom from kindergarten to the third grade (or fifth grade, in some instances). Why, then, do we argue that total immersion in English is the best way for native Spanish speakers to learn English? It is obvious to laypeople that children could learn English faster if they were immersed in it. But bilingual pedagogues disagree, saying that Spanish speakers should first be immersed in Spanish to gain fluency in their native tongue and then gradually be introduced to English until the fifth or sixth grade. All too often the children learn neither language well, and the native Spanish speakers leave school ill-prepared for most jobs that require fluency in English.

Recently California's Board of Education decided to let local school districts decide whether to teach children only in English or to be bilingual, which usually means students receive Spanish-language training. This return of power to local school districts poses problems for Prop. 277, which would ban bilingual instruction altogether and remove all local decision-making authority. The Board of Education's decision to give control to local bilingual bureaucracies means, in effect, that nothing will change even if Prop. 227 passes. If passed, Prop. 227 would deny local choice and all districts would be required to teach in English after a transitional year in bilingual education.

If local control wins out, nothing much will change. Spanish speakers (and others) will be forced to spend three to six years in Spanish-only classrooms with perhaps thirty minutes a day devoted to English. The children will fall further and further behind in English, and most will not be able to pass tests in English in high school. Poor English means fewer opportunities for higher education or skilled jobs. Bilingual education will continue to produce an underclass of Latino school-leavers who cannot compete in an economy that requires skilled people who are proficient in English.

A further tragic consequence will be the creation of ethnic nationalists who, not having been Americanized in the schools, will claim they are victims of Anglo American cultural dominance and demand special rights for Spanish speakers, in effect creating new Quebecs.

Most people do not understand what is at stake. The issue is not whether Spanish and English should be taught equally. It is whether Spanish-language mastery and Latino cultural dominance in the first three to six years of school are necessary in order for a native Spanish speaker to go on to master English. The belief that they are necessary is called "facilitation theory"—a muddle-headed concept of educational psychology, untested in practice, and disproved by over two hundred years of teaching immigrant children through total immersion in English.

The Unz initiative would not do away with Spanish-language teaching entirely and lead to teaching only in English. Prop. 227 calls for a transitional year or two in which the child would be taught in both Spanish and English. After this transition period, the child would move on to English-only classes but keep an hour a day of instruction in his native language as well. Prop. 227 also allows parental consent for a child to remain in Spanish-only classes if the child is not fully prepared for English-only. The evidence is clear—most children learn enough English to move out of bilingual classes in one year, and only a small minority need more than one year.

One would think that giving local school districts control over whether to teach students in English or bilingually would be a good thing. But the history of bilingual education does not give one much hope. Bilingual education has continued against the wishes of many parents, even though it has failed in most U.S. schools. Parents in Los Angeles and New York, for example, had to sue their school systems to get their children taught in English! The debate has overtones of ethnic politics, or Chicanismo. There is a large bureaucracy of administrators, bilingual teachers (they are paid more than regular teachers), psychologists, and textbook publishers at the feeding trough—in California, 1.3 million students attend bilingual classes at a cost of more than $30 million. Don't expect local school districts to turn their backs on these funds. Parents will have to organize and lobby hard to win and also to resist appeals to language and cultural chauvinism. The teachers and principals will say, "Isn't it a shame your child cannot learn his native tongue and Spanish culture!"

Bilingual education has retarded the advancement of Latinos, who have the highest dropout rate of any minority; and they are stuck at the bottom of the economic ladder in the service sector as gardeners, agricultural workers, babysitters, janitors, and busboys. Why? Because of bilingual education.

In conclusion, no economist or social planner can determine with confidence the ideal number of immigrants that the U.S. economy should accept each year. But if it is the nation's political aim to assimilate immigrants into a single nation, annual immigration must be kept in bounds; we suggest not more than two per thousand of the population during any one year (roughly 500,000 a year). For political reasons, immigration policy should also ensure a diversity of immigrants—not too many (perhaps not more than 10 percent of the total) from any one country in every single year. Regular immigration could be supplemented once again by a *braçero* or guest-worker program to assist agribusiness if a real labor shortage were to occur. (A 1998 NSF report denies there is a labor shortage in agriculture.)

We reiterate our preference for an immigration policy designed to attract newcomers with skills, technical qualifications, and capital. We wish to preserve the United States as a free-market society based on the rule of law, a Western, not a "world" nation. We reiterate that assimilation should be the national objective—not the ethnicization of America. We reject race as a criterion for admission. We observe with pleasure that assimilation and intermarriage are ongoing processes. We are pleased that ethnic separatists at U.S. universities have not had much success in converting to their own viewpoints those popular masses for whom the ethnic elites profess to speak. The United States can rightly demand that immigrants be loyal to its language, its laws, its flag, its constitution. Only those who accept this proposition merit welcome. The biggest challenge facing the United States and the new immigrants is adaptation, because the new immigrants are so different from the bulk of earlier immigrants, who came from Europe. The acceptance of immigrants by native-born Americans is crucial to their adaptation. The current rise of an immigrant-baiting mood does not bode well for a quick, peaceful integration of the new immigrants.

The 1996 immigration bills strengthen enforcement measures at the border, but more enforcement authority is needed in the work place and to stop entry at airports, smuggling and document fraud. The INS should process political asylum-seekers and illegals more quickly. All ports of entry must also be strictly watched, and the abuse of claims for political asylum at these ports of entry should be better controlled. Heavy penalties for illegal immigrants who arrive as students, tourists, or businessmen but stay on should also be enforced. Employer sanctions should be repealed as unenforceable. Those who come in illegally should be caught, punished, and deported quickly. Any sort of computer verification system would be expensive and unworkable and could lead to the undesirable use of a national identification card. There should be generous quotas for the admission of skilled immigrants but smaller quotas for refugees and unskilled non-English speakers. Sponsors of immigrants should face tough financial requirements, and immigrants should not be able to receive welfare benefits for ten years.

Congress should reform the policy for legal immigrants, as it has already done for illegals. There should be no more amnesties for illegal immigrants, and family reunification should apply only for youthful members of a nuclear family, not for adult members. Legal immigration should be cut to 400,000—500,000 newcomers a year (still a generous quota). This number should include refugees and skilled immigrants. Affirmative action and bilingual programs should be terminated. Census categories such as "Hispanic" and "Asian" should be replaced by national origin classifications. The time for legal residence for naturalization should be extended to ten years. The children of illegal immigrants born in this country should no longer be automatically entitled to U.S. citizenship. "English only" should be required in the law, in government, in schools, and in the political system. No long-term bilingual education programs should be mandated; a transition year or two could be provided for those who do not speak English, then "English only" in all academic courses; training in foreign languages should also be encouraged. "Becoming proficient in the language of America is a price that any immigrant should want to pay."[102]

APPENDIX I

Alternative Projections of the U.S. Population,
by Race/Ethnicity, 2000–2040 (in millions)

		White	White	Asian	Black	Hispanic	Other
Year	Total	Total	Non-Hispanic				
2000	274.8	224.6	196.7	12.3	35.5	30.6	2.4
2020	322.6	250.6	206.2	23.1	45.7	49.0	3.2
2040	364.3	268.6	205.6	35.0	56.4	69.8	4.1

Source: Barry Edmonston and Jeffrey S. Passel, eds., *Immigration and Ethnicity*, p. 345.

APPENDIX II

**High School Dropouts among Persons 16 to 24 Years Old,
by Race/Ethnicity, October 1975 to October 1994 (percent)**

Year	All Races	Hispanic	White, Non-Hispanic	Black, Non-Hispanic
1975	13.9	11.4	22.9	29.2
1977	14.1	11.9	19.8	33.0
1979	14.6	12.0	21.1	33.8
1980	14.1	11.4	19.1	35.2
1981	13.9	11.4	18.4	33.2
1982	13.9	11.4	18.4	31.7
1983	13.7	11.2	18.0	31.6
1984	13.1	11.0	15.5	29.8
1985	12.6	10.4	15.2	27.6
1986	12.2	9.7	14.2	30.1
1987	12.7	10.4	14.1	28.6
1988	12.9	9.6	14.5	35.8
1990	12.1	9.0	13.2	32.4
1991	12.5	8.9	13.6	35.3
1992	11.0	7.7	13.7	29.4
1993	11.0	7.9	13.6	27.5
1994	10.5	7.7	12.6	30.0

Source: *Mini-Digest of Education Statistics*, 1995 (Washington, D.C.: National Center for Educational Statistics, 1995).

Notes

Preface

1. Since our book has gone to press, two new books of high quality have appeared: Joan Moore and Harry Pachon, *Hispanics in the United States* (Englewood Cliffs, N.J.: Prentice-Hall, 1985), and Alejandro Portes and Robert L. Bach, *Latin Journey: Cuban and Mexican Immigrants in the United States* (Berkeley: University of California Press, 1985).

2. John Higham, "Current Trends in the Study of Ethnicity in the United States," *Journal of Ethnic History* 2, no. 1 (Fall 1982): 5–15.

Chapter 1

The literature on the topics covered in this section is extensive. For a general history, see Matt S. Meier and Feliciano Rivera, *The Chicanos: A History of Mexican Americans* (New York: Hill and Wang, 1972). A militant Chicano viewpoint is put forward in Rodolfo Acuña, *Occupied America: The Chicano's Struggle Toward Liberation* (San Francisco: Canfield Press, 1972). An analysis of Anglo-American racist components in the "manifest destiny" doctrine is provided in Reginald Horsman, *Race and Manifest Destiny: The Origins of American Racial Anglo-Saxonism* (Cambridge, Mass.: Harvard University Press, 1981).

1. For an excellent introduction, see Hubert Herring, *A History of Latin America from the Beginnings to the Present* (New York: Alfred Knopf, 1961). For a case study of the Indians' comparative position under Anglo-American and Spanish-American rule, see Edward H. Spicer, *Cycles of Conquest: The Impact of Spain, Mexico, and the United States on the Indians of the Southwest, 1533–1960* (Tucson: University of Arizona Press, 1961).

2. See the contribution by Manfred Kossock in *Alexander von Humboldt: Eine Festschrift* (East Berlin: Akademie Verlag, 1969), pp. 25–26.

3. Michael P. Costelos, *La primera república federal en el México independiente* (Mexico City: Fondo de Cultura Economica, 1975). For an analysis of the great landowners' role, see, for instance, Charles H. Harris, *A Mexican Family Empire: The Latifundio of Sanchez Navarros, 1756–1867* (Austin: University of Texas Press, 1975).

4. Spicer, *Cycles of Conquest*.

5. Richard Henry Dana, *Two Years Before the Mast: A Personal Narrative of Life at Sea* (Boston: Bates and Lauriat, 1895), p. 162.

6. Leonard Pitt, *The Decline of the Californios: A Social History of Spanish-Speaking Californians, 1846–1890* (Berkeley: University of California Press, 1966), especially pp. 48–68.

7. Dana, *Two Years Before the Mast*, p. 33.

8. Reprinted in David Weber, ed., *Foreigners in Their Native Land: Historical Roots of the Mexican Americans* (Albuquerque: University of New Mexico Press, 1973), p. 53.

9. Jose Maria Sanchez, in Weber, *Foreigners in Their Native Land*, pp. 80–82.

10. Rufus B. Sage, in Weber, *Foreigners in Their Native Land*, pp. 72–73.

11. Cited in Thomas Bailey, *Diplomatic History of the American People* (Englewood Cliffs, N.J.: Prentice-Hall, 1970), p. 259.

12. Alexis de Tocqueville, *Democracy in America* (Garden City, N.Y.: Doubleday, 1969), pp. 654–58. Friedrich Engels was even more outspoken. He insisted that the Americans' seizure of California from the "Lazy Mexicans" was a happy event that served historical progress; cited by Nathaniel Weyl, *Karl Marx: Racist* (New Rochelle, N.Y.: Arlington House, 1979).

13. Juan Bautista Vigil y Alavid, in Weber, *Foreigners in Their Native Land*, pp. 128–29.

Chapter 2

1. Leonard Pitt, *The Decline of the Californios: A Social History of Spanish-Speaking Californians, 1846–1890* (Berkeley: University of California Press, 1966), pp. 48–68.

2. The history of U.S. treatment of western land claims has a considerable literature, including: Thomas Lloyd Miller, *The Public Lands of Texas, 1519–1970* (Norman: University of Oklahoma Press, 1972); J. Bowden, *Spanish and Mexican Land Grants in the Chihuahua Acquisition in El Paso* (El Paso: Western Press, 1971); and Paul W. Gates, "The California Land Act, 1851," *California Historical Quarterly* 50, no. 4 (December 1971): 395–430 (a defense of the U.S. record).

3. Albert Camarillo, *Chicanos in a Changing Society: From Mexican Pueblos to American Barrios in Santa Barbara and Southern California, 1848–1930* (Cambridge, Mass.: Harvard University Press, 1979), pp. 101–41.

4. Presentation by Pedro Castillo, Latin American Studies Association, XI International Congress, Mexico City, September 29–October 11, 1983; Ricardo Romo, *East Los Angeles: History of a Barrio* (Austin: University of Texas Press, 1983).

5. Robert F. Foerster, *The Italian Emigration of Our Times* (New York: Arno Press, 1961), p. 262, and Elzine Thomas, "San Mateo County Historical Association on the Italians in the Bay Area," *San Francisco Examiner*, October 14, 1981, Section C, p. 8.

6. For contrasting views, see Rodolfo Acuña, *Occupied America: The Chicano's Struggle toward Liberation* (San Francisco: Caufield Press, 1972), pp. 46–49, and T. R. Fehrenbach, *Lone Star State: A History of Texas and the Texans* (New York: Collier Books, 1980), pp. 572–74; also see Clarence C. Clendenen,

Blood on the Border: The United States Army and the Mexican Irregulars (New York: Macmillan, 1969), pp. 1–7.

7. For a critical view written from the anticapitalist standpoint, see Roxanne Dunbar Ortiz, *Roots of Resistance: Land Tenure in New Mexico, 1680–1980* (Los Angeles: Chicano Studies Research Center and American Indian Studies Center, 1980).

8. See Matt S. Meier and Feliciano Rivera, *The Chicanos: A History of Mexican Americans* (New York: Hill and Wang, 1972), pp. 96–114, and David Weber, ed., *Foreigners in Their Native Land: Historical Roots of the Mexican Americans* (Albuquerque: University of New Mexico Press, 1973), pp. 209–261.

9. Gilberto Miguel Hinojosa, *A Borderlands Town in Transition: Laredo, 1755–1870* (College Station: Texas A. and M. University Press, 1983).

10. See the entries on "Spaniards" and "Basques" in Stephan Thernstrom, ed., *Harvard Encyclopedia of American Ethnic Groups* (Cambridge, Mass.: Harvard University Press, 1980), and see *Historical Abstracts of the United States: Colonial Times to 1957* (Washington, D.C.: Bureau of the Census, 1957), p. 65. Catalans and Basques had their own respective mother tongues; only outsiders would refer to them as "Spaniards."

11. See Marc D. Angel, *La América: The Sephardic Experience in the United States* (Philadelphia: Jewish Publication Society of the United States, 1982). For the career of Luis de Carvajal y de la Cuera, see I. Harold Scharfman, *Jews on the Frontier: An Account of Jewish Pioneers and Settlers in Early America* (Chicago: Regnery, 1977), pp. 231–2.

12. Louis A. Pérez, *Cuba Between Empires, 1878–1902* (Pittsburgh: Pittsburgh University Press, 1983).

13. The phrase comes from Mark Falcoff, "Fighting Castro," Commentary 22, no. 5 (December 1981): 89–91.

14. See Henry Wells, *The Modernization of Puerto Rico: A Political Study of Changing Values and Institutions* (Cambridge, Mass.: Harvard University Press, 1969). The most recent study is Arturo Morales Carrión, ed., *Puerto Rico: A Political and Cultural History* (New York: W. W. Norton, 1983), see especially his chapter "1898: The Hope and the Trauma," pp. 129–151.

15. Presentation by Virginia E. Sánchez Korrol at the Latin American Studies Association, XI International Congress, Mexico City, September 29–October 1, 1983. And see Virginia E. Sánchez Korrol, *From Colonial to Community: The History of Puerto Ricans in New York City, 1917–1948* (Westport, Conn.: 1983).

16. For figures, see entry on "Puerto Rico" in the 1929 edition of the *Encyclopedia Britannica*, 14th edition, vol. 18, pp. 260–65.

Chapter 3

1. See, for instance, Ramon Eduardo Ruiz, *The Great Rebellion: Mexico, 1905–1924* (New York: W. W. Norton, 1981).

2. Paul S. Taylor, *Mexican Labor in the United States* (Berkeley: University of California Press, 1932), vol. 2, pp. 263–264.

3. Ibid., p. 271.

4. Mark Reisler, *By the Sweat of Their Brow: Mexican Immigrant Labor in the United States, 1900–1940* (Westport, Conn.: Greenwood Press, 1976), p. 167.

5. Ibid., p. 102.

6. Carey McWilliams, *Ill Fares the Land: Migrants and Migrant Labor in the United States* (New York: Arno Press, 1976), pp. 144–145.

7. Reisler, *Mexican Labor*, p. 167, and George C. Kiser and Martha Woody Kiser, eds., *Mexican Workers in the United States: Historical and Political Perspectives* (Albuquerque: University of New Mexico Press, 1979), p. 18.

8. Ricardo Romo, *East Los Angeles: History of a Barrio* (Austin: University of Texas Press, 1983).

9. Louise Año Nuevo Kerr, "Mexican Chicago: Chicano Assimilation Aborted, 1939–1952," in Melvin G. Holli and Peter d'A. Jones, eds., *The Ethnic Frontier: Essays in the History of Group Survival in Chicago and the Midwest* (Grand Rapids, Mich.: William B. Eerdmans Publishing Company, 1977), p. 294.

10. Reisler, *Mexican Labor*, p. 102, and Kerr, "Mexican Chicago," in Holli and Jones, *The Ethnic Frontier*, pp. 294–95.

11. Taylor, *Mexican Labor in the United States*, vol. 2, pp. 270–73, 275.

12. Ibid., p. 275.

13. Ibid., p. 273.

14. Ibid., p. 275.

15. For a tabulated account of Latin American immigration restrictions, see Herbert A. Strauss, "Jewish Emigration from Germany," in *Leo Baeck Institute Year Book* no. 26 (London: Secker and Warburg, 1981), pp. 376–78.

16. The Portuguese began to enter the United States in substantial numbers from the 1870s; by the 1920s, they numbered perhaps 200,000 in all. They settled in three main regions: New England, where they worked in the fishing industry, in factories, and in truck-farming; in central California, where they were prominent as fishermen, farmers, storekeepers, and craftsmen; and in Hawaii, where they initially labored on plantations but later moved into better-paid urban occupations. The great majority of them came from the Azores, the Madeiras, and the Cape Verde islands. These islanders had little sense of attachment to the Portuguese mainland. They were equally split among themselves, the people from Madeira and the Azores inclining to keep aloof from the Cape Verdeans, who were primarily of African or Afro-Portuguese origin. The "new migration" began in the late 1950s; thereafter, Portugal developed into a major source of European immigration into the United States. See Leo Pap, *The Portuguese-Americans* (Boston: G. K. Hall, 1981), and Peter Duignan and L. H. Gann, *The United States and Africa: A History* (New York: Cambridge University Press, 1984).

17. See entry on "Spaniards" in Stephan Thernstrom, ed., *Harvard Encyclopedia of American Ethnic Groups* (Cambridge, Mass.: Harvard University Press, 1980), pp. 948–50. Between 1901 and 1910, 27,935 Spaniards entered the United States; between 1911 and 1920, their number rose to 68,611; it dropped to 28,958 between 1921 and 1930, and to 3,258 between 1931 and 1940.

18. George C. Kiser and Martha Woody Kiser, *Mexican Workers in the United States: Historical and Political Perspectives* (Albuquerque: University of New Mexico Press, 1979), p. 19.

19. In 1884, 213 persons were lynched; of these, 160 were whites and 53 were blacks. Corresponding figures for 1894 were 192 (58 white and 134 black); in 1904, 83 (7 and 76); in 1914, 55 (4 and 51); in 1924, 16 (0 and 16); in 1934, 15 (0 and 15); in 1944, 2 (0 and 2); and in 1954, 0. U.S. Department of Commerce, *Historical Statistics of the United States* (Washington, D.C.: Government Printing Office, 1960), p. 218.

20. Kiser and Kiser, *Mexican Workers*, p. 22.

21. Ibid., p. 19.

Chapter 4

1. A. J. Jaffe, Ruth M. Cullen, and Thomas D. Boswell, *The Changing Demography of Spanish Americans* (New York: Academic Press, 1980), pp. 182–183.

2. Paul Schuster Taylor, *Mexican Labor in the United States* (Berkeley: University of California Press), pp. 61–74.

3. Ibid., p. 74.

4. The phrase comes from Saul S. Friedman, *No Haven for the Oppressed: United States Policy Toward Jewish Refugees, 1938–1945* (Detroit: Wayne State University Press, 1973). Friedman's critique of U.S. immigration policies, though justified, misses the point that the United States was in fact the world's most important haven for Jewish refugees during the Nazi era.

5. According to the Census Bureau instructions, "All persons born in Mexico, or having parents born in Mexico, who are not definitely white, Negro, Indian, Chinese, or Japanese, should be returned as Mexican." The Census Bureau in 1930 counted 1,422,533 "Mexicans." Of these, 541,197 (38 percent) were either native born or of foreign or mixed parentage; only 264,338 (18.6 percent) were native born of native parentage. The 1,422,533 figure equaled 1.2 percent of the total American population. Mark Reisler, *By the Sweat of Their Brow: Mexican Immigrant Labor in the United States, 1900–1940* (Westport, Conn.: Greenwood Press, 1976), p. 99. In fact, the number of Mexicans in the country must have been much larger because the Census Bureau had no way of counting illegal immigrants. The census figures also were biased because the authorities mistakenly attempted to identify Mexicans as a "race" and thereby eliminated from the count thousands of Spanish-speaking people of Mexican origin and European appearance.

6. Abraham Offman, *Unwanted Mexican Americans in the Great Depression* (Tucson: University of Arizona Press, 1974), p. 31.

7. Mark Reisler, *Passing Through Egypt: Mexican Labor in the United States, 1900–1940* (Ph.D. Diss., Cornell University, 1974; published by University Microfilms, Ann Arbor, Michigan, 1975), p. 417.

8. Carey McWilliams, *North from Mexico: The Spanish-Speaking Peoples of the United States* (New York: Greenwood Press, 1968). In this section we have

drawn especially from Carey McWilliams, *Ill Fares the Land: Migrants and Migratory Labor in the United States* (New York: Arno Press, 1976). Paul S. Taylor wrote the six-volume *Mexican Labor in the United States,* published between 1928 and 1934. Emory Stephen Bogardus wrote *The Mexican in the United States* (Los Angeles: University of Southern California Press, 1970).

9. Manuel Garcia y Griego, "The Importation of Mexican Contract Laborers to the United States, 1942–1964: Antecedents, Operations and Legacy," University of California, San Diego, 1981, Program in United States-Mexican Studies, working paper no. 11. Lisbeth Hass, "The Bracero in Orange County, California: A Work Force for Economic Transition." University of California, San Diego, 1981, Program in U.S.-Mexican Studies, working paper no. 29.

10. Matt S. Meier and Feliciano Rivera, *The Chicanos: A History of Mexican Americans* (New York: Hill and Wang, 1972), p. 111.

11. Juan Ramon Garcia, *Operation Wetback: The Mass Deportation of Mexican Undocumented Workers in 1954* (Westport, Conn.: Greenwood Press, 1980), pp. 18–69. According to Garcia, *braceros* in 1957 earned approximately $200 million, half of which went back to Mexico.

12. Congressional Research Service, Library of Congress, 96th Congress, *U.S. Immigration Laws and Policy: 1952–1979: A Report* (Washington, D.C.: Government Printing Office, 1979), p. 33.

13. *Who Was Who in the American Military* (Chicago: Marquis Who's Who, 1975) contains few Hispanic names.

14. Meier and Rivera, *The Chicanos,* p. 186. According to the U.S. Office of Inter-American Affairs Publications, *Norte Americanos de Habla Española en la Guerra* (Washington D.C.: Government Printing Office, c. 1942), 250,000 Spanish-speaking Americans had enlisted at the time of its publication.

15. Information supplied by the Adjutant General's Office, National Guard, Commonwealth of Puerto Rico. During the Korean War, the 296th Combat Group of the Puerto Rico National Guard was activated; elements of the unit were sent to Korea as replacements for the 65th Infantry Regiment. Of the 43,434 Puerto Ricans who served in the forces, 322 died and 582 were killed in action. See also: William Warner Harris, *Puerto Rico's Fighting 65th U.S. Infantry: From San Juan to Chorwau* (San Rafael, Calif.: Presidio Press, 1980).

16. Raul Morin, *Among the Valiant: Mexican-Americans in World War II and Korea* (Alhambra, California: Borden Publishing Company, 1966), pp. 25–33.

17. We have not come across any studies of ethnic prejudice against Hispanic soldiers in World War II. Morris Janowits, "Mobility, Subjective Deprivation, and Ethnic Hostility" (Ph.D. diss., University of Chicago, 1948), p. 122, deals only with anti-Jewish and anti-black prejudice. According to Janowitz' sample, there was less "outspoken and intense" anti-Semitism among combat soldiers (28 percent) and combat-support soldiers (25 percent) than among noncombatant personnel (47 percent). There was more anti-black sentiment among the combat soldiers than among combat-support and noncombatant personnel (40 percent, 21 percent, and 32 percent, respectively) at a time when most black soldiers were segregated and excluded from combat formations. In regard to prejudice in general, the educated and technically well-qualified soldiers in all the world's

armies probably were less subject to racial prejudice than their more poorly educated contemporaries, no matter what their combat status.

18. Rodolfo Acuña, *Occupied America: The Chicanos' Struggle Toward Liberation* (San Francisco: Canfield Press, 1972), pp. 198–208. See also Mauricio Mazón, *The Zoot-Suit Riots: The Psychology of Symbolic Annihilation* (Austin: University of Texas Press, 1984).

19. See U.S. Office of Inter-American Affairs, *Norte Americanos de Habla Española en la Guerra* (Washington, D.C.: Government Printing Office, c. 1942) and Morin, *Among the Valiant.*

20. Morin, *Among the Valiant,* p. 189.

Chapter 5

1. Gordon K. Lewis, *Notes on the Puerto Rican Revolution: An Essay on American Dominance and Caribbean Resistance* (New York: Monthly Review Press, 1975).

2. Manuel Maldonado-Denis, *Puerto Rico: A Social-Historic Interpretation* (New York: Random House, 1972).

3. Earl S. Garver and Ernest B. Fincher, *Puerto Rico: Unsolved Problem* (New York: Elgin Press, 1945), pp. 80–87.

4. Between 1940 and 1964, manufacturing output rose from $27 million to $486 million; trade and commerce from $26 million to $375 million; finance and related service from $25 million to $231 million; and contract construction from $3 million to $2,531 million. See Henry Wells, *The Modernization of Puerto Rico: A Political Study of Changing Values and Institutions* (Cambridge, Mass.: Harvard University Press, 1969), p. 155.

5. Maldonado-Denis, *Puerto Rico,* p. 180.

6. Comparative figures in U.S. dollars in 1958 were: United States, $2,115; Puerto Rico, $1,250; Mexico, $510. *Britannica Book of the Year* (Chicago: William Benton, 1971), p. 388.

7. Wells, *The Modernization of Puerto Rico,* p. 268.

8. Rafael Herandez-Colon, "Reagan's Caribbean Aid," *San Francisco Chronicle,* July 7, 1982, Section C, pp. 4–5.

9. Kal Wagenheim, *Puerto Ricans in the U.S., Report No. 58,* Minority Rights Group, New York, 1982, p. 20. Juan M. García-Passalacqua, *Puerto Rico: Equality and Freedom at Issue* (New York: Praeger, 1984).

10. Raymond Carr, *Puerto Rico: A Colonial Experiment* (New York: Vintage Books, 1984), p. 5.

11. For figures, see Nathan Glazer and Daniel Patrick Moynihan, *Beyond the Melting Pot: The Negroes, Puerto Ricans, Jews, Italians, and Irish of New York City* (Cambridge, Mass.: M.I.T. Press, 1963), p. 320.

12. U.S. Department of Labor. Bureau of Statistics. *A Socio-Economic Profile of Puerto Rican New Yorkers.* Regional Report 46 (Washington, D.C.: The Bureau, 1975).

13. Joseph P. Fitzpatrick, "The Puerto Ricans," in Dennis Laurence Cuddy, ed., *Contemporary American Immigration: Interpretive Essays* (Boston: Twayne Publishers, 1982), pp. 118–45.

14. Jagna Wojcicka Sharff, "Free Enterprise and the Ghetto Family," *Psychology Today* (March 1981): 41–48.
15. Kenneth A. Briggs, "Among Hispanic Catholics, Another Pattern of Practice," *New York Times,* January 9, 1983, section EY, p. 10.
16. Thomas Sowell, *Ethnic America: A History* (New York: Basic Books, 1981), p. 243.
17. "Learning the Hispanic Hustle," *Christian Science Monitor,* May 1, 1980.

Chapter 6

1. *Encyclopaedia Britannica,* "Macropaedia" series (1975), vol. 5, p. 353. To be fair to the *Encyclopaedia,* this interpretation differed strikingly from that given in the *Encyclopaedia Britannica's* preceding (1968) edition's entry on "Cuba," vol. 6, p. 877. The literature on the subject is vast. For Cuban government statistics, see "Cuba": Dirección General de Estadístico, *Compendio Estadístico de Cuba* (La Havana: 1965); Julio Le Rierend, *Historia Económica de Cuba* (La Havana: Editorial Nacional de Cuba, 1965); and Francisco Lopez Segrera, *Cuba: Capitalismo Dependiente y Subdesarrollo, 1910–1959* (La Havana: Casa de las Americas, 1972).
2. Wages for an eight-hour day in the early 1950s were $6.00 Belgium, $4.70 Austria, $2.42 Mexico, and $1.15 Egypt. See Cuban Economic Research Project, *A Study on Cuba: The Colonial and Republican Periods* (Coral Gables: University of Miami Press, 1965), pp. 421, 429. Truth about Cuba Committee, *Facts, Data, and Statistics on Pre-Communist Cuba* (Miami, 1956), passim.
3. Theodore Draper, "The Communist Party of Cuba," in Witold S. Sworakowski, ed., *World Communism: A Handbook, 1918–1965* (Stanford: Hoover Institution Press, 1973), pp. 98–105.
4. Theodore Draper, *Castroism: Theory and Practice* (New York: Praeger, 1965), p. 105.
5. Ibid., p. 107. For a more recent account, and one friendlier to Cuba's attempt to build socialism, see Arthur MacEwan, *Revolution and Economic Development in Cuba: Moving Toward Socialism* (New York: St. Martin's Press, 1981).
6. According to the NAACP, the American blacks' total income stood at $157 billion; of this, $7.6 billion was spent on automobiles, $5 billion on recreation, and $1.3 billion on vacations and pleasure trips—altogether, $13.9 billion. See "NAACP Boycott Strategy," *San Francisco Chronicle,* June 30, 1982, p. 9. The Cuban GNP in 1979 also stood at $13.9 billion.
7. *New York Times,* June 17, 1982, pp. 35–36. For statistics, see also "Jürgen Westphalen, Latein-Amerikas Wirtschaft in der Bewahrungsprobe," *Rissener Rundbrief,* no. 6 (June 1982), p. 2. For a variety of other interpretations, see Loree Wilkerson, *Fidel Castro's Political Programs from Reformism to "Marxism-Leninism"* (Gainesville: University of Florida Press, 1965); Richard R. Fagen, *The Transformation of Political Culture in Cuba* (Stanford University Press, 1965); and Pedro Serviat, *40 Aniversario de la Fundación del Partido Comunista* (Havana: Editorial EIR, 1965).

8. Raul Moncarz and Antonio Jorge, "Cuban Immigration to the United States," in Dennis Laurence Cuddy, ed., *Contemporary American Immigration* (Boston: Twayne Publishers, 1982), pp. 148–49. For an interpretation favorable to Castro, see Yolanda Prieto, "Cuban Migration of the 1960s in Perspective." New York University Center for Latin and Caribbean Studies, 1984, occasional paper no. 46. The author argues that the United States deliberately fostered Cuban emigration in order to destabilize the revolution by depriving Cuba of many skilled people and by persuading world opinion that things were bad under Castro's rule.

9. For statistical details, see Juan M. Clark, "The Exodus from Revolutionary Cuba, 1959-1974: A Sociological Analysis" (Ph.D. diss., University of Florida, 1975), especially pp. 214-15. For political motives, see Richard R. Fagen, Richard A. Brody, and Thomas J. O'Leary, *Cubans in Exile: Disaffection and the Revolution* (Stanford, Calif.: Stanford University Press, 1968) and Lorrin Philipson and Rafael Llerena, *Freedom Flights: Cuban Refugees Talk About Life Under Castro* (New York: Random House, 1981).

10. Between 1961 and 1970, a total of 256,800 Cubans legally entered the United States; between 1971 and 1980, 276,000; between 1981 and 1983, 28,000. Comparative figures for Mexico were, respectively, 443,300; 637,200; and 216,500. For Central America (including El Salvador, Guatemala, and Panama) 97,700; 132,400; and 72,700. For South America 228,300; 284,400; and 107,400. For Spain 30,500; 30,000; and 4,800. See U.S. Department of Commerce, *Statistical Abstracts of the United States 1986* (Washington, D.C.: U.S. Government Printing Office, 1985), p. 86.

11. Douglas Butterworth, *The People of Buena Ventura: Relocation of Slum Dwellers* (Urbana: University of Illinois Press, 1980). See also the review by Roland Alum, "A Study of 'The Culture of Poverty' in Castro's Cuba," *New America*, vol. 14, July–August 1983, p. 12.

12. See Alejandro Portes, "Immigrants' Attainment: An Analysis of Occupation and Earnings Among Cuban Exiles," in Robert M. Hauser et al., eds., *Social Structure and Behavior: Essays in Honor of William Hamilton Sewell* (New York: Academic Press, 1982), p. 21–112.

13. Moncarz and Jorge, "Cuban Immigration to the United States," in Cuddy, *Cuban Migration of the 1960s*, pp. 149–150.

14. Lorrin Philipson and Rafael Llerena, *Freedom Flights* (New York: Random House, 1981), pp. 20–21.

15. Ibid., pp. 43, 138.

16. Sylvia Castellanos, *The Cuban Refugee Problem in Perspective: 1959–1980* (Washington, D.C.: Heritage Foundation, 1980).

17. Antonio Navarro, *Tocayo: The True Story of a Resistance Leader in Castro's Cuba* (Westport, Conn.: Arlington House, 1981).

18. Douglas Gurak, "The Social and Economic Situation of Hispanics: An Overview," in Office of Pastoral Research, Diocese of New York, *Hispanics in New York: Religious, Cultural and Social Experiences*. New York, 1982, vol. 2, pp. 87–147.

19. These figures came from a hitherto unpublished manuscript by Roland A. Alum and Luis Alum, with the assistance of R. Heriberto Dixon, "Impli-

caciones Sociológicas de la Diaspora Cubana," kindly made available to the authors by Dr. Roland A. Alum. Other works by the Alums include, for instance, Roland A. Alum and L. Alum, "On the Assimilation of Cubans in New Jersey," *International Migration Review* no. 41 (Spring 1978): pp. 143–144.

20. For a detailed study, see Eleanor Rogg, *The Assimilation of Cuban Exiles: The Role of Community and Class* (New York: Aberdeen Press, 1974).

21. Robert M. Price, in the *Christian Science Monitor*, October 20, 1980, p. 12. For a recent study of the Cubans, see Thomas D. Boswell and James R. Curtis, *The Cuban-American Experience* (Totowa, N. J.: Rowman and Allanheld, 1984).

22. For an expression of the fear of the spread of Spanish, see Thomas B. Morgan, "The Latinization of America," *Esquire*, May 1983, pp. 47–59.

Chapter 7

1. The 1965 Immigration Act set an annual numerical limit of 170,000 from the Eastern Hemisphere, with no more than 20,000 immigrants from any one country, and a limit of 120,000 on Western Hemisphere immigrants. Certain categories were exempt from numerical limitations, including immediate relatives (parents, spouses, and children) of U.S. citizens and various clauses of special immigrants. The act marked a departure from the old principle that certain Northern European nationalities—British, Germans, and Scandanavians—were more desirable. Between 1968 and 1976, preference quotas were applied only to immigrants from the Eastern Hemisphere. From 1978 onward, the separate hemisphere limits were abolished in favor of a worldwide limit of 290,000. In practice, this worldwide limitation was rendered almost meaningless through the growth of illegal immigration as well as a variety of court decisions that further opened the doors to immigrants. In 1976, for example, a court decision exempted Cuban refugees from numerical limitations; the decision was made retroactive to 1968.

2. Ann Orlov and Reed Ueda, "Central and South Americans," in Stephen Thermstrom, ed., *Harvard Encyclopedia of American Ethnic Groups* (Cambridge, Mass.: Harvard University Press, 1980), pp. 210–17.

3. Willard L. Beaulac, *The Fractured Continent: Latin America in Close-up* (Stanford: Hoover Institution Press, 1980), p. 52.

4. Peter Pauer, "The Market in the Dock," *Policy Review* 10 (Fall 1979): 101–21.

5. Robert A. Alum, "The Dominican Republic," in *Encyclopedia of Developing Nations* (New York: McGraw-Hill, n.d.), pp. 283–97; Eugenia Georges, "New Immigrants and the Political Process: Dominicans in New York," Faculty of Arts and Science, Center for Latin American and Caribbean Studies, occasional paper no. 45, 1984.

6. E. Erik Calonius, "Caribbean Crisis," *Wall Street Journal*, January 7, 1983, pp. 7–8.

7. Thomas K. Morrison and Richard Sinkin, "International Migration in the Dominican Republic: Implications for Development Planning," *International Migration Review*, vol. 16, no. 4 (1981): 819–837.

8. Glenn Hendricks, *The Dominican Diaspora: From the Dominican Republic to New York City—Villagers in Transition* (New York: Teachers College, 1974).
9. For a comparative study of German post-World War II emigration, see Joachim Schops, ed., *Auswanderer: ein deutscher Traum* (Hamburg: Rowohlt Verlag, 1982).
10. *TV Guide*, January 22, 1983, p. 26.
11. Orlov and Ueda, "Central and South Americans," in Thermstrom, ed., *Harvard Encyclopedia of American Ethnic Groups*, pp. 210–17.
12. Poem by Rodolfo "Corky" Gonzales, cited by Stan Steiner, *The Mexican Americans* (New York: Harper and Row, 1970), p. 384.
13. Thomas Sowell, *Ethnic America: A History* (New York: Basic Books, 1981).
14. Barry R. Chiswick, "The Economic Progress of Immigrants: Some Apparently Universal Patterns," in Barry Chiswick, ed., *The Gateway* (Washington, D.C.: American Enterprise Institute, 1982), p. 131, p. 137.
15. Douglas Gurak, "The Social and Economic Situation of Hispanics: An Overview of Puerto Ricans, Dominicans, Cubans, and Mexicans in the United States and New York City," in Office of Pastoral Research, *Hispanics in New York*, New York, 1982, vol. 2, p. 89–152, especially p. 113. The figures for intergroup intermarriage may be compared with those provided by Clyde Mitchell for African mineworkers of differing backgrounds on the Zambian copper belt; see J. Clyde Mitchell, "Aspects of African Marriage on the Copper Belt of Northern Rhodesia," *Rhodes-Livingston Institute Journal* no. 22 (1957): 1–30.
16. A. J. Jaffe, Ruth M. Cullen, and Thomas Boswell, *Spanish Americans in the United States: Changing Demographic Characteristics* (New York: Research Institute for the Study of Man, 1976), especially pp. 22–23.

Chapter 8

1. John Price, *Tijuana: Urbanization in a Border Culture* (South Bend, Ind.: University of Notre Dame Press, 1973), p. 18.
2. Miles Hansen, *The Border Economy: Regional Development in the Southwest* (Austin: University of Texas Press, 1981), pp. 11–12.
3. John W. House, *Frontier in the Rio Grande: A Political Geography of Development and Social Deprivation* (Oxford: Clarendon Press, 1982), pp. 259–260. For a popular representation, written from the standpoint of a local border community, see the informative "Special Report, by the *El Paso Herald-Post*," Summer 1983, entitled "The Border."
4. Cited in Miles Hansen, *The Border Economy: Regional Development in the Southwest* (Austin: University of Texas Press, 1981), pp. 11–12.
5. W. I. Thomas and Florian Znaniecki, *The Polish Peasant in Europe and America: Monograph of an Immigrant Group*, 5 vols. (Boston: The Gorham Press, 1920). For a critique, see Andrew M. Greeley, *The American Catholic: A Social Portrait* (New York: Basic Books, 1977), especially pp. 60–67.
6. Antonio Ugalde et al., *The Urbanization Process of a Poor Mexican Neighborhood* (Austin: University of Texas Press, 1974), a study of a *barrio* in

Ciudad Júarez. For a contrasting view, *Politico-Economic Profile* (South Bend, Ind.: University of Notre Dame Press, 1977), p. 156.

7. Quoted by Tom Miller, *On the Border: Portraits of America's Southwestern Frontier* (New York: Harper and Row, 1981).

8. Ugalde et al., *Urbanization Process*, p. 54.

9. James Stuart and Michael Kearney, "Causes and Effects of Agricultural Labor Migration from the Mixeta of Oaxaca to California," University of California, San Diego, 1981, working papers in U.S. Mexican Studies, no. 28. Roland Mines, *Developing a Community Tradition of Migration: A Field Study in Rural Zacatecas, Mexico and California Settlement Areas*, University of California, San Diego, 1981, monographs in U.S.-Mexican Studies, no. 3. Merilee S. Grindle, ed., *Issues in U.S. Mexican Agricultural Relations: A Binational Consultation*, University of California, San Diego, 1982. Paul Ehrlich et al., *The Golden Door: International Migration, Mexico and the United States* (New York: Wideview Books, 1981), pp. 355–ff.

10. Carlos Salinas de Gotari, *Political Participation, Public Investment and Support for the System: A Comparative Study of Rural Communities in Mexico*, University of California, 1982, Center for U.S-Mexico Studies, research report no. 35. The author found that, contrary to expectations, government investment in rural communities in Mexico actually diminished political support for the government from the beneficiaries of public aid. The author concluded that if the state wants to maximize support, it may have to forgo the strategy of organizing *campesinos* to increase productivity. Development programs must be decentralized; gratitude cannot be expected for development programs not requested by the community.

11. Kenneth D. Roberts, *Agrarian Structure and Labor Migration in Rural Mexico*, University of California, San Diego, 1981, working papers in U.S.-Mexican Studies, no. 30.

12. Dusko Dader, *The Yugoslavs* (New York: Vintage Books, 1979), pp. 80–81.

13. George Kiser and Marth Woody Kiser, eds., *Mexican Workers in the United States: Historical and Political Perspectives* (Albuquerque: University of New Mexico Press, 1979), pp. 215–ff.

14. See Report by David S. North in House of Representatives, *Meetings Before the Subcommittee on Migratory Labor* (Washington, D.C.: Government Printing Office, May 21, 1969).

15. See Manuel Villalpando, "The Socioeconomic impact of illegal aliens in the County of San Diego" (Ph.D. diss., United States International University, 1976), pp. 202–3.

16. Anna-Stinson Ericson, "The Impact of Commuters on the Mexican-American Border Area," in Kiser and Kiser, eds., *Mexican Workers in the United States*, p. 238.

17. Ellwyn R. Stoddard, "Overview," in Ellwyn R. Stoddard, Richard L. Nostrand, and Jonathan P. West, eds., *Borderland Sourcebook: A Guide to the Literature on Northern Mexico and the American Southwest* (Norman: University of Oklahoma Press, 1983), p. 5.

18. Ellwyn R. Stoddard, "Local and Regional Incongruities in Bi-National Diplomacy: Policy of the U.S.-Mexico Border," in Craig Wagner, ed., *Policy*

Perspectives, vol. 2, no. 1, 1982, pp. 111–135; and Ellwyn Stoddard, *Patterns of Poverty Along the U.S.-Mexico Border* (El Paso: University of Texas Center for Inter-American Studies, 1978).

19. Frank J. Call, "Problems and Cooperation between U.S. and Mexican Border Cities," in Richard D. Erb and Stanley R. Ross, eds., *United States Relations with Mexico: Context and Content* (Washington, D.C.: American Enterprise Institute, 1981), pp. 74–85.

Chapter 9

1. See Michael J. Piore, *Birds of Passage: Migrant Labor and Industrial Societies* (New York: Cambridge University Press, 1979), pp. 1–26.
2. David S. North and Marion F. Houston, *The Characteristics and Role of Illegal Aliens in the U.S. Labor Market: An Exploratory Study* (Washington, D.C.: Lipton, 1976).
3. Maurice D. van Arsdol et al., *Non-Apprehended and Unapprehended Undocumented Residents in the Los Angeles Labor Market: An Exploratory Study*, University of California, Los Angeles, Department of Anthropology and Sociology, May 1979, pp. 51, 73.
4. For comparisons, see Kenneth F. Johnson and Miles I. Williams, *Illegal Aliens in the Western Hemisphere* (New York: Praeger Press, 1981).
5. Walter Fogel, "Twentieth-Century Mexican Migration to the United States," in Barry R. Chiswick, ed., *The Gateway: U.S. Immigration Issues and Policies* (Washington, D.C.: American Enterprise Institute, 1982), pp. 199–200.
6. For a discussion, see Frank D. Bean and Allan G. King, *Estimates of the Size of the Illegal Migrant Population of Mexican Origin in the United States: An Assessment and Review* (Austin: Texas Population Research Center Papers, series 5, 1983). For Mexican findings, see the ongoing publications series for the *Encuesta nacional de emigración a la frontera norte del país y los Estados Unidos* (ENEFNEU), which is being published by the Centro Nacional de Información y Estadísticas de Trabajo Mexico in Mexico, D.F. Publications available to us include Miguel Cervera, *Tabla de estancia en Los Estados Unidos para trabajadores Mexicanos indocumentados*, 1979; and Carlos H. Zazueta, *En las puertas del paraíso*, 1980. See also David M. Heer, "What is the Annual Net Flow of Undocumented Mexican Immigrants to the United States?" *Demography* vol. 16, no. 3 (August 1979): 417–423.
7. Johnson and Williams, *Illegal Aliens in the Western Hemisphere*, p. 89.
8. See Julian Samora, *Los Mojados, The Wetback Story* (South Bend, Ind.: University of Notre Dame Press, 1971).
9. See Harry E. Cross and James A. Sandos, *The Impact of Undocumented Mexican Workers on the United States: A Critical Assessment*, paper no. 15 (Washington, D.C.: Batelle Population and Development Program, 1979).
10. See Edwin Harwood, "Can Immigration Laws Be Enforced," *The Public Interest* 27 (Summer 1983): 107–123; "The Crisis in Immigration Policy," *Journal of Contemporary Studies* (Fall 1983): 45–59; and "Alienation: American Attitudes Toward Immigration," *Public Opinion* (June–July 1983): 49–51.

11. David M. Heer, "Latin America Immigration to the United States Since World War 2." (Paper presented at the conference, Crossing The Border: Latin Immigration and the United States Interest, San Diego, Calif., January 31–February 3, 1985).

12. Figures reported in *Christian Science Monitor*, January 27, 1981, p. 9.

13. See Antonio Arias, "Undocumented Mexicans: A Study in the Social Psychology of Clandestine Migration to the United States" (Ph.D. diss., University of California, San Diego, 1981), pp. 25, 170–188, 189.

14. In 1982, for instance, a federal judge in San Francisco enjoined the INS from entering private business properties to search for undocumented workers unless the INS agents have a search warrant or the consent of the owners. See *San Francisco Chronicle*, September 17, 1982, p. 2.

15. We are indebted to our colleague Dr. Edwin Harwood, an American sociologist, for allowing us to use an unpublished paper entitled "Apprehending Deportable Aliens: Are There Viable Policy Options?" Dr. Harwood, who read this chapter, was, at the time of our writing, engaged in a major study of immigration law enforcement in the United States. For assessments of the immigration problem from the Mexican standpoint, see Jorge A. Bustamente, "El Espalda Mojada: Informe de un Observador Participiente," in *Espaldas Mojadas* (Mexico D.F.: Centro de Estudios Sociologicos, No. 6, Colegio de Mexico, 1976).

16. Michael Piore, *Birds of Passage* (New York: Cambridge University Press, 1979), p. 149.

17. For statistics, see Leon F. Bouvier, *The Impact of Immigration on U.S. Population Size* (Washington, D.C.: Population Reference Bureau, Inc., 1981), p. 2.

18. *San Francisco Chronicle*, October 21, 1982, p. 20.

19. Center for Continuing Study of the California Economy, *Projections of Hispanic Population for the United States: 1990 and 2000* (Palo Alto, Calif.: 1982), p. 16.

20. According to Marian E. De Forest, "Mexican Workers North of the Border," *Harvard Business Review* 16 (May–June 1981), p. 150, Spanish-speaking persons in the United States number 13.6 million according to the 1980 census; federal estimates add at least 7.4 million undocumented aliens. Of the total number, about 15 million are of Mexican extraction; one million or more Mexicans enter the United States every year, legally or illegally. Their natural increase (births minus deaths) is about 1.8 percent per year compared to virtually zero percent for the U.S. population as a whole and 1.2 percent for black Americans.

21. Thomas Sowell, *Ethnic America: A History* (New York: Basic Books, 1981), p. 220, and Barry Chiswick, "The Effects of Americanization on the Earnings of Foreign Born," *Journal of Political Economy* 11 (October 1978): 879–922.

22. Julian L. Simon, *What Immigrants Take From, and Give To, the Public Coffers*, faculty working paper no. 730, Champaign-Urbana: University of Illinois, Bureau of Economic and Business Research, 1981, p. 20.

23. See Paul Ehrlich, Loy Bilderback, and Anne H. Ehrlich, *The Golden Gate: International Migration, Mexico and the United States* (New York: Wideview Books, 1981), pp. 344–ff.

24. Figures kindly supplied to us by Barbara Held, a doctoral student at the University of Free Berlin who is preparing a dissertation on Mexican Americans.

25. Julian L. Simon, *What Immigrants Take From, and Give To, the Public Coffers*, faculty working paper no. 730, Champaign-Urbana: University of Illinois, Bureau of Economic and Business Research, 1980, p. 24.

26. Wayne A. Cornelius, "The Future of Mexican Immigrants in California: A New Perspective for Public Policy." (Paper presented at the Woodrow Wilson International Center for Scholars, Washington, D.C., February 27, 1980).

27. American experts in the pseudo-science of eugenics played an important role in shaping the post–World War I immigration laws designed to keep out racially "inferior" stock. The expert eugenics agent for the U.S. House of Representatives Committee on Immigration and Naturalization was H.H. Laughlin, author of a "model law" to prevent the breeding of "inferior" stock. His model law was almost identical to the code drawn up by the Nazis to destroy "incurable" mental patients in their infamous euthanasia campaign. See Allan Chase, *The Legacy of Malthus: The Social Costs of the New Scientific Racism* (Chicago: University of Illinois Press, 1980), pp. 343–50.

28. In 1982, U.S. Ambassador to Mexico John Gavin pointed out in a dispatch to Washington the highly unfavorable consequences of the immigration bill then pending in Congress: "Probably between one and two million Mexicans would be forced to return . . . at a moment [when] Mexico is least capable of generating additional employment." *San Francisco Chronicle*, November 25, 1982, p. 33.

29. Cited by Kal Wagenheim, *Puerto Rico: A Profile* (London: Pall Mall Press, 1970), p. 244.

30. U.S. Senate, *U.S. Immigration Law and Policy 1952–1979 . . .*, Committee on the Judiciary Upon the Formation of the Select Commission on Immigration and Refuge Policy (Washington, D.C.: Government Printing Office, 1979), p. 72.

31. Otis L. Graham, *Illegal Immigration and the New Reform Movement*, FAIR Immigration Papers, no. 2 (Washington, D.C., 1980), p. 10.

32. *Christian Science Monitor*, December 3, 1982, p. 4.

33. For Mexican population growth, see Walter Fogel, "Twentieth-Century Mexican Migration to the United States," in Barry R. Chiswick, ed., *The Gateway: U.S. Immigration Issues and Policies* (Washington, D.C.: American Enterprise Institute for Public Policy Research, 1982), pp. 204–206.

34. David North and Allen LeBel, *Manpower and Immigration Policies in the U.S.: A Special Report of the National Commission for Manpower Policy* (Washington, D.C.: Government Printing Office, 1979).

35. Graham, *Illegal Immigration and the New Reform Movement*.

36. Morton Paglin, *Poverty and Transfer in Kind: A Reevaluation of Poverty in the United States* (Stanford: Hoover Institution Press, 1980), p. 41.

37. Also in 1982, a federal judge ruled in Atlanta that refugees held in an Atlanta penitentiary could settle anywhere in the United States. This decision,

made by U.S. District Judge Marvin Shoob, set aside a policy that had previously restricted settlement in south Florida to refugees with immediate relatives in that part of the country. As a result of the court's decision, every refugee already settled in south Florida could serve as sponsor for his friends and relatives, including distant ones, in prison. Federal and state officials, expressing disappointment at Shoob's decision, explained that the government had previously followed a strict policy of not resettling former prison inmates in such areas as Florida. Florida governor Bob Graham expressed his disagreement on the grounds that refugee policy should be treated as a national concern and that no one state should be unusually burdened.

38. For a detailed discussion, see Roger Conner, *Breaking Down the Barriers: The Changing Relationship Between Illegal Immigration and Welfare*, FAIR Immigration Paper no. IV (Washington, D.C., 1982).

39. Maurice D. Van Arsdol, Jr., et al., *Non-Apprehended and Apprehended Undocumented Residents in the Los Angeles Labor Market: An Exploratory Study* (Los Angeles: University of Southern California, Department of Sociology and Anthropology, 1979).

40. Cited by Roger Conner, "Breaking Down the Barriers," pp. 14–17.

41. *Hispanic Monitor*, May 1984, p. 3.

42. David S. North and Jennifer R. Wagner, *Immigration and Income Transfer Policies in the United States: An Analysis of a Non-relationship* (Washington, D.C.: Center for Labor and Migration Studies, 1982), pp. iv–v.

43. See Julian Simon, "The Overall Effect of Immigrants Upon Natives' Income," University of Illinois, College of Commerce and Business Administration, working paper, 1980.

44. Paul R. Ehrlich, Loy Bilderback, and Anne H. Ehrlich, *The Golden Door: International Migration, Mexico and the United States* (New York: Wideview Books, 1981), pp. 283–296; *The United States Government Manual, 1981–1982* (Washington, D.C.: U.S. Government Printing Office, 1981), pp. 349–350.

45. See Edwin Harwood, "The Crisis in Immigration Policy," *Journal of Contemporary Studies* IV, no. 1 (Fall 1983); Van Arsdol, *Non-Apprehended and Apprehended Undocumented Residents,* pp. 126–127. For a detailed listing of do's and don'ts of immigration, see Pastora San Juan Cafferty et al., *The Dilemma of American Immigration: Beyond the Golden Door* (New Brunswick, N.J.: Transaction Books, 1983), chapter 12. See also F. Ray Marshall, *Illegal Immigration: The Problem, the Solutions,* FAIR Immigration Paper no. 3 (Washington, D.C.: 1982). For comparison, see Kenneth F. Johnson and Miles W. Williams, *Illegal Aliens in the Western Hemisphere* (New York: Praeger Press, 1981).

46. *Christian Science Monitor*, December 3, 1982, p. 8.

47. Pastora San Juan Cafferty et al., *The Dilemma of American Immigration,* pp. 181–ff.

Chapter 10

1. Ernesto Galarza, *Merchants of Labor* (San José, CA: Rosicrucion Press, 1964), p. 336.

2. For the Chicano revival, see, for instance, the essays in National Association for Chicano Studies, *History, Culture and Society: Chicano Studies in the 1980s* (Ypsilanti, Mich.: Bilingual Press, 1983). For the problem of language, see Fausto Avedano, "The Spanish Language in the Southwest: Past, Present, and Future," in Arnulfo D. Trejo, ed., *The Chicanos: As We See Ourselves* (Tucson: University of Arizona Press, 1979), pp. 133–50.

3. Linda S. Lichter, S. Robert Lichter, and Stanley Rothman, "How Show Business Shows Business," *Public Opinion* 18 (October–November 1982): pp. 10–12. The authors' analysis of prime-time entertainment picturing businessmen in 1979–81 showed that only 9 percent of those portrayed in business were represented in a positive fashion. Most businessmen were depicted as wealthy, middle-aged, white males who lived in beautifully furnished estates, were pampered by servants, were animated by greed, were apt to break the law, and lived in idle luxury. Not a single businessman in the study was working class or poor. Even the characters represented in a positive fashion often were portrayed as "good guys" precisely because they were unusual figures in the business world.

4. Jesus Chevaria, "On Chicano History," in Americo Paredes, ed., *Humanidad: Essays in Honor of George I. Sanchez*, monograph 6, Chicano Studies Center Publications, University of California, Los Angeles, 1977, pp. 41–57.

5. See, for instance, the 9:00 PM telecast of December 1981 on KQED, San Francisco.

6. "The Spiritual Plan of Aztlán," (March 31, 1969), reprinted in Armando B. Rendon, *Chicano Manifesto* (New York: Collier Books, 1971), pp. 336–37.

7. Rendon, *Chicano Manifesto*, pp. 9–10, 16, 178.

8. Arnulfo D. Trejo, "As We See Ourselves in Chicano Literature," in Arnulfo D. Trejo, ed., *The Chicanos*, p. 188.

9. Rudolfo Gonzáles, *I Am Joaquín* (Toronto and New York: Bantam Pathfinders, 1972), pp. 10–11, 52, 100.

10. Robert E. Quirk, *Mexico* (Englewood Cliffs, N.J.: Prentice-Hall, 1971), p. 21.

11. See, for instance, Narciso Martinez, *Una historia de la música de la frontera* (Texas-American Border Music, vol. 10, Folloric Records, 9017, Arhoollie Records, El Cerrito, Calif.).

12. Manuel A. Machado, *Listen Chicano: An Informal History of the Mexican American* (Chicago: Nelson Hall, 1978), p. 150.

13. See also *Public Opinion*, 1983.

14. Ibid.

15. See Ron Arias, *"The Road to Tamazunchale," West Coast Poetry Review* 6, vol. 4, no. 4 (1975), and also the introduction by Tomas Rivera. For Gómez-Quinoñes, see, for example, his studies *On Culture*, UCLA-Chicano Studies Center Publications, popular series no. 1, 1977; "Research Notes on the Twentieth Century: Notes on Periodizations 1900–1965," *Aztlán* 1 (Spring 1970): 115–118; "Toward a Perspective on Chicano History, *Aztlán* 2 (Fall 1971): 1–49; "Critique of the National Question, Self-Determination and Nationalism," *Latin American Perspectives* 33 (Spring 1982): 62–83.

16. For a comprehensive guide, see Ellwyn R. Stoddard, Richard L. Nostrand, and Jonathan P. West, *Borderland Source Book: A Guide to the Literature on Northern Mexico and the American Southwest* (Norman: University of Oklahoma Press, 1983).

17. See the section "Ethnicity in America," *Public Opinion* (October–November 1964), especially p. 23. Eighty-one percent of Hispanic respondents stated that they were "very happy" or "pretty happy" with their lives, compared to a national average of 68 percent. See also Nathan Glazer's analysis of these figures, p. 2.

18. John Mirowsky II and Catherine E. Ross, "Minority Status, Ethnic Culture, and Distress: A Comparison of Blacks, Whites, Mexicans and Mexican Americans," *American Journal of Sociology* 86, no. 8: 479–95. According to the *Gallup Report*, no. 234, July 1985, pp. 4–13, "a great deal" or "quite a lot" of confidence in churches was expressed by 66 percent of all respondents and by 67 percent of Hispanic respondents. Corresponding figures for all respondents and for Hispanics concerning banks and banking were 41 percent and 55 percent; newspapers, 35 percent and 44 percent; big business, 31 percent and 36 percent; television, 29 percent and 47 percent; organized labor, 28 percent and 40 percent. The military fared slightly worse in Hispanic opinion than in the overall opinion; a 61 percent approval nationwide, a 57 percent approval among Hispanics. The Supreme Court was approved by 66 percent of all respondents and by 59 percent among Hispanics.

19. Machado, *Listen Chicano,* p. 353.

20. Richard Rodriguez, *Hunger of Memory: The Education of Richard Rodrigues* (New York: Bantam Books, 1983).

21. According to Rodolfo O. de la Garza et al., *The Mexican-American Electorate: A Demographic Profile* (San Antonio Southwest Voter Registration Education Project, 1982), p. 11. Only 5 percent of respondents in the subsamples taken in East Los Angeles and San Antonio, respectively, identified themselves as Chicanos. Of the respondents in San Antonio, 44 percent identified themselves as Mexican Americans or Americans, as did 31 percent in East Los Angeles; 25 percent in San Antonio and 54 percent in East Los Angeles styled themselves Mexicanos, and the rest chose to be called Latinos, Hispanics, etc.

22. By 1982, 89 percent of all citizens of Mexican-American descent and 94 percent of citizens under 26 years of age were either bilingual in Spanish and English or spoke no language other than English. Garza et al., *The Mexican-American Electorate*, p. 13. In the authors' samples, 35 percent had an average family income of $20,000 or more.

23. See, for instance, James Stuart Olson's description: "From the Spanish the Hispanics inherited a spiritual individualism that saw the soul as the most important ingredient of character . . . From Native Americans they acquired a trust for one another, a spiritual communalism, a comfort with the rhythms of nature. The Hispanics judged people according to their inner value, not their political or economic status." James Stuart Olson, *The Ethnic Dimension in American History* (New York: St. Martin's Press, 1979), pp. 377–78.

24. See for instance, Luis Valdez, ed., *Aztlan: An Anthology of Mexican-American Literature* (New York: Alfred A. Knopf, 1972), and Guillermo Her-

nandez, *Canciones de la Raza: Songs of the Chicano Experience* (Berkeley, Calif.: El Sol, 1978). In addition, splendid Mexican-American folklore now found its way into print, for instance, through the work of Americo Paredes of the University of Texas.

25. Rodolfo A. Anaya, *Bless Me Ultima* (Berkeley, Calif.: Quinto Sol Publications, 1972); José António Villareal, *Pocho* (Garden City, N.Y.: Doubleday and Co., 1959); Tomas Rivera, *Y no se lo tragó la tierra: And the Earth did Not Part* (Berkeley, Calif.: Quinto Sol Publications, 1971); Miguel Méndez-M, *Peregrinos de Aztlán* (Tucson, Arizona: Editorial Peregrinos, 1974); Luis Valdez, *Las dos caras del patroncito* (Englewood Cliffs, N. J.: Prentice-Hall, 1972); and Alberto Baltazar Urista, *Floricanto en Aztlán* (University of California, Los Angeles, 1971).

26. Jacinto Quirarte, *Mexican-American Artists* (Austin: University of Texas Press, 1973).

27. Figures from *The World of Learning, 1981–1982* (London: Europa Publications, 1982).

28. Arturo Morales Carrion, *Puerto Rico. A Political and Cultural History* (New York: W.W. Norton, 1983), chapter by Maria Teresa Babin, "A Special Voice: The Cultural Expression," pp. 319–352.

29. Economist Jose Alverez Diaz; architect José María Bens Arrarte; conductor and violinist Alberto Bolet y Tremoleda; noted physician Francisco García Bengochea; economist and labor expert Roberto Eduardo Hernandez Moralez; political scientist Pablo F. Lavin y Padrón; writer-educator and leading expert on Martí (the hero of Cuban independence), Felix Celestino Liazaso y Gonzales; economist Raul Maestri y Arredondo; anthropologist Roland A. Alum; and many others.

30. Other prominent Chicano journals included *Agenda: A Journal of Hispanic Issues* (magazine of the National Council of La Raza, based in Washington, D.C., with analytical and research-based articles on issues of public policy, started in 1973); *Atisbos: Journal of Chicano Research* (Stanford University, founded in 1975, emphasizing quantitative studies); *Aztlán: International Journal of Chicano Studies Research* (Chicano Studies Research Center at UCLA, founded in 1970, a major publication with articles in history, the social sciences, art, literature, and politics); *Caracol: La Revista de la Raza* (published for a time at San Antonio as a tabloid); *Chicana Action Service Center News* (Los Angeles, founded in 1973, for women); *Chicano Law Review* (UCLA School of Law, founded in 1972, emphasizing legal problems affecting Chicanos); *Con Safos: Reflections on Life in the Barrios* (published for a time in Los Angeles); *De Colores: Journal of Chicano Expression and Thought* (Albuquerque, New Mexico, founded in 1973, emphasizing literature, arts, and philosophy); *Encuentro Femenil: The First Chicana Feminist Journal* (published for a time in San Fernando, California); *El Grito: A Journal of Contemporary Mexican-American Thought* (published for a time in Berkeley, Calif., with articles on social, literary, and cultural themes); *Grito del Sol: A Chicano Quarterly* (Berkeley, Calif., founded in 1976, with a literary and social science content); *Journal of Mexican-American History* (started in 1970 at Santa Barbara, Calif.); *Journal of Mexican-*

American Studies (published for a time at Cypress, Calif.); *La Luz* (founded in 1972 at Denver as a magazine of national interest, with a wide range of topics); *Nuestro: The Magazine for Latinos* (published since 1977 in New York City, a general interest magazine); *La Raza Habla* (published for a time at New Mexico State University at Las Cruces); *Regeneración* (published for a time in Los Angeles); *Revista Chicano Riqueña* (founded in 1973, published first at Indiana University and later at the University of Houston; an important publication of interest both to Puerto Rican and Chicano studies, with an emphasis on literature); *Somos* (founded in 1978 at San Bernadino, Calif., as a general magazine); *La Vos de Aztlán* (started in 1968 in Moraga, Calif.). For a fuller listing see Richard Chabran and Francisco Garcia, eds., *Chicano Periodical Index: A Cumulative Index to Selected Chicano Periodicals between 1967 and 1978* (Boston: G.K. Hall, 1981).

31. *Flaco Jimenez y su conjunto*, Arhoolie no. 3007, Arhoolie Records, El Cerrito, California.

32. For example, in 1977 the champions of the World Boxing Association were: heavyweight, Muhammed Ali, Chicago; middleweight, Carlos Monzon, Argentina; jr. middleweight, Eddie Gazo, Nicaragua; welterweight, Carlos Palomino, Mexico; jr. welterweight, Wilfred Benitez, Puerto Rico; lightweight, Roberto Duran, Panama; jr. lightweight, Samuel Serrano, Puerto Rico; featherweight, Aloe Arguello, Nicaragua; and flyweight, Miguel Canto, Mexico.

33. "Latino Film Making is Artistic Renaissance," *Latino* (monthly organ of LULAC), vol. 53, no. 5 (September 1982), p. 8.

34. *Broadcasting Cable Yearbook* (Washington, D.C.: Broadcasting Publications, 1980), pp. B–147, D–90. Nine of these are centered in California, six in Texas, two each in New York and Florida, one each in Illinois and New Mexico, and eight operated in Puerto Rico. See also the informative article by Mercedes de Uriarte, "Battle for the Ear of the Latino," *Los Angeles Times, Calendar Section*, December 14, 1980, pp. 2–7. For a list of Hispanic radio and TV stations, see "Hispanic Employment: A Recruitment Sources Booklet," United States Office of Personnel Management, Hispanic Employment Program, P.O. 1981, pp. 74–83.

35. Felix Frank Gutierrez, "Spanish-Language Radio and Internal Colonialism" (Ph.D. diss., Stanford University, 1976), especially pp. 282–283.

36. Rodolfo O. de la Garza and Robert R. Brischetto, *The Mexican-American Electorate: Information Sources and Policy Orientations* (Southwest Voter Education Registration Project and Hispanic Population Studies Program, University of Texas at Austin, 1982), pp. 4, 12.

Chapter 11

1. Wallace Brown, *The Good Americans: The Loyalists in the American Revolution* (New York: William Morrow, 1969), p. 240.

2. The Community Service Organization (CSO) grew out of a committee formed in 1947 to attempt to get Edward Roybal elected to the Los Angeles City Council. (This attempt failed, but CSO helped him win the election in

1949.) CSO aimed to achieve political representation for groups that were not represented and to help Chicanos learn to help themselves. It maintains a credit union and building association, sponsors language classes, and monitors police actions against Chicanos. CSO obtained little funding from government, but raised money by holding bingo games and similar events.

3. MALDEF also seeks to build an awareness of the Hispanic heritage. In 1973, it formed the Hispanic Education Commission to discuss higher education concerns of the Hispanic communities. MALDEF publishes a quarterly, the *MALDEF Newsletter*. MALDEF also instituted a Lawyer Referral Service and provided grants for the purpose of assisting students to go to law schools. MALDEF became responsible for more than 90 percent of all civil rights litigation affecting Mexican Americans. MALDEF owed much of its financial support to the Ford Foundation, which further assisted minorities through the Ford Foundation Doctoral Fellowships for Black Americans, Mexican Americans, Puerto Ricans, and American Indians (also set up in 1968).

4. NCLR had three major missions: technical assistance and support to Hispanic groups in towns and cities; research and policy analysis and advocacy for Hispanics; and communications and media activities to improve U.S. knowledge of Hispanic heritage and concerns. It also provided support staff and information for local Hispanic groups. Funded originally by the federal government, it drew most of its support from foundations, corporations, and state agencies. The council is the only constituted national Hispanic group in Washington, D.C., but its strength rests on more than one-hundred Hispanic community-based organizations with more than 1 million members throughout the country. The council conducts research on problems facing the Hispanic community (employment, education, etc.). NCLR turned into an active participant in the Hispanic Higher Education Coalition and the Forum of National Hispanic Organizations. Headed in the early 1980s by Raul Yzaguirre, the Council employed some 40 staff officers with field offices in Chicago, Phoenix, and Albuquerque. NCLR also developed the Southwest Voters Registration Education Project which has registered more than 500,000 Hispanic voters. A similar project was started for the midwest in 1982. In 1973, the council co-convened the National Committee on the Concerns of Hispanics and Blacks. The NCLR also publishes a quarterly, *Agenda*, and operates La Raza Production Center to produce Spanish/English radio and TV programs. Before Reagan became President, 75 percent of the council's funds had come from government; thereafter, the proportion dropped to one-third.

5. Sixty percent of ASPIRA's program funding had come from the federal government and 40 percent from other sources. After Ronald Reagan assumed the presidency, the proportion was reversed. ASPIRA of New York provided community-based educational services for the city's Puerto Rican and other Hispanic groups, aimed at training people for jobs. By 1983, ASPIRA leaders claimed that 10,000 a year were being trained in two centers. ASPIRA clubs in high schools encouraged youth to stay in school and gave some instruction in the history and culture of Puerto Rico. The clubs also were concerned with social abuses (drugs, alcoholism, etc.) and personal problems. ASPIRA claimed

a good job-placement record. With a Puerto Rican dropout rate of 40 to 50 percent after age 16, ASPIRA saw this as its main problem. Job training was the next most important function of ASPIRA groups. (Interviews with Mario Anglada, 25 April 1983, New York City.)

6. By the early 1980s, there were nine offices nationwide and the demand for its services was expanding. Funding came from federal, state, and local governments and from the private sector. By the early 1980s, the forum's new president, Dr. Michael Borrero, an economist, sought to reduce the group's dependency on erratic government funding. He looked more to private money in order to diversify the forum's services. He also aimed at putting more emphasis than before on the profit motive in order to develop venture capital for new programs encouraging economic independence and social stability in the Hispanic community. On the national level, the forum supported career services and job placement programs in cities in several states (New York, Illinois, Ohio, and Florida) and in Washington, D.C. For the states, the forum ran, for example, the Hartford Bilingual Career Skills Training Program and the Counseling Unit in Hartford. In New York State, the forum offered a translation bureau to put the state's Department of Social Services literature into Spanish and a training placement program. The New York City program stressed: skills training and placement, bilingual secretaries, clerical and fiscal training, job development, and displaced homemakers services. Marketing research also became of interest to the forum. It planned to reduce the dependency of Puerto Ricans on public funding—by 1983, 30 to 45 percent received public assistance; another 10 to 15 percent were unemployed; and another 20 to 25 percent were underemployed or regarded as an "underclass." These figures graphically demonstrate the plight of the Puerto Rican. The underclass of the young and unskilled families on welfare had little work experience. In the forum's view, they lacked self-confidence, having lost their personal initiative through dependence on the welfare system. (Interview with Dr. Michael Borrero, 25 April 1983, New York City.)

7. Casita Maria, Inc., had been an important part of the South Bronx and East Harlem communities for almost 50 years, providing the neighborhoods with a wide variety of recreational, cultural, educational, and social services. Casita Maria also participated in community planning groups, local school boards, and self-help groups interested in rebuilding inner city areas. The East Harlem Council for Human Services was established in 1964 as the East Harlem Tenant's Council. Since the 1960s it had stood in the vanguard of community development. The council was a community-controlled and ethnically based organization rooted in a firm commitment that those who are in the client population also should be the provider of services. Without sacrificing quality of staff or services, everything possible was done to assure that the client population was represented in project planning and implementation. By 1983, the council functioned as a multiservice social service agency including a health center, senior citizens nutrition program, home attendant services, substance abuse programs, headstart, and family day care facilities.

8. According to figures published by the Defense Department Manpower Data Center, Hispanics in 1981 supplied only 1.1 percent of the officers in the

army; 0.8 percent in the navy; 1 percent in the marines; 1.7 percent in the Air Force; and 1.2 percent in all services. Corresponding figures for blacks were 7.8; 2.7; 4; 4.8; and 5.3./Corresponding figures for "whites" (excluding Hispanics) were 87.2; 93.2; 94.1; 91.1; and 90.4. The figures for enlisted men for Hispanics in the aforementioned categories were: 4.5; 3.1; 5.5; 3.9; 4.1. Blacks: 33.2; 22.0; 16.5; 22.1. Whites: 53.4; 78.8; 70.1; 75.9; and 79.6.

9. Henry B. Gonzales, address to the National Conference on the Emerging Role of the Hispanics, Freedom International Foundation, San Antonio, Texas, March 11–12, 1983.

10. Rudolph O. de la Garza, "The Politics of Mexican-Americans," in Arnulfu D. Trejo, ed., *The Chicanos* (Tucson: University of Arizona, 1980), p. 109.

11. See Joseph S. Roucek and Bernard Eisenberg, eds., *America's Ethnic Politics* (Westport, Conn.: Greenwood Press, 1982), article by Michael V. Balok and James J. Van Patten, "Puerto Ricans," pp. 307–322; James Jennings, *Puerto Rican Politics in New York City* (Washington, D.C.: American University Press, 1977), pp. 190–212.

12. Manuel A. Machado, *Listen Chicano* (Chicago: Nelson Hall, 1981), p. 124.

13. Armando Rendon, *Chicano Manifesto* (New York: Collier Books, 1972), pp. 195–6. For details regarding police abuses in southern Texas, see, for example, Janet Brown and Gerald Colca, *Equal Justice for the Hispanics* (Houston, Texas: Freedom International Foundation, 1982).

14. Cuban organizations included, among others, *Rescate Democrático Revolucionario* (also known as the Cuban Rescue Committee). *Rescate* (founded in 1960) centered on New York; it aimed to unite Cubans of every social class for the purpose of liberating Cuba. The Cuban National Foundation conducted research and publicity for the purpose of gathering and distributing information on the island and on Cubans in exile. The Foundation looked to the creation of a free and democratic Cuba. So did the U.S. Committee for a Free Cuba in Washington, D.C., and the Free Cuba Patriotic Movement (*Movimiento Patriótico Cuba Libre*) in New York (both set up in 1963). The Cuban Representation of Exiles (*Representación Cubana del Exilo*) centered on Miami. *Cuba Independiente y Democrática* (CID) was founded in Caracas in 1980 and operated out of Miami. Its major aim was the establishment of a democratic system in Cuba. Several Latin American countries have endorsed CID, as have such unions as the AFL-CIO. It became heavily involved in radio broadcasting to Cuba; in 1983, 10 radio stations were broadcasting 20 hours a day.

15. Recent examples cited by Peter Brimelow and Stephen J. Markman, "Supreme Irony: The Court of Last Resort," *Harper's* (October 1981), pp. 16–28, include: "A Texas court ordering the expansion of school bilingualism in the teeth of the new administration's policy of de-emphasis; the District of Columbia Appeals Court moving against the proposal that federal employees should pay for their parking; a Tennessee court refusing to allow a reduction of outpatient visits to meet federally imposed spending cuts. On the state level, a Florida court has struck down an attempt to make functional literacy tests a prerequisite for high-school grade changes and graduation; the Massachusetts Supreme Court

has required Boston to keep its school system open although it has already exhausted its budget."

16. Abdin Noboa-Rios, "An Analysis of Hispanic Doctoral Recipients from U.S. Universities, 1953–1973 . . . ," *Metas* 2, no. 2 (Winter 1981–82): 92.

17. Cited by Jesus Chavarria, "The Hispanic Business Economy," address to the *National Conference on the Emerging Role of the Hispanic Community,* Freedom International Foundation, San Antonio, Texas, March 11–12, 1983.

18. Ibid.

19. For leadership within the CPUSA, see Harvey F. Klenr, *Communist Cadre: The Social Background of the American Communist Party Elite* (Stanford: Hoover Institution, 1976), p. 105. Only 1.4 percent of the central committee sample and 1.6 percent of party cadres were of Spanish, Portuguese, Mexican, or Puerto Rican extraction, compared to 31.6 percent and 38.8 percent, respectively, of Eastern European origin. In regard to divisions in communist ranks, by the early 1960s in Mexico, groups as diverse as the Partido Comunista Mexicano, the Partido Mexicano de Trabajadores, the Partido Popular Socialista, the Partido Mexicano Popular, the Partido Socialista Revolucionario, and many others competed for the goodwill of the masses. The militants were equally fragmented in the United States. In Puerto Rico, Marxist groups included the Partido Comunista Puertorriqueño, an orthodox pro-Soviet party with ties to the CPUSA, the Movimiento Obrero Unido, and various others. The most important of the Marxist bodies was the Partido Socialista Puertorriqueño (PSP), which enjoyed considerable backing within various Puerto Rican trade unions. The PSP, founded in 1971, leaned toward Cuba; it called for Puerto Rican independence and an end to the island's "colonial" status. The PSP took steps to bring the issue to the U.N., and its supporters in the United States staged a number of mass demonstrations (for instance, thousands of supporters marched in north Philadelphia at the U.S. Bicentennial). But even the PSP could mobilize no more than 1 percent of the total Puerto Rican vote during the 1976 gubernatorial elections.

20. During the first half of the 1970s, the FBI recorded a total of about 700 terrorist incidents connected with every kind of militant organization. During these five years, 83 policemen and civilians lost their lives—compared to an average of 40,000 homicide victims of crime or private vengeance every year.

21. *Gallup Report: Political Trends*, Princeton, N.J., January 1983, pp. 25–29.

22. Organized as a party, the Young Lords formulated a "13-point program" that called for Puerto Rican liberation; self-determination for all Latinos; liberation of the Third World; an end to racism; equality for women; control by the people of their institutions and land; true education in Afro-Indio culture and Spanish; opposition to capitalism; opposition to the "Amerikkan" military; freedom for political prisoners; support for all liberation forces around the world; self-defense; and socialist society.

23. Cited in Clifford Hauberg, *Puerto Rico and the Puerto Ricans* (New York: Hippocrene Books, 1974), pp. 140–1.

24. For a favorable account, see Peter Matthiessen, *Sal Si Puedes: Cesar Chavez and the New American Revolution* (New York: Delta Books, 1969). For a critique, see Machado, *Listen Chicano*, pp. 97–106.

25. See Peter Nabokov, *Tijerina and the Court House Raid* (Albuquerque: University of New Mexico Press, 1963).

26. Roberto E. Villareal, *Chicano Elites and Non-Elites: An Inquiry into Social and Political Change* (Palo Alto, Calif.: R. and E. Research Associates, 1979), pp. 101–2.

27. Herbert Hirsch, "Political Activation and the Socialization of Support for a Third Party: Mexican-American Children and the Future of La Raza Unide Party," in Z. Anthony Kruszwski, Richard L. Hough, and Jacob Ornstein-Galicia, eds., *Politics and Society in the Southwest: Ethnicity and Chicano Pluralism* (Boulder, Colo.: Westview Press, 1982), pp. 257–8.

28. Armando Navararro, "The Evolution of Chicano Politics," *Aztlán* 5, nos. 1–2 (Spring and Fall 1974): 57–84.

29. For lists of national, local, and state Hispanic organizations, and for evidence of their diversity, see *Hispanic Employment: A Recruitment Sources Booklet* (U.S. Office of Personnel Management, Hispanic Employment Program, Government Printing Office, 1980).

30. Willie Valasquez, cited in "Gap Remains between Potential Votes . . . and Power," *San Jose Mercury*, November 2, 1982, p. 7a.

31. In selected sample studies by Southwest Voter Registration Education Project in Texas, only between 2 and 4 percent of the respondents defined themselves a "radical." See Robert R. Brischetto and Rodolfo O. de la Garza, *The Mexican American Electorate: Political Participation and Ideology* (San Antonio, Texas: Southwest Voter Registration Project, 1983), p. 28.

32. According to a survey published in 1982, 78 percent of black Americans in 1982 considered themselves Democrats, 5 percent Republicans, 15 percent independents, and 3 percent other. Corresponding figures for Hispanic voters were 60 percent, 16 percent, 22 percent, and 3 percent; for Poles, 52 percent, 15 percent, 31 percent, and 3 percent; Scandinavians, 33 percent, 32 percent, 31 percent, and 3 percent; English, Scottish, and Welsh: 33 percent, 33 percent, 30 percent, and 4 percent. *Public Opinion* 5, no. 3 (December 1982, January 1983): 36.

33. Robert Gurwitt, "Widespread Political Efforts to Open New Era for Hispanics," *Congressional Quarterly*, October 23, 1982, pp. 2707–8.

34. Robert R. Brischetto, Anette A. Avina, and Yalanda Doerfler, *Mexican-American Voting in the 1982 Texas General Election* (San Antonio, Texas, Southwest Voter Registration Education Project, 1983), p. 1.

35. Mervin D. Field, "The Four Keys to Bradley's Election Defeat." *San Francisco Chronicle*, February 1, 1983, p. 9.

36. Villareal, *Chicano Elites and Non-Elites*, p. 118.

37. William V. d'Antonio and William H. Form, *Influentials in Two Border Cities: A Study in Community* (South Bend, Ind.: Notre Dame University Press, 1965), p. 30.

38. Roy C. Rodriguez, *Mexican-American Civic Organizations: Political Participation and Political Attitudes* (San Francisco: R. E. Research Associates, 1978), pp. 9–32.

39. See Rodolfo de la Garza, Robert R. Brischetto, *The Mexican American Electorate: A Demographic Profile* (Austin: University of Texas, Southwest Voter Registration Education Project, 1982).

40. Robert R. Brischetto, "Hispanic Poll Results," *National Conference on the Emerging Role of the Hispanic Community*, 1983.

41. *Hispanic Monitor*, vol. 1, no. 10, November 1984, pp. 1–2. For a more detailed breakdown of the Mexican vote in Texas, see *Hispanic Monitor* vol. 1, no. 11, December 1984, p. 3. SIN almost certainly gave too high a figure for Hispanic voters. The Southwest Voter Registration and Education Project, cited by *Hispanic Monitor* (December 1984), put the percentage of Mexican-American Republican voters in Texas at 27 percent, as against SIN's 32 percent. For Hispanic preference regarding Reagan in 1984, see *Gallup Report*, no. 230, November 1984, p. 7.

42. By 1983, a group of Hispanic elected and appointed officials had united under the banner of "Hispanic Force '84" for the purpose of strengthening the Democratic ticket. The new group—composed of Mexican Americans and Cuban and Puerto Rican Americans—had chosen New Mexico's governor Tony Anaya as their chairman. Other prominent members included Miami Mayor Maurice Ferre; Tony Bonilla, president of the League of United Latin American Citizens; and Colorado State Senator Polly Baca Barragan, vice chairperson of the Democratic National Committee. As Anaya put it, the new organization was designed to get Hispanics into key positions, not as spokesmen for Hispanics, but in roles that would speak to society at large.

43. Rodolfo O. de La Garza and Robert R. Brischetto, *The Mexican-American Electorate: Information Sources and Policy Orientation* (Austin: University of Texas, Southwest Voter Education Registration Project and Hispanic Population Studies Program, 1982), p. 25.

44. According to an inquiry made in October 1983, 21 percent of Hispanic respondents wanted the United States to withdraw from the U.N., compared to 12 percent of whites and 10 percent of blacks. Seventy-seven percent of Hispanic respondents wanted a compulsory national identity card, compared to 69 percent of blacks and 66 percent of whites. See *Gallup Report* no. 218, November 1983, pp. 13, 17.

45. By 1983, 55 percent of Hispanics considered taxation either a "great threat" or "somewhat" of a threat, compared to 77 percent of blacks and 74 percent of whites. Sixty-nine percent of Hispanics opposed raising income taxes for the purpose of reducing the federal deficit, compared to 79 percent of both white and black voters. Seventy-five percent of Hispanics considered inflation as a great or somewhat of a threat to national recovery, compared to 78 percent of blacks and 84 percent of whites. *Gallup Report*, pp. 6, 9.

46. See *Gallup Report*, nos. 232–233, January–February 1985, pp. 22–34.

Chapter 12

1. W.E.B. DuBois, cited in Kenneth James King, *Pan-Africanism and Education: A Study of Race, Philanthropy, and Education in the Southern States of America and East Africa* (Oxford: Clarendon Press, 1971), p. 257.

2. Charles Wentworth Dilke, *Greater Britain: A Record of Travel* (Philadelphia: J. B. Lippincott and Co., 1869), pp. 72, 211. Dilke, himself a radical, made these observations in the early 1860s, long before the industrial revolution had made its full impact on U.S. society.

3. For a highly readable account of the Germans, see, for instance, Richard O'Connor, *The German Americans* (New York: Little, Brown, 1968). The fullest recent history is LaVern J. Rippley, *The German Americans* (Boston: Twayne, 1976).

4. See *The Immigration History Newsletter* vol. XIV, no. 1, May 1982, for a bibliographic essay on bilingual education in American schools.

5. For a defense of bilingual education, see, for instance, Manuel H. Guerra, "Bilingualism and Biculturalism: Assets for Chicanos," in Arnulfo D. Trejo, ed., *The Chicanos: As We See Ourselves* (Tucson: University of Arizona Press, 1980), pp. 121–132.

6. Manuel H. Guerra, "Bilingualism and Biculturalism: Assets for Chicanos," in Arnulfo D. Trejo, ed., *The Chicanos: As We See Ourselves* (Tucson: University of Arizona Press, 1980), p. 126.

7. According to the 1971 Report of the U.S. Commission on Civil Rights, only 60 of every 100 Mexican Americans who entered first grade graduated from high school, compared to 86 "Anglos." The situation was no better for Puerto Ricans. Whereas Puerto Ricans in 1965 constituted 25 percent of New York's public school students, they formed barely 4 percent of the City University's enrollment. According to the 1980 census, the educational standards of Hispanic New Yorkers still left much to be desired. (Only 5.9 percent of Hispanics 25 years old and over had completed four years of college; 9.7 percent had attended college for one to three years; 23.9 percent had four years of high school; 20.3 percent had been at high school for one to three years; and 40.2 percent had only an elementary school education.) Hispanics not only have a low rate of college enrollment (4 percent) but also a low rate of receiving a degree (only 2 percent in 1976–77). Between 1976–77 and 1980–81, the percentage of public school professional staff in New York State had increased slowly (from 4.4 percent to 5.1 percent).

8. According to the U.S. Commission on Civil Rights, *Unemployment and Under-employment Among Blacks, Hispanics, and Women* (Washington, D.C.: Clearing House Publication 74, 1982), pp. 5, 43. The figures for 1980 stood as follows: 6 percent of majority males and 5.6 percent of majority females were unemployed: corresponding figures for blacks were 13 percent for both men and women, and 8.1 percent and 10.3 percent for Hispanic men and women, respectively. "Majority" college graduates had an unemployment rate of no more than 1.6 percent for males and 2.4 percent for females. Corresponding figures were 5.5 percent and 3.1 percent for black males and females, respectively. For Hispanics, the corresponding percentages stood at 3.8 percent and 2.8 percent, respectively.

9. Guerra, "Bilingualism and Biculturalism," in Trejo, *The Chicanos*, p. 128.

10. Roger A. Freeman, *The Growth of American Government* (Stanford: Hoover Institution Press, 1975), p. 15.

11. For a detailed description, see David E. Washburn, *Ethnic Studies, Bilingual/Bicultural Education and Multicultural Teacher Education in the United States* (Miami: Inquiry International, 1979).

12. Cited by *MALDEF (Organ of the Mexican American Legal Defense and Educational Fund)*, vol. XII, no. 3 (Fall–Winter 1982), p. 3.

13. For these controversies, see, for instance, Ellwyn Stoddard, *Mexican Americans* (New York: Random House, 1973); Thomas P. Carter and Roberto D. Segura, *Mexican Americans in School: A Decade of Change* (New York: College Board Publications, 1979); and N. Epstein, *Language, Ethnicity, and the Schools: Policy Alternatives for Bilingual-Bicultural Education* (Washington, D.C.: George Washington University, Institute for Educational Leadership, 1977).

14. Colin Greer, *The Great American School Legend: A Revisionist Interpretation of American Education* (New York: Basic Books, 1972).

15. See *Public Opinion* 4, no. 3 (June–July 1981), pp. 20–36. Eighty-three percent of all respondents said that they were extremely proud to be Americans; 65 percent of the black respondents said that they were "extremely proud" to be Americans. Eighty-five percent of whites thought that the United States had a special role to play in the world; 80 percent of the black respondents agreed. Ninety-four percent of the whites thought that the United States was the very best country in which to live; 86 percent of the black respondents agreed. Ninety-one percent of white respondents considered that the private business system in the United States worked better than any other system; 85 percent of black respondents agreed. Seventy-nine percent of all respondents (no separate racial breakdown given for this answer) opposed any measure that would place a top limit of $100,000 on all incomes.

16. Quoted in *Immigration History Newsletter*, May 1982, p. 5.

17. See, for instance, James Ylisea, "Bilingual Bellwether at Bay," *Christian Science Monitor*, October 18, 1982, for a critique of Ronald Reagan's policy.

18. *Public Opinion* 5, no. 3 (June–July 1982): 1–10.

19. U.S. Senate Committee on Labor and Human Resources, hearing, April 23–26, 1982.

20. David Hoffman and Lorenzo Romero, "Spanish Current Flows Into the English Mainstream," *San Jose Mercury*, "Mercury Special Report," November 4, 1981.

21. Abdin Noboa-Rios, "An Analysis of Hispanic Doctoral Recipients," *Metas* vol. 2, no. 2 (Winter 1981-1982), p. 95.

22. Gallup Poll (463–4).

23. Milton L. Barron, ed., *The Blending American: Patterns of Intermarriage* (Chicago: Quadrangle Books, 1972). For intermarriage figures of first- and second-generation Hispanics in New York, see Office of Pastoral Research, *Hispanics in New York*, New York, 1982, vol. 2, p. 133, table 13. All Hispanic groups increased their rate of outgroup marriage, except the Puerto Ricans.

24. See *Christian Science Monitor*, August 25, 1983, p. 12.

25. Robert E. Rossiter, "Bilingual Education: Training for the Ghetto," *Policy Review* 25 (Summer 1983): 36–45.

26. *Ibid.*, p. 467.

27. Mary Ellen Goodman and Alma Beman, "Child's Eye Views of Life in an Urban Barrio," in Nathaniel Wagner and Marsha J. Haugh, eds., *Chicanos: Social and Psychological Perspectives* (St. Louis: C. V. Mosby Co., 1971), pp. 109–19.

28. According to a survey carried out by the Roper Organization in 1982, 66 percent of respondents thought that the English immigrants had been "a good thing" for the United States, 59 percent thought so of the Jews, 46 percent of the blacks, 25 percent of the Mexicans, and 9 percent of the Cubans (the latter mainly a "white group"). Conversely, 59 percent of respondents thought that Cubans had been "a bad thing" for the United States, 34 percent thought so of Mexicans, 16 percent thought so of blacks, 9 percent thought so of Jews, and 6 percent thought so of the English. See *Public Opinion* 5, no. 2 (June–July 1982): 34.

29. See John Mirowsky II and Catherine E. Ross, "Minority Status, Ethnic Culture, and Distress: A Comparison of Blacks, Whites, Mexicans and Mexican Americans," *American Journal of Sociology* 86, no. 1 (July–November 1980): 479–95.

30. *Time*, 30 May 1983, p. 64.

31. *Newcomer High School Yearbook: 1981–1982* (San Francisco); see also Newcomer High School pamphlet, "General Information," and San Francisco Unified School District, *1982–1983: Lau Consent Decree Progress Report* (San Francisco: Office of the Superintendent of Schools, 1982). We are indebted to personal information from Newcomer High School principal Paul Cheng and his staff and Ms. Lupe Tiernan, coordinator of the Intake Center.

32. Jacques Portes, "The Franco-American Reawakening," reprinted from *Le Monde*, November 29, 1982, in *The Guardian* [London], January 3, 1982, p. 18.

33. Calvin Veltman (479).

Chapter 13

1. Thomas Sowell, "Weber and Bakke, and the Presuppositions of 'Affirmative Action,'" in E.E. Block and M.A. Walker, *Discrimination, Affirmative Action and Equal Opportunity, An Economic and Social Perspective* (Vancouver, B.C.: The Fraser Institute, 1982), pp. 39–40.

2. Hispanics gained the mayorality in such cities as Miami (1973), Tampa, Florida (1979), San Antonio (1981), and Denver (1983). Blacks, by contrast, won the mayorality in such leading urban centers as Gary, Indiana (1967), Newark, New Jersey (1970), Detroit (1973), Los Angeles (1973), Washington, D.C. (1974), New Orleans (1978), Atlanta (1981), and Chicago (1983).

3. Chester E. Finn, "Affirmative Action under Reagan," *Commentary*, April 1982, pp. 17–28.

4. Santiago Rodriguez, "Beyond Compliance: A Prescription for Greater Diversity at Stanford University," sent to the president of Stanford University by the University's affirmative action officer, July 23, 1982, and kindly supplied to the authors.

5. "Postal Service's Hispanic Accord," *San Francisco Chronicle*, February 26, 1983, and "U.S. Berkeley Signs Pact . . . " *The Tribune* (Oakland), September 6, 1983, p. B2.

6. Allan Bakke, a white applicant, was rejected in 1973 and 1974 by the University of California at Davis, even though individuals with lower qualifications were accepted because they were members of government-designated ethnic groups. The U.S. Supreme Court later affirmed a decision by the California Supreme Court which had ruled that the University might not exclude candidates in favor of less qualified applicants for racial reasons alone. The judgment, however, rested on technical grounds. The Supreme Court's decision was of an *ad hoc* nature; the Supreme Court thereby preserved its option to consider future affirmative action programs on their merit. The Weber case dealt with the complaint of a white worker, Brian Weber, who was denied admission to a training program set up by Kaiser Aluminum and Chemical Corporation. The plan set aside at least 50 percent of the trainee positions for blacks. Weber sued under the Civil Rights Act, claiming discrimination. He won in the federal district court and again in the court of appeals, but the Supreme Court reversed those decisions. The Court argued that no constitutional issue was involved, because the Kaiser plan was voluntary and did not involve state action. For detailed treatment, see Thomas Sowell, "Weber and Bakke," in Black and Walker, eds., *Discrimination, Affirmative Action and Equal Opportunity*, pp. 37–63.

7. See Christopher Jencks, "Special Treatment for the Blacks?" *New York Review of Books*, March 17, 1983, pp. 12–19.

8. Samuel L. Baily, "The Adjustment of Italian Immigrants in Buenos Aires and New York, 1870–1914," *American Historical Review* 88, no. 2 (April 1983): pp. 281–305.

9. Daniel Yankelovich, *New Rules: Searching for Self-Fulfillment in a World Turned Upside Down* (New York: Random House, 1982), p. 157.

10. Bertell Ollman and Edward Vernoff, eds., *The Left Academy: Marxist Scholarship on American Campuses* (New York: McGraw Hill, 1982).

11. See L. H. Gann and Alvin Rabushka, "Racial Classification: Politics of the Future," *Policy Review* (Summer 1981): pp. 87–94.

12. In 1979, the Subcommittee on Civil and Constitutional Rights of the U.S. House of Representatives Committee on the Judiciary requested detailed information on the numbers of minorities and women serving in the federal judiciary. To collect these data for the subcommittee, the administrative office of the U.S. Court issued a series of guidelines to all courts. One particular guideline, issued on August 23, 1980, promulgated a requirement that federal court employees and judicial officers must thereafter be identified according to a listing of "race/national origin" that included the subgroups "Arabic" and "Hebrew." The new subgroups were to be based, in the words of the circular, "on ethnic, not religious factors." As Senator Daniel Patrick Moynihan pointed out, this was the first time the federal government had ever asked the "Hebrew" employees to be so identified. The agency's request aroused an unanticipated degree of opposition. A new circular, issued to all Equal Employment Opportunity Coordinators on September 26, 1980, backtracked on the grounds that "the

breakdown of the category 'white' to reflect the semitic [sic] subgroups designated as 'Arabic' and 'Hebrew' would not be necessary in the future." This information had been requested merely "in anticipation of a possibility that it might be needed in the future." The agency, however, did not even consider the possibility that such racialist identification might be politically divisive, morally objectionable, and unacceptable to any legislature.

13. The proportions were as follows: San Francisco: percentage of Hispanic people, 12.3; percentage of Hispanic police officers, 8.1. San Jose: percentage of Hispanic population, 22.3; percentage of Hispanic police officers, 16.2. Los Angeles: percentage of Hispanic population, 27.5; percentage of police officers, 13.4. Oakland: percentage of Hispanic population, 9.6; percentage of Hispanic police officers, 8.9. *San Francisco Chronicle*, April 19, 1983, p. 4.

14. Richard Rodriguez, *Hunger of Memory: The Education of Richard Rodriguez* (Toronto: Bantam Books, 1983), p. 151.

15. Walter Williams, "On Discrimination, Prejudice, Racial Income Differentials, and Affirmative Action," in Block and Walker, eds., *Discrimination, Affirmative Action, and Equal Opportunity*, p. 97.

16. John H. Bunzel, "The Politics of Quotas," *Change*, vol. 19 (October 1972): 32.

17. According to a recent Gallup poll, 77 percent of all respondents in 1983 stated that they would be willing to vote for a well-qualified black president nominated by the respondent's party, compared to 38 percent in 1958. See *San Francisco Chronicle*, 18 April 1983, p. 8.

18. Lord Acton, "Political Causes of the American Revolution," in *Essays on Freedom and Power* (New York: Meridian Books, 1955), p. 223.

19. Nathan Glazer, *Ethnic Dilemmas 1964–1982* (Cambridge, Mass.: Harvard University Press, 1983).

Chapter 14

1. According to "Religion in America," Gallup Report, no. 222, March 1984, 44 percent of respondents in 1983 stated that religion was increasing in influence on American life, while 42 percent stated it was losing. Sixty-two percent of respondents expressed "a great deal" or "quite a lot" of confidence in the Church or in organized religion, 53 percent in the military, 51 percent in banking, 42 percent in the Supreme Court, 39 percent in the public schools, 38 percent in newspapers, 28 percent in Congress, 28 percent in big business, 26 percent in organized labor, and 25 percent in television. Ninety-five percent of teenagers believed in a personal God. Eighty-seven percent would welcome changes leading to more respect for authority, 82 percent for more emphasis on self-expression, 80 percent for more emphasis on traditional family ties, 78 percent on technological improvements. Sixty-four percent of teenagers, 61 percent of the adults, and 36 percent of the opinion leaders believed that the Church provided adequate answers to the moral needs of individuals. See the *Gallup Report*, pp. 23, 27, 42, 74, 75. For a more recent appraisal of religiosity in the U.S., see "Religion in America," *Gallup Report*, no. 233, May 1985.

2. Joan W. Moore and Alfred Cuellar, *Mexican Americans* (Englewood Cliffs, N.J.: Prentice-Hall, 1970), pp. 85–87.

3. Rev. Frank Ponce, "Hispanic Catholics in the United States: An Overview," in Dr. Virgilio Elizondo et al., *Los Católicos en los Estados Unidos* (New York: Centro Católico Pastoral para Hispanos del Noroeste, 1980), p. 51.

4. Interview with Mario Paredes of the Northeast Center for Hispanics, New York City, April 24, 1983, and Pablo Sedillo, executive director, U.S. Catholic Conference, Secretariat for Hispanic Affairs, Washington, D.C., June 29, 1983.

5. Office of Pastoral Research, Archdiocese of New York, *Hispanics in New York: Religious, Cultural and Social Experiences*, New York, 1982, vol. 1, pp. 81–85.

6. Ibid., pp. 71–78.

7. Figures cited in the Northeast Catholic Pastoral Center for Hispanics, *The Hispanic Community: The Church and the Northeast Center for Hispanics* (New York: Northeast Catholic Pastoral Center for Hispanics, 1982), p. 20.

8. *Gallup Report*, no. 23, May 1985, p. 20.

9. Office of Pastoral Research, Archdiocese of New York, *Hispanics in New York: Religious, Cultural and Social Experiences,* New York, 1982, vol. 1, p. 26.

10. The Secretariat had numerous functions; it maintained a publishing house, a language institute, and a pastoral institute to train people. It established a National Hispanic Resource Center in that city as well as a Mexican-American Cultural Center in San Antonio. But, basically it was the Secretariat that set policies for the U.S. Catholic Church serving Hispanics. Responsibilities and operations were parceled out to these various regional centers. The Secretariat also established a pastoral ministry for the migrant farmworkers and their families which coordinates the work of the dioceses and provides knowledge about the farmworker.

11. Office of Pastoral Research, Archdiocese of New York, *Hispanics in New York: Religious, Cultural and Social Experiences,* New York, 1982, 2 vols.

12. *The Hispanic Community, the Church and the Northeast Center of Hispanics*, pp. 22–23.

13. Andrew M. Greeley, "Immigration and Religious Ethnic Groups," in Barry R. Chiswick, ed., *The Gateway* (Washington, D.C.: American Enterprise Institute, 1982), pp. 159–192. See also Andrew M. Greeley, *The American Catholic: a Social Portrait* (New York: Basic Books, 1977), pp. 50–68.

14. Antonio Steven Arroyo, *Prophets Denied Honor: An Anthology on the Hispanic Church of the United States* (Maryknoll, New York: Orbis 1980), p. 9.

15. Virgilio P. Elizondo, *Los Católicos Hispanos en los Estados Unidos* (New York: Spanish American Printing Corporation, 1980), p. 70.

16. According to *Hispanics in New York*, vol. 1, p. 42, only 30 percent of the Protestants favored church involvement in politics, compared to 53 percent of Catholics. For a general critique of the bishops' position, see J. Brian Benestad, *The Pursuit of a Just Social Order: Policy Statements of the U.S. Catholic Bishops* (Washington, D.C.: Ethics and Policy Center, 1982). For divided views on the Simpson-Mazzoli bill, see Cecilio J. Morales, "Where has the Catholic Church Been?" *Pacific News Service*, June 1984, p. 9.

17. *Hispanics in New York*, vol. 1, p. 83.

Chapter 15

1. Karel D. Bicha, "Hunkies: Stereotyping the Slavic Immigrant, 1890–1920," *Journal of American Ethnic History* 2, no. 1 (Fall 1982): 27.
2. U.S. Department of Justice, Federal Bureau of Investigation, "Uniform Crime Reports: Crime in the United States" (Washington, D.C.: Government Printing Office, 1982), p. 182. Of the arrests made in 1981, 10.6 percent were Hispanics. Hispanics, however, accounted for 17.4 percent of those arrested for drunkeness.
3. Alan Parachini, "The Cantina Culture," *The World*, June 12, 1981.
4. Ellwyn R. Stoddard and Gustavo M. Quesach, "Health and Health Care," in Ellwyn R. Stoddard et al., eds., *Borderland Source Book* (Norman: University of Oklahoma Press, 1983), p. 249.
5. James M. Schaefer, "Firewater Myths Revisited: Review of Findings and Some New Directions," *Journal of Studies on Alcohol*, supplement no. 9 (January 1981): 99–117. Jerrold E. Levy and Stephen J. Kunitz, "Economic and Political Factors Inhibiting the Use of Basic Research Findings in Indian Alcoholism Programs," ibid., pp. 60–72.
6. David L. Strong, "Social Functions of an Alcoholism Treatment Program," ibid., pp. 207–210.
7. Marlene Dobkin de Rios and Daniel J. Feldman, "Southern Californian Mexican American Drinking Patterns," *Journal of Psychedelic Drugs* 9, no. 2 (1981): 151–158.
8. Robert Guinn, "Alcohol Use Among Mexican American Youth," *Journal of School Health* (February 1978): 90–91.
9. George E. Vaillant, *The Natural History of Alcoholism* (Cambridge, Mass.: Harvard University Press, 1983).
10. Strong, "Social Functions of an Alcoholism Treatment Program," p. 235.
11. Monica Herrera Smith, "Exploring the Re-Entry and Support Services for Hispanic Offenders," National Conference on Law Enforcement and Criminal Justice, Washington, D.C., 1980, p. 143.
12. Church of Scientology, *What is Scientology* (Los Angeles: The Church, 1978), p. 333; see p. 238–259 for a statistical breakdown of the social characteristics of a selected sample of church adherents.
13. Joan W. Moore and Robert Garcia, *Homeboys: Gangs, Drugs, and Prisons in the Barrios of Los Angeles* (Philadelphia: Temple University Press, 1978), pp. 18–28.
14. Interview by Bob Strauss with officer Phil Burten, *The Reporter* (Stanford School of Business), May 6, 1983, p. 5. According to FBI statistics, "Uniform Crime Reports: Crime in the United States," 1982, p. 160, heroin- and cocaine-related offenses formed 12.9 percent of all drug-related arrests; marijuana-related offenses formed 7.2 percent; synthetic drugs formed 3.6 percent.
15. Richard B. Craig, "Illegal Drug Traffic," in Ellwyn R. Stoddard et al., eds., *Borderlands Source Book*, pp. 209–213. Janet Brown and Gerald Colca,

Equal Justice for Hispanics (Houston, Texas: Freedom International Foundation, 1983), pp. 57–58.

16. *The Church and the Northeast Center for Hispanics* (New York: Northeast Catholic Pastoral Center for Hispanics, 1982), p. 20, *The Hispanic Community.*

17. Mario Rendon, "Transcultural Aspects of Puerto Rican Mental Illness in New York," *International Journal of Social Psychiatrics* 20, nos. 1–2 (Spring–Summer 1974): pp. 18–24.

18. Robert E. Roberts, "Prevalence of Psychological Distress among Mexican Americans," *Journal of Health and Social Behavior* 21, no. 2 (June 1980): 134–145.

19. Rodolfo O. de la Garza and Robert R. Brischetto, *The Mexican-American Electorate: A Demographic Profile* (San Antonio Southwest Voter Registration Project, 1982), p. 8.

20. William S. Aron, Norman Alger, Ricardo T. Gonzales, "Chicanoizing Drug Abuse Programs," *Human Organization* 33, no. 4 (Winter 1974): 388–390.

21. The British weekly food ration in 1948 stood at 13 ounces of meat, 1 1/2 ounces of cheese, 6 ounces of butter or margerine, 1 ounce of cooking fat, 8 ounces of sugar, 2 pints of milk, and 1 egg. See Arthur Marwick, *British Society Since 1945* (London: Allen Lane, 1982), p. 74.

22. Elliot M. Heiman and Martin W. Kahn, "Mental Health Problems in a Barrio Health Center," *International Journal of Social Psychology* 21, no. 3 (Autumn 1975): 197–203.

23. Rosina M. Becerra, Marvin Karno, and Javier Escobar, eds., *Mental Health and Hispanic Americans: Clinical Perspectives* (New York: Grune and Stretton, 1982), p. 89.

24. According to surveys published in *Public Opinion* no. 2 (April–May 1983): 30–31, the percentage of respondents wanting to legalize the use of marijuana dropped from 30 to 21 percent between 1977 and 1982. (This shift went along with changing attitudes toward divorce. Between 1978 and 1982, the percentage of respondents wanting stricter divorce laws rose from 44 to 54 percent.)

Chapter 16

1. For a comparison between the American and Rhodesian frontier situations, see L. H. Gann, *A History of Southern Rhodesia: Early Days to 1933* (London: Chatto and Windus, 1964), p. 105.

2. Paul Johnson, *Modern Times: The World from the Twenties to the Eighties* (New York: Harper and Row, 1983), pp. 209–212.

3. In 1981, according to the FBI Uniform Crime Reports, the total arrest rate per 100,000 inhabitants was 4,795; for cities with a population of 250,000 and over, it was 6,816; for suburbs, 3,994; and for rural counties, 3,229.

4. For details see Jonathan Rubinstein, *City Police* (New York: Farrar, Straus, and Giroux, 1973), especially pp. 353–7.

5. See Peter L. Sissons, *The Hispanic Experience of Criminal Justice* (New York: Fordham University Press, 1979), p. 16.

6. Wayne A. Cornelius, Leo R. Chavez, and Jorge G. Castro, eds., *Mexican Immigrants and Southern California: A Summary of Current Knowledge*, University of California, San Diego, Center for U.S.-Mexican Studies, research report series no. 36, 1982, pp. 74–75.

7. An investigation of 101 delinquent and 101 nondelinquent youngsters, conducted in San Juan, Puerto Rico, all drawn from similar socioeconomic backgrounds, concluded that poverty in and of itself did not cause crime. See Franco Ferracuti, Simon Dinitz, and Esperanza de Benes, *Delinquents and Non-Delinquents in a Puerto Rican Slum Culture* (Columbus: Ohio State University Press, 1975).

8. See, for instance, Lewis Yablonsky, *The Violent Gang* (Baltimore: Penguin Books, 1966), a study based on the investigation of ethnically mixed gang activity on the upper West Side of Manhattan.

9. For a detailed discussion of crime from the free market standpoint, see James Q. Wilson, ed., *Crime and Public Policy* (San Francisco: I.C.S. Press Institute for Contemporary Studies, 1983).

10. Paul Garcia, "Bilingual Programming: A Viable Alternative in Corrections, Part B," *National Hispanic Conference on Law Enforcement and Criminal Justice*, Washington, D.C., July 1980, appendix 1. Garcia matched the prison population in New York State with the shifting rates of unemployment from 1952 to 1974. He found an extraordinary correlation between the fluctuating figures for the number of persons jailed each year and the unemployment index for fifteen months earlier. Since the highest percentages of unemployment were found among Hispanic youths, Hispanic youngsters were more tempted to take to crime than the rest, quite irrespective of the welfare payments to which the poor of all races were entitled.

11. Between 1850 and 1890 the number of criminal convictions in England and Wales dropped from 20,537 to 8,157, compared to 17,800 cases of aggravated assault alone in San Francisco in 1970. See *Whitaker's Almanac* (London, 1912), p. 489, and U.S. Department of Justice, *Criminal Victimization Surveys: 13 American Cities* (Washington, D.C., 1975).

12. "The New Ellis Island," *Time*, June 13, 1983, pp. 18–21. Between 1970 and 1983, the estimated number of selected ethnic groups in Los Angeles County increased as follows: Mexicans, 822,300 to 2,100,000; Salvadorans, less than 2,000 to 200,000; Guatemalans, less than 2,000 to 50,000; Filipinos, 33,500 to 150,000; and Koreans, 8,900 to 150,000.

13. Annie M. Gutierrez, "Hispanic and Undocumented Aliens—Will Those Who Are Not Injured Be as Indignant as Those Who Are?" *National Hispanic Conference on Law Enforcement and Criminal Justice*, Washington, D.C., July 1980, pp. 11–24.

14. Alfredo Mirandé, "The Chicano and the Law: An Analysis of Community Police Conflict in an Urban Barrio," *Pacific Sociological Review* 24, no. 1 (1981): 65–86. Twenty-three percent of the respondents feared attacks in their immediate neighborhood; they were most likely to call for strengthened police powers. Twenty-eight percent of respondents thought attacks in their own neighborhoods extremely unlikely; they were less inclined to be sympathetic to the police.

15. See, for instance, Richard L. Strout, "U.S. Border Patrol Fights Fund Cuts on Capitol Hill," *Christian Science Monitor*, March 4, 1981, p. 7. In 1982, the INS requested $385 million for fiscal year 1982, an increase of only $9 million. Stanford University's total expenditure, 1979–1980, was $318.4 million.

16. The publications of the U.S. Commission on Civil Rights with regard to women, minorities, and poor people in general is too extensive to be summarized in a footnote or even to be fully listed in the bibliography. Particularly noteworthy as a critique of the INS is U.S. Commission on Civil Rights, *The Tarnished Golden Door: Civil Rights Issues In Immigration* (Washington, D.C.: Government Printing Office, September 1980).

17. Alfredo Mirandé, "Fear of Crime and Fear of the Police in a Chicano Community," *Sociology and Social Research* 64, no. 4 (June 1980): 538.

18. Armando Morales, *Ando Sangrando (I Am Bleeding): A Study of Mexican-American Police Conflict* (Fair Lawn, N.J.: R. E. Burdick, 1972).

19. For a summary of the inquest, see Appendix 11, "Inquest of Salazar's death," in Julian Samora and Patricia Vandel Simon, *A History of the Mexican-American People* (South Bend, Ind.: Notre Dame, University of Notre Dame Press, 1977), pp. 231–234. For a general discussion, see Armando Morales, "Chicano Police Riots," in Nathaniel Wagner and Marsha Haug, eds., *Chicanos: Social and Psychological Perspectives* (St. Louis: C. V. Mosby, 1971), pp. 184–205.

20. Statement reprinted in Janel Brown and Gerald Colca, *Equal Justice for Texas Hispanics* (Houston, Texas: Freedom International Foundation, 1983), p. 11. See also U.S. Commission on Civil Rights, *Mexican Americans and the Administration of Justice in the Southwest* (Washington, D.C.: Government Printing Office, 1981).

21. Brown and Colca, *Equal Justice for the Texas Hispanics,* p. 9.

22. See the analysis of Los Angeles rioting in Armando Morales, "Chicano Police Riots," in Wagner and Haug, eds., *Chicanos,* pp. 185–186.

23. Nathan Glazer and Daniel Patrick Moynihan, *Beyond the Melting Pot: The Negroes, Puerto Ricans, Jews, Italians, and Irish of New York City* (Cambridge, Mass.: M.I.T. Press, 1963), p. 122.

24. Joan Petersilia, *Racial Disparities in the Criminal Justice System* (Santa Monica, Calif.: Rand Corporation, 1983).

25. Agenor L. Castro, "Bilingual Programming, A Viable Alternative in Corrections, Part A," *National Hispanic Conference on Law Enforcements and Criminal Justice,* Washington, D.C., July 1980, pp. 99–100.

26. Peter H. King and Carol Pogash, "Youth Gangs Thrive in the City," *San Francisco Examiner,* special report, May 2, 1981, pp. 8–9.

27. Christopher Rand, *The Puerto Ricans* (New York: Oxford University Press, 1958), pp. 88–96.

28. For a detailed study, see Joan Moore and Robert Garcia, *Homeboys, Gangs, Drugs and Prisons in the Barrios of Los Angeles* (Philadelphia: Temple University Press, 1978).

29. Edward Murguia, *Chicano Intermarriages: A Theoretical and Empirical Study* (San Antonio, Texas: Trinity University Press, 1982), p. 47.

30. Yablonski, *The Violent Gang,* p. 244.

31. R. Theodore Davidson, *Chicano Prisoners: The Key to San Quentin* (New York: Holt, Rinehart and Winston, 1974).

32. Cited in Marshall Ingwerson, "Los Angeles Gangs: Rumbles of Reform," *Christian Science Monitor*, June 15, 1981.

Chapter 17

1. See Joe Cobb, *Issues, The Candidate's Briefing Book*, chapter 11, "Immigration," (Washington D.C.: Heritage Foundation, 1996).

2. The numbers were (in thousands) 1941–1950: 1,035; 1951–1960: 2,515; 1961–1970: 3,322; 1971–1980: 4,493; 1981–1990: 7,338; 1991–1993: 3,705. (See Cobb, *Immigration*, p. 10).

3. According to the Bureau of the Census, the Hispanic population exceeded 20 million by 1990. That is, six out of ten Hispanics, or 12.6 million were of Mexican origin; 2.3 million were of Puerto Rican descent, 1.1 million of Cuban provenance, 2.5 million of Central or South American origin, and 1.6 million of other Hispanic origins. Two-thirds of all Hispanics live in three states— California, Texas, and New York.

4. Jeffrey S. Passel, "Illegal Immigration to the United States," in Wayne A. Cornelius et al., eds., *Controlling Immigration: A Global Perspective* (Stanford, Calif.: Stanford University Press, 1994), p. 114. Also see Frank D. Bean, Barry Edmonton, and Jeffrey S. Passel, eds., *Undocumented Migration to the United States: IRCA and the Experience of the 1980s* (Santa Monica, Calif.: Rand Corporation, 1990); Michael Fix, ed., *The Paper Curtain: Employer Sanctions: Implementation, Impact, and Reform* (Santa Monica, Calif.: Rand Corporation, 1991); Edwin Harwood, *In Liberty's Shadow: Illegal Aliens and Immigration Law Enforcement* (Stanford, Calif.: Hoover Institution Press, 1986); Barry Edmonton and Jeffrey S. Passel, eds., *Immigration and Ethnicity: The Integration of America's Newest Arrivals* (Washington, D.C.: Urban Institute, 1995); L. H. Gann and Peter Duignan, *The Hispanics in the United States: A History* (Boulder, Colo.: Westview Press, 1986); Maldwyn Allen Jones, *American Immigration* (Chicago, Ill.: University of Chicago Press, 1992); Julian L. Simon, *The Economic Consequences of Immigration* (Oxford: Basil Blackwell, 1989).

5. Carlos Hamann, "Tex-Mex," *New Republic*, Apr. 15, 1966, pp. 14–18.

6. Jose Cuello, "Latinos and Hispanics: A Primer on Terminology," Wayne State University, unpublished paper.

7. George Will, "Why Multiracial Census Options Are a Good Thing," *San Francisco Chronicle*, October 6, 1997.

8. "Immigration," *American Enterprise*, Jan.–Feb. 1994, pp. 97–100.

9. *The Immigration Briefing Book* (Washington D.C.: Carrying Capacity Network, 1994); Molly Ivins, "Our Problems Aren't Caused by Immigrants," *San Francisco Chronicle*, Apr. 26, 1996.

10. Celia W. Dugger, "A Woman's Plea for Asylum Puts Tribal Ritual on Trial," *New York Times*, Apr. 15, 1996, p. 1.

11. Yeh Ling-Ling and Gil Wong, "Why It's Time to Limit Immigration," *San Francisco Chronicle*, Mar. 17, 1996.

12. Jonathan Tilove, "Poll of 4 States: Hispanic-Americans Yield Surprises," *Jersey Journal*, Mar. 4, 1996, p. 12.

13. President Johnson's Message to Congress," *Keesing's Contemporary Archives*, Sept. 20–27, 1995, p. 21083.

14. Cited by George Will, "Discomforting Truths about Bilingual Ballots," *San Francisco Chronicle*, May 2, 1996.

15. Michael Tomasky, "Reaffirming Our Actions," *Nation*, May 13, 1996, pp. 21–23.

16. See Alfredo Corchado's article in the *Dallas Morning News*, October 29, 1996.

17. William Branigin, "Congress Finishes Major Legislation Immigration, Focus on Borders not Benefits," *Washington Post*, October 1, 1996. For details of the left-right coalition that prevented true immigration reform in 1996, see John B. Judes, "Huddled Elites," *New Republic*, December 23, 1996.

18. *Immigration News* 3, no. 10 (October 1996): 1–3.

19. German authorities estimate that the approximately 500,000 illegals who work there may cost Germany $65 billion in lost taxes and social welfare contributions every year. Undocumented jobs are most often in construction, sanitation, and the food industry. Claims for political asylum have shot up all over Western Europe. Germany has been hardest hit; and in Great Britain in 1989, 2,900 people applied for asylum; in 1995 the number was 50,000. Both Germany and Britain have tightened the immigration rules and deny political asylum to more people—Britain denied 94 percent of applications for political asylum in 1997. Germany had 86,000 applications through September 1997, 6.3 percent fewer than in the same period in 1995.

20. Interview with Herman Kahn, *Conservative Digest*, Sept. 1983, pp. 36–38. "False Bad News vs. Truly Bad News," *Public Interest*, no. 65 (Fall 1981): 71–89. For a detailed discussion of *Global 2000 Report to the President*, see "The Global 2000 Juggernaut," Institutional Analysis, Washington, D.C.: Heritage Foundation, 1983.

21. Julian L. Simon, "Resources, Population, Environment: An Oversupply of Bad False News," *Science* 208 (June 27, 1980): 1421–1437. See also Simon, *Economic Consequences of Immigration*.

22. Julian L. Simon, *Immigration and Economic Facts* (Washington, D.C.: Cato Institute, 1995).

23. Thomas Sowell, *Ethnic America: A History* (New York: Basic Books, 1981), p. 220; and Barry Chiswick, "The Effects of Americanization on the Earnings of Foreign Born," *Journal of Political Economy* 11 (Oct. 1978): 879–922.

24. Letter by T. J. Rodgers, president and CEO of Cypress Semiconductor, to Senator Spencer Abraham, Feb. 26, 1996, kindly communicated to the authors by Mr. Rodgers.

25. "The Best Americans?" *Economist*, Nov. 26, 1994, reporting on the "Index of Leading Immigration Indicators," Manhattan Institute, 1994.

26. Julian L. Simon, "Public Expenditure on Immigrants to the United States: Past and Present," *Population and Development Review* 22, no. 1 (Mar. 1996): 99–110.

27. Paul Rich, "Mexican Neoliberal Nightmares: Tampico Is Not Taiwan," *Journal of Interamerican Studies* 37, no. 4 (Winter 1995): 173–90.

28. John Tanton, "Rethinking Immigration Policy," Washington D.C., FAIR, 1980, p. 13.

29. B. Meredith Burke, "An Environmental Impact Statement for Immigration," *Wall Street Journal*, Apr. 1, 1993, p. A15.

30. Peter Brimelow, *Alien Nation: Common Sense about America's Immigration Disaster* (New York, Random House, 1995).

31. Lawrence Auster, "Massive Immigration Will Destroy America," *Insight*, Oct. 3, 1994, p. 18.

32. Roy Beck, *The Case against Immigration: The Moral, Economic, Social and Environmental Reasons for Reducing U.S. Immigration Back to Traditional Levels* (New York: W. W. Norton, 1996), p. 246; Nathan Glazer, ed., *Clamor at the Gates: The New American Immigration* (San Francisco: Institute for Contemporary Studies, 1985); Chilton Williamson, Jr., *The Immigration Mystique: America's False Conscience* (New York: Basic Books, 1996).

33. See Edward P. Lazear, *Culture Wars in America*, Essays in Public Policy series (Stanford, Calif.: Hoover Institution Press, 1996).

34. Peter Skerry, *Mexican-Americans: The Ambivalent Minority* (New York: Free Press, 1993, p. 367).

35. Patrick J. McDonnell et al., "Latinos Make Strong Showing at the Polls," *Los Angeles Times*, Nov. 8, 1996.

36. Reported in Michael McCabe, "Historically Black East Palo Alto Now Moving toward a Latino Majority," *San Francisco Chronicle*, May 14, 1996, p. A4.

37. See *Washington Post*, Feb. 10, 1998, p. A02.

38. John Miller, "The Naturalizers," *Policy Review*, July–Aug. 1996, p. 31.

39. George J. Borjas and Lynette Hilton, *Immigration and the Welfare State: Immigrant Participation in Means-Tested Entitlement Programs* (Cambridge, Mass.: National Bureau of Economic Research, 1995), pp. 2–3; George J. Borjas, *Immigration and Welfare 1970–1990* (Cambridge, Mass.: National Bureau of Economic Research, 1994).

40. Georges Vernez and Kevin McCarthy, "Public Costs of Immigration. Testimony before the Subcommittee on Immigration and Claims," U.S. House of Representatives, Rand Corporation, CT 133, Apr. 1995.

41. Michael Fix, Jeffrey S. Passel, and Wendy Zimmerman, "The Use of SSI and Other Welfare Programs by Immigrants. Testimony before the U.S. Senate Subcommittee on Immigration. February 6, 1996," Washington D.C.: Urban Institute.

42. Norman Matloff, "The Adverse Impacts of Immigration on Minorities," testimony to House Judiciary Committee, Subcommittee on Immigration, Apr. 5, 1995 (updated Nov. 19, 1995).

43. Norman Matloff, *Welfare Use among Elderly Chinese Immigrants*, testimony to the Senate Judiciary Committee, Subcommittee on Immigration, Feb. 6, 1996 (updated Mar. 11, 1996).

44. Norman Matloff, "A Critical Look at Immigration's Role in the U.S. Computer Industry," Mar. 22, 1996, paper submitted to the Hoover Institution Workshop on Immigration.

45. Cited by Matloff, "Adverse Impacts of Immigration on Minorities," p. 13.

46. June Marie Nagle, "Immigrants on the Move: How Internal Migration Increases the Concentration of the Foreign-Born," *Backgrounder* (Washington, D.C.: Center for Immigration Studies, 1996).

47. L. H. Gann and Alvin Rabushka, "Racial Classification: Politics of the Future," *Policy Review* (Summer 1981), Hoover Institution Reprint series, no. 45.

48. Rosalie Pedalino Porter, Introduction to Charles L. Glenn, "What Does the National Research Council Study Tell Us About Educating Language Minority Children?" *READ Abstracts Research and Policy Review*, May 1997, pp. 1–2, a review of the National Research Council Study, "Improving Schooling for Language Minority Children: A Research Agenda."

49. See article in *Los Angeles Times*, Aug. 1, 1997, p. A16.

50. Carey Goldberg, "Hispanic Households Struggle as Poorest of the Poor in the U.S.," *New York Times,* Jan. 30, 1997. See also the Census Bureau's figures for 1996; median household incomes in 1996 were: for Asian Americans, $43,276, for African Americans, $23,482, for Hispanics (of any race) $24,906, and for whites, $37,161. These figures were roughly the same in 1995, except for Hispanics, whose income rose 5.8 percent in 1996.

51. Ibid.

52. See article in *Los Angeles Times*, Feb. 13, 1998.

53. See article in *Washington Post*, Feb. 13, 1998, p. A10.

54. See Philip Martin, *Rural Migration News* (Apr. 1997).

55. In Anne-Marie O'Connor, *Los Angeles Times*, Aug. 12, 1997, reporting on the University of Houston's Center for Immigration Research study, *Death at the Border*.

56. See Elsa C. Arnett, *Philadelphia Inquirer*, Jan. 19, 1998.

57. See Blaine Harden and Jay Mathews, "New Mix Enlivens N.Y. Melting Pot," *Washington Post*, May 26, 1997.

58. See article by David Gonzalez, *New York Times*, July 28, 1997.

59. See William H. Carlile, *Christian Science Monitor*, Aug. 6, 1997, p. 1.

60. Thaddeus Herrick and James Finkerton, *Houston Chronicle*, Oct. 20, 1996.

61. Ibid.

62. See Michael Totty's article in the *Wall Street Journal*, Jan. 7, 1998.

63. Ibid.

64. See article by Patrick Reddy in the *San Francisco Chronicle*, Sept. 17, 1996.

65. See V. Edward Taylor, Philip J. Martin, and Michael Fix, *Poverty and Prosperity: Immigration and the Changing Face of Rural California* (Lanham, Md.: University Press of America, 1997).

66. Roger Waldinger and Mehdi Bozorgmehr, eds., *Ethnic Los Angeles* (New York: Russell Sage Foundation, 1996).

67. See article by Patrick J. McDonnell in the *Los Angeles Times*, Dec. 10, 1996.

68. See Jodie Wilgoren in the *Los Angeles Times*, Nov. 23, 1997.

69. William Branigin, "Immigration Issues Await New Congress," *Washington Post*, Nov. 18, 1996.

70. See Stephen A. Camorotta, "Separate Questions on Immigration," *San Diego Union-Tribune,* Jan. 17, 1997.

71. See Philip Martin, *Rural Migration News* (Apr. 1997).

72. "Immigration," *American Enterprise*, p. 97.

73. Tilove, "Poll of 4 States," p. 12.

74. See Edwin Harwood, *In Liberty's Shadow* (Stanford, Calif.: Hoover Institution Press, 1986).

75. *Sacramento Bee*, Nov. 13, 1994.

76. See *Los Angeles Times*, May 1, 1997.

77. See article by Walter Branigin, *Washington Post*, Oct. 24, 1996.

78. See Eric Schmitt, "Breakup of Immigration Service Urged by Advisory Panel," *New York Times,* Aug. 5, 1997.

79. *Wall Street Journal*, May 16, 1997, p. 1.

80. Patrick J. McDonnell, *Los Angeles Times,* July 30, 1997.

81. See article by Patrick J. McDonnell in the *Los Angeles Times*, Sept. 24, 1996.

82. Mark Krikorian, "Who Deserves Asylum?" *Commentary*, June 1996, p. 54,

83. Associated Press, "Global Refugee Flow Declining," May 19, 1997.

84. William Branigin, "White House Leadership Sought on Refugee Matters," *Washington Post*, Jan. 7, 1997.

85. See *Christian Science Monitor*, Mar. 1, 1995, p. 11.

86. Ibid.

87. See Jorge Amselle, ed., *The Failure of Bilingual Education, 1996* (Washington, D.C.: Center for Equal Opportunity, 1997.)

88. Ibid.

89. Lazear, *Culture Wars in America.*

90. Glen Garvin, *"Loco, Completamente Loco," Reason*, Jan. 1998, p. 3.

91. Ibid., pp. 5–6.

92. Ibid., p. 7.

93. John H. Miller, "Bilingual Bullies," *National Review*, Feb. 23, 1998, pp 34–35.

94. Ibid., pp. 14–15.

95. Ibid., pp. 15–20.

96. Rodolfo Acuña, *Occupied America: The Chicano's Struggle toward Liberation* (San Francisco: Canfield Press, 1972).

97. See Scott McConnell, "American No More," *National Review*, Dec. 31, 1997, pp. 30–35, for an excellent survey of this topic.

98. Ibid., p. 35.

99. Ruth Wisse, "Shul Daze," *New Republic*, May 27, 1996, p. 19. According to the 1990 U.S. census, the U.S. population stood at 253,451,585. In 1975 the total number of legal immigrants amounted to 386,194. By 1993 this figure had more than doubled, to 904,922 (not counting illegals). An annual immigration rate of two per thousand would still admit more than half a million every year. Reduced immigration would facilitate the assimilation of immigrants in this country. If necessary, the number of legally admitted newcomers could be increased.

100. Zig Layton-Henry, *The Politics of Immigration: Immigration, 'Race' and 'Race' Relations in Post-war Britain* (Oxford: Basil Blackwell, 1992), pp. 223–24.

101. Charlie Breitrose, "Immersed en Español," *Palo Alto Weekly*, Mar. 18, 1998, pp. 18ff.

102. *Issues '96*, p. 355; for reforms of the U.S. immigration see chap. 11, pp. 333–57.

Select Bibliography

Here is listed only a small portion of the more recent books listed in the text. For more complete references, see the Notes.

Acosta, Mercedes; Corten, Andrés; Duarte, Isis; and Vilas, Carlos María. *Imperialismo y clases sociales en el Caribe.* Buenos Aires: Cuenca Ediciones, 1973.

Acuna, Rodolfo, et al., eds. *The Mexican American and the Law.* New York: Arno Press, 1974.

Acuna, Rodolfo. *Occupied America: The Chicanos' Struggle Toward Liberation.* San Francisco: Canfield Press, 1972.

Alvarado, Arturo R. *Crónica De Aztlán: A Migrant's Tale.* Berkeley, Calif.: Quinto Sol Publications, 1977.

Anaya, Rodolfo A. *Bless Me Ultima.* Berkeley, Calif.: Quinto Sol Publications, 1972.

Anderson, Robert W. *Party Politics in Puerto Rico.* Stanford: Stanford University Press, 1965.

Anderson, Theodore. *The American Experience.* Toronto: Ontario Institute for Studies in Education, 1972.

Archdiocese of New York: Office of Pastoral Research. *Hispanics in New York: Religious, Cultural and Social Experiences: Hispanos en Nueva York: Experiencias Religiosas, Culturales y Sociales.* New York: Office of Pastoral Research, 1982.

Arias, Ron. *"The Road to Tamazunchale": A Novel.* Reno, Nev.: West Coast Poetry Review, 1975.

Arroyo, Antonio Steven. *Prophets Denied Honor: An Anthology on the Hispanic Church in the United States.* Maryknoll, N.Y.: Orbis, 1980.

Atkins, G. Pope. *Arms and Politics in the Dominican Republic.* Boulder, Colo.: Westview Press, 1981.

Balderrama, Francisco E. *In Defense of La Raza: The Los Angeles Consulate and the Mexican Community.* Tucson: University of Arizona Press, 1982.

Barron, Milton L., ed. *The Blending American: Patterns of Intermarriage.* Chicago: Quadrangle Books, 1972.

Becerra, Rosina; Karns, M. Arvin; and Escobar, Javier; eds. *Mental Health and Hispanic Americans: Clinical Perpectives.* New York: Grune and Stratton, 1982.

Bell, Ian. *The Dominican Republic.* Boulder, Colo.: Westview Press, 1980.

Bernardino, Stephanie. *The Ethnic Almanac.* New York: Doubleday, 1981.

Bernstein, Blanche. *The Politics of Welfare: The New York City Experience.* New York: Abt Books, 1982.

Blatt, Irwin B. *A Study of Culture Change in Modern Puerto Rico.* Palo Alto, Calif.: R. and E. Research Associates, 1979.

Block, Walter E., and Walker, Michael A., eds. *Discrimination, Affirmative Action, and Equal Opportunity.* Vancouver, B.C.: Fraser Institute, 1982.

Boswell, Thomas D., and Curtis, James R. *The Cuban-American Experience: Culture, Images, and Perspectives.* Totowa, N.J.: Rowman and Allanheld, 1984.

Bowden, A. J. *Spanish and Mexican Land Grants in the Chihuahua Acquisition in El Paso.* El Paso, Texas: Western Press, 1971.

Burma, John A., ed. *Mexican Americans in the United States: A Reader.* Cambridge, Mass.: Schenkman Publishing Company, 1970.

Bustamente, Jorge A. *Espaldas mojadas: Materie prima para la expansión del capital norteamericano.* Mexico D.F.: Centro de Estudios Sociológicos, Colegio de Mexico, 1976.

Butterworth, Douglas. *The People of Buena Ventura: Relocation of Slum Dwellers in Post Revolutionary Cuba.* Urbana: University of Illinois Press, 1980.

Cafferty, Pastora San Juan; Chiswick, Barry R.; Greeley, Andrew M.; and Sullivan, Teresa A. *The Dilemma of American Immigration: Beyond the Golden Door.* New Brunswick, N.J.: Transaction Books, 1983.

Cafferty, Pastora San Juan, and McCready, William C. *Hispanics in the United States: A New Social Agenda.* New Brunswick, N.J.: Transaction Books, 1985.

Camara, Fernando, and van Kemperer, Robert, eds. *Migration Across Frontiers: Mexico and the United States.* Albany: New York State University, 1979.

Camarillo, Albert. *Chicanos in a Changing Society: From Mexican Pueblos to American Barrios in Santa Barbara and Southern California, 1848–1930.* Cambridge, Mass.: Harvard University Press, 1979.

Camp, Roderic A. *Mexican Political Biographies, 1935–1981.* Tucson: University of Arizona Press, 1982.

Cardoso, Lawrence A. *Mexican Emigration to the United States, 1897–1931. Socioeconomic Patterns.* Tucson: University of Arizona Press, 1980.

Carr, Raymond. *Puerto Rico: A Colonial Experiment.* New York: Vantage Books, 1984.

Carrion, Arturo Morales. *Puerto Rico: A Political and Cultural History.* New York: W.W. Norton, 1983.

Carter, Thomas P. *Mexican Americans in School: A History of Educational Neglect.* Princeton, N.J.: College Entrance Examination Boards, 1970.

Casavantes, Edward J. *A New Look at the Attributes of the Mexican American.* Albuquerque, N.M.: Southwestern Cooperative Educational Laboratory, 1969.

Castaneda, Alfredo; Ramirez III, Manuel; Cortés, Carlos E.; and Barrera, Mario; eds. *Mexican Americans and Educational Change.* New York: Arno Press, 1974.

Castles, Stephen, and Kosack, Godula. *Immigrant Workers and Class Structure in Western Europe.* London: Oxford University Press, 1973.

Chabran, Richard, and García-Ayvems, Francisco, eds. *Chicano Periodical Index: A Cumulative Index to Selected Chicano Periodicals Between 1967 and 1978.* Boston: G.K. Hall, 1981.

Chase, Allan. *The Legacy of Malthus: The Social Cost of Scientific Racism.* Chicago: University of Illinois Press, 1980.

Chiswick, Barry R., ed. *The Gateway: U.S. Immigration Issues and Policies.* Washington, D.C.: American Enterprise Institute, 1982.

Clark, Juan M. *The Exodus from Revolutionary Cuba, 1959–1974: A Sociological Analysis.* Ph.D. dissertation, University of Florida, 1975.

Cline, Howard F. *The United States and Mexico.* Cambridge, Mass.: Harvard University Press, 1963.

Comptroller General of the United States. *Report to Congress, Puerto Rico's Political Future, A Divisive Issue With Many Dimensions.* Washington: U.S. General Accounting Office, 1981.

Cordasco, F., and Buccioni, E. *Puerto Rican Children in Mainland Schools.* Methuchen, N.J.: Scarecrow Press, 1968.

Cornelius, Wayne A. *Los Norteños: Mexican Migrants in Rural Mexico and the United States.* Berkeley: University of California Press, 1980.

Cornelius, Wayne A. *Building the Cactus Curtain: Mexico and U.S. Responses, from Wilson to Carter.* Berkeley: University of California Press, 1980.

Cornelius, Wayne A. *Mexican Migration to the United States: Causes, Consequences, and U.S. Responses.* Cambridge, Mass.: Migration Study Group, Center for International Studies, 1977.

Cornelius, Wayne A. *Politics and the Migrant Poor.* Stanford: Stanford University Press, 1975.

Corwin, Arthur F., ed. *Immigrants and Immigrants' Perpectives on Mexican Labor Migration to the United States.* Westport, Conn.: Greenwood Press, 1978.

Cross, Harry E., and Sandos, James A. *Across the Border: Rural Development in Mexico and Recent Migration to the United States.* Berkeley: University of California Institute of Governmental Studies, 1981.

Cuban Economic Research Project. *A Study on Cuba: The Colonial and Republican Periods. The Socialist Experiment, Economic Structure, Institutional Development, Socialism and Collectivism.* Coral Cables, Fla.: University of Miami Press, 1965.

Cuddy, Dennis Lawrence, ed. *Contemporary American Immigration.* Boston, Mass.: Twayne Publishers, 1982.

Cue Canovas, Agustín. *Los Estados Unidos y el México Olvidado.* Mexico D.F.: Costa-Amic, 1970.

D'Antonio, William V., and Form, William H. *Influentials in Two Border Cities: A Study in Community.* South Bend: University Press of Notre Dame, 1965.

Davidson, R. Theodore. *Chicano Prisoner: The Key to San Quentin.* New York: Holt, Rinehart and Winston, 1974.

De Leon, Arnoldo. *The Tejano Community, 1836–1900.* Albuquerque, N.M.: University of New Mexico Press, 1982.

Diaz-Briquets, Sergio, and Perez, Lisandro. *Cuba: The Demography of Revolution.* Washington, D.C.: Population Reference Bureau, 1981.

Dinnerstein, Leonard; Nichols, Roger L.; and Reimers, David M. *Natives and Strangers: Ethnic Groups and the Building of America.* New York: Oxford University Press, 1979.

Dominquez, Virginia R. *The Caribbean: Its Implications for the United States.* New York: Foreign Policy Association, 1981.

Draper, Theodore. *Castro's Revolution: Myths and Realities.* New York: Praeger, 1962.

Draper, Theodore. *Castroism: Theory and Practise.* New York: Praeger, 1965.

Ehrlich, Paul R.; Bilderback, Loy; and Ehrlich, Anne H. *The Golden Door: International Migration: Mexico and the United States.* New York: Wideview Books, 1981.

El Plan de Santa Barbara: A Chicano Plan for Higher Education. Analyses and Positions by the Chicano Coordinating Council on Higher Education. Santa Barbara, Calif.: La Causa Publications, 1970.

Elizondo, Virgilio P.; Ponce, Frank; Flores, Patrick L.; and Sanchez, Robert F. *Los Católicos Hispanos en Los Estados Unidos.* New York: Spanish American Printing Corp., 1980.

Erb, Richard D., and Ross, Stanley R., eds. *United States Relations with Mexico: Context and Content.* Washington, D.C.: American Enterprise Institute, 1981.

Fagen, Richard R. *The Transformation of Political Culture in Cuba.* Stanford: Stanford University Press, 1969.

Fagen, Richard R.; Brody, Richard A.; and O'Leary, Thomas. *Cubans in Exile: Disaffection and the Revolution.* Stanford: Stanford University Press, 1968.

Fehrenbach, T.R. *Lone Star: A History of Texas and the Texans.* New York: Collier Books, 1968.

Fernandez, Raul. *The U.S.-Mexican Border: A Political-Economic Profile.* South Bend, Ind.: University of Notre Dame Press, 1977.

Ferracuti, Franco; Dinitz, Simon; and Brenes, Esperanza de. *Delinquents and Non-Delinquents in a Puerto Rican Slum Culture.* Columbus: Ohio State University Press, 1975.

Fitzpatrick, Joseph P. *Puerto Rican Migrants.* Englewood Cliffs, N.J.: Prentice-Hall, 1971.

Fitzpatrick, Joseph P., and Gurak, Douglas T. *Hispanic Intermarriage in New York City.* New York: Hispanic Research Center, Fordham, 1979.

Flores, Ernest Yutze. *The Nature of Leadership for Hispanics and Other Minorities.* Saratoga: Century Twenty One Publishing, 1981.

Friedlander, Stanley L. *Labor Migration and Economic Growth: A Case Study of Puerto Rico.* Cambridge, Mass.: MIT Press, 1965.

Galarza, Ernesto. *Merchants of Labor: The Mexican Bracero Story. An Account of the Managed Migration of Mexican Farm Workers in California, 1942–1960.* Santa Barbara, Calif.: McNally and Loftin, 1969.

Garcia Cantu, Gaston. *Las Invasiones Norteamericanas en México.* Mexico, D.F.: Editorial Era, 1971.

Garcia y Griego, Manuel. *The Importation of Mexican Contract Labor to the United States, 1942–1964: Antecedents, Operations, and Legacy.* San Diego: University of California, San Diego, 1981.

Garcia, F. Chris, ed. *La Causa Política.* South Bend, Ind.: University of Notre Dame Press, 1974.

Garcia, Juan Ramon. *Operation Wetback: The Mass Deportation of Mexican Undocumented Workers in 1954.* Westport, Conn.: Greenwood Press, 1980.

Garcia, Mario T. *Desert Immigrants: The Mexicans of El Paso, 1880–1920*. New Haven: Yale University Press, 1981.

Garver, Earl S., and Fincher, Ernest B. *Puerto Rico: Unsolved Problems*. Elgin, Ill.: Elgin Press, 1945.

Glazer, Nathan, and Moynihan, Daniel Patrick. *Beyond the Melting Pot: The Negroes, Puerto Ricans, Jews, Italians, and Irish of New York City*. Cambridge, Mass.: M.I.T. Press, 1963.

Golden, Marita. *Migrations of the Heart*. Garden City, New York: Anchor Press, 1983.

Gomez-Quiñones, Juan, and Camarillo, Albert. *Selected Bibliography for Chicano Studies*. Los Angeles: Chicano Studies Center Publications, 1975.

Gonzales, Rodolfo. *I am Joaquín: Yo soy Joaquín. An Epic Poem*. Toronto and New York: Bantam Pathfinders, 1972.

Gonzalez, Antonio J. *Economía política de Puerto Rico*. San Juan: Editorial Cordellera, 1967.

Grebler, Leo; Moore, Joan M.; and Guzman, Ralph C. *The Mexican-American People. The Nation's Second Largest Minority*. New York: Free Press, 1970.

Greeley, Andrew M. *The American Catholic: A Social Portrait*. New York: Basic Books, 1977.

Greenberg, Bradley S.; Burgoon, Michael; Burgoon, Jedee K.; Korzenny, Felipe. *Mexican Americans and the Mass Media*. London: Ablex Publishing Corporation, 1982.

Halperin, Maurice. *The Rise and Decline of Fidel Castro: An Essay in Contemporary History*. Berkeley: University of California Press, 1972.

Halsell, Grace. *The Illegals*. New York: Stein and Day, 1978.

Handlin, Oscar. *The Distortion of America*. Boston: Little, Brown, 1981.

Handlin, Oscar. *The Uprooted*. Boston: Little, Brown, 1973.

Hansen, Marcus Lee. *The Immigrant in American History*. New York: Harper Torch Books, 1964.

Hansen, Niles. *The Border Economy: Regional Development in the Southwest*. Austin: University of Texas Press, 1981.

Hanson, Earl Parker. *Puerto Rico: Ally for Progress*. New York: Van Nostrand, 1962.

Harris, William Warner. *Puerto Rico's Fighting 65th U.S. Infantry From San Juan to Chorwan*. San Rafael, Calif.: Presido Press, 1980.

Hauberg, Clifford A. *Puerto Rico and the Puerto Ricans: A Study of Puerto Rican History and Immigration to the United States*. New York: Hippocrene Books, 1974.

Hendricks, Glenn. *The Dominican Diaspora: From the Dominican Republic to New York City—Villagers in Transition*. New York: Teachers College, 1974.

Hennesey, James T. *American Catholics: A History of the Roman Catholic Community in the United States*. New York: Oxford University Press, 1981.

Hennesy, Alistair. *The Frontier in Latin American History*. Albuquerque: University of New Mexico Press, 1978.

Herring, Hubert. *A History of Latin America: From the Beginnings to the Present*. New York: Alfred A. Knopf, 1961.

Hirsch, Herbert, and Gutierrez, Armando. *Learning to Be Militant: Ethnic Identity and the Development of Political Militance in a Chicano Community.* San Francisco: R. and E. Research Associates, 1977.

Hispanic Employment: Recruitment Sources Booklet. United States Office of Personnel Management, Hispanic Employment Program. Washington D.C.: Government Printing Office, 1980.

Hoffman, Abraham. *Unwanted Mexican Americans in the Great Depression.* Tucson: University of Arizona Press, 1974.

Holli, Melvin G., and Jones, Peter d'A., eds. *The Ethnic Frontier: Essays in the History of Group Survival in Chicago and the Midwest.* Grand Rapids, Mich.: 1977.

House, John W. *Frontier on the Rio Grande: A Political Geography of Development and Social Deprivation.* New York: Oxford University Press, 1982.

Jaffe, A.J.; Cullen, Ruth M.; and Bosell, Thomas D. *The Changing Demography of Spanish Americans.* New York: Academic Press, 1980.

Jamail, Milton H. *The United States-Mexican Border: A Guide to Institutions, Organizations and Scholars.* Tucson: University of Arizona, Latin American Center, 1980.

Jennings, James. *Puerto Ricans in Politics in New York.* Washington, D.C.: Catholic University Press of America, 1977.

Johnson, Kenneth F., and Ogle, Nina M. *Illegal Mexican Aliens in the U.S.* Washington, D.C.: American University Press, 1978.

Johnson, Kenneth F., and Williams, Miles W. *Illegal Aliens in the Western Hemisphere: Political and Economic Factors.* New York: Praeger, 1981.

Johnson, Roberta Ann. *Puerto Rico: Commonwealth or Colony?* New York: Praeger, 1980.

Johnson, Harry S., and Hernandes, William J., eds. *Educating the Mexican Americans.* Valley Forge: Judson Press, 1970.

Kiser, George C., and Kiser, Martha Woody. *Mexican Workers in the United States: Historical and Political Perspectives.* Albuquerque: University of New Mexico Press, 1979.

Knight, Franklin W. *The Caribbean: The Genesis of a Fragmented Nationalism.* New York: Oxford University Press, 1978.

Kruszewski, Z. Anthony; Hough, Richard L.; and Ornstein-Galicia, Jacob, eds. *Politics and Society in the Southwest: Ethnicity and Chicano Pluralism.* Boulder, Colo.: Westview Press, 1982.

Kwartler, Richard, ed. *Behind Bars: Prisons in America.* New York: Vintage Books, 1977.

Langley, Lester D. *The United States and the Caribbean, 1900-1972.* Athens: University of Georgia Press, 1980.

Lewis, Gordon K. *Notes on the Puerto Rican Revolution: An Essay on American Dominance and Caribbean Resistance.* New York: Monthly Review Press, 1974.

Lewis, Gordon K. *Puerto Rico: Freedom and Power in the Caribbean.* New York: Monthly Review Press, 1963.

Lewis, Oscar. *La Vida: A Puerto Rican Family in the Culture of Poverty.* New York: Random House, 1965.

Lewis, Sasha G. *Slave Trade Today: American Exploitation of Illegal Aliens.* Boston: Beacon Press, 1979.

Lopez Segrera, Francisco. *Cuba: Capitalismo Dependiente y subdesarrollo, 1910-1959.* La Havana: Casa de las Americas, 1972.

Lopez y Rivas, Gilberto. *Chicano, o la explotación de "la raza."* Mexico, D.F.: Editorial Imprenta Casa, 1969.

Lopez y Rivas, Gilberto. *Los Chicanos: Una minoría nacional explotada.* Mexico, D.F.: Editorial Nuestro Tiempo, 1971.

Lopez, Adalberto. *Puerto Ricans: Their History, Culture, and Society.* Cambridge, Mass.: Schenkman Publishing Company, 1980.

MacEwan, Arthur. *Revolution and Economic Development in Cuba: Moving Toward Socialism.* New York: St. Martin's Press, 1981.

Machado, Manuel A. *Listen Chicano: An Informal History of the Mexican American.* Chicago: Nelson Hall, 1981.

Maciel, David, and Bueno, Patricia. *La Historia del pueblo chicano, 1848-1910.* Mexico, D.F.: Sepsetenta, 1974.

Madsen, William. *The Mexican Americans of South Texas.* New York: Holt, Rinehart, and Winston, 1964.

Maldonado-Denis, Manuel. *The Emigration Dialectic: Puerto Rico and the U.S.A.* New York: International Publishers, 1980.

Maldonado-Denis, Manuel. *Puerto Rico: A Socio-Historic Interpretation.* New York: Random House, 1972.

Martinez Masden, Edgar, comp. *Literatura Puertoriqueña Antología General* 2 vols. Rio Piedras, San Juan: 1970-1971.

Mathews, Thomas. *Puerto Rican Politics and the New Deal.* Gainesville: University of Florida Press, 1960.

Matthews, Herbert. *The Cuban Story.* New York: Braziller, 1961.

Matthiesen, Peter. *Sal si puedes: Cesar Chavez and the New American Revolution.* New York: Random House, 1969.

McWilliams, Carey. *Ill Fares the Land: Migrants and Migratory Labor in the United States.* Boston: Little, Brown and Company, 1942.

McWilliams, Carey. *North from Mexico: The Spanish-Speaking People of the United States.* New York: Greenwood Press, 1968.

Meier, Matt S., and Rivera, Feliciano. *Dictionary of Mexican American History.* Westport, Conn.: Greenwood Press, 1981.

Meier, Matt S., and Rivera, Feliciano. *The Chicanos: A History of Mexican Americans.* New York: Hill and Wang, 1972.

Mendez, M. Miguel. *Peregrinos de Azátlan: Literatura Chicana.* Tucson, Ariz.: Editorial Peregrinos, 1974.

Miller, Eugene Willard, and Miller, Ruby M. *Middle America and the Caribbean: A Bibliography on the Third World.* Monticello, Ill.: Vance Bibliographies, 1982.

Miller, Mark J. *Foreign Workers in Western Europe: An Emerging Political Force.* New York: Praeger, 1981.

Miller, Mark J., and Martin, Philip L. *Administering Foreign Worker Programs: Lessons from Europe.* Lexington, Ky.: D.C. Heath, 1981.

Miller, Tom. *On the Border: Portraits of America's Southwestern Frontier*. New York: Harper and Row, 1981.

Mills, C. Wright. *Listen Yankee: The Revolution in Cuba*. New York: McGraw-Hill, 1960.

Mirande, Alfredo, and Enriquez, Evangelina. *The Mexican-American Woman*. Chicago: University of Chicago Press, 1981.

Mitchell, Sir Harold Paton. *Caribbean Patterns: A Political and Economic Study of the Contemporary Caribbean*. Edinburgh: Chambers, 1972.

Moore, Joan W., and Cuellar, Alfred. *Mexican Americans*. Englewood Cliffs: Prentice-Hall, 1970.

Moore, Joan W., and Garcia, Robert. *Homeboys: Gangs, Drugs, and Prisons in the Barrios of Los Angeles*. Philadelphia: Temple University Press, 1978.

Moore, Joan, and Pachón, Harry. *Hispanics in the United States*. Englewood Cliffs, N.J.: Prentice-Hall, 1985.

Morales, Armando. *Ando-Sangrando (I Am Bleeding): A Study of Mexican-American Police Conflict*. Fairlawn, N.J.: R.E. Burdick, 1972.

Morin, Raul. *Among the Valiant: Mexican Americans in World War II and Korea*. Alhambra, Calif.: Borden Publishing Company, 1966.

Murguia, Edward. *Chicano Intermarriage: A Theoretical and Empirical Study*. San Antonio, Texas: Trinity University Press, 1982.

Navarro, Antonio. *Tocayo: The True Story of a Resistance Leader in Castro's Cuba*. Westport, Conn.: Arlington House, 1981.

Needler, Martin C. *Mexican Politics: The Containment of Conflict*. New York: Praeger, 1982.

New York City Department of City Planning. *Puerto Rican Population and Households*. New York, 1982.

New York Department of City Planning. *The Puerto Rican New Yorkers: A Recent History of Their Distribution, Population and Household Characteristics*. New York, 1982.

North, David S. *The Border Crossers: People Who Live in Mexico and Work in the United States*. Washington, D.C.: TransCentury Corporation, 1970.

North, David S., and Houston, Marion F. *The Characteristics and Role of Illegal Aliens in the U.S. Labor Market: An Exploratory Study*. Washington, D.C.: Linton.

Northeast Catholic Pastoral Center for Hispanics. *The Hispanic Community, the Church and the Northeast Center for Hispanics*. New York, 1982.

O'Leary, Thomas J.; Brady, Richard A.; and Fagan, Richard R. *Cubans in Exile: Disaffection and the Revolution*. Stanford: Stanford University Press, 1968.

Olson, James Stuart. *The Ethnic Dimension in American History*. New York: St. Martin's Press, 1979.

Ortiz, Roxanne Dunbar. *Roots of Resistance: Land Tenure in New Mexico 1680-1980*. Los Angeles: Chicano Studies Research Center and American Indian Studies Research Center, 1980.

Paredes, Américo, comp. *Mexican-American Authors*. Boston: Houghton Mifflin Company, 1972.

Paredes, Américo. *"With His Pistol in His Hand": A Border Ballad and Its Hero*. Austin: University of Texas Press, 1958.

Payne, Anthony. *The Politics of the Caribbean Community, 1961-1979*. New York: St. Martin's Press, 1979.

Peach, Ceri; Robinson, Vaughan; and Smith, Susan; eds. *Ethnic Segregation in Cities*. Athens: University of Georgia Press, 1982.

Peraza Sarausa, Fermin. *Personalidades Cubanas: Cuba en el Exilio*. Gainesville: University of Florida Press, 1965.

Perkins, Whitney T. *Constraints of Empire: The United States and Caribbean Interventions*. Westport, Conn.: Greenwood Press, 1981.

Petersilia, Joan. *Racial Disparities in the Criminal Justice System*. Santa Monica, Calif.: Rand Corporation, 1983.

Philipson, Lorrin, and Llerena, Rafael. *Freedom Flights: Cuban Refugees Talk About Life Under Castro*. New York: Random House, 1981.

Piore, Michael. *Birds of Passage: Migrant Labor and Industrial Societies*. New York: Cambridge University Press, 1979.

Piri, Thomas. *Down These Mean Streets*. New York: Alfred A. Knopf, 1967.

Pitt, Leonard Marvin. *The Decline of the Californios: A Social History of the Spanish-Speaking Californians, 1846-1890*. Berkeley: University of California Press, 1966.

Portes, Alejandro, and Bach, Robert L. *Latin Journey: Cuban and Mexican Immigrants in the United States*. Berkeley: University of California Press, 1985.

Price, John A. *Tijuana: Urbanization in a Border Culture*. South Bend, Ind.: University of Notre Dame Press, 1973.

Quirarte, Jacinto. *Mexican-American Artists*. Austin: University of Texas, 1973.

Quirk, Robert E. *Mexico*. Englewood Cliffs, N.J.: Prentice-Hall, 1971.

Rand, Christopher. *The Puerto Ricans*. New York: Oxford University Press, 1958.

Ravitch, Diane. *The Troubled Crusade: American Education, 1945-1980*. New York: Basic Books, 1983.

Reisler, Mark. *By the Sweat of Their Brow: Mexican Immigrant Labor in the United States, 1900-1940*. Westport: Greenwood Press, 1976.

Rendon, Armando B. *Chicano Manifesto: The History and Aspirations of the Second Largest Minority in America*. New York: Collier Books, 1972.

Ridge, Martin, ed. *The New Bilingualism: An American Dilemma*. Los Angeles: University of Southern California Press, 1981.

Rivera de Alvarez, Josefina. *Diccionario de Literatura Puertoriqueña*. San Juan: Instituto de Cultura Puertoriqueña, 1970.

Rivera, Edward. *Family Installments: Memories of Growing Up Hispanic*. New York: William Morrow and Company, Inc., 1982.

Rivera, Tomas. *Y no se lo tragó la tierra (...And the Earth did not Part)*. Berkeley: Quinto Sol Publications, 1971.

Rodriguez, Richard. *Hunger of Memory: The Education of Richard Rodriguez*. New York: Bantam Books, 1982.

Rogg, Eleanor. *The Assimilation of Cuban Exiles: The Role of Community and Class*. New York: Aberdeen Press, 1974.

Rolf, Eric, and Hansen, Edward C. *The Human Condition in Latin America*. New York: Oxford University Press, 1971.

Romo, Ricardo. *East Los Angeles: History of a Barrio.* Austin: University of Texas Press, 1983.

Ross, Stanley R. *Views Across the Border: The United States and Mexico.* Albuquerque: University of New Mexico Press, 1978.

Rothschild, Joseph. *Ethnopolitics: A Conceptual Framework.* New York: Columbia University Press, 1981.

Roucek, Joseph S., and Eisenberg, Bernard, eds. *America's Ethnic Frontier.* Westport, Conn.: Greenwood Press, 1981.

Samora, Julian, and Simon, Patricia Vanotel. *A History of the Mexican-American People.* South Bend: University of Notre Dame Press, 1976.

Samora, Julian; Bustamente, Jorge A.; and Cardenas, Gilbert. *Los Mojados: The Wetback Story.* South Bend: University of Notre Dame Press, 1971.

Sánchez Korrol, Virginia E. *From Colonia to Community: The History of Puerto Ricans in New York City, 1917–1984.* Westport, Conn.: Greenwood Press, 1983.

Serviat, Pedro. *40 Aniversario de la fundación del Partido Comunista . . .* Havana: Editorial EIR, 1965.

Sexton, Patricia Cayo. *Spanish Harlem: An Anatomy of Poverty.* New York: Harper and Row, 1965.

Shafer, Robert Jones, and Mabry, Donald. *Neighbors—Mexico and the United States: Wetbacks and Oil.* Chicago: Nelson Hall, 1981.

Simon, Julian L. *The Ultimate Resource.* Princeton, N.J.: Princeton University Press, 1981.

Smith, Peter H. *Mexico: The Quest for a U.S. Policy.* New York: The Foreign Policy Association, 1980.

Sosnick, Stephen H. *Hired Hands: Seasonal Farm Workers in the United States.* New York: McNally and Loften West, 1979.

Soto, Pedro Juan. *Spiks: Stories.* Translated by Victoria Ortiz. New York: Monthly Review Press, 1973.

Sowell, Thomas. *Essays and Data on American Ethnic Life.* Washington: The Urban Institute, 1979.

Sowell, Thomas. *Ethnic America: A History.* New York: Basic Books, 1981.

Spicer, Edward. *Cycles of Conquest: The Impact of Spain, Mexico, and the United States on the Indians of the Southwest.* Tucson: University of Arizona Press, 1962.

Steinberg, Stephen. *The Ethnic Myth: Race, Ethnicity, and Class in America.* New York: Atheneum, 1981.

Steiner, Stan. *La Raza: The Mexican Americans.* New York: Harper and Row, 1970.

Stoddard, Ellwyn R.; Nostrand, Richard L.; and West, Jonathan P.; eds. *Borderland Source Book: A Guide to the Literature on Northern Mexico and the American Southwest.* Norman: University of Oklahoma Press, 1983.

Stoddard, Ellwyn. *Mexican Americans.* New York: Random House, 1973.

Thernstrom, Stephen, ed. *Harvard Encyclopedia of American Ethnic Groups.* Cambridge: Harvard University Press, 1980.

Trejo, Arnulfo D., ed. *The Chicanos: As We See Ourselves.* Tucson: University of Arizona Press, 1980.

U.S. Bureau of the Census. *Census of Population: 1970, Persons of Spanish Origin. Final Report.* Washington, D.C.: U.S. Government Printing Office, 1973.

U.S. Bureau of the Census. *Statistical Abstract of the United States.* Washington, D.C.: U.S. Government Printing Office, published annually from 1878 onward.

U.S. Commission on Civil Rights. *Puerto Ricans in the Continental United States: An Uncertain Future.* Washington, D.C.: Government Printing Office, 1976.

U.S. Commission on Civil Rights. *El Boricua: The Puerto Rican Community in Bridgeport and New Haven.* Washington, D.C.: Government Printing Office, 1973.

U.S. Commission on Civil Rights. *The Tarnished Golden Door: Civil Rights Issues in Immigration.* Washington, D.C.: Government Printing Office, 1980.

U.S. Commission on Civil Rights. *Unemployment and Underemployment among Blacks, Hispanics, and Women.* Washington, D.C.: Government Printing Office, 1982.

U.S. Department of Commerce: Bureau of the Census. *Historical Statistics of the United States: Colonial Times to 1957.* Washington, D.C.: U.S. Government Printing Office, 1960.

U.S. Department of Justice: Law Enforcement Assistance Administration. *National Hispanic Conference on Law Enforcement and Criminal Justice, July 28–30, 1980.* Washington, D.C.: 1980.

U.S. Department of Labor: Bureau of Census Statistics. *A Socio-Economic Profile of Puerto Rican New Yorkers.* Regional Report No. 46. New York, 1975.

Urista, Alberta Baltazar (Alurista). *Floricanto en Aztlán.* Los Angeles: Aztlan Publications, 1971.

Valdez, Armando; Camarillo, Albert; and Almaguer, Tomas; eds. *The State of Chicano Research on Family, Labor, and Migration: Proceedings of the First Stanford Symposium on Chicano Research and Public Policy.* Stanford, Calif.: Center for Chicano Research, 1983.

Valdez, Luis. *Las dos caras del patroncito.* Englewood Cliffs, N.J.: Prentice-Hall, 1972.

Vasquez, Carlos, and García y Griego, Manuel, eds. *Mexican-U.S. Relations: Conflict and Convergence.* Berkeley: University of California Press, 1983.

Vidal, Mirta. *Chicanas Speak Out: New Voice of La Raza.* New York: Pathfinder Press, 1971.

Villareal, Roberto E. *Chicano Elites and Non-Elites: An Inquiry into Social and Political Change.* Palo Alto: R. and E. Research Associates, 1979.

Wagenheim, Kal, ed., with Wagenheim, Olga Jiménez de. *The Puerto Ricans: A Documentary History.* New York: Praeger, 1973.

Wagenheim, Kal. *Puerto Rico: A Profile.* London: Pall Mall, 1970.

Wagner, Nathaniel; Haugh, Marsha J.; and Hernández, Carrol A., eds. *Chicanos: Social and Psychological Perspectives.* 2nd ed. Saint Louis: Mosby, 1976.

Washburn, David E. *Ethnic Studies, Bilingual/Bicultural Education and MultiCultural Teacher Education in the United States.* Miami: Inquiry International, 1979.

Wasserman, Paul, and Morgan, Jean, eds. *Ethnic Information Sources of the United States.* Detroit: Gale Research Company, 1976.

Weber, David J. *The Mexican Frontier, 1821-1846: The American Southwest Under Mexico.* Albuquerque: University of New Mexico Press, 1982.

Weber, David, ed. *Foreigners in Their Native Land: Historical Roots of the Mexican Americans.* Albuquerque: University of New Mexico Press, 1973.

Weintraub, Sydney, and Ross, Stanley R. *The Illegal Alien From Mexico: Policy Choices for an Intractable Issue.* Austin: University of Texas, Mexico-United States Border Research Program, 1980.

Wells, Henry. *The Modernization of Puerto Rico: Political Study of Changing Values and Institutions.* Cambridge, Mass.: Harvard University Press, 1969.

Wiarda, Howard J., and Kryzanek, Michael J. *The Dominican Republic: A Caribbean Crucible.* Boulder, Colo.: Westview Press, 1982.

Wilkerson, Loree A.R. *Fidel Castro's Political Programs from Reformism to Marxism-Leninism.* Gainesville: University of Florida Press, 1965.

World Bank. *The Dominican Republic: Its Main Economic Problems.* The Bank, Caribbean Regional Office, 1978.

Index

political power, 213-214, 224-225
  See also Cuba
Cuban Studies/Estudios Cubanos,
  198
Cugat, Xavier, 200
Cultural imperialism, 13
Customs Brokers Association, 146
CUOM. *See* Confederación de
  Obreros Mexicanos
Dana, Richard Henry, 12
Deganiwidah-Quetzalcoatl
  University (D.Q.U.), 189
Democratic party
  Hispanic support, 54-55, 210,
  230, 231, 424(n42)
Demography, 156-157
  Hispanics, 433(n12)
  See also Assimilation; Population
  growth
Denver, 41, 60, 155, 156
Department of Health and Human
  Services, 254
Department of Justice, 169. *See also*
  Immigration and Naturalization
  Service
Department of Labor, 160, 169
Department of Labor and
  Commerce, 169
Department of Migration (Mexico),
  46-47
Department of Texas (U.S. Army),
  24
Deportation. *See* Repatriation
  programs
Depression, Great effects, 48-55
Deukmejian, George, 221
Dewey, George, 29
Diaz, Angel Giberto, 301
Diáz, Porfirio, 33
Dilemma of American Immigration,
  The, 174-175, 177

Discrimination, 36, 162, 253, 263,
  295, 428(n6)
  in California, 21, 23, 49-50
  against Puerto Ricans, 82-83, 195
  reverse, 257-258. See also
  Prejudice
Dominican Republic, 114-115, 116,
  225, 273. *See also* Dominicans
Dominicans, 276, 283
  immigration, 114-118
  in New York, 116, 117-118
  welfare users, 165-166
  See also Dominican Republic
Down These Mean Streets, 195
D.Q.U. *See* Deganiwidah-
  Quetzalcoatl University
"Dragons," 306
Drug traffic, 131, 134, 287-292, 307

Eagle Pass, 142
East Harlem, 79
East Harlem Council for Human
  Services, 92, 210, 420(n7)
East Harlem Tenants' Council. *See*
  East Harlem Council for Human
  Services
East Los Angeles, 40, 211-212, 287,
  307
Economic advancement, 123-125
  Cubans, 105-106, 107-108, 109
  Mexicans, 49-50
  and politics, 215-216, 224-225
  Puerto Ricans, 79, 92-93
  spending power, 216-217
  veterans, 63-65
  See also Businesses; Employment;
  Middle class
Ecuadoreans, 317
Editorial Universitaria, Universidad
  de Puerto Rico, 194
Education, xiii, 103, 114, 123, 168,
  204, 235